PERSO[illegible]
GRO[illegible]

BEHA[illegible]

[illegible]enth Edition

Annual Editions
A Library of Information from the Public Press

Karen G. Duffy [illegible]
Michigan State Uni[illegible] psychology at SUNY at Geneseo. She sits on the executive board of the New York State Employees Assistance Program and is a certified community and family mediator. She is a member of the American Psychological Society and the Eastern Psychological Association.

Cover illustration by Mike Eagle

The Dushkin Publishing Group, Inc.
Sluice Dock, Guilford, Connecticut 06437

The Annual Editions Series

Annual Editions is a series of over 55 volumes designed to provide the reader with convenient, low-cost access to a wide range of current, carefully selected articles from some of the most important magazines, newspapers, and journals published today. Annual Editions are updated on an annual basis through a continuous monitoring of over 300 periodical sources. All Annual Editions have a number of features designed to make them particularly useful, including topic guides, annotated tables of contents, unit overviews, and indexes. For the teacher using Annual Editions in the classroom, an Instructor's Resource Guide with test questions is available for each volume.

VOLUMES AVAILABLE

Africa
Aging
American Government
American History, Pre-Civil War
American History, Post-Civil War
Anthropology
Biology
Business Ethics
Canadian Politics
China
Commonwealth of Independent States
Comparative Politics
Computers in Education
Computers in Business
Computers in Society
Criminal Justice
Drugs, Society, and Behavior
Dying, Death, and Bereavement
Early Childhood Education
Economics
Educating Exceptional Children
Education
Educational Psychology
Environment
Geography
Global Issues
Health
Human Development
Human Resources
Human Sexuality
India and South Asia
International Business
Japan and the Pacific Rim
Latin America
Life Management
Macroeconomics
Management
Marketing
Marriage and Family
Microeconomics
Middle East and the Islamic World
Money and Banking
Nutrition
Personal Growth and Behavior
Physical Anthropology
Psychology
Public Administration
Race and Ethnic Relations
Social Problems
Sociology
State and Local Government
Third World
Urban Society
Violence and Terrorism
Western Civilization, Pre-Reformation
Western Civilization, Post-Reformation
Western Europe
World History, Pre-Modern
World History, Modern
World Politics

Library of Congress Cataloging in Publication Data
Main entry under title: Annual editions: Personal growth and behavior. 1993/94.
1. Personality—Periodicals. 2. Adjustment (Psychology)—Periodicals. I. Duffy, Karen G., *comp.* II. Title: Personal growth and behavior.
155′.2′05 75–20757 ISBN 1–56134–210–6

Thirteenth Edition

Manufactured by The Banta Company, Harrisonburg, Virginia 22801

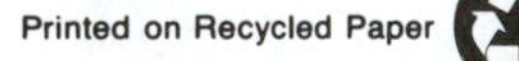
Printed on Recycled Paper

Editors/Advisory Board

Members of the Advisory Board are instrumental in the final selection of articles for each edition of Annual Editions. Their review of articles for content, level, currentness, and appropriateness provides critical direction to the editor and staff. We think you'll find their careful consideration well reflected in this volume.

To the Reader

In publishing ANNUAL EDITIONS we recognize the enormous role played by the magazines, newspapers, and journals of the *public press* in providing current, first-rate educational information in a broad spectrum of interest areas. Within the articles, the best scientists, practitioners, researchers, and commentators draw issues into new perspective as accepted theories and viewpoints are called into account by new events, recent discoveries change old facts, and fresh debate breaks out over important controversies.

Many of the articles resulting from this enormous editorial effort are appropriate for students, researchers, and professionals seeking accurate, current material to help bridge the gap between principles and theories and the real world. These articles, however, become more useful for study when those of lasting value are carefully *collected, organized, indexed,* and *reproduced* in a *low-cost format*, which provides easy and permanent access when the material is needed. That is the role played by *Annual Editions*. Under the direction of each volume's *Editor*, who is an expert in the subject area, and with the guidance of an *Advisory Board*, we seek each year to provide in each *ANNUAL EDITION* a current, well-balanced, carefully selected collection of the best of the public press for your study and enjoyment. We think you'll find this volume useful, and we hope you'll take a moment to let us know what you think.

Have you ever watched children on a playground? Some children are reticent; they sit demurely watching the other children play and shun becoming involved when invited to join the others. Other children readily and happily interact with their playmates. Some of these children take turns, share their toys, and follow the rules of the playground. Others are bullies who brazenly taunt the playing children and take the others' possessions. What makes each child so different? Do childhood behaviors forecast adult behaviors? Can children's antisocial behaviors be changed?

These questions are not new. Laypersons and social scientists alike have been curious about human nature for thousands of years. The answers to our questions, though, are incomplete at present because attempts to address these issues are relatively new or just developing. Psychology, the science that can and should answer such questions about individual differences, and which is the primary focus of this book, is only about 100 years old. One hundred years may seem old to you, but it is comparatively young when other disciplines are considered. Mathematics, medicine, and philosophy are thousands of years old.

Via psychology and related social sciences, this anthology will help you explore the issues of individual differences, etiology, and personality change as well as other issues concerning human nature. The purpose of this anthology is to compile the newest, most complete and most readable articles that examine individual behavior and adjustment as well as the dynamics of personal growth and interpersonal relationships. The articles in this book offer interesting insights into both the real and scientific worlds, a blend welcomed by most of today's researchers.

This anthology is revised each year and reflects both traditional viewpoints and emerging perspectives on people's behavior. Thanks to the editorial board's valuable advice, this edition has been completely revised. Those of you familiar with past editions will notice that all articles in the current edition are dated 1985 or newer, with most of the articles from the 1990s.

Annual Editions: Personal Growth and Behavior 93/94 is comprised of six units, each of which serves a distinct purpose. The first unit is concerned with issues related to self-identity. For example, one theory addressed in this anthology, humanism, hypothesizes that self-concept, our feelings about who we are and how worthy we are, is the most valuable component of personality. A contrasting perspective, behaviorism, maintains that there exist no such entities as self-concept or personality. The second unit provides information on *how* and *why* a person develops in a particular way. In other words, what factors determine or direct individual growth: physiology, heredity, experience, or some combination of all factors. The third unit pertains to problems commonly encountered in the different stages of development: infancy, childhood, adolescence, adulthood, and old age. The fourth and fifth units are similar in that they address problems of adjustment—problems that occur in interpersonal relationships and problems created for individuals by their social settings. For example, unit four contains articles on topics such as anger, conflict, and codependency while unit five includes articles on the pace of American life, the use of social distance, feminism, and racism. The final unit focuses on adjustment, or how most people cope with some of these and other problems.

As has been true in the past, your feedback on this edition would be particularly valuable for future revisions. Please take a moment to fill out and return the article rating form on the last page. Thank you.

Karen Grover Duffy

Karen Grover Duffy
Editor

Contents

Unit 1

Becoming a Person: Seeking Self-Identity

Eight selections discuss the psychosocial development of an individual's personality. Attention is given to values, life-styles, and the self-concept.

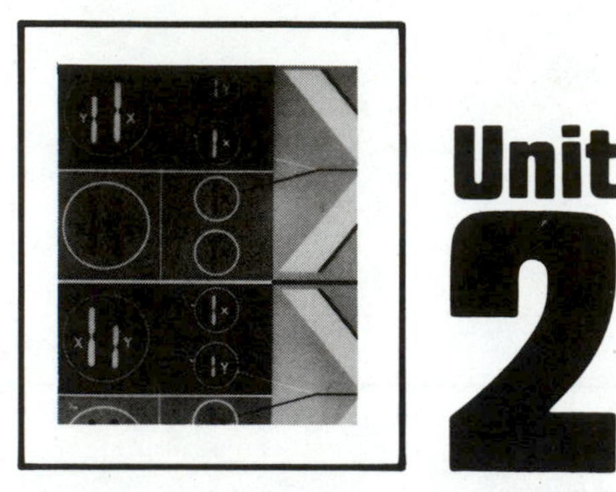

Unit 2

Determinants of Behavior: Motivation, Environment, and Physiology

Ten articles examine the effects of nutrition, culture, genes, and chemically sponsored emotions on an individual's behavior.

The concepts in bold italics are developed in the article. For further expansion please refer to the Topic Guide, the Index, and the Glossary.

Problems Influencing Personal Growth

Twelve articles consider aging, development, self-image, depression, and social interaction and their influences on personal growth.

The concepts in bold italics are developed in the article. For further expansion please refer to the Topic Guide, the Index, and the Glossary.

Unit 4

Relating to Others

Eight articles examine some of the dynamics involved in relating to others. Topics discussed include friendship, jealousy, the importance of family ties, and self-esteem.

Unit 5

Dynamics of Personal Adjustment: The Individual and Society

Seven selections discuss some of the problems experienced by individuals as they attempt to adjust to society.

Unit 6

Enhancing Human Adjustment: Learning to Cope Effectively

Twelve selections examine some of the ways an individual learns to cope successfully within today's society. Topics discussed include therapy, depression, stress, and interpersonal relations.

Topic Guide

This topic guide suggests how the selections in this book relate to topics of traditional concern to students and professionals involved with the study of personal growth and behavior. It is useful for locating articles that relate to each other for reading and research. The guide is arranged alphabetically according to topic. Articles may, of course, treat topics that do not appear in the topic guide. In turn, entries in the topic guide do not necessarily constitute a comprehensive listing of all the contents of each selection.

TOPIC AREA	TREATED IN:
Adolescence	24. Girls' Self-Esteem Is Lost on Way to Adolescence 25. Children in Gangs
Aging	5. Erikson, In His Own Old Age, Expands His View of Life 27. Silent Saviors
Alcoholism	35. No Life To Live
Anger/Aggression	31. Art of Anger Difficult for Women to Master 33. How Anger Affects Your Health
Attitudes	16. Tapping the Healing Power of Positive Thinking
Behaviorism	7. Embattled Giant of Psychology Speaks His Mind 8. Town B. F. Skinner Boxed
Brain, Brain Chemistry, Brain Damage	12. Mapping the Brain 13. 1990–2000, Decade of the Brain 15. The Face as Window and Machine for Emotions
Bystander Apathy	44. When Bystanders Just Stand By
Childhood	3. Self-Esteem: The Keystone to Happiness 9. Same Family, Different Lives 19. Clipped Wings 20. Is Your Baby Getting Enough Stimulation? 21. Putting Children First 22. I'm OK, They're OK 23. Children After Divorce
Codependency	35. No Life To Live
Conflict	34. Resolving Conflicts
Criminality	56. Hitting Bottom Can Be the Beginning
Culture/Society	39. Pace of Life 40. American Man in Transition 41. Blame It on Feminism 42. Taking Sides Against Ourselves 45 How Much Is Enough?
Death	29. Bright Lights, Big Mystery 30. Euthanasia: What Is The "Good Death"?
Defenses	49. What Good Is Feeling Bad?
Depression	23. Children After Divorce 51. Winning the War on Clinical Depression
Development	5. Erikson, In His Own Old Age, Expands His View of Life
Drug Use/Drug Abuse	25. Children in Gangs 35. No Life to Live
Emotions	15. Face as Window and Machine for the Emotions 16. Tapping the Healing Power of Positive Thinking 17. Doctors Find Comfort Is a Potent Medicine
Families	9. Same Family, Different Lives 21. Putting Children First 22. I'm OK, They're OK 35. No Life to Live
Genetics	10. What a Child Is Given 11. Born or Bred?
Groups	43. Groupthink: Taking Easy Way Out of a Tough Decision 44. When Bystanders Just Stand By
Helping	44. When Bystanders Just Stand By
Homosexuality	11. Born or Bred?
Humanism/ Humanistic Psychology	1. Last Interview with Abraham Maslow 7. Embattled Giant of Psychology Speaks His Mind
Marriage	36. What Happy Couples Do Right 37. Friends Forever
Mental Illness/ Emotional Disorders	13. 1990–2000, Decade of the Brain 46. Mental Health Checkup 47. Listening Cure 51. Winning the War Against Clinical Depression 53. Secret Illness 54. Who Am I? 55. Awakenings: Schizophrenia
Middle Age	26. Reaching the Child Within Us
Natural Selection	4. Oedipus Wrecked
Oedipus Complex	4. Oedipus Wrecked

Becoming a Person: Seeking Self-Identity

A baby sits in front of a mirror and looks at herself. A chimpanzee sorts through photographs while its trainer watches carefully for the chimp's reaction. What do each of these events share in common? "Nothing," you say. Wrong! Both are examples of techniques utilized to investigate self-concept.

The baby has a red dot on her nose. The researchers watch to see if the child reaches for the dot in the mirror or touches her own nose. In recognition of the fact that the image she sees in the mirror is her own, the baby touches her real nose, not the nose in the mirror.

The chimpanzee has been trained to sort photographs into piles of human or animal pictures. If the chimp has been raised with humans, the researcher wants to know into which pile (animal or human) the chimp will place its own picture. Is the chimp's concept of itself animal or human? Or does the chimp have no concept of self at all?

These research projects are designed to investigate how self-concept develops. Most psychologists believe that people develop a personal identity or sense of self—a sense of who they are, their likes and dislikes, their characteristic feelings and thoughts, and an understanding of why they behave as they do. Self-concept is knowledge of gender, race, age, self-worth and much more. Strong positive or negative feelings are usually attached to this identity. Psychologists are studying how and when this sense of self develops. Most psychologists do not believe that infants are born with a sense of self, but rather that children slowly develop self-concept as a consequence of their experiences.

This section of the book delineates some of the popular viewpoints regarding how the sense of self and personality develop and how or whether they guide behavior. This knowledge of how self develops provides an important foundation for the rest of the units in this book. In this unit, then, we are going to explore the major theories or forces in psychology: self or humanistic psychology, psychoanalysis, trait theory, and behaviorism. For most theories, we will also examine related research, applications, or concepts in a companion article.

The first two articles are devoted to humanistic psychology. In the first article, "The Last Interview of Abraham Maslow," Maslow, a founder of humanistic psychology, discusses the evolution of his theory. In the interview, he discusses his philosophy of human nature and its potential for peaceful living and other positive outcomes for humans. The second article is the companion article. In "Hey, I'm Terrific!" what self-esteem is and its history as a concept in psychology is detailed. One of the conclusions is that self-esteem is an overworked concept in today's literature.

The next article, "Self-Esteem: The Keystone to Happiness," relates to one of the most important aspects of self-concept, self-esteem. Individuals high in esteem seem to glide through life's bad moments and report that they are quite happy the rest of the time. Low self-esteem individuals are often unhappy and are sometimes suicide-prone. The article also provides some self-tests as well as guidelines for raising children with high esteem.

The next two articles relate to psychoanalysis, a theory and form of therapy to which humanism was a reaction. The main proponent of psychoanalysis was Sigmund Freud, who believed that individuals possess a dark, lurking unconscious that often motivates negative behaviors. Bruce Bower, in "Oedipus Wrecked," pits Freudian concepts against Darwinian concepts and determines that each perspective adds to our understanding of human nature. Finally, in the second article in this series on psychoanalysis, Erik Erikson's version of psychosocial development is revealed. Parts of his theory appear Freudian, development in stages for example, while others are unique to Erikson.

The next article in the unit offers an alternative viewpoint known as the trait or dispositional approach. Trait theories in general hold that our personalities are comprised of various traits that may or may not be held together by a self-concept. In the sixth article, "Personality: Major Traits Found Stable Through Life," the author claims that most personality traits remain constant over time, in contrast with the growth theory of Maslow and the psychosocial theory of Erikson.

Be aware that there are psychologists who are convinced that people do not possess a sense of self. Individuals do not ever really come to "know" themselves. Instead, actions at the moment are based either on past learning experiences or on immediate stimuli in their

Unit 1

environments. There is no self-concept upon which people regularly rely or reflect. The remaining articles are about the work of a very influential contemporary behaviorist, B. F. Skinner. Skinner claims there indeed is no self-concept that directs behavior. In "Embattled Giant of Psychology Speaks His Mind," Skinner explains his work and argues against his critics, especially humanists. A companion article, "The Town B. F. Skinner Boxed," describes a whole community that has become a laboratory for Skinnerian or behavioral principles.

Looking Ahead: Challenge Questions

Does the sense of self develop the same way in each individual? Are there various aspects of self, such as gender, that develop faster than other aspects?

Is self-concept stable or does it seem to change regularly? What events create change?

Do you think there is such a thing as a personality trait? How could you demonstrate the existence of a trait? Do you think personality remains stable over a lifetime?

Does self-concept or psychosocial development guide behaviors? What behaviors does each influence?

Suppose someone developed on a desert island with no human contact. What might this individual be like? How might the person appear to others who have been raised in civilization?

Is self a uniquely human concept? Could animals develop a sense of self? How would you test animals for self-concept?

How and when do you think children develop a sense of self? How do people show others that they have a sense of self?

What do you think is responsible for guiding our behavior, our past reinforcement history, self-concept, or our traits?

What would a community based on Skinnerian or behavioral principles be like? How would this contrast with a humanistic community, for example?

Do you believe in the concept of the unconscious? Why? Describe the concepts that are important in each of these theories: humanistic, psychoanalytic, trait, and behavioral theory? Which theory do you think is best and why?

The Last Interview of ABRAHAM MASLOW

Edward Hoffman, Ph.D.

About the author: *Edward Hoffman received his doctorate from the University of Michigan. A clinical psychologist on New York's Long Island, he is the author of several books, including* The Right to be Human: A Biography of Abraham Maslow *(Tarcher).*

When Abraham Maslow first shared his pioneering vision of a "comprehensive human psychology" in this magazine in early 1968, he stood at the pinnacle of his international acclaim and influence.

His election as president of the American Psychological Association some months before capped an illustrious academic career spanning more than 35 productive years, during which Maslow had steadily gained the high regard—even adulation—of countless numbers of colleagues and former students. His best-known books, *Motivation and Personality* and *Toward a Psychology of Being*, were not only being discussed avidly by psychologists, but also by professionals in fields ranging from management and marketing to education and counseling. Perhaps even more significantly, Maslow's iconoclastic concepts like peak experience, self-actualization, and synergy had even begun penetrating popular language.

Nevertheless, it was a very unsettling time for him: Recovering from a major heart attack, the temperamentally restless and ceaselessly active Maslow was finding forced convalescence at home to be almost painfully unbearable. Suddenly, his extensive plans for future research, travel, and lecturing had to be postponed. Although Maslow hoped for a speedy recovery, frequent chest pains induced a keen sense of his own mortality. As perhaps never before, he began to ponder his career's accomplishments and his unrealized goals.

In 1968 Psychology Today was a precocious one-year-old upstart, but such was its prestige that it was able to attract perhaps the country's most famous psychologist for an interview.

Maslow likely regarded the PT interview as a major opportunity to outline his "comprehensive human psychology" and the best way to actualize it. At 60, he knew that time permitted him only to plant seeds (in his own metaphor) of research and theory—and hope that later generations would live to see the flowering of human betterment. Perhaps most prescient at a time of global unrest is Maslow's stirring vision of "building a psychology for the peace table." It was his hope that through psychological research, we might learn how to unify peoples of differing racial and ethnic origins, and thereby create a world of peace.

Although the complete audiotapes of the sessions, conducted over three days, disappeared long ago under mysterious circumstances, the written condensation that remains provides a fascinating and still-relevant portrait of a key thinker at the height of his prowess. Intellectually, Maslow was decades ahead of his time; today the wide-ranging ideas he offers here are far from outdated. Indeed, after some twenty-odd years, they're still on the cutting edge of American psychology and social science. Emotionally, this interview is significant for the rare—essentially unprecedented—glimpse it affords into Maslow's personal history and concerns: his ancestry and upbringing; his mentors and ambitions; his courtship, marriage, and fatherhood; and even a few of his peak experiences.

Maslow continued to be puzzled and intrigued by the more positive human phenomenon of self-actualization. He was well aware that his theory about the "best of humanity" suffered from methodological flaws. Yet he had become ever more convinced of its intuitive validity, that self-actualizers provide us with clues to our highest innate traits: love and compassion, creativity and aesthetics, ethics and spirituality. Maslow longed to empirically verify this lifelong hunch.

In the two years of his life that remained, this gifted psychologist never wrote an autobiography, nor did he ever again bare his soul in such a public and wide-ranging way. It may have been that Maslow regarded this unusually personal interview as a true legacy. More than 20 years later, it remains a fresh and important document for the field of psychology.

Mary Harrington Hall, for PSYCHOLOGY TODAY: A couple of William B. Yeats's lines keep running through my head: "And in my heart, the daemons and the gods wage an eternal battle and I feel the pain of wounds, the labor of the spear." How thin is the veneer of civilization, and how can we understand and deal with evil?

Abraham H. Maslow: It's a psychological puzzle I've been trying to solve for years. Why are people cruel and why are they nice? Evil people are rare, but you find evil behavior in the majority of people. The next thing I want to do with my life is to study evil and understand it.

PT: By evil here, I think we both mean destructive action without remorse. Racial prejudice is an evil in our society which we must deal with. And soon. Or we will go down as a racist society.

Maslow: You know, when I became A.P.A. president, the first thing I wanted to do was work for greater recognition for the Negro psychologists. Then I found that there were no Negroes in psychology, at least not many. They don't major in psychology.

PT: Why should they? Why would I think that psychology would solve social problems if I were a Negro living in the ghetto, surrounded by despair?

Maslow: Negroes have really had to take it. We've given them every possible blow. If I were a Negro, I'd be fighting, as Martin Luther King fought, for human recognition and justice. I'd rather go down with my flag flying. If you're weak or crippled, or you can't speak out or fight back in some way, then people don't hesitate to treat you badly.

PT: Could you look at evil behavior in two ways: evil from below and evil from above? Evil as a sickness and evil as understood compassionately?

Maslow: If you look at evil from above, you can be realistic. Evil exists. You don't give it quarter, and you're a better fighter if you can understand it. You're in the position of a psychotherapist. In the the same way, you can look at neurosis. You can see neurosis from below—as a sickness—as most psychiatrists see it. Or you can understand it as a compassionate man might: respecting the neurosis as a fumbling and inefficient effort toward good ends.

PT: You can understand race riots in the same way, can't you?

Maslow: If you can only be detached enough, you can feel that it's better to riot than to be hopeless, degraded, and defeated. Rioting is a childish way of trying to be a man, but it takes time to rise out of the hell of hatred and frustration and accept that to be a man you don't have to riot.

PT: In our society, we see all behavior as a demon we can vanquish and banish, don't we? And yet good people do evil things.

Maslow: Most people are nice people. Evil is caused by ignorance, thoughtlessness, fear, or even the desire for popularity with one's gang. We can cure many such causes of evil. Science is progressing, and I feel hope that psychology can solve many of these problems. I think that a good part of evil behavior bears on the behavior of the normal.

PT: How will you approach the study of evil?

Maslow: If you think only of evil, then you become pessimistic and hopeless like Freud. But if you think there is no evil, then you're just one more deluded Pollyanna. The thing is to try to understand and realize how it's possible for people who are capable of being angels, heroes, or saints to be bastards and killers. Sometimes, poor and miserable people are hopeless. Many revenge themselves upon life for what society has done to them. They enjoy hurting.

PT: Your study of evil will have to be subjective, won't it? How can we measure evil in the laboratory?

Maslow: All the goals of objectivity, repeatability, and preplanned experimentation are things we have to move toward. The more reliable you make knowledge, the better it is. If the salvation of man comes out of the advancement of knowledge—taken in the best sense—then these goals are part of the strategy of knowledge.

PT: What did you tell your own daughters, Ann and Ellen, when they were growing up?

Maslow: Learn to hate meanness. Watch out for anybody who is mean or cruel. Watch out for people who delight in destruction.

PT: How would you describe yourself? Not in personality, because you're one of the warmest and sweetest men I've ever met. But who are you?

Maslow: I'm someone who likes plowing new ground, then walking away from it. I get bored easily. For me, the big thrill comes with the discovering.

PT: Psychologists all love Abe Maslow. How did you escape the crossfire?

Maslow: I just avoid most academic warfare. Besides, I had my first heart attack many years ago, and perhaps I've been unconsciously favoring my body. So I may have avoided real struggle. Besides, I only like fights I know I can win, and I'm not personally mean.

PT: Maybe you're just one of the lucky few who grew up through a happy childhood without malice.

Maslow: With my childhood, it's a wonder I'm not psychotic. I was the little Jewish boy in the non-Jewish neighborhood. It was a little like being the first Negro enrolled in the all-white school. I grew up in libraries and among books, without friends.

Both my mother and father were uneducated. My father wanted me to be a lawyer. He thumbed his way across the whole continent of Europe from Russia and got here at the age of 15. He wanted success for me. I tried law school for two weeks. Then I came home to my poor father one night after a class discussing "spite fences" and told him I couldn't be a lawyer. "Well, son," he said, "what do you want to study?" I answered: "Everything." He was uneducated and couldn't understand my passion for learning, but he was a nice man. He didn't understand either that at 16, I was in love.

PT: All 16-year-olds are in love.

Maslow: Mine was different. We're talking about my wife. I loved Bertha. You know her. Wasn't I right? I was extremely shy, and I tagged around after her. We were too young to get married. I tried to run away with her.

PT: Where did you run?

Maslow: I ran to Cornell for my sophomore year in college, then to Wisconsin. We were married there when I was 20 and Bertha was 19. Life didn't really start for me until I got married.

I went to Wisconsin because I had just discovered John B. Watson's work, and I was sold on behaviorism. It was an explosion of excitement for me. Bertha came to pick me up at New York's 42nd Street library, and I was dancing down Fifth Avenue with exuberance. I embarrassed her, but I was so excited about

Watson's behaviorist program. It was beautiful. I was confident that here was a real road to travel: solving one problem after another and changing the world.

PT: A clear lifetime with built-in progress guaranteed.

Maslow: That was it. I was off to Wisconsin to change the world. I went there to study with psychologist Kurt Koffka, biologist Hans Dreisch, and philosopher Alexander Meiklejohn. But when I showed up on the campus, they weren't there. They had just been visiting professors, but the lying catalog had included them anyway.

Oh, but I was so lucky, though. I was young Harry Harlow's first doctoral graduate. And they were angels, my professors. I've always had angels around. They helped me when I needed it, even fed me. Bill Sheldon taught me how to buy a suit. I didn't know anything of amenities. Clark Hull was an angel to me, and later, Edward L. Thorndike.

PT: You're an angelic man. I've heard too many stories to let you deny it. What kind of research were you doing at Wisconsin?

Maslow: I was a monkey man. By studying monkeys for my doctoral dissertation, I found that dominance was related to sex, and to maleness. It was a great discovery, but somebody had discovered it two months before me.

PT: Great ideas always go in different places and minds at the same time.

Maslow: Yes, I worked on it until the start of World War II. I thought that working on sex was the easiest way to help mankind. I felt if I could discover a way to improve the sexual life by even one percent, then I could improve the whole species.

One day, it suddenly dawned on me that I knew as much about sex as any man living—in the intellectual sense. I knew everything that had been written; I had made discoveries with which I was pleased; I had done therapeutic work. This was about 10 years before the Kinsey report came out. Then I suddenly burst into laughter. Here was I, the great sexologist, and I had never seen an erect penis except one, and that was from my own bird's-eye view. That humbled me considerably.

PT: I suppose you interviewed people the way Kinsey did?

Maslow: No, something was wrong with Kinsey. I really don't think he liked women, or men. In my research, I interviewed 120 women with a new form of interview. No notes. We just talked until I got some feeling for the individual's personality, then put sex against that background. Sex has to be considered in regard to love, otherwise it's useless. This is because behavior can be a defense—a way of hiding what you feel—particularly regarding sex.

I was fascinated with my research. But I gave up interviewing men. They were useless because they boasted and lied about sex. I also planned a big research project involving prostitutes. I thought we could learn a lot about men from them, but the research never came off.

PT: You gave up all your experimental research in these fields.

Maslow: Yes, around 1941 I felt I must try to save the world, and to prevent the horrible wars and the awful hatred and prejudice. It happened very suddenly. One day just after Pearl Harbor, I was driving home and my car was stopped by a poor, pathetic parade. Boy Scouts and old uniforms and a flag and someone playing a flute off-key.

As I watched, the tears began to run down my face. I felt we didn't understand—not Hitler, nor the Germans, nor Stalin, nor the Communists. We didn't understand any of them. I felt that if we could understand, then we could make progress. I had a vision of a peace table, with people sitting around it, talking about human nature and hatred, war and peace, and brotherhood.

I was too old to go into the army. It was at that moment I realized that the rest of my life must be devoted to discovering a psychology for the peace table. That moment changed my whole life. Since then, I've devoted myself to developing a theory of human nature that could be tested by experiment and research. I wanted to prove that humans are capable of something grander than war, prejudice, and hatred. I wanted to make science consider all the people: the best specimen of mankind I could find. I found that many of them reported having something like mystical experiences.

PT: Your work with "self-actualizing" people is famous. You have described some of these mystical experiences.

Maslow: Peak experiences come from love and sex, from aesthetic moments, from bursts of creativity, from moments of insight and discovery, or from fusion with nature.

I had one such experience in a faculty procession here at Brandeis University. I saw the line stretching off into a dim future. At its head was Socrates. And in the line were the ones I love most. Thomas Jefferson was there. And Spinoza. And Alfred North Whitehead. I was in the same line. Behind me, that infinite line melted into the dimness. And there were all the people not yet born who were going to be in the same line.

I believe these experiences can be studied scientifically, and they will be.

PT: This is all part of your theory of metamotivation, isn't it?

Maslow: But not all people who are metamotivated report peak experiences. The "nonpeakers" are healthy, but they lack poetry and soaring flights of the imagination. Both peakers and nonpeakers can be self-actualized in that they're not motivated by basic needs, but by something higher.

PT: Real self-actualization must be rare. What percentage of us achieve it?

Maslow: I'd say only a fraction of one percent.

PT: People whose basic needs have been met, then, will pursue life's ultimate values?

Maslow: Yes, the ultimate happiness for man is the realization of pure beauty and truth, which are the ultimate values. What we need is a system of thought—you might even call it a religion—that can bind humans together. A system that would fit the Republic of Chad as well as the United States: a system that would supply our idealistic young people with something to believe in. They're searching for something they can pour all that emotion into, and the churches are not much help.

PT: This system must come.

Maslow: I'm not alone in trying to make it. There are plenty of others working toward the same end. Perhaps their efforts, aided by the hundreds of youngsters who are devoting their lives to this, will develop a new image of man that rejects the chemical and technological views. We've technologized everything.

PT: The technologist is the person who has fallen in love with a machine. I suppose that has also happened to those in psychology?

Maslow: They become fascinated with the machine. It's almost a neurotic love. They're like the man who spends Sundays polishing his car instead of stroking his wife.

PT: In several of your papers, you've said that you stopped being a behaviorist when your first child was born.

Maslow: My whole training at Wisconsin was behaviorist. I didn't question it until I began reading some other sources. Later, I began studying the Rorschach test.

At the same time, I stumbled into embryology and read Ludwig von Bertalanffy's *Modern Theories of Development*. I had already become disillusioned with Bertrand Russell and with English philosophy generally. Then, I fell in love with Alfred North Whitehead and Henri Bergson. Their writings destroyed behaviorism for me without my recognizing it.

When my first baby was born, that was the thunderclap that settled things. I looked at this tiny, mysterious thing and felt so stupid. I felt small, weak, and feeble. I'd say that anyone who's had a baby couldn't be a behaviorist.

PT: As you propose new ideas, and blaze new ground, you're bound to be criticized, aren't you?

Maslow: I have worked out a lot of good tricks for fending off professional attacks. We all have to do that. A good, controlled experiment is possible only when you already know a hell of a lot. If I'm a pioneer by choice and I go into the wilderness, how am I going to make careful experiments? If I tried to, I'd be a fool. I'm not against careful experiments. But rather, I've been working with what I call "growing tip" statistics.

With a tree, all the growth takes place at the growing tips. Humanity is exactly the same. All the growth takes place in the growing tip: among that one percent of the population. It's made up of pioneers, the beginners. That's where the action is.

PT: You were the one who helped publish Ruth Benedict's work on synergy. What's it about?

Maslow: That it's possible to set up social institutions that merge selfishness and unselfishness, so that you can't benefit yourself without benefiting others. And the reverse.

PT: How can psychology become a stronger force in our society?

Maslow: We all should look at the similarities within the various disciplines and think of enlarging psychology. To throw anything away is crazy. Good psychology should include all the methodological techniques, without having loyalty to one method, one idea, or one person.

PT: I see you as a catalyst and as a bridge between many disciplines, theories, and philosophies.

Maslow: My job is to put them all together. We shouldn't have "humanistic psychology." The adjective should be unnecessary. I'm not antibehaviorist. I'm antidoctrinaire.

PT: Abe, when you look back on your own education, what kind would you recommend for others?

Maslow: The great educational experiences of my life were those that taught me most. They taught me what kind of a person I was. These were experiences that drew me out and strengthened me. Psychoanalysis was a big thing for me. And getting married. Marriage is a school itself. Also, having children. Becoming a father changed my whole life. It taught me as if by revelation. And reading particular books. William Graham Sumner's *Folkways* was a Mount Everest in my life: It changed me.

My teachers were the best in the world. I sought them out: Erich Fromm, Karen Horney, Ruth Benedict, Max Wertheimer, Alfred Adler, David Levy, and Harry Harlow. I was there in New York City during the 1930s when the wave of distinguished émigrés arrived from Europe.

PT: Not everyone can have such an illustrious faculty.

Maslow: It's the teacher who's important. And if this is so, then what we are doing with our whole educational structure—with credits and the idea that one teacher is as good as another? You look at the college catalog and it says English 342. It doesn't even bother to tell you the instructor's name, and that's insane. The purpose of education—and of all social institutions—is the development of full humaneness. If you keep that in mind, all else follows. We've got to concentrate on goals.

PT: It's like the story about the test pilot who radioed back home: "I'm lost, but I'm making record time."

Maslow: If you forget the goal of education, then the whole thing is lost.

PT: If a rare, self-actualizing young psychologist came to you today and said, "What's the most important thing I can do in this time of crisis?", what advice would you give?

Maslow: I'd say: Get to work on aggression and hostility. We need the definitive book on aggression. And we need it now. Only the pieces exist: the animal stuff, the psychoanalytic stuff, the endocrine stuff. Time is running out. A key to understanding the evil which can destroy our society lies in this understanding.

There's another study that could be done. I'd like to test the whole, incoming freshman class at Brandeis University in various ways: psychiatric interviews, personality tests, everything. I want to follow them for four years of college. For a beginning, I want to test my theory that emotionally healthy people perceive better.

PT: You could make the college study only a preliminary, and follow them through their whole life span, the way Lewis Terman did with his gifted kids.

Maslow: Oh yes! I'd like to know: How good a father or mother does this student become? And what happens to his/her children? This kind of long-term study would take more time than I have left. But that ultimately doesn't make any difference. I like to be the first runner in the relay race. I like to pass on the baton to the next person.

Hey, I'm Terrific!

The latest national elixir—self-esteem—is supposed to cure everything from poor grades to bad management. Instead, it gives feeling good a bad name.

If you're like most Americans, chances are you never thought you were at risk for low self-esteem. Sure, you felt bad at your kids' school's Career Day when you were the only parent who didn't own his own company. But unless your family psychometrician has administered a Coopersmith Self-Esteem Inventory or the Kaplan Self-Derogation Scale you probably never imagined that a negative self-image might be holding you back in life. You just thought you were no good.

But now you know that there are no bad people, only people who think badly of themselves. You know that "if you really joyfully accept yourself . . . nothing can make you unhappy," in the words of Father John Powell, a specialist in "psychotheology" at Loyola University of Chicago. You know that even famous, successful people like writer Gloria Steinem ("Revolution From Within: A Book of Self-Esteem") have to battle "inner feelings of incompleteness, emptiness, self-doubt and self-hatred." Negative thoughts afflict even paragons of achievement like athlete Michael Jordan, author of this poignant confession in the "self-esteem corner" of the Children's Museum of Denver: "I wish I came in first more often." Ordinary people obviously wish the same thing for themselves. Although only one in 10 Americans believes he personally suffers from low self-esteem, according to a NEWSWEEK Gallup Poll, more than 50 percent diagnose the condition in someone else in their families. And, of course, deviant behavior is prima facie evidence of self-image problems, as in the case of a man being sought in Montgomery County, Md., for a series of rapes. Citizens have been warned by police to be on the lookout for a man in his 30s with a medium build and "low self-esteem."

As a concept, self-esteem can be traced to Freud, who used the term ego ideal. Shame, the emotional expression of low self-esteem, has been a hot topic among therapists in recent years, and is the subject of a new book ("Shame: The Exposed Self") by a prominent developmental psychologist, Michael Lewis. But as a paradigm for analyzing almost every problem in American society, self-esteem is clearly a product of today's relentless search for ever more fundamental and unifying laws of nature. Self-esteem is the quark of social science, a way to make sense of the wildly proliferating addictions, dependencies and 12-step programs jostling for air time on "Donahue." Low self-esteem is a meta-addiction, a state that seems to underlie afflictions as diverse as bulimia and performance anxiety. "People saw that self-esteem was a component of so many other things—teenage pregnancies, dropouts, drugs, school success—and they were hoping we'd found one solution to many problems," says psychoanalyst Nancy E. Curry of the University of Pittsburgh. People always hope that; it's what keeps publishers going, not to speak of religions.

As the distinction between therapy and the rest of American life has eroded, the concept of self-esteem has established itself in almost every area of society. The bulletin of The National Council for Self-Esteem, Self-Esteem Today, lists 10 national and regional conferences this year aimed at extirpating negative self-images from society. Most people, thanks to "Doonesbury," know that California appointed a state commission to promote self-esteem. But the idea is also very big in places like Minnesota (home of the "Very Important Kid" program for "encouraging self-esteem in 3–6 year olds") and in Maryland, where a state task force counted more than 1,000 ways in which citizens were already working to improve the self-esteem of their fellow students, government workers, business executives and cellmates. An outfit called High Self-Esteem Toys Corp. has brought out a fashion doll named Happy To Be Me, whose scale measurements of 36-27-38 are intended to represent a more realistic ambition for a human being than Barbie's exotic mannequin's figure, with its 18-inch waist and 33-inch hips.

Churches have discovered that "low self-esteem" is a less off-putting phrase to congregants than "sin." When Peewee Herman was arrested last year, Jesuit scholar William O'Malley partially exonerated him with the observation that "masturbation isn't the problem, it's lack of self-esteem." (Going further, a Presbyterian Church committee on "human sexuality" last year actually recommended masturbation in cases of severe self-image deficiency. Its example was a man confined to a wheelchair who gains "self-esteem" from the use of an electric vibrator. The committee's report was rejected.)

Businesses have begun to realize that improving employees' self-esteem, usually known in this context as "empowerment," can be a more effective motivator than expensive, old-fashioned "raises." "Self-esteem is a basic building block on which personal effectiveness is based," says management-training consultant Dave Ehlen, head of Wilson Learning Corp. America's corporate managers—the same group whose excessive salaries are elsewhere regarded as a national scandal—have to be made to "believe in themselves . . . to feel good about what they are and where they are going." How does this work in practice? Nancy Stephan, a Minneapolis consultant, was called in to help a medium-size company suffering from a communication problem: the president was yelling at his subordinates. She diagnosed this as a lack of executive self-esteem. By teaching him to "talk to people in a caring way," the company's problem was solved! "Relationships have improved tremendously," Stephan says. They're not actually making any more money, "but they're communicating on a whole different level."

Nowhere has the concept taken root as firmly as in education. Toddlers are encouraged to "reach their full potential" in self-esteem day-care centers. High-school drug and alcohol programs now emphasize self-esteem, on the theory, according to New Hampshire school administrator James Weiss, that "if youngsters feel good about themselves, those temptations won't be so strong." Of course, there are still some kinks to work out. Pamela Smart, the New Hampshire schoolteacher convicted of having her husband murdered, met her teenage lover at a "Project Self-Esteem" workshop in Winnacunnet High School.

The San Diego city school system voted last year to abolish failing grades, a move that was widely misconstrued as an effort to legislate failure itself out of existence. That was not precisely the intention; under the proposal, a student who didn't complete the work would have to repeat the course, but only the subsequent passing grade would show on his record. Nevertheless an outraged public rescued the "F" before the plan could take effect. In any case, it's not clear why anyone believes that too many failing grades are the problem in American schools. Psychologist Harold Stevenson of the University of Michigan found that American schoolchildren rank far ahead of students in Japan, Taiwan and China in self-confidence about their abilities in math. Unfortunately, this achievement was marred by the fact that Americans were far behind in *actual performance* in math. Japanese parents "don't lavish praise on their children—they're concerned they will end up thinking too much about themselves, and not enough about the group," says Lewis. The difference between the cultures "is that the Japanese are trying to be proud, and we're trying to be happy." A new comparison of math and science achievement by schoolchildren in 20 countries, released last week, also showed Americans ranking near the bottom.

As a theory of behavior, self-esteem has intuition on its side, if not necessarily a monopoly on convincing research. It seems to make sense that people who have a low opinion of themselves are more likely to seek momentary pleasures in drugs or sex. Many criminologists believe that delinquency results from youth with low self-esteem trying to show off—a "performance for an audience," in the words of Martin Gold of the University of Michigan's Institute for Social Research. Inevitably, the evidence for this tends to be somewhat anecdotal. The best anecdote is Lewis's account of adolescent boys in a reform school who would punch the offender in the face when one of them passed gas. But does it necessarily follow that "people with low self-esteem confuse being in the presence of someone who farts with the different situation of actually being farted upon"? And what should the nation do about it, anyway?

As a general prescription for child-rearing, self-esteem is unassailable. To develop it, says child psychiatrist Dr. Stanley Greenspan, children need "a constant and loving caregiver . . . a fundamental sense of safety and security." Who could be against that? "A sense of self, grounded in a sense of personal competence and supported by people who think I am a valuable and worthy person, is a requisite for productive learning to occur," says Linda Darling-Hammond, a professor of education at Columbia Teachers College. That also seems intuitively obvious to most Americans today—although 70 years ago it was equally obvious to many educators that schools had to break down children's "sense of self," the better to fill their heads with facts.

But what is it? Like most things that are intuitively obvious, though, self-esteem can be hard to demonstrate empirically. A recent survey of the literature estimated that more than 10,000 scientific studies of self-esteem have been conducted. Researchers have measured it with more than 200 different tests. (Typically, respondents are asked to agree or disagree with statements such as, "On the whole, I am satisfied with myself.") There isn't even agreement on what it is. Greenspan defines it, tautologically enough, as "the innermost sense of self-worth and value." "I think of it as related to three things: confidence, competence and relationships," says Rutgers University psychologist Maurice Elias, clarifying matters only somewhat. Even the National Council has been unable to agree on a single definition, according to executive director LeRoy Foster, after polling 100 teachers and coming up with "27 distinctly different answers."

The programs aimed at cultivating self-esteem also have a fairly homegrown air about them. "There's a huge self-esteem industry out there, and a lot of it is nonsense," says Lillian Katz, president-elect of the National Association for the Education of Young Children. Everyone gives lip service to the notion that self-esteem must arise from within, from a genuine sense of achievement and worth. But the actual impact of the self-esteem movement has been an explosion of awards, gold stars and happy-face stickers for the most routine accomplishments of childhood. Most children's sports teams now automatically give trophies just for showing up, with the result that the average 12-year-old's bedroom is as cluttered with honors as Bob Hope's den. In Woodland Hills, Calif., the Halsey Schools (nursery through grade 3) holds an awards ceremony *every six weeks*. Each child who enters the Denver Children's Museum is directed to the "self-esteem corner," handed a paper flag and a supply of positive adjectives to trace and stamp on it. The adjectives are supposed to spell out the child's name, so if she happens to be, say, Phyllis, she can anoint herself Patient or Perky, but not Awesome.

A nation of flatterers: And what if Phyllis happens to be Pompous, or just a Pill? There is no self-criticism corner; the museum's goal according to promotion director Leslie McKay is for children to leave "feeling good about themselves." If children are actually fooled by this stuff, the country is in worse shape than anyone imagined. Katz, who is also a professor of education at the University of Illinois, holds to the old-fashioned notion that self-esteem must follow, not precede, real accomplishment. "I'm getting so sick of these empty slogans," she says, citing an example of an Illinois school decked out with a giant banner reading: WE APPLAUD OURSELVES. "Schools have established award structures—the happy helper of the week, the reader of the week. Teachers think that if they don't do this stuff, the kids won't do the work, but that's ridiculous. We don't need all this flattery. No other country does this."

This is not a prescription for never saying anything nice to children. Children do need encouragement; the problem is that like so much else in life, it is distributed inequitably. "Praise has to be connected with values, with the development of character," says Curry. "Kids need authentic feedback, not praise for walking across the room without falling over." "Too many teachers forget to give children credit for the things they did right, rather than focusing on X-ing what they did wrong," says Darling-Hammond. "We should be remedying that—rather than encouraging Yuppies to be more obnoxious with their kids."

But who wants to be bothered waiting for a child to do something right, when it's so much simpler just to praise him all the time? The Self-Esteem movement hunts down negative thoughts with a holy zeal, a single-minded dedication to knocking some self-esteem into these kids' heads. "101 Ways to Make Your Child Feel Special," by well-known parenting authority Vicki Lansky, recommends that you "tell your child how nice he or she looks . . . even if plaid pants are being worn with a striped shirt!" Do parents really have to suspend judgment to that degree? She also recommends blowing up your child's photo to poster size and hanging it in his room, just the thing if you want to raise a kid with the ego of a rock star. In a pamphlet called "Celebrate Yourself," the Corporation for Public Broadcasting points out that even "handsome 6-foot 1-inch actor Kevin Costner" sometimes criticizes himself: "I wish I were smart . . . more disciplined . . . and better read." If Harold Bloom said this, he would have a self-esteem problem. But a movie star? Isn't Costner just expressing an honest criticism and setting a laudable goal for improvement? Evidently not; this is dismaying evidence that "all of us—even very successful people—put ourselves down."

Self-esteem is a common prescription for African-American youth, who bear the particular burden of a heritage of racial prejudice. "The decks are really stacked against some minorities," says Dr. Alan Stoudemire, a psychiatrist at the Emory Clinic in Atlanta. "They receive powerful messages from family or teachers or society that they are not as good as everyone else." In the absence of real solutions to this problem, slogans and exhortations are being tried instead. Jesse Jackson's famous chant distills the philosophy of self-esteem to its minimalist essence: "I am . . . Somebody!" Others are a trifle more specific. When Jacqueline Ponder, the principal of Atlanta's East Lake Elementary School, noticed that the boys in her classrooms were neglecting to carry books and hold doors for their teachers, she diagnosed the problem as low self-esteem and prescribed a motto: "I Am a Noble African-American Boy!" "Once they have their self-esteem," Ponder asserts, "they don't need anything else. They *are*. And all they have to do is develop that which they are."

As far as the case for self-esteem goes, that says it all. It is a matter less of scientific pedagogy than of faith—faith that positive thoughts can make manifest the inherent goodness in anyone, even 10-year-old boys. Americans are notoriously partial to this brand of naive optimism. As long ago as the 1920s, the French therapist Emile Coué wowed this nation with his formula for self-improvement, based on daily repetitions of the mantra "Every day in every way I am getting better and better." Norman Vincent Peale gave self-esteem (or "positive thinking") a religious dimension. His accounts of industrialists, golf pros and similar role models triumphing over adversity through faith sold millions of books in the 1950s. In the 1980s, the concept got its fullest expression from California television preacher Robert H. Schuller. From the pulpit of the Crystal Cathedral, Schuller preaches an explicit gospel of self-esteem, which he defines as "the human hunger for the divine dignity that God intended to be our emotional birthright. People who do not love themselves," Schuller asserts, "can't believe in God."

"Like a lot of other words, self-esteem is sort of 'religiously correct' today," agrees Father John E. Forliti, vice president of the University of Saint Thomas in Minnesota. The notion may put off anyone old enough to remember when "Christian" as an adjective was often followed by "humility." But American churches, which once did not shrink from calling their congregants wretches, have moved toward a more congenial view of human nature. The Roman Catholic parish of St. Joan of Arc in Minneapolis is packed every Sunday in part because it won't turn anyone away, including homosexuals and divorced Catholics remarried outside the church. "There's no sense that you broke some law or rule and that you're not good enough," says parish administrator Peter Eichten. In Warren, Mich., the nondenominational Church of Today preaches a doctrine of "empowerment," based on the belief that "the great sin is not the things that people typically see as sins, it's not living up to their own potential." At first glance this seems like a terrific deal for people who *like* doing "the things that people typically see as sins." But self-esteem has a catch to it: like "grace," if you're living an immoral life, by definition you don't have it. The point is not to abolish ethical distinctions. Wrong actions hurt oneself or others, and no one with real self-esteem would do anything like that. That's why chastising sinners is considered counterproductive: it makes them feel worse about themselves.

The man most responsible for putting self-esteem on the national agenda is not a clergyman or philosopher, but a California state assemblyman named John Vasconcellos, Democrat from San Jose. In his own life Vasconcellos, 59, is a walking advertisement for the importance of self-esteem. He was raised by strict, attentive parents who set high standards for him. This is one of the biggest risk factors for self-esteem problems, next to lax, indifferent parents who don't demand enough. He was college valedictorian, a successful lawyer and politician. Overachievement is a very common sign of low self-esteem, next to underachievement. Yet he was also a troubled legislator, going for three years without cutting his hair and engaging in hostile outbursts against colleagues. Self-esteem problems often contribute to aggression, except when they result in passivity.

The big picture: Psychotherapy helped Vasconcellos correct his own self-esteem shortfall. Then one day in 1983 he stumbled on a theory linking teen pregnancy with low self-esteem. "All of a sudden, the

America Seems to Feel Good About Self-Esteem

How important are the following in motivating a person to work hard and succeed? (percent saying "very important")

89%	Self-esteem / the way people feel about themselves
77%	Family duty or honor
49%	Responsibility to community
44%	Fear of failure
35%	Status in the eyes of others

Is too much time and effort spent on self-esteem?

63%	Time and effort spent is worthwhile
34%	Time and effort could be better spent on work

Who would you say has low self-esteem?

	TOTAL	18 to 29 years old	30 to 49 years old	50 or more years old
Me, personally	**10%**	**7%**	**8%**	**15%**
Spouse	**8%**	**8%**	**7%**	**9%**
Child	**13%**	**3%**	**17%**	**15%**
Other relative	**33%**	**30%**	**46%**	**21%**

Do you think never giving F's in school to maintain self-esteem and eagerness to learn is a . . .

68% Bad idea | **26%** Good idea

Which situations would make you feel very bad about yourself?

	18 to 29 years old	30 to 49 years old	50 or more years old
Not being able to pay your bills	**51%**	**57%**	**80%**
Being tempted into doing something immoral	**48%**	**57%**	**77%**
Having an abortion (if male, your wife or girlfriend having an abortion*)	**60%**	**56%**	**69%**
Getting a divorce	**57%**	**52%**	**73%**
Losing your job	**50%**	**53%**	**65%**
Feeling you had disobeyed God	**47%**	**49%**	**71%**
Being noticeably overweight	**39%**	**29%**	**42%**
Doing something embarrassing in public	**26%**	**25%**	**50%**
Being criticized by someone you admire	**19%**	**19%**	**39%**

*Total saying "yes" includes 67% of women, 55% of men. In a differently worded question 10 years ago, 66% of women but only 36% of men said having an abortion would make them feel very bad.

For this NEWSWEEK Poll, The Gallup Organization interviewed 612 adults by telephone Jan. 15-16. The margin of error is plus or minus 5 percentage points. Some "Don't know" and other responses not shown.

pattern just loomed large," Vasconcellos said. "Maybe violence, drug addiction, crime and other problems were also a product of the same thing."

Eager to share this insight, Vasconcellos helped create a state task force on "self-esteem and personal and social responsibility." Its conclusion—that "lack of self-esteem is central to most personal and social ills plaguing our state and nation"—has inspired five states and nearly all 58 California counties to set up self-esteem task forces. Several groups are urging national legislation. This is a remarkable instance of adopting as a goal of public policy something that is quintessentially private and introspective. It is one thing for the state to discourage welfare dependency, for instance, by requiring recipients to get jobs. It is a big—and thus far unexamined—step for the state to try to do the same thing by tinkering directly with citizens' psyches.

And if it does, it ought at least to be sure it knows what it's doing. Most of what people believe about the public-policy implications of self-esteem come from the task-force report, "Toward a State of Esteem." The report's "key finding" was that "self-esteem is the likeliest candidate for a *social vaccine* [emphasis in original], something that empowers us to live responsibly and that inoculates us against the lures of crime, violence, substance abuse, teen pregnancy, child abuse, chronic welfare dependency and educational failure."

A lot less attention has been paid to the scientific papers prepared for the task force, which were published separately as "The Social Importance of Self-Esteem." Can self-esteem cut drug abuse? The scientists concluded that "there is a paucity of good research, especially studies that could link the abuse of alcohol and drugs with self-esteem." Is it implicated in child abuse? "There is insufficient evidence to support the belief in a direct relation between low self-esteem and child abuse." Crime and violence? "Self-esteem may be positively *or* negatively correlated with aggression." Teen pregnancy? Somewhat embarrassingly, two studies linked *high* self-esteem with increased sexual activity by teens. But there was evidence that girls with high self-esteem were more likely to use contraceptives. Admitting the findings were inconclusive, the authors went on to write that "our approach is to make the strongest case possible, given the research, for the existence of a causal link between self-esteem and teenage pregnancy. We conclude, therefore, that low self-esteem does contribute to the risk of an adolescent pregnancy."

That does seem a remarkable admission in an academic paper, and at least one of the task-force members refused to sign the final report in part because of the gap between the research results and the report's sweeping conclusions. Vasconcellos regards this as pettifoggery. Such criticism comes from "those who only live in their heads, in the intellectual." The research, he says, did what it was supposed to do; it "confirms our intuitive knowledge."

So why be a pedant? How much better it is to think positive thoughts. If you don't have any, the Public Broadcasting pamphlet can supply some, including a list of eight body parts (arms, nose, teeth . . .) and 22 attributes (funny, mature, awesome . . .) it's possible to feel good about. Think of the Halsey Schools, where the word "bad" is never spoken, where everyone gets an award every year, where kindergarten children learn to count by being handed pictures of objects and *told how many there are instead of figuring it out themselves.* Ask yourself: wouldn't it be nice if life were really like this?

And what's going to happen to those kids when they find out it's not?

JERRY ADLER *with* PAT WINGERT *in Washington,* LYNDA WRIGHT *in Los Angeles,* PATRICK HOUSTON *in Minneapolis,* HOWARD MANLY *in Atlanta,* ALDEN D. COHEN *in New York and bureau reports*

SELF-ESTEEM: THE KEYSTONE TO HAPPINESS

"There are few experiences in life that equal the wonderful feelings of self-satisfaction."

Ralph Hyatt

Dr. Hyatt, Psychology Editor of USA Today, *is professor emeritus of psychology, Saint Joseph's University, Philadelphia, Pa.*

UNDERSTANDING the human personality is fascinating, but difficult. Not only are there hundreds of personal characteristics to consider as they interplay with one another, but the creativity and stamina of researchers truly are tested in their attempts to study them scientifically. Just when one seems securely tied down, it slips and slides away. Yet, there's no doubt about its existence.

Self-esteem is one of those esoteric personality variables. Simply, it refers to the general value you place on who you are. When you don't like yourself very much, esteem is low. You hunch your back, you see the world as overwhelming, there's a tendency to grovel, and you're sensitive. With high esteem, your back is straight, you walk briskly, speech is confident, nothing seems too much, and negatives roll off your back.

How does your self-esteem measure up? The following selected thoughts, feelings, and behaviors, if they tend to recur, may hint at your esteem sensitivities:

- Choosing to sit in the last row of a classroom.
- Blaming yourself for almost everything.
- Self-consciousness when approaching a group of peers.
- Embarrassment at dressing improperly.
- Not sharing an idea in a group for fear of saying something stupid.
- Inner panic at being called upon at a meeting.
- Believing that you constantly are being taken advantage of by others.
- Feeling wimpy when someone quickly pulls into *your* parking space.
- Wondering why you frequently are misunderstood by friends.
- Being turned on by flashy clothing, jewelry, automobiles, and/or home furnishings.
- Bragging about your activities, successes, children, etc.
- Loudly expressing your ideas, attracting attention in crowds.
- Feeling ill after being told that you don't look well.

Those with adequate esteem ordinarily select any classroom seat that is comfortable, do not fret about their party dress the morning after, enjoy sharing ideas with a group, and feel sufficiently comfortable with themselves so as not to overreact to the statements and actions of others, especially strangers.

Self-esteem runs on a continuum from low to high. There are days and occasions when you'll feel a loss of confidence and somewhat insecure. Overwork, fatigue, failures, and tension tend to lower esteem. In the main, however, what you think of yourself is fairly constant. It influences how you act and react. Even though others may not use the term esteem—they may call you moody, sensitive, boisterous, or shy—it affects how you are perceived and accepted by family and friends.

Given the perennial popularity of self-help books, one easily could conclude that the esteem deficit outruns, by far, America's combined budget and trade deficits. Werner Erhardt, the wizard of EST, convinced us in the 1970's that our esteem needed a thorough overhaul. Now, he transmits the same message to baby-boomers. He probably can prove his thesis most convincingly by pointing to the vast numbers who flock to his seminars.

John Vasconcellos, a California legislator, attributes crime, drug abuse, and adolescent pregnancy to low self-esteem. He and a task force he formed recommend that teachers and welfare workers receive training in self-esteem to combat these and other social problems. Interestingly, Vasconcellos became a believer only after personally experiencing a variety of psychotherapeutic approaches, including encounter groups and individual counseling. His present level of self-esteem is great. What's good for him, he holds, should be of value to others.

There are those who differ, however. Journalist Charles Krauthammer, in an essay in *Time* magazine (Feb. 5, 1990), decries that American 13-year-olds, compared to similarly aged youth in Korea, Spain, Britain, Ireland, and Canada, came in last on a standardized math test. The real shocker is that they ranked *first* in their self-estimates—that is, how proficient they believe they are in mathematics. They feel good even about things they don't know. In other words, they have learned esteem, but not basic math! Krauthammer concludes: "The pursuit of good feeling in education is a dead end. The way to true self-esteem is through real achievement and real learning."

Labels and tattoos

From birth onward, perhaps even prenatally, self-esteem is influenced by events around you. Parents often glibly "train" their children by calling them weird, odd, stupid, or clumsy. Being "good" or "bad" easily is inculcated. Verbal and non-verbal messages are "stamped in." When labels stick, they become tattoos. These are the basic rules for labels and tattoos:

- Labels can be positive or negative.
- The younger you are when labeled, the stronger the imprint.
- The more powerful the imprint, the greater the holding power.
- The more you are given the same label, the stickier it is.
- Parents can label their offspring more effectively than anyone else.
- The larger the number of people giving the same label—siblings, friends, teachers—the greater the stickiness.
- Life experiences—opportunities and stresses, successes and failures—print significant labels, with tattoo potential.

Depending on your health, intelligence, family patterns, physical attractiveness, social experiences, special talents and skills, and school achievement, self-esteem develops from the day you are born. With a reasonable number of pluses in many of these areas, esteem can withstand a fair amount of stress without faltering. With shaky developmental experiences, vulnerability to even minor stressors increase and self-esteem dips.

There are two additional considerations. It's fine to stretch for your goals and expect success. However, if expectations are too lofty, you're flirting with failure. Don't develop goals that are "a piece of cake" or unrealistically high. Establish objectives which you have to reach for, but are achievable.

Second, don't overlook your genetic makeup. You very well may be "built" to be quiet, introverted, and sensitive. Some personality traits associated with vulnerability—shyness, for example—can not be blamed universally on poor parenting skills, a rural background, sibling rivalry, economic deprivation, etc. Inborn temperament may be as influential as learning.

What can you do about it? First, admit that you tend to be highly vulnerable. Then, select stressors carefully whenever you have that luxury. Don't overreach. Make a point of objectively assessing your tender emotions, when they do blossom, giving enough power to the possibilities of hypersensitivity. Unless it is perfectly clear otherwise, give the other person the benefit of the doubt before you attack or shrink away. When similar situations occur in the future, attempt to pre-empt your touchiness by recalling past insights. Finally, evaluate how the behaviors of others may be changing, as you alter your sensitivity reactions to them.

No one is suggesting that it will be easy. After all, you are battling a basic social approach that has been going on and has been reinforced for years. In fact, you may not have been totally aware of the nuances of your behaviors and tender feelings. By taking small steps and not expecting too much of yourself all at once, your self-esteem eventually can be elevated.

The necessary exchanges between a child's biology and the environment bring into clear relief the exquisite skills necessary for parenting. No wonder that the "wisdom of Solomon" often is required. Self-esteem frequently is made or broken by parental interventions. Here are some tips:

Raise your child in an atmosphere of acceptance. However, not everything he or she does should be considered "correct" or "good." Differentiate between the behavior and the child. Psychologist Carl Rogers coined the term "unconditional positive regard." He urged that we do not place conditions of worth on the child ("If you do this, I will not love you"). Confidence in your love usually equips your child with the strength and insights to understand why you can not accept some of his or her behaviors.

Give your children enough room to think for themselves. Allow your offspring opportunities for learning how to solve problems independently, barring a potential catastrophe. Afterwards, a calm, respectful conversation about the problem-solving process could be meaningful as you encourage another try, perhaps an alternate approach.

When necessary, be clear and firm about the rules. Children must be prohibited from injuring themselves or others. They must learn to eat, sleep, and do other things on time. There are occasions when a crisp command is required. Be sure, however, to explain the reasons for the rules and/or the limitations on their behavior. Children thrive on reasonable structure in their lives. When you correct them, describe more efficient ways of acting.

No matter how exasperated you become, do not belittle your children or label them negatively. Parents are not saints. There are times when we lose our cool. Explain to the child why you are annoyed. Step away a bit, cool off, then, together, formulate a constructive plan for dealing with the problem. Try not to yell—that places you in a weaker psychological position with the child. It also teaches him or her an ineffective way of dealing with annoyances. Yelling erodes esteem for both of you.

Don't forget to reinforce good things positively. We sometimes become so intense about teaching youngsters not to do wrong that we overlook the multiple occasions when they perform well. These are not necessarily restricted to academic achievements or exceptional accomplishments. They can include such everyday nice things as constructing an airplane model, playing cooperatively with friends, sitting quietly and enjoying television, interacting positively with a sibling, etc. Hug and kiss them, state how much you love them, and share your pride in them.

There are few experiences in life that equal the wonderful feelings of self-satisfaction. Genuine satisfaction can be derived only by meeting reasonable standards we have set for ourselves. As children, good feelings about self are largely a result of healthy home relationships. As adults, a positive self-image depends more on living consistently with our fundamental values and beliefs. A context of love helps considerably at all developmental levels.

Abraham Maslow, the noted humanistic psychologist, considered self-esteem as a core psychological need for humans—not a want, but a necessity, like food and oxygen. One might add that self-esteem is the keystone of happiness.

Oedipus Wrecked

Freud's theory of frustrated incest goes on the defensive

BRUCE BOWER

Poor Oedipus Rex. Twice he has achieved royal status, only to have the red carpet rudely pulled out from under him. First, as described in a play written by the 5th century B.C. Greek dramatist Sophocles, Oedipus triumphantly ascended to the throne of ancient Thebes. Master of all he surveyed, the new king then hit rock bottom. Upon learning that he had unwittingly killed his father and married his mother, Oedipus gouged out his own eyes.

Much later, Sigmund Freud honored the tragic king by dubbing the central theory of psychoanalysis the Oedipus complex. Freud proposed that all toddlers direct their first sexual longings at the opposite-sex parent and consequently aim their first feelings of intense rivalry toward the same-sex parent. Healthy psychological development requires a resolution and redirection of these urges, the Viennese psychiatrist asserted. Dressed in his Freudian finery, Oedipus strutted into the 20th century and seized the imaginations of psychoanalysts, social scientists, artists, writers and other observers of the human condition.

Now, however, the Oedipus complex shows its own flair for tragedy, as it falls from grace among many of Freud's intellectual progeny and faces empirical challenges from psychologists and other researchers influenced by Charles Darwin's theory of evolution.

"The Oedipus complex clearly has waned in popularity and credibility, both within psychoanalysis and within the culture at large," contends psychiatrist Bennett Simon of Harvard Medical School in Boston. Simon describes psychoanalytic "confusion and disagreement" over the Oedipus complex in the

July-September JOURNAL OF THE AMERICAN PSYCHOANALYTIC ASSOCIATION.

Evolutionary psychologists and anthropologists, who view social behavior as the outgrowth of evolution by natural selection, generally respect Freud's intellectual contributions but consider the Oedipus complex a misguided explanation of conflict between parents and children. Natural selection – the preservation in a species of genetically based traits that best contribute to the survival and reproduction of individuals and their genetic relatives – has produced typical forms of parent-child conflict that have nothing to do with incestuous desires, according to evolutionary investigators.

The Oedipus complex produced unease and dissension among psychoanalysts almost from the start, Simon points out. Freud first laid out the basis of the theory – without mentioning Oedipus by name – in *The Interpretation of Dreams* in 1900. He then elaborated the concept in works such as *Totem and Taboo* (1913), in which he proposed that the little boy's urge to kill his father and mate with his mother stemmed from one or more incidents of actual father murder carried out by Stone Age men. Ancient homicides of fathers by sons – an idea since rejected by anthropologists – ushered in incest taboos, religion and culture, Freud argued.

In perhaps his most controversial Oedipal formulation, Freud described different paths of healthy sexual and moral development for girls and boys. Oedipal urges lead to castration anxieties in boys, who then resolve the dilemma by turning to the father for moral and religious guidance, resulting in a strong "superego," or conscience, he maintained. Freud made no secret of his difficulty in explaining female development, but suggested that girls experience penis envy, which creates anger at the mother and a subsequent turn to the father. Without the intense unconscious push males get from Oedipally derived castration fears, the female superego ends up weaker than that of males, Freud posited.

By the late 1920s, some prominent psychoanalysts questioned the alleged inferiority of the female conscience and downplayed the role assigned to the Oedipal complex. Freud's closest protege, Otto Rank, noted the "anti-Oedipal" tendency displayed by children trying to keep their parents together when divorce loomed, and cautioned against the rigid application of the Oedipus complex to individual patients. One current school of psychoanalytic thought rejects Freud's assertion that the Oedipus complex occurs universally, arguing instead that psychologically disturbed parents sometimes stir up incestuous and intensely competitive feelings in their children.

Other psychoanalysts cast off conflict and sexuality as the prime Oedipal movers and shakers. For instance, psychiatrist E. James Lieberman of George Washington University School of Medicine in Washington, D.C., contends that Sophocles' "Oedipus Rex" emphasizes themes of family love and altruism, not the hostility and fear described by Freud. In the play, Oedipus grew up with adoptive parents whom he dearly loved, and only left them when told of his incestuous and homicidal fate by an oracle, Lieberman observes. At the time of his departure, Oedipus did not know that the oracle's prophecy referred to his biological parents.

"Legal or biological paternity needs a human relationship to give it significance," Lieberman writes in the June HARVARD MENTAL HEALTH LETTER. "Oedipus really loved his [adoptive] father. The moral of the drama is that honest, loving family ties are the best defense against dire prophecy and the greatest security in an uncertain world."

True enough, respond evolutionary theorists, but mounting evidence indicates that even loving parents and their children encounter important conflicts that fall outside the realm of incestuous desire. Two theories guide the evolutionary approach. The first, proposed by Finnish anthropologist Edward Westermarck in 1891, holds that natural selection has endowed humans and other animals with an unconscious mental tendency to avoid inbreeding and its harmful genetic effects on offspring. This mental "adaptation" automatically motivates sexual avoidance among individuals raised together in the same family or group, regardless of the degree to which their genetic backgrounds match, Westermarck argued.

A second model, developed since 1974 by Harvard University sociobiologist Robert L. Trivers and several others, maintains that natural selection has produced children, daughters and sons alike, who generally covet more attention, help and other resources than parents – and mothers in particular – reasonably can offer, especially as additional offspring enter the family. The result: occasional parent-child friction and sibling rivalries even in the most tranquil families.

An analysis of homicides within families fits the Darwinian perspective better than Freud's Oedipal scenario of childhood rivalry with the same-sex parent, report Canadian psychologists Martin Daly and Margo Wilson, both of McMaster University in Hamilton, Ontario, in the March 1990 JOURNAL OF PERSONALITY. Their review of all reported murders of children by their parents and all murders of parents by their children in Canada between 1974 and 1983, and in Chicago between 1965 and 1981, finds no evidence of a same-sex bias in killings of children during the Oedipal phase (ages 2 to 5). Whether the mother or father committed the murder, the proportion of male to female victims remains nearly even. And no evidence of same-sex bias in the physical abuse of young children by mothers versus fathers turns up either, the researchers observe.

At all ages except during the Oedipal years, sons outnumber daughters as murder victims, more often at the hands of their fathers, Daly and Wilson note. Impoverished parents make up the bulk of child murderers, they add.

Adolescent boys display the greatest likelihood of murdering a parent, particularly the father. This trend probably reflects rivalries over the use and control of family property, Daly and Wilson suggest.

Freud collapsed two distinct father-son rivalries into one, the two psychologists conclude: an early conflict over access to the mother that does not involve sexual rivalry, and a later rivalry during adolescence – often seen in nonindustrial, polygynous societies – involving competition for women other than the mother or the control of family wealth.

"The Oedipus complex clearly has waned in popularity and credibility, both within psychoanalysis and within the culture at large"

Freud — and many scholars in his wake — also erred in assuming that all human societies retain explicit taboos against incest within the immediate family, contends anthropologist Nancy W. Thornhill of the University of New Mexico in Albuquerque. Incest rules primarily exist to regulate mating between in-laws and cousins rather than close genetic relatives, who show little interest in incest, Thornhill concludes in the June BEHAVIORAL AND BRAIN SCIENCES.

Thornhill tracked information on mating and marriage rules in the ethnographies of 129 societies — from the 16th-century Incas to the 20th-century Vietnamese — stored at the Human Relations Area Files in New Haven, Conn., a research arm of Yale University. Only 57 of the societies — less than half — specified rules against nuclear family incest, whereas 114 societies designated rules to control mating or marriage with cousins, in-laws or both, Thornhill reports.

Rules regulating mating between in-laws serve as checks on paternity and obstacles to female adultery, mainly in the societies that require a woman to live with her husband and his relatives upon marriage, the New Mexico researcher argues. Only 14 of the ethnographies describe societies that require a man to live with his wife and her relatives upon marriage, and most of those societies either lack rules regarding in-law mating or mete out mild punishments for an infraction of the rules, she adds.

Rulers of stratified societies enforce sanctions against cousin marriage and inbreeding in order to secure their lofty positions by discouraging the concentration of wealth and power within families other than their own, Thornhill notes. In non-stratified societies, with no central rulers and relatively equal distribution of food and other resources, dictums against cousin unions foil the accumulation of wealth in extended families and maintain the level social playing field trod by most men, in her view.

In Thornhill's survey of worldwide societies, the more highly stratified the society, the more kin outside the immediate family fall under inbreeding regulations. However, rulers in stratified societies rarely observe those rules and frequently marry their own relatives — although they may not mate with them — in the quest to consolidate their power, Thornhill points out.

Although increasing reports in the United States and elsewhere of parent-child incest seem to demonstrate strong — indeed, sometimes overpowering — Oedipal urges within the nuclear family, appearances prove deceiving, according to Thornhill. In fact, data on incest cases tend to support Westermarck's theory, she says. For instance, studies in the United States and Canada find that step-fathers, not genetic fathers, most often initiate incest, and typically had no regular contact with a youthful victim during the first few years of the child's life. Reports of incest between genetic fathers and their daughters involve sexual intercourse far less often than incest between step-fathers and daughters, Thornhill says.

Sexual intercourse between close genetic relatives rarely occurs because natural selection has molded a human psyche that promotes paternity concerns in men and the striving for status and resource control through social competition in both sexes, Thornhill proposes. Cultural and moral taboos against incest sprang from these psychological foundations.

Psychoanalysts — psychiatrists and psychologists who undergo special clinical training and receive psychotherapy based on Freud's theories — remain largely ignorant of the evolutionary theories about family conflict, even as their enthusiasm for the Oedipus complex subsides, says psychologist Malcolm O. Slavin of Tufts University Counseling Center in Medford, Mass. Slavin, a trained psychoanalyst, uses an evolutionary perspective in his psychotherapy.

"Fathers and children engage in much competition and rivalry over the mother's scarce time and resources, even in loving families," Slavin asserts. "It's often hard for family members to reconcile this conflict with the love and support they give to one another."

Family conflict swirls in a cauldron of deception forged by natural selection, Slavin argues. Men who successfully seek additional or more desirable mates, and women who attract the best marriage prospects often employ deception to mislead same-sex competitors and maximize the deceiver's perceived attractiveness, he says. What's more, deception works best when the deceiver remains unaware of his or her true motives and cannot give the strategy away. Thus, according to Slavin, evolution has promoted the psychological repression, or unconscious stowing away, of disturbing thoughts, fantasies and selfish motives.

"We're never motivated to reveal ourselves fully to others or to ourselves," he maintains.

Some psychoanalytically oriented researchers, however, see no reason to discard Freud's theory of the Oedipus complex. They believe it works in concert with evolutionary tendencies to discourage incest.

Evolutionary or sociobiological theories address the reproductive concerns that have fostered incest avoidance in the human species, while psychoanalytic theory explains how individual development further blocks the possibility of incest, asserts anthropologist Robert A. Paul of Emory University in Atlanta. Freud argued that the child normally represses erotic feelings toward an opposite-sex parent or sibling out of fear of reprisal from the same-sex parent, Paul says. Freud's emphasis on the child's experience in the family and Westermarck's focus on natural selection provide complementary explanations of the rarity of incest, he remarks.

"The human superego is a powerful part of this 'incest avoidance complex,'" adds anthropologist David H. Spain of the University of Washington in Seattle. The largely unconscious influence of the child's emerging moral conscience as a result of Oedipal conflicts helps explain why most of the societies studied by Thornhill require no explicit incest taboos, Spain contends.

Thornhill disagrees. The traditional Freudian view assumes intense sexual attractions naturally occur among family members, while evolutionary theories present evidence of sexual repugnance among close genetic relatives, she says.

Freud, who considered his theories a preliminary step toward a scientific psychology, might extract a certain intellectual excitement from the debate surrounding the Oedipus complex. "Mediocre spirits demand of science the kind of certainty which it cannot give, a sort of religious satisfaction," he wrote to his friend Princess Marie Bonaparte toward the end of his life. "Only the real, rare, true scientific minds can endure doubt, which is attached to all our knowledge."

Erikson, In His Own Old Age, Expands His View of Life

In partnership with his wife, the psychoanalyst describes how wisdom of the elderly is born.

Daniel Goleman

In his ninth decade of life, Erik H. Erikson has expanded the psychological model of the life cycle that he put forward with his wife, Joan, almost 40 years ago.

Their original work profoundly changed psychology's view of human development. Now, breaking new ground, they have spelled out the way the lessons of each major stage of life can ripen into wisdom in old age. They depict an old age in which one has enough conviction in one's own completeness to ward off the despair that gradual physical disintegration can too easily bring.

"You've got to learn to accept the law of life, and face the fact that we disintegrate slowly," Mr. Erikson said.

On a recent afternoon, in a rare interview, they sat in their favorite nook in a bay window of Mrs. Erikson's study on the second floor of their Victorian house near Harvard Square in Cambridge, Mass. "The light is good here and it's cozy at night," Mrs. Erikson told a visitor.

Although Mr. Erikson has a comfortable study downstairs, and Mrs. Erikson, an artist and author in her own right, has a separate workroom, they prefer to spend their time together in this quiet corner, in the spirit of their lifelong collaboration.

Mr. Erikson, who never earned an academic degree (he is usually called Professor Erikson), deeply affected the study of psychology. Many believe that his widely read books made Freud pertinent to the struggles of adult life and shaped the way people today think about their own emotional growth. He gave psychology the term "identity crisis."

When Mr. Erikson came to this country in 1933 from Vienna, he spoke little English. Mrs. Erikson, a Canadian, has always lent her editorial hand to those writings of her husband on which she did not act as co-author.

As Mr. Erikson approaches 87 years of age and Mrs. Erikson 86, old age is one topic very much on their minds.

Their original chart of the life cycle was prepared in 1950 for a White House conference on childhood and youth. In it, each stage of life, from infancy and early childhood on, is associated with a specific psychological struggle that contributes to a major aspect of personality.

In infancy, for instance, the tension is between trust and mistrust; if an infant feels trusting, the result is a sense of hope.

In old age, according to the new addition to the stages, the struggle is between a sense of one's own integrity and a feeling of defeat, of despair about one's life in the phase of normal physical disintegration. The fruit of that struggle is wisdom.

"When we looked at the life cycle in our 40's, we looked to old people for wisdom," Mrs. Erikson said. "At 80, though, we look at other 80-year-olds to see who got wise and who not. Lots of old people don't get wise, but you don't get wise unless you age."

Originally, the Eriksons defined wisdom in the elderly as a more objective concern with life itself in the face of death. Now that they are at that stage of life, they have been developing a more detailed description of just what the lessons of each part of life lend to wisdom in old age. For each earlier stage of development they see a parallel development toward the end of life's journey.

For instance, the sense of trust that begins to develop from the infant's experience of a loving and supportive environment becomes, in old age, an appreciation of human interdependence, according to the Eriksons.

"Life doesn't make any sense without interdependence," Mrs. Erikson said. "We need each other and the sooner we learn that the better for us all."

The second stage of life, which begins in early childhood with learning control over one's own body, builds the sense of will on the one hand, or shame and doubt on the other. In old age, one's experience is almost a mirror image of what it was earlier as the body deteriorates and one needs to learn to accept it.

In "play age" or preschool children, what is being learned is a sense of initiative and purpose in life, as well as a sense of playfulness and creativity, the theory holds.

Two lessons for old age from that stage of life are empathy and resilience, as the Eriksons see it.

"The more you know yourself, the more patience you have for what you see in others," Mrs. Erikson said. "You don't have to accept what people do, but understand what leads them to do it. The stance this leads to is to forgive even though you still oppose."

The child's playfulness becomes, too, a sense of humor about life. "I can't imagine a wise old person who can't laugh," said Mr. Erikson. "The world is full of ridiculous dichotomies."

At school age, the Erikson's next stage, the child strives to become effective and industrious, and so develops a sense of competence; if he or she does not, the outcome is feelings of inferiority.

HUMILITY IN OLD AGE

In old age, as one's physical and sensory abilities wane, a lifelong sense of effectiveness is a critical resource. Reflections in old age on the course one's life has taken—especially comparing one's early hopes and dreams with the life one actually lived—foster humility. Thus, humility in old age is a realistic appreciation of one's limits and competencies.

The adolescent's struggle to overcome confusion and find a lifelong identity results in the capacity for commitment and fidelity, the Eriksons hold. Reflections in old age on the complexity of living go hand in hand with a new way of perceiving, one that merges sensory, logical and esthetic perception, they say. Too often, they say, people overemphasize logic and ignore other modes of knowing.

"If you leave out what your senses tell you, your thinking is not so good," Mrs. Erikson said.

In young adulthood, the conflict is between finding a balance between lasting intimacy and the need for isolation. At the last stage of life, this takes the form of coming to terms with love expressed and unexpressed during one's entire life; the understanding of the complexity of relationships is a facet of wisdom.

"You have to live intimacy out over many years, with all the complications of a long-range relationship, really to understand it," Mrs. Erikson said. "Anyone can flirt around with many relationships, but commitment is crucial to intimacy. Loving better is what comes from understanding the complications of a long-term intimate bond."

She added: "You put such a stress on passion when you're young. You learn about the value of tenderness when you grow old. You also learn in late life not to hold, to give without hanging on; to love freely, in the sense of wanting nothing in return."

In the adult years, the psychological tension is between what the Eriksons call generativity and caring on the one hand and self-absorption and stagnation on the other. Generativity expresses itself, as Mrs. Erikson put it, in "taking care to pass on to the next generation what you've contributed to life."

Mr. Erikson sees a widespread failing in modern life.

"The only thing that can save us as a species is seeing how we're not thinking about future generations in the way we live," he said. "What's lacking is generativity, a generativity that will promote positive values in the lives of the next generation. Unfortunately, we set the example of greed, wanting a bigger and better everything, with no thought of what will make it a better world for our great-grandchildren. That's why we go on depleting the earth: we're not thinking of the next generations."

UNDERSTANDING GENERATIVITY

As an attribute of wisdom in old age, generativity has two faces. One is "caritas," a Latin word for charity, which the Eriksons take in the broad sense of caring for others. The other is "agape," a Greek word for love, which they define

The Completed Life Cycle

In the Eriksons' view, each stage of life is associated with a specific psychological conflict and a specific resolution. In a new amplification, lessons from each of the earlier stages mature into the many facets of wisdom in old age, shown in column at right.

Conflict and resolution	Culmination in old age
Old Age Integrity vs. despair: wisdom	Existential identity; a sense of integrity strong enough to withstand physical disintegration.
Adulthood Generativity vs. stagnation: care	Caritas, caring for others, and agape, empathy and concern.
Early Adulthood Intimacy vs. isolation: love	Sense of complexity of relationships; value of tenderness and loving freely.
Adolescence Identity vs. confusion: fidelity	Sense of complexity of life; merger of sensory, logical and aesthetic perception.
School Age Industry vs. inferiority: competence	Humility; acceptance of the course of one's life and unfulfilled hopes.
Play Age Initiative vs. guilt: purpose	Humor; empathy; resilience.
Early Childhood Autonomy vs. shame: will	Acceptance of the cycle of life, from integration to disintegration.
Infancy Basic trust vs. mistrust: hope	Appreciation of interdependence and relatedness.

as a kind of empathy.

The final phase of life, in which integrity battles despair, culminates in a full wisdom to the degree each earlier phase of life has had a positive resolution, the Eriksons believe. If everything has gone well, one achieves a sense of integrity, a sense of completeness, of personal wholeness that is strong enough to offset the downward psychological pull of the inevitable physical disintegration.

Despair seems quite far from the Eriksons in their own lives. Both continue to exemplify what they described in the title of a 1986 book, "Vital Involvement in Old Age." Mr. Erikson is writing about, among other things, the sayings of Jesus. Mrs. Erikson's most recent book, "Wisdom and the Senses," sets out evidence that the liveliness of the senses throughout life, and the creativity and playfulness that this brings, is the keystone of wisdom in old age.

"The importance of the senses came to us in old age," said Mr. Erikson, who now wears a hearing aid and walks with a slow, measured dignity.

In her book, Mrs. Erikson argues that modern life allows too little time for the pleasures of the senses. She says: "We start to lose touch with the senses in school: we call play, which stimulates the senses and makes them acute, a waste of time or laziness. The schools relegate play to sports. We call that play, but it isn't; it's competitive, not in the spirit of a game."

The Eriksons contend that wisdom has little to do with formal learning. "What is real wisdom?" Mrs. Erikson asked. "It comes from life experience, well digested. It's not what comes from reading great books. When it comes to understanding life, experiential learning is the only worthwhile kind; everything else is hearsay."

Mr. Erikson has been continuing a line of thought he set out in a Yale Review article in 1981 on the sayings of Jesus and their implications for the sense of "I," an argument that takes on the concept of the "ego" in Freudian thought.

"The trouble with the word 'ego' is its technical connotations," Mr. Erikson said. "It has bothered me that 'ego' was used as the translation of the German word 'Ich.' That's wrong. Freud was referring to the simple sense of "I."

The Eriksons contend that wisdom has little to do with formal learning.

Another continuing concern for the Eriksons has been the ethics of survival, and what they see as the urgent need to overcome the human tendency to define other groups as an enemy, an outgrowth of the line of thinking Mr. Erikson began in his biography of Gandhi.

Mr. Erikson was trained in psychoanalysis in Vienna while Freud was still there, and worked closely with Freud's daughter Anna in exploring ways to apply psychoanalytic methods to children. That expertise made him welcome at Harvard, where he had his first academic post.

There he began the expansion of Freud's thinking that was to make him world famous. By describing in his books "Childhood and Society" and "Identity and the Life Cycle" how psychological growth is shaped throughout life, not just during the formative early years that Freud focused on, Mr. Erikson made a quantum leap in Freudian thought.

Over the years since first coming to Harvard, Mr. Erikson has spent time at other universities and hospitals, including Yale in the late 1930's, the University of California at Berkeley in the 40's, the Austen Riggs Center in Stockbridge, Mass., in the 50's, and again at Harvard through the 60's. Until last year, the Eriksons lived in Marin County near San Francisco, but it is to Cambridge that they returned.

One lure was grandchildren nearby. Their son Kai, with two children, is a professor of sociology at Yale, and their daughter Sue, with one child, also lives nearby.

Informally, Mr. Erikson still continues to supervise therapists. "The students tell me it's the most powerful clinical supervision they've ever had," said Margaret Brenman-Gibson, a professor of psychology in the psychiatry department at Cambridge City Hospital, a part of Harvard Medical School.

In Cambridge, the Eriksons share a rambling three-story Victorian with three other people: a graduate student, a professor of comparative religion and a psychologist. The housemates often take meals together.

"Living communally," said Mrs. Erikson, "is an adventure at our age."

Personality: Major Traits Found Stable Through Life

Daniel Goleman

Studies challenge theories that see transitions.

The largest and longest studies to carefully analyze personality throughout life reveal a core of traits that remain remarkably stable over the years and a number of other traits that can change drastically from age to age.

The new studies have shown that three basic aspects of personality change little throughout life: a person's anxiety level, friendliness and eagerness for novel experiences. But other traits, such as alienation, morale and feelings of satisfaction, can vary greatly as a person goes through life. These more changeable traits largely reflect such things as how a person sees himself and his life at a given point, rather than a basic underlying temperament.

One of the recently completed studies followed 10,000 people 25 to 74 years old for nine years. Another involved 300 couples first tested in 1935. The studies are joined by a new analysis of more than two dozen earlier studies of lifetime personality and a study of twins that looks at the genetic contribution.

The recent work poses a powerful challenge to theories of personality that have emphasized stages or passages—predictable points in adult life—in which people change significantly.

The new research is "a death knell" for the passage theories of adult personality, in the view of a researcher who conducted one of the new studies. "I see no evidence for specific changes in personality due to age," said the researcher, Paul T. Costa Jr. "What changes as you go through life are your roles and the issues that matter most to you. People may think their personality has changed as they age, but it is their habits that change, their vigor and health, their responsibilities and circumstances—not their basic personality."

But the new work has not made converts of the theorists who see adult life through the framework of passages. Rather they assert that simple pencil and paper tests cannot discern the richness inherent in the maturing personality. A theory proposed by Daniel Levinson, a psychologist at Yale University, suggests a series of sometimes troubled transitions between psychological stages; Erik Erikson coined the term "identity crisis" for the difficulties some young people have in settling on a life course.

Proponents of the most recent studies say, however, that the notion of passages, built on clinical interviews, was never objectively tested.

Some of the strongest evidence for the stability of the core personality throughout adulthood comes from a study by Dr. Costa and Robert McCrae, psychologists at the National Institute on Aging in Baltimore. They interviewed thousands of people in 100 places throughout the United States in 1975, and again in 1984.

The researchers found virtually no change in the three key personality traits. Their report in a recent issue of the Journal of Gerontology asserts that a person who was calm and well-adjusted at 25 years of age would remain so at 65, while a person who was emotionally volatile at 25 would be about the same at 65. Their findings represented averages, however, and could not reflect the changes in some individuals that might have been brought on by, for instance, psychotherapy or a personal catastrophe.

ONLY THE FORM CHANGES

"There is no evidence of any universal age-related crises; those people who have crises at one point or another in life tend to be those who are more emotional," said Dr. Costa. "Such people experience some degree of distress through most of life; only the form of the trouble seems to change."

A mellowing in midlife, found by other studies, has now been shown to relate more to a muting of some of a person's more extreme feelings than to any change in the overall pattern of personality.

The new studies find no increase in irritability with aging. "The stereotype that people become cranky and rigid as they age does not hold up," said Dr. Costa. "The calm, outgoing, adventurous young person is going to stay that way into old age, given good health. Those who are dogmatic and closed to experience early in life remain that way."

The greatest changes in core personality occur in childhood and from adolescence to early adulthood, according to Dr. Costa. "After 25, as William James said, character is set in plaster," he said. "What does change is one's role in life, and the situations that influence your temporary behavior one way or another."

Support for Dr. Costa's large study comes from a recent study of twins that found an important genetic influence on the three main traits. Early childhood experiences, the investigators concluded, are not the main influence in shaping the most persistent of personality traits, though they may shape them to some degree, as they do all personality.

In this study of 203 pairs of twins at Indiana University, the researchers, Michael Pogue-Geile and Richard Rose, administered a personality test when the subjects were 20, and again when they were 25. The researchers were looking to see whether fraternal twins changed in the same ways as identical twins in that time, which is one of the stages of turbulent transition proposed by some theorists. If a particular trait is genetically determined it will tend to change more similarly in identical twins than it will in fraternal twins.

There was evidence of significant genetic influence on the three main personality traits of anxiety or emotionality, friendliness and openness to new things.

Life experience also shaped these basic traits. But it had a far greater influence on other personality traits, including alienation, morale and feelings of satisfaction. These traits change so much over the course of adult life that there is virtually no relationship between their levels when a person is in his 20's and when he is in his 60's, according to James Conley, who studied 300 couples who were tested in 1935, 1955 and 1980, when the researchers were able to interview 388 of the original 600 men and women.

"If you try to predict how alienated or satisfied with life people will be in their later years from how they seem in college, you will fail abysmally," he said.

Dr. Conley is among those finding that the three basic traits change little over a lifetime. In addition to the study of couples, he has reviewed data from more than two dozen other long-term personality studies.

Some personality traits may make certain crises in life more probable. For instance, the study of couples suggests that specific combinations of personality in a marriage are explosive. Over the course of 45 years, the highest probability of divorce occurred in those marriages where both the husband and wife were emotionally volatile and the husband had little impulse control.

"The evaluations in 1935, by five friends, of the personalities of an engaged couple was highly predictive of which marriages would break up," Dr. Conley said, "If you have a couple with emotional hair triggers, and where the husband philanders, gambles, drinks, or loses jobs, a break-up is almost certain. Some marriages broke up right away: some took 45 years to end. Data from younger couples suggests that today the dangerous combination of personalities is the same, except now it can be either the wife or the husband whose impulsiveness triggers the trouble."

Critics say the new studies lack necessary subtlety.

Walter Mischel, a psychologist at Columbia University, wrote an influential article in 1968 arguing that the variation in expression of a given trait from situation to situation is so great that the notion of personality traits itself was of little use in accounting for how people behave.

VARIATIONS WITH SITUATION

"There is lots of evidence for the stability of some traits, such as extroversion, over time," Dr. Mischel said in a recent interview. "But the same person may be quite outgoing in some circumstances, and not at all in others."

Kenneth Craik, a psychologist at the University of California at Berkeley, said, "The belief for 10 to 15 years after Mischel's critique was that the situation determined far more than personality about how people behave." Now, within the last few years, he said, "personality and situation are seen by most researchers as having about equal influence."

Researchers are concluding that the influence of one situation or another on how a person acts may also create the impression that personality itself changes more than is the case; apparent changes in personality may actually reflect temporary circumstances.

"Any trait can vary with the moment," said Seymour Epstein, a personality psychologist at the University of Massachusetts at Amherst. "You need to look at the person in many situations to get a stable rating of that trait."

And people seem to differ in how much situations affect their actions, according to research by Mark Snyder, a psychologist at the University of Minnesota. In "Public Appearances, Private Reality," published recently by W.H. Freeman & Company, Dr. Snyder reviews evidence showing that some people are virtual chameleons, shaping themselves to blend into whatever social situation they find themselves, while others are almost oblivious to the special demands and expectations of differing situations, being more or less the same person regardless of where they are.

The situation-oriented, Dr. Snyder has found, are skilled at social roles: At a church service, they display just the right combination of seriousness and reserve; at a cocktail party they become the friendly and sociable extrovert.

Those less affected by situations are more consistent in their behavior, putting less effort into role-playing: They have a smaller wardrobe, wearing the same clothes in more situations, than do the situation-oriented.

It is as though each type were playing to a different audience, one inner, the other outer, says Dr. Snyder.

Those adept at situations flourish in jobs where they deal with a range of different groups, Dr. Snyder reports.

Embattled Giant of Psychology Speaks His Mind

Daniel Goleman
Special to The New York Times

B.F. Skinner, the architect of behaviorism, battles 'grave mistakes' in rival approaches.

CAMBRIDGE, Mass.—B.F. Skinner is a creature of carefully shaped habit. At the age of 83, he has fashioned a schedule and environment for himself that is in perfect keeping with his theories of behavioral reinforcement.

Dr. Skinner's personal Skinner box—his own self-contained environment of positive reinforcements—is his basement office in his home here, a 1950's flat-top set among charming New England-style saltboxes.

"I spent a lot of time creating the environment where I work," Dr. Skinner said as he recently led a visitor through the home where he and his wife, Yvonne, live. "I believe people should design a world where they will be as happy as possible in old age."

Burrhus Frederic Skinner, the chief architect of behaviorism, uses the office to marshal a crusade against what he sees as grave mistakes in psychology that have left his own once pre-eminent theories in decline.

Behaviorism holds that people act as they do because of the rewards and punishments—positive and negative reinforcements—they have received. The mind and such things as memory and perception cannot be directly observed, and so, in Dr. Skinner's view, are unworthy of scientific study.

Much of Dr. Skinner's efforts now aim at meeting two major challenges to behaviorism: brain science, the study of links between brain and behavior, and cognitive psychology, the study of how the mind perceives, thinks and remembers and how goals and plans influence behavior.

During the recent visit, Dr. Skinner, known to colleagues as Fred, was in the midst of preparing a talk week at psychology's major annual convention.

It is to maximize his productivity in such writing, and to conserve energy in his later years, that Dr. Skinner has designed this environment. He sleeps in the office, in a bright yellow plastic tank just large enough for the mattress it contains, a small television and some narrow shelves and controls. The bed unit, which bears some resemblance to a sleeper on a train, is one of those used by the Japanese in stacks in tiny hotel rooms, Dr. Skinner explained.

The office-bedroom suits Dr. Skinner's habits well: he goes to bed each night at 10 P.M. sleeps three hours, then rolls out of bed to his nearby desk, where he works for one hour. Then he goes back to bed for another three hours, getting up to begin his day at 5 A.M.

POSITIVE REINFORCEMENT: MUSIC

In these early morning hours Dr. Skinner puts in about three hours of writing, which he considers to be his main work. After his writing, he walks a mile or so to his office at Harvard University, where he answers mail and attends to other business. And then, for reinforcement, he spends the afternoon listening to music—which he loves—on the quadrophonic tape deck in his office.

This schedule, with its work output and rewards, allows Dr. Skinner to continue to act as the undisputed leader of modern behaviorism. As such, he fights a continuing battle for his ideas on many fronts, many of which he touched on in the wide-ranging interview.

"I think cognitive psychology is a great hoax and a fraud, and that goes for brain science, too," Dr. Skinner said. "They are nowhere near answering the important questions about behavior."

Dr. Skinner is still vigorous in arguing his cause. In addition to the speech opposing cognitive psychology he is giving at the annual meeting of the American Psychological Association, next month he will publish in the American Psychologist an article attacking not only cognitive psychology, but also other enemies of his brand of behaviorism: humanistic psychology and other nonbehaviorist psychotherapies.

Humanists, Dr. Skinner writes in his article, have attacked behaviorism as undermining people's sense of freedom and have denounced its claims that the environment determines what people achieve. And, he writes, psychotherapists—apart from those who practice a behaviorist approach—rely too much on inferences they make about what is supposedly going on inside their patients, and too little on direct observation of what they do.

The use of punishment is another issue Dr. Skinner still feels impassioned about. He is an ardent opponent of the use of punishment, such as spanking, or using "aversives"—such as pinches and shocks—with autistic children.

"What's wrong with punishments is that they work immediately, but give no long-term results," Dr. Skinner said. "The responses to punishment are either the urge to escape, to counterattack or a stubborn apathy. These are the bad effects you get in prisons or schools, or wherever punishments are used."

One of the ways Dr. Skinner feels behaviorist techniques have been under-appreciated is in the failure of teaching machines to find wide acceptance in the schools. The machines, which can be computerized, break a topic like division or Russian history into small, manageable concepts, and methodically teach each so a student gets the reinforcement of knowing he has mastered it before moving on to the next.

The learning devices had a great advantage over the classroom teacher, according to Dr. Skinner. "Schools were invented to extend a tutor to more than one student at once," Dr. Skinner said. "That's O.K. with three or four, but when you have 30 or more in a classroom, the teacher is no longer able to give the student the reinforcement of a 'right' before moving on to the next task."

Such machines are widely used now in industrial education, but are not widely used in schools.

REWARDS OF WORK

Dr. Skinner continues to act as a social philosopher, a role he played most prominently with his 1948 book "Walden Two," which described a behaviorist utopia. In an article last year in the American Psychologist in which he examined "What is Wrong With Daily Life in the Western World," Dr. Skinner charged that common practices had eroded the natural relationship between what people do and the pleasing effects that would reinforce their activities.

For instance, in Dr. Skinner's view, fixed salaries do not reinforce workers because they are paid whether or not they do more than the minimum job. If workers were paid on a commission or by the piece their pay would be a direct reinforcer for their labors, and they would work with more effort and pleasure, according to behaviorist principles.

Another aspect of modern life Dr. Skinner criticizes, in all seriousness, is labor-saving devices, such as dishwashers or frozen dinners, which he sees as depriving people of the small satisfactions that accomplishing something brings. "We've destroyed all the reinforcers in daily life," said Dr. Skinner. "For example, if you wash a dish, you've accomplished something, done something that gives you a pleasing result. That is far more reinforcing than putting the dishes in with some powder and then taking them about again."

The device for which Dr. Skinner may be most famous, the original "Skinner box," was a large glass-enclosed, climate-controlled baby crib with equipment to keep infants amused and well-exercised. Dr. Skinner is still pained by the rumors that his daughters, who used the box, became psychotic or suicidal as a result. Today one daughter is an artist and writer living in London, and the other is a professor of educational psychology at Indiana University; both are married.

When Dr. Skinner first began in the 1930's and 1940's to develop the principles of what he calls "radical behaviorism"—to distinguish it from the earlier theories of Pavlov and Watson—he argued that a scientific psychology could only study behavior that can be directly observed. For that reason, Skinnerian behaviorists have studied the laws of learning through observing responses such as the pecking of a pigeon, and avoided the "black box" of the inner workings of the mind.

In recent decades, though, advances in devices for monitoring faculties such as attention have spurred studies linking the brain and mental activity. If he were starting his research today, Dr. Skinner was asked, would he avail himself of these techniques?

"If I had it all to do again, I would still call the mind a black box," Dr. Skinner said. "I would not use any of the new techniques for measuring information processing and the like. My point has always been that psychology should not look at the nervous system or so-called mind—just at behavior."

For Dr. Skinner, the mind is irrelevant to understanding why people behave as they do. In his view, most assumptions about mental life made by laymen and psychologists alike are based on fallacies. In his address next week before the American Psychological Association, he will argue that all the words that describe mental activities actually refer to some behavior.

"No one invented a word for mental experience that comes from the mind," Dr. Skinner said. "They all have their roots in a reference to action.

"To contemplate, for instance, means to look at a template, or picture. 'Consider' comes from roots meaning to look at the stars until you see a pattern. 'Compare' means to put things side by side to see if they match."

"All the words for mental experience go back to what people do," Dr. Skinner continued. "Over thousands of years, people have used these terms to express something that goes on in their bodies. But these are action terms; they do not mean that these things are going on inside the mind."

"The cognitive revolution is a search inside the mind for something that is not there," Dr. Skinner said. "You can't see yourself process information; information-processing is an inference from behavior—and a bad one, at that. If you look carefully at what people mean when they talk about the mind, you find it just refers to how they behave."

One of the major disputes between the cognitive and behaviorist viewpoints is whether a person's actions are guided by goals and plans, or whether they are a result of that person's history of rewards and punishments. For Dr. Skinner, there is no question. "Behavior is always reinforced behavior," he said.

Despite their differences with other points of view, behaviorists are influential in many psychology departments, and the school of thought remains prominent, particularly among those who are trying to apply its principles in areas like psychotherapy, industrial motivation and remedial education. From the 1930's through the 1960's, behaviorism dominated academic psychology; in the 1960's the so-called cognitive revolution began and would go on to sweep psychology.

There is no precise estimate of the numbers of behaviorists, although there are 1,228 members of the division of the psychological association that is devoted to behaviorist research and applications. The strongholds of behaviorism tend to be in colleges in the South and Midwest, according to Kurt Salzinger, a psychologist at Polytechnic University in Brooklyn who is the new president of the behaviorist division.

Dr. Skinner concedes that behaviorism is on the decline while the cognitive school of thought is increasingly popular among psychologists. There is now a move afoot to reconcile the two approaches.

"Behaviorism was right in saying the task of psychology is to account for what people do, but wrong in ruling out talking about what's going on in the head that generates what people do," said Stephan Harnad, one of the editors of a collection of Dr. Skinner's major papers, along with more than 150 comments by leading scholars. The book is scheduled to be published this winter by the Cambridge University Press.

He considers much of recent psychology to be 'a great hoax and a fraud.'

"That left behaviorists only able to talk about a person's history of rewards and punishments," Dr. Harnad said. "But that accounts for almost nothing of what we can do—our perception, our being able to remember something and our speech. This calls for a cognitive theory."

As the field evolves, an increasing number of behaviorists are violating Dr. Skinner's tenets by studying mental activity. "My major research now is a collaborative project with a cognitive scientist," said Richard Herrnstein, a psychologist who is a former colleague of Dr. Skinner at Harvard University. "We're studying how organisms perceive shapes; we're doing studies of pigeons, humans and computers. I'm pretty comfortable with much of the cognitive school, and I consider myself a behaviorist."

The Town B. F. Skinner Boxed

In the dusty reaches of the Mexican desert, a handful of utopians are trying to prove that what worked for the psychologist's pigeons can work for humans, too.

Steve Fishman

Steve Fishman is a contributing editor.

Lately Ivan, who is two years old, has been emitting some undesirable verbal behavior.

Where Ivan lives, the Code of Children's Behavior is quite explicit about what is desirable: Orderliness and cleanliness, for example; singing, laughing, dancing. And speaking positively.

"Great!" "I like it." "I'm happy"—these are the kinds of statements Ivan should be making. But Ivan has been negative. Linda, the leader of the committee on children's behavior, reports that he has been saying things like "The sky is not blue," or "You can't run," or "No, that is not yours, that is everyone's"—which could be considered desirable "sharing behavior," if it weren't for all the other negatives.

It's Thursday night and the committee is holding its weekly meeting in the children's house, where the community's four youngest children live. In these get-togethers, the adults discuss everything about the kids, from how they ought to behave to what medical care they should receive to how long their hair should be. The eleven adults listening to Linda's recitation of Ivan's negatives—two biological parents and nine "behavioral" parents—sit in the dining room clumped around the long, low children's table.

Linda explains that for the past week, the grownups who care for the youngest children have been wearing counters around their necks—little silvery devices like those that ticket takers use to click off the number of people entering a theater. Every time Ivan, who has brown bangs, brown eyes, and a voice that penetrates like a foghorn, has emitted a negative verbal behavior, *click*. "I don't like the beans." *Click*. "It's too cold outside." *Click*.

Linda holds up a piece of peach-colored graph paper with penciled peaks: Ivan has averaged 18 negative verbal behaviors per day. She poses the crucial question: "Should we intervene now to correct Ivan's behavior?"

WELCOME TO LOS HORCONES, a tiny enclave in the barely hospitable stretches of Mexico's Sonora Desert, 175 miles south of the U.S. border. Here 26 adults and children are attempting to live according to the teachings of the late Harvard behaviorist Burrhus Frederic (B.F.) Skinner—one of the most widely recognized and most often maligned of psychologists.

In the cultural lab they call home, this outpost community of Mexicans has been at it for 17 years, experimenting with Skinner's ideas, working away on themselves and their children. So that no visitor will miss the point, there is this welcome sign at the edge of their land, written in both Spanish and English: "We apply the science of behavior to the design of a new society."

The idea, first Skinner's and now theirs, is as ambitious as it sounds: By the methodical application of the science of behaviorism, the little band at Los Horcones believes it can transform selfish human beings into cooperative, sharing ones.

Until his death this past August, B.F. Skinner argued that his psychology was both potent and practical. His fundamental discoveries, made 55 years ago, rest on this idea: If any particular behavior is reinforced, it will continue. If not, it will cease.

For pigeons, Skinner found, reinforcement came in the form of dry, hard food pellets. What a hungry pigeon wouldn't do for the promise of a pellet! Climb stairs, peck a key 10,000 times, even guide a missile—which Skinner demonstrated to U.S. Army officials in World War II.

Give Skinner some lab time—he was one of psychology's first great experimenters—and he'd figure out which reinforcers, administered how often and for how long, would not only make people share but make them *like* to share. "We can *make* men adequate for group living," boasted the protagonist in Skinner's classic 1948 utopian novel, *Walden Two*.

Over the past two decades, Skinner's behaviorism and his

From *Health* (formerly *In Health*), January/February 1991, pp. 50-57.

ideas about what motivates people have largely been supplanted in the world of academic psychology. The trend now is toward cognitive psychology, which concentrates on the unconscious causes of human behavior, processes that cognitive psychologists say cannot or should not be subject to systems of reward and punishment.

But in this desert proving ground, behaviorism is as alive as the tarantulas that take up guard on the drainpipes, as hardy as the boa constrictors that swallow live rabbits whole. In the children's house and the other whitewashed bungalows of the community of Los Horcones, behaviorism still has a shot.

"It's true," says Juan Robinson, the community's coordinator of adult behavior. "A person can be made to enjoy what he did not at first enjoy."

Take Ivan.

IVAN'S BIOLOGICAL PARENTS, Luciano Coronado Paredes, 26, and Maria Guadalupe Cosio de Coronado, 26, better known as Lucho and Lupita, sit in the tiny children's chairs with the other adults. They met elsewhere, but heard about Los Horcones and were married here. They vowed to put the community first. "If you ever decide to leave, just go, don't even tell me," said Lupita. Both Ivan and his brother Sebastian, aged four, were born at Los Horcones, and live together in the children's house.

Lucho and Lupita are tired after a long day's work, and remain quiet even when the subject is their younger son. Lucho, in fact, peruses a book on rabbits while Linda's discussion goes on. "Did you know," he asks a neighbor, "that rabbits eat their food twice?" No one is really worried about Ivan. It is just behavior, after all. Ivan used to cry when he wanted something, instead of asking for it. That took but a few weeks to correct.

An approach is suggested for Ivan's negative emissions—straightforward Skinnerian science. When Ivan says something positive, he'll be reinforced with attention—hugs and kisses, pats on the head, and M&Ms. His negative comments will be ignored (but still counted with the clickers). Punishment isn't shunned out of principle; it is just, as Skinner saw it, that the consequences can turn out to be troublesome.

Linda (the children all call her La Linda) asks if everyone agrees. In the community's open family, all decisions must be made unanimously. One by one, the adults, all of whom are considered parents, nod. "Adults are difficult to change," says a parent. "Pigeons and children are easy."

B. F. SKINNER experimented on pigeons and also on rats. In his crucial experiments of the 1930s, he demonstrated that by offering a simple food pellet as a "reinforcer"—a term first used by the famed Russian physiologist Ivan Pavlov—he could condition laboratory rats to press a bar when a light came on, to hold it down for as long as 30 seconds, and to keep pressing harder.

To Skinner, humans were bigger and more complex but not fundamentally different from lab animals. For the right reinforcers, he claimed, they would do almost anything.

Critics denounced Skinner's science, when it came to humans, as simplistic, manipulative, and reductionist—as well as downright unflattering. They argued that people, unlike pigeons, have rich inner lives and complex, hidden motivations. What, for goodness' sake, of a person's free will? cried the critics. Skinner harrumphed. Free will, he said, was illusory. He preferred to talk about the predictability of people.

The late psychologist wasn't, however, a cold, impersonal manipulator. Rather, he seems to have been as cheery and optimistic as a handyman who says, Hey, I can fix that. After his wife complained that the first years of child-rearing were hell, he devised the "baby tender," a glass-enclosed, temperature-controlled crib that eliminated the need to change the baby's clothes so often. His own daughter tried it out and became the notorious baby in the "Skinner box." After noticing how dull his other daughter's grammar school was, Skinner built a "teaching machine," decades ahead of today's interactive learning systems.

In the same problem-solving spirit, the late behaviorist sat down in 1947 and in seven weeks wrote the book outlining his plan to ease society's woes through behaviorism. In Skinner's utopia, 1,000 citizens work four hours a day for no money, share their children, develop their artistic talents. As literature, *Walden Two* is a bore, freighted with long arguments between the proselytizing Frazier and his skeptical foil, a character named Castle. But the ideas have had a long life.

The book became a staple of college psychology classes as behaviorism flourished in the 1950s and 1960s. Two million copies are in print today. To a disposed mind, it can read like a do-it-yourself kit.

IN THE LATE 1960S, Juan Robinson, a handsome young middle-class Mexican (descended from a Scottish grandfather), was a university psychology student in Mexico City. Robinson read *Walden Two* and quickly became a convert.

In 1972, on the dusty edge of the Mexican town of Hermosillo, he and his wife, Mireya Bustamente Norberto, then 21, decided to give behaviorism a practical try. They founded a school for retarded children, many of them so unmanageable that their parents were prepared to ship them to an institution. Subjected to behavioral techniques, the 20 students fell into line.

Consider the case of Luis, an autistic teen who threw as many as three tantrums a day. Did Luis sit quietly? Very nice, the behaviorists said, and handed him a coin. Shake hands? Very good. Another coin. Do anything but throw a fit? One more coin. Merchant Luis began bartering half hours of appropriate behavior—he even did chores!—for coins redeemable for meals, and his tantrums virtually ceased. "We can modify antisocial behavior," Juan concluded, "in three months."

At the end of the school day, Juan and Mireya hosted gatherings. Linda (La Linda), just 19, a volunteer at the school, attended; **so did her husband, Ramon Armendariz, 21. Juan, old man of the group at 24, would break out his copy of *Walden Two* and read aloud. Juan's voice is high and breathy, like the sound produced by blowing air into a Coke bottle. Night after night, his audience listened to that eerie hoot go on about how, with the aid of Skinner's science, a new society could be formed.**

Among the small following, the idea started to take. They would start a community called Los Horcones—or "the pillars"—of a new society, nothing less. It would be a living experiment, a "cultural lab." They would be the researchers, they and their children the pigeons. Together they'd take Skinner's behaviorism another step down the road.

They drafted a Code of Adult Behavior—41 pages in a green

The little band at Los Horcones believes it can transform human nature. "Adults are difficult to change," says a resident. "Pigeons and children are easy."

plastic binder, written in a style about as lively as a traffic ticket's—and in it they spelled out the details of the communitarian lifestyle. All adults would be parents to all children. Residents would be discouraged from saying "mine" and encouraged to say "ours"—as in "This is our daughter," even if one was not a blood relation. If an adult was working and a child asked a question, the adult would drop everything and explain what was going on. In addition, the older children would serve as teachers for the younger ones. Casual sex would not be considered a good example for "our" children.

In general, residents were to keep the community in mind at all times. They had to stop getting satisfaction from receiving more—whether pie or praise—and start getting excited about giving more. "Have approving thoughts about others" was a key dictum. The worst adjective that could be applied to someone at Los Horcones was "individualistic."

In all, six young urban friends gave up the career track in society—"the outside"—and moved to the countryside to build houses and to farm. They knew nothing about these endeavors, and Ramon recalls that for a few moments in 1973, the idea of building a new society with these ragtag city kids seemed like a very silly idea. It was dawn and the brand new behaviorists found themselves circling a fawn and white Guernsey cow, trying to figure out how to milk it.

IN 1980, THE CITIZENS of Los Horcones departed that first desolate site for the current patch of desert: an even more remote 250 acres of brush, cactus, and mesquite, 40 miles from Hermosillo. The new land might as well have been a stretch of concrete. They dug a small reservoir and carved out irrigation ditches to compensate for the parching lack of rain, and they hauled in trees. With a mania for systems, they not only planted but numbered every one of them. "Orderliness," Mireya says with a chortle, "is reinforcing."

Today Los Horcones is an oasis. "Everywhere you look, there we have done something," says Lucho. Vegetables grow in flawless stripes on seven acres. Orchards produce grapefruits as big as melons and lemons the size of baseballs. There are pigs, rabbits, chickens, 13 cows, electric milking machines, and a cheese factory. The community is, in fact, 75 percent food self-sufficient, buying only such staples as rice and flour. They have a Caterpillar tractor, trucks, and a school bus converted into a touring vehicle—sleeps nine—for occasional group forays to the outside world.

There's a basketball court and a plaza where they hold pig roasts and dances for guests from Hermosillo. They've dug a swimming hole, called Walden Pond, and built wood and metal shops. There's a dormitory for the dozen or so mentally impaired children they care for, which earns them cash to buy supplies. Luis is still there, helping to milk the cows for coins. The huge main house has a living room, communal dining room, and an office featuring a couple of computers. A lab contains cages of cooing pigeons used in behavioral experiments.

This has taken considerable work, far more than the four hours a day Skinner projected in his book. "I did like to play sports, but for me, it's not so important now," says Lucho, who, as all the adults do, works six and a half days a week. What's important to him now? "Building a building, fixing a toilet," he says simply.

The only space an adult can call his or her own at Los Horcones is one of the 25 assigned white stucco residences, each no more than a bedroom. Meager quarters for a private life, but the idea, after all, was to build a place where people shared not only space but belongings and emotions. The bedrooms are starkly utilitarian, with perhaps a table, an overhead fan—and no closets.

That's because the clothes at Los Horcones belong to everybody and are stored in one building: rows of jeans, neatly pressed and arranged by size, rows of shirts on hangers. First come, first served; too bad what goes best with your eyes. "I have four or five shirts I like," says Ramon. "I don't care who uses them. How could you build a community on sharing and be worried about who uses shirts?"

At first, it's fair to say, newcomers couldn't believe they had to do this clothes-swap thing. Even those dedicated to the design of a new society found it strange to see someone else in the clothes they were wearing yesterday.

And yet, in the long run, sharing clothes has turned out to be one of the easier things to adjust to. Some of the less tangible behaviors have been tougher to master. The main hurdle for the individual and for the new society is this: How can someone who's been reared to believe that if you don't look out for yourself, no one else will, suddenly believe that other people's happiness is your happiness, too?

"It's like being born again," says Juan.

But how to be reborn?

FORTUNATELY, A DAY AT LOS HORCONES is chock-full of strategies. Every activity can, it seems, be a form of reinforcement. Not only do the residents pick beans side by side, and take turns cooking together, they hold meetings to air any thoughts about how everyone behaved during the picking and cooking.

If you don't show up where you are supposed to, or if your tone of voice is too authoritarian, someone will take note of it. Alcohol, and even coffee, are allowed only in moderation because they aren't good for you. The place is like a big self-improvement camp, with lots of monitors. Lucho wrote in his notebook how many times his coworker was late for his shift at the cheese factory. That way, he said, there would be no argument when they were both sitting down with the behavior coordinator, trying to improve the situation.

If the extended family's kindhearted badgering can't haul a newcomer into line, there are, of course, other weapons for promoting utopia in the desert. That's where Skinner's science comes in. "That's right," says Juan, "we have the technology to change behavior."

In theory, no behavior is beyond the technology's reach. One woman—who prefers to remain anonymous, so we'll call her Susan—was interested in improving her relationship with her husband, so she designed a self-management program. She translated relationship-with-husband into graphable entities—positive verbal contacts, or PVCs, and negative verbal contacts, NVCs. She collected the data on a notepad she hid in her pocket, and after nine days she checked her chart: on average, 3.5 PVCs and 1.8 NVCs per day. Secretly, she also tallied her husband's

Here, the clothes belong to everyone. How could you build a community based on sharing and be worried about who wears what shirt?

communications. His score: 2.5 PVCs and 1.5 NVCs.

For Susan, or anyone, to learn a new behavior, it's essential to figure out what reinforces that behavior. Busi, 15 years old, taught Sebastian, just four, how to read in an astonishingly quick 15 hours. As he sounded out words, syllable by syllable, she patted his head and pushed a few of his reinforcers, Fruit Loops, into his mouth. But pats and sweets don't work for everybody. There is also the "participative reinforcer." To reward someone for cooking a nice meal, you not only applaud—though they like applause here—you offer to help afterwards with the dishes.

The most reliable reinforcer, though, is what the behaviorists at Los Horcones call a "natural" one, in which the person practicing a new behavior is reinforced by the consequences of that behavior. When Linda, for instance, discovered that she didn't run to other people's babies when they cried, she made herself run. The babies smiled in her arms, which, she explained, reinforced her response, naturally.

Susan, too, chose a natural reinforcer: her husband's response. She set a goal for herself: She would emit seven PVCs a day, and drop her NVCs to zero. Her husband had no idea about this particular behavior management program—it's hard to always know who's managing whose behavior at Los Horcones—but Susan noted that his PVCs increased to almost eight a day and his NVCs fell to zero. Both their PVCs up, Susan felt a lot better about their relationship.

PVCs? NVCs? They make lovely points on a graph, but are they love? It's not a distinction that behaviorists are troubled by. They're interested in observable behavior, not hidden recesses of the psyche. "How can you see what is inside except by the outside product?" explains Linda. "Anyone can imagine that if you, as a wife, have more pleasing interactions with your husband, you feel like he loves you more."

Despite the behaviorist lingo and the laboratory overtones, there is a bit of common sense to all this. A baby's smile can make someone feel good. And many people know that lending a hand, the essence of "participative reinforcement," or making tender comments, as Susan did to increase her PVCs, brings returns in good will. The difference is that at Los Horcones, these insights are applied in a deliberated system.

What's more, in a community that's also a behaviorism laboratory, reinforcers are the object of methodical study. Every morning, Linda experiments with the little ones. One current topic: Can children learn to consider future consequences? Linda doles out the investigative tool: M&M's. "you can eat it now," she tells the two- through seven-year-olds, "but if you wait until I say 'eat,' you get another." On a wall are the graphs she has charted; the lines reveal that the children will wait up to four minutes.

Los Horcones may, in fact, be one of the most self-studied communities in history. The results of the group's self-scrutiny, 20 papers, have been published in academic journals over the past 15 years—each signed communally, of course: "Los Horcones." The articles have examined the steps the community has taken to make its system of government by consensus more democratic, or revealed some of the reinforcers they've discovered to be most effective in motivating people to clean their rooms (candy and praise for a 14-year-old) or help harvest the crops (participation rather than sweets).

Still, when it comes to human overhaul, there are sticky areas. Even the technology, apparently, cannot always correct a history of individualistic living. Jealousy, for instance. That most individualistic of emotions, which says this is mine and not yours, seems to be stubborn as hell.

At Los Horcones possessiveness is discouraged. You aren't supposed to waltz into the dining room where the kids slide from one adult's lap to another's and check that your child or your husband has enough of Lupita's special rabbit-garlic stew on his or her plate. Spouses rarely sit together, often don't acknowledge each other, and a visitor doesn't at first know who the pairs are. One couple who became too much of a couple, walking hand in hand and generally behaving like honeymooners, was booted out. The community may be sexually monogamous, but it is emotionally polygamous. "You're married to everyone," Lupita explains.

"Yes, I had jealousy," says Ramon. "I went to Juan, the behavior manager. Here, your problem is everybody's. We had long meetings about it. It helped, though I think behaviors that you have when you are an adult you can't entirely get rid of."

CLEARLY, THE BRIGHTEST HOPES for the redesigned society are the people without an individualistic past, those who have benefited from the technology starting at the earliest stages of their lives: the children. If anyone is to carry out the caring and cooperative ideal, it ought to be those who have grown up here. "I never wanted kids before this," says Ramon, who is the father of four. "I didn't think I had anything to offer them, not until Los Horcones."

The children receive an enormous amount of attention from lots of adults. They're bright and outgoing, and from all appearances, feel capable and loved and useful. Skinner himself, who met the youngsters on several visits they paid to the United States, approved. "They've done wonderful things with their children," he said.

The first wave of the community's children are teenagers now. They have spent weekends with friends from the outside, and have had their friends visit them at Los Horcones. They know their upbringing has been different, but they dismiss the issue with a big shrug.

Ask them, for instance: If you had a problem, would you go to your mother?

"Sometimes when I have a problem I go to La Linda because she is the coordinator of child behavior," says Esteban, 12, son of Juan and Mireya.

Or you could ask: Who won the game of Monopoly?

"I think we all did," one child says. " We were all rich."

Or, Wouldn't you like a little pocket money?

Another shrug, confused, like when you try to explain something to a cat. "I have the money I need," says a teenager named Javier. "Whenever I go to town, they give me some money to buy a soda or something."

Or, Wouldn't you like to live somewhere else?

"I can't stand to stay away more than a couple of days," says Busi, her hands filled with fruit from the orchard.

Still, when it comes to human overhaul, there are sticky areas. Jealousy, for instance. The community may be sexually monogamous, but it is emotionally polygamous.

None of the kids can; but none have had to. That may all change. The teenagers may soon be sent to Tucson, Arizona, to a branch of the community to be opened there, so they can enroll at the University of Arizona—not for a diploma, just to attend classes and learn. The prospect of this exodus makes some nervous, and not just the kids.

Who knows how many of the five teenagers will return? Or will these behaviorally brought up young people make their lives elsewhere?

"I accept both possibilities," says Juan.

WALDEN TWO was a community of a thousand people; Los Horcones hovers at 25 to 30, and can seem at times on the verge of depopulating. They would like to boost the population to 100 or 200; that would be much more reinforcing. Then at mid-day, children could greet workers with fresh lemonade and maybe a band would be playing.

"Then, even the people we lost would return," says Ramon. As it is now, members, even those who share the ideals, fall away, beyond the reach of the technology. Over the past 17 years, 60 people have come and gone—from South America, the United States, even as far away as Europe. Perhaps some were simply lonely, or seeking food and shelter, or curious because they'd heard about the community or seen an ad. (Yes, Los Horcones advertised in the local newspaper.) They stayed a few months or a couple of years, and drifted away. Leaving is the worst anticommunitarian behavior, and yet, it would seem, the toughest to change.

Last spring, just as the counter revealed that four in five of tiny, horn-voiced Ivan's commentaries were positive, Lupita and Lucho packed up their sons and left for Lupita's family home in Hermosillo. Lucho said he had wearied of trying, against his nature, to put the community first, whether by working more or organizing better. Lupita was torn, but followed her husband.

Lucho had succeeded through behavioral self-management in giving more approval to the kids, but he had never found a program that would make him think less often of his family and himself. "I just didn't want to change for what the community was offering me," he says. "It was simply that."

It was an awful failure of the technology—that was the shared analysis of the members who remained, though the discussions weren't so analytical. There were tears. The departure was like a divorce, an angry divorce.

With the exception of one founder who stayed 12 years before leaving, Lupita and Lucho had been there longer than any of the dozens who had passed through. But years spent at the community were evidently no guarantee of continued commitment.

Outside Los Horcones, Lucho said, things seemed easier. "Here it's not the same as starting a new society and defining everything. Here, the rules of the game are easy. I feel energized to do something. I think this energy I got at Los Horcones, and I am thankful for that." He got other things, too, like knowledge of how to make cheese, which is the business he and Lupita have chosen to go into for themselves—competing, of all things, for Los Horcones's customers.

Maybe Lucho would have liked some other reinforcers: additional time for himself, more trips outside the community, perhaps a few more economic incentives?

"If there had been those, I would have felt much better," Lucho said after he left.

And now, into this 17-year-old utopia, new "experimental" reinforcers soon may be creeping: credits for work, and paid vacations. That's what Los Horcones is considering. "People won't try to live communitarianly if they are not earning something more individualistic," says Juan pragmatically.

Individual rewards for living together? It sounds against the grain. Could behaviorism have pecked up against its limits?

"With investigation, you rise above the limits," says Juan, faithful as Skinner's *Walden Two* hero, Frazier. "We must investigate in more detail the variables that control these problems."

As the late great experimenter himself might have said: Back to the lab.

Not only do the residents pick beans together, and share kitchen duties, they meet to discuss how everyone behaved during the picking and cooking.

Determinants of Behavior: Motivation, Environment, and Physiology

On the front pages of every newspaper, in practically every televised newscast, and on many magazine covers, the problems of substance abuse haunt us. Innocent children are killed when caught in the crossfire of guns of drug lords. Prostitutes selling their bodies for drug money spread the deadly AIDS virus. The white-collar middle manager loses his job because he embezzled company money to support his cocaine habit.

Why do people turn to drugs? Why doesn't all of the publicity about the ruination of human lives diminish the drug problem? Why can some people consume two cocktails and stop while others feel helpless against the inebriating seduction of alcohol? Why do some people crave heroin as their drug of choice when others crave marijuana?

The causes of individual behavior, such as drug abuse or drinking, are the focus of this section. If physiology, either biochemistry or genes, is the determinant of our behavior, then solutions to such puzzles as alcoholism lie in the field of psychobiology (the study of behavior in relation to biological processes). However, if experience as a function of our environment and learning histories creates personality and causes subsequent behavior, normal or not, then researchers must take a different tack and explore features of the environment responsible for certain behaviors. A third explanation involves some complex interaction between experience and biology. If this interaction accounts for individual characteristics, then scientists have a very complicated task ahead of them.

Conducting research designed to unravel the determinants of behavior is difficult. Scientists must call upon their best design skills to develop studies that will yield useful and replicable findings. A researcher hoping to examine the role of experience in personal growth and behavior needs to be able to isolate one or two stimuli or environmental factors that seem to control a particular behavior. Imagine trying to sufficiently delimit the complexity of the world so that only one or two events would stand out as the causes of an individual's alcoholism. Likewise, researchers interested in psychobiology also need refined, technical knowledge. Suppose a scientist hopes to show that a particular form of mental illness is inherited. One cannot merely examine family histories, since family members can learn maladaptive patterns from one another. The researcher's ingenuity will be challenged; intricate techniques such as comparing children to their adoptive parents, as well as to their biological parents, must be used. Volunteer subjects will be difficult to find, and even then, the data may be hard to interpret.

The articles in this section are meant to familiarize you with a variety of hypothesized determinants of behavior. The first article, "Same Family, Different Lives" by Bruce Bower, offers an attempt to disentangle the effects of environment versus genetics. In other words, the article

Unit 

examines the nature-nurture controversy. However, Bower concludes that neither of these is as important as *how* the individual construes or perceives his or her experience in the family. No two children, he suggests, will have exactly the same perceptions of the same family. "What a Child Is Given" examines studies of adopted children and identical twins to reveal what parts of personality are inherited. Deborah Franklin suggests that predilections rather than full-blown traits seem to be what are inherited.

The next article examines the nature-nurture controversy in more detail. "Born or Bred?" examines what the causes of homosexuality might be. Interesting new research suggests that preference for same-sex partners might be more genetic than learned, contrary to what most researchers first thought.

The role of the brain in our personality development is explored in "Mapping the Brain." The article incorporates information about mapping the brain, brainteasers for the reader to try, and discussion of how various parts of the brain function to contribute to thought, language, and, most importantly for us, emotions. In "1990–2000, The Decade of the Brain," the role of the brain in mental disorders and addictions is reviewed.

Related to this, our anthology next offers an article on biochemistry, another factor believed by scientists to be important in determining our personalities. Janet Hopson, in "A Pleasurable Chemistry," suggests that endorphins are fundamental to many different behaviors, such as the ability to experience fun.

The next three articles describe emotions and their influence on our well-being. Emotions are closely tied to motivation or our desire or need to perform certain behaviors. When we experience a positive emotion, we enjoy it, and we are motivated to prolong its pleasantness. When we experience a negative affect, such as grief, we want the pain terminated as quickly as possible.

In the first article on emotions, Robert Zajonc, in "The Face as Window and Machine for the Emotions," first describes past theories about the origin of emotions and then reveals his controversial hypothesis that feedback from facial muscles drive our emotions. In the second article, Nick Gallo takes this notion a step further. He suggests that positive emotions and attitudes affect our whole physical being. Gallo hypothesizes that positive attitudes positively influence our health; negative attitudes and emotions have an adverse impact on our being. Gallo reviews these premises in "Tapping the Healing Power of Positive Thinking." The selections on emotions are rounded out by an article demonstrating that others can generate positive and negative reactions in us; thus others can affect our physical and mental health. Daniel Goleman, the author of "Doctors Find Comfort Is a Potent Medicine," reports that social and emotional support from others helped ill patients, some waiting for heart transplants, to survive better than patients who received no social support.

The final article in this unit examines the self-sabotage or self-defeating behaviors that keep individuals from meeting their goals. "Barriers to Success" provides a number of steps to help confront and resolve these often subtle issues.

In summary, then, this unit covers factors that determine our behavior, whether the factors be internal to us, as in genetics and physiology, or external, such as our environment and those around us.

Looking Ahead: Challenge Questions

Based on your experience observing children, what would you say most contributes to their personal growth: physiological factors or environmental factors?

Besides sex differences and homosexuality, can you think of other psychological phenomena that would be interesting or worth examining to determine what factors contribute to them?

Robert Zajonc's facial feedback hypothesis is a controversial one. First explain the hypothesis. Do you feel that it is valid and can you offer concrete evidence to support your answer?

How can we map the brain? Do you know the various parts of the brain? Can you relate certain parts to certain behaviors?

Endorphins are neurochemicals. Do you know of other important neurochemicals? What are their functions?

Does the mind control the body? Do you think there is a link between mental state and bodily illness?

Name some bona fide sex differences. What stereotypical differences are usually untrue? Where do sex differences originate?

How important do you think inheritance is in substance abuse? In mental illness? In homosexuality? Do you think if these behaviors are physiological, they will be easier to treat than if they are environmentally induced?

Heart attack victims and those awaiting transplants seem to benefit from social support. What other individuals do you think might benefit from support from others?

Same Family, Different Lives

Family experiences may make siblings different, not similar

BRUCE BOWER

Psychologists uncovered a curious feature of military morale during World War II. Those in branches of the service handing out the most promotions complained the most about their rank. The investigators cited "relative deprivation" as an explanation for the trend — it's not what you have, but what you have compared with others in the same situation.

Relative deprivation achieves a more profound influence through the daily battles and negotiations that constitute life in the nuclear family, maintain researchers in human behavioral genetics. Each child in a family harbors an exquisite sensitivity to his or her standing with parents, brothers and sisters, and thus essentially grows up in a unique psychological environment, according to these investigators. The result: Two children in the same family grow to differ from one another in attitudes, intelligence and personality as much as two youngsters randomly plucked from the population at large.

While one-of-a-kind experiences and perceptions of family life combine with each child's genetic heritage to create pervasive sibling differences, shared genes — which account for half the genes possessed by all siblings save for identical twins — foster whatever similarities they display, argue scientists who apply behavioral genetics to child development.

The emphasis on children's diverse experiences cultivating sibling differences seems ironic coming from scientists dedicated to estimating the genetic contribution to individual development. Yet behavioral genetic data provide a compelling antidote to the increasingly influential notion among psychiatrists that defective genes and broken brains primarily cause mental disorders, asserts psychologist Robert Plomin of Pennsylvania State University in University Park, a leading researcher in human behavioral genetics. Ongoing studies also challenge the assumption of many developmental psychologists that important family features, such as parental education, child-rearing styles and the quality of the marital relationship, affect all siblings similarly, Plomin adds.

"What runs in families is DNA, not shared experiences," Plomin contends. "Significant environmental effects are specific to each child rather than common to the entire family."

In a further challenge to child development researchers, Plomin and psychologist Cindy S. Bergeman of the University of Notre Dame (Ind.) contend that genetic influences substantially affect common environment measures, such as self-reports or experimenter observations of family warmth and maternal affection. "Labeling a measure environmental does not make it environmental," they conclude in the September BEHAVIORAL AND BRAIN SCIENCES. "We need measures . . . that can capture the individual's active selection, modification and creation of environments."

Not surprisingly, the trumpeting of "non-shared" sibling environments and the questioning of traditional measures of the family milieu have drawn heated rebukes from some psychologists. In particular, critics claim that behavioral genetics studies rely on statistical techniques that inappropriately divvy up separate genetic and environmental effects on individual traits, rather than examining more important interactions between genes and environment.

Human behavioral genetics use family, adoption and twins studies to estimate the importance of genes and environment to individual development. Family studies assess the similarity among genetically related family members on measures of intelligence, extroversion, verbal ability, mental disturbances and other psychological traits. Adoption studies obtain psychological measures from genetically related individuals adopted by different families, their biological parents, and their adoptive parents and siblings. Researchers assume that similar scores between adoptees and biological parents reflect a greater genetic contribution, while adoptees showing similarity to adoptive parents and their children illuminate environmental effects. Twin studies compare the resemblance of identical twins on various measures to the resemblance of fraternal twins on the same measures. If heredity shapes a particular trait, identical twins display more similarity for it than fraternal twins, behavioral geneticists maintain.

Psychologist John C. Loehlin of the University of Texas at Austin directed a twin study published in 1976 that greatly influenced human behavioral genetics. Averaging across a broad range of personality measures obtained from 514 identical and 336 fraternal pairs of twins culled from a national sample of high school seniors, Loehlin's group found a

From *Science News*, December 7, 1992, pp. 376-378. Reprinted with permission from *Science News*, the weekly newsmagazine of science.

correlation of 0.50 for identical twins and 0.28 for fraternal twins.

Correlations numerically express associations between two or more variables. The closer to 1.0 a correlation figure reaches, the more one variable resembles another — say, one twin's IQ and the corresponding twin's IQ. A correlation of zero between twin IQs would signify a complete lack of resemblance, with twin pairs as different in intelligence scores as randomly selected pairs of youngsters.

The Texas researchers doubled the difference between identical and fraternal twin correlations to obtain a "heritability estimate" of 0.44, or 44 percent, an estimate of how much genes contribute to individual differences. This means that genes accounted for just under half of the individual personality differences observed in the sample of twins. Thus, environment accounted for slightly more than half of the twin's personality variations.

A further finding intrigued the scientists. The correlation on personality measures for identical twins only reached 0.50, suggesting the environment orchestrated one-half of their personality differences. Since these twins carried matching sets of genes and grew up in the same families, only "non-shared" family experiences could account for such differences, Loehlin's group argued.

Subsequent twin and adoption studies carried out in Colorado, Minnesota, Sweden and England confirmed the importance of the non-shared environment for most aspects of personality, as well as intelligence and mental disorders such as schizophrenia, Plomin asserts. He and psychologist Denise Daniels of Stanford University reviewed much of this data in the March 1987 BEHAVIORAL AND BRAIN SCIENCES, followed by a book on the subject written with Penn State psychologist Judy Dunn titled *Separate Lives: Why Siblings Are So Different* (1990, Basic Books).

All the correlations and heritability estimates boil down to a simple point, Plomin maintains: Allegedly shared family influences, such as parent's emotional warmth or disciplinary practices, get filtered through each child's unique perceptions and produce siblings with strikingly diverse personalities. For example, a shy 9-year-old who gets picked on by schoolmates will react differently to an emotional, permissive mother than a gregarious 7-year-old sibling who attracts friends easily.

Many factors divide sibling's perceptions of family life, Plomin says, including age spacing, peer and school experiences, accidents, illnesses, random events and — to a lesser extent — birth order and sex differences.

Each sibling's temperament and behavior also generate specific perceptions and responses from parents that further shape non-shared environments, he argues.

As researchers in molecular genetics vigilantly pursue genes that predispose people to a variety of mental disorders, psychiatrists should not neglect the importance of the environment specific to each child in a family, contends Plomin and two colleagues — psychiatrist David Reiss of George Washington University in Washington, D.C., and psychologist E. Mavis Hetherington of the University of Virginia in Charlottesville — in the March AMERICAN JOURNAL OF PSYCHIATRY.

The three researchers bluntly warn psychiatrists enamored of the new genetic techniques that biology alone cannot explain the development of serious mental disorders. For example, a large, ongoing study in Sweden — conducted by Plomin and several other researchers — has found that when one identical twin develops schizophrenia, the other twin contracts the disorder about one-third of the time. Heredity shoulders considerable responsibility for fomenting schizophrenia, Plomin acknowledges, but an individual's experience of family life, peers and chance events plays at least as strong a role in triggering the devastating fragmentation of thought and emotion that characterizes the disorder.

Research directed by George Washington's Reiss, and described in his article with Plomin and Hetherington, suggests non-shared experiences protect some siblings, but not others, from alcoholism when one or both parents drink alcohol uncontrollably. Family members often shield the protected child from alcoholic behavior during that child's most cherished family practices, such as Christmas celebrations, Reiss' team finds. In this way, the protected sibling gradually learns to minimize brushes with the corrosive effects of alcoholism within and outside the family, the investigators observe. Upon reaching adolescence and adulthood, the protected sibling maintains limited family contacts to avoid the influence of an alcoholic parent and often marries a non-alcoholic person.

Given the importance of non-shared environments, developmental researchers need to study more than one child per family and devise better measures of children's perceptions of family experiences, Plomin contends. He and Bergeman find that several self-report tests currently used to assess the home environment largely ignore unique individual experiences within the family and rely on measures that show substantial genetic influence. In one case they cite, unpublished data from a study of 179 reared-apart twin pairs (both identical and fraternal) and 207 reared-together twin pairs indicate that genes account for one-quarter of the individual differences plumbed by the widely used Family Environment Scales, which is generally regarded to measure environmental influences. These scales include ratings of emotional warmth, conflict, cohesion and cultural pursuits within the family.

Even the time children spend watching television — a seemingly vacuum-sealed environmental measure employed in many studies — significantly stems from genetically influenced characteristics, Plomin and his colleagues argue in the November 1990 PSYCHOLOGICAL SCIENCE. Parental restrictions do not exert strong effects on children's television viewing, since about 70 percent of parents put no limits on how much time their offspring can spend watching the tube, they state.

Plomin's team tested 220 adopted children three times, at 3, 4 and 5 years of age, as well as their biological and adoptive parents, younger adopted and non-adopted siblings, and control families with no adopted children. Biological parents and their children adopted by others spent a surprisingly similar amount of time watching television, indicating an important genetic influence on the behavior, Plomin's team asserted. Shared home environment, such as the television viewing habits of parents, also influenced children's television time, but to a lesser extent.

The results do not imply that some people follow a genetic imperative to sit glassy-eyed in front of the television for hours, day after day. "We can turn the television on or off as we please, but turning it off or leaving it on pleases individuals differently, in part due to genetic factors," the investigators conclude.

Some scientists who have long labored to understand family influences on psychological development take no pleasure in the conclusions of behavioral genetics researchers. Psychologist Lois W. Hoffman of the University of Michigan in Ann Arbor offers a critique of research highlighting sibling differences in the September PSYCHOLOGICAL BULLETIN.

Behavioral genetics tends to overestimate sibling differences because it concentrates on self-reports of personality traits, rather than on observations of coping skills and social behavior typically relied upon by developmental psychologists, Hoffman holds. A child may exaggerate differences from siblings on self-reports, whereas behavioral observations by experimenters may turn up sibling similarities in aggression or other attributes, she maintains.

Even in behavioral genetics research, significant sibling similarities apparently due to shared family environment turn up in political and religious beliefs and in general interests such as music, Hoffman adds.

Some family environments may more easily produce similarities among siblings than others, she argues. When both parents share the same values, attitudes and child-rearing styles, the chances increase that their pattern of behavior will rub off on all their children, in Hoffman's opinion.

Behavioral genetics researchers also incorrectly assume that only strong correlations between the personalities of adoptive parents and their adopted children reflect an environmental influence, the Michigan psychologist contends. Parental influences can weaken parent-child correlations on all sorts of personality measures, she points out. For instance, domineering, powerful parents may produce an anxious child, and an extremely self-assured, professionally successful parent may make a child feel inadequate.

Behavioral genetics comes under additional fire for its reliance on statistics that treat genetic and environmental influences on personality separately. This approach simply lacks the statistical power to pick up the interactions between genes and environment that primarily direct physical and psychological development, rendering current research in human behavioral genetics meaningless, argues Canadian psychologist Douglas Wahlsten of the University of Alberta in Edmonton. Much larger samples might begin to pick up such interactions, he adds.

Behavioral geneticists rely on statistics derived from a technique known as analysis of variance (ANOVA). This method is used throughout psychology to calculate whether a significant relationship, or correlation, exists between experimental variables by comparing variations in individual scores from a group's average value. Statisticians developed ANOVA in the 1920s as a way to estimate whether different types and amounts of fertilizer substantially increased the yield of various agricultural crops.

When applied to human personality and behavior, an ANOVA-based approach treats heredity and environment as mutually exclusive influences on personality, Wahlsten argues. Psychologists possess no conclusive test of interactions between genes and environments. But evidence of their interplay – as in the widely accepted theory that specific genes combine with particular family experiences to produce a psychotic disorder – may begin to emerge in behavioral genetics studies employing samples of 600 or more individuals, Wahlsten maintains. Mathematical formulas used in conjunction with ANOVA stand a better chance of ferreting out gene-environment interactions in extremely large samples, Wahlsten concludes in the March 1990 BEHAVIORAL AND BRAIN SCIENCES.

Psychologist Daniel Bullock of Boston University takes a bleaker view of ANOVA, citing its neglect of the intertwined forces guiding personality development. "The special status of ANOVA in psychology is an utter anachronism," he contends. "Many past claims by behavioral geneticists are unreliable."

Plomin rejects such charges. "To say that genetic and environmental effects interact and therefore cannot be disentangled is wrong," he states.

Twin and adoption studies consistently find strong separate effects of genes and non-shared environments on personality and other developmental measures, even when researchers painstakingly seek out possible interactions of nature and nurture, Plomin points out. Investigators may devise more sensitive statistical tests to illuminate cooperative ventures between genes and family experiences, but that will not invalidate the insights of behavioral genetics, he maintains.

That includes the discovery that what parents do similarly to two children does not importantly influence personality or problem behavior in the long run; rather, each child's perceptions of what goes on in the family prove critical. Appreciating the differences of offspring based on their individual qualities, with minimal preferential treatment of one child over another, seems a good general rule for concerned parents, Plomin says. Parents should recognize that siblings as well as "only children" harbor a keen sensitivity to their standing within the family, he adds.

"If we are reasonable, loving, but not perfect parents, the children will grow up to be themselves – all different but okay," says psychologist Sandra Scarr of the University of Virginia, a behavioral genetics researcher. "Children experience us as different parents, depending on their own characteristics, and we simply cannot make them alike or easily spoil their chances to be normal adults."

WHAT A CHILD IS GIVEN

We have long accepted that chromosomes form our physical selves. Now, scientists say they also provide a blueprint for personality.

Deborah Franklin

Deborah Franklin, who lives in San Francisco, is a staff writer at Hippocrates magazine.

On the August morning in 1971 when Marietta Spencer first met the birth family of her adopted son, Paul, she was prepared to be nervous. In the four years that she had worked as a social worker for the Children's Home Society of Minnesota, in St. Paul, Spencer had arranged and guided many such meetings. She had seen firsthand the fears and confusion stirred up when strangers, joined at the heart by adoption, examine the potent ties among them. But what Spencer wasn't prepared for, as she and Paul and the rest of the family spent a day swapping stories with a score of her son's birth relatives in their home in northern Germany, was how familiar all these strangers would seem.

It was more than physical appearance, she decided, though Paul's tall, slight build, blue eyes and narrow smile were echoed throughout the birth family, who had not seen the boy since they had arranged for his adoption 17 years earlier. It had more to do with the way one of the birth mother's brothers tossed a pillow up atop a bookcase to punctuate a joke, and with the jokes themselves—no slapstick here, only very dry, occasional one-liners. The conversational tone was familiar, too—mostly quiet and spare of excess emotion.

Like Paul, a gifted pianist, they reserved their passion for music; three of the birth mother's brothers had played for years in the local orchestra. In this German family of the woman who had died soon after giving birth to Paul, Spencer saw striking reflections of her son's personality.

"I felt such a tremendous sense of relief, as I realized, of course, this is Paul, here are the roots of who he is," she recalls.

For Paul, the encounter sparked a friendship that he pursued, returning again to visit the family on his own. For Spencer, it hammered home a lesson that scientific studies of the last 20 years have validated: A newborn child is not a formless bit of clay waiting to be shaped by parents or anybody else.

Rather, the core of many behaviors and most personality traits—the determinants of whether we're shy or extroverted, even the kinds of jokes we find funny and the kinds of people we like—seem largely embedded in the coils of chromosomes that our parents pass to us at conception. The question today is no longer whether genetics influence personality, but rather how much, and in what ways?

The answers, emerging in the last few years primarily from long-term studies of twins and adopted children, bring increasing clarity to the nature/nurture debate: While environmental forces *can* help shape temperament, it is apparently equally true that genes can dictate an individual's response to those environmental forces.

The cumulative evidence also suggests that it's not full-blown personality traits that are inherited, but rather predilections. And, in an interesting turnabout, that information has already begun to change the process of adoption itself. At many adoption agencies, a child is no longer passed from one family to another like a closely held secret. Instead, birth parents fill out lengthy questionnaires that probe not only their medical histories, but also their interests, talents and goals; that information is presented to the adoptive parents as a part of the child's birthright.

Spencer is unsentimental about the value of this information.

"A genetic history—psychological as well as medical—is something like a child's washing instructions," she ways. "When you buy a sweater, you want to know all about its fabric content. How much more important is it to know everything you can about the care and feeding of the child you are about to nuture?"

Not long ago, such views were scandalous. James Watson, Francis Crick and Maurice Wilkins were awarded a 1962 Nobel Prize for puzzling out the structure of the human genetic code, and the medical discoveries that their work has spawned—genetic clues to Tay-Sachs disease, sickle-cell anemia and hemophilia, for example—have been universally heralded. But the notion that psychological traits and behavioral disorders may also be genetically rooted has had more difficulty escaping the pall of Nazi experiments in eugenics during World War II.

Irving Gottesman, a psychologist at the University of Virginia, has studied genetic influences in intelligence, criminality and mental illness for 30 years and has some chilling memories. "At one point, I was invited to speak at the University of Texas," he says. "When I arrived, there were flyers all over campus with the title of my talk and a large swastika, implying that my work was somehow fascist." Gottesman, who is Jewish and lost several members of his family in the Holocaust, was both unnerved and outraged.

"That was the moment I first realized that it's important to say not only what I believe but what I don't believe," he says, "and to explain not only what the results of my studies mean, but also what they don't mean."

Many political activists of the 1960's and 70's, wary that genetic theories might ultimately be used to justify social inequality, attacked anyone who suggested that it wasn't within the DNA of each person to be a mathematical genius, a concert pianist or a gifted statesman. "Potential" was the buzzword; any mention of limits was deemed reactionary. It was all right to talk to your veterinarian about a sweet-tempered pup, but heaven forbid you should suggest that your child had an inherent nature. Still, even then, in a few psychology departments scattered around the world, researchers were stubbornly chipping away at the idea that every aspect of personality is learned.

It is within the family that the alchemy of nurture and nature works its strongest magic, and it is by studying families—of twins and adopted children—that behavioral geneticists have best succeeded in untangling those forces. Thomas J. Bouchard at the University of Minnesota heads one of the most dramatic of such studies.

Since 1979, Bouchard has specialized in the examination of adult identical and fraternal twins who were separated soon after their birth and reared in separate families, separate worlds. To date, he has found about 100 twin pairs—60 of them identical—and has brought each to his laboratory for a week of tests.

These days, when newspapers carry stories every other week of scientists closing in on the gene that causes one or another illness, such as cystic fibrosis or Huntington's disease, it is tempting to think of all genetic research in terms of test tubes and bits of chopped-up DNA. But those aren't a behavioral geneticist's tools. Bouchard does take many physical measurements—of heart rhythms, brainwave patterns and motor skills, for example—but most of his tests are done with pencil and paper.

He finds that identical twins reared in completely different families and communities answer the 15,000 questions he asks in remarkably similar ways. In fact, in questions that reveal traits as diverse as leadership ability, traditionalism or irritability, for example, they respond just as identical twins would who grew up in the same family. When measuring traditionalism—a composite trait that includes showing respect for authority, endorsing strict child-rearing practices and valuing the esteem of the community—the similarities between twins reared in different families were striking.

What elevates these findings above the level of what Mark Twain, borrowing from Disraeli, disparaged as "lies, damned lies, and statistics," is that these are very well-controlled statistics. By focusing on identical twins reared apart, Bouchard has found individuals who have all of their genes—and perhaps only their genes—in common. The clincher is that he and his colleagues run the same battery of tests on three other types of twins: identical pairs raised in the same families, fraternal twins reared together and fraternal twins reared apart.

Remember that identical twins arise from the fertilization of a single egg that splits in half shortly after conception, while fraternal twins are the product of *two* fertilized eggs. Identical twins have in common all their genes; fraternal twins, on average, half. By comparing the degree of similarity among twins in each of these four categories, Bouchard is able to look trait by trait and see how much each is influenced by genetics. In measuring I.Q., for example, Bouchard found that identical twins reared apart were more similar than fraternal twins reared together.

Adoptions lend insight—what do we get from nature and what from nurture?

Internationally, there are two other major, ongoing studies of identical twins reared apart—one in Sweden, the other in Finland—encompassing more than 7,000 pairs of twins all told. Together with earlier, smaller studies, this research has allowed behavioral geneticists to begin to speak confidently about the influence of genes on a number of human characteristics.

Though the debate over the value of intelligence quotient tests continues, for example, there is ample evidence that whatever it is they measure is in large part inherited. Studies of some 100,000 children and adults internationally suggest that genes are 50 percent to 70 percent responsible for an individual's I.Q. "That's not to say that you can't reduce anybody's I.Q. to zero if you hit them over the head hard enough," says John C. Loehlin, a behavioral geneticist at the University of Texas at Austin. Physical or psychological abuse, malnutrition or even a lack of intellectual stimulation can act as environmental bludgeons to native intelligence. However, Loehlin adds, "The idea that, if raised in the same environment, we would all have the same I.Q. has pretty much been laid to rest."

The findings are trickiest to understand where what we call personality is concerned. Research of the last decade shows that genetics are as influential as environment on characteristics as varied as extraversion, motivation for achievement, leadership, conscientiousness and conservatism. But whether some traits are more genetically controlled than others is much harder to tease apart. Like Bouchard and others, Robert Plomin, a developmental psychologist at Pennsylvania State University, is trying to do just that in a study of nearly 700 pairs of Swedish twins.

"The interesting question today," says Plomin, "is, 'Are there any traits that *aren't* significantly affected by genetics?' " He thinks he has found one: agreeableness, or as he calls it, "niceness"—whether a person is more trusting, sympathetic and cooperative, or cynical, callous and antagonistic. "We found that where a person tends to fall on that scale is much more influenced by environment—mostly early environment—that by genes," Plomin says, "and as a parent, I find that very reassuring."

The same studies continue to shed light on behavioral disorders such as alcoholism—a particularly complicated area of inquiry, since research shows that "situational" alcoholism caused by environmental factors such as war and unemployment skews the findings.

Men appear to be much more susceptible to the disorder than women; an alcoholic father is a strong indicator of a possible problem in a son. Conventional wisdom holds that about 25 percent of the male relatives of alcoholics are problem drinkers themselves, as compared with less than 5 percent of the general population. Perhaps the best evidence for a genetic link comes from a 1987 adoption study in Sweden, which found that the adopted sons of alcoholic birth fathers were four times more likely to grow up to be alcoholic than were members of a control group. A smaller study of adopted daughters of alcoholic birth mothers found they were three times more likely to have the disorder.

Recent adoption and twin studies also suggest that there's a genetic link to most—but not all—forms of schizophrenia. The likelihood that a child or sibling of someone with schizophrenia will develop the disorder is about 12 percent—12 times higher than the risk for everyone else—and if one identical twin has schizophrenia, the other has a 50 percent chance of developing the illness. Researchers suspect that a constellation of genes, working in combination with environmental forces, triggers the disease.

Both adoptive and twin studies confirm that clinical depression, particularly the bipolar manic-depressive variety, has a strong genetic component. According to one of the largest studies, in Denmark in 1977, if one identical twin suffers from bipolar manic depression, the other has a 79 percent likelihood of having the same disorder. Among fraternal twins, that correlation is only 19 percent.

The genetic study of criminality has replaced the study of I.Q. as the most controversial area of behavioral genetics. It is also one of the most speculative. In the mid-1960's, a theory was put forward, based on several studies of felons, that men with an extra Y choromosome were more aggressive than the average male. But further research disproved the finding. More recent adoption and twin studies, says Gottesman, indicate that if there *is* a genetic component to criminal behavior, it is slight.

Marietta Spencer's second-floor office at the Children's Home Society overlooks a shaded avenue on the residential fringe of St. Paul. On her way upstairs after lunch one afternoon last spring, she walked through the examining room, where a nurse gently prodded and poked a line-up of infants, waiting for adoption, who had been brought to the society by their foster mothers for routine check-ups. Spencer paused to play with a strikingly serious 3-month-old girl. After getting a smile from the child, she moved on.

"Even at this age, children have such obviously different temperaments," Spencer said. "Every child comes into the world with a genetic history. You can't expect them to let go of that, like so much baggage, just because they've been adopted into a new family."

These views were confirmed in the mid-1970's, Spencer said, when "people who had been adopted as children were coming back to us for more information. Some wanted to meet their birth parents, but many just wanted to know more about them, as a way of knowing more about themselves." Even if sympathetic, most adoption workers at the time had little information to offer. Disorders like depression, schizophrenia and alcoholism carried a much stronger social stigma then, and were commonly thought to be either failures of character or environmentally induced. Rather, the emphasis was on integrating the child into the new family as quickly as possible, and for some families that even meant denying the child was adopted.

To help the adopted learn more about their backgrounds, Spencer assembled a team of social workers whose main job was and continues to be detective work; they've answered 1,600 requests for information since 1977. They locate birth parents wherever possible, discreetly contact them and—if and when the individuals are willing—fill in the history of the adopted child.

Twins, raised apart and together, form the basis for the new findings.

"Anything that might be even partially inherited, and provide useful information for the adopted person, we'll ask about," Spencer says. She steps into her office and pulls open a file drawer filled with folders detailing the lives of her clients.

One particularly thick file belongs to Robert Morse. He and his family weren't much interested in questions of personality when they sought Spencer's help eight years ago; they were afraid for the boy's life. Though apparently healthy when adopted soon after birth, Morse, now 21, nearly died at age 5 from a bout with Crohn's disease, an intestinal disorder that kept him from absorbing nutrients from food. He recovered, but went on to develop arthritis at 12. The pain was so intense that at times he couldn't walk.

"I was starting to feel like a time bomb," Morse remembers, "wondering what was going to happen to me next." While hospitalized, he had plenty to wonder about. Without any medical history to work from, doctors were forced to perform painful test after painful test to come up with a definitive diagnosis of juvenile chronic arthritis, which has sometimes been associated with Crohn's disease.

"They asked if we had any illness like this in the family," Morse recalls. "All we knew from my records was that my birth mother was of Swedish extraction and allergic to hollyhocks."

Spencer, whose agency had arranged the adoption, had more information, which eventually led her to Sally Boyum, a 39-year-old whose avocation is acting. In 1967, on the day of her fiancé's funeral—he had drowned in a boating accident—Boyum had discovered she was pregnant. Grief-stricken, she arranged for an adoption. Though she didn't think to mention it at the time of the adoption—"Both Jim and I had always been so healthy"—there was a history of Crohn's disease and intestinal illness in her family. Several of her close relatives, Boyum would later learn, had bone abnormalities and the same type of arthritis as Morse.

"At first I didn't want to meet with Sally, and she didn't push it," Morse says. "I had the medical information, and that was enough." But after a few weeks of gentle encouragement from his parents, he changed his mind.

"Apparently Jim—my birth father—was a terrible tease, and so am I," Morse says. "Both my folks have a good sense of humor, but teasing—calling up on the phone and pretending to be someone else, for example—that's a kind of joking that I do, but they don't" The list goes on. "At school, or in the fraternity, I've always been a coalition-builder—it's one of the things I do best," says Morse, "and that's a role that Sally plays too." Then there's acting—a love of playing to the crowd that for Sally Boyum is also a passion.

One piece of information, Morse says, has changed his life: Many members of both sides of the family struggled with alcoholism. "Like a lot of kids in college, I used to go out and drink a lot on the weekends," he says. "Now I know that's a danger for me, and I've stopped."

MARY ANNE MAISER, WHO SUPERVISES SOCIAL WORKERS at the Children's Home Society, works in an office dotted with photographs of her three daughters, the oldest of whom, Laura, is adopted. "At the time my husband and I adopted Laura, social workers were taught—and taught clients—that each baby is a tabula rasa," Maiser says. "But by the time Laura was a year old, I knew something was wrong." She was an extremely difficult child, even alienated.

Over the years, the family sought help from a therapist. It wasn't until age 17 that Laura was diagnosed with bipolar disorder, or manic-depressive illness. Around that time, after two years of trying, Maiser was able to get more information about Laura's birth family; she had been adopted through a different agency in another state. The agency revealed that within months of Laura's adoption, her biological father had been hospitalized. "You can guess the diagnosis," Maiser says. "Bipolar disorder and schizophrenia."

If she had been given the information earlier, would it have made a difference? Maiser's voice gets tight and her mouth forms a resolute line. "Laura had so much pain and went undiagnosed for so long," she says. "She didn't just need family therapy, she needed lithium."

Despite such testimonials, some people still argue that wrapping an adopted child in genetic history does more damage than good. Laura had only about a 15 percent chance of inheriting her biological father's illness. If the disorder had never appeared, might not the label itself have twisted her life?

Marietta Spencer dismisses such objections: "Everyone I have ever worked with has said it is always better to know the history than not to know. Because, believe me, it's the parents who *don't* know who imagine the worst if they have a child who seems to be troubled."

For his part, Plomin thinks it's at least as important to tell adoptive parents that the birth father was an alcoholic as to alert them to their child's tiny risk of inheriting a rare disease. "Even if you have a genetic vulnerability," he points out, "you don't become an alcoholic unless you drink a lot over a long period. If you have the genetic history ahead of time, and you see the symptoms developing, you may be more likely to get help early."

If adoption agencies are going to do everything they can to maximize the chances of harmony in a family, should they perhaps go one step further and take temperamental factors into account when "matching" a child to new parents?

Spencer, while stressing that genetic history isn't the *only* factor to consider in an adoption, thinks it shouldn't be ignored. "Adoption, like marriage, is a process of family building, and empathy is very important," she says.

While Spencer might have a point, Plomin says, accurately predicting whether family members will be sympathetic or antagonistic to each other—in essence, predicting the chemistry of relationships—is much more difficult than she imagines. And even if adoption workers could give long, detailed personality tests to both sets of parents, they would still be a long way from predicting the baby's temperament.

Moreover, Plomin cautions, the current infatuation with genetic influences has obscured the very real importance of environment in human development. "More and more, I find myself standing up before funding committees and the public to say, 'Hey, wait a minute everybody, hold on. It's not *all* genetic."

In fact, Plomin's most recent research suggests that the influences of genes and the environment may be intractably intertwined. He asked participants in the Swedish twin study, who were an average of 59 years old, to fill out questionnaires about their parents, siblings and childhood experiences. The questions were phrased so as to get at the respondents' perceptions of their families—how cohesive, or emotionally demonstrative the families were, for example, or how much stress parents had placed on achievement, organization, discipline or culture.

The results were striking: identical twins reared in different families described their early childhood environments as remarkably similar—almost as similar as if they had been raised in the same family. Fraternal twins, on the other hand, even when raised in the same family, described that family very differently.

"You can interpret the finding in one of two ways," Plomin says. "Maybe, because of their identical genes, identical twins perceive their environment in a quite similar way—sort of like looking at the world through the same shade of gray- or rose-colored glasses. But it is also possible—and we think quite likely—that their parents and others respond to them similarly because of genetically influenced quirks of personality that they share."

In matters of human development, 'It's not* all *genetic,' as one researcher stresses. 'The trait develops via the environment,' says another.

Bouchard is finding much the same thing in his study; . . . He cites the example of one pair of identical twins from Britain, now middle-aged, who were separated soon after birth. One was adopted by a working-class family with little time or money for books. The other grew up exposed to a rich library as the daughter of a university professor. "From early childhood, both women loved to read," Bouchard says. "One had only to walk out into the living room and pull books off the shelf. The other went every week to the library and came home with a huge stack. Though one had to work a little harder at it than the other, they both ended up creating functionally similar environments."

However, "if one of those women had been raised in a family with *no* access to libraries, she would have been dramatically different from her sister," he explains. "The trait develops via the environment."

If the behavioral geneticists are right, then those who fear the tyranny of biological determinism can rest a little easier. Genes aren't the sole ingredient of the personality soup, they are merely the well-seasoned stock. That message should be liberating for all parents—and children.

BORN OR BRED?

Science and psychiatry are struggling to make sense of new research that suggests that homosexuality may be a matter of genetics, not parenting

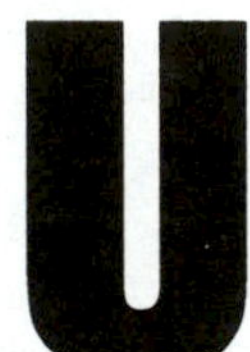ntil the age of 28, Doug Barnett* was a practicing heterosexual. He was vaguely attracted to men, but with nurturing parents, a lively interest in sports and appropriate relations with women, he had little reason to question his proclivities. Then an astonishing thing happened: his identical twin brother "came out" to him, revealing he was gay. Barnett, who believed sexual orientation is genetic, was bewildered. He recalls thinking, "If this is inherited and we're identical twins—what's going on here?" To find out, he thought he should try sex with men. When he did, he says, "The bells went off, for the first time. Those homosexual encounters were more fulfilling." A year later both twins told their parents they were gay.

Simon LeVay knew he was homosexual by the time he was 12. Growing up bookish, in England, he fit the "sissy boy" profile limned by psychologists: an aversion to rough sports, a strong attachment to his mother, a hostile relationship with his father. It was, LeVay acknowledges, the perfect Freudian recipe for homosexuality—only he was convinced Freud had cause and effect backward: hostile fathers didn't make sons gay; fathers turned hostile because the sons were "unmasculine" to begin with.

Last year, LeVay, now a neuroscientist at the Salk Institute in La Jolla, Calif., got a chance to examine his hunch up close. What he found is still reverberating among scientists and may have a profound impact on how the rest of us think about homosexuality. Scanning the brains of 41 cadavers, including 19 homosexual males, LeVay determined that a tiny area believed to control sexual activity was less than half the size in the gay men than in the heterosexuals. It was perhaps the first direct evidence of what some gays have long contended—that whether or not they choose to be different, they are born different.

Doug Barnett, meanwhile, got an opportunity to make his own contribution to the case. Two years ago he was recruited for an ambitious study of homosexuality in twins, undertaken by psychologist Michael Bailey, of Northwestern University, and psychiatrist Richard Pillard, of the Boston University School of Medicine. Published last December, only months after LeVay's work, the results showed that if one identical twin is gay, the other is almost three times more likely to be gay than if twins are fraternal—sugesting that something in the identical twins' shared genetic makeup affected their sexual orientation.

Many people have welcomed the indication that gayness begins in the chromosomes

In both studies, the implications are potentially huge. For decades, scientists and the public at large have debated whether homosexuals are born or made—whether their sexual orientation is the result of a genetic roll of the dice or a combination of formative factors in their upbringing. If it turns out, indeed, that homosexuals are born that way, it could undercut the animosity gays have had to contend with for centuries. "It would reduce being gay to something like being left-handed, which is in fact all that it is," says gay San Francisco journalist and author Randy Shilts.

But instead of resolving the debate, the studies may well have intensified it. Some scientists profess not to be surprised at all by LeVay's finding of brain differences. "Of course it [sexual orientation] is in the brain," says Johns Hopkins University psychologist John Money, sometimes called the dean of American sexologists. "The real question is, when did it get there? Was it prenatal, neonatal, during childhood, puberty? That we do not know."

Others are sharply critical of the Bailey-Pillard study. Instead of proving the genetics argument, they think it only confirms the obvious: that twins are apt to have the same sort of shaping influences. "In order for such a study to be at all meaningful, you'd have to look at twins raised apart," says Anne Fausto Stirling, a developmen-

*Not his real name.

tal biologist at Brown University, in Providence, R.I. "It's such badly interpreted genetics."

In the gay community itself, many welcome the indication that gayness begins in the chromosomes. Theoretically, it could gain them the civil-rights protections accorded any "natural" minority, in which the legal linchpin is the question of an "immutable" characteristic. Moreover, it could lift the burden of self-blame from their parents. "A genetic component in sexual orientation says, 'This is not a fault, and it's not your fault'," says Pillard.

Yet the intimation that an actual gene for gayness might be found causes some foreboding. If there is a single, identifiable cause, how long before some nerdy genius finds a "cure"? Many scientists say it's naive to think a single gene could account for so complex a behavior as homosexuality. Yet at least three research projects, one of them at the National Institutes of Health, are believed to be searching for a "gay gene" or group of genes. LeVay, for one, thinks a small number of sex genes may be isolated, perhaps within five years: "And that's going to blow society's mind."

For some people, it is not too great a leap from there to Nazi-style eugenics. In the nightmare scenario, once a gay fetus is detected in utero, it is aborted, or a genetic switch is "flipped" to ensure its heterosexuality. The gay population simply fades away. Would mothers permit such tampering? Even parents who've come to terms with their child's homosexuality might. "No parent would choose to have a child born with any factor that would make life difficult for him or her," says Laurie Coburn, program director of the Federation of Parents and Friends of Lesbians and Gays (ParentsFLAG).

On this subject, feelings are seldom restrained. But cooler voices can be heard, mainly those of lesbians. Many of them say their choice of lesbianism was as much a feminist statement as a sexual one, so the fuss over origins doesn't interest them. "It's mostly fascinating to heteros," says one gay activist. On the whole, lesbians are warier of the research, and their conspicuous absence from most studies angers them. "It's part of the society's intrinsic sexism," says Penny Perkins, public-education coordinator for Lambda Legal Defense and Education Fund, which works to promote lesbian and gay men's rights. Frances Stevens, editor in chief of Deneuve, a lesbian news magazine, admits her personal history supports biological causes; although she came from a wholesome "Brady Bunch" family, she knew she was gay "from day one." But she is skeptical of the studies, she says. "My response was: if the gay guy's [hypothalamus] is smaller, what's it like for dykes? Is it the same size as a straight male's?" That's something researchers still have to find out.

Gay men have their own reasons to be irate: as they see it, looking for a "cause" of homosexuality implies it is deviant and heterosexuality is the norm. When John De Cecco, professor of psychology at San Francisco State University and editor of the Journal of Homosexuality, began one of his classes recently by suggesting students discuss the causes of homosexuality, someone called out, "Who cares?" and the class burst into applause.

All the same, homosexuals must care deeply about how the straight world perceives them. History has taught them that the consequences of those perceptions can be deadly. Over the centuries they have been tolerated or reviled, enfranchised or oppressed. According to John Boswell's 1980 book, "Christianity, Social Tolerance and Homosexuality," things didn't turn truly nasty until the 13th century, when the church, on the heels of a diatribe from Saint Thomas Aquinas, began to view gays as not only unnatural but dangerous.

In our own century of *sex et lux,* beginning with Sigmund Freud, psychiatrists ascribed male homosexuality to unconscious conflicts and fixations that have their roots in early childhood. (Freud was always foggier on female sexuality.) But that view was officially dropped in 1973, when more stringent diagnostic standards—and the lobbying of gay activists—persuaded the American Psychiatric Association to expunge homosexuality from the list of emotional disorders. The decision was bitterly disputed; 37 percent of APA members voted against it in a 1974 referendum. But younger psychiatrists now are taught that rather

SIMON LEVAY

A grieving scientist's labor of love convinces him that biology is destiny

In the long-running debate over whether homosexuality begins in the genes or the nursery, Simon LeVay was an unlikely champion for the genetic side. As a homosexual himself (with a homosexual brother), he seemed a textbook-perfect product of nurture. "When I look back," he says, "I definitely see things that went along with being gay: not liking rough sports, preferring reading, being very close with my mother." And the classic clincher—"I hated my father as long as I can remember." By Freudian lights, that should have made an open-and-shut case for nurture. But LeVay believed even then that nature comes first. "My point would be that gays are extremely different when they're young and as a *result* they can develop hostile relationships with their fathers. It's just a big mistake to think it's the other way around and the relationships are causative."

An Englishman with a Ph.D. in neuroanatomy, LeVay spent 12 years at Harvard before moving on to the Salk Institute to pursue his field of research—which, ironically, included the influence of environment on development. But when his lover of 21 years, Richard Hersey, died of AIDS, LeVay went into a deep depression. Hospitalized for two weeks, he began reevaluating his goals. "It makes you think what your life is about," he says. Around that time, a UCLA lab announced its finding that a portion of the male hypothalamus that regulates sex was more than twice as large as women's. Suddenly, it seemed to LeVay there was a thesis to pursue: was it also larger than that of gays? "I felt if I didn't find anything, I would give up a scientific career altogether."

After nine months' work, LeVay did find that in at least one group of gays, the sex-regulating area was smaller than in straight men. The work brought him instant fame and a round of talk shows, where he's often obliged to contend with the unconvinced. But he thinks it's worth it, if it promotes the idea that homosexuality is a matter of destiny, not choice. "It's important to educate society," he says. "I think this issue does affect religious and legal attitudes." From here on he'll be spreading the word as codirector of the West Hollywood Institute for Gay and Lesbian Education, on leave from Salk. The new institute opens in September as one of the first free-standing schools for homosexual studies. LeVay may have to abandon research. But he's still on the compassionate course he set out on after the death of his lover.

than trying to "cure" homosexuals, they should help them feel more comfortable about themselves.

LeVay resolved to look for sex differences in the brain after the slow, wrenching death from AIDS of his companion of 21 years (box). He'd been impressed by a study done by a UCLA graduate student, Laura Allen, working with biologist Robert Gorski, showing that a portion of the hypothalamus in the brains of males was more than twice as large as that of women. LeVay's report, published in the journal Science on Aug. 30, 1991, was based on his own yearlong study of the hypothalamus in 41 cadavers, including 19 self-avowed homosexual men, 16 heterosexual men and 6 heterosexual women. All the homosexuals had died of AIDS, as had seven of the heterosexuals—including one of the women. What emerged with almost startling clarity was that, with some exceptions, the cluster of neurons known as INAH 3 (the third interstitial nucleus of the anterior hypothalamus, which LeVay calls "the business end as far as sex goes") was more than twice as large in the heterosexual males as in the homosexuals, whose INAH 3 was around the same size as in the women. In the sensation that greeted the report, its cautious wording was all but ignored. "What I reported was a difference in the brain structure of the hypothalamus," says LeVay. "We can't say on the basis of that what makes people gay or straight. But it opens the door to find the answer to that question."

One of the major criticisms of the study was that AIDS could have affected the brain structure of the homosexual subjects. LeVay has been able to field that one by pointing out that he found no pathology suggesting such damage either in gay or straight men who died of the disease. Later, in fact, he examined the brain of a homosexual who died of lung cancer, and again found INAH 3 much smaller.

The trickier question is whether things might work the other way around: could sexual orientation affect brain structure? Kenneth Klivington, an assistant to the president of the Salk Institute, points to a body of evidence showing that the brain's neural networks reconfigure themselves in response to certain experiences. One fascinating NIH study found that in people reading Braille after becoming blind, the area of the brain controlling the reading finger grew larger. There are also intriguing conundrums in animal brains. In male songbirds, for example, the brain area associated with mating is not only larger than in the female but varies according to the season.

Says Klivington: "From the study of animals, we know that circulating sex hormones in the mother can have a profound effect on the organization of the brain of the fetus. Once the individual is born, the story gets more complex because of the interplay between the brain and experience. It's a feedback loop: the brain influences behavior, behavior shapes experience, experience affects the organization of the brain, and so forth."

LeVay knows he is somewhat vulnerable on that score. Because his subjects were all dead, he knew "regrettably little" about their sexual histories, besides their declared or presumed orientation. "That's a distinct shortcoming of my study," he concedes. Did the gay men play the passive or aggressive roles in sex? Were some bisexual, another variable, and could that have affected their neuron clusters? To find answers, LeVay plans next to study living subjects with the new MRI (magnetic resonance imaging) technology. But he remains convinced that biology is destiny. "If there are environmental influences," he says, "they operate very early in life, at the fetal or early-infancy stage, when the brain is still putting itself together. I'm very much skeptical of the idea that sexual orientation is a cultural thing."

The Bailey-Pillard twin study had its own shortcomings. The numbers alone were impressive. The researchers found that of 56 identical twins, 52 percent were both gay, as against 22 percent of fraternal twins, who have somewhat weaker genetic bonds. (Of the adoptive, nongenetically related brothers in the study, only 11 percent were both gay.) The suggestion of a shared genetic destiny is strong, but many critics have wondered: what about the discordant twins—those where only one was homosexual? Many in the study were not only discordant, but dramatically different.

Most sexuality studies use the Kinsey

ANNETTE BRENNER

For parents, a child's 'coming out' can lead to painful episodes of soul-searching

Annette E. Brenner remembers joking when her oldest son was 4 that she'd approve his marrying outside the family's faith as long as he married a woman. When he "came out" to her and her husband at 17, one of her first reactions was to try to "negotiate" him out of his gayness. She offered him a car, a house, if only he would wait and try marriage. He was at boarding school in Connecticut at the time, and she was convinced it was "just a stage." She remembers thinking, "Sure, this week you're a homosexual. Enjoy the experiment, have fun. Next week you'll be a Hare Krishna." Then she became enraged. "What is this kid doing to me?" she'd ask herself. What was he doing to his grandparents, his brother and sister?

Years of gay activism haven't made coming out much easier on parents. At the Chicago-area office of ParentsFLAG (parents and Friends of Lesbians and Gays), the national support organization Brenner joined, parents often call in tears. Some, she says, have had nervous breakdowns over the news of their child's homosexuality. Brenner had a terrible time accepting her son's revelation. For a while she wondered about the Freudian explanation. "We replayed his whole life" looking for some environmental reason, she says. She wondered whether she had been too domineering. They sent him to a therapist, only to be told he was comfortable with his gayness. Finally, they came to terms with it, too—her husband more easily than she did. She understands now why her son had such a poor self-image at school, why he endured falling grades and bouts of depression.

Her son is 28 now, and he brings his lover home for visits. "He's happy because his family accepts him," says Brenner. Still, she frets about AIDS, and she knows he hasn't been tested. He's been "bashed" a couple of times—and she worries about his physical safety. Even seeing how content her son is, Brenner says, "Had I known that I was to have a gay child, I would probably not want to have a gay child."

At FLAG, parents are firmly behind any research that implicates biology as the source of gayness. It assuages the raging guilt some of them feel that they might be responsible. "Especially if my child gets AIDS," says Brenner, "can you imagine what that would be like?" Probably, it would be shattering. Gays may come out and get on with their lives, often happily. But for parents, the doubts and the dread never seem to stop.

scale, which rates orientation on a seven-point spectrum from strictly heterosexual to exclusively homosexual. The study found that most of the discordant identical twins were at opposite ends of the Kinsey spectrum. How could two individuals with identical genetic traits and upbringing wind up with totally different sexual orientation? Richard Green, a noted UCLA researcher of homosexuality, says he believes research should focus on that finding, which he deems "astounding." Although Pillard and Bailey are certain that biology plays the dominant role, Bailey acknowledges: "There must be something in the environment to yield the discordant twins."

What that might be is uncertain. None of the usual domineering-mother, distant-father theories has been conclusively shown to determine sexuality. Meanwhile the case for biology has grown stronger. "If you look at all societies," says Frederick Whitam, who has researched homosexuality in cultures as diverse as the United States, Central America and the Philippines, "homosexuality occurs at the same rates with the same kinds of behavior. That suggests something biological going on. The biological evidence has been growing for 20 or more years."

"Something in the environment," "something biological"—the truth is, the nature-nurture argument is no longer as polarized as it once was. Scientists are beginning to realize there is a complex interplay between the two, still to be explored. June Reinisch, director of the Kinsey Institute, prefers to think we are only "flavored, not programmed." Genetics, she says, only give us "a range of outcomes."

'There are talk shows where people still say, homosexuality is an abomination, it's vile.'

Novelist Jacquelyn Holt Park

Should it really matter to gays what makes them gay? Whitam says it does matter. In a 1989 study of attitudes toward gays in four different societies, those who believed homosexuals "were born that way" represented a minority but were also the least homophobic. Observes Whitam: "There is a tendency for people, when told that homosexuality is biological, to heave a sigh of relief. It relieves the families and homosexuals of guilt. It also means that society doesn't have to worry about things like gay teachers."

For the most part, gays remain doubtful that even the strongest evidence of biological origins will cut much ice with confirmed homophobes. Many find the assumption naive. "Our organization considers the studies useless," says Dr. Howard Grossman, a gay doctor who heads New York Physicians for Human Rights. "It's just like the military—you can show them a thousand studies that show gay soldiers aren't a security risk and they still don't care."

The doctor's pessimism is not unwarranted. Jacquelyn Holt Park, author of a moving novel about the sorrows of growing up lesbian in the sexually benighted 1940s and '50s, is just back from a 9,000-mile book tour where she was astonished to find how little has changed. "There are talk shows," says Park, "where fundamentalists and the like still say [homosexuality] is an abomination, it's vile. They said, 'You're not black, blacks can't change their color, but you can change.' I guess these new studies might address some of those feelings."

Even within the enlightened ranks of the American Psychoanalytic Association there is still some reluctance to let homosexual analysts practice. As arrested cases themselves, the argument goes, they are ill equipped to deal with developmental problems. The belief that homosexuality can and should be "cured" persists in some quarters of the profession.

Others are exasperated by that view. Richard Isay, chairperson of the APA's Committee on Gay, Lesbian and Bisexual Issues, is convinced analysis can be more damaging than beneficial to gays. "I still see many gay men who come to me after they've been in analysis where the therapist has been trying to change their orientation," he says. "That's extremely harmful to the self-esteem of a gay man." Isay thinks the approach, instead, should be to try to clear away "roadblocks" that may interfere with a gay's ability to function.

Perhaps the most voluble spokesman for

MIKE

Through therapy, a gay widower seeks an end to a lifestyle of cruising

"Mike" is a 49-year-old widower who was married for 18 years and has a teenage son. Although he says he loved his wife, he was secretly cruising gay bars during his marriage and engaging in short-term homosexual encounters. After his wife died, he found his way to Dr. Joseph Nicolosi, whom he consulted for eight months.

"I went on binges, just like an alcoholic would do. [After my wife died] Saturday nights were terrible. I'd go to a heterosexual bar and end up jumping in my car and going to some bath or gay bar. I was at a point in my life whether either I was a homosexual and I was going to be open and public about it, or I was not going to be a homosexual and be otherwise. I was in the pits. Whatever I was doing was not making me happy. I was not going to continue living the lie that I was living.

"I kept searching for somebody to help me, but you always heard that nothing could be done about this and anybody who came to your attention was usually a gay therapist. I was more than in a closet, I was in a coffin. I had never revealed this to anybody before. I never trusted anybody. In the very first session [with Dr. Nicolosi], I realized we were on the same wavelength.

"I never had a man in my life who taught me how to be a man. I never had a role model. I realize how my dad's failure to be present for me screwed me up. I was very angry toward my dad. And I never knew why. I [also] felt I'd been castrated by women. When I got into therapy, the resentment toward my mother was far greater than toward my dad. There was a lot of anger, a lot of deep feeling at not having your mother accept your maleness. When I started loving myself, when I started to know who I was, my maleness came with it." (*Six months after completing therapy, Mike says he has not had any homosexual encounters. Does he feel "cured"?*)

"I would have to answer, yes, I still do sometimes have homosexual feelings. But I don't get upset if I get them because I understand them now. Now Saturday night comes and goes and I don't even think about it."

the "fix it" school is Charles Socarides, a New York City analyst who claims a flourishing practice in turning troubled homosexuals into "happy, fulfilled heterosexuals." To Socarides, the only biological evidence is "that we're anatomically made to go in male-female pairs." Thus he "reconstructs" patients' lives to learn why they can't mate with opposite-sex partners. There can be many reasons, he says: "abdicating fathers, difficult wives, marital disruptions." From there, he "opens up the path" to hetero happiness, for which, he says, one gratified customer cabled him recently: "The eagle has landed."

Some psychiatrists still see the removal of homosexuality from the official list of emotional disorders as a mistake. (Instead, it was innocuously identified as "sexual orientation disturbance.") "Psychology and psychiatry have essentially abandoned a whole population of people who feel dissatisfied with their feelings of homosexuality," says psychologist Joseph Nicolosi, author of "Reparative Therapy of Male Homosexuality" *(Jason Aronson. 1991).* In graduate school, says Nicolosi, he found the stance was that if a client came in complaining about his gayness, the therapist's job was to teach him to accept it. "It was like the old joke of the patient who tells the doctor his arm hurts when he bends it and the doctor advises him not to bend it."

'Psychology and psychiatry have abandoned a whole population of people who feel dissatisfied with homosexuality.'

Psychologist Joseph Nicolosi

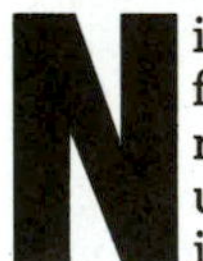

Nicolosi tries to do more than that for his patients, most of them men in their 20s and 30s who are unhappy with their homosexuality. As director of the Thomas Aquinas Psychology Clinic in Encino, Calif., he tries to bolster his patients' sense of male identity, which he sees as crucial to their orientation. The biological evidence is inconclusive, Nicolosi says; there is much more proof for familial causes of homosexuality. "Research has shown repeatedly that a poor relationship with a distant, aloof father and an overpossessive, domineering mother could cause homosexuality in males," he says.

In fact, some of that research, dating back to the 1950s, has been discredited because of faulty techniques, among other problems. Nicolosi is at any rate modest in his own claims. No cures as such, but "a diminishment of homosexual feelings" to the point where some patients can marry and have families. How long is treatment? "Probably a lifetime process," he says.

With the debate over origins still going strong, comes one more exhibit in evidence. Recently, Bailey and Pillard divulged just a tidbit from their not-yet-published study of lesbian twins. Finding enough females for the study took twice as long as their earlier project, says Bailey, but apparently it was worth the effort. "If there are genes for homosexuality, they're not gender blind," he says. Lesbians in the study had more lesbian sisters than they did gay brothers.

Nature? Nurture? Perhaps the most appropriate answer comes from Evelyn Hooker, who showed in an important 1950s study that it is impossible to distinguish heterosexuals from homosexuals on psychological tests. Hooker takes the long view of the search for origins. "Why do we want to know the cause?" she asks. "It's a mistake to hope that we will be able to modify or change homosexuality . . . If we understand its nature and accept it as a given, then we come much closer to the kind of attitudes which will make it possible for homosexuals to lead a decent life in society." The psychiatric profession heeded Hooker when it stopped calling homosexuality an illness. At 84, her voice has grown fainter, but the rest of us could do worse than listen to her now.

DAVID GELMAN *with* DONNA FOOTE *in Los Angeles,* TODD BARRETT *in Chicago,* MARY TALBOT *in New York and bureau reports*

MAPPING THE BRAIN

With powerful new devices that peer through the skull and see the brain at work, neuroscientists seek the wellsprings of thoughts and emotions, the genesis of intelligence and language. They hope, in short, to read your mind.

If you have one of 1,000 test copies of this magazine, sometime while you read this article a specially embedded microchip will give you a mild electric shock. If you have an ordinary copy, there is no danger.

Deep inside your brain, a little knob-shaped organ no bigger than a chickpea is going like gangbusters right now (at least if you're the gullible type). The organ is called the amygdala, and when neuroscientists gave volunteers a version of this warning—that sometime during an experiment they might receive an electric shock—the nerve cells in the volunteers' amygdalae lit up like telephone lines during the World Series earthquake. How did the scientists know? They were reading their volunteers' minds—by mapping their brains.

It seems only fitting that, with 1492 in the air, one of the greatest uncharted territories in science is finally attracting its own cartographers. The terrain is the gelatinous three-pound world called the Brain, and the map makers' sextants are devices that stare right through the solid wall of the skull. The maps they are slowly piecing together will carry labels even more provocative than the 15th century's "Disappointment Islands." They will show, with the precision of the best atlas, the islands of emotion and the seas of semantics, the land of forethought and the peninsula of musical appreciation. They will show, in short, exactly where in the brain cognition, feelings, language and everything else that makes us human comes from.

It's called a functional map of the brain, and it is one of the grandest goals of what Congress and President George Bush have declared the "Decade of the Brain." The neuroscientists might actually achieve it, thanks to the technologies that open windows on the mind. With 100 billion cells—neurons—each sprouting about 1,000 sylphlike fingers to reach out and touch another, it's quite a view. "The brain is the last and greatest biological frontier," says James Watson, codiscoverer of the double helix that is DNA. In a book from the National Academy of Sciences released last month entitled "Discovering the Brain," Watson calls it "the most complex thing we have yet discovered in our universe."

To make sense of the jungle of neurons and swamps of gray matter, it won't be enough to take snapshots with, say, a CAT scanner. Computer-assisted tomography produces lovely pictures of brain structure, but can't distinguish between a live brain and a dead one. The challenge for brain cartography is to move beyond structure—all the cranial continents have been identified—to create a detailed diagram of which parts do what. For that, the map makers rely on an alphabet soup of technologies, from PETs to SQUIDs (page 49), that pinpoint neural activity in all its electrical, magnetic and chemical glory.

Each technique adds a different piece to the neural puzzle. Some magnetic imaging, for instance, is so spatially precise it can distinguish structures as small as a millimeter, but is much too slow to reveal the sequence in which different clumps of neurons blink on during a thought. But together, the technologies are yielding a map as detailed as that expected to be drawn for human DNA—though much more interesting. For instance, neuroscientists thought that the cerebellum was the patron saint of the clumsy, the region that controls balance and coordination and so keeps people from stumbling. New studies suggest that the cerebellum may also house the memory of rote movements: touch-typing or violin fingering may originate in the same place as the command not to trip over your own two feet. "Perhaps the brain can package a task very efficiently, even take it out of the conscious world [of the cortex] and just run the program unconsciously," speculates neurologist John Mazziotta of the University of California, Los Angeles. The mapping expeditions have also perked up philosophy. Once again, eminent thinkers are dueling over whether the mind is anything more than the brain.

The lofty abilities of the brain reside in the cortex, the quarter-inch-thick cap of grooved tissue that runs from the eyebrows to the ears. The cortex consists of two hemispheres, a left and a right, each composed of four distinct lobes (diagram, next page) and connected by a highway of fibers called the corpus callosum. Studies of patients with brain lesions, as well as electrical stimulation of conscious patients during brain surgery, have pinpointed scores of regions that seem to specialize in particular jobs. Some make sense of what the eyes see. Others distinguish irregular from regular verbs. But research on brain-damaged people always runs the risk that they aren't representative. The power of the new imaging techniques is that they peer inside the minds of the healthy. "They allow us to study how the living brain performs sophisticated mental functions," says neuroscientist Eric Kandel of Columbia University. "With them, we can address the most complicated questions in all science."

Some of the maps confirm what studies of brain-damaged patients had already shown. Last November, for instance, research-

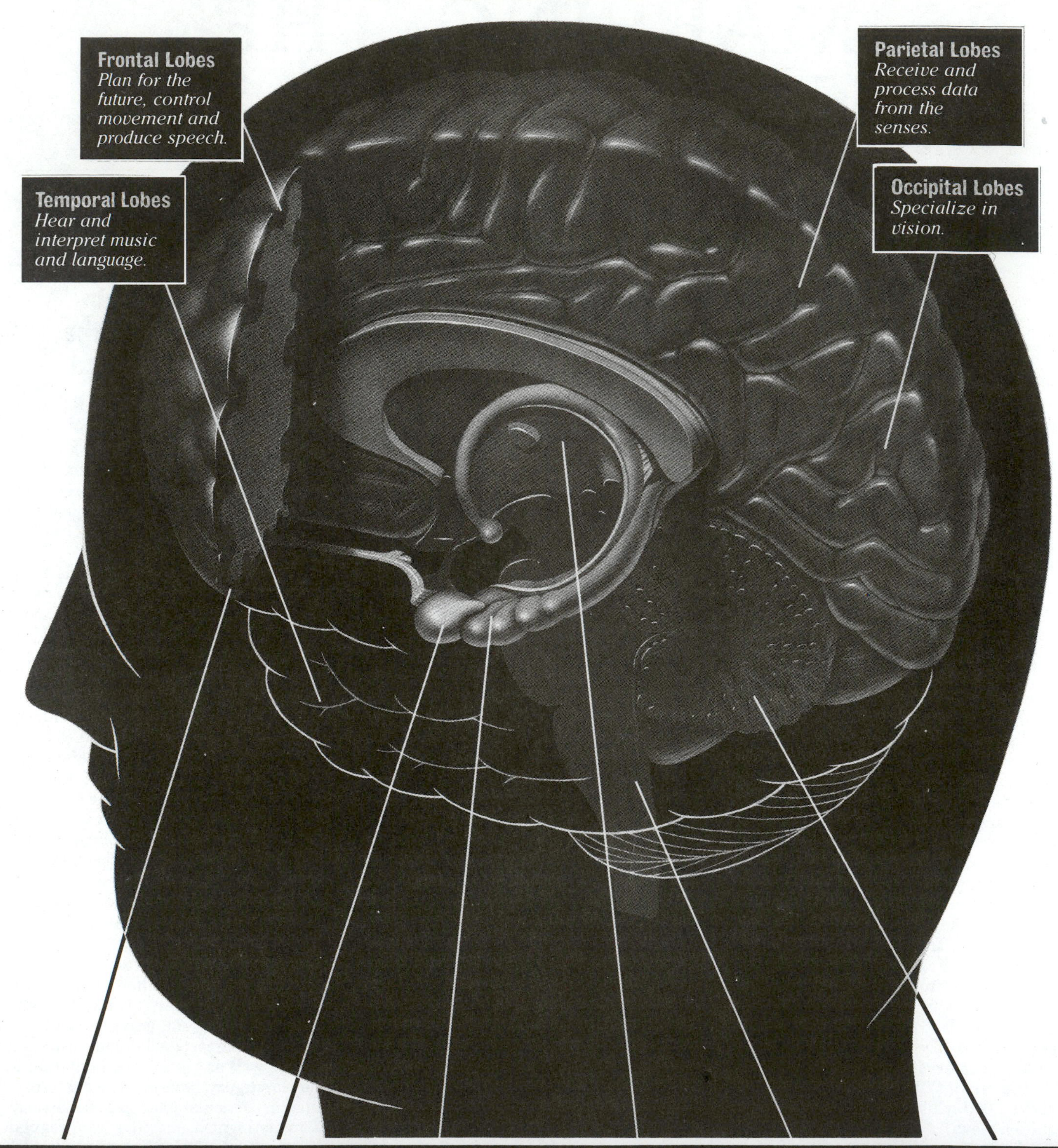

Cerebral Cortex *Covers the four lobes that make up the left and right hemispheres of the brain. It is just a few millimeters thick.*

Amygdala *Generates emotions from perceptions and thoughts.*

Hippocampus *Consolidates recently acquired information, somehow turning short-term memory into long term.*

Thalamus *Takes sensory information and relays it to the cortex.*

Brainstem *Controls automatic body functions like breathing. It is the junction between the brain and the spine.*

Cerebellum *Governs muscle coordination and the learning of rote movements.*

ers reported on a PET (positron emission tomography) study confirming that the hippocampus, a little sea-horse-shaped structure deep inside the brain, is necessary for forming and retrieving memories of facts and events (Newsweek, Nov. 25, 1991). That's just what studies of amnesiacs had found. But while confirmation of old notions is nice, what the brain mappers really want is to stumble upon a Northwest Passage, connections that were totally unexpected, symphonies of neurons that had gone completely unheard. PET may do that. For a PET scan, volunteers are injected with radioactive glucose. Glucose, the body's fuel, mixes with the blood and wends its way to the brain. The more active a part of the brain is, the more glucose it uses. PET sensors arrayed around the head of a volunteer, who sits in a modified dentist's chair with his head behind black felt to keep out distractions, pinpoint the source of the radioactivity, and hence the heightened activity. They send the data to computers that produce two-dimensional drawings showing the neural hot spots.

PET is hardly the only technique to discover that the brain is organized in weird ways. Take music—as a team at New York University did. It has pioneered the use of the SQUID (superconducting quantum interference device), which senses tiny changes in magnetic fields. (When neurons fire, they create an electric current; electric fields induce magnetic fields, so magnetic changes indicate neural activity.) The device looks like a hair dryer from hell. When the NYU scientists aimed a SQUID at a brain listening to various notes, they found an eerie reflection of the black and white keys on a piano. NYU physicist Samuel Williamson and psychologist Lloyd Kaufman saw not only that the brain hears loud sounds in a totally different place from quieter sounds, but also that the areas that hear tones are laid out like a keyboard. "The distance between brain areas that hear low C and middle C is the same as the distance between areas that hear middle C and high C—just like on a piano," says Williamson.

In another unexpected find, brain systems that learn and remember faces turn out to reside in a completely different neighborhood from those that learn and recall man-made objects. The memory of a face activates a region in the right part of the brain that specializes in spatial configurations. The memory of a kitchen spatula, in contrast, activates areas that govern movement and touch. "What counts is how the brain acquires the knowledge," says neuroscientist Antonio Damasio of the University of Iowa College of Medicine. "The brain lays down knowledge in the very same systems that are engaged with the interactions"—in the case of a spatula, the memory resides in that part of the cortex that originally processed how the spatula felt and how the hands moved it.

Imagine four squares and form them into an "L." Now imagine two squares side by side. Fit the pieces into a smooth rectangle.

An area near the left side of the back of your head snapped to attention, especially if you're doing this without pencil and paper. It's one of the brain's centers for spatial reasoning—no surprise there. The astonishing thing is how hard it works. At the Brain Imaging Center at UC, Irvine, Richard Haier had volunteers play the computer game Tetris while in a PET scanner. In Tetris, players move and rotate squares, in various configurations such as an "I" or an "L," to create a solid block. This year, Haier found that people used lots of mental energy while learning Tetris, but after practicing for several weeks their brains burned much less energy—even though their scores had improved 700 percent. "Watching someone play Tetris at an advanced level, you might think, 'That person's brain must really be active'," says Haier. However, "[their] brains were actually not working as hard as when they played for the first time." Even more intriguing, the greater a volunteer's drop in the energy his brain used, the higher his IQ.

Intelligence, then, may be a matter of efficiency—neural efficiency. Smart brains may get away with less work because they use fewer neurons or circuits, or both. Conversely, when a less smart brain thinks, lots of extraneous or inefficient neural circuits crackle. Intelligence, in this model, is a function not of effort but of efficiency. Intelligence "may involve learning what brain areas *not* to use," says Haier.

One key to intelligence may be "pruning." At birth, a baby's brain is a rat's nest of jumbled neurons. It uses up more and more glucose until the child is about 5, when it is roughly twice as active as an adult's. Then glucose use and the number of circuits plummet until the early teen years. This is called neural pruning, and Haier speculates it's the key to neural efficiency. More intelligent people may get that way by more pruning, which leaves remaining circuits much more efficient. Might pruning explain the link between genius and madness? "Overpruning may result in the high intelligence often associated with creativity, but hyperpruning may result in psychopathology," suggests Haier. No one has a clue as to why some brains prune their circuits like prize bonsai and others let them proliferate

WINDOWS ON THE MIND?

Each scanning device has strengths and weaknesses. PET accurately tracks brain function, but can't resolve structures less than .5 inch apart. MRI can't detect function, but can distinguish structures even .05 inch apart.

MRI
Magnetic resonance imaging snaps detailed images of brain

PET
Positron emission tomography tracks blood flow, a proxy for brain activity

SQUID
Superconducting quantum interference device picks up magnetic fields,a mark of brain action

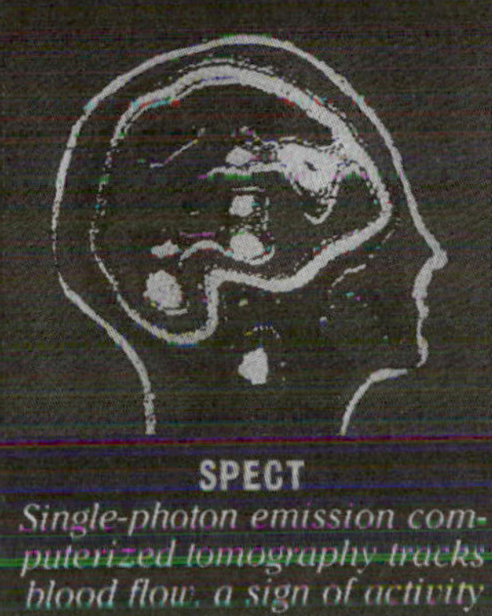

SPECT
Single-photon emission computerized tomography tracks blood flow, a sign of activity

EEG
Electroencephalogram, an early brain-monitoring technique, detects electrical activity

like out-of-control wisteria. Edward Scissorhands, call Dr. Frankenstein.

Decide whether any words in this sentence rhyme. Now name an animal with a very long neck.

Your vision center, at the back of your head right behind your eyes, has been buzzing with activity as you read. That's to be expected. But until recently, scientists thought that all language skills—reading, writing and rhyming—were contained within a single brain circuit. They were wrong. Naming and reading are governed from two different places. You can thank several clusters of neurons scattered across the cortex for coming up with "giraffe"; that's where naming comes from. But these clusters are not necessarily involved in reading. Similarly, regions that process spoken language, midway back on the left side of your head, told you that no words in the sentence rhymed. That spot had been basically dormant until then: contrary to psych texts, words do not have to be pronounced in the mind's ear in order for the brain to assign them a meaning. In the new model, the brain processes words by sight *or* sound. The result goes to the left frontal lobe, which imparts meaning to information received by either sense.

That finding undercuts psychologists' certainty that language is processed like a football play. Scholars had thought that to speak aloud a written word, the printed word had to pass from the visual cortex that saw it to the area that decoded it. From there, it was lateraled to the area in the frontal lobe that pronounces it. Touchdown! "The surprise is that when you see a word, and say it, it doesn't pass through the auditory part of the brain at all," says neuroscientist and PET pioneer Marcus Raichle of Washington University in St. Louis. "The old idea was that before you could say a word, the brain must change a visual code into a sound code. We don't see that at all." In fact, auditory areas of the brain are not active when one speaks, says Raichle: "You don't listen to what you say in the same way that you hear what others say."

COURTESY HAIER & BUCHSBAUM (TOP & MIDDLE), COURTESY BUCHSBAUM (BOTTOM)

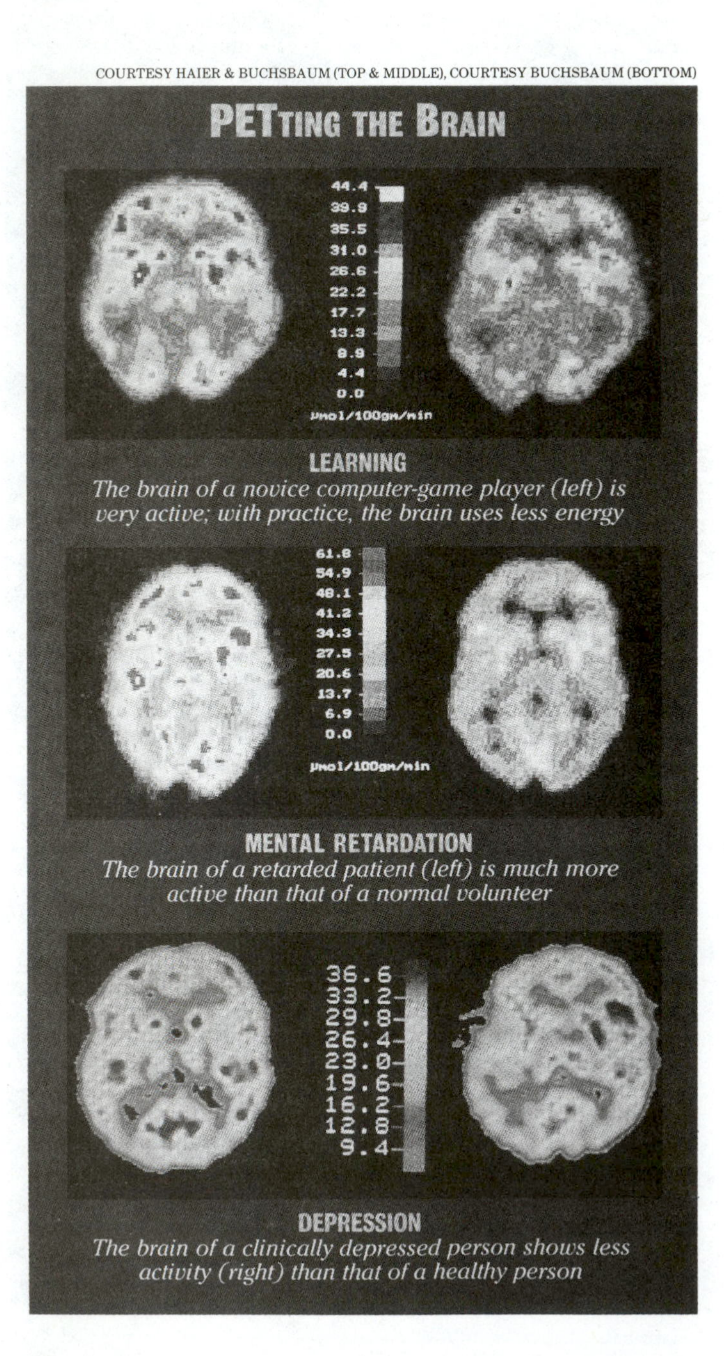

LEARNING
The brain of a novice computer-game player (left) is very active; with practice, the brain uses less energy

MENTAL RETARDATION
The brain of a retarded patient (left) is much more active than that of a normal volunteer

DEPRESSION
The brain of a clinically depressed person shows less activity (right) than that of a healthy person

Board. Tweal. Nlpfz.

Your visual cortex is still on the job, seeing words. But so are areas way outside the vision centers. To get at the great questions of language, Raichle and colleagues started small—with single words. As words flashed by on a computer screen, one per second, the PET volunteers' visual cortex lit up, as expected. But so did dime-size clusters of neurons way outside the vision centers, on the left side of the brain. Perhaps they hold the meanings of words. Call it Semantic Central. These same areas lit up when the volunteers saw nonwords that nevertheless obeyed rules of English—"tweal"—as if the brain were scrambling to assign a meaning to something that by all rights should have one. These semantic areas stayed dark when the volunteers saw consonant letter strings—*nlpfz.* Since babies aren't born knowing which letters form words and which don't, the brain has apparently learned what conforms to rules of English spelling and what does not. And it has carved out special zones that do nothing but analyze these rule-obeying strings of letters.

Supply a verb for each noun: pencil, oven, broom. And tell which animals in this list are dangerous: tapir, lion, lamb.

Two clusters in your cerebral cortex lit up. One, in the left frontal lobe, kicks in when the brain deals with meanings. But it gets bored easily. If you were asked to supply verbs for the same nouns, or analyze the same animals, over and over, the region wouldn't lift a neuron: it seems to play a role only "in the acquisition of a new skill, in this case linguistic," says Raichle. Then it bows out. The brain can still provide "write" for "pencil," but seems to do so on automatic pilot. In addition, to focus on the word problems, the "anterior cingulate gyrus" turns on, as it does whenever "subjects are told to pay attention," says Raichle. It also shines with activity when researchers ask volunteers to read words for colors—red, orange, yellow—written in the "wrong" color ink, such as "red" written in blue. Some neural arbiter must choose which processing center, that for reading "red" or naming blue, to activate. As the brain tries to resolve the conflict, the front of something called the cingulate cortex, located an inch or so beneath the center line of the front of the scalp, positively glows.

Scans make it clear that the brain is a society of specialists. Different grape-size regions process proper but not common nouns, for instance. Not only that, separate zones also harbor tiny fragments of a larger idea, says Antonio Damasio. It can be an idea as lofty as Truth or as mundane as silver candlesticks. The Ph.D.s haven't figured out Truth yet, but they think they have a pretty good idea how your mind's eye sees the candlestick. PET scans show that these fragments come together in time but not in space, thanks to an as-yet-undiscovered maestro that takes the disparate tones and melds them into perfect harmony.

Fragments of knowledge are scattered around the brain, especially in the back of the cortex. Areas closer to the front contain what Damasio calls "combinatorial codes," which assemble information from the rear. Damasio has christened these "convergence zones"; their location varies from one person to the next. A convergence zone recalls where in the back office the different attributes of the candlestick are stored. When it's time to reconstruct the silver candlestick, the convergence zone activates all the relevant storage sites simultaneously. One bundle of nerves sends in a pulse that means "silver," another shoots out "cylinder shaped," another offers "burns." "Our sensory experiences happen in different places," says Damasio. "There must be an area where the facts converge."

PETs have seen clues to convergence zones in people who, because of brain lesions, cannot name famous faces. They register a flicker of recognition, but deny they know whose face it is. The knowledge exists, says Damasio, but is "unavailable to consciousness." The lesion has apparently disrupted the links between the memories for various parts of a face—the shapes of its features, the tone of its skin—tucked away in the right part of the cortex and the memory of the name in another back office. The fragments remain, but the convergence zone cannot bring them together.

Sing "Row, Row, Row Your Boat." Lift your finger when you come to a four-letter word.

If you're female, tiny spots on both sides of your brain light up. If you're male, only one side does. That's the kind of map Cecile Naylor of the Bowman Gray School of Medicine saw when she scanned brains of people who had been marked with a radioactive tracer that homes in on active areas. In one task, they listened to words and raised a finger when they heard one four letters long. Women's mental acrobatics were all over the brain; men's were compartmentalized. In women but not in men, some areas associated with vision lit up. "You wonder if females are using more of a visual strategy than males," says Naylor. Perhaps they see the spelled word in their mind's eye and then count letters.

New windows into the brain are ready to open. Robert Turner of the National Institutes of Health recalls "the awe-inspiring experience" of lying inside a colossal MRI (magnetic resonance imaging) magnet as images flashed on and off before his eyes. The machine recorded changes in his brain that came 50 milliseconds apart. "You can see different areas light up at different times," marvels Turner. NYU uses five SQUIDs to spy on the brain; the Japanese are hard at work on a 200-SQUID array. At Massachusetts General Hospital, researchers are putting the finishing touches on "ecoplanar MRI," which snaps a picture of the brain in just 45 milliseconds. The brain's cartographers are poised to glimpse thoughts, feelings and memories as they spring from one tiny clump of cells, ignite others and blossom into an idea or a passion, a creative leap or a unique insight. When they do, science may truly have read the mind.

SHARON BEGLEY *in St. Louis with* LYNDA WRIGHT *in Los Angeles,*
VERNON CHURCH *in New York and* MARY HAGER *in Washington*

1990–2000 The Decade of the Brain

The consummate computer. Three pounds of pinkish grey tissue shaped like a walnut. The most complex living structure on Earth. The last frontier in biology.

The human brain has been described as all these things. But it is so much more, it now seems, that it defies comparison.

For the brain is also a chemical factory. It has astounding capacity for change and repair. And it is infinitely more complex than any machine to which it has been compared.

"In my opinion, at this stage, there is no reasonable similarity," says Dr. Murray Goldstein, director of the National Institute of Neurological Disorders and Stroke.

Furthermore, he adds, "It's just amazing how well it works."

Bit by bit, research of the past few decades has contributed perhaps 95 percent of what is known about the brain. But that is only enough, really, to disprove the old myths and clarify the "right questions."

We still don't know where intelligence comes from, or what memory is, or why the brain focuses on certain problems and ignores others. But now we have the basic knowledge and technology to find out.

The challenge has galvanized scientists, in part because, despite the brain's overall reliability, so many brain processes can go awry.

Nearly 1 in 4 Americans are affected each year by one or more neurological or psychiatric disabilities, in which abnormal structure or function in their brain results in abnormal movements, sensory loss, thought processes, or emotions.

How this happens is becoming increasingly clear. Scientists are coming to understand the complexity of the interplay of parts within the brain, the full extent of the organ's capabilities and control.

HOW THE BRAIN "TALKS"

The basic mechanisms of the brain are common to all humans, but the particular circuitry that develops in an individual depends on genetic heritage or environment, often both.

The brain communicates by means of electrical and chemical messages, with impulses transmitted among any number of nerve cells (neurons) up to 80 times a second. With up to 100 billion neurons, the brain has almost limitless capacity to form circuits or networks and store and process information.

When a neuron is stimulated, it communicates with a neighbor by releasing a chemical called a neurotransmitter, which crosses the tiny gap between cells (the synapse) and locks onto specialized receptors on the target cells. This sparks a new message.

More than 40 different neurotransmitters have been identified, each with different functions. Some command a new impulse, while others stop or modify the process. A cell thus may be deluged with different messages, the sum of which directs its activity.

This delicately balanced process is easily upset; a frequent cause is the wrong amount of a neurotransmitter.

Lack of one (acetylcholine) is linked to the memory loss of Alzheimer's disease. Too little dopamine leads to the tremor of Parkinson's disease, while too much

Appreciation is expressed to the National Foundation for Brain Research for excerpts entitled "1990-2000: The Decade of the Brain."

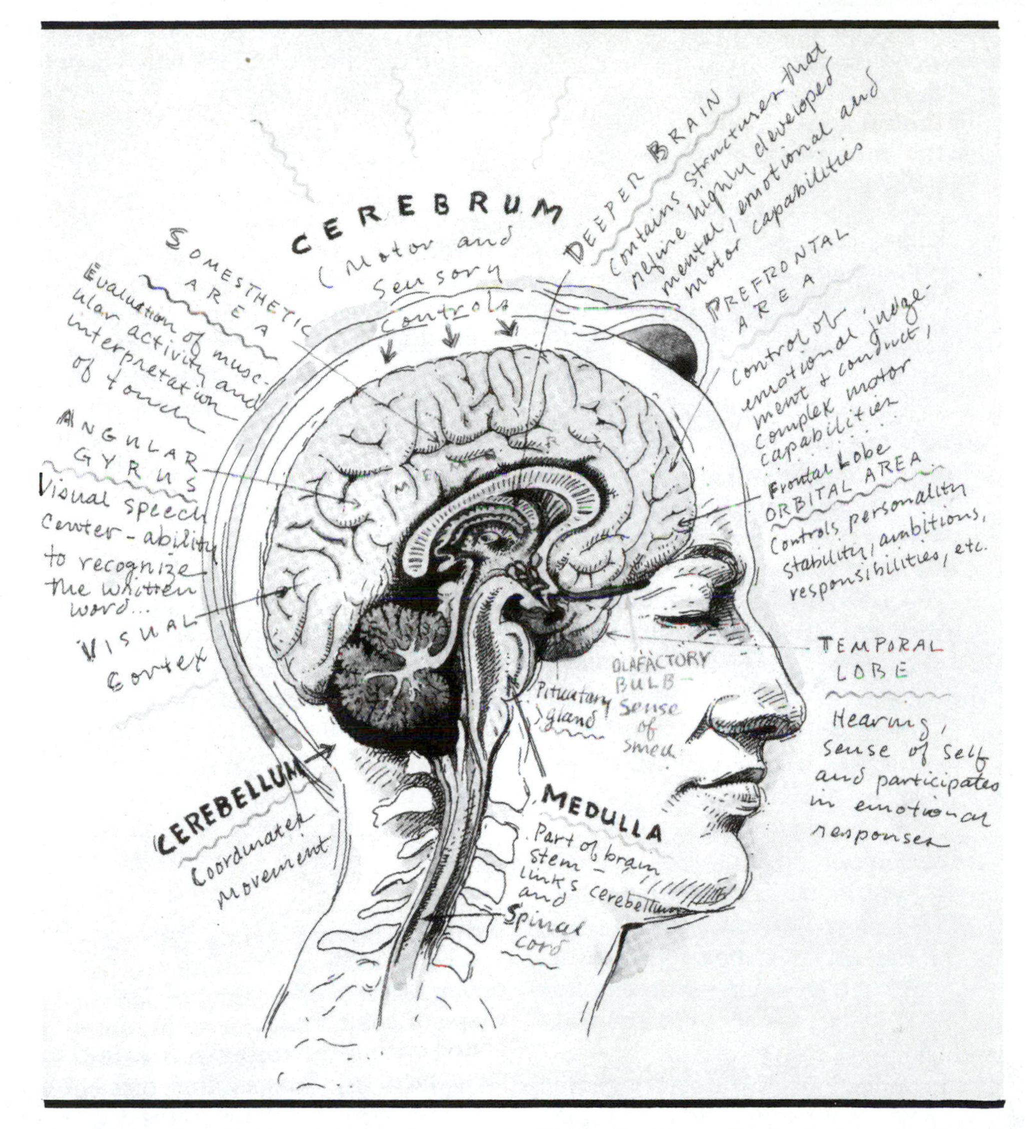

seems to be a factor in schizophrenia.

A stroke may tip the balance fatally, killing cells by shutting off oxygen supplies and then flooding the region with chemicals. Or, messages may be short-circuited by loss of the neurons' insulation, as occurs in multiple sclerosis.

Other neuronal disorders appear for reasons now unknown. Cell activity may suddenly storm out of control, with clusters of impulses firing at up to six times the normal rate. The result is an epileptic seizure.

Neurotransmitters are among the chemicals produced through the activities of genes, the heredity material contained in the body's cells. An estimated 1,000 human heredity disorders have some effect on the brain, and many of the 650 neurologic disorders are a direct result of gene defects.

A few genes or gene markers implicated in neurologic and mental disorders have been isolated, including those responsible for chemical abnormalities in muscular dystrophy and Gaucher's disease. Of all genetic disorders, one-fourth affect the brain and the central nervous system.

Scientists have also found a gene linked to abnormal brain deposits found in Alzheimer's and Down's syndrome, and they are closing in on genes implicated in manic-depression, schizophrenia, dyslexia, alcoholism, and in Huntington's disease.

But neurotransmitters and genes explain only the basic mechanics of brain function. More intriguing—and mysterious—processes control how the organ's parts work together to create a functioning human being.

BRAIN AND BEHAVIOR

As a famous psychologist once said, "There is no phenomenon, however complex, which when closely examined will not turn out to be even more complex."

This is especially true for how the brain forms the mind. We can begin to understand by examining the parts of the brain, and how they work and interact.

The most obvious features are the two halves of the cerebrum, which controls intellect. The left hemisphere generally processes speech, language comprehension, mathematics, and logic. The right mediates nonverbal ability, such as musical and emotional expression, and visual-spatial judgment.

The bundle of fibers connecting the hemispheres, the corpus callosum, enables us to consciously use information collected by both sides. If the fibers are severed, input to one hemisphere is available to the other only on a subconscious level. It is as if the hemispheres operate independently.

In fact, there seem to be a number of separate cognitive systems in the brain. But we are consciously aware of only one—the verbal system which some call the "interpreter." Some activities and changes in the older, deeper parts of the brain are interpreted as "feelings" or "moods;" malfunction in these areas may contribute to mental disorders such as depression.

The convoluted tissue covering the cerebrum is the cortex, which processes all sorts of disparate information. This occurs in precisely organized columns of cells. Exactly how is a mystery, but different sections of the cortex coordinate voluntary movement, sensation, hearing, speech, and vision.

When individual neurons sense particular features of a stimulus, such as shape or color, these pieces are integrated within the cortex into a complete picture. Sensory loss can be overcome in part, through electrical stimulation of the proper area of the cortex—creating, for example, sensations of light in a blind individual.

The frontal lobe of the cortex appears critical in creative problem-solving, which often is used as a measure of intelligence. Intelligence, it is theorized, is at least partly hereditary, and it may be related to the richness of nerve cell connections in the cortex. More experienced animals have more connections in some areas.

The temporal lobe processes hearing, speech and a sense of personal integration. Seizures in this area may trigger bizarre sensations, such as out-of-body experiences or a compulsive need to write or draw. Abnormally high metabolism in this area is associated with some cases of panic disorder.

The parietal lobe registers sensory information and communicates with movement-control centers. This area is crucial in physical orientation. The occipital lobe processes vision.

Deep inside the brain is the limbic system, which mediates powerful aspects of our humanity such as emotions, sex and defense drives, and memory. It also contributes, through connections with sensory areas of the cortex, to cognition.

The limbic system has many components, including the hypothalamus, the master control center, so called because it helps regulate feeding, fighting, and reproduction, among other things. Other parts include the thalamus and the amygdala. The thalamus helps relay messages from muscles and sense organs. Chronic alcoholics may suffer damage in both these areas.

The amygdala helps process the emotional significance of sensory information.

Another part of the limbic system, the hippocampus, helps convert temporary memory to permanent form.

Human memory isn't perfect even under the best of circumstances; "normal" people tend to forget—or can't retrieve—almost half of what they learned only four days before.

Memory appears to be regulated by multiple neurochemical systems. Long-term memories apparently consist of both changes in certain cells and oft-repeated patterns of activation in certain circuits.

Deeper still in the brain are the basal ganglia, which help with voluntary movement. In Parkinson's disease, cells die from a region that apparently adjusts nerve signals passing from the brain's command centers to the muscles. The cause of the cell death is unknown. But the disease illuminates the brain's capacity to compensate for loss. Some 80 percent of these cells must be lost before symptoms appear.

Beneath and behind all these structures are the cerebellum, which helps integrate movement, and the brain stem. This is the primitive instinct center, coordinating involuntary activities such as breathing, heart rate and sleep cycles. It also may be a site where anxiety originates.

THE BRAIN AND MENTAL ILLNESS

Many people, according to a survey a few years back, think mental illness comes from emotional weakness, bad parenting, or sin. And some clinicians still focus primarily on psychological conflicts. But, mental illness, it turns out, is at least partly physical. "Two decades of research have shown that these are diseases and illnesses like any other diseases and illnesses. They just happen to involve the brain," says Dr. Lewis Judd, director of the National Institute of Mental Health. "And as our knowledge of the brain has expanded dramatically, so has our ability to treat mental disorders," he says.

Of course, experience and social/psychological factors still play a considerable role; but the shift in thinking has been nothing less than revolutionary.

The change has brought hope for the 1 in 5 Americans who suffer from mental illness. Neuropsychiatric research has already made mental disorders such as manic-depressive illness and many anxiety disorders highly treatable. And it is expected to improve treatments significantly in the coming decade.

Scientists now believe many forms of mental illnesses result from an inherited predisposition to a brain disorder, which may be triggered by environmental stresses. The illness then is maintained through a deepening cycle of biological and psychological/behavioral problems.

A similar process may underlie other behavioral disorders, specifically addictions. For instance, some forms of alcoholism, and also manic-depression, panic disorder, and schizophrenia, run in families, and are associated with particular brain abnormalities. Less is known about drug abuse, but some researchers suspect that a similar interaction of biological and environmental factors is at work. Additional evidence supports the commonality of mental illness and addictions, in that these conditions often coexist. And, in at least one case, a drug that appears to block the cycle of a mental illness (manic depression) appears promising in treating addiction (to cocaine).

BRAIN ABNORMALITIES IN MENTAL ILLNESS

If you are depressed—an increasingly common condition—you are likely to have abnormal brain chemistry involving the neurotransmitters serotonin and norepinephrine.

If you have dyslexia (a learning disability), you may have misfiring cells in the cortex.

If you have panic disorder, you may have metabolic abnormalities in the temporal lobe.

Such biological clues ultimately may lead to improved treatments for these and other mental disorders.

Substantial research efforts are being focused on schizophrenia, one of the most costly and disabling mental disorders.

While the disease strikes less than 1 percent of the population (1.5 million Americans have it), 300,000 new cases are diagnosed each year, and the toll is tragic. Despite efforts to encourage community living, these patients occupy one-fourth of all hospital beds.

Although heredity plays a role, even among identical twins (who have the same genes) sometimes only one twin develops the disease and shows abnormal brain structure.

Schizophrenia usually develops in early adulthood, a period when stress-sensitive brain structures mature. Perhaps a brain injury acquired very early in life does not exert its effects until this time.

In this disease, symptoms such as social withdrawal appear to be linked to structural abnormalities, while symptoms such as hallucinations are associated with neurochemical changes and are more responsive to medications. Because schizophrenia affects the cortex, the intellect is disturbed. So are emotions, possibly because the disrupted neurochemical system links the cortex to the limbic system.

BRAIN ABNORMALITIES AND ALCOHOLISM

One in 10 adults abuses or is dependent on alcohol. They may have an inherited predisposition. Brain electrical activity is abnormal not only in certain types of alcoholics, but also in their young sons, who are prone to developing the disease by early adulthood.

Drinking alcohol alters neurotransmitter systems temporarily. The pleasant state aroused by drinking (as blood-alcohol level is rising), is linked to increased release of dopamine in the brain. The first step toward alcoholism is physical tolerance. This is a biological process similar to that which underlies learning: Chronic exposure alters cells and transmitter activity, creating a new "normal" state.

The next step is dependence. Alcohol reduces activity of the transmitter system that inhibits firing of brain cells. Once the brain has adapted to the reduction, the removal of alcohol may result in convulsive discharges—and withdrawal symptoms such as seizures. This encourages continued alcohol use.

Chronic use leads to dramatic damage, including brain shrinkage (atrophy), and tissue loss in a region associated with short-term memory. This helps explain why alcoholics often have trouble with problem-solving, abstract thinking, certain kinds of movement, and difficult memory tasks.

The cortex (the intellectual processing center) appears especially vulnerable to the effects of alcohol. Even abstinent alcoholics have multiple deficits in processing circuits. However, the brain apparently has some capacity to rebound. After five years of abstinence, brain atrophy is reduced, and performance improves in reasoning, memory, and visual-spatial ability.

THE BRAIN AND COCAINE ADDICTION

Although use of illicit drugs appears to be declining in the United States, the estimated number of Americans who frequently use cocaine has risen by 33 percent in recent years.

In fact, according to a recent Congressional survey, 1 in 100 Americans is addicted to cocaine.

The drug is extraordinarily addictive. Cocaine affects circuits involved in pleasure—within seconds of use.

Researchers now believe cocaine disrupts the cycle of a brain chemical that periodically stimulates certain neurons. The net effect is continual stimulation, and overexcitation of the limbic system.

Cocaine addicts may have a deficiency in their internal chemical reward system, making it difficult for them to achieve "natural highs." This might encourage them to seek artificial highs through drugs.

DEVELOPMENTAL DISORDERS

Developmental disorders of the brain can create serious problems for children—including mental deficiency, autism, developmental language disorders, learning disabilities (including dyslexia), cerebral palsy and disorders affecting attention and behavior. These create life-long problems, often being the cause of school dropout, unemployment, homelessness, drug abuse, and violence.

TRAUMA

Approximately a half-million persons, especially young males, require hospitalization for head injury each year. 10,000 persons suffer a traumatic spinal cord injury. And brain damage from strokes leaves thousands permanently disabled and many with late-life dementia.

THE FUTURE

In the last two decades, the human brain has been systematically taken apart and its cells, circuits, and chemicals have been studied in minute detail. As a result of the knowledge gained millions of people with brain-related disorders that were once untreatable can now be helped.

Many questions remain, but scientists are beginning to put the brain back together, to understand better how the collective parts make us human.

Scientists now know that damaged nerve cells exhibit "neuroplasticity," that is, they are able to recover and grow new connections under particular conditions, suggesting that the human brain is much more adaptable than previously thought. Special substances found within the brain, such as nerve growth factor and others, create the best conditions for this process of repair and may some day be used as drugs to help the injured brain regain its normal functions.

Continued advances should enable us to:

OVERCOME AND PREVENT SENSORY LOSS

Already, electronic systems can mimic brain signals.

Such devices can stimulate arm muscles, enabling quadriplegics to grip items with their hands. Or, they can stimulate auditory nerves, enabling the deaf to hear.

It may not be long before the blind can detect crude images, through stimulation of the visual cortex.

What is more, electronic systems eventually will be fully implanted, leaving no cumbersome parts outside the body.

Scientists also hope to reduce the need for such devices. Every 5 minutes, a victim of head or spinal cord injury is doomed to permanent damage. But there may be ways to prevent that damage.

Recent findings indicate, for example, that high doses of steroids can prevent permanent spinal cord damage if administered early enough. Why this happens is not yet clear.

Other treatments may come from blocking the body's process of releasing natural painkillers after a spinal cord injury—paradoxically, the body's natural painkillers seem to increase spinal cord damage.

REVERSE BRAIN DAMAGE

While adult songbirds can grow new brain cells (in the brain region responsible for song) adult humans cannot; yet, there is growing cause for hope in reversing brain damage.

The mature human brain is adaptable enough to form new connections that comprise memories; and, it is able to repair itself, scientists now know, under particular conditions.

By implanting certain types of healthy tissue into some areas of the damaged brain, scientists have been able to reverse some symptoms of Parkinson's disease.

Furthermore, tissue implants in animals produce new nerve fibers and improve movement disorders. The grafts enable nerve cells to grow through scar tissue and connect with other cells.

The grafts may serve as surrogate chemical pumps; or, they may be involved in the mysterious process by which genes switch growth processes on/off during youth.

These early successes hold out hope for ever more dramatic discoveries—and patient recoveries.

Recently, scientists for the first time halted the cell death associated with neurological disease. They now can look forward to replacing dead cells with living implants.

In fact, researchers now have grown living human brain cells in culture. These cells can be used in research—on drug safety and how neurons work—and possibly as brain implants.

MAP HUMAN THOUGHT, ABILITIES, AND LEARNING—AND THEIR DISORDERS

Imaging techniques now enable scientists to pinpoint abnormalities within the living brain, and, by observing patient symptoms, to learn what functions these brain regions control.

These techniques are producing "maps" of the brain in health and disease. Thanks to positron emission tomography (PET), for example, scientists are learning where metabolism goes awry in brain illnesses and can understand the genesis of symptoms in Huntington's disease.

With magnetic resonance imaging (MRI), researchers can detect pathologies associated with multiple sclerosis, schizophrenia, trauma, stroke, and dementing diseases such as Alzheimer's and hydrocephalus. Many of these are currently treatable and are cured by neurosurgeons performing delicate operations on the brain.

Now, researchers are mapping even the most elusive processes such as thought and musical talent, in almost unimaginable detail.

By generating two-dimensional computerized maps from MRI scans, researchers are "unfolding" the convoluted cortex covering the brain.

The "brainprinting" technique, which can be performed on living subjects serially over time, is expected to help reveal many secrets of intellectual processing.

Is musical or athletic ability, for example, linked to the size of a particular region of the cortex? Does IQ test performance correlate with certain structural patterns?

Brainprinting could become a specific diagnostic tool, enabling doctors to predict, for example, particular deficits in a patient's thought processes after a stroke. Now, they simply have to wait and see.

DEVELOP MORE EFFECTIVE AND SAFER TREATMENTS

The combination of basic scientific advances and modern technology has revolutionized medicine, perhaps nowhere as much as in the surgical and medical treatment of brain-related disorders.

Brain operations that appeared impossible a generation ago now are routine for neurosurgeons, and the future outlook is similarly incredible.

Using computerized axial tomography (CAT scans), surgeons now can localize a tiny target within the brain precisely, either to irradiate a tumor or to remove a lesion.

As researchers come to understand neurochemical deficiencies associated with disease, they will be able to treat some of these conditions with tiny chemical pumps implanted in the brain.

Laser beams already can be aimed at abnormal tissue, and can cut and vaporize it with extreme precision. Eventually, lasers will be used to join severed vessels or nerves, in a process similar to the welding of metal.

Meanwhile, new generations of safer, more effective, treatments for mental illnesses will emerge from knowledge of how brain chemical systems work.

Natural compounds will be re-engineered so they can fine-tune the brain, to restore balance to mood and to check memory and thinking impairments. The ability to perform demanding, every-day memory tasks diminishes dramatically over the adult life span, perhaps by as much as 50%. Such a decrease is distressing to many mature adults, particularly those engaged in intellectually challenging activities. There is now reason to believe that this "Age Associated Memory Impairment" can be corrected and treated.

Drugs targeted at brain stress circuits may prevent mental disorders and even the development of arthritis in vulnerable individuals, while manipulations of sleep/wake cycles, light, and temperature will be developed into new therapies for mood disorders.

Neurosurgeons have developed methods of precise techniques of focused radiation to obliterate small vascular malformations and brain tumors. Stereotactic surgery allows the precise localization to remove tiny brain tumors located deeply within the central parts of the brain. Genetic engineering is developing newer techniques to modify growth and development of brain tumors and within the next decade major advances are expected in the treatment of presently incurable brain tumors.

The potential of brain and spinal cord tissue implants will alter the treatment and outcome of head injuries, spinal cord injuries causing paraplegia and quadriplegia, as well as diseases causing dementia, such as Alzheimer's disease.

Strokes are the third leading cause of death and major cause of disability. The outlook for patients has improved with the understanding of the role of aspirin and TPA in medical treatment, and the use of microneurosurgery to increase blood flow to the brain.

OVERCOME AND PREVENT DISORDERS OF THINKING AND BEHAVIOR

Two decades of research progress has already made many once-feared mental illnesses such as major depression, manic-depressive illness, and many anxiety disorders much more manageable, although little can now be done to prevent them.

As knowledge of the brain's role in specific mental disorders increases, so should the capacity to treat and prevent them more effectively.

For example, researchers have now shown abnormal activity in deep brain structures and certain areas of the cortex in obsessive compulsive disorder (OCD) and have identified medications that are effective in reducing symptoms of OCD. They have also developed animal models that potentially can be used to screen new OCD medications systematically and study their effects on the brain.

Since there seems to be a hereditary component to OCD, with better understanding of the genetic mechanisms involved, it may be possible to identify and treat some people at risk of the disorder before their symptoms ever appear. And as knowledge grows about the abnormal neurotransmitter systems and brain areas involved, more precisely targeted medications can be developed, with fewer side effects.

Similarly, mounting evidence that schizophrenia is a brain disease—one that may originate early in development—has sparked the search to identify both genetic and environmental factors, such as viral infections, that may combine to injure the developing brain. Researchers are also exploring biological and environmental factors that may trigger clinical illness in vulnerable young adults. These promising new lines of study are paving the way for novel approaches to preventing and treating schizophrenia.

A new medication for schizophrenia has already offered renewed hope to thousands of patients who could not respond to older treatments, and many more therapeutically important developments are bound to follow.

A Pleasurable Chemistry

Endorphins, the body's natural narcotics, aren't something we have to run after. They're everywhere.

Janet L. Hopson

Janet L. Hopson, who lives in Oakland, California, gets endorphin highs by contributing to Psychology Today.

Welcome aboard the biochemical bandwagon of the 1980s. The magical, morphine-like brain chemicals called endorphins are getting a lot of play. First we heard they were responsible for runner's high and several other cheap thrills. Now we're hearing that they play a role in almost every human experience from birth to death, including much that is pleasurable, painful and lusty along the way.

Consider the following: crying, laughing, thrills from music, acupuncture, placebos, stress, depression, chili peppers, compulsive gambling, aerobics, trauma, masochism, massage, labor and delivery, appetite, immunity, near-death experiences, playing with pets. Each, it is claimed, is somehow involved with endorphins. Serious endorphin researchers pooh-pooh many or most of these claims but, skeptics notwithstanding, the field has clearly sprinted a long way past runner's high.

Endorphin research had its start in the early 1970s with the unexpected discovery of opiate receptors in the brain. If we have these receptors, researchers reasoned, then it is likely that the body produces some sort of opiate- or morphine-like chemicals. And that's exactly what was found, a set of relatively small biochemicals dubbed "opioid peptides" or "endorphins" (short for "endogenous morphines") that plug into the receptors. In other words, these palliative peptides are sloshing around in our brains, spines and bloodstreams, apparently acting just like morphine. In fact, morphine's long list of narcotic effects was used as a treasure map for where scientists might hunt out natural opiates in the body. Morphine slows the pulse and depresses breathing, so they searched in the heart and lungs. Morphine deadens pain, so they looked in the central and peripheral nervous systems. It disturbs digestion and elimination, so they explored the gut. It savages the sex drive, so they probed the reproductive and endocrine systems. It triggers euphoria, so they scrutinized mood.

Nearly everywhere researchers looked, endorphins or their receptors were present. But what were they doing: transmitting nerve impulses, alleviating pain, triggering hormone release, doing several of these things simultaneously or disintegrating at high speed and doing nothing at all? In the past decade, a trickle of scientific papers has become a tidal wave, but still no one seems entirely certain of what, collectively, the endorphins are doing to us or for us at any given time.

Researchers do have modern-day sextants for their search, including drugs such as naloxone and naltrexone. These drugs, known as opiate blockers, pop into the endorphin receptors and block the peptides' normal activity, giving researchers some idea of what their natural roles might be. Whatever endorphins are doing, however, it must be fairly subtle. As one researcher points out, people injected with opiate blockers may feel a little more pain or a little less "high," but no one gasps for breath, suffers a seizure or collapses in a coma.

Subtle or not, endorphins are there, and researchers are beginning to get answers to questions about how they touch our daily lives—pain, exercise, appetite, reproduction and emotions.

•ANSWERS ON ANALGESIA: A man falls off a ladder, takes one look at his right hand—now cantilevered at a sickening angle—and knows he has a broken bone. Surprisingly, he feels little pain or anxiety until hours later, when he's home from the emergency room. This physiological grace period, which closely resembles a sojourn on morphine, is a common survival mechanism in the animal world, and researchers are confident that brain opiates are responsible for such cases of natural pain relief. The question is how do they work and, more to the point, how can we make them work for us?

The answers aren't in, but researchers have located a pain control system in the periaquaductal gray (PAG), a tiny region in the center of the brain, and interestingly, it produces opioid peptides. While no one fully understands how this center operates, physicians can now jolt it with electric current to lessen chronic pain.

One day in 1976, as Navy veteran Dennis Hough was working at a hospital's psychiatric unit, a disturbed patient snapped Hough's back and ruptured three of his vertebral discs. Five years later, after two failed back operations, Hough was bedridden with constant shooting pains in his legs, back and shoulders and was depressed to the point of suicide. Doctors were just then pioneering a technique of implanting platinum electrodes in the PAG, and Hough soon underwent the skull drilling and emplacement. He remembers it as "the most barbaric thing I've ever experienced, including my tour of duty in Vietnam," but the results were worth the ordeal; For the past seven years, Hough has been able to stimulate his brain's own endorphins four times a day by producing a radio signal from a transmitter on his belt. The procedure is delicate—too much current and his eyes flutter, too little and the pain returns in less than six hours. But it works dependably, and Hough not only holds down an office job now but is engaged to be married.

Researchers would obviously like to find an easier way to stimulate the brain's own painkillers, and while they have yet to find it, workers in many labs are actively developing new drugs and treatments. Some physicians have tried direct spinal injections of endorphins to alleviate postoperative pain. And even the most cynical now seem to agree that acupuncture works its magic by somehow triggering the release of endorphins. There may, however, be an even easier path to pain relief: the power of the mind.

Several years ago, neurobiologist Jon Levine, at the University of California, San Francisco, discovered that the placebo effect (relief) based on no known action other than the patient's belief in a treatment) can itself be blocked by naloxone and must therefore be based on endorphins. Just last year Levine was able to quantify the effects: One shot of placebo can equal the relief of 6 to 8 milligrams of morphine, a low but fairly typical dose.

Another line of research suggests that endorphins may be involved in self-inflicted injury—a surprisingly common veterinary and medical complaint and one that, in many cases, can also be prevented with naloxone. Paul Millard Hardy, a behavioral neurologist at Boston's New England Medical Center, believes that animals may boost endorphin levels through self-inflicted pain and then "get caught in a self-reinforcing positive feedback loop." He thinks something similar may occur in compulsive daredevils and in some cases of deliberate self-injury. One young woman he studied had injected pesticide into her own veins by spraying Raid into an intravenous needle. This appalling act, she told Hardy, "made her feel better, calmer and almost high."

Hardy also thinks endorphin release might explain why some autistic children constantly injure themselves by banging their heads. Because exercise is believed to be an alternate route to endorphin release, Hardy and physician Kiyo Kitahara set up a twice-a-day exercise program for a group of autistic children. He qualifies the evidence as "very anecdotal at this point" but calls the results "phenomenal."

•RUNNER'S HIGH, RUNNER'S CALM: For most people, "endorphins" are synonymous with "runner's high," a feeling of well-being that comes after an aerobic workout. Many people claim to have experienced this "high," and remarkable incidents are legion. Take, for example, San Francisco runner Don Paul, who placed 10th in the 1979 San Francisco Marathon and wound up with his ankle in a cast the next day. Paul had run the 26 miles only vaguely aware of what turned out to be a serious stress fracture. Observers on the sidelines had to tell him he was "listing badly to one side for the last six miles." He now runs 90 miles per week in preparation for the U.S. men's Olympic marathon trial and says that when he trains at the level, he feels "constantly great. Wonderful."

Is runner's high a real phenomenon based on endorphins? And can those brain opiates result in "exercise addiction"? Or, as many skeptics hold, are the effects on mood largely psychological? Most studies with humans have found rising levels of endorphins in the blood during exercise.

However, says exercise physiologist Peter Farrell of Pennsylvania State University, "when we look at animal studies, we don't see a concurrent increase in the brain." Most circulating peptides fail to cross into the brain, he explains, so explaining moods like runner's high based on endorphin levels in the blood is questionable. Adds placebo expert Jon Levine, "Looking for mood changes based on the circulating blood is like putting a voltmeter to the outside of a computer and saying 'Now I know how it works.' " Nevertheless, Farrell exercises religiously: "I'm not going to waste my lifetime sitting around getting sclerotic just because something's not proven yet."

Murray Allen, a physician and kinesiologist at Canada's Simon Fraser University, is far more convinced about the endorphin connection. He recently conducted his own study correlating positive moods and exercise—moods that could be blocked by infusing the runner with naloxone. Allen thinks these moods are "Mother Nature's way of rewarding us for staying fit" but insists that aerobic exercisers don't get "high." Opioid peptides "slow down and inhibit excess activity in the brain," he says. "Many researchers have been chasing after psychedelic, excitable responses." The actual effect, he says, is "runner's calm" and extremes leading to exhaustion usually negate it.

In a very similar experiment last year, a research team at Georgia State University found the mood-endorphin link more elusive. Team member and psychologist Wade Silverman of Atlanta explains that only those people who experience "runner's high" on the track also noticed it in the lab. Older people and those who ran fewer, not more, miles per week were also more likely to show a "high" on the test. "People who run a lot—50 miles per week or more—are often drudges, masochists, running junkies," says Silverman. "They don't really enjoy it. It hurts." For optimum benefits. Silverman recommends running no more than three miles per day four times a week.

Silverman and Lewis Maharam, a sports medicine internist at Manhattan's New York Infirmary/Beekman Downtown Hospital, both agree that powerful psychological factors—including heightened sense of self-esteem and self-discipline—contribute to the "high" in those who exercise moderately. Maharam would still like to isolate and quantify the role of endorphins, however, so he could help patients "harness the high." He would like to give people "proper exercise prescriptions," he says, "to stimulate the greatest enjoyment and benefit from exercise. If we could encourage the 'high' early on, maybe we could get people to want to keep exercising from the start."

The questions surrounding exercise, mood and circulating endorphins remain. But even if opioids released into the bloodstream from, say, the adrenal glands don't enter the brain and give a "high" or a "calm," several studies show that endorphins in the blood do bolster the immune system's activity. One way or the other, regular moderate exercise seems destined to make us happy.

•APPETITE CLOCKS AND BLOCKS: Few things in life are more basic to survival and yet more pleasurable than eating good food—and where survival and pleasure intersect, can the endorphins be far behind? To keep from starving, an animal needs to know when, what and how much to eat, and researchers immediately suspected that opioid peptides might help control appetite and satiety. People, after all, have long claimed that specific foods such as chili peppers or sweets give them a "high." And those unmistakably "high" on morphine or heroin experience constipation, cravings and other gastrointestinal glitches.

Indeed, investigators quickly located opiate receptors in the alimentary tract and found a region of the rat's hypothalamus that—when injected with tiny amounts of beta endorphin—will trigger noshing of particular nutrients. Even a satiated rat will dig heartily into fats, proteins or sweets when injected with the peptide. Neurobiologist Sarah Leibowitz and her colleagues at Rockefeller University produced this result and also founa that opiate blockers would prevent the snack attack—strong evidence that endorphins help regulate appetite. The opiates "probably enhance the hedonic, pleasurable, rewarding properties" of fats, proteins and sweets—foods that can help satiate an animal far longer than carbohydrates so it can survive extended periods without eating.

Intriguingly, rats crave carbohydrates at the beginning of their 12-hour activity cycles, but they like fats, proteins or sweets before retiring—a hint that endorphins control not just the nature but the timing of appetites. Leibowitz suspects that endorphins also help control cravings in response to stress and starvation, and that disturbed endorphin systems may, in part, underlie obesity and eating disorders. Obese people given opiate blockers, for example, tend to eat less; bulimics often gorge on fat-rich foods; both bulimics and anorexics often have abnormal levels of endorphins; and in anorexics, food deprivation enhances the release of opiates in the brain. This brain opiate reward, some speculate, may reinforce the anorexic's self-starvation much as self-injury seems to be rewarding to an autistic child.

Researchers such as Leibowitz are hoping to learn enough about the chemistry of appetite to fashion a binge-blocking drug as well as more effective behavioral approaches to over- or undereating. In the meantime, people who try boosting their own endorphins through exercise, mirth or music may notice a vexing increase in their taste for fattening treats.

•PUBERTY, PREGNANCY AND PEPTIDES: Evolution has equipped animals with two great appetites—the hunger for food to prevent short-term disintegration and the hunger for sex and reproduction to prevent longer-term genetic oblivion. While some endorphin researchers were studying opioids and food hunger, others began searching for a sex role—and they found it.

Once again, drug addiction pointed the way: Users of morphine and heroin often complain of impotence and frigidity that fade when they kick their habits. Could natural opioids have some biochemical dampening effect on reproduction? Yes, says Theodore Cicero of Washington University Medical School. Endorphins, he says, "play an integral role—probably the dominant role—in regulating reproductive hormone cycles."

This formerly small corner of endorphin research has "exploded into a huge area of neurobiology," Cicero says, and researchers now think the opioid peptides help fine-tune many—perhaps all—of the nervous and hormonal pathways that together keep the body operating normally.

Cicero and his colleagues have tracked the byzantine biochemical loops through which endorphins, the brain, the body's master gland (the pituitary), the master's master (the hypothalamus) and the gonads exchange signals to ensure that an adult animal can reproduce when times are good but not when the environment is hostile. Cicero's work helped show that beta endorphin rules the hypothalamus and thus, indirectly, the pituitary and gonads.

The Washington University group also sees "a perfect parallel" between the brain's ability to produce endorphins and the onset of puberty: As the opioid system matures, so does the body sexually. A juvenile rat with endorphins blocked by naloxone undergoes puberty earlier; a young rat given opiates matures far later than normal and its offspring can have disturbed hormonal systems. Cicero calls the results "frightening" and adds, "there couldn't possibly be a worse time for a person to take drugs than during late childhood or adolescence."

Endorphins play a critical role in a later reproductive phase, as well: pregnancy and labor. Women in their third trimester sometimes notice that the pain and pressure of, say, a blood pressure cuff, is far less pronounced than before or after pregnancy. Alan Gintzler and his colleagues at the State University of New York Health Science Center in Brooklyn found that opioid peptides produced inside the spinal cord probably muffle pain and perhaps elevate mood to help a woman deal with the increasing physical stress of pregnancy. Endorphin activity builds throughout pregnancy and reaches a peak just before and during labor. Some have speculated that the tenfold drop from peak endorphin levels within 24 hours of delivery may greatly contribute to postpartum depression.

•CHILLS, THRILLS, LAUGHTER AND TEARS: Just as the effects of morphine go beyond the physical, claims for the opioid peptides extend to purely esthetic and emotional, with speculation falling on everything from the pleasure of playing with pets and the transcendence of near-death experiences to shivers over sonatas and the feeling of well-being that comes with a rousing laugh or a good cry.

Avram Goldstein of Stanford University, a pioneer in peptide research, recently collected a group of volunteers who get a spine-tingling thrill from their favorite music and gave them either a placebo or an opiate blocker during a listening session. Their shivers declined with the blocker—tantalizing evidence that endorphins mediate rapture, even though the mechanics are anyone's guess.

Former *Saturday Review* editor Norman Cousins may have spawned a different supposition about endorphins and emotion when he literally laughed himself out of the sometimes fatal disease ankylosing spondylitis. He found that 10 minutes of belly laughing before bed gave him two hours of painfree sleep. Before long, someone credited endorphins with the effect, and by now the claim is commonplace. For example, Matt Weinstein, a humor consultant from Berkeley, California, frequently mentions a possible link between endorphins, laughter and health in his lectures on humor in the workplace. His company's motto: If you take yourself too seriously, there's an excellent chance you may end up seriously ill.

Weinstein agrees with laughter researcher William Fry, a psychiatrist at Stanford's medical school, that evidence is currently circumstantial. Fry tried to confirm the laughter-endorphin link experimentally, but the most accurate way to assess it would be to tap the cerebrospinal fluid. That, Fry says, "is not only a difficult procedure but it's not conducive to laughter" and could result in a fountain of spinal fluid gushing out with the first good guffaw. Confirmation clearly awaits a less ghoulish methodology. But in the meantime, Fry is convinced that mirth and playfulness can diminish fear, anger and depression. At the very least, he says, laughter is a good aerobic exercise that ventilates the lungs and leaves the muscles relaxed. Fry advises patients to take their own humor inventory, then amass a library of books, tapes and gags that dependably trigger hilarity.

Another William Frey, this one at the University of Minnesota, studies the role of tears in emotion, stress and health. "The physiology of the brain when we experience a change in emotional state from sad to angry to happy or vice versa is an absolutely unexplored frontier," Frey says. And emotional tears are a fascinating guidepost because "they are unique to human beings and are our natural excretory response to strong emotion." Since all other bodily fluids are involved in removing something, he reasons, logic dictates that tears wash something away, too. Frey correctly predicted that tears would contain the three biochemicals that build up during stress: leucine-enkephalin, an endorphin, and the hormones prolactin and ACTH. These biochemicals are found in both emotional tears and tears from chopping onions, a different sort of stress.

Frey is uncertain whether tears simply carry off excess endorphins that collect in the stressed brain or whether those peptides have some activity in the tear ducts, eyes, nose or throat. Regardless, he cites evidence that people with ulcers and colitis tend to cry less than the average, and he concludes that a person who feels like crying "should go ahead and do it! I can't think of any other physical excretory process that humans alone can do, so why suppress it and its possibly healthful effects?"

All in all, the accumulated evidence suggests that if you want to use your endorphins, you should live the unfettered natural life. Laugh! Cry! Thrill to music! Reach puberty. Get pregnant. Get aerobic. Get hungry, Eat! Lest this sound like a song from *Fiddler on the Roof*, however, remember that stress or injury may be even quicker ways to pump out home-brew opioids. The bottom line is this: Endorphins are so fundamental to normal physiological functioning that we don't have to seek them out at all. We probably surf life's pleasures and pains on a wave of endorphins already.

Test yourself by imagining the following: the sound of chalk squeaking across a blackboard; a pink rose sparkling with dew; embracing your favorite movie star; chocolate-mocha mousse cake; smashing your thumb with a hammer. If any of these thoughts sent the tiniest tingle down your spine, then you have have just proved the point.

The Face as Window and Machine for the Emotions

Do we smile because we are happy? Or, are we happy because we smile? New studies suggest that both may be true.

Robert Zajonc

Robert Zajonc is the Charles Cooley Distinguished Professor of Social Sciences and director of the Institute for Social Research. He presented the 1989–90 LS&A Distinguished Senior Faculty Lectures, from which this article was prepared.

Emotions are fundamental psychological processes that participate in nearly all aspects of our behavior. Because emotions are the essential ingredients of reinforcement, they are basic to learning and conditioning: a behavior that removes an organism from danger or results in a positive outcome will be repeated. Emotions are also basic to perception and cognition: we attend to what is significant, and what is significant *is* so because of its relation to emotion.

All emotional experiences involve a sudden and vigorous change in the nervous system; we are *always* in a state of emotion, and what we know of emotion is simply a change from one state to another. Some stimuli, such as strong sensory events, are intrinsically capable of evoking emotional reactions. But *any* stimulus can become emotional under particular circumstances: the harmless ticking of a clock is felt as a real threat is we believe it is connected to a bomb fuse.

The bodily manifestation of emotion can be noted in muscular action in the face and other parts of the body, in posture and movement, in modulation of voice patterns, in breathing patterns, and certainly in language. The subjective aspect of emotion is feeling. But where does feeling come from and what is its nature? What is *it* that we feel when we feel sad or angry? For we do feel *something,* since *to feel* is a transitive verb.

The traditional view of the relationship between feeling and expression holds that expression of emotion is the manifestation of an internal subjective state, the externalization of the feeling. The 19th-century psychologist William James had a more radical view. He described the process as the other way around. According to James,

> the more rational statement is that we feel sorry because we cry, angry because we strike, afraid because we tremble, and not that we cry, strike, tremble, because we are sorry, angry, or fearful, as the case may be.

Can both views be correct? My research suggests that the answer to this question may be Yes. We are now learning that the face can display our internal states *and* can itself cause changes in our feelings. How and why it does both is the subject of this article.

The face as a window of the emotions

Psychologists inherited from philosophers the assumption of a mind-body dualism, a dualism that persists in some form to this day. Aristotle's classic remark is unambiguous:

> Mental character . . . conditioned by the state of the body; and contrariwise the body is influenced by the affections of the soul.

Significant parallels between animals and humans imply the existence of cross-cultural uniformity in emotional expressions. Darwin was the first to undertake a systematic study of this. His classic book is called *The Expression of Emotions in Man and Animals.* He may also have been the first to use the mail questionnaire. He sent a large number of letters to military men, government officials, missionaries, and his friends who lived in distant parts of the British Empire, asking them in a series of very clear questions if the people in those areas expressed grief by weeping, joy by laughing, and so on. The results of his survey led him to accept the proposition of cross-cultural universality of emotional expression.

My colleagues at the Survey Research Center, however, would dismiss Darwin's research, not only because it was unrepresentative, but because it gave more answers about the observers than about those they observed: They could describe what they saw, but they could not judge what the people they were observing actually felt. In fact,

From *LSAmagazine* (University of Michigan), Vol. 14, No. 1, Fall 1990, pp. 17-21. Reprinted by permission of the author.

recent cross-cultural comparisons indicate that while there are several uniformities, there are also considerable differences. It now seems that although there is a good deal of agreement among Americans, Brazilians, Chileans, Argentineans, and Japanese in the facial configuration expressing *happiness* (agreement ranges between 95 and 100 percent), there is much less agreement about the expression that might stand for *fear*.

Different cultures clearly have different display rules. If you grew up in Italy, you are more likely to let your face readily manifest your internal states than if you went to an English public school. Clearly, Darwin exaggerated the universality of emotional expression, but there is, nevertheless, considerable uniformity among what appear to be facial *manifestations* of emotion.

The face is a very special organ, the major instrument of social interaction. Its muscles are capable of countless expressive configurations, all having meaning for others. Observe people in conversation, and you will note that the important thing is not the exchange of knowledge, but the *dance of emotions*, with each participant displaying emotion so as to evoke a particular emotion in the other; the exchange of pure cognitions occurs rarely.

Because of its crucial role in the display of emotion, the face is also a very special perceptual object. It is readily accessible to perception and is very easy to identify and remember. Faces presented for only 150 milliseconds can be judged quite reliably for attractiveness. In fact, specialized cells in the brain have been discovered—in the temporal sulcus—that respond only to faces. These cells do not respond to hands; they do not respond to feet, nor to any other parts of the body, and they do not respond to items of clothing or to flowers. They respond only to faces.

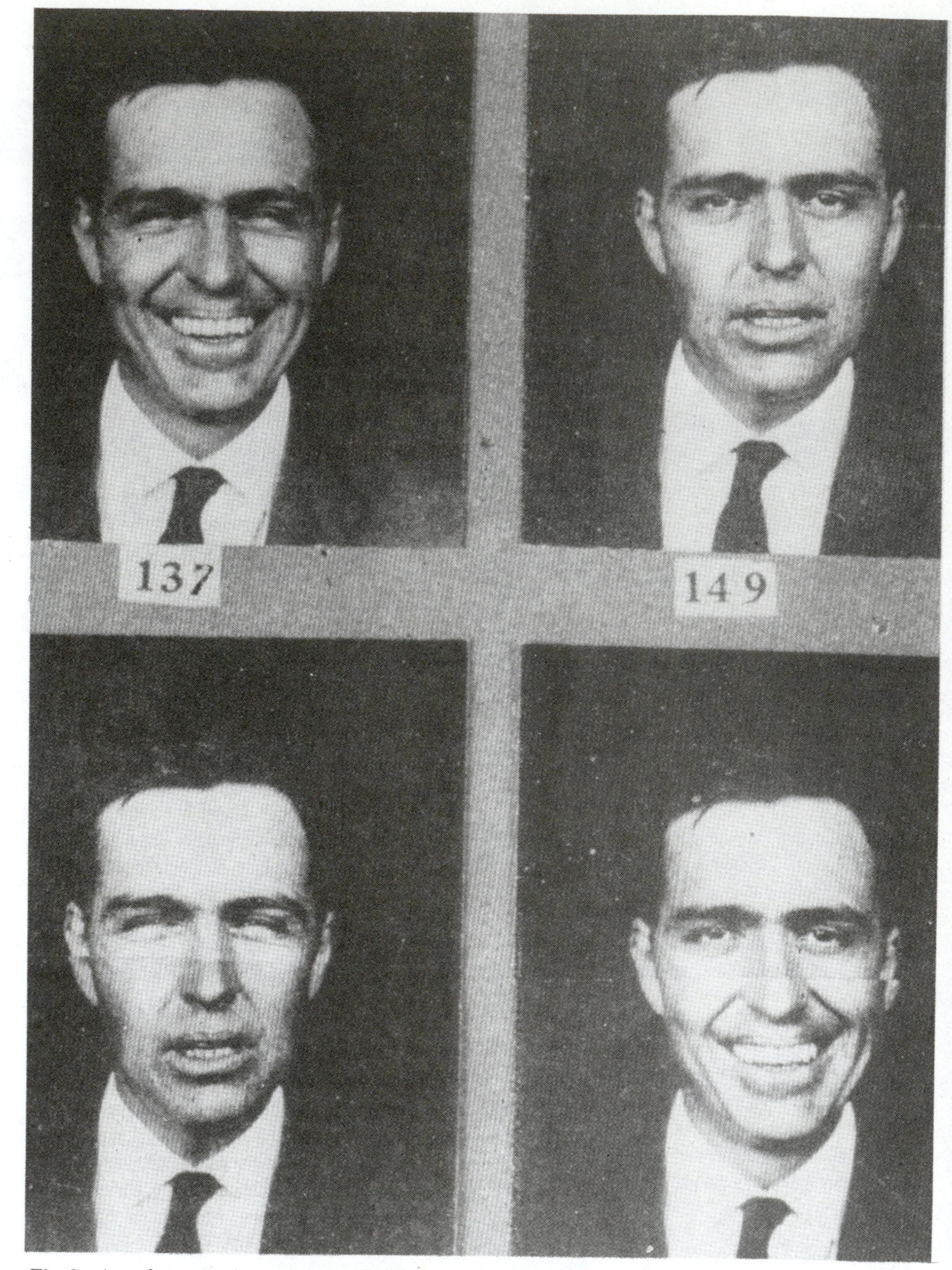

Fig.1. Are the eyes the window of the soul? When photographs of happy and sad faces are cut in half and the halves exchanged, it is obvious that the bottom half of the face dominates the expression.

A common supposition is that the eyes are the window of the soul and thus best communicate emotion. St. Jerome (A.D. 342–420) said that "the face is the mirror of the mind, and eyes, without speaking, confess the secrets of the heart." Not so: in an experiment many years ago, photographs of happy and sad faces were cut in half horizontally and the halves exchanged (fig.1). It is obvious from this experiment that the bottom of the face dominates the expression. When you put a sad mouth on smiling eyes, you get a sad countenance; when you put a smiling mouth on sad eyes, you get a happy countenance.

Why *are* particular facial expressions associated with particular emotions? Why do we contract the major zygomatic muscle when we are happy? Why don't we pucker instead? This is the question that motivated Darwin's study.

Darwin proposed that emotional expression was an adaptive process that evolved by natural selection. When one bird screeches in distress, other birds are alerted and can be saved from a predator. When an attacker bears its teeth, the attacked animal might leave the territory without a fight, thus preserving both. However, although Darwin began his famous book by asking why particular facial actions accompany particular emotional states, he never came up with an answer; he simply ended with the assertion that the evidence he reviewed proved once again that man descended from lower animal forms.

The next important figure in the debate is William James, who, as noted earlier, turned previous conceptions of emotion and expression upside down. James wrote:

> My theory . . . is that the bodily changes follow directly the perception of the exciting fact, and that our feelings of the same changes as they occur *is* the emotion. . . . Common sense says, we lose our fortune, are sorry and weep; we meet a bear, are frightened and run; we are insulted by a rival, are angry and strike. . . . The hypothesis here to be defended says that this order of sequence is incorrect.

When James spoke of "bodily changes," he meant mainly "visceral changes," but he also included respiratory, cutaneous, and circulatory effects as sources for feedback that produces the subjective feeling. Note that this sequence is totally inconsistent with Darwin's idea of emotional expression arising from selective pressures. One can communicate an internal state by outward gesture *only* if that state has already been felt. If the internal state is to *follow* the gesture—the crying, the striking, the trembling—it would be quite difficult to explain the adaptive value of particular expressions.

Of course, James was immediately attacked by several people, whose experiments indicated that the sequence he described did not adequately explain emotion. However, I propose that although James was wrong in his belief that visceral changes are necessary as the basis for our feelings, he may have been right in disputing the traditional classical sequence. Our research suggests that feelings are in fact controlled by hypothalamic temperature, and that the face can cause changes in our feeling states because it can act to control temperature in the area of the brain that is crucially implicated in emotion: the hypothalamus.

The face as a machine of the emotions

"*Expression* of emotions" is the commonly accepted phrase; but note that the very word "expression" is in itself a theory, in that it implies that an internal state is manifested externally. By using this word we commit ourselves to a theory that feelings have to precede a related outward action, as well as to the idea that internal states seek externalization—hence the word *suppression*. But if, as I suggested, the face can *cause* internal changes as well as register them, these terms are somewhat misleading. More neutral terms would be *facial action* or *facial efference*.

I was compelled to come to the conclusion that facial action can precede and even *cause* feelings, on the basis of our recent studies, which were stimulated by a book written in 1907 by Israel Waynbaum, a Russian immigrant to France who wrote only one book, and that one hardly known.

Waynbaum, a physician, argued that facial gestures in general, and emotional gestures in particular, have regulatory and restorative functions for the vascular system of the head. He observed first, that all emotional experiences produce a considerable disequilibrium of the vascular process. Second, he noted the curious fact that the main carotid artery is divided at the neck into two arteries, the internal, which supplies the brain, and the external, which supplies the face and skull.

Waynbaum conjectured that this strange configuration exists to allow the facial branch of the artery to act as a safety valve. The muscles of the face could, he thought, press against facial arteries and thus shunt blood away from the brain in case of oversupply and allow greater inflow when the supply is insufficient. In other words, he thought of the facial muscles as tourniquets.

Waynbaum's theory makes better sense than Darwin's in explaining several kinds of facial efference. Darwin argued that we blush because blood rushes to those parts of the body that are under intense scrutiny of others. Those more sensitive to this scrutiny will blush more easily than others; therefore women and children blush more readily than men—an interesting idea, but it isn't obvious what adaptive value such behavior would have. Waynbaum, on the contrary, suggested that blushing results when there is danger of blood flooding the brain. In these cases, blood is shunted away to the face, which becomes flushed. We blush when we are embarrassed and cannot run or hide. Energy is mobilized for flight or fight; blood surges up, but the energy cannot be released, and the face takes it up to prevent congestion to the brain.

It is not surprising that, based on turn-of-the-century physiology, several of Waynbaum's assumptions are questionable and others are outright wrong. Because arterial flow can be controlled directly by vasodilators and vasoconstriction, it is unlikely to be much affected by muscular action of the face.

Nevertheless, much of Waynbaum's thinking can be useful. Facial muscles might not have a significant effect on arteries, but they can affect venous flow. More importantly, by interfering with or facilitating the cooling process of the brain, facial action might alter the temperature of blood entering the brain. Facial action can produce changes in brain blood temperature, which, in turn, has significant hedonic consequences. Such a process may in turn have subjective effects through its impact on the neurochemical activity in the brain. For example, if a certain action of facial muscles results in changing the temperature in a particular brain region that is active in releasing norepinephrine, then norepinephrine might be either partially blocked or released, with subsequent calming or excitation effects. If the action releases serotonin, the action will be an antidepressant. (The absence of serotonin is associated with depressive states.)

To be sure, the conjecture that changes in brain temperature can influence brain neurochemicals associated with subjective emotional states still needs empirical documentation, but it is consistent with the fact that *all* biochemical processes are affected by temperature. Cooling of the brain is a crucial physiological function. The brain is an organ that cannot tolerate temperature variations as readily as other organs, and its cooling relies heavily on heat exchange, whereby venous blood, cooled by evaporation, exchanges heat with the arterial blood entering the brain. In addition, brain temperature is controlled by the temperature of venous blood that reaches the cavernous sinus, a venous configuration enveloping the internal carotid just before the latter enters the brain (fig.2).

The cooling function of the cavernous sinus has been verified by experiments with animals. The near panic felt by people whose nasal airways must be packed and the great discomfort experienced by anyone with extreme nasal congestion suggest that nose breathing serves another function besides air intake. In each of these cases the cooling action of the cavernous sinus is severely restricted. It seems likely, therefore, that the cooling action of the cavernous sinus has an important influence on the subjective state of an individual.

I must say here that we really don't know exactly how the cavernous sinus does its job, but we do know that the temperature of the blood before it enters the brain is about .3°C warmer than after it has passed through the cavernous sinus.

To summarize:

1. Subjective feeling states—feeling good and feeling bad—are the result of neurochemical activity of the brain.
2. Neurochemical activity that is implicated in emotion is temperature-sensitive.
3. Therefore, changes in brain temperature can modulate neurochemical activity of the brain and will be experienced as changes in feeling states.
4. The metabolic activity of the brain produces considerable amounts of heat, and the brain, therefore, requires continuous cooling.
5. Hypothalamic cooling depends on the temperature of the arterial blood supplying it.
6. The temperature of the arterial blood that supplies the brain is cooled by the cavernous sinus, a venous structure that surrounds the internal carotid artery.
7. Facial veins, including those from the nasal airways, drain into the cavernous sinus, or they can drain into the external jugular vein, and they carry cooled blood, which cools the internal carotid artery.
8. Both breathing patterns and facial muscular action control the temperature and the flow in the veins that empty into the cavernous sinus.
9. Because the metabolic activity of the brain requires continuous cooling, the absence of cooling is felt as discomfort and negative affect, whereas increased cooling is felt as pleasurable and positive affect.

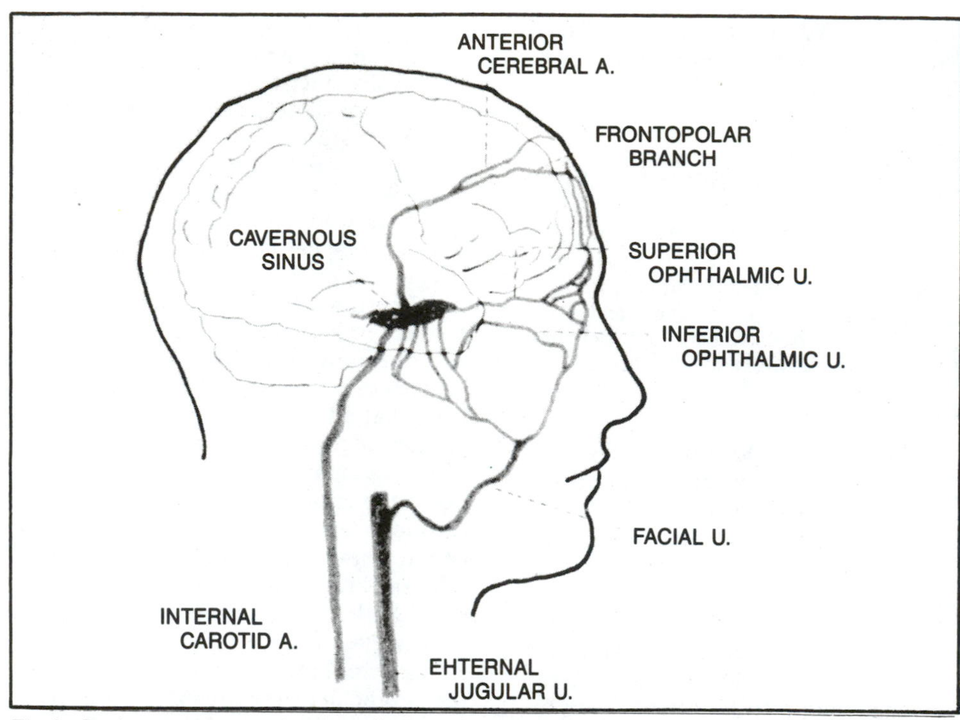

Fig.2. Brain temperature is controlled by the temperature of venous blood that reaches the cavernous sinus, a venous configuration enveloping the internal carotid just before the latter enters the brain.

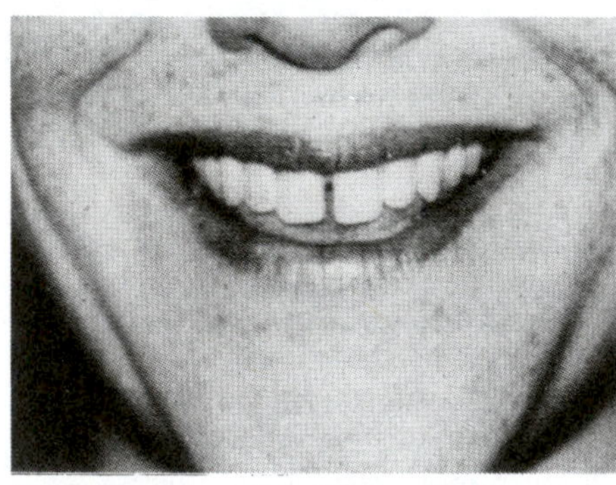
Fig.3. Person saying "cheese."

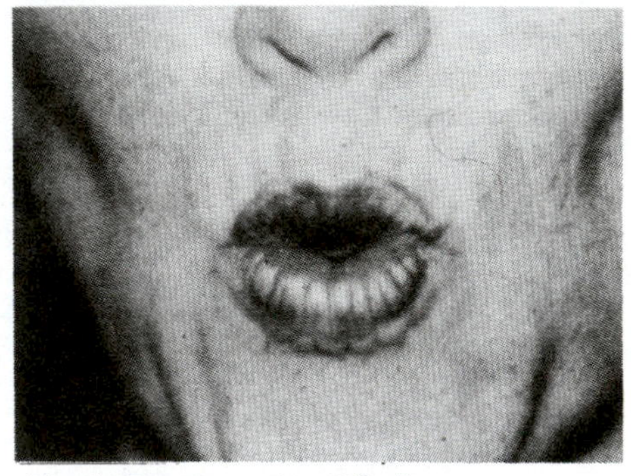
Fig.4. Person saying "für."

This, then, is a process that connects subjective feeling states in the emotions to bodily processes—a form of resolution to the mind-body problem. In recent experimental work we examined the connections between facial expressions and feeling states. We wanted to learn whether facial action alone, without accompanying emotional excitation, can change subjective states. Can facial action have hedonic consequences?

Look at the expressions on the faces in figures 3 and 4. One's first impression is that they are indications of a felt emotion. In fact, the subject is saying "cheese" (fig.3) and "für" (fig.4). A number of experiments have now shown that the expressions accompanying phonetic actions that resemble positive emotional expressions (such as saying "cheese") generate lower temperatures and positive affect, while those accompanying phonetic actions that resemble negative emotional expressions (saying the German "für") generate higher temperatures and negative affect. In one study, German subjects read stories containing many instances of the German umlaut (the phoneme *ü* [ue]), which requires action the opposite of a smile; they also read stories that did not contain many umlauts. When they read the stories with the many *ü*'s, their forehead temperatures were elevated and the concurrent feelings were negative; in contrast, when they read the other stories, temperatures remained normal and feelings neutral.

Further experiments invited subjects to breathe what they supposed were subtle odors and to indicate whether the odors were pleasant or unpleasant. In fact, the air they breathed was either slightly heated or slightly cooled. The result was that the subjects' forehead temperatures went down with cooled air and up with warm air. More important, these changes were correlated with positive and negative feelings. Experiments with animals substantiated these findings.

The varied roles of sneezing, sucking, and smiling

If the vascular theory of hedonic states makes any sense, it is reasonable to suppose that universality of emotional facial action evolved not because it served a communicative function, as Darwin argued, but because it was a useful regulator of brain temperature. As an added attraction, it also became an emotional language. Viewed in this light, the smile is similar to a sneeze, which is a regulatory process and tells us something about the internal state of the sneezer. The sneeze is present in humans and many animals and is cross-cultural, but it is not an emotional expression; we don't sneeze to inform those around us of a difficulty in our respiratory system.

Another line of research is exploring the link between brain temperature and emotion in a different way. It turns out that the metaphors "hothead," "boiling mad," and "cool as a cucumber" are not altogether accidental. Forehead temperature, which is very diagnostic of brain temperature, is higher for a person expressing anger than for one with a neutral expression. Extensive research has also shown that aggression and negative affect occur more readily when ambient temperature is high. In one example, students gave an instructor more negative ratings under conditions of high temperature than in moderate temperature.

Why do we scratch our heads when we are confused? Why do we rub our chins? Why do some people bite their

Kissing may be pleasurable not because the mouth is an erogenous zone, but because it forces breathing through the nose.

fingernails, or pens or pencils? Why do people chew gum? My answer to these questions is that these movements may help cool brain blood by moving cooled blood to the cavernous sinus more efficiently.

Thumb-sucking may be a prime example of this. Sucking is a powerful unlearned action that is very hard to extinguish, even after the reinforcement and obvious incentives are long gone. Why? Sucking is an activity that forces nasal breathing—deep nasal breathing that can cool the brain quite efficiently—and it is not unlikely that this releases endorphins, for it seems to have a pacifying effect. Cooling of the brain is particularly important for infants, whose brain produces 80 percent of body heat. So, there are two reasons for sucking: sucking for milk, which is indeed a reflex that is probably a result of natural selection pressures; and sucking that results in cooling of the brain and brings a different kind of satisfaction.

Kissing, too, may be pleasurable not because the mouth is an erogenous zone, as Freud suggested, but because it forces breathing through the nose. Likewise with screaming and cringing: they have an effect on venous blood flow, which changes brain temperature and perhaps releases endogenous opiates that act as analgesics. Weight lifters scream not to communicate the effort they are making, but to relieve the pain.

Tapping the Healing Power of Positive Thinking

How emotions help—or hurt

Nick Gallo

Consider these three brief stories:

• A young mother crawls through a burning house to save her child, not realizing until both have escaped that she has severe burns over most of her back.

• A teenage boy worries so much about his parent's impending divorce that he develops severe stomach pains and must be hospitalized.

• A middle-aged cancer patient lies hopelessly ill in a hospital bed laughing at a stream of humorous books, articles, and movies—which he will later credit for his recovery.

Scientists have long accepted the validity of the first two scenarios. During periods of crisis, the mind is fully capable of turning off pain. And severe emotional turmoil commonly leads to physical symptoms of illness.

What is still open to debate is the third situation. Yet dozens of studies have led researchers tantalizingly close to agreeing that laughter can heal and that hostility can kill. Here's a report on the latest thinking about how your attitudes and emotions can be a force for health—good or bad.

MIND OVER MATTER?

More than a decade ago, Norman Cousins wrote *Anatomy of an Illness*, a personal story of his recovery from a supposedly irreversible disease. In it, he championed the healing value of life-affirming emotions, such as hope, love, faith, a strong will to live, a sense of purpose, and a capacity for fun.

In recent years, his anecdotal account has been supported by scientific studies. Researchers point to a cluster of emotions and attitudes that seem to be linked to improved health.

Sheldon Cohen, Ph.D., a psychologist at Carnegie Mellon University in Pittsburgh, collected data from a five-year study of 400 people exposed to the common cold. Early results indicate that psychological factors influence your odds of infection.

Fighting spirit. A British study of women with breast cancer reports that women with a "fighting spirit" are more than twice as likely to be alive and well 10 years later than women who hold a helpless, hopeless attitude.

Solid marriage, friendships. Social support seems to contribute to health and lifespan, according to a nine-year survey of 7,000 people. The group with strong social ties—marriage, friendship, group membership—had lower death rates than those who were isolated.

Love, compassion. In a Harvard study, students who were shown a film designed to inspire feelings of love and caring experienced an increase in an antibody that protects against upper respiratory infection.

MIND UNDERMINES MATTER, TOO

Just as positive emotions help health, negative attitudes and emotions seem to undermine one's health. For example, a review of 99 Harvard University graduates who completed personality questionnaires in 1946 found that students who had been most pessimistic at age 25 experienced more severe illnesses at middle-age.

Researchers point to other unhealthy emotions:

Depression. At the University of Chicago, psychologist Richard Shekelle followed the health histories of 2,020 middle-aged Western Electric plant employees and found that those who had been depressed were twice as likely to later die from cancer.

Cynicism and hostility. Researchers at Duke University contend that people with a cynical or hostile attitude are five times more likely to die before age 50 than their calmer, more trusting counterparts.

Loneliness. Rates of illness and death tend to be higher among single and divorced individuals, suggesting that loneliness takes its toll on the immune system.

Stress. Increased illness rates among the recently bereaved suggest that chronic stress affects health. In a study at Ohio State University, medical students nearing exam time suffered a drop in the fighter cells that help the body combat infections.

Reprinted from *Better Homes and Gardens* magazine, November 1991, pp. 68, 70.

THE MEANING OF IT ALL

Not everyone is convinced that these statistical associations prove much. How exactly does a positive or negative attitude influence whether you get sick? How can a thought protect you against germs?

Two general theories exist, says David Spiegel, M.D., professor of psychiatry and behavioral sciences at Stanford University. First, people who have a positive mental outlook or strong social support tend to take better care of themselves. They're more likely to go to the doctor regularly, adopt a healthful diet, and avoid smoking, drug use, and other self-destructive behavior.

The second, more radical, idea is that a person's thoughts and emotions act directly on the immune system, the body's disease-fighting brigade. Studies seem to show that emotions may directly stimulate the production of brain chemicals that enhance—or undermine—the immune system.

Beyond the test tube. Various researchers wonder if these effects mean much outside a laboratory. Dr. George Solomon, a UCLA psychiatrist involved in mind-body research, notes that people can lose quite a bit of immune function—in terms of white blood cell counts—and still stay healthy.

Other medical experts claim that any psychological effect would pale in comparison to the biology of a disease such as cancer. Such factors as the type of tumor, its stage, the patient's age, and the treatment are more important than state of mind, believes University of Pennsylvania psychologist Barrie Cassileth, Ph.D., whose studies of cancer patients have not found a link between attitude and length of survival.

Even supporters of mind over health admit that the ultimate value of a positive attitude is unproven. "No matter how probable it seems that the mind influences the immune system, we still don't have enough actual evidence," says Steven Locke, M.D., assistant professor of psychiatry at Harvard Medical School and coauthor of *The Health Within* (New American Library, 1986).

MAKING IT WORK FOR YOU

Although we don't understand the exact connection between health and attitude, research does offer clues on using your mind to stay healthy.

Think positively. University of Pennsylvania psychologist Martin Seligman, Ph.D., author of *Learned Optimism* (Knopf, 1991), believes that your outlook may affect your health.

More than two decades ago he proposed a concept called "learned helplessness." His studies showed that rats who received mild but inescapable shocks wouldn't even try to escape punishment when they were later placed in a box in which they could avoid the shocks. They'd surrendered willpower after deciding that whatever they did didn't matter.

Some humans, too, may lose hope quickly and become passive and depressed when crises strike.

How do you explain a setback to yourself? For some the response is: "It's me; it's going to last forever; it's going to undermine everything I do," says Dr. Seligman. Others are able to say and believe: "It was just circumstances; it's going away quickly, and besides, there is much more in life."

By reviewing and challenging your automatic first thoughts, it's possible to change the habit of saying destructive things to yourself when you suffer disappointments, he says.

"One of the most significant findings in psychology in the last 20 years is that individuals can choose the way they *think*," says Dr. Seligman.

Redford Williams, M.D., a behavioral medicine expert at Duke University and author of *The Trusting Heart* (Times Book, 1989), believes that how you think and feel *about others* affects your health. His studies of Type A people—overcompetitive, hard-driving, hurried—show that hostility ups your odds of heart disease.

In his 12-step program toward a trusting heart, he advises people to reduce their anger and cynical mistrust of others, learn to treat others with kindness and consideration, and to be assertive, not aggressive, in threatening situations.

Other researchers believe there is a health benefit to having some personal control over your surroundings. In a study by psychologists Ellen Langer and Judith Rodin, a group of nursing-home residents who were given a set of responsibilities and greater decision-making showed improvements in health and activities within three weeks. After 18 months, the death rate of this "self-responsibility" group was half that of the other group.

Reach out. One long-range study showed that people with social contact—volunteer work, community activities, support groups—lived longer and were healthier than isolated people.

Use mind-body techniques. Meditation, biofeedback, and numerous other unconventional therapies may help turn on the inner healer. In one study at New England Deaconess Hospital's Mind/Body Clinic, relaxation techniques helped nearly 80 percent of patients with hypertension to either lower their blood pressure or reduce drug dosage. Other studies have used hypnosis to improve the quality of life for cancer patients.

Few experts call these techniques potential cures for illness. "They are meant to complement medicine, not replace it," says Dr. Locke. Yet most doctors agree that a positive attitude—whether optimism or a fighting spirit—plays a role in recovery from illness. And although the evidence is still coming in, there's good reason to believe that a positive outlook on life helps protect you from illness.

Doctors Find Comfort Is a Potent Medicine

Support can be more effective than chemotherapy.

Daniel Goleman

"Comfort always, cure rarely," was a motto of medicine in times long gone, when bedside manner was far more potent than any medicines.

Now, in a movement that counters the rush to high-technology, high-turnover medicine, some physicians are urging that the lost art of comforting be revived. They are spurred by a steady march of scientific findings demonstrating how heavily patients' emotional states can affect the course of their diseases.

For example, among 100 patients preparing to go through bone marrow transplants for leukemia, 13 were found to be highly depressed and 12 of them indeed died within a year of the transplant. But 34 out of the 87 who were not depressed were still alive after two years, a recent study at the University of Minnesota showed.

Of the patients who felt they had strong emotional support from their spouses, family or friends, 54 percent survived the transplants after two years. But the two-year survival rate of those who said they had little social support was only 20 percent.

In another study, 122 men were evaluated for the pessimism or optimism they had felt at the time of suffering a heart attack. Their state of mind was found to be a better predictor of death from heart attack eight years later than were any of the standard medical risk factors, including damage to the heart in the first episode, artery blockage, cholesterol levels or blood pressure. Of the 25 most pessimistic men, 21 had died after eight years; of the 25 most optimistic, just 6 died.

And in a study done at Mount Sinai Hospital in New York City and Northwestern University Medical School in Chicago, elderly patients admitted for a fractured hip were also checked for and given mental health care if they needed it. They left the hospital two days sooner, on average, than patients who, as is standard in most orthopedic units, received care only for their fractures.

"Physicians absolutely should take their patients' emotional state into account when they treat them for medical problems," said Dr. James Strain, a psychiatrist at Mount Sinai who is the main author of this study, which was published in The American Journal of Psychiatry in August. "There's a tremendous amount of psychiatric difficulty among medical patients."

No one is suggesting that emotional distress outweighs biological factors in disease or that psychological help can replace medical care. But the bottom line from these and other new studies seems to be that attending to patients' emotional distress along with ordinary medical care can add an extra margin of healing in many cases.

To be sure, the very idea that emotions can play any role at all in disease is anathema to many people in the field of medicine. That notion, a much-cited 1985 editorial in The New England Journal of Medicine proclaimed, is nothing but "folklore."

But more and more medical researchers are finding the new data too compelling to ignore. Many scientists interviewed cited as particularly convincing a 1990 Stanford University study that found that women with advanced breast cancer who were in support groups lived twice as long as did other women with equivalent illness and medication.

Adding 18 Months of Life

What has caught the interest of cancer specialists about the Stanford findings is that the support groups added an average 18 months to the women's lives, appreciably longer than any of the chemotherapy medications they were also taking could have been expected to offer, given the advanced stage of their cancer. More than a half-dozen experiments in four countries are now under way to repeat the Stanford study, with as many more studies in the planning stages.

Like the Stanford results, many of the most intriguing findings are from small clinical experiments. To confirm their validity, such findings must be repeated by other researchers. Some of the early findings are part of converging lines of evidence pointing to the importance of emotions in health and disease.

For example, the study of pessimists and heart attacks is one of a series done by different researchers on people's attitudes and their health. In one of the first, reported by Dr. Martin Seligman at the University of Pennsylvania in 1988, members of the Harvard University classes of 1939 to 1944 were evaluated as being pessimistic or optimistic on the basis of essays they had written in college about their wartime experiences.

Pessimism and Chronic Disease

"Pessimists" tend to explain setbacks in their lives as resulting from some trait of theirs that cannot change and will blight other things, too. By contrast, "optimists" tend to explain an unfortunate turn of events as resulting from something in the situation that can be changed, rather than as their fault.

The more pessimistic the Harvard men had been as students, the more likely they were to have got a serious chronic disease like atherosclerosis by the age of 45.

Medical scientists are already looking for possible physical mechanisms that could link people's emotional states to their state of health.

"The search for mechanisms in the next generation of studies will have to range widely," Dr. Strain said. "One of the simplest hypotheses is that patients who are anxious, depressed or confused just don't follow instructions. Another possibility is that if you are slowed down, anxious or depressed, there may be a physiological effect on the healing process."

Dozens of research teams are pursuing the possibility that negative emotional states may adversely affect the ability of the immune system to fight disease. Although some of these researchers have established that anxiety and depression can hamper the activity of crucial cells within the immune system, no research has yet been able to show that these changes are clinically significant for the course of disease or healing.

Another explanation why optimistic patients may do better is simply that doctors and nurses may treat emotionally disturbed patients differently.

"If patients are recalcitrant or tired, nurses may back off," Dr. Strain said. "In our study of hip fracture patients, they sometimes sent depressed patients to physical therapy just once a day instead of twice."

Effects of Giving Up

By the same token, "pessimistic people are less likely to change habits that might be damaging to their health," said Gregory Buchanan, a psychologist at Beth Israel Hospital in Boston who did the study of pessimism and heart attacks while a graduate at the University of Pennsylvania. "If pessimists think, 'What's the point of trying—it won't matter,' then they are less likely to make the effort to exercise or try to control the stress in their lives."

Dr. Eduardo Colon, a psychiatrist at the University of Minnesota, said his own study showing that depression in recipients of bone marrow transplants for leukemia led to a high death rate "raises more questions than it answers."

Noting that the bone marrow transplants are psychologically trying as well as physically difficult, Dr. Colon said, "If you're depressed, you may not do the things that could help you recover—get out of bed and move around, care for mouth sores the treatment causes, and so on. Or it may make you less compliant in taking your medication. Or, perhaps, the depression may cause changes in the immune system." His study was published in the current issue of Psychosomatics.

Treating the mind can save money. In Dr. Strain's experiment at Mount Sinai, a psychiatrist evaluated every hip fracture patient. The shorter hospital stays of those who received psychiatric care led to a savings of $178,572. The cost of the psychiatric care was just $21,760.

Conversely, emotionally distressed patients stay longer in hospitals, according to Dr. George Fulop, also of Mount Sinai. Studying 59,259 men and women who came for surgery to two hospitals in 1984, he found that those with problems like extreme anxiety or depression stayed eight days longer in the hospital on average than did untroubled patients.

Link to Emotional Problems

According to a recent door-to-door survey of more than 18,000 men and women in five cities, a large majority of people with medical complaints also have emotional problems. Of those who had five or more physical complaints, 63 percent reported psychological problems as well.

In 50 percent of the cases, the problems were severe enough to qualify for a psychiatric diagnosis like depression. But among people who did not have so many physical problems, the rate of psychiatric disorders was 7 percent, Dr. Gregory Simon and Dr. Michael VonKorff of the University of Washington Medical School in Seattle reported in this month's issue of The American Journal of Psychiatry.

But they said people suffering with both physical and psychological symptoms were likely to mention only their physical problems to their doctors. They urged that doctors address both kinds of problems, noting that failing to recognize emotional distress leaves out half the treatment.

"Doctors are very bad at identifying distressed patients," said Dr. Deborah Roter, a psychologist at Johns Hopkins University who has been training physicians to deal with emotional distress in their patients.

In a study of 69 physicians, Dr. Roter, working with Dr. Judith Hall, a psychologist at Northeastern University in Boston, taped all their office visits for a week. Two-thirds of the physicians had gone through eight hours of training to improve their ability to listen with empathy and to deal with patients' emotional distress.

Effects of Empathy Training

Their patients were independently assessed for their level of distress before they saw the doctors. Then researchers phoned the patients two weeks, three months and six months after their visit to the doctor.

Of the 340 patients identified as most distraught while waiting to see their doctors, "those whose doctors went through the training were significantly less distressed even six months later than were those whose doctors treated them as usual," Dr. Roter said.

"Physicians usually don't ask patients about their emotional state, and typically feel they have no time or training for handling distress," Dr. Roter said. "For their part, patients are afraid it's not a legitimate topic for them to bring up. But it should be."

Barriers To Success

How to examine your self-defeating tactics and overcome the hurdles between you and your goals.

BRUCE A. BALDWIN

Bruce A. Baldwin is a practicing psychologist and author who heads Direction Dynamics in Wilmington, North Carolina, a consulting service that specializes in promoting quality of life. For busy achievers, Dr. Baldwin has written It's All in Your Head: Lifestyle Management Strategies for Busy People.

When you create goals for yourself, you define what you want out of life. You set about achieving what is important to you. To do this, though, requires a base of successful experiences that have created confidence and a sense of personal control—feelings not always easy to acquire.

Setting and achieving personal goals, however, contributes to emotional well-being, and defining realistic personal goals provides a core of personal meaning from which motivational energy is generated. Frequently, men and women without realistic personal goals develop low self-esteem, and over time they often become lethargic and depressed.

Some men and women have realistic personal goals, but just don't seem to be able to reach them. Although these individuals have the skills and opportunities needed to succeed, they are very frustrated. They do not understand why they can't quite reach their goals, and the personal consequences are negative. The problem here is subtle and often difficult to resolve unless the dynamics involved are understood.

The problem lies within the individual. Rationalizing failure or blaming others for lack of success is human nature. Resistance to success, however, is a personal problem and must be addressed within the individual. To accomplish this, the person must accept full responsibility for his or her behavior.

A pattern to the problem is obvious. Almost always, resistance to success involves a pattern of behavior that is repeated. Sometimes self-sabotage is seen only in specific kinds of situations. In other people the problem is more generalized and emerges more or less across the board.

The reason for self-sabotage is often not in conscious awareness. It would be easy to assume that resistance to success always involves self-defeating acts that are calculated and conscious. While this is occasionally true, more often such patterns operate just below conscious awareness.

The result is failure and lowered self-esteem. No one feels good about repeatedly failing to reach personal goals. Self-sabotage results in erosion of self-esteem and feelings about one's own competence. Over time, motivation to try again often diminishes.

Resistance to success, often beginning in childhood or adolescence, does not necessarily end once adulthood is reached. When resistance does continue in adulthood, the individual's potential is never reached because of self-sabotage. Negative gossip, condescending remarks, put-downs, or even name-calling by family members may develop and make matters worse.

Resistance to success is a most frustrating experience for everyone involved. The problem of self-sabotage and resistance to success *can* be resolved, but first, other dimensions of what is actually taking place must be examined.

The Mechanisms of Resistance

When we recognize self-sabotage, the next level of understanding is to define how personal defeat is carried out. Self-sabotage is manifested through a few well-defined patterns of behavior. While these patterns tend to be quite consistent within individuals, they are often clouded by rationalizations, denials, blaming, and other forms of minimizing.

Each mechanism of resistance serves several psychological purposes. First, the individual never makes an active personal decision to attain a goal or not to do so. Second, each mechanism of resistance gives the individual a built-in excuse, so the decision to proceed (or not) is made by others. The individual escapes responsibility for making that decision or reaching a goal. Here's how it's done.

Choosing an inappropriate peer group. Most of us are influenced by our peer groups. When an individual consistently gravitates toward a peer group that has low academic/work motivation, that legitimizes illegal behavior, or that consistently manifests socially inappropriate values, then a problem develops.

Becoming physically sick. The common personal sabotage technique of becoming physically incapacitated can be observed as early as kindergarten, and it can easily persist into adulthood. Some men and women fake an illness to avoid specific situations that may be stressful or psychologically threatening. More often, an actual illness results from the intense emotional

From *USAir Magazine*, June 1992, pp. 18, 19, 22, 23, 25. This article is adapted from B. A. Baldwin's "It's All in Your Head: Lifestyle Management Strategies for Busy People," *Direction Dynamics*, 1985. The book is available from *Direction Dynamics*, 309 Honeycutt Dr., Wilmington, NC 28412 for $11.70 postpaid (NC residents should add 6% sales tax).

turmoil being experienced. Common symptoms include palpitations, severe headaches, diarrhea, nausea, faintness or fainting, dizziness, hyperventilation, and generalized gastrointestinal upset. These symptoms justify avoiding key situations.

Procrastinating until it's too late. Procrastination involves habitually putting off obtaining necessary information, filling out applications, or informing key people of a personal desire or decision. Eventually, this creates a situation where a decision is made for the individual, as for example, when a deadline passes. Such procrastination reflects an individual's inability to make an important decision.

Behaving inappropriately in key situations. Everyone goofs up now and then. But when a consistent pattern of making serious mistakes in critical situations is clear, then an underlying problem involving resistance to success may be present. Inappropriate behaviors include drinking too much at dinner with a potential employer, arriving late for an interview, or making inappropriate remarks that are overheard. The person behaves in ways that prevent a successful outcome. Self-recrimination or rationalizations result, but the real problem remains unaddressed.

Starting strong, giving up at the end. Someone who manifests this pattern typically makes a wonderful start toward reaching a goal. While progress early on is steady, as goal attainment nears, persistence wanes and energy output steadily declines. Why? Because the closer one is to reaching a goal, the more one's underlying ambivalence about achieving it rises to the surface. Toward the end, underlying resistance becomes so strong and performance so impaired that goal attainment is either significantly compromised or sabotaged completely.

The Road to Success

Within each self-sabotaging individual is a personal dilemma that produces resistance to success in life. Usually, the problem is not technical competency or a lack of intellectual ability. This is what is so frustrating. It is also what makes it so difficult for friends, family, and colleagues who know the potential of such individuals and see it not being used. The effect on everyone is disappointment. The long-term effect on the individual is serious self-doubt, damaged self-esteem, and feelings of failure.

While many negative feelings result from lack of progress toward success, deep down in each one of these men and women also lies a secret sense of relief. Why? Because each one has not faced a fear within. Self-sabotage has neatly allowed them to avoid facing important personal issues. While these emotional issues frequently have their **origins in the family during the developmental years, part of the problem is that they are not consciously aware of these fears.**

Perhaps you recognize yourself in this description. Until critical issues within are resolved, you will continue to be frustrated by internal blocks that impede development of personal maturity and professional success. Here are a number of steps to help confront and resolve these often subtle personal issues.

Define your pattern of avoidance. Uncover the mechanisms of sabotage that are present and determine under what conditions they emerge to impede progress toward personal goals. If possible, pinpoint the very first time that the problem occurred.

Select and dissect one representative incident. If one stands out above all others, use it. If not, then choose a recent example that is still fresh in your memory. Take a few moments to write down exactly what happened before, during, and after the self-sabotage.

Clearly articulate the underlying fear. Ask yourself these questions: "What fear do I associate with success or reaching my personal goals?" "What consequences of success did I avoid through self-sabotage?" Say your answers out loud. The fears usually involve threats to self-image or key relationships.

Look for the origins of your fear. It is helpful to understand where your fear began. Because family dynamics are often involved, try to trace your avoidance pattern back as far as you can. Try to understand the fear, but be careful not to blame others for your problem.

Make an active decision about your directions. This is absolutely critical in breaking this pattern. Decide actively to go forward. If, once considered, the payoffs do not seem to be worth it, then actively decide to stay right where you are. The key is to articulate your decision to yourself.

Obtain support and encouragement. Talk over your decision with one good friend who you know will be objective and have your best interests in mind. Avoid those people who may be part of the problem, who are habitually negative, or who may allow their own interests to influence any support they give you.

Inform others of your decision. After carefully considering all options, let others know what you have decided. This may be the most frightening part of all. Don't vacillate or ask others for permission. Instead, inform them of your decision and your future intentions.

Follow through with direct action. With the positives of your decision firmly in mind, do what you've said you'll do. Recognize that every decision involves something gained and something lost. Don't dwell on the loss. Make yourself do whatever is necessary to implement what you've decided.

When you have completed these steps, you've broken your pattern of self-sabotage. You have overcome unresolved issues from the past and have freed yourself to determine your future. As a result, you've not only reestablished direction for your life, but you've also re-created a sense of internal control, and your self-esteem has increased because you are no longer failing. Winston Churchill once commented, "It's a mistake to look too far ahead. Only one link in the chain of destiny can be handled at a time." You've now broken a negative link to the past and are free to forge your destiny—one link at a time.

Problems Influencing Personal Growth

At each stage of development from infancy to old age, humans are faced with new challenges. The infant has the rudimentary sensory apparatus for seeing, hearing, and touching, but needs to begin coordinating stimuli into meaningful information. For example, early in life the baby begins to recognize familiar and unfamiliar people and usually becomes attached to those who are the primary caregivers. As a toddler, the same child must master the difficult skills of walking, talking, and toilet training. This energetic, mobile, and sociable child also needs to learn the limits set by others on his or her behavior. As the child matures, not only do physical changes continue to take place, but the child's family composition may change when siblings are added, parents divorce, or mother decides to work outside the home. Playmates become more influential, and others in the community, such as day-care workers and teachers, also have an increasing impact on the child. The child eventually may spend more time in school than at home. The demands in this new environment require that the child sit still, pay attention, learn, and cooperate with others for long periods of time, something perhaps never before required of the child.

In adolescence the child's body changes noticeably. Peers may pressure the individual to indulge in activities never before attempted (such as consumption of illegal drugs or premarital sex). Adolescent youths are often said to be faced with an identity crisis. The older teenager and the young adult must choose among career, education, and marriage. The pressures of work and family life exact a toll on less mature youths while others are satisfied with the workplace and home.

Adulthood and middle age may bring contentment or turmoil as individuals face career peaks, empty nests, advancing age, and perhaps the deaths of loved ones. Again, some individuals cope more effectively with these events than do others.

At any step in the developmental sequence, unexpected stressors challenge individuals. Stressors include major illnesses, accidents, natural disasters, economic recessions, and family and other personal crises. It is important to remember, however, that an event need not be negative to be stressful. Any major life change may cause stress. As happy as weddings, new babies, and job promotions may be, they too can be stressful because of the changes in daily life they require. Each crisis and each change must be met and adjusted to if the individual is going to move successfully to the next stage of development. Some individuals continue along their paths unscathed; others do not fare so well.

This unit examines major problems in various stages of life from childhood to old age. The first article begins with prenatal life. In "Clipped Wings," the results of a recent report on the deleterious effects of drugs, alcohol, and other substances on the fetus are shared with the reader. Even before life commences, there exist problems for development. The second article addresses infancy. Babies need a certain amount of stimulation for intellectual, perceptual, and social development to progress normally. In "Is Your Baby Getting Enough Stimulation?" Bettye Caldwell examines how much is enough stimulation for babies of different ages.

Developmentally, the life era called childhood occurs next, so the third article in this unit looks at changes in our society that affect all of our children. "Putting Children First" focuses primarily on changes in the family, particularly negative changes, but it also alludes to other societal changes that again are not positive for American children. The author, William Galston, would be remiss if he did not offer solutions to these situations, which he does.

In "I'm OK, They're OK," noted psychologist Faye Crosby discusses the effects of working mothers on their children. She shatters the myth that mothers who work damage their children. Her data also demonstrate that work affects positively both mothers and fathers, too.

A problem of late childhood is addressed in "Children After Divorce" by Judith Wallerstein. While many studies have focused on the immediate effects of divorce on young children, Wallerstein reviews research which shows that a parental divorce in early life follows the child for years, and the child later has difficulty establishing long-term, intimate relationships.

Late childhood and adolescence are also the focus of "Girls' Self-Esteem Is Lost on Way to Adolescence, New Study Finds" by Suzanne Daley. Daley explores psychologist Carol Gilligan's research on self-esteem of adolescent girls. Gilligan contends that girls enter adolescence with robust, positive self-images but emerge with poor images and lowered life expectations. Daley also examines why this is the case. In "Children in Gangs," Carl Rogers investigates youth gangs that often attract teen members. He reveals why youth gangs are on the rise and why the average member's age is declining.

Adulthood is probed in this unit as well. In "Reaching

Unit 3

the Child Within Us," Ashley Montagu challenges the reader to maintain the childlike quantities of flexibility, playfulness, and so on, despite the vagaries of adulthood and middle age.

Millions of grandparents are raising their grandchildren because their own adult children are victims of violence, drugs, and other traumas, and this issue is addressed in "Silent Saviors." Being parents the second time around is a challenge but one that provides the grandchildren with opportunities and love they otherwise might not have.

In the article "The Miracle of Resiliency," David Gelman notes that despite the myriad of problems that face American children, some children are remarkably adaptable. Scientists are studying these children to learn how to assist other not-so-fortunate children.

The ultimate developmental stage is death. Death is a topic that fascinates yet frightens most of us. Studies of the near-death experience are helping us understand what the afterlife holds for us and is the topic of "Bright Lights, Big Mystery." Death, in fact, speeding death via euthanasia, is the topic of "Euthanasia: What Is the 'Good Death?' " the last article in this unit. In this article the pros and cons of ending life early are examined.

Looking Ahead: Challenge Questions

Individuals face challenges at every stage of development. What are some challenges typical of each stage that have not been mentioned in the reader? Is any one stage more demanding than the others? Why?

If drugs and other substances have detrimental effects on the fetus, should we hold addicted parents responsible for the care and treatment of their addicted and deformed infants? What other factors besides drugs and alcohol influence prenatal life?

How can we enhance children's early development? Providing sufficient stimulation is one means; can you think of others?

The book examines parental divorce. What are some of the effects of this problem on American children? What are some other problems and their effects on the child not mentioned in the readings?

Are there lessons we can learn from other cultures that we might incorporate into our childrearing methods? Are there strategies and techniques we could teach them?

What seems to be causing the rash of teen suicides, gang violence, and eating disorders in American youths?

When children join gangs, why do they join? Why is the average age of gang members declining?

Nearly everyone fears death. Is this a sign of poor coping? How might people learn to cope better with the prospect of their own or another's death?

CLIPPED WINGS

The Fullest Look Yet at How Prenatal Exposure to Drugs, Alcohol, and Nicotine Hobbles Children's Learning

LUCILE F. NEWMAN AND STEPHEN L. BUKA

Lucile F. Newman is a professor of community health and anthropology at Brown University and the director of the Preventable Causes of Learning Impairment Project. Stephen L. Buka is an epidemiologist and instructor at the Harvard Medical School and School of Public Health.

SOME FORTY thousand children a year are born with learning impairments related to their mother's alcohol use. Drug abuse during pregnancy affects 11 percent of newborns each year—more than 425,000 infants in 1988. Some 260,000 children each year are born at below normal weights—often because they were prenatally exposed to nicotine, alcohol, or illegal drugs.

What learning problems are being visited upon these children? The existing evidence has heretofore been scattered in many different fields of research—in pediatric medicine, epidemiology, public health, child development, and drug and alcohol abuse. Neither educators, health professionals, nor policy makers could go to one single place to receive a full picture of how widespread or severe were these preventable causes of learning impairment.

In our report for the Education Commission of the States, excerpts of which follow, we combed these various fields to collect and synthesize the major studies that relate prenatal exposure to nicotine, alcohol, and illegal drugs* with various indexes of students' school performance.

The state of current research in this area is not always as full and satisfying as we would wish. Most of what exists is statistical and epidemiological data, which document the frequency of certain high-risk behaviors and correlate those behaviors to student performance. Such data are very interesting and useful, as they allow teachers and policy makers to calculate the probability that a student with a certain family history will experience school failure. But such data often cannot control for the effects of other risk factors, many of which tend to cluster in similar populations. In other words, the same mother who drinks during her pregnancy may also use drugs, suffer from malnutrition, be uneducated, a teenager, or poor—all factors that might ultimately affect her child's school performance. An epidemiological study generally can't tell you how much of a child's poor school performance is due exclusively to a single risk factor.

Moreover, the cumulative damage wrought by several different postnatal exposures may be greater than the damage caused by a single one operating in isolation. And many of the learning problems that are caused by prenatal exposure to drugs can be compounded by such social factors as poverty and parental disinterest and, conversely, overcome if the child lives in a high-quality postnatal environment.

All of these facts make it difficult to isolate and interpret the level and character of the damage that is caused by a single factor. Further, until recently, there was little interest among researchers in the effects of prenatal alcohol exposure because there was little awareness that it was affecting a substantial number of children. The large cohort of children affected by crack is just now entering the schools, so research on their school performance hasn't been extensive.

What does clearly emerge from the collected data is that our classrooms now include many students whose ability to pay attention, sit still, or fully develop their visual, auditory, and language skills was impaired even before they walked through our schoolhouse doors. On the

*The full report for the ECS also addressed the effect on children's learning of fetal malnutrition, pre- and postnatal exposure to lead, and child abuse and neglect.

From *American Educator*, Spring 1991, pp. 27-33, 42. Adapted from "Every Child a Learner: Reducing Risks of Learning Impairment During Pregnancy and Infancy," supported by the Exxon Educational Foundation, published by the Education Commission of the States.

brighter side, the evidence that many of these impairments can be overcome by improved environmental conditions suggests that postnatal treatment is possible; promising experiments in treatment are, in fact, under way and are outlined at the end of this article.

1. Low Birthweight

The collection of graphs begins with a set on low birthweight, which is strongly associated with lowered I.Q. and poor school performance. While low birthweight can be brought on by other factors, including maternal malnutrition and teenage pregnancy, significant causes are maternal smoking, drinking, and drug use.

Around 6.9 percent of babies born in the United States weigh less than 5.5 pounds (2,500 grams) at birth and are considered "low-birthweight" babies. In 1987, this accounted for some 269,100 infants. Low birthweight may result when babies are born prematurely (born too early) or from intrauterine growth retardation (born too small) as a result of maternal malnutrition or actions that restrict blood flow to the fetus, such as smoking or drug use.

FIGURE 1
DISTRIBUTION OF LIVE BIRTHS BY BIRTHWEIGHT AND RACE, 1980

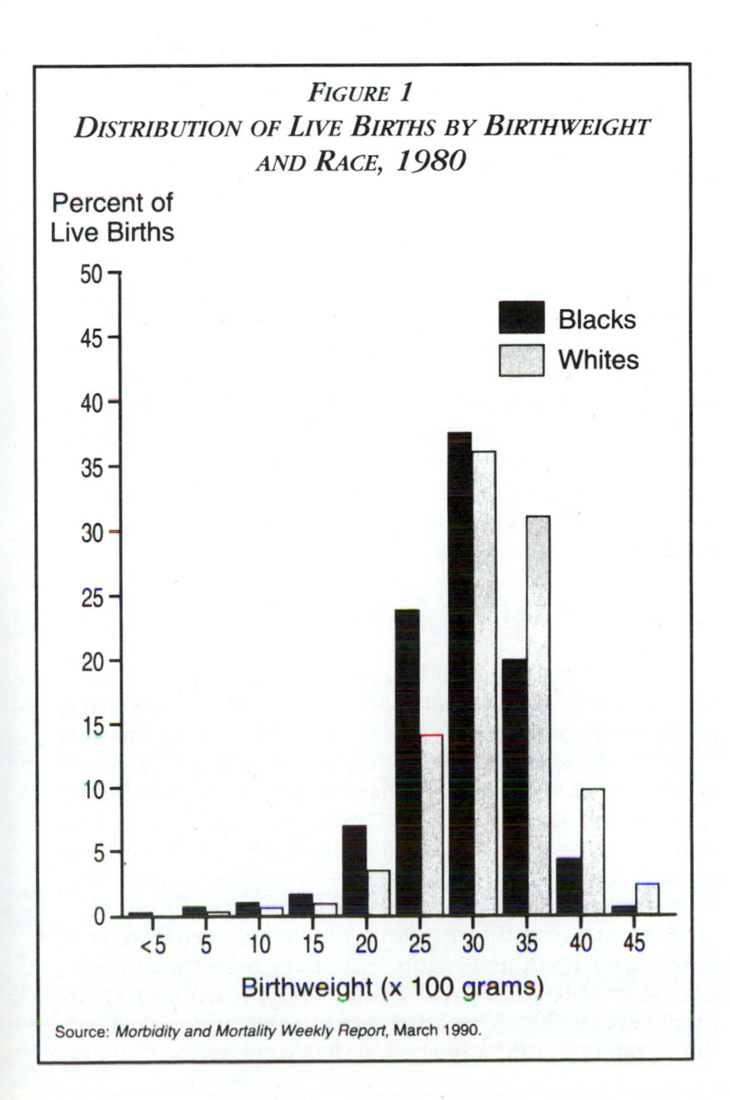

Source: *Morbidity and Mortality Weekly Report*, March 1990.

In 1987, about 48,750 babies were born at very low birthweights (under 3.25 lbs. or 1,500 grams). Research estimates that 6 to 8 percent of these babies experience major handicaps such as severe mental retardation or cerebral palsy (Eilers et al., 1986; Hack and Breslau, 1986). Another 25 to 26 percent have borderline I.Q. scores, problems in understanding and expressing language, or other deficits (Hack and Breslau, 1986; Lefebvre et al., 1988; Nickel et al., 1982; Vohr et al., 1988). Although these children may enter the public school system, many of them show intellectual disabilities and require special educational assistance. Reading, spelling, handwriting, arts, crafts, and mathematics are difficult school subjects for them. Many are late in developing their speech and language. Children born at very low birthweights are more likely than those born at normal weights to be inattentive, hyperactive, depressed, socially withdrawn, or aggressive (Breslau et al., 1988).

FIGURE 2
RELATION OF BIRTHWEIGHT TO VARIOUS MEASURES OF SCHOOL FAILURE AMONG CHILDREN AGED 4-17

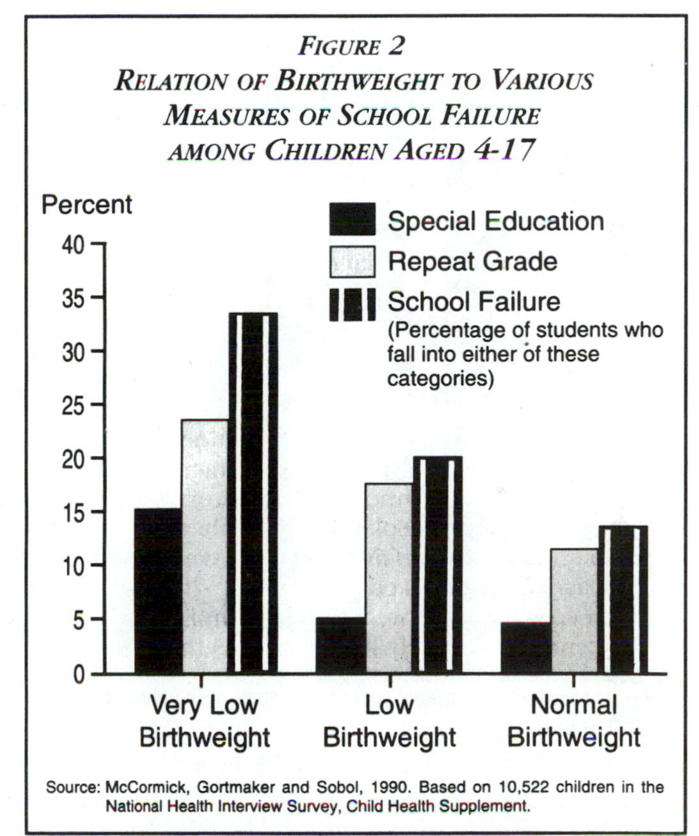

Source: McCormick, Gortmaker and Sobol, 1990. Based on 10,522 children in the National Health Interview Survey, Child Health Supplement.

New technologies and the spread of neonatal intensive care over the past decade have improved survival rates of babies born at weights ranging from 3.25 pounds to 5.5 pounds. But, as Figures 2 and 3 show, those born at low birthweight still are at increased risk of school failure. The increased risk, however, is very much tied to the child's postnatal environment. When the data on which Figure 2 is based are controlled to account for socioeconomic circumstances, very low-birthweight babies are approximately twice, not three times, as likely to repeat a grade.

FIGURE 3
RELATION OF BIRTHWEIGHT TO INTELLIGENCE AND ACHIEVEMENT SCORES AT AGE 7

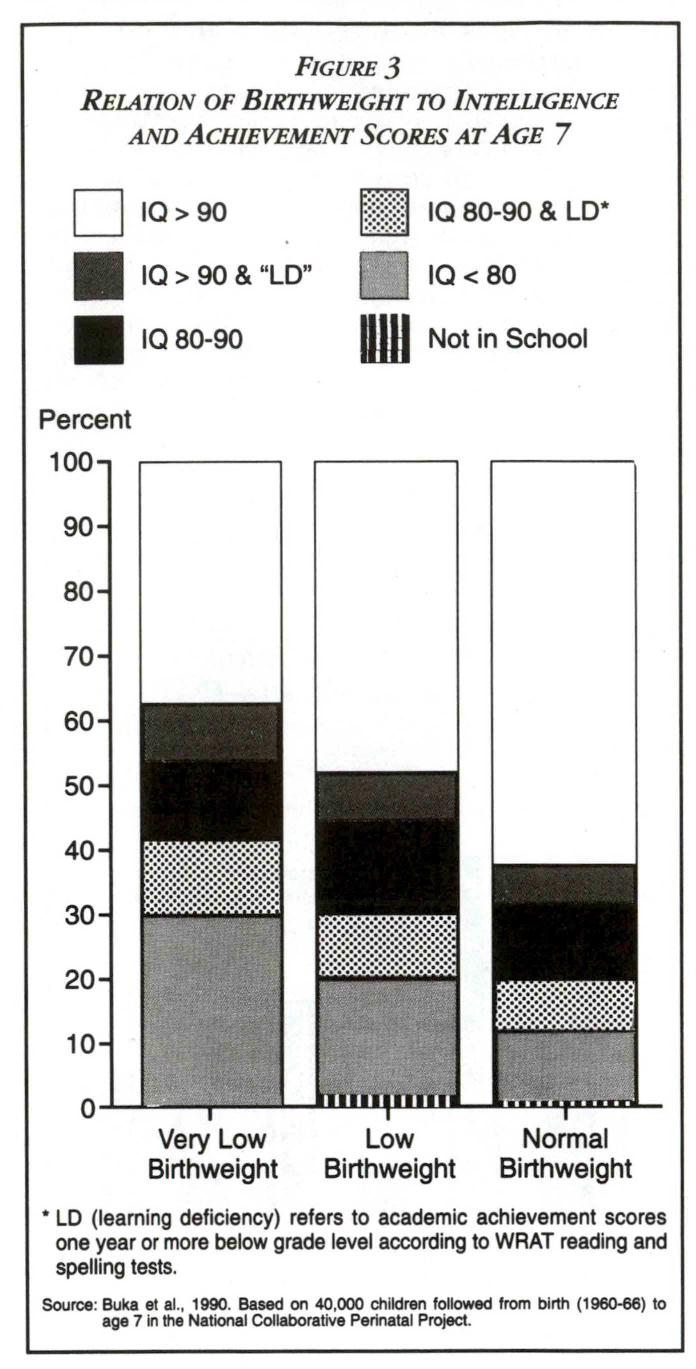

* LD (learning deficiency) refers to academic achievement scores one year or more below grade level according to WRAT reading and spelling tests.

Source: Buka et al., 1990. Based on 40,000 children followed from birth (1960-66) to age 7 in the National Collaborative Perinatal Project.

Indeed, follow-up studies of low-birthweight infants at school age have concluded that "the influence of the environment far outweighs most effects of nonoptimal prenatal or perinatal factors on outcome" (Aylward et al., 1989). This finding suggests that early assistance can improve the intellectual functioning of children at risk for learning delay or impairment (Richmond, 1990).

2. Maternal Smoking

Maternal smoking during pregnancy has long been known to be related to low birthweight (Abel, 1980), an increased risk for cancer in the offspring (Stjernfeldt et al., 1986), and early and persistent asthma, which leads to, among other problems, frequent hospitalization and school absence (Streissguth, 1986). A growing number of new studies has shown that children of smokers are smaller in stature and lag behind other children in cognitive development and educational achievement. These children are particularly subject to hyperactivity and inattention (Rush and Callahan, 1989).

Data from the National Collaborative Perinatal Project on births from 1960 to 1966 measured, among other things, the amount pregnant women smoked at each prenatal visit and how their children functioned in school at age seven. Compared to offspring of nonsmokers, children of heavy smokers (more than two packs per day) were nearly twice as likely to experience school failure by age seven (see Figure 4). The impact of heavy smoking is apparently greater the earlier it occurs during pregnancy. Children of women who smoked heavily during the first trimester of pregnancy were more than twice as likely to fail than children whose mothers did not smoke during the first trimester. During the second and third trimesters, these risks decreased. In all of these analyses, it is difficult to differentiate the effects of exposure to smoking before birth and from either parent after birth; to distinguish between learning problems caused by low birthweight and those caused by other damaging effects of smoking; or, to disentangle the effects of smoke from the socioeconomic setting of the smoker. But it is worth noting that Figure 4 is based on children born in the early sixties, an era when smoking mothers were fairly well distributed across socioeconomic groups.

One study that attempted to divorce the effects of smoking from those of poverty examined middle-class children whose mothers smoked during pregnancy (Fried and Watkinson, 1990) and found that the infants showed differences in responsiveness beginning at one week of age. Later tests at 1, 2, 3, and 4 years of age showed that on verbal tests "the children of the heavy smokers had mean test scores that were lower than those born to lighter smokers, who in turn did not perform as well as those born to nonsmokers." The study also indicated that the effects of smoke exposure, whether in the womb or after birth, may not be identifiable until later ages when a child needs to perform complex cognitive functions, such as problem solving or reading and interpretation.

3. Prenatal Alcohol Exposure

Around forty thousand babies per year are born with fetal alcohol effect resulting from alcohol abuse during pregnancy (Fitzgerald, 1988). In 1984, an estimated 7,024 of these infants were diagnosed with fetal alcohol syndrome (FAS), an incidence of 2.2 per 1,000 births (Abel and Sokol, 1987). The three main features of FAS in its extreme form are facial malformation, intrauterine growth retardation, and dysfunctions of the central nervous system, including mental retardation.

There are, in addition, about 33,000 children each year who suffer from less-severe effects of maternal alcohol use. The more prominent among these learning impairments are problems in attention (attention-deficit disorders), speech and language, and hyperactivity. General school failure also is connected to a history of fetal alcohol exposure (Abel and Sokol, 1987; Ernhart et al., 1985). Figure 5 shows the drinking habits of women of childbearing age by race and education.

When consumed in pregnancy, alcohol easily crosses the placenta, but exactly how it affects the fetus is not well known. The effects of alcohol vary according to how far along in the pregnancy the drinking occurs. The first trimester of pregnancy is a period of brain growth and organ and limb formation. The embryo is most susceptible to alcohol from week two to week eight of development, a point at which a woman may not even know she is pregnant (Hoyseth and Jones, 1989). Researchers have yet to determine how much alcohol it takes to cause problems in development and how alcohol affects each critical gestational period. It appears that the more alcohol consumed during pregnancy, the worse the effect.

Figure 4
Relation of Maternal Cigarette Smoking during Pregnancy and Various Measures of School Failure and Learning Deficiency at Age 7

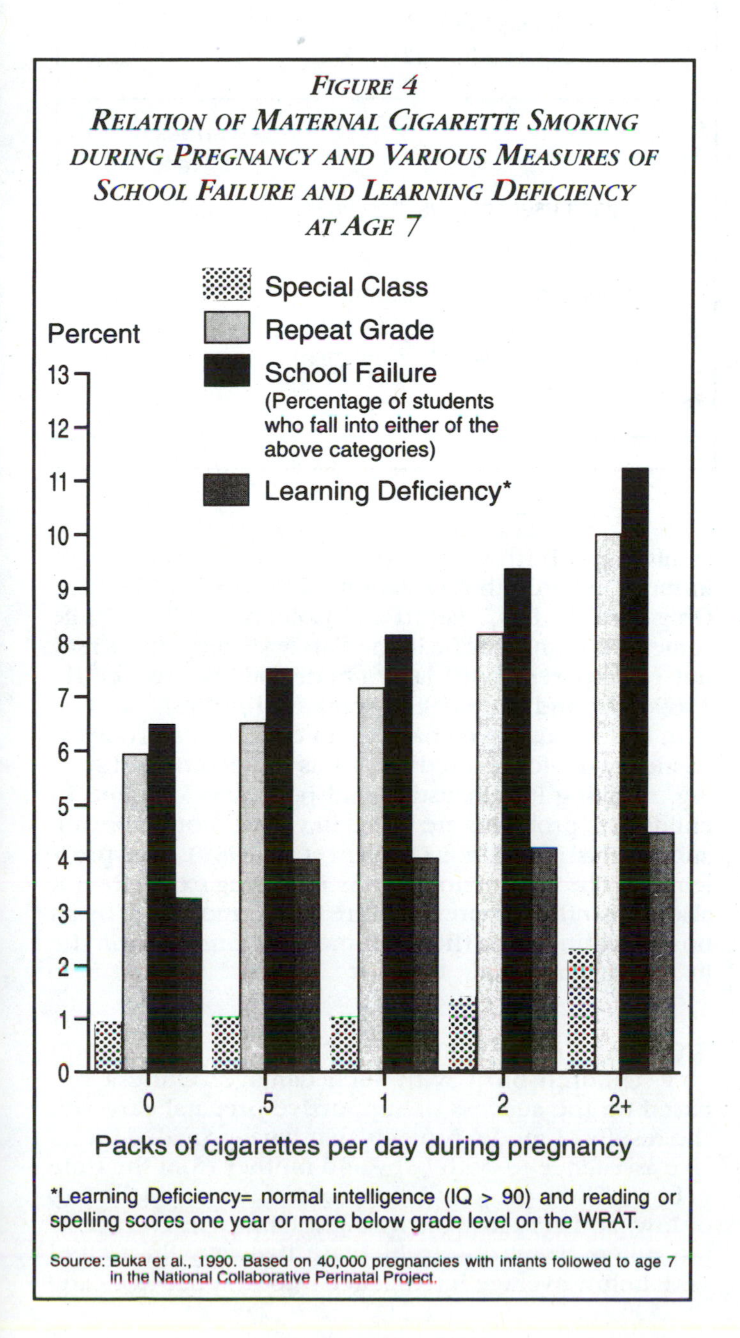

*Learning Deficiency= normal intelligence (IQ > 90) and reading or spelling scores one year or more below grade level on the WRAT.

Source: Buka et al., 1990. Based on 40,000 pregnancies with infants followed to age 7 in the National Collaborative Perinatal Project.

And many of the effects do not appear until ages four to seven, when children enter school.

Nearly one in four (23 percent) white women, eighteen to twenty-nine, reported "binge" drinking (five drinks or more a day at least five times in the past year). This was nearly three times the rate for black women of that age (about 8 percent). Fewer women (around 3 percent for both black and white) reported steady alcohol use (two drinks or more per day in the past two weeks).

Figure 5
Drinking Habits of Women Aged 18-44, by Age, Race, and Education Level, 1985

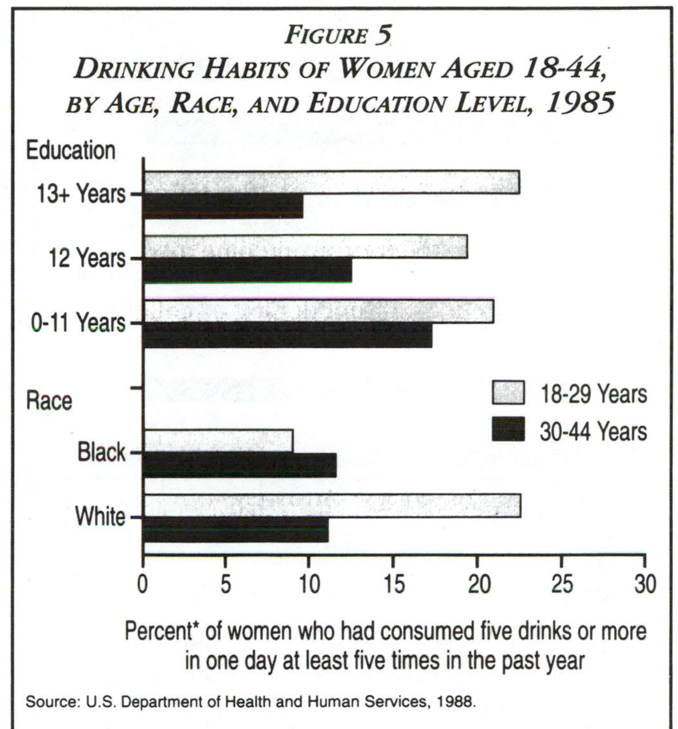

Source: U.S. Department of Health and Human Services, 1988.

4. Fetal Drug Exposure

The abuse of drugs of all kinds—marijuana, cocaine, crack, heroin, or amphetamines—by pregnant women affected about 11 percent of newborns in 1988—about 425,000 babies (Weston et al., 1989).

Cocaine and crack use during pregnancy are consistently associated with lower birthweight, premature birth, and smaller head circumference in comparison with babies whose mothers were free of these drugs (Chasnoff et al., 1989; Cherukuri et al., 1988; Doberczak et al., 1987; Keith et al., 1989; Zuckerman et al., 1989). In a study of 1,226 women attending a prenatal clinic, 27 percent tested positive for marijuana and 18 percent for cocaine. Infants of those who had used marijuana weighed an average of 2.8 ounces (79 grams) less at birth and were half a centimeter shorter in length. Infants of mothers who had used cocaine averaged 3.3 ounces (93 grams) less in weight and .7 of a centimeter less in length and also had a smaller head circumference than babies of nonusers (Zuckerman et al., 1989). The study concluded that "marijuana use and cocaine use during pregnancy are each independently associated with impaired fetal growth" (Zuckerman et al., 1989).

In addition, women who use these substances are like-

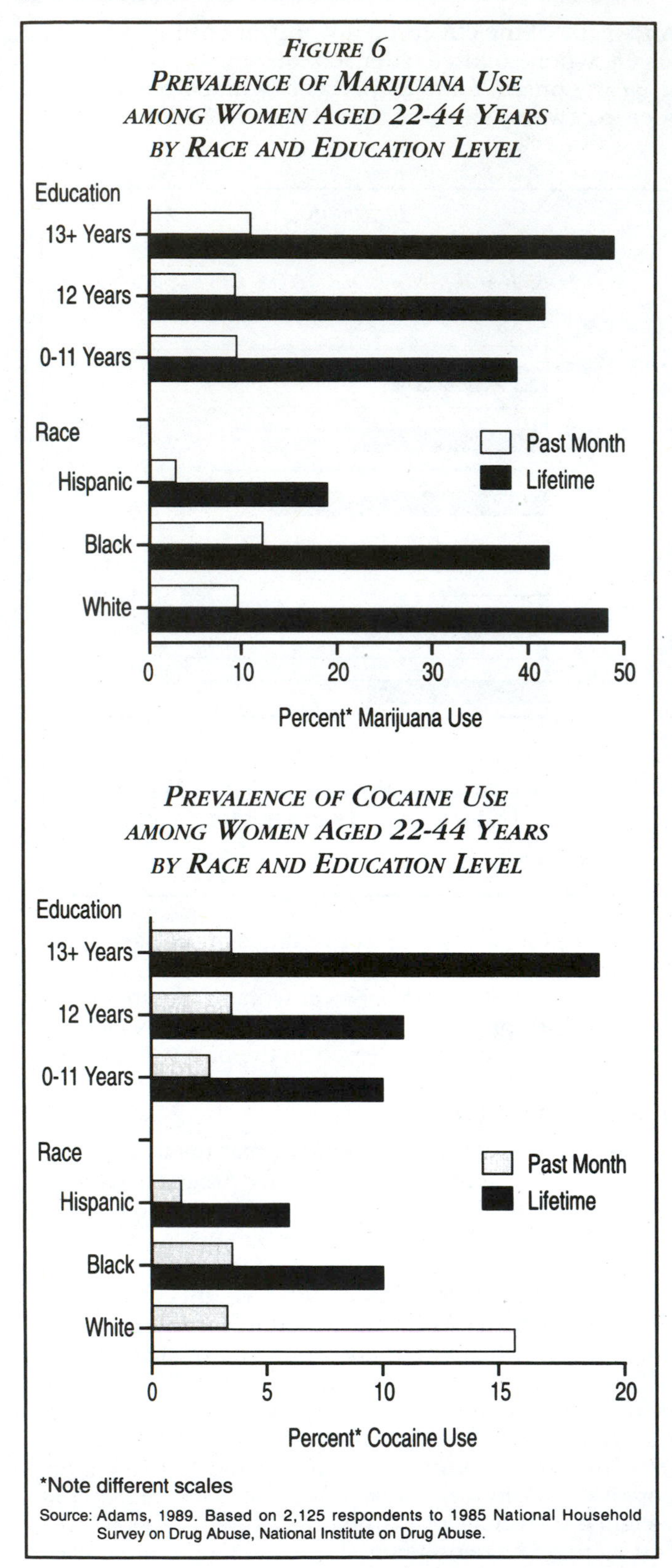

ly to smoke and to gain less weight during pregnancy, two factors associated with low birthweight. The cumulative effect of these risk factors is demonstrated by the finding that infants born to women who gained little weight, who had smoked one pack of cigarettes a day, and who tested positive for marijuana and cocaine averaged nearly a pound (14.6 ounces or 416 grams) smaller than those born to women who had normal weight gain and did not use cigarettes, marijuana, and cocaine (see Table 1). The effect of these substances on size is more than the sum of the risk factors combined.

Like alcohol use, drug use has different effects at different points in fetal development. Use in very early pregnancy is more likely to cause birth defects affecting organ formation and the central nervous systems. Later use may result in low birthweight due to either preterm birth or intrauterine growth retardation (Kaye et al., 1989; MacGregor et al., 1987; Petitti and Coleman, 1990). While some symptoms may be immediately visible, others may not be apparent until later childhood (Weston et al., 1989; Gray and Yaffe, 1986; Frank et al., 1988).

TABLE 1
INFANT WEIGHT DIFFERENCES ASSOCIATED WITH SUBSTANCE ABUSE

Substance Use During Pregnancy at One Prenatal Clinic:

N = 1,226
Marijuana (n = 330) (27%)
Cocaine (n = 221) (18%)

	Birthweight difference:
Marijuana users only vs. non-users	– 2.8 oz.
Cocaine users only vs. non-users	– 3.3 oz.
Combination users (marijuana, cocaine, one pack of cigarettes a day, low maternal weight gain) vs. non-users	–14.6 oz.

Source: Zuckerman et al., 1989.

In infancy, damaged babies can experience problems in such taken-for-granted functions as sleeping and waking, resulting in exhaustion and poor development. In childhood, problems are found in vision, motor control, and in social interaction (Weston et al., 1989). Such problems may be caused not only by fetal drug exposure but also by insufficient prenatal care for the mother or by an unstimulating or difficult home environment for the infant (Lifschitz et al., 1985).

WHAT CAN be done to ameliorate the condition of children born with such damage? Quite a bit, based on the success of supportive prenatal care and the results of model projects that have provided intensive assistance to both baby and mother from the time of birth. These projects have successfully raised the I.Q. of low- and very-low birthweight babies an average of ten points or more—an increase that may lift a child with below-average intelligence into a higher I.Q. category (i.e., from retarded to low average or from low average to average). Generally known as either educational day care or infant day care, these programs provide a developmentally stimulating environment to high-risk babies and/or intensive parent support to prepare the parent to help her child.

In one such program based at the University of California/Los Angeles, weekly meetings were held among staff, parents, and infants over a period of four years. By the project's end, the low-birthweight babies had caught up in mental function to the control group of normal birthweight children (Rauh et al., 1988). The Infant Health and Development Project, which was conducted in eight cities and provided low-birthweight babies with pediatric follow-up and an educational curriculum with family support, on average increased their I.Q. scores by thirteen points and the scores of very-low birthweight children by more than six points. Another project targeted poor single teenage mothers whose infants were at high risk for intellectual impairment (Martin, Ramey and Ramey, 1990). One group of children was enrolled in educational day care from six and one-half weeks of age to four and one-half years for five days a week, fifty weeks a year. By four and one-half years, the children's I.Q. scores were in the normal range and ten points higher than a control group. In addition, by the time their children were four and one-half, mothers in the experimental group were more likely to have graduated from high school and be self-supporting than were mothers in the control group.

These studies indicate that some disadvantages of poverty and low birthweight can be mitigated and intellectual impairment avoided. The key is attention to the cognitive development of young children, in conjunction with social support of their families.

Is your baby getting enough stimulation?

If you know what to look for, you can tell whether your child's emotional and intellectual needs are being met each day

Bettye Caldwell

Your baby's smile is bright with joy, and her eyes are brimming with intelligence and curiosity. Of course you want to nurture all that promise! The question is, how can you be sure your child is getting enough stimulation from you and her caregiver without pushing her too much?

What do babies really need?

One thing that never changes is the fact that whatever babies require must be provided through the good graces of others. Playthings are important, but people, especially adults, are primary.

It also helps to understand that babies actually have four birthdays, not just one, during the first year. These occur roughly every three months. As each milestone is reached, babies' needs change in subtle but important ways.

First quarter (birth to three months): Basic comfort and stability. During these early weeks, babies need peace and quiet and predictability in order to adjust to life outside the uterus. Your baby's physiological needs (food, sleep, warmth) are powerful and need prompt attention. But certain types of stimulation are also important, such as gentle rocking and stroking, smiling and talking. After her eyes begin to focus efficiently, she needs interesting things to look at—particularly faces—and little toys like rattles and rings to try to grasp and hold.

She'll smile at you if you prompt her with a close-up view of your own smiling face. And she'll let you know you are doing the right thing by settling into a stable routine.

Second quarter (three to six months): The right playthings. Babies really "come to life" during this time. Your infant will enjoy being busy—thrashing her arms and legs if on her back; lifting her head and fingering designs on the mat if placed on her stomach; swiping at objects dangled over her; picking up and mouthing small toys. To vary your baby's experiences and keep her interested, let her spend time strapped safely in her infant seat and placed securely on a couch or table so she can see what's going on. When an adult or older child walks by, she'll love to follow the movements with her eyes and head. She gurgles and drools, and if you lean over, smile and answer her gurgles, she'll be beside herself with joy and gurgle some more. Above all, she needs adults to interact with her. She also still needs rattles and other small toys or household items (a connected set of measuring spoons, for instance) to play with, and she likes things that provide interesting sounds and sights, like spinning musical tops and windup mobiles. To provide exercise and keep her from getting bored, let her spend some of her waking time on her stomach on a firm surface. This helps her learn to hold her head steady and practice movements she will use later to crawl and walk.

Third quarter (six to nine months): Special people to play with. A common expression used to describe a baby at this time is "He's become a person!" No longer "just a baby," he's a unique personality. Now he needs even more stimulation from a few special people like his parents, his caregiver and not too many others. Just anybody won't do any longer. Your infant's emotional attachment to these adults was developing during the previous quarter, but now it is present in all its demanding glory. Let your mother or a neighbor try to pick her up and she'll probably howl in protest. Toys that formerly seemed intriguing may be ignored unless you play too. To keep her interested and amused, squeeze a rubber toy that makes a sound and then place it slightly out of her reach. You'll see her grab for it and try to reproduce the sound.

During this quarter, your baby begins to see the world from an upright position; she sits up by herself. She makes sounds frequently and is starting to shape distinct syllables. To encourage this language development, you, her daddy and her caregiver should talk to her often and respond whenever she produces a recognizable sound. She also needs plenty of opportunities to crawl around and explore as much as possible.

Fourth quarter (nine to 12 months): Outings and other experiences. Just as your child displayed her personality during the third quarter, she now begins to impress you with her developing mind. She needs a lot of action and to participate in exciting events to keep from getting bored. Actually, everything that happens seems exciting and challenging. For instance, she'll pursue a ball that rolls under the sofa—things are no longer "out of sight, out of mind." She'll want toys to put together and take apart; these will encourage her beginning awareness of structure and function. Now she can demand a particular food, not by words, but by expressions of distinct displeasure if the "wrong" one is offered.

But, most miraculously, she's beginning to understand dozens of phrases such as: "Want to go?" "Where's Daddy?" "Come to Mommy." And slowly, she's forming a few words herself. Be sure not to lose the opportunity to let her understand what these words mean—speak them again in the appropriate context. Saying "Let's get you some juice out of the refrigerator" while reaching for the apple juice is a good example of a full language lesson.

At the risk of oversimplifying, we might say that in the first quarter your baby needs comfort and stability more than stimulation; in the second, plenty of playthings and responsive people; in the third, just a few special people to make the playthings seem important; and in the fourth, interesting experiences—people and playthings brought together in little fast-moving scenarios. The key is to watch your child—she'll give out the necessary signals as to what she wants and needs.

Can all these things come together in child care?

Of course they can. But not unless your caregiver (or the center teachers) knows a great deal about the type of stimulation babies need and how to provide it. Over the past decade child care advocates have worked hard to get states to require that providers have some training in child development. Although some progress has been made, many states are still without these standards. Many Americans seem to feel that "just anybody can take care of a baby." Not so in countries like France, where caregivers who are responsible for infants must first be fully trained as nurses and then as specialists in early-childhood education and care.

Even in states where licensing requirements mandate some training or experience for all caregivers, many providers seem to stimulate their charges randomly, putting out toys just so something is available, without thinking about what babies in each age-group really need.

To make sure your baby gets the right kinds of experiences in child care, you need to take three essential steps:

Check credentials. Be sure to find out what kind of training the person has (or people have) who will spend time with your baby throughout the day. If you're putting her in a center, see if at least one person in her room has a degree in early-childhood development or a CDA (Child Development Associate) certificate. Don't hesitate to ask to see certificates.

If you prefer family day care, make every effort to locate a provider who is either registered or licensed. Ask about the most recent training event she has attended and whether it dealt with infants. (These sessions are available in most states about once every three months and are run by the state agency that's responsible for regulating child care.) Attendance at such an event suggests that the provider is interested in giving the best care possible to her charges.

> **Many providers seem to randomly put out toys without thinking about what a baby really needs.**

If you are considering hiring a nanny, by all means ask to see proof of early-childhood training. Ask for her references and be sure to check them out.

Watch what goes on. The second, and probably most important, thing to do is to carefully observe what goes on at the place in which you plan to enroll your child.

Although it may be difficult to arrange, try to spend an entire day, or at least a full morning, there. If the potential caregiver objects to such a visit, scratch that person from your list. If you are invited to observe, note the amount and kind of stimulation provided the infants. What toys are available? Are the babies propped in front of the television to watch the soaps? (They shouldn't be!) Are they given toys small enough for them to grasp and manipulate but safe enough for them to put in their mouths (no small parts!), or less appropriate things such as big plastic trucks or other jumbo toys that are too big for infants to play with? Does the caregiver play individually with each baby at least briefly? (She should.) And, depending on the ages of infants in her care, does she do the kinds of things described earlier as appropriate for each quarter of the year? Does she hold the tiny ones? Does she respond when they gurgle and smile? Or does she ignore them while you are there and talk only to you? Are the older ones allowed to crawl around and explore? (They need to.)

PUTTING CHILDREN FIRST

WILLIAM A. GALSTON

William A. Galston, the author most recently of Liberal Purposes: Goods, Virtues, and Diversity in the Liberal State *(Cambridge University Press), teaches at the University of Maryland, College Park. He is an advisor to the Washington, D.C.-based Progressive Policy Institute and a co-editor of* The Responsive Community, *a new journal that seeks a better balance between rights and responsibilities. This article is an expanded version of an essay that appeared in the December 2, 1991, issue of* The New Republic, *with material drawn from* Putting Children First: A Progressive Family Policy for the 1990s *by Elaine Ciulla Kamarck and William A. Galston, published by the Progressive Policy Institute.*

THE AMERICAN family has changed dramatically in the past generation, and it is children who have paid the price. From Ozzie and Harriet to the Simpsons, from one breadwinner to two, from child-centered nuclear families that stayed together for the sake of the children to the struggling one-parent families of today; the revolution in the American family has affected us all. Divorce rates have surged, and child poverty has risen alarmingly. The signs are everywhere around us that America's children are suffering—economically, educationally, and emotionally. Although this fact is obvious, indeed increasingly obtrusive, it has hardly been discussed by intellectuals and policy elites until quite recently. Several broad forces—racial conflict, feminism, the culture of individual rights—help explain this odd silence.

The story begins in 1965, with the publication of Daniel Patrick Moynihan's *The Negro Family: The Case for National Action,* which identified the breakdown of the black family as a growing obstacle to racial progress. Although intended as the analytical backdrop to major federal initiatives, it was received as a call for quietism, even as a subtle relegitimation of racism. Black civil rights leaders and white liberal scholars argued that the emphasis on family structure would inevitably divert attention from economic inequalities and would justify "blaming the victims" for the consequences of discrimination. As William Julius Wilson has argued, this enraged response had the consequence of suppressing public debate over, and serious scholarly inquiry into, the relation between black family structure and the problems of the ghetto poor—suppressing it for an entire generation.

Feminism also contributed to the silence. The postwar American women's movement began as a criticism of the 1950s family. "Liberation" meant leaving the domestic sphere for the world of work outside the home. It also meant denying traditional theories of gender difference that seemed to legitimate inequalities of resources, power, and self-respect. To be equal was to be the same: to compete on the same terms as men, with the same focus on individual separateness and independence. As Sylvia Ann Hewlett argues, the unquestionable moral force of the feminist movement muted the voices of those who, though dubious about its denial of gender differences and deeply concerned about its consequences for the well-being of children, did not wish to be accused of a disguised effort to ratify the patriarchal or chauvinist status quo.

Then there was the cultural upheaval of the 1960s, which yielded an ethic of self-realization through incessant personal experimentation, the triumph of what has been termed "expressive individualism." An increasingly influential therapeutic vocabulary emphasized the constraints that relations could impose on personal growth and encouraged adults to turn inward toward the self's struggles for sovereignty, to view commitments as temporary or endlessly renegotiable—to behave, in effect, like adolescents. This vocabulary was anything but hospitable to the discourse of parental continuity, commitment, and self-sacrifice.

A related legacy of the generation just past has been an impoverishment of moral vocabulary. What some regard as a descent into relativism is more accurately

Reprinted with permission from the Summer 1992 issue of the *American Educator,* pp. 8-13, 44-46, the quarterly journal of the American Federation of Teachers.

characterized as the relentless expansion of morality understood as the articulation of the rights of individuals. This development is not alien to the American experience, and it is not wholly to be deplored. Rights, after all, do support self-respect and offer protection against evils. Still, we now know that there is a difficulty: Although systems of rights can guide some spheres of life tolerably well, they can obscure and distort others. In particular, the effort to understand family relations as the mutual exercise of rights led to a legal and emotional cul-de-sac.

There is growing recognition that we must place the family at the center of our thinking about social issues and children at the center of our thinking about the family.

IN RECENT years, however, the climate has changed. Debates within the black community, and among social democrats as well as conservatives, have helped to relegitimate the discussion of the links between family structure and a range of social ills. To acknowledge such links, it is not necessary to sever the causal connections between structural inequalities at the political and economic level and disintegration at the family level, or to focus exclusively on the "culture of poverty." The point is, rather, that the cultural effects of past discrimination can take on a life of their own, that they can persist even in the face of changing opportunity structures.

The women's movement is changing, too. In place of equality understood as sameness, feminists such as Sara Ruddick, Carol Gilligan, and Jean Bethke Elshtain have embraced categories of difference, nurturance, and care. Martha Albertson Fineman insists that public policy "recognize and accommodate the positive and lasting nature of mothers' ties to their children." Surely this style of feminist argument will prove far more compatible with traditional understandings of the family than anyone could have predicted a decade ago.

And even broader cultural changes are under way, provoked by demographic shifts. Baby boomers who delayed marriage until their thirties have discovered that the moral universe of their young adulthood is not a suitable place for parents with young children. Others have discovered that the casting off of binding relationships is not necessarily the path to liberation and happiness. A generation that once devoted itself to the proliferation of rights and the expression of individuality has begun haltingly to explore counterbalancing notions of responsibility and community; several polls have documented rapid shifts during the past two years in public attitudes toward a range of family issues.

The most important shift is a welcome expansion of concern beyond narrow bounds of race and class. For too long, worries about children and families focused on such issues as teenage pregnancy, dire deprivation, and collapsing marriage rates. These are serious problems, but they are disproportionately characteristic of the ghetto poor. Such measurements, in other words, enabled the American middle class, scholars as well as citizens, to believe that families and children were someone else's problem. But with increased attention to the clash between work and family, to parental time deficits, and to the impact of divorce, the middle class can no longer sustain such an illusion. The decay of the family is its problem, too. The children of the middle class are also at risk; and its choices can be just as shortsighted, self-indulgent, and harmful to the young as any ever contemplated in the culture of poverty.

THESE RECENT trends are at last producing important changes at the level of national politics. For decades, the revolution in the American family evoked a polarized reaction: Liberals talked about structural economic pressures facing families and avoided issues of personal conduct, and conservatives did just the reverse. Liberals habitually reached for bureaucratic responses, even when they were counter-productive, and conservatives reflexively rejected government programs even when they would work.

Both are wrong. Traditional conservatives' support for families is largely rhetorical; their disregard for new economic realities engenders a policy of unresponsive neglect—expressed for example, in President Bush's misguided veto of the Family Leave Act. Conversely, traditional liberals' unwillingness to acknowledge that intact two-parent families are the most effective units for raising children has led them into a series of policy cul-de-sacs.

Recently, however, this clash of conflicting worldviews has begun to give way to a new spirit of accommodation. As E.J. Dionne Jr. has observed, recent proposals for pro-family tax reform reflect the realization that both values and dollars count. Many younger conservatives are addressing social problems long neglected by their movement. Many younger Democrats, meanwhile, are looking for new forms of nonbureaucratic, choice-based public activism as a supplement to the frequently cumbersome and intrusive institutions of the welfare state. There is growing recognition that we must place the family at the center of our thinking about social issues and children at the center of our thinking about the family. We need policies that support and compensate families as they carry out their critical social role—providing for the economic and moral well-being of children. As we will see, a large body of evidence supports the conclusion that in the aggregate, the intact two-parent family is best suited to this task. Making this premise our point of departure takes us toward policies that *reinforce* families and away from bureaucratic approaches that seek to *replace* family functions.

To avoid misunderstanding, I want to make it clear that a general preference for the intact two-parent family does not mean that this is the best option in every case. Nor does it mean that all single-parent families are somehow dysfunctional; that proposition would diminish the achievements of millions of single parents who are struggling successfully against the odds to provide good homes for their children. Rather, the point is that at the level of statistical aggregates and society-wide phenomena, significant differences do emerge between one-parent and two-parent families, differences that can and should shape our understanding of social policy.

I DO NOT mean to suggest that the renewed emphasis on the family is solely the product of cultural and ideological change. Equally important is a broad process of social learning—a growing (and increasingly painful) awareness of the consequences of the choices that we already have made, individually and collectively, over the past generation.

The economic facts are distressing. As Hewlett summarizes the data: Among all children eighteen years and under, one in five is poor, nearly twice the poverty rate for the elderly; among children younger than six, the rate is almost one in four; among children in families headed by adults younger than thirty, one in three; among black children, almost one in two. And noneconomic trends are no less stark. In the past quarter-century, the amount of time that parents spend with their children has dropped by 40 percent, from thirty hours a week to just seventeen; and there is no evidence that these remaining shreds of parental availability represent "quality time." On the contrary: As social historian Barbara Whitehead reports, "Increasingly, family schedules are intricate applications of time-motion principles."

These stress-filled lives reflect changes in the economy that have prompted momentous shifts in the labor force in this country. Since 1973, under the pressure of declining productivity and mounting international competition, family incomes have stagnated while the relative costs of a middle-class existence—in particular, of homeownership, health care, and higher education—have soared. Wage prospects have grown increasingly dismal, especially for young people with no more than a high school education. The surge of women into the work force may have begun three decades ago as a cultural revolt against household roles experienced as stifling, but it has been sustained by increasingly urgent economic necessity. Today two-thirds of all mothers with children younger than eighteen do at least some work outside the home, as do more than one-half of all mothers with children under five.

For tens of millions of American families, the second income means the difference between keeping and losing a tenuously maintained middle-class way of life. To be sure, some adjustments at the margin are possible: Young families can live in smaller houses and stop eating at restaurants. Still, the hope of many moral traditionalists that the 1950s family can somehow be restored flies in the face of contemporary market forces. The tension between remunerative work and family time will not be overcome in the foreseeable future—unless increased income from nonmarket sources allows parents with young children to do less work outside the home. Many thoughtful conservatives are coming to the realization that they must choose between their vision of a well-ordered family and their desire for smaller, less costly government.

THESE TENSIONS and others have clearly taken their toll. Test scores are down, and not just the much-discussed SATs. At BellSouth in Atlanta, for example, only about 10 percent of job applicants can pass exams that test basic learning ability, versus 20 percent a decade ago. Theft, violence, and the use of illicit drugs are far more prevalent among teenagers than they were thirty years ago; and the rate of suicide among teenagers has tripled.

It is tempting to dismiss these data as one sided, or to interpret them as mere cyclical variations within longer-term stability. After all, virtually every generation in every culture has complained of a decline of the family. But this is an alibi. We must face the fact that the conditions we take for granted are the product of a social revolution that has rapidly unfolded over just the past three decades. And at the heart of this revolution lie changes in family structure.

In thirty years, the percentage of children born outside of marriage has quintupled, and now stands at 18 percent for whites and 63 percent for blacks. In this same period, the divorce rate has tripled, as has the percentage of children living with only one parent. Of white children born in the early 1950s, 81 percent lived continuously until the age of seventeen with their two biological parents; the projected rate for children born in the early 1980s is 30 percent. The corresponding rate for black children has fallen from 52 percent in the 1950s to only 6 percent today.

These structural shifts are responsible for a substantial portion of child poverty. As David Ellwood has observed, "[t]he vast majority of children who are raised entirely in a two-parent home will never be poor during childhood. By contrast, the vast majority of children who spend time in a single-parent home will experience poverty." As Ellwood showed in *Poor Support,* in any given year, fully 50 percent of children in one-parent families will experience poverty, versus 15 percent for those in two-parent families; 73 percent of children from one-parent families will experience poverty at some point during their childhood, versus 20 percent for children from two-parent families; 22 percent of children from one-parent families will experience persistent poverty (seven years or more), versus only 2 percent from two-parent families.

These data suggest that the best anti-poverty program for children is a stable, intact family. And this conclusion holds even for families headed by younger parents with very modest levels of educational attainment. For married high school graduates with children, the 1987 poverty rate was 9 percent, versus more than 47 percent for families headed by female high school graduates. Even for married high school dropouts with children, the poverty rate was 25 percent, versus more than 81 percent for families headed by female high school dropouts. Overall, Frank Furstenberg Jr. and Andrew Cherlin conclude, the differences in family structure go "a long way toward accounting for the enormous racial disparity in poverty rates. Within family types, black families are still poorer than white families; but the racial gap in poverty shrinks considerably when the marital status of the household head is taken into account."

'The vast majority of children who are raised entirely in a two-parent home will never be poor during childhood. By contrast, the vast majority of children who spend time in a single-parent home will experience poverty.'

TO BE SURE, the causal arrow could point in the opposite direction: differences in family structure might be thought to reflect differences in economic status. Wilson offered an influential statement of this counterthesis in *The Truly Disadvantaged:* Reduced black marriage rates reflect dramatically higher rates of black male unemployment, which reduces the "male marriageable pool"—under the assumption that "to be marriageable a man needs to be employed." But the most recent research offers only modest support for this hypothesis. Robert Mare and Christopher Winship find that changes in employment rates among young black males account for only 20 percent of the decline in their marriage rates since 1960; they speculate that the various family disruptions of the past three decades may be self-reinforcing.[1] Though Wilson continues to defend the validity of his thesis for the hard-hit central cities of the Northeast and Midwest, he is now willing to say that "the decline in marriage among inner-city blacks is not simply a function of the proportion of jobless men . . . it is reasonable to consider the effects of weaker social structures against out-of-wedlock births."

Along with family non-formation, family breakup is a potent source of poverty, especially among children. According to a recently released Census Bureau study by Susan Bianchi, who identified and tracked twenty thousand households, it turns out that after their parents separate or divorce, children are almost twice as likely to be living in poverty as they were before the split. The gross income of the children and their custodial parent (usually the mother) dropped by 37 percent immediately after the family breakup (26 percent after adjustment for the decline in family size) and recovered only slightly after sixteen months. These findings support the arguments of scholars who have long contended that divorce under current law spells economic hardship for most custodial parents and their minor children.

As Furstenberg and Cherlin show in their admirably balanced survey of current research, there are at least three sets of reasons for this outcome: Many women bargain away support payments in return for sole custody of their children or to eliminate the need to deal with their former spouses; when awarded, child support payments are on average pitifully inadequate; and many fathers cough up only a portion (at best) of their required payments. A Census Bureau report from the mid-1980s showed that of mothers with court-ordered support payments, only half received all of what they were owed, a quarter received partial payments, and the remaining quarter got nothing at all.

IF THE economic effects of family breakdown are clear, the psychological effects are just now coming into focus. As Karl Zinsmeister summarizes an emerging consensus, "There is a mountain of scientific evidence showing that when families disintegrate children often end up with intellectual, physical, and emotional scars that persist for life. . . . We talk about the drug crisis, the education crisis, and the problems of teen pregnancy and juvenile crime. But all these ills trace back predominantly to one source: broken families."

As more and more children are reared in one-parent families, it becomes clear that the economic consequences of a parent's absence (usually the father) may pale beside the psychological consequences—which include higher than average levels of youth suicide, low intellectual and educational performance, and higher than average rates of mental illness, violence, and drug use.

Nowhere is this more evident than in the longstanding and strong relationship between crime and one-parent families. In a recent study, Douglas Smith and G. Roger Jarjoura found that "neighborhoods with larger percentages of youth (those aged 12 to 20) and areas with higher percentages of single-parent households also have higher rates of violent crime."[2] The relationship is so strong that controlling for family configuration erases the relationship between race and crime and between low income and crime. This conclusion shows up time and time again in the literature; poverty is far from the sole determinant of crime.

While the scarcity of intact families in the ghetto is largely a function of the failure of families to form in the first place, in the larger society the central problem is family disintegration, caused primarily by divorce. This pervasive phenomenon has effects that are independent of economics. It is to these studies that we now turn.

In 1981, John Guidubaldi, then president of the National Association of School Psychologists, picked a team of 144 psychologists in thirty-eight states, who gathered long-term data on seven hundred children, half from intact families, the other half children of divorce. Preliminary results published in 1986 showed that the effects of divorce on children persisted over time and that the psychological consequences were significant even after correcting for income differences.[3]

The problems engendered by divorce extend well beyond vanishing role models. Children need authoritative rules and stable schedules, which harried single parents often have a hard time supplying. As Guidubaldi puts it, "One of the things we found is that children who had regular bedtimes, less TV, hobbies and after-school activities—children who are in households that are orderly and predictable—do better than children who [did] not. I don't think we can escape the conclusion that children need structure, and oftentimes the divorce household is a chaotic scene."

The results of the Guidubaldi study have been confirmed and deepened by Judith Wallerstein's ten-year study of sixty middle-class divorced families. Among her key findings:

- Divorce is almost always more devastating for children than for their parents.
- The effects of divorce are often long lasting. Children are especially affected because divorce occurs during their formative years. What they see and experience becomes a part of their inner world, their view of themselves, and their view of society.
- Almost half the children entered adulthood as worried, underachieving, self-deprecating, and sometimes angry young men and women.
- Adolescence is a period of grave risk for children in divorced families; those who entered adolescence in the immediate wake of their parents' divorces had a particularly bad time. The young people told us time and again how much they needed a family structure, how much they wanted to be protected, and how much they yearned for clear guidelines for moral behavior.[4]

Furstenberg and Cherlin offer a nuanced, but ultimately troubling, account of the noneconomic consequences of divorce. For most children, it comes as an "unwelcome shock," even when the parents are openly quarreling. In the short-term, boys seem to have a harder time coping than girls, in part because of an "escalating cycle of misbehavior and harsh response between mothers and sons." Girls more typically respond with internalized disruption rather than external behavior—with heightened levels of anxiety, withdrawal, and depression that may become apparent only years later. These differences reflect the fact that divorce almost always means disrupted relations with the father. It is difficult to overstate the extent of the disruption that typically occurs. Even in the period relatively soon after divorce, only one-sixth of all children will see their fathers as often as once a week, and close to one-half will not see them at all. After ten years, almost two-thirds will have no contact.

These findings are less than self-interpreting, Furstenberg and Cherlin point out, because they must be compared with the effects on children of intact but troubled families. On the one hand, various studies indicate that the children of divorce do no worse than children in families in which parents fight continuously. On the other hand, a relatively small percentage of divorces result from, and terminate, such clearly pathological situations. There are many more cases in which there is little open conflict, but one or both partners feels unfulfilled, bored, or constrained. Indeed, the onset of divorce in these families can intensify conflict, particularly as experienced by children. As Nicholas Zill observes, "Divorces tend to generate their own problems."

Given the profound psychological effects of divorce, it is hardly surprising to discover what teachers and administrators have known for some time: One of the major reasons for America's declining educational achievement is the disintegrating American family. And if we continue to neglect the crisis of the American family, we will have undercut current efforts at educational reform.

Untangling just what it is about family structure that makes for high or low educational achievement is a difficult task. Clearly the economics of the family have a great deal to do with achievement; children from poor families consistently do less well than do children from non-poor or well-to-do families. Nevertheless, income is clearly not the whole story. When studies control for income, significant differences in educational achievement appear between children from single-parent families and children from intact families.

For example, a study conducted under the auspices of the National Association of Elementary School Principals and the Institute for Development of Educational Activities shows that family background has an important effect on educational achievement above and beyond income level—especially for boys. Lower-income girls with two parents, for instance, score higher on achievement tests than do higher-income boys with one parent. At the very bottom of the achievement scale are lower-income boys with one parent.[5]

WHAT SHOULD be our response to these developments? The recent literature suggests three broad possibilities. First, we may applaud, with Judith Stacey, the demise of the traditional (rigid, patriarchal) family and the rise of "postmodern" (flexible, variegated, female-centered) arrangements, which are allegedly far more consistent with egalitarian democracy. Second, we may accept Jan Dizard and Howard Gadlin's suggestion that moral change (in the direction of autonomy) and economic change (in the direction of a two-earner, postindustrial economy) have rendered obsolete the older model of the private family; in its place, they advocate a dramatically expanded public sphere on the Swedish model that assumes many of the private family's functions. And third, there is the response, neither postmodern nor socialist, that might be called neotraditional.

It goes something like this. A primary purpose of the family is to raise children well, and for this purpose stably married parents are best. Sharply rising rates of divorce, unwed mothers, and runaway fathers do not represent "alternative lifestyles." They are, instead, most truly characterized as patterns of adult behavior with profoundly negative consequences for children. Families have primary responsibility for instilling traits such as discipline, ambition, respect for the law, and regard for others; and it is a responsibility that cannot be discharged as effectively by auxiliary social institutions such as public schools. This responsibility entails a sphere of legitimate parental authority that should be bolstered—not undermined—by society. It requires personal sacrifice and the delay of certain forms of gratification on the part of parents. It means that government should devote substantial resources to stabilizing families and to enhancing their child-rearing capacity. But at the same time it must minimize bureaucratic cost, complexity, and intrusiveness, working instead to broaden family choice, opportunity, and responsibility.

The willingness to join the languages of economics and morals, and to consider new approaches to old goals, is increasingly characteristic of public discussion of the family. As Barbara Whitehead notes, this approach suffuses the recent report of the National Commission on Children. The volume edited by David Blankenhorn, Steven Bayme, and Jean Bethke Elshtain is particularly strong along the moral dimension. To be sure, it is easy for this stance to give the appearance of ineffectual exhortation. The editors of *The New York Times* assert that the commission's final report "swims in platitudes." Still, there are eminently practical ways of embedding moral concerns in policies and institutions. Richard Louv argues for moral change focused on the community as much as the individual. He urges us to reweave the tattered "web" of social relationships—parent-school ties, neighborhoods, communal child care arrangements, and the like—that provide a supportive environment for families and help nurture children. Although Louv emphasizes the importance of civil society, he does not imagine that the web can be adequately repaired without major changes in public policy.

Here Louv joins an emerging consensus that differs over details but not over essentials. The point is not to be driven to make a false choice between moral and economic concerns, but rather to combine them in a relation of mutual support. It might well be argued, for example, that the government has a responsibility not to tax away the money that families need to raise children. Four decades ago, the United States had a disguised family allowance: In 1948 the personal exemption was $600 (42 percent of per-capita personal income), while today's personal exemption is only 11 percent of per-capita income. This meant that a married couple at the median income with two minor dependents paid only 0.3 percent of their 1948 income in federal income taxes, compared to today's 9.1 percent. The 1948 couple's total tax bill (federal, state, and Social Security) was 2 percent of personal income. Today that total comes to about 30 percent.

Thus, one proposal now gaining support is to raise the personal exemption from the current $2,050 to at least $4,000, and perhaps eventually to $7,500. To make this more affordable, the bulk of the increase could be targeted to young children, and the increase could be phased out for upper-income taxpayers. Another approach, endorsed by the National Commission on Children, would create a $1,000 tax credit for each child; low-income families that owe no taxes would receive a cash payment for the amount of the credit. (To avoid potentially perverse incentives, this proposal should be coupled with a broader program of welfare reform.)

Reducing the tension between work and family will take changes in the private as well as the public sector. Hewlett, Louv, and many others argue for a "family-oriented workplace" with far more adaptable schedules: more flexible hours, greater opportunities for working at home and communicating by computer, for part-time employment, and for job sharing. Resistance to these changes reflects primarily the ignorance or the obduracy of middle-aged male managers, not negative impact on corporate balance sheets. Much the same is true of unpaid leave for parents following the birth of a child. Studies at the state level indicate that the costs and disruptive effects of such leaves, even when legally mandatory, are minimal. President Bush's opposition to federal family leave legislation is increasingly indefensible.

Adequate reward for labor force participation represents another important link between morals and public policy. If we believe that the presence of a parent who works outside the home furnishes a crucial moral example for his or her children, then surely the community has a responsibility to ensure that full-time work by a parent provides a nonpoverty family income. As Robert Shapiro of the Progressive Policy Institute has argued, the most efficient way to accomplish this goal would be to expand the Earned Income Tax Credit and tie it to family size.

This emphasis on the use of the tax code to promote family opportunity and responsibility is characteristic of a political outlook that has been called "neoprogressive." This is not to suggest that traditional liberal approaches are in every case misguided. Some of them—prenatal care, WIC (the nutrition program for poor women, infants, and children), childhood immunization, and Head Start—efficiently promote the well-being of children and families, and the political consensus supporting their expansion now stretches from KidsPac (a liberal, children-oriented political action committee) and the Children's Defense Fund to the Bush administration and the corporate-based Committee for Economic Development. And yet the neoprogressives are more willing than the traditional liberals to re-examine the programs of the past and to distinguish between what works and what doesn't.

If THE PRIVATE and public sectors must assume greater responsibility for the well-being of families with children, so must parents. In particular, the moral obligation to help support one's biological children persists regardless of one's legal relationship to them, and the law is fully justified in enforcing this obligation. The 1988 Family Support Act requires states to collect the Social Security numbers of both parents (married or unmarried) at birth, to increase efforts to establish contested paternity, to use (as at least rebuttable presumptions) their guidelines concerning appropriate levels of child support, and to move toward collecting all new support awards through automatic payroll deductions.

These are steps in the right direction, but they don't go far enough. Mary Ann Glendon has argued powerfully that a "children first" principle should govern our spousal support and marital property law:

> The judges' main task would be to piece together, from property and income and inkind personal care, the best possible package to meet the needs of children and their physical guardian. Until the welfare of the children had been adequately secured in this way, there would be no question of, or debate about, "marital property." All assets, no matter when or how acquired, would be subject to the duty to provide for the children.[6]

Moreover, the state-level reforms mentioned above do nothing to address what is in many cases the chief impediment to support collection: fathers moving from state to state to slow or avoid apprehension. Conflicting state laws and a morass of administrative complexity discourage mothers from pursuing their claims across jurisdictions. Ellwood and others have called for the federalization of the system, with payroll deductions remitted to, and support payments drawn from, a centralized national fund. The U.S. Commission on Interstate Child Support, created by Congress to develop a blueprint for reform, is considering this idea.

Even when child support is collected regularly from absent parents who can afford to provide it, payments are typically set too low to avoid tremendous disruption in the lives of custodial mothers and their children. Writing from very different perspectives, Lenore Weitzman, Martha Albertson Fineman, and Furstenberg and Cherlin converge on the conclusion that the laws and the practices of many states leave men in a far more favorable situation after divorce. Furstenberg and Cherlin cite approvingly a proposal to require noncustodial fathers to pay a fixed proportion of their income, 17 percent to 34 percent, depending on the number of minor children; the adoption of this standard nationwide would raise total child support due by roughly two-thirds. Fineman advocates a need-based approach that would (she argues) yield better results for women and children than would ostensibly egalitarian standards.

During the past generation, the presumption in favor of awarding mothers custody of their children has been replaced in many cases by the presumption of equal claims. This development has generated a rising number of joint custody arrangements that do not, on average, work out very well. It has also worsened the post-divorce economic status of custodial mothers and their children: Because women tend to view custody as a paramount issue, they often compromise on economic matters to avoid the custody battle made possible by the new, supposedly more egalitarian, legal framework. And here, too, scholars from various points on the ideological spectrum are converging on the conclusion that the traditional arrangement had much to recommend it. They propose a "primary caretaker" standard: judges should be instructed to award custody of young children to the parent who has (in the words of a leading advocate) "performed a substantial majority of the [direct] caregiving tasks for the child."

THESE AND similar proposals will help custodial mothers and their children pick up the pieces after divorce, but they will do little to reduce the incidence of divorce. For Furstenberg and Cherlin, this is all that can be done: "We are inclined to accept the irreversibility of high levels of divorce as our starting point for thinking about changes in public policy." Hewlett is more disposed to grasp the nettle. While rejecting a return to the fault-based system of the past, she believes that the current system makes divorce too easy and too automatic. Government should send a clearer moral signal that families with children are worth preserving. In this spirit, she suggests that parents of minor children seeking divorce undergo an eighteen-month waiting period, during which they would be obliged to seek counseling and to reach a binding agreement that truly safeguards their children's future.

The generation that installed the extremes of self-expression and self-indulgence at the heart of American culture must now learn some hard old lessons about commitment, self-sacrifice, the deferral of gratification, and simple endurance. It will not be easy. But other sorts of gratifications may be their reward. Perhaps the old morality was not wrong to suggest that a deeper kind of satisfaction awaits those who accept and fulfill their essential human responsibilities.

REFERENCES

[1]Mare, Robert D. and Winship, Christopher, "Socio-economic Change and the Decline of Marriage for Blacks and Whites." In *The Urban Underclass*, edited by Christopher Jencks and Paul Peterson. Washington, D.C.: The Brookings Institute, 1991.

[2]Smith, Douglas A., Jarjoura, G. Roger, "Social Structure and Criminal Victimization." In *Journal of Research in Crime and Delinquency*, Vol. 25, No. 1, February 1988.

[3]Guidubaldi, J., Cleminshaw, H.K., Perry, J.D., Nastasi, B.K., and Lightel, J., "The Role of Selected Family Environment Factors in Children's Post-Divorce Adjustment." In *Family Relations*, Vol. 35, 1986.

[4]Wallerstein, Judith S., and Blakeslee, Sandra, *Second Chances: Men, Women, and Children a Decade after Divorce*. New York: Ticknor and Fields, 1989.

[5]Sally Banks Zakariya, "Another Look at the Children of Divorce," *Principal Magazine*, September 1982, p. 35. See also, R.B. Zajonc, "Family Configuration and Intelligence," *Science*, Vol. 192, April 16, 1976, pp. 227-236. In a later and more methodologically sophisticated study, the authors try to define more completely what it is about two-parent families that make them better at preparing students for educational success. Income clearly stands out as the most important variable; but the close relationship between one-parent status, lower income, and lack of time for things like homework help and attendance at parent teacher conferences—to name a few of the variables considered—led the authors to say that "the negative effects of living in a one-parent family work primarily through other variables in our model." Ann M. Milne, David E. Myers, Alvin S. Rosenthal, and Alan Ginsburg, "Single Parents, Working Mothers, and the Educational Achievement of School Children," *Sociology of Education*, 1986, Vol. 59 (July), p. 132.

[6]Glendon, Mary Ann, *Abortion and Divorce in Western Law*. Cambridge, MA: Harvard University Press, 1987 (pp. 93-95).

I'm OK, They're OK

Working women and their children are not only surviving the balancing act, they're thriving. Reassuring research from the ground-breaking book 'Juggling'

Faye J. Crosby, PhD

Faye J. Crosby, PhD, is a professor of psychology and chair of the psychology department at Smith College.

I asked Laura, one of the 50 people I interviewed for my research on working mothers, "Would you say that you ever experience difficulty combining your different life roles?" Even before the last words had left my mouth, she started laughing. "Ever? They all conflict right now," she replied. Then she enumerated the stresses in her life—her husband's bad health, her pregnancy with a second child, her parents' divorce, her still-wobbly law practice, her worries about finances.

Had I not asked more questions, I might have concluded, mistakenly, that Laura—and working mothers like her—was suffering under the weight of too many roles. Fortunately, I did ask: "What do you see as the advantages of juggling?" Laura answered, "It keeps life interesting. I think it makes you feel so much more whole to be able to do all these things. It proves to me that I am a capable individual, somebody who can handle the role of mothering and everything else too. And even more than that, I think my time away from my son actually works to his advantage and mine. Because we have this space away from each other, I'm thrilled whenever I see him, and he is always excited to see me."

When I asked Laura if she had ever thought about what life would be like if she did not play all her current roles, she replied, "Well, it certainly would be different, wouldn't it? I'm thrilled with the mother role. It's something I've always wanted. The role of wife—that would be a hard one to give up. I'm the kind of person who needs a mate. And my role as a lawyer gives me a great sense of accomplishment. So my different roles all contribute to one another. And right now I feel pretty good about them all. Life feels good. I know there are going to be more conflicts, but I feel a great sense of accomplishment."

In fact, a sense of accomplishment or fulfillment was mentioned by many of the women I interviewed. One labor organizer joked about "being so exhausted that I am constantly looking forward to retirement" and yet observed: "I feel that if I retired right now, I would look back on my life and say 'Ah, this has really been satisfying. It has been satisfying to do everything.' "

My research is not the first to show that most women feel enriched as well as stressed by juggling occupational and domestic responsibilities. Indeed, nearly 20 years ago sociologist Cynthia Fuchs Epstein began to investigate the positive aspects of juggling. Her subjects were female lawyers.

The women Epstein interviewed over the years did not benefit from flextime or organized child care. Some of them could afford household help so that they could delegate labor. But they made all the decisions. And almost without exception, they were subject to subtle and blatant prejudice in their professional lives. Yet, in spite of these hurdles, the lawyers managed to combine their professional careers and family lives with success and vigor.

The same sense of purpose and satisfaction has been noted by other researchers. According to Lisa Silberstein, a psychologist at Yale University who studied 20 dual-career couples, many women feel stimulated and enriched by continuing their careers during their children's early years. When they do not give in to a culturally sanctioned sense of guilt, they are filled with excitement and self-esteem.

Both Silberstein and Epstein studied middle-class and professional women. Many researchers have speculated that juggling is less rewarding for less affluent women. But the evidence shows that working-class women also enjoy working outside the home, derive a sense of satisfaction and self-esteem from paid labor and dislike housework. In the mid-1970s, sociologist Myra Marx Ferree interviewed 135 married women living in a working-class neighborhood in Massachusetts. Most of the women were in long-term marriages. More than half were employed outside the home. Ferree found that 92 percent of the part-time workers and 83 percent of the full-time workers were satisfied with their lives, while only 74 percent of the housewives were.

What are the benefits of combining roles? Here are the most important ones that I uncovered in my research:

Better emotional health: Why are so many women depressed? The question has propelled a veritable mini-industry of research. The American Psychological Association has even established a task force on Women and Depression. We are beginning to find answers.

Biology is one of them. Hormones may play a major role in certain types of depression—such as the postpartum blues. But biology alone does not cause depression. Social roles are also important. Researchers have uncovered links between life roles and mental illness. Here are some pieces of the puzzle:

- There is a strong association between stress and depression, and research shows that women simply face more stress than men.
- Stress is most common among the financially insecure. Many more women than men in our country are economically disadvantaged.

Now add to those basic observations two others:

- In the so-called traditional family, wives are much more likely than their husbands to experience depression. Conversely, wives in dual-earner families do *not* suffer more depressions than their husbands.
- Employed women are not exempt from stress and depression, but employed women tend to recover emotionally from major traumas more rapidly than housewives do. Thus, when a marriage dissolves or finances take a turn for the worse, everyone feels bad—but among housewives, the painful emotions linger longer and are more severe than among jugglers.

All of these findings point in one direction. It seems that traditional restrictions on women's life roles increase the problems women face. To be a housewife is often to be burdened, isolated and psychologically hampered.

Greater personal happiness: In quest of hard evidence about whether multiple roles enhance a woman's psychological well-being, a team at Wellesley College's Center for Research on Women interviewed more than 200 women living in a suburb of Boston. In their sample of middle-class women, researchers Grace Baruch and Rosalind Barnett found that the more life roles a woman played, the less depressed she was. The jugglers in the sample also exhibited higher self-esteem than other women. And they took a great deal of pleasure in life—more than women with fewer life roles. The point is this: Life's different roles all contribute to one another.

Another study documented the link between multiple roles and well-being. It found that employment and marriage shielded people from depression. Unemployed women and men were more depressed than employed women and men; unmarried people were more depressed than married people.

So the bulk of research has shown that jugglers are happier than others. By and large, the more roles, the greater the happiness. Parents are happier than nonparents, and workers are happier than nonworkers. Married people are much happier than unmarried people. And married, working parents are generally at the top of the emotional totem pole.

Better family life: Not only do jugglers feel happier than other women about themselves, jugglers also feel happier with other aspects of their lives. Involvement in many roles seems to increase their satisfaction with each one. Having an occupation helps people to be contented with their domestic situations. Even though they sacrifice leisure time and sleep, employed women often enjoy their domestic pursuits more than housewives do. Employed women also express greater marital satisfaction.

Each Role Should Be Satisfying

We must, of course, resist oversimplification. Good mental health is not automatically assured by multiple life roles. The quality of each role also influences well-being.

Woe to the woman who has a bad marriage and a miserable job. Neither role will help make the other one more bearable. Such was the predictable conclusion of an intensive study of 43 Boston women living in poverty. All of them exhibited fairly high levels of depression. The poorer the woman, the more likely she was to be depressed. For these women, each role—including marriage—brought many obligations but few benefits. It is only when roles contain enough reward that women benefit by combining public and private responsibilities.

Recognizing that the nature—and quality—of a woman's various roles matters at least as much as their number leads us to another qualifier: There is a limit to how many different roles any woman can juggle. Nobody is able to do everything.

Just as we need to encourage women to test life's many options, we also need to acknowledge the real limits of energy and resources. It would be pointless and cruel to prescribe role combination for every woman at each moment of her life. Life has its seasons. There are moments when a woman ought to invest emotionally in many different roles, and other moments when she may need to conserve her psychological energies.

Opening Our Ears and Eyes

As I waded through the voluminous research reports in the social and medical sciences, I wondered about a curious discrepancy. The beneficial effects of juggling are well documented, and yet, outside a small circle of scholars on college campuses, few laypeople know about these satisfactions. Why haven't women been clamoring for more information about how others like themselves struggle with and benefit from a life composed of many parts?

The answer came in a memory. Some years ago I organized a conference on women and multiple roles. My good friend Dana provided weeks of physical and emotional help preparing for the conference. Minutes before the first speaker was scheduled to talk, Dana whispered, "Faye, I feel really ambivalent. On the one hand, I'm hoping to learn all sorts of tips that could help me juggle my different demands. But on the other, something in me does not want to learn how the truly competent woman does it all. Something in me wants to learn that there are no truly competent women, or at least no women who are managing any better than I am."

Curiously, it was Dana's fear of inadequacy that kept her from realizing her own wonderful competence as a working mother and wife. To liberate Dana from that fear, she needed dispassionate and cumulative information. I trust that she will not be the only woman to find comfort and validation in the new research that shows that having many roles leads to a rich and satisfying life.

What About the Kids?

It's all well and good, of course, to rejoice in the satisfactions of our juggling lives. But working mothers want to know how well their kids are doing, too. Numerous studies confirm that when children have good child care, there are no deficits—and many rewards.

With the help of my kids and friends, I have identified the six special benefits of having a juggler for a mother.

1. Intimate contact with father: Men certainly do not do their share of laundry, cooking, shopping, cleaning and general household maintenance. They do not even do their share of child care. But the child of two working parents has at least a little better chance than most children to see Dad in an apron.

When asked what effect employment had on the father-child relationship, 58 percent of the young mothers in a sample of middle-class Caucasians replied that the effect was unequivocally positive. An even higher percentage of men in the sample agreed. Another study, this time of Chicano families, found that maternal employment was strongly associated with a shift in the family toward egalitarian child care patterns. When the mother worked, the father shed some of the trappings of patriarchy.

2. Increased contact with the work world: Rigid separations between work and home are harder to maintain when the mother works in the office as well as the kitchen. When I was a child, I saw the inside of my father's office about twice a year. My children see the inside of my office several times a week. It's given them a richer, broader view of the world and a more realistic understanding of what I do—and what life will be like when they grow up. My son Tim has been coming to work with me since he was a week old. He's now thoroughly familiar with my office. In fact, in the building where I currently work, there's a machine that dispenses chocolate milk, and Tim's comment when I told him that I was writing this book was: "Tell them about how the best part of your job is the chocolate milk."

3. Contact with other children and with care outside the home: Sandra Scarr, Commonwealth Professor of Psychology at the University of Virginia; Edward F. Zigler, Sterling Professor of Psychology and director of the Bush Center in Child Development and Social Policy at Yale University; Kathleen McCartney, associate professor of psychology at the University of New Hampshire, and other researchers have found that children who attend high-quality child care centers show benefits in their intellectual and emotional development as a result of contact with children and adults outside the family. Social resourcefulness and resilience are the hallmarks of some children cared for outside the home. Child care is a positive experience for many girls and boys. As high-quality centers increase, this becomes more frequently true.

4. A more egalitarian view of men and women: A respectable amount of research has now accumulated on the sex-role attitudes of children of housewives and children of employed women. The research shows rather compellingly that children lose some of the rigidity of their sex-role stereotyping when they have mothers who play the provider role as well as the nurturer role. Employed mothers in two-parent families have children who are more egalitarian in terms of gender than the children of other mothers. Other research suggests that children of men who are highly involved in child care retain less rigid sex-role ideologies than do other children.

Children who are free of these stereotypes may be better equipped than other kids to negotiate the traumas of the teenage years. Adolescent girls, for instance, may not place so much emphasis on their looks for self-esteem; they may turn instead to other, more reliable strengths, such as dedication to academic work or development of athletic or artistic skills.

5. Positive self-regard and initiative: Learning how to get about in the world not only makes kids more tolerant, it can increase their self-confidence. Without challenges, children do not strive for excellence. Kids who face tasks they have a good chance of succeeding at develop confidence in their own competence.

Challenges must, of course, be at the right level; if they are too great they stunt growth. There is nothing that disrupts emotional growth so much as foisting inappropriate adult demands on a child. For instance, a youngster who is afraid to stay home alone after school needs to go to an after-school program. But with the right challenges, such as helping with the dinner or laundry at the appropriate age, children gain confidence in their abilities to accomplish things.

6. Money: The last major benefit—and it is, in my book, the most important—concerns finances. There are 12.5 million children in this country who live with a mother and no father. Many of these children depend entirely on the mother's income for their survival. For these children, having a working mother allows them to have basic necessities.

Even when there is a father in the family who brings in money, the mother's money matters to the children. In 1978, the median income of a family in which the husband was the sole earner leveled at just above $17,000. For dual-earner families in that year, median family income reached $21,000. Twelve years later, the median income of a family in which both husband and wife worked full time reached $44,000, almost 40 percent higher than the median family income of the traditional family ($32,000). Women are contributing a higher percentage to family income and boosting that income as never before.

Figures and facts change stereotypes and myths only slowly. Our tendency to discount women's financial contribution to family welfare perpetuates maternal guilt. Why do we ask employed women how they can choose between their jobs and their children when we do not ask men the same question?

It has taken me years to come to see myself as a financial provider, but I am glad to be at that point. So are my children. They are normal kids. They like the things money can buy—basics such as clothing, food and shelter as well as extras like chocolate milk from a machine!

CHILDREN AFTER DIVORCE

WOUNDS THAT DON'T HEAL

Judith S. Wallerstein

Judith S. Wallerstein is a psychologist and author of "Second Chances: Men, Women & Children a Decade After Divorce," published by Ticknor & Fields. This article, adapted from the book, was written with the book's co-author, Sandra Blakeslee, who is a regular contributor to The New York Times.

As recently as the 1970's, when the American divorce rate began to soar, divorce was thought to be a brief crisis that soon resolved itself. Young children might have difficulty falling asleep and older children might have trouble at school. Men and women might become depressed or frenetic, throwing themselves into sexual affairs or immersing themselves in work.

But after a year or two, it was expected, most would get their lives back on track, at least outwardly. Parents and children would get on with new routines, new friends and new schools, taking full opportunity of the second chances that divorce brings in its wake.

These views, I have come to realize, were wishful thinking. In 1971, working with a small group of colleagues and with funding from San Francisco's Zellerback Family Fund, I began a study of the effects of divorce on middle-class people who continue to function despite the stress of a marriage breakup.

That is, we chose families in which, despite the failing marriage, the children were doing well at school and the parents were not in clinical treatment for psychiatric disorders. Half of the families attended church or synagogue. Most of the parents were college educated. This was, in other words, divorce under the best circumstances.

Our study, which would become the first ever made over an extended period of time, eventually tracked 60 families, most of them white, with a total of 131 children, for 10, and in some cases 15, years after divorce. We found that although some divorces work well—some adults are happier in the long run, and some children do better than they would have been expected to in an unhappy intact family—more often than not divorce is a wrenching, long-lasting experience for at least one of the former partners. Perhaps most important, we found that for virtually all the children, it exerts powerful and wholly unanticipated effects.

Our study began with modest aspirations. With a colleague, Joan Berlin Kelly—who headed a community mental-health program in the San Francisco area—I planned to examine the short-term effects of divorce on these middle-class families.

We spent many hours with each member of each of our 60 families—hearing their first-hand reports from the battleground of divorce. At the core of our research was the case study, which has been the main source of the fundamental insights of clinical psychology and of psychoanalysis. Many important changes, especially in the long run, would be neither directly observable nor easily measured. They would become accessible only through case studies: by examining the way each of these people processed, responded to and integrated the events and relationships that divorce brings in its wake.

We planned to interview families at the time of decisive separation and filing for divorce, and again 12 to 18 months later, expecting to chart recoveries among men and women and to look at how the children were mastering troubling family events.

We were stunned when, at the second series of visits, we found family after family still in crisis, their wounds wide open. Turmoil and distress had not noticeably subsided. Many adults were angry, and felt humiliated and rejected, and most had not gotten their lives back together. An unexpectedly large number of children were on a downward course. Their symptoms were worse than they had been immediately after the divorce. Our findings were absolutely contradictory to our expectations.

Dismayed, we asked the Zellerbach Fund to support a follow-up study in the fifth year after divorce. To our surprise, interviewing 56 of the 60 families in our original study, we found that although half the men

From *The New York Times* Magazine, January 22, 1989, pp. 19–21, 41–44. Adapted from *Second Chances: Men, Women & Children a Decade After Divorce*, by Judith S. Wallerstein and Sandra Blakeslee.

and two-thirds of the women (even many of those suffering economically) said they were more content with their lives, only 34 percent of the children were clearly doing well.

Another 37 percent were depressed, could not concentrate in school, had trouble making friends and suffered a wide range of other behavior problems. While able to function on a daily basis, these children were not recovering, as everyone thought they would. Indeed most of them were on a downward course. This is a powerful statistic, considering that these were children who were functioning well five years before. It would be hard to find any other group of children—except, perhaps, the victims of a natural disaster—who suffered such a rate of sudden serious psychological problems.

The remaining children showed a mixed picture of good achievement in some areas and faltering achievement in others; it was hard to know which way they would eventually tilt.

The psychological condition of these children and adolescents, we found, was related in large part to the overall quality of life in the post-divorce family, to what the adults had been able to build in place of the failed marriage. Children tended to do well if their mothers and fathers, whether or not they remarried, resumed their parenting roles, managed to put their differences aside, and allowed the children a continuing relationship with both parents. Only a handful of kids had all these advantages.

We went back to these families again in 1980 and 1981 to conduct a 10-year follow-up. Many of those we had first interviewed as children were now adults. Overall, 45 percent were doing well; they had emerged as competent, compassionate and courageous people. But 41 percent were doing poorly; they were entering adulthood as worried, underachieving, self-deprecating and sometimes angry young men and women. The rest were strikingly uneven in how they adjusted to the world; it is too soon to say how they will turn out.

At around this time, I founded the Center for the Family in Transition, in Marin County, near San Francisco, which provides counseling to people who are separating, divorcing or remarrying. Over the years, my colleagues and I have seen more than 2,000 families—an experience that has amplified my concern about divorce. Through our work at the center and in the study, we have come to see divorce not as a single circumscribed event but as a continuum of changing family relationships—as a process that begins during the failing marriage and extends over many years. Things are not getting better, and divorce is not getting easier. It's too soon to call our conclusions definitive, but they point to an urgent need to learn more.

It was only at the 10-year point that two of our most unexpected findings became apparent. The first of these is something we call the sleeper effect.

A divorce-prone society is producing its first generation of young adults, men and women so anxious about attachment and love that their ability to create enduring families is imperiled.

The first youngster in our study to be interviewed at the 10-year mark was one who had always been a favorite of mine. As I waited for her to arrive for this interview, I remembered her innocence at age 16, when we had last met. It was she who alerted us to the fact that many young women experience a delayed effect of divorce.

As she entered my office, she greeted me warmly. With a flourishing sweep of one arm, she said, "You called me at just the right time. I just turned 21!" Then she startled me by turning immediately serious. She was in pain, she said.

She was the one child in our study who we all thought was a prime candidate for full recovery. She had denied some of her feelings at the time of divorce, I felt, but she had much going for her, including high intelligence, many friends, supportive parents, plenty of money.

As she told her story, I found myself drawn into unexpected intricacies of her life. Her trouble began, typically, in her late teens. After graduating from high school with honors, she was admitted to a respected university and did very well her freshman year. Then she fell apart. As she told it, "I met my first true love."

The young man, her age, so captivated her that she decided it was time to have a fully committed love affair. But on her way to spend summer vacation with him, her courage failed. "I went to New York instead. I hitchhiked across the country. I didn't know what I was looking for. I thought I was just passing time. I didn't stop and ponder. I just kept going, recklessly, all the time waiting for some word from my parents. I guess I was testing them. But no one—not my dad, not my mom—ever asked me what I was doing there on the road alone."

She also revealed that her weight dropped to 94 pounds from 128 and that she had not menstruated for a year and a half.

"I began to get angry," she said. "I'm angry at my parents for not facing up to the emotions, to the feelings in their lives, and for not helping me face up to the feelings in mine. I have a hard time forgiving them."

I asked if I should have pushed her to express her anger earlier.

She smiled patiently and said, "I don't think so. That was exactly the point. All those years I denied feelings. I thought I could live without love, without sorrow, without anger, without pain. That's how I coped with the unhappiness in my parents' marriage. Only when I met my boyfriend did I become aware of how much feeling I was sitting on all those years. I'm afraid I'll lose him."

It was no coincidence that her acute depression and anorexia occurred just as she was on her way to consummate her first love affair, as she was entering the kind of relationship in which her parents failed. For the first time, she confronted the fears, anxieties, guilt and concerns that she had suppressed over the years.

Sometimes with the sleeper effect the fear is of betrayal rather than commitment. I was shocked when another young woman—at the age of 24, sophisticated, warm and friendly—told me she worried if her boyfriend was even 30 minutes late, wondering who he was with and if he was having an affair with another woman. This fear of betrayal occurs at a frequency that far exceeds what one might expect from a group of people randomly selected from the population. They suffer minute to minute, even though their partners may be faithful.

In these two girls we saw a pattern that we documented in 66 percent of the young women in our study between the ages of 19 and 23; half of them were seriously derailed by it. The sleeper effect occurs at a time when these young women are making decisions with long-term implications for their lives. Faced with issues of commitment, love and sex in an adult context, they are aware that the game is serious. If they tie in with the wrong man, have children too soon, or choose harmful life-styles, the effects can be tragic. Overcome by fears and anxieties, they begin to make connections between these feelings and their parents' divorce:

"I'm so afraid I'll marry someone like my dad."

"How can you believe in commitment when anyone can change his mind anytime?"

"I am in awe of people who stay together."

We can no longer say—as most experts have held in recent years—that girls are generally less troubled by the divorce experience than boys. Our study strongly indicates, for the first time, that girls experience serious effects of divorce at the time they are entering young adulthood. Perhaps the risk for girls and boys is equalized over the long term.

When a marriage breaks down, men and women alike often experience a diminished capacity to parent. They may give less time, provide less discipline and be less sensitive to their children, since they are themselves caught up in the maelstrom of divorce and its aftermath. Many researchers and clinicians find that parents are temporarily unable to separate their children's needs from their own.

In a second major unexpected finding of our 10-year study, we found that fully a quarter of the mothers and a fifth of the fathers had not gotten their lives back on track a decade after divorce. The diminished parenting continued, permanently disrupting the child-rearing functions of the family. These parents were chronically disorganized and, unable to meet the challenges of being a parent, often leaned heavily on their children. The child's role became one of warding off the serious depression that threatened the parents' psychological functioning. The divorce itself may not be solely to blame but, rather, may aggravate emotional difficulties that had been masked in the marriage. Some studies have found that emotionally disturbed parents within a marriage produce similar kinds of problems in children.

These new roles played by the children of divorce are complex and unfamiliar. They are not simple role reversals, as some have claimed, because the child's role becomes one of holding the parent together psychologically. It is more than a caretaking role. This phenomenon merits our careful attention, for it affected 15 percent of the children in our study, which means many youngsters in our society. I propose that we identify as a distinct psychological syndrome the "overburdened child," in the hope that people will begin to recognize the problems and take steps to help these children, just as they help battered and abused children.

One of our subjects, in whom we saw this syndrome, was a sweet 5-year-old girl who clearly felt that she was her father's favorite. Indeed, she was the only person in the family he never hit. Preoccupied with being good and helping to calm both parents, she opposed the divorce because she knew it would take her father away from her. As it turned out, she also lost her mother who, soon after the divorce, turned to liquor and sex, a combination that left little time for mothering.

A year after the divorce, at the age of 6, she was getting herself dressed, making her own meals and putting herself to bed. A teacher noticed the dark circles under her eyes, and asked why she looked so tired. "We have a new baby at home," the girl explained. The teacher, worried, visited the house and discovered there was no baby. The girl's story was designed to explain her fatigue but also enabled her to fantasize endlessly about a caring loving mother.

Shortly after this episode, her father moved to another state. He wrote to her once or twice a year, and when we saw her at the five-year follow-up she pulled out a packet of letters from him. She explained how worried she was that he might get into trouble, as if she were the parent and he the child who had left home.

"I always knew he was O.K. if he drew pictures on the letters," she said. "The last two really worried me because he stopped drawing."

Now 15, she has taken care of her mother for the past 10 years. "I felt it was my responsibility to make sure that Mom was O.K.," she says. "I stayed home with her instead of playing or going to school. When she got mad, I'd let her take it out on me."

I asked what her mother would do when she was angry.

"She'd hit me or scream. It scared me more when she screamed. I'd rather be hit. She always seemed so much bigger when she screamed. Once Mom got drunk and passed out on the street. I called my brothers, but they hung up. So I did it. I've done a lot of things I've never told anyone. There were many times she was so upset I was sure she would take her own life. Sometimes I held both her hands and talked to her for hours I was so afraid."

In truth, few children can rescue a troubled parent. Many become angry at being trapped by the parents' demands, at being robbed of their separate identity and denied their childhood. And they are saddened, sometimes beyond repair, at seeing so few of their own needs gratified.

Since this is a newly identified condition that is just being described, we cannot know its true incidence. I suspect that the number of overburdened children runs much higher than the 15 percent we saw in our study, and that we will begin to see rising reports in the next few years—just as the reported incidence of child abuse has risen since it was first identified as a syndrome in 1962.

The sleeper effect and the overburdened-child syndrome were but two of many findings in our study. Perhaps most important, overall, was our finding that divorce has a lasting psychological effect on many children, one that, in fact, may turn out to be permanent.

Children of divorce have vivid memories about their parents' separation. The details are etched firmly in their minds, more so than those of any other experiences in their lives. They refer to themselves as children of divorce, as if they share an experience that sets them apart from all others. Although many have come to agree that their parents were wise to part company, they nevertheless feel that they suffered from their parents' mistakes. In many instances, conditions in the post-divorce family were more stressful and less supportive to the child than conditions in the failing marriage.

If the finding that 66 percent of the 19- to 23-year-old young women experienced the sleeper effect was most unexpected, others were no less dramatic. Boys, too, were found to suffer unforeseen long-lasting effects. Forty percent of the 19- to 23-year-old young men in our study, 10 years after divorce, still had no set goals, a limited education and a sense of having little control over their lives.

In comparing the post-divorce lives of former husbands and wives, we saw that 50 percent of the women and 30 percent of the men were still intensely angry at their former spouses a decade after divorce. For women over 40 at divorce, life was lonely throughout the decade; not one in our study remarried or sustained a loving relationship. Half the men over 40 had the same problem.

In the decade after divorce, three in five children felt rejected by one of their parents, usually the father—whether or not it was true. The frequency and duration of visiting made no difference. Children longed for their fathers, and the need increased during adolescence. Thirty-four percent of the youngsters went to live with their fathers during adolescence for at least a year. Half returned to the mother's home disappointed with what they had found. Only one in seven saw both mother and father happily remarried after 10 years. One in two saw their mother or their father undergo a second divorce. One in four suffered a severe and enduring drop in the family's standard of living and went on to observe a lasting discrepancy between their parents' standards of living.

We found that the children who were best adjusted 10 years later were those who showed the most distress at the time of the divorce—the youngest. In general, pre-schoolers are the most frightened and show the most dramatic symptoms when marriages break up. Many are afraid that they will be abandoned by both parents and they have trouble sleeping or staying by themselves. It is therefore surprising to find that the same children 10 years later seem better adjusted than their older siblings. Now in early and mid-adolescence, they were rated better on a wide range of psychological dimensions than the older children. Sixty-eight percent were doing well, compared with less than 40 percent of older children. But whether having been young at the time of divorce will continue to protect them as they enter young adulthood is an open question.

Our study shows that adolescence is a period of particularly grave risk for children in divorced families. Through rigorous analysis, statistical and otherwise, we were able to see clearly that we weren't dealing simply with the routine angst of young people going through transition but rather that, for most of them, divorce was the single most important cause of enduring pain and anomie in their lives. The young people told us time and again how much they needed a family structure, how much they wanted to be protected, and how much they yearned for clear guidelines for moral behavior. An alarming number of teenagers felt abandoned, physically and emotionally.

For children, divorce occurs during the formative years. What they see and experience becomes a part of their inner world, influencing their own relationships 10 and 15 years later, especially when they have witnessed violence between the parents. It is then, as these young men and women face the developmental task of establishing love and intimacy, that they most feel the lack of a template for a loving relationship between a man and a woman. It is here that their anxiety threatens their ability to create new, enduring families of their own.

As these anxieties peak in the children of divorce throughout our society, the full legacy of the rising divorce rate is beginning to hit home. The new families being formed today by these children as they reach adulthood appear particularly vulnerable.

Because our study was such an early inquiry, we did not set out to compare children of divorce with children from intact families. Lacking fundamental knowledge about life after the breakup of a marriage, we could not know on what basis to build a comparison or control group. Was the central issue one of economics, age, sex, a happy intact marriage—or would any intact marriage do? We began, therefore, with a question—What is the nature of the divorce experience?—and in answering it we would generate hypotheses that could be tested in subsequent studies.

This has indeed been the case. Numerous studies have been conducted in different regions of the country, using control groups, that have further explored and validated our findings as they have emerged over the years. For example, one national study of 699 elementary school children carefully compared children six years after their parents' divorce with children from intact families. It found—as we did—that elementary-age boys from divorced families show marked discrepancies in peer relationships, school achievement and social adjustment. Girls in this group, as expected, were hardly distinguishable based on the experience of divorce, but, as we later found out, this would not always hold up. Moreover, our findings are supported by a litany of modern-day statistics. Although one in three children are from divorced families, they account for an inordinately high proportion of children in mental-health treatment, in special-education classes, or referred by teachers to school psychologists. Children of divorce make up an estimated 60 percent of child patients in clinical treatment and 80 percent—in some cases, 100 percent—of adolescents in inpatient mental hospital settings. While no one would claim that a cause and effect relationship has been established in all of these cases, no one would deny that the role of divorce is so persuasively suggested that it is time to sound the alarm.

All studies have limitations in what they can accomplish. Longitudinal studies, designed to establish the impact of a major event or series of events on the course of a subsequent life, must always allow for the influence of many interrelated factors. They must deal with chance and the uncontrolled factors that so often modify the sequences being followed. This is particularly true of children, whose lives are influenced by developmental changes, only some of which are predictable, and by the problem of individual differences, about which we know so little.

Our sample, besides being quite small, was also drawn from a particular population slice—predominately white, middle class and relatively privileged suburbanites.

Despite these limitations, our data have generated working hypotheses about the effects of divorce that can now be tested with more precise methods, including appropriate control groups. Future research should be aimed at testing, correcting or modifying our initial findings, with larger and more diverse segments of the population. For example, we found that children—especially boys and young men—continued to need their fathers after divorce and suffered feelings of rejection even when they were visited regularly. I would like to see a study comparing boys and girls in sole and joint custody, spanning different developmental stages, to see if greater access to both parents counteracts these feelings of rejection. Or, does joint custody lead to a different sense of rejection—of feeling peripheral in both homes?

It is time to take a long, hard look at divorce in America. Divorce is not an event that stands alone in childrens' or adults' experience. It is a continuum that begins in the unhappy marriage and extends through the separation, divorce and any remarriages and second divorces. Divorce is not necessarily the sole culprit. It may be no more than one of the many experiences that occur in this broad continuum.

Profound changes in the family can only mean profound changes in society as a whole. All children in today's world feel less protected. They sense that the institution of the family is weaker than it has ever been before. Even those children raised in happy, intact families worry that their families may come undone. The task for society in its true and proper perspective is to strengthen the family—all families.

A biblical phrase I have not thought of for many years has recently kept running through my head: "Watchman, what of the night?" We are not I'm afraid, doing very well on our watch—at least for our children. We are allowing them to bear the psychological, economic and moral brunt of divorce.

And they recognize the burdens. When one 6-year-old boy came to our center shortly after his parents' divorce, he would not answer questions; he played games instead. First he hunted all over the playroom for the sturdy Swedish-designed dolls that we use in therapy. When he found a good number of them, he stood the baby dolls firmly on their feet and placed the miniature tables, chairs, beds and, eventually, all the playhouse furniture on top of them. He looked at me, satisfied. The babies were supporting a great deal. Then, wordlessly, he placed all the mother and father dolls in precarious positions on the steep roof of the doll house. As a father doll slid off the roof, the boy caught him and, looking up at me, said, "He might die." Soon, all the mother and father dolls began sliding off the roof. He caught them gently, one by one.

"The babies are holding up the world," he said.

Although our overall findings are troubling and serious, we should not point the finger of blame at divorce per se. Indeed, divorce is often the only rational solution to a bad marriage. When people ask whether they should stay married for the sake of the children, I have to say, "Of course not." All our evidence shows that children exposed to open conflict, where parents terrorize or strike one another, turn out less well-adjusted than do children from divorced families. And although we lack systematic studies comparing children in divorced families with those in unhappy intact families, I am convinced that it is not useful to provide children with a model of adult behavior that avoids problem-solving and that stresses martyrdom, violence or apathy. A divorce undertaken thoughtfully and realistically can teach children how to confront serious life problems with compassion, wisdom and appropriate action.

Our findings do not support those who would turn back the clock. As family issues are flung to the center of our political arena, nostalgic voices from the right argue for a return to a time when divorce was more difficult to obtain. But they do not offer solutions to the wretchedness and humiliation within many marriages.

Still we need to understand that divorce has consequences—we need to go into the experience with our eyes open. We need to know that many children will suffer for many years. As a society, we need to take steps to preserve for the children as much as possible of the social, economic and emotional security that existed while their parents' marriage was intact.

Like it or not, we are witnessing family changes which are an integral part of the wider changes in our society. We are on a wholly new course, one that gives us unprecedented opportunities for creating better relationships and stronger families—but one that also brings unprecedented dangers for society, especially for our children.

Girls' Self-Esteem Is Lost on Way To Adolescence, New Study Finds

Suzanne Daley

Girls emerge from adolescence with a poor self-image, relatively low expectations from life and much less confidence in themselves and their abilities than boys, a study to be made public today has concluded.

Confirming earlier studies that were smaller and more anecdotal, this survey of 3,000 children found that at the age of 9 a majority of girls were confident, assertive and felt positive about themselves. But by the time they reached high school, less than a third felt that way.

The survey, commissioned by the American Association of University Women, found that boys, too, lost some sense of self-worth, but they ended up far ahead of the girls.

For example, when elementary school boys were asked how often they felt "happy the way I am," 67 percent answered "always." By high school, 46 percent still felt that way. But with girls, the figures dropped from 60 percent to 29 percent.

Race as a Factor

"It's really quite staggering to see that this is still going on," said Myra Sadker, a professor at American University in Washington, who has spent most of the last decade studying the way teachers treat girls in the classroom. "No one has taken such a large-scale look at self-esteem before, but we have known of this issue for years. And here you see that it is not going away."

Among the girls, race is apparently a factor in the retention of self-esteem, the survey found. Far more black girls surveyed were still self-confident in high school, compared with white and Hispanic girls, and white girls lost their self-assurance earlier than Hispanic girls.

The subject of girls' self-esteem has emerged relatively recently as a field of study, generating considerable controversy. Some academics say the psychological development process of women differs profoundly from that of men; others disagree.

Dr. Carol Gilligan, a professor of education at Harvard and a pioneer in studying the development of girls, said the survey's findings would force a series of more complex questions about what happens to girls' self-esteem during adolescence.

"This survey makes it impossible to say what happens to girls is simply a matter of hormones," said Dr. Gilligan, an adviser on the development of questions asked in the survey. "If that was it, then the loss of self-esteem would happen to all girls and at roughly the same time.

"This work raises all kinds of issues about cultural contributions," she added, "and it raises questions about the role of the schools, both in the drop of self-esteem and in the potential for intervention."

Sharon Schuster, president of the American Association of University Women, a research and advocacy group, said the association had commissioned the study to draw attention to the plight of girls at a time when education changes is a topic of widespread interest.

Are girls still shortchanged in the classroom?

"Generally, most people feel that girls are getting a good education," Ms. Schuster said. "I think this survey shows that the system has some shortfalls. We wanted to put some factual data behind our belief that girls are getting shortchanged in the classroom."

Based on an index of personal self-esteem created by the responses to such statements as "I like the way I look," "I like most things about myself" and "I wish I were somebody else," the study found that overall, boys had a higher sense of self-esteem than girls in elementary school and retained it better over the years.

The study, conducted by Greenberg-Lake Analysis Group Inc., surveyed 2,400 girls and 600 boys at 36 public schools in 12 communities throughout the country last fall. The children, in grades 4 through 10, were asked to answer written questions in the classroom.

The researchers said the margin of sampling error was plus or minus three percentage points for the girls and plus or minus five percentage points for the boys.

Enough girls were questioned for the researches to draw conclusions about race distinctions, but no such conclusions could be drawn about the boys because there were too few boys included in the survey.

The findings among the girls, combined with the answers that black girls gave regarding their relationships with teachers, prompted the researchers to conclude that black girls drew their apparent self-confidence from their families and communities rather than the school system.

Janie Victoria Ward, a Rockefeller fellow at the University of Pennsylvania who is studying the socialization of black families and was an adviser to the study, said one factor that might help black girls is that they are often surrounded by strong women they admire. Black women are more likely than others to have a full-time job and run a household.

Another factor, she said, may be that black parents often teach their children that there is nothing wrong with them, only with the way the world treats them.

"In order to maintain that high self-esteem they are disassociating from school," said Dr. Ward.

Linda Kerber, a professor of history at the University of Iowa, said she, too, found the results about black girls to be particularly interesting.

"This should encourage white people to look with admiration at the black community," Dr. Kerber said. "So often we look at the black family as a locus of problems, but here we can see that they are doing something right."

Dr. Gilligan of Harvard said that what appeared to be happening to black girls had both good and bad consequences. "The danger is that the black girls will miss the opportunity of school," she said. "You can't just romanticize this."

To some degree, the new study supports the work Dr. Gilligan has been doing in recent years. One of her studies looked intensively at about 100 girls enrolled at a private school outside of Cleveland, and followed their development closely for more than five years.

Dr. Gilligan also found that adolescence is the moment when girls begin to doubt themselves: while 11-year-olds tend to be full of self-confidence, she said, by 15 and 16 they start to say, " 'I don't know. I don't know. I don't know.' "

But Dr. Gilligan said her study was too small to draw broad-based conclusions about race. "We did see some of these things," she said. "But we could not make the kind of generalizations that this survey allows."

The American Association of University Women's survey also examined children's attitudes toward science and mathematics, finding that girls who did poorly in math tended to see their problems as "personal failures," while boys more often attributed their lack of success or interest in math to a sense that the subject "was not useful."

Indeed, young women who like math are more confident about their appearances than are young men, whether they like math or not, the study found.

Children in gangs

The tragedy of inner-city youth drawn into delinquency and drug trafficking

Carl Rogers

CARL ROGERS,
of the United States, is an expert on child and family issues. He serves as the public policy liaison officer for the American National Council on Child Abuse and Family Violence, a U.S. private sector initiative for the prevention and treatment of child abuse, based in Washington D.C.

THE 1980s witnessed the explosive resurgence of an historic American urban social problem: children and youth in gangs. From New York to Los Angeles, from Chicago to Miami, over forty-five American cities have an identified youth gang problem.

The number of youth gangs in the United States is on the rise and their involvement in the drug trade is resulting in dramatic increases in gang-related violence—including homicide—and arrests for criminal activities in almost every American city. The scope and the nature of the problem vary widely from city to city, but it has been estimated that over 50,000 children and youths are gang members in the city of Los Angeles and that there are over 600 youth gangs in California alone.

Popularized in the 1950s musical *West Side Story,* youth gangs have been a recurring social problem in U.S. cities at least since the second half of the nineteenth century. Their emergence and growth, primarily in poor, urban neighbourhoods, were frequently fuelled by successive waves of immigrants arriving in the United States, and were symptomatic of the problems these groups encountered in trying to adapt to a new and at times radically different culture. Today many youth gangs continue to reflect the difficulties of assimilation of immigrant populations.

Youth gangs are usually defined as groups of young people who frequently engage in illegal activity on a group basis. They are usually territorial in nature, identifying with a particular neighbourhood and protecting their "turf" from encroachment by other gangs. Better organized gangs often control economically motivated crime such as burglary, extortion or drug-trafficking at the neighbourhood level. They may also sell "protection" from criminal activity to legitimate merchants. Youth gangs usually identify themselves by a name ("Crips", and "Bloods" are the names of two Los Angeles-based gangs), and may further distinguish themselves by a particular style or colour of clothing, by use of symbols, or by wearing certain kinds of jewellery.

A MILLION DOLLARS A WEEK FROM CRACK

The recent dynamic growth of youth gangs and related violence is directly attributed by most sources to the increased sale of cocaine, particu-

Courtesy of *The UNESCO Courier,* October 1991, pp. 19-21.

larly in the form known as "rock" or "crack". This lucrative illegal activity is helping to transform gangs into drug trafficking criminal organizations. In 1988 Los Angeles police officials acknowledged that they were aware of at least four gangs in their city grossing over $1,000,000 per week through the sale of cocaine. A recent article in the U.S. magazine *Time* ironically noted that the crack cocaine trade may be one of the biggest job programmes for inner city youth in the United States.

One reason why children become involved in drug trafficking is that the laws governing juvenile crime are more lenient than those governing adult crime. Ironically, as the U.S. "war on drugs" has intensified, with both increasing arrests for drug trafficking and more severe penalties for adults convicted of drug-related crime, the value of youth gang members has increased. While an adult convicted of selling drugs in most states is subject to a mandatory prison sentence of anywhere from two years to life imprisonment, a young person under the age of eighteen will seldom be committed to a correctional facility for a first offence, and even if committed is not subject to mandatory sentence lengths. It has become both increasingly profitable and safer for adult criminals to enroll children and youths in the drug trafficking business.

PEEWEES AND WANNABEES

The average age of youth gang members continues to decline. Most experts place the figure at around thirteen to fifteen years of age, while law enforcement officials in Los Angeles, Chicago and other cities note that children as young as nine or ten years are frequently found in today's gangs. These young recruits, often called "peewees" (slang for little members) or "wannabees" (slang for "want to be" gang members), become casually involved with older gang members who live in their neighbourhood, attend their school, or are members of their own families. Initially, younger children may be asked to perform "favours" for older gang members—to watch for police in the neighbourhood, or to deliver packages which may contain drugs, money or weapons. In exchange, the children often receive expensive gifts or money.

As they demonstrate their trustworthiness and reliability, these children assume more difficult and more dangerous roles. Children as young as ten or eleven years of age are frequently involved in gang-related drug trafficking. Younger children are routinely employed as "spotters" watching and reporting on police activity in their neighbourhood to other gang members, as "weapons carriers" for older gang members, or in other roles, and earn anywhere from $200 per week to $100 per day. "Runners", usually slightly older children, may earn up to $300 per day keeping street corner dealers supplied with drugs from a hidden cache. Enterprising youths as young as fifteen or sixteen may advance to the level of street corner dealers, routinely earning between $400 and $1,000 per day. In a particularly good market such as New York City, authorities indicate that dealers can make up to $3,000 per day.

Few dealers, however, work full time, and two different studies in Washington, D.C. would suggest that a street corner dealer's average earnings are more likely to be in the range of $4,000 to $7,000 per month. In contrast, most states in the U.S. set a minimum employment age of sixteen years, and most legal entry-level jobs available to young people pay less than $40 per day, or approximately $800 per month.

Once a child is involved with a gang, it may be virtually impossible for him to quit. Gang membership usually leads to truancy and ultimately dropping out of school, closing off escape from a criminal lifestyle through education. The gang member also finds it difficult to give up a more lucrative lifestyle in exchange for unemployment or employment at minimum wage.

The gang member who attempts to quit is also subject to social pressures to continue his or her involvement. At best, attempting to leave the gang may lead to social ostracism; at worst it may lead to direct intimidation.

IMPOVERISHED INNER-CITY NEIGHBOURHOODS

To truly understand the youth gang problem it is important to understand the social context within which the gangs emerge. First, they are almost universally a product of impoverished urban neighbourhoods, where unemployment routinely exceeds 20 per cent of the workforce and in some cases exceeds 50 per cent. Families consist overwhelmingly of single mothers with children and often rely primarily on public assistance for their livelihood. Nationally, 20 per cent of all children in the United States live in families at or below the established federal poverty level. In many inner-city neighbourhoods this figure approaches 100 per cent. These communities are characterized by generally high crime rates, limited legitimate business activity or employment opportunities, and poorly functioning public education systems.

In contrast to the phenomenon of street children in many Third World countries, or to the problem of runaway or "throwaway" children (children, usually teenagers, expelled from their homes by their parents), most youth gang members live at home with their families. Some parents actively support their child's gang involvement or are totally indifferent, but most parents do care. Even the best intentioned parent, however, can find it difficult, if not impossible, to keep his or her child from becoming involved with a local gang. Every neighbourhood has its history of gang revenge against individual children or their families for resisting the gang. The combined factors of intimidation on the one hand and some financial support on the other eventually result in tacit collusion on the part of these parents. An uneasy truce develops where the parent, while not condoning or supporting the child's gang involvement, nonetheless does little to try to stop this involvement and welcomes the child's periodic financial contributions to the family budget.

So far, the overall public policy approach to this social problem has focused on three broad strategies: suppression of drug use and drug trafficking; suppression of youth gangs; and prevention of youth involvement in gangs. To date, while national statistics suggest an overall decline in the use of illegal drugs, this decline appears to have had little effect on the growth of the gangs or on the frequency of gang-related violence. Similarly, attempts at direct suppression of the gangs through law enforcement activities appear to have had limited effects, despite the mobilization of extensive resources. It is argued by many, however, that these efforts have slowed the growth and spread of gangs. Alternatively, some have suggested that efforts at gang suppression through arrest and detention of gang members actually lead to increased levels of gang-related violence as other gangs compete for control of territories once controlled by the suppressed gang.

Most experts agree that the only viable long-term solution to the problem is to prevent children and youths from getting involved in gangs in the first place. Most current programmes seek to provide support for high-risk children and their families. They focus on children between the ages of six and fourteen, since it appears to be generally agreed that prevention efforts must begin before young people develop well-established patterns of delinquent behaviour or become seriously involved with gangs. Key elements in many of these programmes include the provision of social and recreational activities, and educational assistance, as well as efforts to prevent the children from dropping out of school and to enhance their self-confidence and self-esteem. The success of prevention efforts ultimately depends on whether these children and young people have a sense of hope in their own future and a belief that through their own efforts they can lead useful, productive lives.

Reaching the child within us

ASHLEY MONTAGU

The truth about the human species is that we are intended to remain in many ways childlike; we were never intended to grow "up" into the kind of adults most of us have become. We are designed—in body, spirit, feeling, and conduct—to grow and develop in ways that emphasize rather than minimize childlike traits. By learning to act more like a child, human beings can revolutionize their lives and become for the first time, perhaps, the kinds of creatures their heritage has prepared them to be—youthful all the days of their lives.

What are those traits of childhood behavior that are so valuable yet tend to disappear gradually as human beings grow older? We have only to watch children to see them clearly displayed: Curiosity is one of the most important; imaginativeness; playfulness; open mindedness; willingness to experiment; flexibility; humor; energy; receptiveness to new ideas; honesty; eagerness to learn; and perhaps the most pervasive and the most valuable of all, the need to love. Children ask questions endlessly: "Why?" "What is it?" "What's it for?" "How does it work?" They watch, and they listen. They want to know everything about everything. They can keep themselves busy for hours with the simplest toys, endowing sticks and stones and featureless objects with personalities and histories, imagining elaborate stories about them, building sagas that continue day after day, month after month. They play games endlessly, sometimes carefully constructing the rules, sometimes developing the game as they go along. They accept changes without defensiveness. When they try to accomplish something and fail, they are able to try it another way, and another, until they find a way that works. They laugh—babies smile and laugh before they can even babble—and children laugh from sheer exuberance and happiness. Unless they fear punishment, they tell the truth; they call the shots as they see them. And they soak up knowledge and information like sponges; they are learning all the time; every moment is filled with learning.

Most adults draw back from the unfamiliar.

How many adults retain these qualities into middle age? Few. They tend to stop asking those questions that will elicit information. Not many adults, when confronted with something unfamiliar, ask, as children do: "What is it?" "What's it for?" "Why?" "How does it work?" Most adults draw back from the unfamiliar, perhaps because they are reluctant to reveal ignorance, perhaps because they have become genuinely indifferent to the interesting experiences of life and consider that absorbing something new is simply too much trouble.

Nor can most adults content themselves with simple playthings enriched by the imagination. Witness the enormous growth of industries that cater to the "leisure-time" and "recreational" activities of adults, that manufacture the toys grown-ups need to play: boats, cars, trailers, equipment for camping, hiking, running, tennis, and golf. The list seems endless.

Most adults have lost, too, the ability to laugh

From *Utne Reader*, January/February 1990, pp. 87-90. Abridged from Ashley Montagu's *Growing Young*, 2nd edition (Bergin & Garvey Publishers, an imprint of Greenwood Press, Inc., New York, 1989).

from sheer happiness; perhaps they have lost happiness itself. Adulthood as we know it brings sobriety and seriousness along with its responsibilities. Most adults have also lost the ability to tell the simple truth; many appear to have lost the ability to discern a simple truth in the complex morass they live in.

Perhaps the saddest loss of all is the gradual erosion of the eagerness to learn. Most adults stop any

Celebrate midlife with a ritual

As part of my work as a learning consultant, I have held ritual ceremonies for people who were concerned about reaching midlife. Like many in their 40s and 50s, these people are regretful about losing opportunities and youthful energy, worried about bodily changes, and fearful of losing influence as they grow older. The ritual's purpose is to create a vehicle for expressing concerns and regrets, in the process releasing some of the pain caused by midlife worries as well as moving toward acceptance of growing older, and ultimately gaining new-found peace and empowerment.

I've found rituals to be a very moving experience for participants, and I encourage readers to try their own. Any imaginative person with good listening skills, compassion, experience with symbols, and guidance from resource materials can serve as facilitator. A partial list of resources includes Nancy Cunningham's book *Feeding the Spirit* (Resource Publishing, 160 E. Virginia St., #290, San Jose, CA 95112), Penina Adelman's *Miriam's Well* (Biblio Press, 27 W. 20th St., Room 1001, New York, NY 10011), and Gertrud Nelson's *To Dance with God* (Paulist Press, 997 Macarthur Blvd., Mahwah, NJ 07430).

The following is a brief description of a ceremony for a group of women who recently turned 40. In this particular ritual, the participants were six women who had been friends since high school and who got together a few times a year. We started the evening with a potluck dinner, which allowed people to shed the day's stresses and to renew their bonds. Since it was fall, we celebrated the concept of harvest with each person bringing a dish made from local produce.

We began the ceremony sitting in a circle, stretching and breathing deeply as one by one each woman spoke of a frustrating experience of the day she wanted to release: a fight with a child, arriving late for a meeting. We passed a sprig of sage—which in Indian rituals is used as a purifier—to signify the start of a special event in which we would speak from a deeper, more poetic place in ourselves. I talked about the emotional stages we'd explore (ones similar to those experienced with loss) of grieving, acceptance, and empowerment.

Then the women named all the things they disliked about being 40—varicose veins, wrinkles, needing to go to bed earlier—while tossing a ball to each other. The ball game brought a lightheartedness to the heartfelt disclosures. Ready now to go deeper, we made a centerpiece out of a circle of gray fabric, on which each woman placed a stone she had brought. The women took turns being storytellers, slipping on a full-length black coat to symbolize loss and grieving. I asked them to dive deep inside themselves to find what it was that pained them most about aging, and to begin a story about what they discovered with the phrase "I never thought ________ would happen to me." Their stories revealed the feelings of betrayal midlife can bring. One spoke of priding herself on never needing glasses; yet a doctor recently suggested that "it's not too early to consider bifocals." Another said that she "feels so young, and yet two of my teeth have already died." Another lamented the fading of the passion that formerly inspired her to stay up all night to know its mystery and then to greet the dawn. And as each woman finished her lament, there was a chorus of, "Oh no! Not you, too!" We pounded the floor and wailed and laughed as these common experiences comforted us.

After some time spent writing in journals, which helped everyone process and pay tribute to the losses of midlife, each woman held the stone she had brought. I led a meditation on the agelessness and endurance of the stones, which have witnessed so much on the planet since their creation, and asked people to imagine that they could send their pain into their stone.

Next we changed the centerpiece to a cloth that symbolized harvest, and each woman added the ripe fruit or vegetable she had brought—a metaphor for the bounty that comes with aging—and commented on it. As an example, one noted that her ripe peach would have been hard and tasteless before; now its fragrance fills the air and it is lush and flavorful. Then each added a photo of a woman in her 40s whom she admired. Many photos were of women older than us, and we mused on how our sexist society is slow to recognize a woman for her accomplishments. One photo showed the wizened face of a native woman, another the mother of a participant who continued to have zest for life at 70.

Next we passed around an ear of corn—a symbol of physical nurturing for humans in almost every culture—as each woman told of something she was passing on to the next generation. Each reflected on the experiences and wisdom the years had brought: love of music, the ability to read a story aloud with drama, pride in ethnic heritage, helping people to believe in themselves.

Then, as the women laid on their backs listen-

conscious efforts to learn early in their adulthood, and thereafter never actively pursue knowledge or understanding of the physical world. It is as if they believed that they had learned all they needed to know by the age

The later years can be the happiest of one's life.

of 18 or 22. At this time they begin to grow a shell around their pitiful store of knowledge; from then on they vigorously resist all attempts to pierce that shell with anything new. In a world changing so rapidly that even the most agile-minded cannot keep up, the effect of this shell building on a person is to develop a dislike of the unfamiliar. This hardening of the mind—psychosclerosis—is a long distance from a child's acceptance and flexibility and open-mindedness.

But the qualities of the child are ours to express for all time. Genius, said Baudelaire, is childhood recaptured. The fables we have inherited concerning aging are so old that many accept them as truths beyond refutation. Such myths constitute striking examples of the self-fulfilling prophecy. Senility is a disease, not an inevitable consequence of aging. Physical,

We are intended to remain childlike–curious, flexible, imaginative, playful, honest, open-minded.

physiological, and psychological changes do occur with aging. There is, however, no necessary connection between the aging of the body and the aging of the mind.

Recent research indicates that intellectual ability does not decrease through the eighth decade and that with exercise and training significant gains can be achieved. To remain intellectually active, intellectual stimulation is necessary, and that is what the quality of youthfulness is constantly encouraging: to remain in touch with reality, to soak up from the environment that for which the mind hungers.

The later years can be the happiest of one's life. Many of those who have achieved what others call old age have confessed to feeling embarrassingly young, as if such feeling were something anachronistic, an unexpected freshness. It is the kind of freshness that the long-distance runner experiences when at the peak of fatigue he experiences a second wind that takes him on to the finish line. This kind of freshness can be maintained throughout life; it is not too late to achieve it in one's later years. The earlier one has been encouraged in one's childlike qualities, however, the more likely is one to realize that feeling of unadulterated joy in being alive that the romping child so gloriously feels—perhaps without the physical romping, but with that gaiety of spirit that has enabled one to grow young more effectively and more happily than was ever before possible—the last of life, for which the first was made.

---

ing to soothing background music, I led a meditation that reflected on each part of the body, thanking it for its gifts, e.g., strong arms and legs that take us on journeys, hands that carry out the creativity borne in the heart and mind.

Next, we reflected on other gifts that years and personal growth had brought: As we focused on one woman, each of her friends in turn held a mirror up to her, saying, "I see that the years have given you the gift of ________," gifts such as a great sense of humor, endurance, self-confidence, courage, and patience.

Finally, each woman shared some of the wisdom she had gained from life that could be helpful to others, and then we closed by taking hands and sending a squeeze around the circle, reminding everyone that she could reach back through time to get sustenance from this evening any time she encountered the turning-40 blues.

Rituals for people turning 50 have a different flavor. At this stage, people are generally more accepting of the aging process and more interested in sorting through the emerging patterns in their lives and celebrating the richness of the journey. Ritual components vary: One woman gathered friends and family and described how each person had been instrumental in her life. She made a hoop from the two ribbons each guest brought—one representing a quality they loved in her and the other representing a funny memory they shared. We talked about the three phases women pass through—maiden, creator/mother, and crone—and conjured up images of those in each of us through guided imagery. Another chose to reconnect with the child in her and thank that child for helping her become who she was, and we made masks to invite our own child out. Guests brought a poem or picture that reminded them of the woman who was having her 50th birthday.

Rituals offer a means of viewing life as a journey that offers us many opportunities for transformation. Any moment or event of importance to someone can be acknowledged and explored in a personalized ritual—spontaneous or planned. Thus, if someone you know wants to mark her midlife, consider going beyond those black balloons that say,

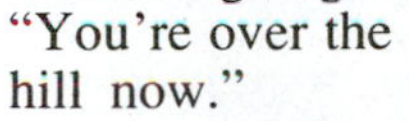

"You're over the hill now."

—Kaia Svien
Special to Utne Reader

Life in the not-so-fast lane

The middle-aging of society will affect the way all Americans live—from the television they watch and the food they eat to the way they spend their precious free time. Here are some statistics to help you chart the course for this coming cultural revolution.

Percent growth in the number of Americans aged 35 to 44 between 1987 and 2000: 27%
Percent growth in the number of Americans aged 45 to 54 between 1987 and 2000: 59%
Percent growth in the number of Americans aged 25 to 34 between 1987 and 2000: -16%
Median age of the U.S. population in 1965: 28.1
Median age in 1985: 31.5
Projected median age in 2005: 37.8
Projected median age in 2030: 41.8
Projected median age in 2080: 43.9
Average annual expenditures for households in 1986: $24,000
Average annual expenditures for households whose head was aged 45 to 54 in 1986: $32,000
Number of companies offering long-term care insurance policies in 1984: 20
Number of companies offering long-term care insurance policies in 1987: 73
Percent of daily newspapers that assigned a reporter to an "aging" beat in 1987: 38
Percent of daily newspapers that carried a regular column on aging in 1987: 47
Number of subscribers to cable TV's Nostalgia Channel since 1985: 5 million
Percentage of luxury car owners who are aged 35 to 54: 41
Percentage of American Express gold card holders who are aged 35 to 54: 42
Number of people in work force per each retiree in 1985: 3.4
In 2030: 2.0
According to the Social Security Administration's intermediate forecast:
The year that Medicare will slip into deficit: 1993
The year that Medicare reserves will be depleted: 1998
The year the federal Social Security disability fund will be exhausted: 2034
The year the federal Social Security pension fund will go broke: 2050
Cost of the nation's disability fund, Medicare, and pension fund as a percent of the nation's taxable payroll in 1985: 14 percent
In 2055: 42 percent
Percent of 18- to 29-year-olds who prefer to spend their leisure time at home: 28
Percent of 30- to 44-year-olds who do: 45
Percent of 45- to 59-year-olds who do: 53
Percent of 18- to 29-year-olds who went to bed before midnight on New Year's Eve 1988: 13
Percent of 30- to 44-year-olds who did: 20
Percent of 45- to 59-year-olds who did: 26
Percent of women aged 18 to 34 who used hair coloring in 1986: 17
Percent of women aged 35 and over who did: 26

—Compiled by Blayne Cutler

Statistics taken from a variety of sources, including Roper Organization polls and Interep Research. For a list of citations, send an SASE to Aging Facts, Utne Reader, 1624 Harmon Pl., Minneapolis, MN 55403.

Silent saviors

Millions of grandparents have stepped into the breach to rescue children from faltering families, drugs, abuse and violent crime

Linda L. Creighton

On a raw, wintry night, Georgie Simmons waited at a hospital in Richmond, Va., for the birth of her first grandson. Nervously pacing the tiled halls, she watched the clock stretch to 4 a.m. Finally a doctor appeared, putting a gentle hand on Georgie's shoulder to guide her to a nursery. There, in an incubator, lay a baby boy, eyes open. Georgie leaned down and whispered, "Welcome to the world, my beautiful grandson." Crying softly, she turned to the doctor and said. "Now I need to say goodbye to my own baby."

Together, they walked down the hall to a darkened room where her 30-year-old daughter, Deborah, shot in the head hours before by a jealous boyfriend, lay comatose, breathing only with the help of a respirator. "You gave him to me," Georgie whispered to her youngest child, "and I'll take care of him." Then the machines that had sustained life long enough for the baby to be born were shut down, and Simmons was left alone with her grief and her grandson.

On that night, DeDongio Simmons became one of the 3.2 million children in the United States who live with their grandparents—an increase of almost 40 percent in the past decade, according to the U.S. Census Bureau. Those, at least, are the known figures; many who are now coming to grips with the trend fear that it could be three to four times worse than that. There is hardly a more frightening leading indicator of the devastation wrought by the nation's manifold social ills, and no class or race is immune. Some 4 percent of all white children in the United States and 12 percent of black children now live with grandparents. Of these, half the families have both grandparents and most of the rest live only with the grandmother. Beyond them are the millions of grandparents who have assumed important part-time child-rearing responsibilities because of the growth of single-parent households and the number of families where both parents work.

The elaborate system of child protection and support agencies throughout the land is more of a hindrance than a help to these beleaguered families. It is very difficult for grandparents to gain unchallenged permanent custody of threatened children. And the financial support they get is less than one third that available to foster families: The national average is $109 per child per month for grandparents who are sole care givers, compared with $371 per child per month for foster parents.

But nothing can really ease the unique burdens these grandparents bear. Many of them are racked by shame and guilt at the fact that their own children have failed as parents—and many blame themselves, wondering where they went wrong as parents. In order to provide safe and loving homes to their grandchildren, some must emotionally abandon their own abusive or drug-addicted children. The stresses are compounded by the fact that some of the children they inherit are among the most needy, most emotionally damaged and most angry in the nation.

There is not a town in America untouched by this version of the extended family. Richmond, capital of the Old Confederacy, is now a very typical home of the nation's new civil wars. It is just like many communities where drugs, crime and financial and emotional distress are splitting families apart and reorganizing them. In the first six months of this year, the city's Juvenile Court handled almost 700 custody cases involving children under 18—many of whom were eventually placed with grandparents.

Richmond's ad hoc way of coping with these problems is fairly typical of other communities. It is the diligence of Wanda Cooper, a resource coordinator at the Richmond Capital Area Agency on Aging, that has begun to convince city officials that special attention must be paid to these new grandparent-led families. In her work visiting homes of senior citizens on fixed incomes, Cooper began to notice more and more small children. She later learned that more than 600 people over 65 were receiving aid to dependent children—the basic welfare program. Now she sees her mission as helping grandparents become parents again and comforting them that they are not alone. It is a message many yearn to hear.

FOGLE FAMILY

Fighting the effects of the drug epidemic is heartbreaking work

Nothing devastated many American families in the 1980s with quite the same malign swiftness as the cocaine epidemic. Katherine Fogle and her two granddaughters are three of its victims. Ask Katherine why she is rearing the girls and she squares off and says, "Drugs." A life rooted in poverty and inner-city hardship has made this 55-year-old strong and unbending. But three of her five children have been stolen from her by drugs, AIDS and hard living, and she is determined her granddaughters will not also be claimed.

That is why, five years ago, Katherine made sure that Melba, then 9, and 2-year-old Katherine, or Kat, were taken

KATHERINE FOGLE, MELBA AND KAT

"I knew I had to take the girls when my daughter looked at me and said, 'Just let me be a junkie.' "

from their cocaine-addicted mother, Penny. For years, Katherine lived across the hall from Penny in a run-down apartment building in New York City and watched her daughter slide into the drug world. Katherine says she had repeatedly tried to intervene, reporting neglect to the child-protection agency, feeding the little girls, washing them and listening for their cries when their mother left them alone. "Melba used to go to school with her clothes turned inside out," says Katherine. "I found out it was because her clothes were so filthy, she was ashamed to wear them right." The animosity between mother and daughter grew until Katherine decided to move home – to Richmond.

But the nightmare only got worse. "I got a phone call from the babies' paternal grandmother, saying Melba was in the hospital. When I asked for what, she broke down and told me Melba, my 9-year-old grandbaby, had gonorrhea. She had been raped." Left by her mother with friends, Melba had been repeatedly assaulted by a young boy. Notified of the rape, the New York Child Welfare Administration placed the girls in protective custody and agreed to let Katherine take them back to Richmond. After nearly five years of extending probationary periods for Penny, authorities finally granted Katherine legal custody of the girls.

In the meantime, Penny had more children, at least two of whom were born drug-influenced. The Sheltering Arms Childrens Service, a private agency that places children throughout the city of New York, contacted Katherine and asked if she would take more of the children to raise. Suffering from diabetes and other health problems, Katherine had to say no. "I'm not physically or mentally capable of taking care of more children," says Katherine. "I held one in my arms and I was tempted. It rode my mind for a long time."

Katherine has refused contact with her daughter for almost five years. And Penny could not be reached for comment for this story. "I'd love to see her get things together, come and take the girls back, but it's just not going to happen," she says. Her eyes soften. "She was my baby, after all." Straightening, she puts her hands together in a firm clasp. "But I just can't think about it that way anymore. I feel like she's just someone I knew." Katherine has come to terms with her own feelings by comforting herself that she did her best as a parent under difficult circumstances: "I never neglected my children, I kept them together. How can I blame myself for what's happened to them?"

In their three-room apartment in a modest, quiet part of Richmond, Katherine holds tight rein on her granddaughters. The girls share a bunk-bedded room. Rising in 6 a.m. darkness, they are on the school bus by 6:45. After-school time and evenings are carefully monitored by Katherine; Melba chafes a bit at not being able to go with friends to places with which Katherine is unfamiliar or to hang out after school talking with friends. "Straight home," says Katherine firmly.

To supplement the $231 a month she receives in ADC benefits, Katherine takes care of a baby during the week. Money for anything extra is tight, and she worries that the girls are being deprived of little extras that give teenagers confidence. On Sundays the three dress in their very best and take a church bus across town to their Baptist church, where they greet everyone by first name and spend the better part of the service waving to friends.

Kat's dark beauty is accentuated by a dazzling grin. At 7, she says she would like to be a teacher when she grows up. She has little memory of her mother, but she listens carefully as Melba speaks of Penny, and it is clear she is curious. "All I know is she's using drugs and she won't take care of us," Kat asserts.

Melba, 14, has inherited her grandmother's grace, but she is a bit uncertain of herself, glancing down as she speaks quietly about her mother: "I love her, but I don't like the things she does. I wish we could be together all in a big house, but I know that probably won't be. I love my grandmother, but I love my mother still, too." Melba talks about the bad things in her life with a steady voice and gaze. "I talked once with a counselor about the rape. But it's just something I need to put behind me." Recently, Melba found letters she had written to her grandmother in Richmond from New York and said: "Mama, I had forgotten what I felt then. It makes me cry now."

Recently, as early evening light began to paint the Richmond streets, Melba walked with her grandmother and sister and giggled self-consciously as a car filled with friends beeped its horn. Safely home, she told her grandmother that night, as she does every night: "Thank you, Mama, for loving me."

MARY AND BRANDY

Some of the worst wounds are the emotional ones that take forever to heal

At 9, Brandy talks a good game. Chin thrust high and eyes narrowed, she does not hold conversations; she challenges. "Yeah, I've got two mothers," she declares. "It's called extra family." Shifting in her seat to face a visitor, she jumps ahead to unasked questions, always ready with a tough reason.

Brandy has had to be strong. She is one of the millions of emotionally scarred and struggling children who must face the fact that their parents couldn't – or wouldn't – care for them. At birth, her mother turned her over to 59-year-old Mary, Brandy's grandmother, and Brandy has lived with her since. Until last year, she thought she had an older sister who lived down the street. Then a neighbor told Brandy the "sister" was her mother. Brandy demanded to know the truth. "I called my daughter and we told her together," says Mary. "I told Brandy, your mother gave birth to you but I raised you. Brandy just sat there and said, 'Now I know.' "

The news had a devastating effect, one Brandy tried desperately to minimize but could not hide. At the William Byrd Community House, where Brandy had been in after-school programs, Elizabeth Moreau says Brandy began to show such hostility toward adults that she felt counseling was in order: "If asked to put away toys, for instance, she would yell, 'You can't make me do anything!' and run out of the room." Her grandmother says Brandy began for the first time to challenge her. "I needed help," says Mary. Finally, this fall, Brandy has begun counseling. "These kids need lots of special care," Mary notes.

This year, for the first time, Brandy gave out two cards on Mother's Day. But her contact with her mother is sporadic and her love and loyalties are defiantly with her grandmother. They asked that their last name not be used here, as Mary has not been able to adopt Brandy.

Bright and a good student, Brandy roller-skates with a hard passion that she hopes will land her in the professionals. But she has more hard roads to travel before she gets to the pros. Mary was diagnosed with emphysema four years ago, and has so far beaten the odds for survival. But she is increasingly tired, and Brandy senses this. "She's talked to me and said she's going to be all right," she says in clipped tones. "She's going to be here to see me get big." Roughly shoving back the bangs that are always in her eyes, she fixes a smile and looks away.

Then the girl with the perfect skin and long black lashes sums up her own soldierly view of life. "There is no such thing as a perfect family," she says. "The only thing I can tell you that's really perfect is heaven." But her time with her grandmother has enabled Brandy to survive and, now, to thrive, and that is a gift that even at 9 she understands. "There are probably some kids who don't feel special living with their grandparents," says Brandy. "I don't have to worry about that because I have a reputation for being very tough. I can beat up anyone in my class who doesn't believe me."

TAYLOR FAMILY

Violent crime turns the world upside down in every way

Until three years ago, Bertha Taylor and her husband, Robert, were living what they felt were their golden years. A respected schoolteacher recently remarried to a successful postal-service truck driver, Bertha was a grandparent for the first time. She and Robert got the usual thrills from visiting her son's 6-month-old baby, Evetta. Then, one night of violence turned their world upside down. Evetta's mother, on her way back from the grocery store, was raped and murdered. Devastated and unable to cope, Bertha's son asked his parents to take Evetta. "Our lives changed completely," says Bertha. "We got her on Saturday, and I thought, 'Lord, what am I going to do? I've got to go to work on Monday.' "

The Taylors became one of the hundreds of thousands of families whose lives were riven by violent crime that year in America. They were financially comfortable and did not have to struggle for the basic needs. "There were a lot of expenses, expenses you never plan for, and I don't know how people making less than our income manage," says Bertha. But there were other things precious to the Taylors—lingering dinners and evenings with friends—that were lost as a baby's schedule took over their lives. "I didn't even have time to go to the bathroom," says Bertha. "Your freedom is gone, your privacy is gone, and you're used to having it." Day care had to be found, and Bertha's work dealing with scores of children all day became exhausting when the end of the day meant a baby waiting for more attention. The marriage underwent stresses neither Bertha nor Robert had expected to con-

BERTHA TAYLOR AND EVETTA

"I believe the death of my daughter-in-law happened for a reason. I thank God for putting little Evetta into our lives. If she left us now, there would be a huge void."

front. "Hey, let me tell you, our sex life changed," she says. "You're tired and you've got no time."

With time, the Taylors adjusted and worked out ways of dealing with Evetta's needs. Robert rises early to dress and feed Evetta while Bertha organizes for her day of work at an elementary school. At night, Bertha prepares dinner, Robert does Evetta's bath and together they read stories to her.

Now 3, Evetta could be a star on a family sitcom, her affection and self-confidence bubbling irrepressibly. Though Bertha says she is not spoiling her, Evetta obviously thrives on her grandparents' doting. She is an addition to their relationship, they say, that they could not have foreseen. "If she left us now," says Bertha, "there would be a huge void."

Bertha's son has maintained close contact with the child, and he plans to marry again next year. Bertha says she wants whatever would make him happy, but she and her husband would like to adopt Evetta. As Bertha braids Evetta's hair, she talks of hoping to see "how this little child grows up and turns out." When night falls, a light comes on beside Evetta's bed in her pink satin and toy-filled bedroom. Her tiny voice chimes in with Bertha's schoolteacher singsong of night prayers, and she adds: "God bless all my mommies, and God bless all my daddies."

TOMAN FAMILY

The burden of poverty is worse when it has to be shared with the young

When the Richmond weather turns cold and bitter, 59-year-old May Toman and her two granddaughters pile blankets onto the worn living-room couch and chairs in their rundown row house. There, around an ancient gas burner, they sleep at night. The upstairs is without heat or electricity—and the leaky kitchen ceiling has already fallen in once. But May is afraid to complain for fear the landlord will raise her $110-a-month rent—a development that could leave them homeless. The girls—Shelly, 8 and Tabatha, 9—make do with thrift-shop clothing, and a steak dinner is a treat remembered for weeks.

Shelly's mother was only 17 when Shelly was born, and soon afterward she and Shelly's father began leaving the baby with friends or near friends, sometimes for long periods without contact. For May, the final straw came when Shelly was 2. May found her alone in the yard one evening. She took Shelly home and called the Richmond Department of Social Services. After an investigation, May got legal custody.

Several years later, May's son, Wayne, ran into marriage problems. When his wife left, he gave his daughter Tabatha, then 7, to his mother and his infant son to his mother-in-law. Tabatha's health had been neglected; her teeth were abscessed. May applied for custody and got it.

The small, frail-looking woman the girls call "Nanny" became their mother, making ends meet by taking in sewing and cutting corners. Up at 7, she walks the girls to school, then cleans house and grocery shops with food stamps. At 3, she meets the girls outside their brick school eight blocks away "so they know there's someone waiting." Together they walk home and do homework until dinner.

One of Shelly's favorite pastimes is studying her baby album, staring intently at the pictures of herself and her mother smiling from behind plastic pages. The album ends abruptly when she is 2, and Shelly turns back to the first page to begin again. She speaks of her Nanny with affection but longs for a reunion with her mother. "I want to live with my mama in a big house," says Shelly, "but I don't really think I'll ever get that." Shelly's mother lives across town and sees Shelly fairly often. But she has another child now, a year old, and says she does not have plans to take Shelly back soon.

Tabatha readily lays her feelings out for inspection: "Well, my daddy lives in the neighborhood, but he can't take me right now. My mama used to call, which made me cry terribly, but she hasn't called now in a long time. She said she was going to send me a birthday card but she never did." Small and polish-chipped fingernails tap determinedly on the table. "I want to stay right here with my Nanny. See, I love my Nanny."

Her father, Wayne, lives next door with two new children and their mother, and though in many ways he and Tabatha are close, he says, "I feel like Tabatha's better off with Nanny."

But Nanny, a high-school dropout with a good deal of worldly wisdom to dispense, is bone weary from trying to make it on $291 a month while solving the typical childhood squabbles and

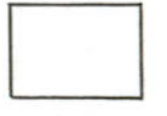

MAY TOMAN, SHELLY AND TABATHA

"I try to explain about our finances, but it's hard for the girls to understand. At least when they go to bed at night, they know they're going to wake up in the same place."

problems of two kids. Her grandchildren are among the 13.4 million American children who live in poverty—1 out of every 5 children.

May is weary, too, of trying to figure out why she and other grandmothers have ended up raising another generation. "Sometimes I feel like I really failed showing my children what kids mean. I raised mine by myself, and I hung on to them hard. Kids don't have a choice about coming into the world, but adults have choices."

May puts a fragile hand to her forehead. "I put my life on hold for 39 years, raising my own children," she says. "Now it's still on hold, but how much life do I have left? Sometimes I feel like I'm just cracking into sharp little pieces that fall to the ground." Then, running a hand through graying hair, she shrugs a smile and says, "Then I just pick up and go on out to do what I have to do."

FOGG FAMILY

Sometimes, the government child-protection system is no friend of kids

Three winters ago, Brian and Stella Fogg left their warm colonial home in Richmond to drive in a dangerous ice storm to South Carolina. Every half-hour they stopped to scrape the windshield, then slid back onto the interstate. Late in the afternoon they pulled into the parking lot of a K mart store in Beaufort. A 2-year-old boy and a 5-year-old girl climbed hesitantly from a waiting car, each clutching a small trash bag filled with personal possessions. They watched as Brian and Stella came to them with arms outstretched and said, "Now you can come home with Grandpa and Granny."

With that, Brian and Stella saved two of their grandchildren, Justine and Brian, from the system meant to protect them. After their parents' separation and inability to care for them, the children were taken into custody by authorities in South Carolina. Unknown to the grandparents, the children were then bounced from foster home to foster home for months, finally landing in a shelter for homeless children.

When the Foggs learned of the children's plight from their son, they immediately tracked down South Carolina child-care workers and asked for the grandchildren. Stella still flushes with anger when she remembers the months of futile pleading. Beaufort County officials have refused to comment on the case.

The Foggs were allowed to visit Justine and little Brian once, with a social worker present in a cramped office. Not having seen them in years, the children at first kept their distance from their grandparents. Finally, Justine walked over, put her hand on her grandmother's knee and said quietly, "I think I remember you now. You took me to see Santa once."

Within two weeks of the Foggs' visit, the South Carolina Department of Social Services, Beaufort County, without notifying Brian and Stella, had moved the children to yet another foster home, where Justine and Brian shared a bed with at least three other children. "I understand that the social services are swamped," says Stella. "But with us ready to take them, there was no reason for those kids to suffer any more."

Weeks passed, though, as the Foggs fought to get custody of the children. They thought they had reached a breakthrough four months into the process when they were told they could pick the children up. But they went before a judge who came to their hearing unprepared. He refused to recognize the Foggs' status and made a decision based on faulty information, granting custody to the Commonwealth of Virginia instead of the grandparents. "There is no continuity in the system, no one really looking out for these kids," says Brian. "We were the only ones trying to save them."

The Foggs thought they were prepared to deal with the kids' problems, but they were surprised at their own resentments. After rearing their four sons, they had settled into a new home, made good friends and were savoring each other's company. Now, with two small children, no financial help and no emotional support, they were not happy. They were angry at their son and his wife, and initially argued about whether taking the children was possible. Brian had suffered a bout with cancer, their home had to be remortgaged to support the children and their social life evaporated. "We asked ourselves, is this going to break up our 30-year marriage?" Stella notes. "But we felt we had no choice."

Their income was cut by a third because Brian reduced his business travel schedule as an equipment specialist for the postal service. They had to pay for extra medical insurance because no local doctor would accept Medicaid patients, and they struggled with the children's emotional scars. Justine's cries for help came when she threatened to burn down the house or rip down the curtains. "There were lots of good days," says Stella. "But never a day when we said we're happy to be doing this."

STELLA AND BRIAN FOGG WITH LITTLE BRIAN AND JUSTINE

"Social-service bureaucrats gave us no help at all. I called my congressman, everyone I could think of, and they still balked at giving us the children."

Three years later, the Foggs say it is never an easy life but they have come to terms with the sacrifices they've had to make and now feel their lives are richer. "Some of our friends say we're crazy, that they would never do this," says Stella. "But if we hadn't done this, in 15 years there might have been a knock on our front door and a young man standing there saying, 'I'm your grandson. Where were you when I needed you, when I lay in bed at night crying for someone to help me?' " The Foggs say that if their son and daughter-in-law's situation does not change soon, they want to adopt Brian and Justine.

On a recent Sunday afternoon, the fireplace in the Foggs' living room snapped with dry logs. Stella brought in a tray filled with tea and hot chocolate, and in her still strong Scottish burr called the kids in from the yard. Racing each other through the leaves, Justine and Brian bounded up the stairs. With small, dirt-dusted hands, they lifted mugs to their lips and stuffed cookies in their mouths. But when Justine talked about what family means and what it is like to live with grandparents, her childishness fell away. "The foster homes were really bad. Mostly the people weren't mean but they didn't like me. And I didn't understand that my parents didn't take care of me. I just thought I got taken away."

Staring at a place on the table, she rested her head in her hand for a moment, then looked up and with an intensity beyond her 8 years said: "At first when I came here to live, I felt kind of sad. I didn't know them. But they act like another kind of parent. They're like they had me out of their own stomachs."

SEXTON FAMILY

After a child has been neglected, the best kind of love is the simple kind

Several weeks ago, 4-year-old James came home from kindergarten crying hysterically. A boy in his class had been given a BB gun, and in a moment of childish bravado told James that he was coming to his house to shoot his parents. Perhaps another 4-year-old boy might have met the challenge with a "Yeah? I'll shoot yours back." But for James, the idea of losing parents is no empty threat. He was taken from his biological parents after he was physically abused. Now James's grandparents, Charlotte and Eddie Sexton, are his parents, and he is afraid of losing them.

From the beginning, say the Sextons, they were worried about the care of James. Neighbors had complained about the baby's treatment. After James's parents showed up at the Sextons' house one afternoon with year-old baby James, asking to leave him, the Sextons readily consented. Desperate to protect the child, Charlotte and Eddie called the Richmond Department of Social Services and, eventually, James was awarded to them on a finding of neglect.

James lived with the Sextons for a year, and then his parents petitioned the court, showing proof of a job and a new apartment. This time the judge ordered James returned to his parents. "It really looked like they had turned around, so how can you keep James from them?" says Charlotte now. "But we felt like our hearts had been ripped out."

CHARLOTTE AND EDDIE SEXTON WITH JAMES

"You have to earn the right to be called Mommy or Daddy. We're trying to. James knows when he's with us, we won't let anyone else hurt him."

Within a short period, the daughter's husband was jailed for four months in the Richmond City Jail for petit larceny. Almost a year to the day that James was returned to his parents, a social worker called the Sextons to say that he was in a hospital emergency room, with head injuries from a belt buckle. Could they please come to get James?

James has been with the Sextons now for over a year, and they want very much to keep him. "Every child has the birthright to be with his mother and father," says Charlotte. "But sometimes, with some parents, someone has to say 'Enough.' We have reached that point."

"Nobody hands you a pamphlet and says, 'Here, this is what you do when your kid dumps his child,' " says Charlotte. But that didn't stop the Sextons from becoming attached to James. "At first you build a wall," she says. "The longer he's with you, the wall starts to fall." They found free counseling to help deal with James's tantrums and chair throwing, in the process refining their parenting style. "I never felt I had to tell my kids I loved them, I thought they knew," says Charlotte. "With James, we had to start over, like with a baby, nurturing and showing him how much we cared." Now, their parenting combines some pretty tough old-fashioned strictness with newly learned techniques like "time out" to cope with his outbursts.

Charlotte is only 45, and her homespun temperament seems perfect for raising children. Her husband, Eddie, is partial to plaid shirts that do not quite conceal a burly physique kept strong by his work in a tractor-trailer-tire shop, and though his speech is rare, it is sharp and funny. On an annual income of just over $20,000 they feel financially lucky, treating James to burgers or subs occasionally and making Christmas special. "There are times we rob Peter to pay Paul," says Eddie. "But we're OK. Sometimes at the end of the month we actually have 30 or 40 dollars left in the account."

Although James has not yet spoken about his past, he talked for the first time this month about his little brother and sister, a 9-month-old and a 2-year-old still living with his parents. Perhaps he wishes they could be with him.

WHAT GRANDPARENTS WANT

Surer ways to save kids

If grandparents who have become parents again could wave a magic wand, at the top of their wish list would be a liberalization of the laws regulating child custody. Most feel that parental rights are given too much weight in clear-cut cases when custody should be changed. The number of times parents can appeal to get children back should be limited, they say, and it should be possible for grandparents to apply for adoption earlier.

Financially, grandparents suffer an enormous burden, one that might be relieved if resources available to them were more in line with those offered to foster parents. Some states have created "kinship care" programs under which relatives caring for children receive the same amounts as foster parents. Under current rules, though, grandparents are only eligible for such benefits if they give custody of the children to the state. In effect, this makes the grandparents "foster parents" of their own grandchildren, and most grandparents are reluctant to cede their authority to the government. In Los Angeles this month, a child whose aunt was forced to return him to the foster-care system because of financial difficulties was beaten to death in a foster home.

Nationally, there are more than 150 support groups for grandparents. If you want help organizing such a group or finding out what your rights are, here are some organizations that can help:

- GAP: Grandparents as Parents. Sylvie de Toledo, Psychiatric Clinic for Youth, 2801 Atlantic Avenue, Long Beach, CA 90801, (213) 595-3151.
- Grandparents Raising Grandchildren. Barbara Kirkland, P.O. Box 104, Colleyville, TX 76034, (817) 577-0435.
- Second Time Around Parents. Michele Daly, Family and Community Services of Delaware County, 100 W. Front Street, Media, PA 19063, (215) 566-7540.

EPILOGUE

It has been nearly a year since the murder of Georgie Simmons's daughter Deborah. For Georgie and her grandson, life has gone on. These days, DeDongio is a curly-topped smiler who lights up at the sound of his grandmother's voice. He will be walking soon. There is not much chance he will ever get to know his father, who has been convicted and sentenced to life plus 36 years for killing Deborah. Georgie says justice was done, but not for DeDongio.

This season is excruciating because for Georgie it brings back memories of last year's celebrations with her pregnant daughter, especially how Deborah enjoyed eating extra pie at Thanksgiving. And Georgie remembers how excited Deborah was at Christmas when she got a new sweater. This year, Georgie has not yet decorated her house the way she has just after Thanksgivings in times past. But she says she will soon, for DeDongio.

In the meantime, they make regular pilgrimages to Mount Calvary Cemetery in Richmond, where Deborah is buried. Last month, as darkness fell, Georgie wrapped her grandson tightly in a blanket to fight the wind and they made their way across the rows of modest headstones. They stopped at a spot marked by wilted flowers and, as she shifted the blanket, DeDongio's tiny face peeked into the cold. "This is your mama's place," Georgie said softly as the boy gazed up at her. Reaching into her pocket, she took out a small pair of booties and bent to lay them on the grave. "I'm sorry I haven't got you a stone yet, my baby, but I needed the money for DeDongio." For a moment she stood quite still. Then the baby began to cry, and Georgie bundled him up thoroughly again. With one last glance back, she turned into the wind to carry her grandson home.

the MIRACLE OF RESILIENCY

DAVID GELMAN

A prominent child psychiatrist, E. James Anthony, once proposed this analogy: there are three dolls, one made of glass, the second of plastic, the third of steel. Struck with a hammer, the glass doll shatters; the plastic doll is scarred. But the steel doll proves invulnerable, reacting only with a metallic ping.

In life, no one is unbreakable. But child-health specialists know there are sharp differences in the way children bear up under stress. In the aftermath of divorce or physical abuse, for instance, some are apt to become nervous and withdrawn; some may be illness-prone and slow to develop. But there are also so-called resilient children who shrug off the hammer blows and go on to highly productive lives. The same small miracle of resiliency has been found under even the most harrowing conditions—in Cambodian refugee camps, in crack-ridden Chicago housing projects. Doctors repeatedly encounter the phenomenon: the one child in a large, benighted brood of five or six who seems able to take adversity in stride. "There are kids in families from very adverse situations who really do beautifully, and seem to rise to the top of their potential, even with everything else working against them," says Dr. W. Thomas Boyce, director of the division of behavioral and developmental pediatrics at the University of California, San Francisco. "Nothing touches them; they thrive no matter what."

There are sharp differences in the way children bear up under stress

Something, clearly, has gone right with these children, but what? Researchers habitually have come at the issue the other way around. The preponderance of the literature has to do with why children fail, fall ill, turn delinquent. Only recently, doctors realized they were neglecting the equally important question of why some children *don't* get sick. Instead of working backward from failure, they decided, there might be as much or more to be learned from studying the secrets of success. In the course of looking at such "risk factors" as poverty, physical impairment or abusive parents, they gradually became aware that there were also "protective factors" that served as buffers against the risks. If those could be identified, the reasoning went, they might help develop interventions that could change the destiny of more vulnerable children.

At the same time, the recognition that many children have these built-in defenses has plunged resiliency research into political controversy. "There is a danger among certain groups who advocate nonfederal involvement in assistance to children," says Duke University professor Neil Boothby, a child psychologist who has studied children in war zones. "They use it to blame people who don't move out of poverty. Internationally, the whole notion of resiliency has been used as an excuse not to do anything."

The quest to identify protective factors has produced an eager burst of studies in the past 10 or 15 years, with new publications tumbling off the presses every month. Although the studies so far offer no startling insights, they are providing fresh perspectives on how nature and nurture intertwine in childhood development. One of the prime protective factors, for example, is a matter of genetic luck of the draw: a child born with an easygoing disposition invariably handles stress better than one with a nervous, overreactive temperament. But even highly reactive children can acquire resilience if they have a consistent, stabilizing element in their young lives—something like an attentive parent or mentor.

The most dramatic evidence on that score comes not from humans but from their more researchable cousins, the apes. In one five-year-long study, primate researcher Stephen Suomi has shown that by putting infant monkeys in the care of supportive mothers, he could virtually turn their lives around. Suomi, who heads the Laboratory of Comparative Ethology at the National Institute of Child Health and Human Development, has been comparing "vulnerable" and "invulnerable" monkeys to see if there are useful nurturing approaches to be learned. Differences of temperament can be spotted in monkeys before they're a week old. Like their human counterparts, vulnerable monkey infants show measurable increases in heart rate and stress-hormone production in response to threat situations. "You see a fairly consistent pattern of physiological arousal, and also major behavioral differences," says Suomi. "Parallel patterns have been found in human-developmental labs, so we feel we're looking at the same phenomena."

Left alone in a regular troop, these high-strung infants grow up to be marginal figures in their troops. But by putting them in the care of particularly loving, attentive foster mothers within their first four days of life, Suomi turns the timid monkeys into social lions. Within two months, they become bold and outgoing. Males in the species Suomi has been working with normally leave their native troop at puberty and eventually work their way into a new troop. The nervous, vulnerable individuals usually are the last to leave home. But after being "cross-fostered" to loving mothers, they develop enough confidence so that they're first to leave.

Once on their own, monkeys have complicated (but somehow familiar) patterns of alliances. Their status often depends on whom they know and to whom they're related. In squabbles, they quickly generate support among friends and family members. The cross-fostered monkeys grow very adept at recruiting that kind of support. It's a knack they somehow get through interaction with their foster mothers, in which they evidently pick up coping styles as well as information. "It's essentially a social-learning phenomenon," says Suomi. "I would argue that's what's going on at the human level, too. Evidently, you can learn styles in addition to specific information."

In the long run, the vulnerable infants not only were turned around to normality, they often rose to the top of their hierarchies; they became community leaders. Boyce notes there are significant "commonalities" between Suomi's findings and studies of vulnerable children. "The implications are that vulnerable children, if placed in the right social environment, might become extraordinarily productive and competent adult individuals," he says.

Children, of course, can't be fostered off to new parents or social conditions as readily as monkeys. Most resiliency research is based on children who have not had such interventions in their lives. Nevertheless, some of the findings are revealing. One of the definitive studies was conducted by Emmy E. Werner, a professor of human development at the University of California, Davis, and Ruth S. Smith, a clinical psychologist on the Hawaiian island of Kauai. Together, they followed 698 children, all descendants of Kauaiian plantation workers, from their birth (in 1955) up to their early 30s. About half the children grew up in poverty; one in six had physical or intellectual handicaps diagnosed between birth and age 2. Of the 225 designated as high risk, two thirds had developed serious learning or behavior problems within their first decade of life. By 18 they had delinquency records, mental-health problems or teenage pregnancies. "Yet one out of three," Werner and Smith noted, "grew into competent young adults who loved well, worked well, played well and expected well."

Some of the protective factors the two psychologists identified underscore the nature-nurture connection. Like other researchers, they found that children who started out with robust, sunny personalities were often twice lucky: not only were they better equipped to cope with life to begin with, but their winning ways made them immediately lovable. In effect, the "nicer" the children, the more readily they won affection—both nature and nurture smiled upon them. There were also other important resiliency factors, including self-esteem and a strong sense of identity. Boyce says he encounters some children who even at 2 or 3 have a sense of "presence" and independence that seem to prefigure success. "It's as if these kids have had the 'Who am I' questions answered for them," he says.

Researchers can spot differences of temperament in monkeys before they're a week old

One of the more intriguing findings of the Kauai research was that resilient children were likely to have characteristics of both sexes. Boys and girls in the study tended to be outgoing and autonomous, in the male fashion, but also nurturant and emotionally sensitive, like females. "It's a little similar to what we find in creative children," observes Werner. Some other key factors were inherent in the children's surroundings rather than their personalities. It helped to have a readily available support network of grandparents, neighbors or relatives. Others note that for children anywhere, it doesn't hurt at all to be born to well-off parents. "The advantage of middle-class life is there's a safety net," says Arnold Sameroff, a developmental psychologist at Brown University's Bradley Hospital. "If you screw up, there's someone to bail you out."

In most cases, resilient children have "clusters" of protective factors, not just one or two. But the sine qua non, according to Werner, is a "basic, trusting relationship" with an adult. In all the clusters in the Kauai study, "there is not one that didn't include that one good relationship, whether with a parent, grandparent, older sibling, teacher or mentor—someone consistent enough in that person's life to say, 'You count,' and that sort of begins to radiate other support in their lives." Even children of abusive or schizophrenic parents may prove resilient if they have had at least one caring adult looking out for them—someone, as Tom Boyce says, "who serves as a kind of beacon presence in their lives."

Such relationships do the most good when they are lasting. There is no lasting guarantee for resiliency itself, which is subject to change, depending on what sort of ups and downs people encounter. Children's ability to cope often improves naturally as they develop and gain experience, although it may decline after a setback in school or at home. Werner notes that around half the vulnerable children in the Kauai study had shaken off their previous problems by the time they reached their late 20s or early 30s. "In the long-term view, more people come through in spite of circumstances. There is an amazing amount of recovery, if you don't focus on one particular time when things are falling apart."

Ironically, this "self-righting" tendency has made the resiliency issue something of a political football. Conservatives have seized on the research to bolster their case against further social spending. "It's the politics of 'It's all within the kid'," says Lisbeth Schorr, a lecturer in social medicine at Harvard Medical School whose book, "Within Our Reach: Breaking the Cycle of Disadvantage," has had a wide impact in the field. "The conservative argument against interventions like Operation Head Start and family-support programs is that if these inner-city kids and families just showed a little grit they would pull themselves up by their own bootstraps. But people working on resilience are aware that when it comes to environments like the inner city, it really doesn't make a lot of sense to talk about what's intrinsic to the kids, because the environment is so overwhelming."

There are kids from adverse situations who do beautifully and seem to rise to their potential

So overwhelming, indeed, that some researchers voice serious doubts over how much change can be brought about in multiple-risk children. Brown's Sameroff, who has been dealing with poor inner-city black and white families in Rochester, N.Y., says the experience has left him "more realistic" about what is possible. "Interventions are important if we can target one or two things wrong with a child. So you provide psychotherapy or extra help in the classroom, then there's a lot better chance." But the children he deals with usually have much more than that going against them—not only poverty but large families, absent fathers, drug-ridden neighborhoods and so on. "We find the more risk factors the worse the outcome," says Sameroff. "With eight or nine, *nobody* does well. For the majority of these children, it's going to involve changing the whole circumstance in which they are raised."

Others are expressing their own reservations, as the first rush of enthusiasm in resiliency research cools somewhat. "A lot of the early intervention procedures that don't follow through have been oversold," says Emmy Werner. "Not everyone benefited equally from such programs as Head Start." Yet, according to child-development specialists, only a third of high-risk children are able to pull through relatively unaided by such interventions. Says Werner: "At least the high-risk children should be guaranteed basic health and social programs."

Interestingly, when Suomi separates his vulnerable monkeys from their foster mothers at 7 months—around the same time that mothers in the wild go off to breed, leaving their young behind—the genes reassert themselves, and the monkeys revert to fearful behavior. According to Suomi, they do recover again when the mothers return and their new coping skills seem to stay with them. Yet their experience underscores the frailty of change. Boyce, an admirer of Suomi's work, acknowledges that the question of how lasting the effects of early interventions are remains open. But, he adds, programs like Head Start continue to reverberate as much as 15 years later, with reportedly higher school-completion rates and lower rates of delinquency and teen pregnancies.

Boyce recalls that years ago, when he was at the University of North Carolina, he dealt with an 8-year-old child from an impoverished, rural black family, who had been abandoned by his mother. The boy also had "prune-belly syndrome," an anomaly of the abdominal musculature that left him with significant kidney and urinary problems, requiring extensive surgery. But he also had two doting grandparents who had raised him from infancy. They showered him with love and unfailingly accompanied him on his hospital visits. Despite his physical problems and loss of a mother, the boy managed to perform "superbly" in school. By the age of 10, when Boyce last saw him, he was "thriving."

Children may not be as manageable or resilient as laboratory monkeys. If anything, they are more susceptible in the early years. But with the right help at the right time, they can overcome almost anything. "Extreme adversity can have devastating effects on development," says psychologist Ann Masten, who did some of the groundbreaking work in the resiliency field with her University of Minnesota colleague Norman Garmezy. "But our species has an enormous capacity for recovery. Children living in a hostile caregiving environment have great difficulty, but a lot of ability to recover to better functioning if they're given a chance. That's a very important message from the resiliency literature." Unfortunately, the message may not be getting through to the people who can provide that chance.

Bright Lights, Big Mystery

Near-death experiences have become a cottage industry—but how real are they?

JAMES MAURO

"No wonder. No wonder. No wonder."

It's hard, talking to Barbara Harris, not to believe in near-death experiences. Even though she speaks of a Star Wars-like "force" pervading her DNA; even though she describes encountering "a cloud of bubbles, each one representing a different moment of my life"; even though she says her experience led her to a realization about herself that she never had before.

"No wonder I am the way I am," she gasps.

Barbara Harris is like the eight million other Americans who, according to a recent poll by George Gallup, Jr., claim to have had a near-death experience (NDE). They have all had visions of lights, tunnels, and dead relatives greeting them and taking them to a place of beauty, warmth, and peace. And they all say they have been profoundly changed by the experience.

Despite literally thousands of stories such as Harris's, however, science is not yet a true believer: There exists no absolute proof that such experiences are more than the product of fancy, fear, or fever. Indeed, almost all of the research to date relies upon anecdotes reported by "NDErs" rather than empirical corroboration of the events.

Stories of an afterlife have been captivating people ever since the sixth century, when Pope Gregory the Great wrote *Dialogues*, a collection of wonder-tales that included reports of return from death. Although each has the earmarks of a morality tale—with visions of hell instead of heaven—many also contain such elements of modern NDEs as "shining" angels and personality transformations.

But it wasn't until 1975, when psychiatrist Raymond Moody, M.D., wrote a book called *Life After Life*, that fascination with the subject became widespread. Coining the phrase "near-death experience," Moody reported story after story about the same, now-familiar encounter. The book intrigued a cross-section of curious individuals who begged to know more about what to expect when they die.

Fifteen years later, there are no new answers, but there *is* a spate of new books containing, mostly, more anecdotes. There is also a growing acceptance by the scientific community that something may be happening to these eight million people. Regardless of whether they are "meeting God" or simply hallucinating, NDErs routinely report that they have undergone a personality transformation—usually in the form of decreased anxiety about death, less concern with material matters, and a general feeling of peace about their lives.

It is this phenomenon that has finally attracted researchers. Rather than attempting to prove the existence of an afterlife, they have begun to study NDEs in order to learn more about brains, minds, and that elusive quality called well-being. If NDErs have truly benefited from their experience, perhaps they have something to teach us that might advance therapeutic

"There were people I knew who were lit from within. I felt myself pulled toward this bright light. It was so forceful, warm and loving. I never felt anything so peaceful and beautiful."

methods for all kinds of problems—from the dilemmas of suicidal patients to the enduring pain of those who have been abused as children. And possibly, along the way, we just might learn something about what happens when we die.

A Real "Event" or Mass Hysteria?

What exactly constitutes a near-death experience? By examining thousands of reports, researchers such as Seattle pediatrician Melvin Morse, M.D., have identified the common elements that define the experience. In his book, *Transformed by the Light* (Villard; 1992), he lists nine traits that generally characterize a "full-blown" NDE:

1) A sense of being dead: the sudden awareness that one has had a "fatal" accident or not survived an operation.

2) Peace and painlessness: a feeling that the ties that bind one to the world have been cut.

3) An out-of-body experience: the sensation of peering down on one's body and perhaps seeing the doctors and nurses trying to resuscitate.

4) Tunnel experience: the sense of moving up or through a narrow passageway.

5) People of Light: being met at the end of the tunnel by others who are "glowing."

6) A Being of Light: the presence of a God-like figure or a force of some kind.

7) Life review: being shown one's life by the Being of Light.

8) Reluctance to return: the feeling of being comfortable and surrounded by the Light, often described as "pure love."

9) Personality transformation: a psychological change involving loss of the fear of death, greater spiritualism, a sense of "connectedness" with the Earth, and greater zest for life.

Although Morse's compilation of characteristics is drawn from the self-reports of NDErs, that doesn't mean there's nothing to them. In fact, evidence of their validity may be found in the startling consistency of such reports:

"I felt myself floating up, out of my bed. Looking down, I could see myself lying there, motionless."

"I moved through something dark and churning. I guess you could call it a tunnel, or a passageway."

"Suddenly there were people around me, some I knew, who were lit from within. I turned and felt myself pulled toward this bright light. It was so forceful, warm and loving. I never felt anything so peaceful and beautiful."

Yet there are enough variations to lead critics to discount NDEs as mere hallucinations. Morse relates the following story of a 45-year-old Midwestern teacher:

"I entered into a dark tunnel and suddenly I was in a place filled up with love and a beautiful, bright light. The place seemed holy. My father, who had died two years earlier, was there, as were my grandparents. Everyone was happy to see me, but my father told me it was not my time and I would be going back. Just as I turned to go, I caught sight of Elvis! He was standing in this place of intense bright light. He just came over to me, took my hand and said: 'Hi Bev, do you remember me?'."

If such experiences are real and not hallucinations, critics argue, why does Elvis appear in the place commonly inhabited by God? And what about those who see Jesus? Or Buddha? Or children who report seeing pets or parents not yet dead?

Simply stated, there are common elements shared by all NDErs. These seem to be intrinsic to the experience, and usually include the sense of leaving one's body, of traveling through a tunnel, and of seeing a bright light. Along with this so-called core experience come secondary embellishments, which account for the differences in NDE reports. The descriptions of various details and people are more personal aspects of NDEs, which are derived from an individual's life course and cultural background—what they have learned from their religious practices and what their image is of God and heaven.

To some researchers, the symbols serve to help make sense of the experience. Whereas a bright white light and a feeling of warmth and peace might not fully convey the notion that one has "died," the point is driven home in greetings by dead relatives or pets, as well as a personification of God as Buddha or Jesus—even Elvis Presley. For the Midwestern teacher, Elvis may have inspired the same awe in her life that she felt when she met the Light.

That still leaves open the question whether NDEs are a uniquely Western experience. Does a woman from Boise, say, have the same type of experience as an African farmer? Morse cites the work of Dr. Nsama Mumbwe of the University of Zambia. The African physician wondered whether NDEs were strictly an American phenomenon, and, if not, how the accounts of Third World subjects would differ from those of Westerners.

Studying 15 NDErs in Lusaka, Zambia, Mumbwe found that all had had the same core experience as those in other parts of the world.

That isn't to say there aren't cultural differences:

- Many of the Africans interpreted the event as somewhat evil; half thought the experience signified that they were somehow "bewitched." Another called it a "bad omen."
- Among 400 Japanese NDErs, many reported seeing long, dark rivers and beautiful flowers, two common symbols that frequently appear as images in Japanese art.
- East Indians sometimes see heaven as a giant bureaucracy, and frequently report being sent back because of clerical errors!
- Americans and English say they are sent back for love or to perform a job.
- Natives of Micronesia often see heaven as similar to a large, brightly lit American city with loud, noisy cars and tall buildings.

To Morse and other investigators, these experiences are not as different as they seem. It is merely the individual *interpretations* that differ. Many report that their

NDEs are, like dreams, "difficult to put into words." That forces them to borrow images from personal experience and apply them to their NDE. And the discrepancies found in reports do not signify mass hysteria or hallucinations. On the contrary, the similarities across a wide variety of cultures, ages, and religions support the idea that being near death not only triggers a specific type of experience, but that the experience is "transcendental"—that there is entry into another dimension of being.

A Trip of the Brain or a Journey of the Mind?

There has long been a "medical-school bias"—as Morse puts it—against near-death experiences. Dismissed for years as hallucinations, patients' stories were routinely ignored by their doctors, and grant money for research has been scarce.

Slowly, however, the once-taboo subject is coming under the neuropsychiatric microscope. Decades ago, before the advent of modern neuroscience, the famous Canadian neurosurgeon Wilder Penfield identified an area of the brain that gives rise to near-death experiences. When he electrically stimulated certain sites of the temporal lobe, patients reported retrieving vivid memories as if they were actually "seeing" them. The findings prompted some researchers to search for a neurophysical explanation for NDEs—as some episode of temporal-lobe dysfunction. The implication of this line of investigation is that NDEs take place entirely within the brain, courtesy of some chemical shift or misfiring neuron.

Researchers have pursued endorphins as a cause of the euphoria and visions of heaven; compression of the optic nerve by lack of oxygen as a cause of the tunnel image; and, most recently, the neurotransmitter serotonin, putatively released by the stress of dying, to explain the typical NDE phenomena. But a direct cause-and-effect relationship has yet to be established.

What *is* known is that people who have a large number of paranormal experiences, such as NDEs, also have a higher incidence of anomalous temporal-lobe functioning. "Not abnormal," insists Vernon Neppe, M.D., director of the division of neuropsychiatry at the University of Washington, who developed a set of questions designed to stimulate the temporal lobe of the brain. "Just different. If you stimulate certain areas of the temporal lobe, you'll get certain reactions. And those subjects with some paranormal experience will react differently."

The finding suggests that some people have a pattern of brain functioning that allows them to experience NDEs. But it does not indicate whether or not these experiences are transcendental—that is, whether the event is a journey into afterlife or a blip in the firing of brain cells. If a spiritual journey occurs entirely in the brain, however, does that make it any less a transformative phenomenon?

Other researchers have attempted to explore whether actually being near death is essential to experience an NDE. Ian Stevenson, M.D., and Justine Owens, Ph.D., of the University of Virginia's Institute for Personality Studies, wondered whether some of those reporting NDEs—and all of their characteristic traits—were not actually near death at the time of their experience, but simply *believed* they were? Surely, they argued, someone who wasn't really dying couldn't transcend into an afterlife, and therefore their experience couldn't be "real."

Stevenson studied the medical records of 40 patients who had reported NDEs, and found that more than half were not close to death at all. He suggested that "the belief of being about to die had been the principal precipitant of their experiences"(*Omega*, Vol. 20, 1989–90). In other words, a psychological reaction to trauma—what the teams calls "fear-death"—had sparked their NDE.

But Stevenson and Owens didn't stop there. They then interviewed 58 NDErs—30 of whom (52 percent) had not actually been near death (*Lancet*; Vol. 336). What they found startled them: A significantly greater number of patients who actually *were* near death reported elements of the core experience—including the bright light—than those who were not. Rather than supporting the psychological explanation, the results actually gave support to the transcendental interpretation. Those who were in a physical state wherein they might transcend into death appeared to do so; the others did not.

Still, whether near-death experiences are neurochemically induced hallucinations, psychological reactions to fear, or transcendental encounters may be moot. As one researcher puts it, in our search for firm answers we may be "overestimating the tether of mind to body."

Encounter-Prone Personalities

For Psychologist Kenneth Ring, Ph.D., author of *The Omega Project* (Morrow, 1992), research into NDEs began with a very down-to-earth approach. He wanted to determine whether there are any dis-

NDEs—Real or Imagined?

"I was on the operating table when all of a sudden I felt myself being pulled upward, slowly at first, then faster and faster. Suddenly I was in a black tunnel, and at the end was a light. As I got closer to it, it got brighter and brighter. It wasn't like any light I could describe to you. It was beautiful.

When I was almost at the end, the light was so bright it surrounded me and filled me with a total love and joy. I felt intensely pure, calm, and reassured. I just wanted to stay there forever."

"I was floating up near the ceiling and saw myself on my bed. I felt no pain, like an observer between two worlds. In time it seemed as though the ceiling was paved with clouds, and the air seemed sprinkled with gold dust.

It became very bright, and I found myself standing at the entrance to a very long canopy made of blue and silver rays. A powerful light was at the other end, and I felt other presences who were joyous with my coming. Then a doctor started banging on my chest and I opened my eyes."

—From Transformed by the Light *(Villard), copyright © 1992 by Melvin Morse, M.D.*

tinguishing features between people who remember and report paranormal encounters and those who do not.

He quickly discovered an extraordinary similarity in the backgrounds of those who had near-death experiences. There was, he says, "a consistent tendency for them to report a greater incidence of childhood abuse and trauma."

One common response to such trauma is dissociation—a psychological phenomenon in which a person separates from a reality that is too painful to process by conscious means, and retreats into a world of their own invention.

In fact, Ring acknowledges that those with histories of child abuse score higher on measures of dissociation, or even develop serious dissociative disorders such as multiple personality. (He cites reports of UFO abductions as possible examples of children dissociating, or "tuning out" from the reality of being abducted by a stranger and forced into an unfamiliar car.)

He sugggests that NDErs are dissociating from the trauma of being near death. But that, for him, does not invalidate the spiritual nature of the experience. Yes, these people are dissociating, he acknowledges, but he sees it as a pathway to another dimension.

"The ability to dissociate makes you more receptive to alternate realities," he explains. "You are dissociating in response to trauma, so you are more likely to register an NDE as a conscious event." By developing a dissociative response style as a psychological defense, you are more able to tune into other realities as well—becoming what Ring calls "an encounter-prone personality."

And that leads back to Barbara Harris, who had her own NDE—actually two experiences within a week—in 1975. A fall in a swimming pool exacerbated her congenital sclerosis and eventually left her in traction, lying immobile in a therapeutic contraption called a circle bed. When a breathing machine failed to allow her to exhale, Harris felt herself "being blown up like a balloon, and then...total blackness.

"Soon, I felt hands and arms around me, and then my grandmother's chest. I experienced myself through my grandmother. It was so much more than words; there was a perfect sharing between the two of us. The darkness was churning and I felt my hands expanding. I could hear a low, droning noise. All of a sudden I was back in my own body."

Afterward, regaining consciousness, she didn't tell anyone about her experience because, she says, "I didn't want to be sedated."

Her second experience was more intense. "I felt myself separating again; saw myself, as if in a bubble. I was one-year-old, in my crib, crying. I kept looking back and forth between my real self lying in bed and as this baby. And the second or third time I turned around, I saw this God-force, if you want to call it that. It moved through me, pervaded my DNA, held me up.

"As soon as I acknowledged it, we moved toward the baby, and it was as though it became part of a cloud of bubbles—each one being a different moment in my life. I relived all the abuse I suffered as a child at the hands of my mother. But I felt detached, the way I did as a kid, and I felt a realization of something I didn't know before. All my adult life I felt like a piece of dirt on somebody else's shoe, and I never knew why. And yet, re-experiencing all of those moments, I realized I had chosen to believe I was bad. I understood why I always felt so worthless.

"And my first thought, watching all this abuse, was, No wonder I am the way I am."

Harris was transformed by her experience: She speaks of acquiring a "general realization about the way everything works." Her experience led her, fittingly, to become a respiratory therapist, and to work with dying patients. She feels she may indeed have something to offer others who are suffering without knowing why.

Yet the question remains: Was Harris, in the face of great pain and trauma, merely dissociating from reality and into a world of her own invention, the way she admits doing as a child in the face of her mother's abuse? Does the coupling effect—her linking of her NDE and the recollection of abuse—reveal a pattern of dissociation, of simply tuning out reality? Or, as she puts it, did her earlier experience with dissociation leave her with a special "pathway" or channel through which she was able to reach such other-worldly levels?

"Yes, I am dissociating," she admits, "but I am also out of my body and I am someplace else. My real separation and tuning out was my misery all my life. When I had my NDE, it was easier for me to slip out of my body because *I already knew how.* The ability was there to let go. And what I experienced was a sense of who I really am—the person I would have been had I not been abused. I had forgotten her, the part of me that remained intact. The part of me that is the spark of God."

Like Ring and other investigators, Harris believes that childhood dissociation may provide the adult with a kind of "road map" to be followed later, a receptiveness to paranormal experiences. As proof that she did indeed leave her body, she recalls overhearing a nurse's conversation that in fact took place in another room—while she was confined to her circle bed. The conversation was later confirmed by those present.

The Transformative Question

Of all aspects of near-death experiences, personality change is the one most scrutinized for insight into what is actually occurring. It attracts researchers of all persuasions. There are those who feel that the only "real" NDE is one that transforms its subjects. And there are others who are concerned merely with what can be learned from those transformations.

"The public wants to know where they go when they die," contends John Sappington, M.D., professor of psychology at Augusta (Georgia) College. "As scientists, we can't answer that question. Nevertheless, there are ways to study NDErs as a group, things we can learn from them and possibly apply to a therapeutic situation which would benefit a client."

For Sappington and others, the issue is not whether the person is actually meeting God, but why NDErs routinely seem better adjusted, more at peace and content with themselves and the world after their experience. Disregarding, for the time being at least, how they got that way, and focusing on the changes themselves, psychologists would like to borrow this new-found sense of well-being and utilize it in therapy.

Reports are highly consistent and common: "I understand things so much more" and "My senses all seem heightened." Subjects claim "sudden knowledge and comprehension of complex mathematical theorems." Psychologist Ring has identified a consistent set of value and belief changes. They include:

- a greater appreciation for life
- higher self-esteem
- greater compassion for others
- a heightened sense of purpose and self-understanding
- desire to learn

- elevated spirituality
- greater ecological sensitivity and planetary concern
- a feeling of being more intuitive, sometimes psychic.

He also observes "psychophysical changes," including:

- increased physical sensitivity
- diminished tolerance to light, alcohol, and drugs
- a feeling that their brains have been "altered" to encompass more
- a feeling that they are now using their "whole brain" rather than just a small part.

NDErs undergo radical changes in personality, and their significant others—spouses, friends, relatives—confirm these changes, reports Bruce Greyson, M.D., clinical psychiatrist and associate professor at the University of Connecticut. Like Sappington, he is concerned with what can be learned from such new outlooks on life.

Specifically, Greyson wondered whether they could be of help to those of his private clients who were suicidal. "Suicide is generally unthinkable among near-death experiencers," he says. "They exude a peace about death which is very comforting." And yet, ironically, he found, "their experience imparts a sense of purpose to those with thoughts of suicide." Those who are suicidal come away with a "renewed hope in life itself, which actually helps them to go on with their own lives," reports Greyson.

Whether such experiences can be used regularly in therapy is another matter. First, there needs to be some objective evidence that NDErs are indeed changed by their experience. He would like to see more first-hand accounts of what the subjects felt *before* their NDE. Lacking such information, he says, "we have to rely on the person to tell us that he or she has changed, rather than seeing it for ourselves."

One approach could be standardized psychological testing of patients who for medical reasons may find themselves in near-death situations. For example,

"The light was so bright it surrounded me and filled me with a total love and joy. I felt intensely calm; I just wanted to stay there forever."

Greyson thinks patients suffering from cardiac arrhythmia would be ideal. They often undergo a process known as cardioversion, in which their hearts are stopped for a brief period by a massive electrical charge intended to correct the irregular beating. Many of those who undergo cardioversion report NDEs.

"What I'd like to do is interview each patient before and after this procedure," Greyson explains. And, in order to confirm reports of an out-of-body experience—patients often say they floated above the operating table—he would "even plant targets near the ceiling to determine whether or not the subject actually saw them when they rose from their bodies." (Such research of arrhythmia patients is, in fact, about to get underway at the University of Wisconsin.)

Those who report out-of-body experiences often tell of listening in on conversations which took place in another room, or being aware of an event (such as the tipping-over of a tray of operating instruments) that they could not have been witness to inside their bodies. If an unconscious patient later describes the ceiling targets, however, Greyson and others would take it as hard evidence that out-of-body experiences are real.

The Big Question

What, in the end, are near-death experiences? And exactly how far can research go in trying to answer that question?

"People with NDEs routinely report that they had an omniscient feeling—a brief conclusion that they were everywhere at once and that time had no meaning," says John Sappington. "I can't help but wonder what is happening to these people—do they tend toward histrionics in general, or have they had access to information that transcends the beyond?

"Of course we're never going to provide hard proof of an afterlife," he laments. "As a scientist, I find it frustrating that I can't empirically test all these theories. The big question—is there life after death—is still going to remain a mystery."

EUTHANASIA

What is the "good death"?

The easing of death is one of the next big items on the modern agenda. There is more than one way of setting about it

IT IS the scene modern man dreads. He is in a hospital, desperately ill and alone. By his side is a respirator, supplementing his breathing with a regular sigh of its own. Tubes run into his nose and stomach, carrying fluids that keep him alive. As death approaches, he has lost control of his life.

Modern medicine affords marvellous cures; it keeps men and women alive longer than they could have hoped for even half a century ago. Yet, when life is prolonged, there is all the more chance that it will end in debilitation, dementia and dependence. The old used to be snatched away by pneumonia, "the old man's friend", or by a heart attack; now pneumonia can be cured with antibiotics, and stopped hearts can be pounded back to life with cardio-pulmonary resuscitation. Man can cheat death.

But the cheating brings with it a crowd of questions. Should people be kept alive who, without intervention, would surely die? Should patients be allowed to choose for themselves whether or not to go on living? Should doctors become ministers, not of cures, but of easeful death? How are life, and death, to be valued?

All religions, and all legal codes, have long upheld the principle that life is sacred and ought to be preserved. To that, hospitals and institutions of medicine add their conviction that death is a failure. These presumptions still carry enormous weight, both in courts and on the wards. To put it in bluntly secular form, the state has an interest in preserving its subjects. This principle was stated most plainly in the case of *Cruzan v Director, Missouri Department of Health,* a case that went before the American Supreme Court in 1989.

The state as prolonger of life

Nancy Cruzan, the victim of a car crash, had been in a "persistent vegetative state" for six years. Her parents went to the Missouri state court to seek permission to have her feeding tube removed; the court refused. Missouri law required "clear and convincing" evidence of the patient's own wishes. Cruzan had told friends, in casual college chats, that she did not want to live "like a vegetable"; but Missouri did not think that convincing enough.

The state, citing its "unqualified interest in life", set itself up as Cruzan's proxy and protector, deciding on her behalf that her best interests would be served by continuing to live. The Supreme Court narrowly ruled in Missouri's favour, and Cruzan lived until a county court judge ruled last December (on new evidence of her wishes) that the tube should be disconnected.

Between 5,000 and 10,000 Americans are now being kept alive in circumstances, and with prognoses, much like Cruzan's. The very slight chance of cure (a few patients have, in fact, recovered) is enough to keep treatment going. Most would be dead if they had not been revived, as Cruzan was, with the tubes and chest-pounding and electric shocks of cardio-pulmonary resuscitation.

Doctors still presume that resuscitation—life at all costs—is what patients and families want. In the case of terminal patients, that assumption is increasingly wrong. Public opinion, both in America and outside it, is overwhelmingly on the side of withdrawing all "invasive" and "extraordinary" treatment in such cases.

If courts and hospitals decide otherwise, it is not always on the ground of preserving life for its own sake. They wish, sometimes, to protect the patient's interests against those of the family. Families are not always united, disinterested and loving. Although few American states have withdrawal-of-treatment codes as restrictive as Missouri's, all accept that it is the state, not the family, that best guarantees in a thoroughly disinterested way the interests of the patient. And there are times—as when, for example, Christian Scientists refuse life-saving blood transfusions for their children—when the public may agree with that.

Yet what are a patient's best interests, and how are they to be discovered? Against the principle of state interest looms the equally weighty principle of autonomy: a person's right to privacy and the direction of his own life. In the end, autonomy decides most cases of "right-to-die": but it is a principle that may sometimes lean towards life, not death. Can anyone say, on behalf of a patient unable to speak for himself, that his life is not worth living?

Much of the confusion could be avoided if people made their wishes known before the final crisis. In "living wills", people specify before their deaths which treatments they do not wish to receive if their condition becomes terminal, and name a proxy to see that their wishes are respected.

Such wills are catching on in America and Europe, and are slowly (too slowly) becoming standardised, so that both patient and doctor can be sure that they intend the same thing. Their greatest drawback is that they short-circuit the process of deliberation between doctor and patient about the course of a disease, and make a pre-emptive decision that may subsequently be regretted. That may explain why, in a survey carried out by the American Medical Association in 1988, 56% of adults had discussed with their families what they wanted to do if they lapsed into irreversible coma; but only 15% had got as far as filling out a living will.

Undoubtedly, such wills would help hospitals and nursing homes in one respect: they would provide a means of rationing expensive treatment and scarce beds. The terminally ill now account for 20-30% of hospital expenditure, yet no amount of money is going to make them better. Doctors tend to shy away these days from the principles of "utility" and cost-worthiness. Instead, they argue a principle of "justice".

If certain patients have enjoyed a good run, and are near the end of it, their claim to live longer is less than that of somebody who has just begun. If the elderly people in question are willing to make that altruistic point on paper, they might save hospitals some distressing dilemmas. They might even make the same point on health-insurance forms, paying a lower premium in exchange for volunteering to forgo the most expensive kinds of care.

Not just a mechanical device

These stratagems, however, do not avoid the central problem of what kind of value can be put on a life. Is an old life, fully lived, *ipso facto* worth less than a young life yet to reach its potential? Is an unconscious life like Nancy Cruzan's, in which the heart beats but the brain is dormant, *ipso facto* worth less than a conscious one?

To say yes suggests that human life is essentially a biological function, or the expression of a personality; that it loses its value, like a mechanical device, when it ceases to work well. Few people would go that far. Legislation now before the European Parliament stresses that human life "is founded on dignity and spirituality". It also insists, however, that human life "cannot be reduced merely to natural functions." This is a two-edged argument. On the one hand, life is clearly more than functions. On the other, if life appears to have sunk so far, should it be kept going at all?

Euthanasia, in Greek, means "the good death": the active intervention of a doctor, usually at the patient's request, to bring that patient's life to an end. Even when asked for, euthanasia is illegal everywhere. In the United States it counts as assistance in a suicide; in Britain it is classed as attempted murder. In Holland, where since 1973 the practice has been winked at, the statutory penalty is up to 12 years in prison.

Yet a majority of people in all these countries (70% in America, 75% in Britain) approves of being "helped to die" *in extremis*, and judgments in the courts are coming to reflect that softer attitude. In Holland most doctors in recent euthanasia cases have been given suspended sentences. In Britain last year a brother and sister were given a conditional discharge for attempting to kill their mother, terminally ill with cancer, by altering the controls on the machine that was dosing her with pain-killers.

Such public cases are clearly the tip of the iceberg. According to a new study (to be published in September by the Free Press in New York) by Carl Gomez, an American doctor, deaths by euthanasia in Holland are estimated at anything between 2,000 and 6,000 a year, or 5-15% of all deaths. Typically, the cause of death will be entered in the medical records as "cardiac arrest", and a mere 6% of cases will be reported, as legally they should be, to the public prosecutor.

In America and the rest of Europe the percentage of deaths by euthanasia is assumed to be much smaller, yet medical people often say that "it happens all the time". They may not be right. Doctors in Holland usually administer euthanasia with a strong injection of barbiturates, sometimes followed by curare. Doctors elsewhere tend to increase the measured dose of opiates, sometimes with the intention of killing the patient but often in the hope of bringing less pain, despite the risk of death.

As many as 70% of all deaths in hospital are already preceded by a decision to withdraw some form of care. That too, on a hectic ward, may often seem like killing. Most doctors do not see a distinction between withdrawal of extraordinary forms of treatment (sometimes called "passive" euthanasia) and the active version. The intent, they argue, is the same: to hasten death. If the diagnosis subsequently proves wrong, and the action mistaken, the regret will be the same. Neither action can be reversed. A doctor's whole training is to preserve life; both interventions go against it.

The British Medical Association and its American counterpart insist that this conclusion is wrong. In the case of withdrawing certain treatments, a doctor or a patient decides that since there is no reasonable hope of recovery there is no moral obligation—and no point—in continuing on a course that brings the patient no benefit. The decision is not to end a life, but to allow the disease to take its natural course. Hence the official medical view: the disease, not the doctor, is the agent of death.

The term "artificial means" is another stumbling-block. According to the moral theologians (and most doctors), artificial means include resuscitation, respirators, dialysis machines and antibiotics. But what of the feeding tubes that sustained Nancy Cruzan? Of the 39 American states that have "living will" laws, nearly half specifically exclude artificial feeding from the treatments that may be refused. To remove feeding tubes seems, to many, a deliberate act of killing, bringing with it a particularly nasty death. But if terminal patients who cannot breathe can be taken off respirators with the blessing of moralists, there is no logic in keeping alive with intravenous drips terminal patients who cannot swallow.

The chief criterion is the quality of care that can be given once extraordinary means are removed. This is, for the most part, inexpensive but time-consuming care: feeding if possible, comforting, counselling and—above all—alleviating pain. Death is no longer held back, but neither is it forced forward. The essential role of the doctor, to care for his patient, continues. Regard for the life that is left continues. This is not the same as actively bringing about the death of a person whose life is "no longer worth living."

Clearly the decision to go on through the dark, and not to ask for death, is easier in some cases than others. The terminal cancer patient sees his end close; if he is in pain, his pain can now be virtually eliminated. It is in cancer treatment that the hospice movement (started in Britain, now spreading all over the world) has had its finest victories.

Most patients in hospices or in the care of home-visiting hospice teams have cancer in its final stages; a growing number have AIDS or motor-neurone disease. Dame Cecily Saunders, director of St Christopher's Hospice in London and a founder of the modern hospice movement, feels that hospice principles of counselling, relieving pain and reassuring the dying have certainly countered, and probably defeated, demands for euthanasia from cancer patients. She also admits that it is difficult to apply the same techniques to the long-term disabled, to stroke victims or to those with Alzheimer's disease. They can be helped to live in the hope of cure; but both a cure, and their deaths, may be years away.

In Michigan last year a woman was helped to die because she had learnt she had Alzheimer's disease, and could not face the future. Janet Adkins was 55, and still healthy. She was allowed the use of a "suicide machine" invented by a doctor, Jack Kevorkian, which enabled her to inject into her bloodstream saline solution, thiopental and potassium chloride. Dr Kevorkian stood by and watched. Arguing for Adkins later, he insisted that she could not be condemned to a life of increasing dementia and loss of personality.

Many people would agree. The problem lies, again, in what constitutes an "unbearable" life. The Dutch have gone this way before. Their informal guidelines for euthanasia begin carefully enough: there must be "a concrete expectation of death". But Dutch courts have also allowed euthanasia where there is "unbearable suffering", "psychic suffering" and "potential disfigurement of personality". These are not medical terms; they rely on the subjective judgment of patient and doctor. Most controversially, Dutch courts have also justified euthanasia on grounds of "necessity".

Modern euthanasia, it is said, is saved from that slippery slope both by its voluntary nature and by the professionalism of doctors. Officials of the Voluntary Euthanasia Society in Britain, as well as the Hemlock Society in America, emphasise that a patient's trust in his doctor is confirmed by the ultimate trusting act of putting his life at the doctor's disposal. (Those who cannot ask for themselves must have appointed a proxy, in a living will, to do it for them.) Those same officials stress that they are not condoning suicide, either *in extremis* or in general.

They want euthanasia to be an "option" of last resort; something, they often say, "to keep in a drawer". And they want that option to be legalised, for an eminently sensible reason: if it were legalised, it could be both overt and properly regulated.

Euthanasia is most likely to reach the statute book in Washington state, where Proposition 119 (on the ballot this November) would allow a mentally competent patient with a terminal illness to seek a doctor's help to kill himself. Once given the opinion of two doctors that he would die within the next six months, he would be able to obtain a lethal dose of barbiturates. (That would rule out euthanasia for long-term disabilities, and Alzheimer's.) Similar proposals exist in Oregon, Washington, DC, California and Florida. A committee of the European Parliament has adopted a resolution—still awaiting debate by the full parliament—that would allow doctors to accede to repeated requests from competent patients who wanted help to end their lives.

The prospect for most of this legislation remains dim. Many doctors, as well as voters and legislators, feel deeply ambivalent about it. Many Dutch doctors, for example, are opposed to pending legislation that would let them perform euthanasia provided they told the police. Although they would like clearer guidelines, these doctors still want what Dr Gomez calls a "private space" within the public law, a place where doctor and patient can make their decision without intrusion. The very idea of that "private space" implies, first, a breach in the law, in which acts can be performed covertly and possibly without accountability; and, second, that a conscious decision to die or to dispense death is one in which society as a whole has no interest.

Bringing death home

In the present century the developed countries have increasingly hidden death away. Three-quarters of all deaths occur in hospital, behind screens or in separate rooms. A quarter occur with no close relative present. In the developed world—with the exception of the Latin countries—mourning has been abbreviated, and the bereaved no longer mark themselves out with black clothes or armbands. Each man is an island, it seems, whose death is largely his own affair.

Yet society has a legitimate interest in death. Not many years ago the whole village, not just the dying man's family, gathered round to give him strength. If societies can no longer agree on the meaning or purpose of death (or whether it has any meaning at all), they can still construct sensible and comforting legislation to allay the fears of the dying about what will happen in what is left for them of this world.

First, they could recognise the right of the terminally ill to decide their own treatment. This would be done by a standardised document, filled in on admission to hospital if not before; by the routine appointment of a proxy with durable power of attorney; and by continuing consultation with a doctor, so that the dying could always change their minds. Where there can be no statement of intention (as with infants), the basis of decision would be the balance of burdens and benefits to the patient of a certain course of treatment.

The patient's right to decide his treatment would stop short of the right to request death. If no extraordinary means were used to prolong life, death would not be unnecessarily delayed. His life, meanwhile, would be made as comfortable as possible. He would receive, as of right, control of pain, therapy if necessary, counselling, and food and water to the extent that these could be taken normally.

He would not need to remain in hospital. At the moment, health-insurance and social-security payments are skewed towards hospital care. These could be redirected, with appropriate safeguards, towards care at home by community teams trained in hospice techniques and working together with the patient's general practitioner. GPS themselves should be trained to counsel the dying and encouraged, as in the old days, to make home visits. Churches and neighbours could be mobilised, as in the old days, to share the burden of comforting. With all this, euthanasia could—and should—remain illegal. If it were ruled out, the dying would not feel there was an "easier" or "quicker" route they ought to take, and it would not be offered to them.

To civilise death, to bring it home and to make it no longer a source of dread, is one of the great challenges of the age. These changes would be a first step on that road. The road leads not to total control of dying (as it should not), but to acceptance and understanding. Gradually, dying may come to hold again the place it used to occupy in the midst of life: not a terror, but a mystery so deep that man would no more wish to cheat himself of it than to cheat himself of life.

Relating to Others

People in groups can be seen everywhere: couples in love, parents with their children, teachers and students, gatherings of friends, church groups, theatergoers. People have a great influence on one another when they congregate in groups. Groups spend a great deal of time communicating with members and nonmembers. The communication can be intentional and forceful, such as when protesters demonstrate against a totalitarian government. Or communication can be more subtle, such as when fraternity members consume large quantities of beer, and a new brother conforms merely to follow the crowd, perhaps drinking to the point of illness.

In some groups the reason a leader emerges is clear—perhaps the most skilled individual in the group is elected leader by the group members. In other groups, for example, during a spontaneous nightclub fire, the rapidly emerging, perhaps self-selected, leader's qualities are less apparent. Nonetheless the followers flee unquestioningly in the leader's direction.

Some groups such as corporations issue formal rules in writing; discipline for rule breaking is also formalized. Other groups such as families possess fewer, less formal rules and disciplinary codes, but the rules are important and quickly learned by their members nonetheless.

Unit 4

Some groups are large, but seek more members, such as nationalized labor unions. Other groups seek to keep their groups small and somewhat exclusive, like teenage cliques. There are groups that are almost completely adversarial with other groups. Conflict between youth gangs is receiving much media attention today. Other groups pride themselves on their ability to remain cooperative with similar groups, such as when families band together in a neighborhood crime watch.

Psychologists are so convinced that interpersonal relationships are important to the human experience that they have intensively studied human relations. There is ample evidence that contact with other people is a necessary part of human existence. Research has shown that most individuals do not like being isolated from other people. In fact, in laboratory experiments where subjects experience total isolation for extended periods, some subjects begin to hallucinate the presence of others. In prisons, solitary confinement is often used as a form of punishment because it is so aversive. Other research has shown that people who must wait under stressful circumstances prefer to wait with others, even if they are total strangers, rather than wait alone.

This unit begins with articles about men and women and their relationships to others. In the first, "Art of Anger Difficult for Women to Master," Barbara Sullivan discusses why women feel uncomfortable expressing angry feelings, and what they must do to act on anger in productive ways. The companion article, "Do You Know Who Your Friends Are?" addresses men's relationships with other people, especially their friends. Men seem to have difficulty becoming emotionally attached to others; Larry Letich suggests six strategies men can use to make and keep friends.

The next article describes how our behaviors affect those around us as well as ourselves. Type A individuals, for instance, often manifest hostility to others. However, this hostile behavior sometimes has deleterious effects on their own health, or so suggests the article "How Anger Affects Your Health."

In the article "Resolving Conflicts: Step by Step," the reader is introduced to creative handling of conflict with others. Sandra Arbetter outlines five steps to help us with conflict resolutions. Sometimes, instead of conflicting with others, we become overly dependent on them. Melinda Blau, in "No Life to Live," describes the phenomenon of codependency—how to recognize it, and how to disentangle oneself from it.

Since many relationships are happy and problem-free, this unit ends with articles on positive relationships. "What Happy Couples Do Right," by Scott Winokur, contains a "formula," a seemingly simple one, for keeping romantic relationships upbeat. Bruce Baldwin showcases married relationships and describes how to maintain a positive relationship with one of the most important persons in our lives, our marital partner.

Continuing this series of articles on interpersonal relations, "The Dance of Intimacy," by Harriet Goldhor Lerner, relates to intimate relationships. The author contends that we need to feel comfortable with ourselves first and then, and only then, can we be involved in or improve an existing relationship.

Looking Ahead: Challenge Questions

Are there other interpersonal processes besides conflict, codependency, and friendship that would be important to study in our society? Do you think that the same social processes are operative in all societies, or do societies differ greatly?

Why do women have a difficult time managing anger? When is anger healthy; when is it destructive?

Can opposite sex friends relate as well as same-sex friends? Do you think men really have a harder time making friends with other men than women have with other women?

Describe some recent conflicts you have recently had with others. What do these conflicts have in common; how are they different?

What is codependency? What treatment is available for the codependent? What would you suggest to someone in a destructive or pathological relationship?

Do you think it is possible to find happiness by oneself (without an intimate partner)? How so? What are the benefits of an intimate relationship? What are the disadvantages? What do couples need to do to develop positive, friendly relationships?

Art of anger difficult for women to master

Barbara Sullivan

Chicago Tribune

CHICAGO—Patricia Adams, a reporter for a news magazine, could feel the rage rising as she started reading an article she had written. Although the article had her byline, it had been rewritten by her editor in such a way that it bore little resemblance to her original. Worse, the editing had made the article inaccurate.

"First, I felt disbelief and then I was absolutely furious," she said. "I could not believe he had done this. But I knew I could not call him right away because I had to sort out the emotionalism. I didn't want to cry.

"It was two days before I talked to him. My anger by that time had not diminished one whit, but it was a cold anger as opposed to the hot anger.

"I knew exactly what I wanted to say and I said it. At first, he kept trying to justify his actions, and then he tried to get off the track. But I kept getting right back to it (the subject). I did not cry and I did not get emotional. Our relationship since then has been fine, and it hasn't happened again."

By almost any measure, Adams is a successful woman and has much in her life to feel good about. But her ability to get angry that week—to recognize her anger and then clearly express it without tears and without emotion—filled her with an intense feeling of accomplishment.

It was a breakthrough because she was aware that it's difficult for herself and most women to even allow themselves to get angry in the first place, much less use that anger constructively as a powerful tool to get their point across.

Uncomfortable with anger

Anger is not an emotion most women feel comfortable with or handle well.

Women traditionally have been raised not to feel or express anger. They are the pleasers, the peacemakers, the guardians of the home. Conversely, men are raised to know it's OK to get angry, to be aggressive.

Historically, said Chicago therapist Jo Lief, "men were given permission to go out and shoot the beasts, and women were objects, wearing their housedresses and girdles and accommodating (male) authority."

But as difficult as it is, anger is increasingly being recognized as the force that will allow women to become successful in the workplace and to improve their personal relationships.

Well-used anger is power, and that power can change not only women's lives but, obviously, the lives of the people they work with and live with as well.

Well-used anger is not temper-tantrum anger, in which people fling objects through the air or yell and scream at each other, or become fragmented and tearful. Well-used anger is anger that's recognized and acted upon. It's used to state and possibly change a situation that is unacceptable.

"There's been a taboo against women's anger," says Menninger Foundation therapist Harriet Lerner, author of the best-selling *The Dance of Anger* (Harper & Row, $8.95). "Women can become angry for other causes, such as against drunk drivers, but there has been a powerful taboo against women using their anger on behalf of their own self.

"But never, never will a woman be successful, either in the workplace or in her relationships, if she's not able to feel her anger, speak to important issues and take a clear position."

A stereotypical response

Although women are making strides toward channeling anger, they are still newcomers to it, and the stereotype of the angry woman is of a woman who has succumbed to negative, non-rational emotions and has thus become ineffectual.

It's a stereotype that has been prevalent both in the workplace and in personal relationships.

For example, picture this real-life scenario of a couple driving down a road.

He's driving, and another driver, a woman, refuses to make room for him to change lanes. He rolls down the window and yells, "You dumb broad, move over."

His female companion is enraged. She grabs the closest available object, which happens to be a box of tissue, and throws it at him while yelling at him to never use the term "dumb broad" again.

He gives her a long, appraising look, and then comments that if there's one thing he dislikes, it's women who lose their tempers. Of the two of them, he continues, he is the stable one.

The more emotional she becomes at

HOW TO CHANNEL ANGER, MAKE USE OF IT

Chicago Tribune

Anger is a powerful emotion. Likewise, it can be a powerful tool for achievement, both in the workplace and in personal relationships.

But learning to channel anger into appropriate, powerful behavior is a skill that doesn't always come naturally. Here is a set of recommendations compiled from comments made by Menninger Foundation therapist Harriet Lerner, who has written extensively on anger, and Evanston psychologist Robert Mark, a corporate consultant on matters of executive development and corporate conflict.

- Don't react quickly. Slow down when a situation arises that makes you angry. Be sure the anger is justified for that particular situation and isn't related to a prior situation.
- Give yourself time to determine what you want to accomplish by communicating your anger. Move from anger to a clear plan of what you want, and when you are ready to speak up, talk specifics, not generalities.
- Shift from feeling to doing. You may feel that you've been hurt, but the point is to use that awareness of being hurt to do something about it.
- Don't accuse. It's better to say something like "I don't like the way things are going," rather than "Why are you doing this to me?" People don't want to hear blame being cast on them, and doing that will raise the intensity level rather than accomplish a change.
- Know what your bottom line is. Are you prepared to negotiate or compromise, or is the situation that has provoked your anger intolerable to the degree you are ready to walk if changes aren't made?
- Don't cloud the issue with emotionalism.
- It's important, especially in personal relationships, to focus on what is needed to change a situation rather than focusing on guilt.
- Be prepared for countermeasures when you express anger.
- And finally, some specific advice for men, according to Robert Mark: "They need to develop their facility for listening and responding. They need to broaden their perspective and reconnect to the emotional part of themselves. Men have these abilities, but, until now, they haven't had to use them in the workplace."

this assessment, the cooler and more calculating he becomes.

Finally, she actually finds herself wondering if she is, indeed, wrong, and her anger becomes suffused with self-doubt and guilt.

Going along to get along

"It's very hard for women to clarify their anger," said Lerner. "Often a woman will go along with a situation for a long time, and then she'll explode, blow up. But too often exploding is just part of a repetitive, unproductive pattern, and then business goes on as usual.

"Anger should be used to define a new position in a relationship pattern, a position that does not mean self-betrayal."

Psychologists such as Lerner stressed the importance of understanding the real source of the anger.

For example, the car passenger was angry at the immediate situation. More important, she had a deep, long-felt but never-expressed anger at what she perceived as the man's hostility toward all women, both in his professional and personal life.

She could not use her anger to change him.

But, by stating clearly and unemotionally how she felt about the situation, she could change her role in the relationship. In time, she did this; the relationship ended.

Anger creates separation

That might not be a so-called "happy ending," and it's one of the reasons women so often sit on their anger or fail to even recognize it. Women have traditionally identified themselves through their relationships, their connections with other people. Expressing anger creates a separation—even if it's only temporary—between themselves and the other person. The result of anger can be aloneness.

"Many women go right from sadness to forgiveness, skipping anger completely," said Evanston clinical psychologist Robert Mark. "And the reason they skip anger is because they're afraid of abandonment.

"Being assertive and expressing anger has its costs. One cost is that the culture we live in still wants to see women as sweet and nice.

"Second, just because a woman is capable of expressing anger—of knowing where she stands and what she wants and asserting herself—doesn't mean that the other people in her world are going to like it."

So to get ahead and feel good about themselves professionally and personally, women must feel and use anger, but they have to do it carefully. It's like walking on eggshells.

On top of that, there are few role models. Past generations of women turned anger inward; depression, sadness and guilt were the unhappy results. And finally, women's anger, even when expressed appropriately, is viewed far more critically than men's anger.

"People react very differently to men's anger and women's anger. Imagine the Boston Tea Party, if it had been women who threw that tea overboard. They would have been written up as a group of hysterical, strident, immature women in the throes of PMS (premenstrual syndrome)," Lerner said.

"It's a big problem for women," acknowledged Wilma Smelcer, the first female senior vice president at Continental Bank. "They can't let their emotions show because that's unprofessional. This probably applies to men, too, but I think women have to be more careful."

A learned expression

"Anger—how to express it—is something I've learned," Smelcer said. "I had to learn it. And when I feel anger, I step back and say, 'All right, what is the real reason why I'm feeling angry?'

"Because sometimes it has to do with other things that have gone on during the week rather than what's happening right now. Once I get through that process, I have to decide whether it's appropriate to react strongly to the situation. You have to stay calm, but you cannot be a wimp."

Smelcer talked about a woman she knew several years ago, who held a high-pressure managerial job.

"She was seen crying one day. No one knew what the reason was, why she was crying, but (the crying) took on a life of its own.

"Every time her name came up about something, there was the impression that this was an emotional, mercurial woman rather than a professional."

Roadblocks exist even when women transform teary anger into lucidly expressed anger. The status quo has a habit of being comfortable, and when women start expressing anger, they are changing that status quo.

"Say you're in a relationship and you want to make a change," Lerner said. "So you, the woman, make it clear you are not going to continue in a certain pattern any longer.

"There is almost certainly going to be a countermove. The other person probably won't want that change. And when there's a countermove, the anger is probably going to intensify."

Finding the bottom line

"So women have to know what their bottom-line position is," Lerner said. "The bottom line is using anger to make very clear what the acceptable limits are, and saying, 'I can no longer tolerate this in the job or in the marriage.' If you know you cannot survive without the job or marriage, you have to navigate within the situation."

Such a bottom-line position—the possibility of anger ending a relationship or job—can strike fear in the strongest of women.

"Women are still terrified—they want approval and love, and they fear that they'll lose that if they get angry," said Evanston, Ill., therapist Linda Randall. "I still hear women saying, 'I'm afraid to be angry.' "

Betty Cook (not her real name) was desperately afraid of that bottom-line position.

The suburban homemaker was afraid, and she also had trouble feeling any anger. She got depressed and sad, but not angry. For most of her 26 years of marriage, she negotiated carefully, trying to change abusive situations without drawing the final line.

"I had always felt that he was right, that he was smarter—I was raised like that. I would think, 'All right, I'll try this for one more year and see if things change.'

"Then the year would be over and I'd just keep rolling along. We kept going in the same circle. It's hard to break out of that.

"He was verbally abusive and physically abusive at times to the boys. He would order me to leave the room (when he became physically abusive to the sons), and I would."

Counseling helped

They started family counseling, but he participated for only a short time. She continued by herself.

"It gave me strength. I started taking stands. Quiet stands, but stands. He (her husband) had problems when I didn't agree with him. He said he was uncomfortable and wanted things back the way they had been. I could not go back."

After 26 years, she got to the bottom line. She told her husband she wanted a divorce.

But she said she still isn't sure what anger is all about. She understands guilt and sadness, she said, but she still doesn't understand anger, or particularly feel that anger is a good thing.

"I defused things and I walked away a lot. But I always felt, and still do, that getting angry would be losing control. I don't want to ever lose control."

It may be a matter of definition, of semantics. Anger was never part of her vocabulary. But, call it what you will, she channeled her emotions into an understanding of what she wanted—and didn't want—and clearly stated that understanding to her husband.

Complicated emotion

"Expressing anger doesn't mean a hysterical, histrionic display of rage," said Robert Mark. "It means going up to someone and saying, 'This is what I want.'

"It's complicated—anger is very complicated," Lerner said. "But women are learning about anger and how to use it. It's changing the way all of us live."

Do you know who your friends are?

Why most men over 30 don't have friends and what they can do about it

Larry Letich

Larry Letich is currently working to create a new magazine about men's issues and progressive politics for a broad audience. People interested in learning more about this project can contact him at 125 Myrtle Av., Cedar Grove, NJ 07009.

"You gotta have frieeends," sang Bette Midler. But most men past the age of 30 don't have friends—not really. They have colleagues and work buddies, golf partners and maybe a "couple" friend or two, where the bond is really between the wives. If they say they *do* have a best friend, often it turns out to be an old friend whom they see or speak to once every few years.

Sadly, for most men in our culture, male friendship is a part of their distant past. One man spoke for many at a recent men's conference in Montclair, N.J., when he lamented, "I haven't made a new friend in 25 years."

Why is this so? All sorts of theories are thrown around, from "homophobia" to the absurd idea that men are biologically geared to competitiveness, which precludes friendship. But the major reason for the shortage of true friendship among men in America is that our culture discourages it.

Male friendship is idealized in the abstract (think of *Butch Cassidy and the Sundance Kid* and numerous other "buddy movies"), but if a man manages to have any true emotional attachment to another man, a lot of subtle pressures are placed on him to eliminate it. The most obvious time this happens is when a man gets married (especially if he's still in his 20s). Think of the impression that comes to mind from a thousand movies and TV shows about the guy who "leaves his wife" for the evening to "go out with the guys." Invariably, the other guys are shown as both immature *and* lower-class, losers who'll never amount to anything in life. The message is clear—no self-respecting middle-class man hangs out regularly with his friends.

In fact, friendship between men is rarely spoken of at all. Instead, we hear about something called male bonding, as if all possible non-sexual connection between men is rooted in some crude, instinctual impulse. More often than not, male friendship, reduced to male bonding, is sniggered at as something terribly juvenile and possibly dangerous.

This denigration of male friendship fits well into Reagan- and Thatcher-style capitalism. The decline in blue-collar jobs and the great white-collar work speed-up of the 1980s made no man's job safe. And money—not the richness of a man's relationship with family, friends, and community—became even more so the universally accepted value of a man's worth.

In this system, men (at least those men without golden parachutes) are put in the position of constantly, and often ruthlessly, competing with all other men for the limited number of positions higher up the ladder—or even to hold onto their jobs at all. Men are encouraged not to trust one another, and are frankly told never to band together. (For example, in most places it is a serious faux pas, and often a dismissable offense, simply to tell a fellow worker what you make for a living; supposedly it is "bad for morale.") Naturally, this keeps men—and women, too—constantly knocking themselves out for the next promotion rather than demanding real changes, like cutting the CEO's million-dollar salary down to size.

Given the kind of sterile, high-pressure work environments men are expected to devote themselves to, it's not surprising that the ideal American man is supposed to feel little or no passion about anything. As Robert Bly has pointed out, the most damaged part of the psyche in modern man is the "lover," meaning not just the ability to make love,

20 questions for men

Ask your friends what it means to be masculine

THERE IS NO HOW-TO GUIDE TO THE PROCESS OF BECOMING A FULL-summed and spirited man. To suggest there are techniques to achieve authentic manhood would be to devalue the dignity we can achieve only by struggling to become conscious and compassionate.

In one sense the voyage of self-discovery is solitary, but that doesn't mean you have to take it all alone. The most powerful resource we have for transforming ourselves is honest conversation between men and men, women and women, men and women.

To start a leaderless men's group, reach out to one person who seems ripe for friendship and risk being candid about your feelings and needs. Go slowly in gathering your community. It is important to collect a group of men with whom you can be candid.

The agenda of a group will emerge naturally from the concerns of the members. Gradually, the group will share experiences, stories, and feelings, and learn how to challenge, pursue, and nurture. Some of the following questions, all of which are best asked in a small group or with a partner, may help you focus your reflections and deal creatively with issues that are central for men.

1. How did you learn to be a man? Were there different rules for boys and girls in your family? What was your father's ideal of masculinity? Femininity? Your mother's?

2. Who were your early heroes and role models? What characters from books, movies, or television programs presented you with images of men you imitated?

3. What kind of ceremonies or symbolic activities marked your passage from boyhood into manhood? Who initiated you into the male mysteries—father, brother, uncle, grandfather, the gang?

4. How, ideally, would you initiate your son into manhood? What would you say to him about the difficulties and joys of being a man?

5. What is hardest about being a man? What do you resent? What expectations and roles have informed and deformed your life?

6. What pleasures and privileges do you enjoy as a man?

7. In what ways do women have it easier? Harder?

8. How competitive do you feel with other men? To feel okay about yourself do you need to be one-up, to be smarter, more powerful, more accomplished than the men around you?

9. Are you afraid men would despise you or take advantage of you if they knew your hidden weaknesses?

10. What is power? Is there a difference between strength and power?

11. Do you consciously strive to accumulate power? How?

12. If power is defined as the ability to overcome resistance and get what you want, what means do you use to achieve your desires? Physical? Financial? Sexual? Mental? Imagination? Moral? Spiritual? Willpower? Do you try to influence or intimidate others, to seduce or persuade? How do you *feel* when you use various types of power?

13. In what circumstances do you feel powerless? Impotent? What do you do when you can't control the situation?

14. Do you empower others? How?

15. Under what conditions are you most at ease sexually? One-night stands? Long-term relationships? Marriage? Is sex best with or without love?

16. How much performance anxiety accompanies sex?

17. How do you deal with conflicts with women? Do you bully and intimidate? Do you shrink and withdraw when you encounter female anger?

18. What are the factors in your personal and work life that cause the most stress?

19. What are your professional and economic goals? What do you want to make, do, create? What are your personal, family, and communal goals? More time? More intimacy? More service? Are you shortchanging your work, your family, your friends, yourself, your community? What interests, enthusiasms, and passions have you never taken the time to pursue?

20. Do a life review. Are you a success? A failure? How do you measure success and failure?

—Sam Keen

but the ability to love life, to feel, to be either tender or passionate. But passion—and with it the capacity for intimacy—is absolutely essential for friendship.

It's also not surprising that our society's ideal man is not supposed to have any emotional needs.

For American men, maintaining one's lawn is more important than maintaining one's friendships.

Since few men can actually live up to that ideal, it's considered acceptable, even laudable, for him to channel all his emotional needs in one direction—his wife and children. A man who has any other important emotional bonds (that are not based on duty, such as an ailing parent) is in danger of being called neglectful, or irresponsible, or weak, because forging emotional bonds with others takes time—time that is supposed to be spent "getting ahead."

Small wonder that the only friendships allowed are those that serve a "business" purpose or those that can be fit effortlessly into one's leisure time. Maintaining one's lawn is more important than maintaining one's friendships. In keeping with this, there are no rituals and no respect given a man's friendships. When was the last time you heard a grown man talk proudly about his best friend?

Despite all these obstacles, it *is* possible to develop a real male friendship—the kind men remember from their childhood, high school, college, or military days—after the age of 30. My best friend today, with whom I share a deep and abiding bond, is a man I met five years ago when I was 30. But to forge real male friendships requires a willingness to ***recognize* that you're going against the grain, and the *courage* to do so. And it requires the sort of** conscious, deliberate campaign worthy of a guerrilla leader. Here are step-by-step guerrilla tactics to forge, maintain, and deepen male friendships in a hostile environment:

1. **First, you have to want it.** Sounds simple and obvious, but isn't. You have to want it badly enough to work at getting it, just as you would a job or a sexual relationship. Right away, this causes anxiety, because it goes against the male self-sufficiency myth. You have to remind yourself *often* that there's nothing weird or effeminate about wanting a friend. Let your wife and children know about your quest. It's good for your sons, especially, to know what you're trying to do. They might even have some good suggestions!

2. **Identify a possible friend.** Men in men's groups and others who seem in some way to be questioning society's view of masculinity and success are possible candidates. Don't look for men so upstanding and "responsible" they never have a second to themselves. Stuart Miller, author of the book *Men & Friendship*, suggested in a recent interview reconnecting with your old friends from childhood or adolescence.

3. **Be sneaky.** Once you've identified the guy you want to make your friend, do you say, "Hey, I want to be your friend, let's do lunch?" No. One of you will probably soon get threatened and pull away. Instead, get involved in a project with him, preferably non-work-related. For my best friend Mike and me, it was a newsletter we were working on. You need structured time just to be together, feel each other out, and get used to each other without the pressure of being "friends."

4. **Invite him to stop for a beer or a cup of coffee.** Ask personal questions. Find out about his wife, his children, his girlfriend, his job. Find out what's really bugging him in his life. Look for common likes and dislikes. And risk being personal about yourself as well. Do this several times, each time risking a little more honesty.

5. **Call just to get together** after a few months of this. Arrange to get together at least once a month, even if only for a few hours. Expect to always be the caller and arranger, especially in the beginning.

6. **Sit down and talk about your friendship.** It may take some time to reach this point. But while it's typical for men to leave things unsaid, this step is crucial. In a society that treats friendships as replaceable, you have to go against the tide by declaring the value of this special friendship between you. Only then will it survive life's stresses, such as a serious disagreement or one of you moving away.

How anger affects your health

Anger is a universal emotion, and when in the thrall of its physical symptoms—the pounding heart, the sweating palms, the rising blood pressure—most people can well believe that anger causes illness, particularly for those who live with chronic suppressed anger that boils over from time to time. Yet anger is not only universal, but can also be useful. For example, it can lead a person to struggle against injustice. It can get a voter to the polls. It can lead a parent to defend (or to instruct) a child. On the down side, it can lead to violent and antisocial behavior. For many years, scientists have looked for links between anger and heart attack, stroke, and high blood pressure, or between chronic hostility and cancer. Scores of studies have been carried out—some leading to dead ends. It's hard to isolate and study anger, which can result from real situations, such as hardship and poverty, or can sometimes seem groundless to the casual observer. Whether a person vents or suppresses anger may alter its effects.

Nevertheless, some plausible theories have begun to emerge. For example, recent research suggests that chronic anger may be more damaging to women than to men, at least in women who habitually suppress their anger. Yet when men are forced to suppress chronic anger day after day, their health suffers too. According to Dr. Leonard Syme of the University of California at Berkeley, the answer may well be that *a lack of control over the situations that cause anger,* rather than hostility itself, determines the long-term health effects of anger.

Hostility and the coronary arteries

The idea that personality and heart disease might be linked was formalized in 1969 with the concept of "Type A." Two California cardiologists, Dr. Meyer Friedman and Dr. Ray Rosenman, presented evidence that men with a certain kind of hard-driving, aggressive, competitive, tense, and hostile personality were at risk for chronic chest pain or angina (a word with the same root as anger) and for heart attack. The Framingham Heart Study, an important and large-scale investigation of the risk factors for heart disease—and one of the few that included women—also provided evidence that Type A personality puts a person at risk, not only men in white collar jobs, but women as well. But to the surprise of many researchers, subsequent studies were contradictory and failed to confirm the link between Type A behavior and heart disease. Careful study stripped away aggressiveness, tenseness, and competitiveness as risk factors for heart attacks. A recent 22-year follow-up by Dr. David Ragland and Dr. Richard Brand of the University of California at Berkeley indicated that Type A behavior was not related to heart attack deaths. Smoking and high blood pressure were far more important risks than personality or behavior.

Thus more than 20 years after Type A was introduced, most investigators have given up on it. What does continue to interest many of them, however, is just one component of Type A—anger, or more specifically the tendency to look at the world with cynicism and hostility. A recent study conducted by Dr. Redford Williams at Duke University Medical Center returned to the subject of heart attack and anger. It found that those identified as hostile personalities when they were 19 years old had significantly higher levels of total cholesterol and lower levels of beneficial HDL cholesterol at age 42 and were thus at higher risk for heart attack.

Dr. Williams and his colleagues hypothesized that hostility can actually affect blood cholesterol levels, or—a very different thing—that it simply leads to bad health habits. Other researchers, too, have conjectured that hostile people may adopt a "why bother" attitude: "Why be careful about my diet, why exercise, why take care of myself when things are so rotten anyhow?" And yet this line of thought hasn't panned out either. Williams's new evidence for a link between hostility and heart disease is called into question by equally good evidence that no such link exists. For example, a new study led by Dr. Dianne Helmer at the University of California at Berkeley found no significant link between hostility (as measured by standardized psychological tests among 158 people hospitalized for coronary angiograms) and heart disease. Hostility, the study concludes, does not predict heart disease. Other studies have had mixed results.

Women and anger: a taboo?

But other researchers are still on the trail. If not Type A or hostility, what about suppressed anger? If not heart disease, what about other diseases? And another question that remains alive is whether anger—if it poses health risks—might have different effects on women than on men. In 1985, in *The Dance of Anger*, Harriet Lerner of the Menninger Clinic in Topeka, Kansas, suggested that women's anger was a taboo topic for scientific investigators.

Some studies have appeared since then, however. For example, Dr. Mara Julius of the University of Michigan has reanalyzed the data from a long-term study of a Michigan community (the Tecumseh Community Health Study). How men and women in this study coped with anger had been measured by such questions as this: "If your spouse or an authority figure such as a policeman yelled at you for something you hadn't done, how would you react?" Possible answers ranged from "I wouldn't feel annoyed" to "I'd get angry and protest." Women—but not men—who suppressed their anger in such confrontations had a higher mortality rate over time. In fact, women who suppressed their anger in confrontations with their spouses had twice the mortality risk as other women, even when other factors such as high blood pressure and smoking were considered. Among couples, if both husband and wife suppressed anger, mortality rates went up among women but not men. Among men, only those who suppressed their anger *and* had high blood pressure had a higher risk of dying.

Thus Dr. Julius concluded that suppressing anger was a risk factor for heart disease and cancer in women. Her work also suggests that women may handle anger differently from men and thus be affected in special ways by suppressing it.

Blowing up may not help, either

But venting anger may not be any better than suppressing it. At the University of Tennessee, a small study of 87 middle-aged women investigated anger levels, and found that angry women tended to be pessimistic about themselves, to lack social support, to be overweight, to sleep poorly, and to lead sedentary lives. These women also believed that they could not control their problems and could do nothing about them. The angriest women were also more likely to have health problems already. It's not clear, of course, whether the anger results from this unhappy life-style, which is definitely not conducive to good health, or is simply another symptom of unhappiness. Researchers noted that many of the issues that made these women angry were not easy to modify. They also found that "contrary to popular wisdom, which recommends ventilation of anger," the women whose health seemed most adversely affected by anger were not suppressors of anger, but those who "directed it outward." In other words, blowing your stack may merely make you feel worse. And as a rule, no matter how justified the outburst, it doesn't promote social ties or provoke sympathetic reactions.

Thus for these women at least, the choice between suppressing or venting anger may be irrelevant. It may not be anger that makes people sick, or even the way they express it, but the inability to deal effectively with the situations that anger them. Recent studies of occupational stress have sug-

Managing anger: easier said than done

In 1989 Dr. Redford Williams of Duke University Medical Center wrote *The Trusting Heart*, subtitled *Great News About Type A Behavior*. In it he agreed that Type A behavior is not "toxic," but claimed that hostility is. He suggested several stress-management techniques to cope with anger, among them:

- Monitor your cynical thoughts by keeping a log of situations that stir you up.
- Try stopping cynical thoughts.
- Put yourself in the other person's shoes.
- Instead of yelling angrily, try to be assertive, calm, and clear about what's bothering you.

Good advice. But though the observation may be cynical, a person who can do all that is not too bad off to begin with. It's hard to develop a "trusting heart" if you have reasons not to be trustful. Whether to suppress or express anger, and how best to express it, depends inevitably on the circumstances and the other people involved. Managing uncontrollable angry outbursts in oneself or in a family member may require counseling, meditation, life-style changes, or other kinds of long-term psychological help.

Learning from the soaps

Some suggestions for managing anger from the Institute for Mental Health Initiatives (IMHI) may be helpful. A few years ago, recognizing that "people who have some skill at managing their anger are less likely to... suffer from emotional disorders such as depression, or grow up to be early victims of heart disease or stroke," IMHI undertook a study of how anger is handled on daytime TV soap operas. These shows have an audience of 20 million people, most of them women. In 1986 researchers analyzed how anger was presented on 12 daytime dramas on the three major networks. Finding that anger too often resulted in violence on the soaps, they drafted guidelines for producers and writers about healthier ways of portraying anger. No one knows just how effective these efforts have been, but according to surveys completed in 1990, IMHI found that anger has increasingly been portrayed on soaps not as an emotion felt by "bad" people but as a normal emotion that even likeable people exhibit and can deal with constructively. In addition, women have been increasingly portrayed as effective at handling anger. These ideas could conceivably be helpful for some viewers. Out of this research IMHI developed anger-management techniques that emphasize such tips as these:

- Recognize your own anger and that of others.
- Empathize with a person expressing anger.
- Always listen carefully to what an angry person is telling you.
- Try to express respect along with the anger.
- Notice your own reactions, especially your physical reactions.
- Focus your attention on the present problem, and avoid thinking of old grudges or wounds.

IMHI has developed pamphlets and workshop materials on anger for children, teenagers, and adults. For more about their programs, write to them at 4545 42nd Street NW, Suite 311, Washington, D.C. 20016, or call 202-364-7111.

gested that anger can loom large and can adversely affect health among men as well as women, especially when there's nothing they can do about their situation.

Men and anger: they are not immune

The health effects of anger on men may perhaps be gauged from some recent occupational research. Driving a big-city bus fits every criterion for a high-strain job (that is, one with high workload demands but little sense of control): pressure to meet a schedule, physical discomfort, high noise levels, unruly or hostile passengers to be dealt with, heavy traffic, the risk of a crash or breakdown. In addition, a virtual requirement of the job is some ability to suppress anger—to be courteous to the public under stressful conditions. According to a recent unpublished paper by Gary Evans of the University of California at Irvine, over 20 studies of bus drivers in various cities reveal that they have an elevated death rate from heart disease and are more prone to suffer from gastrointestinal disorders and musculoskeletal disorders, such as bad backs. They retire earlier than other civil servants, too, usually because of medical disabilities. A study of 1,428 San Francisco bus drivers (male, mostly nonwhite) supplied one puzzling piece of information: those who scored low on the stress scale—that is, who perceived their jobs as unstressful—tended to have high blood pressure more often than those who recognized the strain they worked under.

Human emotions are hard to study scientifically. Still, it does appear that suppression of anger—when a person has no other choice—is linked to ill health.

RESOLVING CONFLICTS
STEP BY STEP

Sandra R. Arbetter, M.S.W.

Jenny couldn't believe how right the world felt. She and Danny had made up. Her mother had stopped nagging her. And her teacher had given her an A on her book report. What had happened to make them all change?

It all started with a speaker who had come to talk to the Students for the Environment club. Instead of talking about the ozone layer or acid rain, the speaker talked about the need for opposing groups in the town to come to an agreement on the proposed building of a multistory parking garage next to a downtown park. "The problem won't be solved until we resolve the conflicts with those who have opinions different from ours," he told the students, who had been attending city council meetings where there was heated debate on the issue.

Then he talked about what kept people from understanding one another. Jenny couldn't help but see herself in some of the things he said, and it got her to thinking about the conflicts she'd been having lately. She was angry at Danny for spending so much time with the guys. She was angry at her mother for expecting her to make dinner every Tuesday. And she was angry at her teacher for giving her a C in English.

The speaker said that there is nothing basically wrong with conflict. Most people have disagreements from time to time. "Conflicts, in fact, are a way to grow," he said. "Every time we face up to a problem and resolve it, we grow as individuals. We learn to get along better with other people and to take responsibility for our own actions."

Then he came to the part that really made Jenny think. He listed some basic assumptions about life that many people hold. Because these assumptions are not reasonable, they can lead people into conflicts.

Don't Assume

1. *I must have everything my way.* That was Jenny. If she didn't have the last word, she felt others would get in control. So what? Maybe it would be OK to let someone else lead the way for a change.

2. *I must be excellent at everything.* That was Jenny, too. She thought that if she weren't perfect she'd be perfectly awful; there was nothing in between. But no one is perfect and no one but Jenny expected her to have all the answers all the time.

3. *People must be fair to me.* Jenny was big on fairness. If her sister got a new shirt, then Jenny thought she should have one, too. If her friend got an A for a six-page report, then Jenny should, too.

4. *I have no control over the way I feel or act.* Jenny had no problem with this one. She knew there was a difference between feelings and actions and that she had the power to control her actions. Long ago she learned not to blame anyone else for her behavior. Back in third grade, she had told her teacher. "Tommy made me laugh." Both she and Tommy had to write 50 sentences.

5. *I must be liked by everyone.* Jenny didn't like everyone; why should they all like her? Did she *want* everyone to like her? Well, maybe. Did she *need* everyone to like her? Of course not.

The Five Steps

After Jenny thought about what the speaker at the club meeting had said, she was motivated to resolve conflicts with those around her. The speaker had outlined some steps that many experts have agreed upon.

Step 1: Identify the Problem

The first step is to identify the problem. Sometimes it's obvious, sometimes it's not. Jenny and her mother had been arguing about making dinner on Tuesdays. Her mom works that night, but Jenny said she's too busy. The problem wasn't just who would make dinner. The problem was that things had changed a lot since Jenny's mom went to work. Jenny missed the way it used to be, when she could count on her mom always being home and having time to take care of everything.

After talking it over with her mom, they agreed Jenny would make dinner on Tuesdays but be able to choose one weeknight when she wouldn't have any cooking or cleanup chores at all.

Jenny's conflict with Danny went below the surface, too. She realized that she didn't want him to be with the guys because she thought his best friend didn't especially like her. During one silly fight, she admitted this to Danny. He laughed and said his friend thought that Jenny didn't like *him.* After laughing about this, the three of them got together for a movie and had a good time, and soon Jenny was feeling much more comfortable about Danny having more time with his friends.

Sometimes the problem needs to be viewed in a new way. That's called *reframing*. If you put a new frame on a picture, the picture looks different. If you put a new meaning on a problem, the problem looks different, too. If the child you're babysitting cheats at a game you could say he's a sore loser. Or you could reframe it with more understanding and say he's afraid to fail.

Step 2: Look for Solutions

The second step in conflict resolution is to look for possible solutions. Think of lots of them, even if they seem nutty. Good solutions often come from this random brainstorming.

In her conflict about her English grade, Jenny considered boycotting the class, asking her parents to talk with the teacher, redoing the report, accepting the C grade, or talking with her teacher about why she felt she deserved a better grade.

There are some possibilities that are just wishful thinking. Many people hope for some magical rescue—somehow, by someone. They think this might come from their parents, their friends, or people in authority.

Another unrealistic possibility is that if we ignore the problem it will go away. It seldom does, and it often gets worse. Another myth is that it will work to be aggressive—to hurt someone physically, say cruel things, or get revenge. Aside from being unkind, these tactics aren't effective in the long run.

Step 3: Choose One

Third step: Choose the best solution. What's a good solution? It's effective and socially acceptable. It solves the problem, does not hurt anyone or interfere with their rights, and satisfies both parties. There should be no winners or losers; both sides should feel as if they have achieved something. That's called a win-win solution.

Steps 4 and 5: Act, Evaluate

The fourth step is to act. Follow through on one of the solutions.

Finally, evaluate how well your approach solved the problem. If it turns out to be ineffective, don't look on that as a failure. It just means you've eliminated one approach and you're ready to try another. We learn by our mistakes.

At every step, communication is important. Communication doesn't mean just telling someone what *you* want. It means listening to what *they* want. It means establishing eye contact and being sensitive to body language. Bob Woolf, author of *Friendly Persuasion*, says it means not making demands (try suggestions instead) or ultimatums.

Jenny used these guidelines to resolve conflicts at home and at school. The environment club used them in presenting its arguments at the city council meeting. Where can we go from here?

Consider the Consequences

Sometimes feelings get so intense you have the impulse to lash out suddenly, without considering the consequences. Roger Fisher, author of *Getting Together*, gives some hints for impulse control:

- Be aware of your feelings. Although some people are ashamed of their angry, sad, or jealous feelings, you are entitled to any feelings you have. If you're angry, admit it to yourself and express your feeling.
- Take a break if feelings get too hot to handle. Divert yourself. Do something else or go somewhere else.
- Count to 10 slowly. It will give you at least 10 seconds to cool off and think about your approach.
- Consult with someone who has a calming effect on you.

No Life to Live

Codependents take over other people and forsake themselves

Melinda Blau

Melinda Blau *is a New York–based writer who reports frequently on mental health and family issues.*

For the four years Laura* was involved with Mike, a verbally abusive heavy drinker, he kept telling her she ought to leave him. Rather than ending the relationship or even worrying about herself, Laura reassured *him* instead.

"I never got on him for his drinking," she says. "I used to excuse him a lot, apologize for his behavior. Some days I'd shave him. I'd let him hide out in my house. I wouldn't even tell his brother and his father." Her love and devotion didn't work. One night, after telling Laura he loved her, Mike hung up the phone and shot himself.

*Names have been have been changed to protect people interviewed about personal experiences.

Ellen spent 15 years preoccupied with her son's drug addiction, which began when the boy was in high school. Gradually, her life narrowed down to activities designed to keep her son from using. "I'd take him to the movies, even though it wasn't a movie I wanted to see—or even what I wanted to be doing with my time. I'd take him away on vacations—well into his 20s." All those years of turmoil and endless defeats only delayed her son's getting the kind of help he really needed—and kept Ellen from living her own life.

Laura thought her love could keep Mike alive, and Ellen sincerely believed she could stop her son from using drugs. Both examples illustrate behavior many mental health professionals have come to label "codependency." Countless others like Laura and Ellen spend years obsessing over a spouse, child, friend or co-worker—always worrying, manipulating, trying to control. They take over other people's responsibilities, clean them up when they get sick, make excuses for their behavior, even lie for them. These "codependents" don't realize that as the people they're trying to protect plunge deeper into their particular addiction, they, too, are traveling downward on a parallel and equally deadly path.

Codependency—actually an old concept adapted by the substance abuse treatment field—has become a buzzword for our times, not surprising in our addiction-ridden society. "There are 40 million codependents in the U.S.," estimates Aileen Clucas, nursing clinical coordinator at the Smithers Alcoholism Treatment and Training Center in New York City. This figure is extrapolated from frequently cited statistics that each of the 10 million alcoholics in the country affects at least four people.

Chances are, that estimate is low. Today codependency is recognized in families and relationships held in thrall to alcohol or drugs, chronic medical problems, mental illness, as well as other kinds of compulsive behavior, such as eating disorders, gambling, sex addiction, workaholism and compulsive spending. In fact, treating codependency has become a burgeoning industry. Self-help books stretch along bookstore shelves and two have been on *The New York Times'* best seller list; there are conferences, workshops, national organizations, rehabs, treatment centers and self-help groups, and 12-step recovery programs modeled after Alcoholics Anonymous (see "Help Yourself: A Guide to Peer Support Groups").

And with good reason. "Codependency is just as lethal as alcoholism or drug addiction," says Clucas. "You see hypertension, ulcers, drug and alcohol abuse, depression, suicide—all as a result of chronic codependency." Codependents use many of the same defense mechanisms as addicted people to excuse their own behavior—or ignore it. They rationalize: "I stayed home from work because I had housework to do, not because I was trying to keep an eye on Bill." And they deny both the addict's or drinker's problem and their own reaction to it: "He wasn't really that drunk or out of control—after all, it *was* his birthday."

Codependents even protect their "supply," much the same way an addict protects his supply of alcohol or drugs, Clucas explains. In this case, the "drug" is the other person. For example, a codependent will forgo dinner plans with a friend in favor of being with the addict. "The progression is similar to the addict's. In the end, the codependent's world becomes smaller and smaller as finally everything revolves around the addict."

Definitions of codependency abound. San Francisco psychiatrist Timmen Cermak, a pioneer in treating the adult children of alcoholics, sums it up: "When codependents die, they see someone else's life flash before them!"

Definitions of codependency abound, but Cermak sums it up: "When codependents die, they see someone else's life flash before them!"

Many experts refer to codependency as a "disease," like alcoholism, but Dr. Cermak says "it fits into the category we call 'personality traits disorders.' " He cites typical characteristics: Codependents change who they are and what they feel to please others; they feel responsible for meeting other people's needs; they have low self-esteem; they're frequently driven by their own compulsions—cleaning, eating, sex, sometimes substance abuse—as well as their partners'.

Cermak points out that the degree of codependency varies: "Just about everyone has some of it," he says. "It can be universal in its minor form, but it can also intensify and take over someone's life. The more thoroughly codependent a person is, the less they feel they have any choice."

Peter Topaz, a New York City family therapist who treats alcoholics and addicts, eschews the codependency label altogether and criticizes the great "marketing" effort alcoholic treatment providers have launched to promote it. Of course, it exists, Topaz says, but he prefers to put the stress on the disabled family, not necessarily the codependent alone. Within the family system, Topaz asserts, "As one person becomes more dysfunctional or altered, it has an impact on all the other family members. It's a ripple effect.

"You can't just keep the focus on the drug," Topaz adds. "Everyone's bound up, and nothing is accomplished unless you get the whole system to change." He mentions a 38-year-old woman who called recently, wanting to know how to get her husband to stop using cocaine and alcohol. "She's tried the typical things—yelled at him, denied him sex. She makes threats but can't follow through."

Typically, codependents like this woman think one way of controlling another's substance abuse is by exerting pressure, nagging or getting angry. Instead, says Topaz, she should try to get him and the whole family in for treatment. "Provoking" behavior gives an addict reason to get high. I may make him feel rebellious, guilty, depressed or hopeless.

Most codependents are also "enablers." They support their partners in a number of ways: They accept excuses just to avoid conflict, fail to follow through on threats, and bail the person out of tough spots, both emotionally and financially. As a result, the addict is encouraged to continue indulging, and is also protected from the consequences of his or her actions. Meanwhile, the codependent, tangled in this disaster, gets sicker, too.

The good news is there *is* help out there—for codependents as well as addicts. In the last decade, as thousands of alcoholics, addicts and other people with compulsive behavior disorders have begun to fight their addictions, there is a new awareness of the need to treat the addict by looking at all the members of a family—an approach known as "systems" psychology. To help loosen the unholy bond that ties addict and codependent, the recovery industry has taken codependents under its wing. Certainly, one should assume a "buyer beware" attitude, but it's reassuring to know others are dealing with the same problem.

Fatal Distraction

It wasn't always that way. Pia Mellody, a nurse and consultant to The Meadows in Wickenburg, AZ, a treatment center for addicts and codependents, is the author of *Facing Codependency* (Harper & Row, $10.95). In her book she talks about wrestling with her own codependency during the late '70s, long before it was so fashionable—or even recognized. "In those days," she says, "the counselors blamed how I was feeling on being married to someone chemically dependent—but I knew my symptoms were too sick, sometimes sicker than the alcoholic's. While working with the family members of drug addicts and alcoholics, I discovered that they had the same symptoms as me."

The common thread in alcoholic and other dysfunctional families is that both spouse and children maintain a precarious balance, keeping the focus on the addicted person, unwittingly supporting the habit and ignoring their own needs. Codependents also breathe life into the illusion that all their problems are caused by the addict—and that if they could somehow "fix" the other person, everything would be fine. But it doesn't necessarily work that way. In fact, when the alcoholic or addict goes into recovery, that's when spouses usually have to start looking at their own problems.

Unless codependents get help by going into therapy themselves and attending support groups, the vicious cycle will continue. Children who come from alcoholic homes have a

HELP YOURSELF: A GUIDE TO PEER SUPPORT GROUPS

Since the first Alcoholics Anonymous group was founded in 1935, peer-supported, 12-step recovery programs have been formed for people with virtually every type of addictive and compulsive behavior and, like AA's companion program, Al-Anon, for family and friends affected by them as well. Such groups have no professionals to guide them, although someone "chairs" each meeting. A donation, a dollar or less, is requested but not mandatory.

Below are three major support groups that deal with general codependency issues. Many groups overlap; if you feel comfortable in a particular type of meeting, it's probably right for you. More specific programs, like Nar-Anon (people affected by drug abuse), O-Anon (eating disorders) or Gam-Anon (gambling) can be found by looking up their companion groups (Narcotics Anonymous, Overeaters Anonymous and Gamblers Anonymous) in local phone directories. Or send an SASE to the National Self-Help Clearinghouse, 33 W. 42nd St., Room 620N, New York, NY 10036.

■ Al-Anon: Established in 1951 for families and friends of alcoholics, the more than 30,000 worldwide groups now attract anyone affected by someone else's drinking as well as people not in relationships with alcoholics but who want to learn why they tend to seek such people out. Alateen is for young people affected by alcoholism. Contact: Al-Anon Family Group Headquarters, P.O. Box 862, Midtown Station, New York, NY 10018-0862; 800-356-9996.

■ Codependents Anonymous (CoDA): Founded in 1986, this relatively new fellowship, for "men and women whose common problem is an inability to maintain functional relationships," already has over 1,500 meetings in more than 48 states and six other countries. Contact: Codependents Anonymous, P.O. Box 33577, Phoenix, AZ 85067-3577; 602-277-7991.

■ Adult Children of Alcoholics (ACA): Though these groups theoretically are for children who've grown up in alcoholic homes, you'll hear "I'm a child of a dysfunctional home" in these meetings as well. Not surprisingly, some of the issues raised here are related to codependency. Contact: Adult Children of Alcoholics, P.O. Box 3216, Torrance, CA 90505 (send an SASE for a printed meeting guide in your area); 213-534-1815.

---

greater chance, some estimate as much as 50%, of marrying substance abusers. Their early experience leaves them tragically prepared to serve as someone's mirror image.

"Both my parents were alcoholic. Then I found out that in every relationship I was in, the man was an alcoholic too," says Maureen, a 29-year-old alcoholism counselor who has been dealing with her own codependency for the last eight years. "At first, I only went into therapy because I needed help coping; then I realized I had to look at some of my own behavior patterns." Today Maureen is in both group and individual therapy and goes to Al-Anon, a self-help group for families and friends of alcoholics, based on the same 12-step program AA follows.

The Three C's

"There's no recipe for recovery," says Melody Beattie, author of what has become the unofficial bible for self-help seekers, *Codependent No More* (Harper/Hazeldon, $9.95). "The key is to find your own healing process—and the proof is if it's working." Depending on the person's needs and what he or she can afford, some type of therapy may be in order. Beattie is also an advocate of programs like Al-Anon and believes recovery begins with step one: "We admitted we were powerless over alcohol and that our lives had become unmanageable." Paradoxically, power starts with admitting your are powerless.

At such support-group meetings there are no professionals. People talk about how hard it is to change time-worn habits of relating to the alcoholic or addict; how they're great at taking care of others, but don't have a clue about meeting their own needs. Hearing it all for the first time can be overwhelming, which is why it's wise to try at least six meetings before deciding you're in the wrong place.

Whether it's the solace of knowing others feel the same way, the vulnerability and honesty expressed in "the rooms," as many refer to the meetings, or the belief that "a power greater than ourselves could restore us to sanity," as the second step reads, few dispute the benefits of regularly attending a 12-step program.

One slogan reminds, "It works if you work it." That means using the "tools" of the program: going to meetings, reading all the literature, nourishing one's spiritual life. "Codependents need to learn how to stand still for a minute, instead of running to *do* or *control*, so they can determine what they're feeling—to learn to act instead of react," Aileen Clucas explains. Spirituality, she says, means "being loving to yourself and connected to your higher self—your intuition—and respecting it."

Which is why taking time for yourself—many do it through prayer and meditation—is recommended for quieting the obsessive chatter in the codependent's head. It's also why slogans like, "Easy does it" and "Think" are popular at meetings. And it's why the concepts of surrender, detachment and letting go are repeated constantly, reminding codependents that they can't control someone else's behavior, they can only deal with their own anxiety and fear.

Naturally, many codependents deny they need help. "I resented it," admits Jane, recalling the first time she was advised to go to Al-Anon. "Why should I go, I thought? I'm the one who's had to put up with all of this—all my life, in fact." Jane had a schizophrenic mother and married an alcoholic.

Al-Anon and other support groups encourage people like Jane to focus on their own behavior. These programs also exhort parents and spouses to remember the Three C's: You didn't *cause* it, you can't *control* it, and you can't *cure* it. However, you can change your own behavior so it no longer supports the addict's abuses. With an addicted person, there's almost nothing you can do until you get help yourself.

Caroline's route to Al-Anon was slightly different. In AA since her early 20s, she also joined Al-Anon because she was in a relationship with an alcoholic and her life was still unmanageable. "After I got sober my behavior was just as crazy," Caroline admits. "I was terrified of new situations. I had low self-esteem. I made people feel guilty or responsible for me." A self-described "people addict," Caroline feels Al-Anon has been the key to her recovery. She learned that her substance abuse was only a symptom of much more deeply rooted pain. "Today I realize I was trying to take care of my pain by taking care of other people," she says.

Breaking the Unholy Bond

Peer support programs aren't for everyone—nor are they necessarily all the help a person needs. Treatment facilities mandate sessions for the whole family, so that substance abusers and codependents can finally begin to see how they affect one another. Ongoing couple or family therapy is often advised as well. The idea is to help people recognize and then disrupt the unhealthy patterns that have developed as a result of years of adapting to someone else's disease.

In addicted family systems, Peter Topaz explains, roles get confused. If the substance abuser is an adult, he or she has been pushed out of the adult role—the codependent has literally taken control—so the balance has to be restored. When a child is addicted, parents have to reclaim their authority as adults, setting limits and offering loving guidance, but not trying to control the child's substance abuse.

It may be hard to accept the idea, but it's not the codependent's job to directly help the alcoholic stay dry, stop the overeater from eating, or keep the gambler from the gaming table. What's more, even if the addict is in treatment, if family members don't also change *their* behavior, there's a good chance the person will relapse and start using again because the system is still supporting it.

"When my son was 15, a psychiatrist told me I should help him out even more than I already was. That's the opposite of what he needed," says a rueful Ellen, who spent years buffeted by a mental health network woefully ignorant about addiction and codependency. Today, Ellen and her husband are in family therapy with their son, the young man is in a therapy group with other addicts, and all three work with individual therapists as well. Ellen now sees how her efforts to "keep my son straight" inadvertently prevented him from facing his drug abuse. "We've learned that although we didn't create the problem, we became a part of it—and until we were disentangled, there would be no solution."

Some codependents opt for more intensive help in the form of short-term inpatient programs. For example, the Caron Foundation, a comprehensive addiction treatment center in Wernersville, PA, offers two such packages, one for adult children of alcoholic or other dysfunctional homes and another for codependents who are in current relationships with alcoholics and are first beginning to accept that they too need help. In both groups, participants are led through various experiential techniques such as "family sculpturing," in which they reenact painful scenes from childhood.

"I can't tell you what in fact works," admits Ann Smith, corporate director of family services for the Caron Foundation, and author of *Grandchildren of Alcoholics* (Health Communications, $8.95). She suspects, however, "It's the safety and opportunity to vent old, repressed feelings and hook up with the past—the group experience is very nurturing, not confrontational."

Liz, a graduate of Caron's five-day Adult Children of Alcoholics program, remarks, "It changed my life. I could finally get angry about my childhood. I'd been programmed to believe I couldn't change things." The 36-year-old associate TV director recalls a former relationship so blatantly codependent that there were no mirrors in the house: "I'd get up in the morning and say, 'How do I look?' and if the other person hesitated for a second, I'd change my clothes and my whole

CODEPENDENCY CHECKLIST

If you identify with some of the following statements, you may wish to visit one of the self-help groups listed on the preceding page.

1. I find myself "covering" for another person's alcohol or drug use, eating or work habits, gambling, sexual escapades or general behavior.

2. I spend a great deal of time talking about—and worrying about—other people's behavior/problems/future, instead of living my own life.

3. I have marked or counted bottles, searched for a hidden "stash," or in other ways monitored someone else's behavior.

4. I find myself taking on more responsibility at home or in a relationship—even when I resent it.

5. I ignore my own needs in favor of meeting someone else's.

6. I'm afraid that if I get angry, the other person will leave or not love me.

7. I worry that if I leave a relationship or stop controlling the other person, that person will fall apart.

8. I spend less time with friends and more with my partner/child in activities I wouldn't normally choose.

9. My self-esteem depends on what others say and think of me, or on my possessions or job.

10. I grew up in a family where there was little communication, where expressing feelings was not acceptable, and where there were either rigid rules or none at all.

day would be ruined. Today I don't need someone else as my mirror."

To be sure, some short-term codependency programs can be catalytic, but recovery is a process, not an event. Several caveats are in order for those seeking help. Any program that doesn't provide referrals for after-care groups or individual therapy, suggesting that the work is over when you leave, is totally irresponsible.

"There's no panacea. You can't fix these kinds of problems in five or 10 days," Topaz maintains. He also points out that graduates of these programs—and people who attend support groups as well—may just learn to *talk* about what they do, while their *behavior* remains the same. Indeed, many people in recovery dot their conversations with phrases like, "I'm bottoming out on my control issues," meaning that focusing on other people is no longer staving off the pain. "The words become another form of relief," Topaz says. "These people refuse to look inside themselves."

Dr. Cermak, who is developing psychiatric criteria for the diagnosis and treatment of codependency, has other concerns: "I'm distressed by inpatient treatment programs that don't define codependency. How do they evaluate if the person has been helped?"

Many other experts agree with Cermak's belief that not all counselors who treat alcoholics are equipped to deal with codependency. Though knowledgeable about addictions, they often lack child development training and the expertise to understand, no less handle, transference and countertransference reactions. These can occur when the client's buried feelings are projected onto the therapist or when the opposite happens because the therapist hasn't dealt with those issues in his or her own life.

Above all, recovery is a complex process. "I didn't realize I had to work for it," admits 23-year-old Jennifer, whose penchant for unavailable men is linked to a compulsive-overeater father and a workaholic mother. Jennifer had been in therapy and then spent four weeks in a codependency treatment center. "When I came home, despite a new openness, I started repeating old behavior."

It takes what it takes. A year later, continuing with individual therapy and regularly attending Al-Anon, Jennifer is learning to share her feelings. She's also beginning to recognize her own needs and act for herself. Today she knows she has choices—and she dares to imagine what many recovering codependents hope for: "I can feel a healthy relationship coming!"

what happy couples do right

Yes, there are reasons some marriages flourish when others fail. New studies can even predict what makes love last . . . and how you and your husband can grow closer.

Scott Winokur

Scott Winokur, a California-based newspaper reporter, often writes about human behavior.

Suppose there were a formula for happy marriage—would you follow it? Of course—who wouldn't?—especially if that formula were backed up by hard evidence that proved its success.

Well, the astonishing news is that such a formula now exists, thanks to pioneering research done with thousands of couples around the country. Psychologist Howard J. Markman, Ph.D., director of the Center for Marital and Family Studies at the University of Denver, is so confident about the lessons learned that he asserts scientists can now evaluate couples about to get married "and predict, with eighty percent accuracy, who will be divorced six or seven years later." If evaluating couples in ongoing relationships, the accuracy of predicting happiness in the future jumps to ninety percent, Dr. Markman says.

Giant-size claims, certainly. But Dr. Markman and others say that new scientific developments have made this possible. Using sophisticated monitoring equipment on couples in mock living-room labs, psychologists are able to analyze not only every word that passes between husband and wife, but nuances of tone, body language and facial expression. When these results are studied, patterns emerge that tell us what happy couples are doing right and what others are doing wrong—in short, the formula for lasting love we've all been waiting for.

*NAMES CHANGED TO PROTECT PRIVACY

Secrets of lasting love

You can't feel like newlyweds forever—or can you? Dr. Markman insists that love and attraction *don't* naturally diminish over time; they are attacked and overcome by negative feelings that grow out of destructive fights.

So what are the thorny issues that cause couples to battle each other? Religion? Money? Childrearing? Not at all. "It's the inability to negotiate almost embarrassingly small issues, like keeping dishes in the sink or dropping socks on the floor, that ultimately tears most at the fabric of a marriage," explains Dr. Markman.

Why is this so? Because, according to psychologist Clifford I. Notarius, Ph.D., of Washington, D.C.'s Catholic University, it matters less *what* couples fight about than *how* they fight about it. Since issues like dripping faucets come up daily—while big ones emerge far less frequently—the little things offer far more opportunity for couples to tangle. The key to a strong marriage, then, is being able to resolve a conflict without leaving scars.

But how can this be done? In comparing the sparring styles of unhappy pairs to those of happy couples, researchers have developed the following "rules."

Don't run from strife Happy couples may disagree vehemently, but they don't shut their partner out. When one spouse brings up an issue, the other listens attentively. From time to time, the listener will paraphrase what the other says ("You're worried about our overspending?") to make sure the message is understood.

In contrast, unhappy husbands or wives often withdraw when faced with a dilemma. John M. Gottman, Ph.D., professor of developmental psychology at the University of Washington, calls this "stonewalling" because a partner not only refuses to talk, but even tenses up his whole body or turns his face away.

More men than women are stonewallers—which may be out of self-defense, since new studies suggest that men are more stressed out by any emotional disruption. Whatever the reason for men's avoidance of conflict, women hate it. In fact, in one study, women rated stonewalling second only to physical violence as the male behavior most repugnant to them.

Give up the put-downs It may sound old-fashioned, but it's true—thriving couples are *polite* to each other. "Talking to each other graciously may be one of the most positive things couples can do," observes Dina Vivian, Ph.D., associate director of the University Marital Therapy Clinic, State University of New York at Stony Brook.

Unhappy couples, on the other hand, may employ such nasty tactics as character assassination ("You don't want a better job because you're lazy") and hostile mind-reading ("You don't call when you're going to be late because you don't care that I stay awake worrying").

What's more, unhappy pairs even have

women in love: what we do better than men

If you feel you do a lot more of the work when it comes to making your marriage run smoothly—you're right. Couple researchers say that women have more relationship skills: ● Women are better communicators. They're comfortable sharing their feelings and being psychologically intimate. And that's the critical ingredient in any successful relationship. ● Women are quick to sense trouble and steer around it—for example, by avoiding confrontations, or by refocusing the discussion before it escalates into all-out warfare. ● Women are far less likely to tune out or withdraw from a conflict than men are. ● You've heard of premature ejaculation? Well, there's such a thing as premature problem-solving, and men are much more prone to that, too. They jump to conclusions and try to force solutions before they've heard their partners out. Women, on the other hand, care deeply about being understood and making sure they understand.

contempt for their partner's feelings ("You can't drive me to the airport because the traffic signs are too confusing? You've gotta be kidding!"). Contempt will poison a relationship whether a couple has been together four months or 40 years, says Dr. Gottman. And even if contempt isn't put into words, it does just as much damage when it's expressed as an irritated tone of voice.

Don't dwell on downers Happy couples argue, too. But when they do, they stick closely to the relevant issues—and try to end the fight.

Clashes for well-matched couples will go on only so long before one partner refocuses the exchange ("Look, let's just decide who's going to drive Molly to gymnastics. Later we can talk about the question of private time for each of us.") or calms the other down ("Let's take a break. We're both too upset to discuss this reasonably right now.").

Fights also escalate because one partner, in anger, makes a hurtful comment. But in stable couples, the other partner won't always retaliate when unfairly provoked. Instead, they find ways to defuse tension:

He: I was really looking forward to a decent meal!

She: Your hours are so unpredictable I can't plan one.

He: There's no choice. I'm under a lot of pressure at work.

She: Yeah, okay. Well, for tonight, let's order a pizza. Sausage or pepperoni?

In other words, says Dr. Notarius, "it's not how you get *into* arguments, but how you exit them." For unhappy couples, there is no exit. Every spat is a slippery slope—one unkind word leads to another:

He: I guess my mistake was looking forward to a nice dinner.

She: If you came home on time, you might have gotten one. You care more about your job than me.

He: Somebody's gotta make a living.

She: It wouldn't be you if I didn't work like a dog to put you through school!

Experts call this sort of runaway spleen-venting the strongest predictor of separation and divorce over time. Says Dr. Notarius: "The couple exchanges criticisms and stops listening to each other." Indeed, there can be ten or more fast and furious exchanges within the space of a minute or two. Worse, the couple often veers off into heated, unproductive fighting over tangential or old, unresolved issues. The result of such "kitchen-sinking" is that nothing gets resolved—and negative feelings rage.

Think like a winner A history of success in resolving conflicts breeds confidence in a couple and makes further success likely, scientists say.

Unhappy couples, on the other hand, expect to continue to fail. Researchers found that when unhappily married men and women who hadn't seen each other all day were

love builders...

● Listening well Couples who remain open to what their partners are trying to say are more likely to stay together. This doesn't mean you must agree all the time, but it does mean you shouldn't *resist* a different point of view.

● Solving problems Negotiating the 1,001 bumps in the road of daily life is crucial to a relationship's success. Happy couples find solutions to problems; they don't use fights merely as forums for hurting each other's feelings.

● Showing respect Let your partner know that you value his individuality and you stand behind him. That means banish sarcasm and sniping and other kinds of rudeness.

...and busters

● Shutting down Doomed pairs can't communicate well because they don't really try to listen—they mostly try to contradict. Every dispute becomes an opportunity to bring up any problem that has ever occurred in the relationship (kitchen-sinking), or to withdraw (stonewalling).

● Sweating the small stuff Couples who are virtually certain to break up can't seem to find a relaxed, reasonably efficient way of figuring out how to settle differences as small as which movie to see or whose friends to visit. Eventually, their inability to negotiate does them in, no matter how much in love they *think* they may be.

● Lashing out Couples who get drawn into clashes where they quickly begin to name-call or show contempt for the other's point of view will not only fail to solve their immediate problem, they likely won't make it as a couple.

called together to a lab to discuss a problem, they registered dramatic signs of stress—elevated heart rates, more rapid respiration and increased perspiration. Convinced that an irresolvable conflict lies ahead, their bodies shift into distress modes in advance, says Dr. Gottman and his psychophysiologist colleague, Robert Levenson, Ph.D., of the University of California, Berkeley.

Nor can distressed couples readily draw on memories of good times together. In a study at the University of Washington in Seattle, scientists found that unhappy couples selectively "forgot" up to half the positive experiences they had shared! "It's almost as if once you become unhappy, there's a negative mind-set that allows you to better remember the negative things and forget the positive," says psychologist K. Daniel O'Leary, Ph.D., director of the University Marital Therapy Clinic, SUNY at Stony Brook.

Teach yourself tenderness A happy byproduct of the new research is that couples can be taught to nurture what's good in their relationships and unlearn destructive habits. There are programs and seminars offered at marital-studies centers and through private psychologists and clergy around the country. (For a program near you, contact PREP, University of Denver, Center for Marital and Family Studies, Denver, CO 80208.)

"We don't argue about trite things anymore, like John's lateness or my housekeeping," says Kass Patterson, 30, of Denver, a graduate of Dr. Markman's PREP (Prevention and Relationship Enhancement Program). Kass, a legal secretary, and her husband, John, a 33-year-old food-service sales representative, took the five-week program of two-hour training sessions just before they married. Though the couple felt they were already "pretty good" together, they fought frequently. "We'd argue and, at some point, one of us would storm out of the room, with nothing resolved," Kass says.

Each PREP session taught a new skill. "Listening was a big one for us," says Kass. To help them control their impulses to cut each other off, the psychologists had them use a prop—a piece of carpet—and only the person with the prop had "the floor," and could speak. Before getting "the floor," a partner had to prove he or she really had listened by paraphrasing.

one couple's fight: will the marriage win?

Experts say they can now predict if a couple will stay together based just on their style of arguing. Let's listen to a couple from Long Island, New York—they're in their twenties, and together they earn slightly over $30,000—arguing about money. Ask yourself: is a breakup inevitable, or can they stay together? Then compare your observations with those of psychologist Howard Markman, Ph.D., director of the Center for Marital and Family Studies at the University of Denver.

WHAT THEY SAID:

HE: You think money grows on a tree.

SHE: You just fly off the handle whenever I want to discuss our finances.

HE: You never catch on, though. We make only X amount of dollars—you can't go buying dishwashers. Somebody's got to pay for that, you know.

SHE: It always seems like I'm the bad guy. We're always going to have bills. Everybody has bills.

HE: I know. But I don't like bills and I'll do what I can to avoid them. I'm breaking my butt. When do I enjoy life? When I'm sixty years old? We got bills now. Let's get them cleared up.

SHE: You'd be bitching about something else. You want me to look at your way of thinking. You never look at mine.

HE: I can't afford your way! I don't have a checkbook that doesn't quit, I'm sorry. Curtail it a little bit. It'll help. Just a little bit here, a little bit there.

SHE: I don't spend it on myself. That's another thing that drives me crazy. When I get any money, it goes to food shopping.

HE: You buy nonsense things. You buy a pool for the dog! I mean the dog needs a pool? I've had millions of dogs. They never had pools!

SHE: You're talking about ten dollars.

HE: It was more than ten dollars because I went to the store and looked and it was about twenty dollars.

SHE: It was not! It was twelve ninety-nine and the sticker is still on it. . . . You bought the dog a nine-dollar bone! When *you* spend money, it's fine. When I spend it, it's a different story. (Voice shaking) It's *always* the way.

AN EXPERT'S ANALYSIS

"This is an example of what I'd call 'destructive arguing,'" says Dr. Markman. "It's as if they're running two parallel tapes here. Someone should be saying, 'Hold it. Stop the action. This discussion isn't going well.'

"He starts off with hostile mind-reading: 'You think money grows on a tree.' That usually precipitates a defensive reaction, and that's what happened here ('You just fly off the handle if I want to discuss money'). He could have said 'How do you feel about money?' rather than assuming he knows.

"Of course, she defends herself, but then mind-reads, too, in a hostile way—'You want me to look at your way of thinking.'"

Despite all this, Dr. Markman believes the couple may not be in serious trouble—not yet, anyway.

"They need to work on their communication and arguing style, but there are some good signs here, too. There's no terrible verbal or physical abuse and both partners stay constructively engaged in the process. Neither is withdrawing."

WHAT THEY SHOULD HAVE SAID:

HE: Why do we argue about money all the time? Maybe we have very different ideas about it.

SHE: I find it hard to talk about because you seem to get upset whenever I raise the subject.

HE: If I do, it's because I have the feeling you don't really accept the fact that there's only so much. If we buy something on credit, somebody's got to pay for that eventually.

SHE: I understand that as well as you do. But you have to spend money to live. Everybody has bills.

HE: I know. But I don't like bills and I'll do what I can to avoid them. I'm working hard now. When do I enjoy life? When I'm an old man?

SHE: I can sympathize with that. Can we figure out a way to buy what we need for the house? After all, I'm not talking about spending money on myself. I'd like a little credit for that.

HE (laughing): Sure! But please just don't ever buy something like a pool for the dog again!

SHE (laughing): Okay, I promise I won't—as long as you stop buying him expensive bones at the pet store!

HE: It's a deal.

THE HAPPY/HEALTHY CONNECTION

A happy marriage isn't only more satisfying emotionally—it may keep you healthy.

"A bad marriage is a double whammy," says Ohio State University psychologist Janice Kiecolt-Glaser, Ph.D. "You lose your major source of support and replace it with a major source of stress."

This is what happens physiologically, scientists believe: When couples fight, they arouse their autonomic nervous systems, which, in turn, affect the functioning of their endocrine glands. Hormones produced by those glands—for example, cortisol, a stress hormone—then suppress their immune systems. Hours or days later, both unhappy people might find themselves reaching for cold medicine.

Scientists don't believe occasional spats do physical harm. Rather, it's chronic fighting that overstimulates your hormones. Studies show that people in troubled relationships or newly separated from their mates have poorer immune systems than men and women in satisfactory marriages. "Separated individuals suffer about thirty percent more acute illnesses and visit the doctor about thirty percent more frequently than married adults," report Dr. Kiecolt-Glaser and coresearcher (and husband) Ronald Glaser, Ph.D., a psychophysiologist.

A stressful marriage takes a shocking toll on women's health. Says psychologist John Gottman, Ph.D., of the University of Washington, "Women in troubled marriages are more prone to respiratory symptoms, gastrointestinal problems, skin problems, genital and urinary problems. Also, they become more fatigued and they have more psychological problems."

For men, the stress assault is more focused—but perhaps more damaging. Since men tend to withdraw when marital troubles loom, they become lonely. And that, it's been shown, makes them more prone to cardiovascular problems.

The prescription for good health: keep your marriage happy.

Kass and John also practiced the XYZ Exercise, in which individuals frame misgivings as expressions of feeling—"In situation X when you do Y, I feel Z"—rather than to hurl blame. For example, instead of crying "You sonofabitch! My friends always said you couldn't be trusted!" a woman might say, "When we're at a party and you spend the entire evening looking at other women, I feel awful."

When a marriage needs more than just fine-tuning, a more vigorous program may be needed. Isabel and Gene Hopper* contacted the University Marital Therapy Clinic at Stony Brook, New York, when their marriage was on the verge of collapse. They fought about everything and resolved nothing. They were accepted for a 20-week program of one-hour sessions.

First, the Hoppers' therapist focused on the "positives" in the couple's relationship—artifacts of the love that originally brought them together. Whenever appropriate, she reminded the couple that there were things besides their children that made their relationship worth saving.

Additionally, the Hoppers made a "wish list" of little things they'd like to see the other do during the week ahead—kiss hello, take a shower together, have dinner together on weekends.

This intensive therapy is intended to offset the impact of past fights and disappointments. As the Hoppers, who saved their marriage, have discovered, research-based therapy can revive the bonds of love and help couples believe again in the joys of lasting love.

Friends Forever

In your most important relationship—your marriage—friendship is easily neglected. Here's how to put the spark into your life again.

BRUCE A. BALDWIN

Dr. Bruce A. Baldwin is a practicing psychologist and author who heads Direction Dynamics in Wilmington, North Carolina, a consulting service specializing in promoting quality of life. For busy men and women, Dr. Baldwin has written It's All in Your Head: Lifestyle Management Strategies for Busy People.

Do you remember when you first met your spouse? You enjoyed just being together, laughing, telling jokes, talking about everyday things happening in your lives. Your relationship and your friendship were so strong, and you understood each other so well.

For many couples factors develop through the years that begin to undermine that once-close friendship. As lives become more complicated and pressured, couples can easily drift into a lifestyle in which they slowly grow apart.

This, combined with unrelenting demands on time and energy, often leaves both partners feeling alone and without support. A serious question may cross each partner's mind: "What am I doing here? I don't feel good, and my marriage is nothing more than an empty shell." The remedy for such a situation is to once again build a solid friendship within the marriage.

Ironically, in the most important relationship in your life—your marriage—friendship is at once easily neglected and difficult to maintain. Furthermore, the quality of friendships with others outside of marriage may be suffering, too. Many people have completely forgotten not only the vital importance of being good friends with a spouse, but also how to be a friend to someone else. Learning the basics of friendship can enhance your life by bringing a deeper meaning to all of your relationships.

Good Friends Stay in Touch with One Another.

Friendship implies a continuing relationship in which both parties involved make consistent **efforts to maintain. With a friend who is not a spouse, these efforts might** involve quality time spent together, telephone calls, cards on special occasions, and dropping in just to say "Hi." To neglect these special efforts is to risk allowing the relationship to wither and possibly disappear entirely. This is exactly what happens with many once-good friends who say, "We just grew apart over the years."

The same situation can happen with a spouse. It is surprisingly easy to drift apart emotionally while living together. One of the most critical aspects of friendship is that a friend is frequently in your thoughts in positive ways. But with inadvertent changes in priorities and hectic lifestyles, your daily focus shifts to tasks being accomplished, not on staying in touch with your spouse. Your friendship together begins to wither and will eventually die unless you make the effort to reestablish it.

To counter this chain of events, communicate that you care and that you are aware of your spouse. Here are specific suggestions to put into practice right away.

Verbally express interest in your spouse. To remain best friends with your spouse, communicate, "I am interested in you as a person." Make it a point to ask your spouse about his or her day, inquire about what was read or seen, and engage in other forms of small talk that transcend career and parental roles.

Touch base every day. This coordination function is a necessary part of busy lifestyles. Take a few moments every day to get signals straight about schedules and activities, and who has to be where when. Taking a few moments to coordinate also prevents conflict and frustration.

Let your spouse know where you are. Be sure to let your spouse know where you are going and when you will be back. It's courteous and caring to let your spouse know when you'll be late. A cheerful hello coming in and a caring goodbye when going out certainly helps a friendship, too.

Good Friends Share Themselves and Their Experiences.

Good friends share both the good and the bad. This is the intimacy part of any relationship and is perhaps one of the deepest and most rewarding aspects. Without this kind of personal sharing, you may have an acquaintance, but you certainly

From *USAir Magazine*, May 1992, pp. 16, 18, 20-21, 24-26. This article is adapted from B. A. Baldwin's "It's All in Your Head: Lifestyle Management Strategies for Busy People," *Direction Dynamics*, 1985. The book is available from *Direction Dynamics*, 309 Honeycutt Dr., Wilmington, NC 28412 for $11.70 postpaid (NC residents should add 6% sales tax).

don't have a good friend. With their thoughts, feelings, and experiences, good friends create an openness that deepens the bond between them.

In many marriages the husband-wife relationship deteriorates so that when feelings are shared, they are extremely negative in tone. Thoughts become critical or cynical, and experiences related focus only on problems and frustrations. Or little sharing at all takes place because of the sense that a partner doesn't really care.

To bring back the many benefits of openness and positive sharing, you must first of all want to share yourself with your partner. With time and a little effort, relating openly becomes easier. Here are three good ways to begin.

Banter with your spouse. Tell your spouse the latest joke you heard, or relate a thought you had about something important to you. Take a moment to describe a fond childhood memory that popped into your mind.

Create interesting things to talk about and share. People doing interesting things have interesting things to share. Create new and stimulating experiences for yourself or with your partner. Doing so also breaks you out of deadening routines.

Keep your vision of the future alive. Young couples talk constantly about their future together. Often, this vision dies from neglect. To keep your future together, talk often about what "we" want and how "we" are going to get there. Such sharing helps solidify the partnership in your marriage.

Good Friends Are Supportive During Troubled Times.

This is what makes a true friend. Almost everyone has had an unfortunate experience in which a so-called friend just wasn't supportive in a time a great emotional need. Under such circumstances, the relationship either ends outright or becomes much more superficial. Friends must always be there for one another, not only during the good times, but also during times of emotional turmoil or personal crisis. To have such a friend in times of need is a wonderful source of strength.

Typically, couples experience many small problems along with some major crises during their years together. Little frustrations can often be handled on one's own. It is absolutely necessary, however, to be a true friend to your partner in personal crises—during the death of a parent or a loved one, serious health problems, or loss of a job, for example. To be a source of strength when such crises occur takes time, energy, and commitment. Keep the following practices in mind.

SMALL ACTS OF KINDNESS AND LOVING WORDS ALLOW A PARTNER TO GROW AND TO LOVE OPENLY.

Make yourself available to listen. Let your partner take the initiative, then do lots of listening. Make it a point to be immediately available no matter what else is going on. Don't try to give advice or solve problems; just be there and be attentive.

Touch in supportive ways. A hug, holding hands, and sitting close are all important aspects of supporting your spouse in times of need. You don't have to say a thing. Communicate that you care in physically and emotionally supportive ways.

Take initiative to show you care. Communicate to your spouse that you know there is a problem and that you care enough to make life a bit easier because of it. Cooking a special dinner, doing more to keep the kids occupied, or arranging time alone all help immensely during times of crisis.

Friends Consistently Validate One Another.

Good friends communicate a very simple message: "I like you, and being with you makes me feel good." It is this dimension that makes a friendship attractive. It is also absolutely critical in maintaining a strong day-to-day friendship.

In a marriage, this kind of positive validation is more difficult to maintain over the years. As stresses and pressures build, negative feelings within are more easily expressed, and that upbeat way of relating disappears. Cautiousness and outright defensiveness impede open communication. Time spent together is less personally satisfying, and enjoyment of that time diminishes.

This is best exemplified by a marital partner who says, "I still love my spouse, but I'm not sure I like him/her much anymore." If you've had such feelings, it's past time to reestablish your friendship with your partner. Start by putting these three suggestions into practice.

Cheerfully acknowledge your partner when you come home. Make it a point to greet your partner when you first get home after work with a cheerful welcome. Then proceed to make small talk for just two or three minutes. A hug at this time wouldn't hurt a bit, either.

Compliment your spouse every day. Complimentary remarks give a wonderful feeling, and by making them an important part of your day, you begin to focus on and notice positive things about your partner.

Flirt and horse around with your spouse. Flirting is a wonderful, validating way to relate, and it needn't end in the bedroom. It simply says, "You're still attractive to me."

Deep Trust Always Exists Between Friends.

As any friendship deepens, a corresponding openness about experiences and feelings develops. To be open in this way also requires vulnerability—letting another person know about personal doubts and sensitivities. While it is very healthy to share your feelings with a good friend, such information must always be respected, and the vulnerability it entails must never be violated.

If such trust is not kept, the friendship usually ends.

Trust is the bedrock of deep emotional intimacy between husband and wife. Over time, marriage partners become aware of the other's vulnerabilities. As life becomes more pressured and the marital relationship becomes strained, two critical questions arise. First, do the marriage partners make it a point to keep their relationship open enough to share their innermost thoughts and feelings? Second, do these same spouses respect their partner's vulnerabilities enough not to use them in hurtful ways? If the answer to both of these questions is not a truthful "yes," then trust in that relationship has been impaired.

When repeated marital betrayal has occurred, intimacy in that relationship has been damaged. Both husband and wife suffer because they cannot risk being hurt by being too open with each other. To rebuild the trust necessary for intimacy, consider these suggestions.

Never hit below the belt. One of the surest ways to shut down intimate communication in a relationship is to use a personal sensitivity to hurt your partner when you are angry. Always respond in mature, nonpunitive ways when conflict occurs—even if your partner doesn't do so.

Do not gossip about your partner. Too many husbands and wives talk about their spouses to friends, relatives, and acquaintances. When such information exchange is positive and upbeat, no problems arise. When it is disparaging or reveals intimate information, it's a betrayal of marital trust.

Do not be judgmental with your partner. Being able to say anything to your best friend and knowing you will not be rejected is clearly one of the best qualities of any friendship. When you accept your spousal friend without judging or rejecting, intimate communication will stay open.

Friends Can Let Go and Have Fun Together.

Good friendships do not focus exclusively on problems or emotionally intimate discussion. While openness to deeper relating must occur, time should be spent just having fun together—playing a strenuous game of tennis, sitting quietly enjoying small talk, laughing together over lunch, or dancing the night away. Good friends can let go to enjoy good times spent together knowing that they are deeply accepted and that they will be there for one another when tough times come.

As married life becomes busier, humor often fades, and no time remains for fun. Stressed and tired, couples feel overwhelmed with responsibilities. Often, they are simply too pooped to go out except for obligatory social functions. Such men and women may completely forget how to relax and enjoy lighthearted times together. Fun, though, is not only energizing, but also a powerful tool in relieving stress. When such quality time becomes a marital priority, a home environment of warmth and laughter replaces one filled with negativity.

GIVE UP TRYING TO CHANGE YOUR PARTNER OR CHANGING FOR YOUR PARTNER.

You and your partner may need to relearn how to let go, because if all you see each day is work and more work, is it all worth it? Here are suggestions to help you both get away from it all and appreciate one another again.

Make sure you have regular time alone as a couple. After children come, finding time to be alone together becomes more difficult. Older children should be trained to respect "couple time" at home. Get a sitter and go out alone together regularly just to have some fun.

Do not contaminate good times with work. When you do spend time alone, do not take work along. Do not make notes or make/take telephone calls. Turn off your beeper; turn on the telephone answering machine. Never talk about work or what you have to do tomorrow.

Friends Accept and Respect One Another.

A good friendship is never static; it is a fluid relationship that exists over time as two people encounter different life experiences and changes. The base of such a relationship is a deep acceptance of one another along with encouragement as life circumstances evolve. Positive change is not discouraged, nor is there an implication that both must stay the same for the relationship to continue. Such acceptance also permits good friends to give one another feedback and different perspectives without defensiveness or a feeling of rejection.

Love and acceptance should never be conditional. Too often, husbands and wives want their partners to be someone other than who they really are. The result is that a spouse is not truly accepted and nurtured as a unique human being. The choice of the individual on the receiving end of such a conditional relationship is a no-win situation—that is, to be oneself and be rejected or to give up being oneself to meet a spouse's expectations.

Whether expressed overtly or subtly, such a nonaccepting attitude or set of expectations drives a wedge in the relationship that tends to deepen with the years. It is to your mutual benefit to change in positive ways for yourself and your marital friendship. Here are ways to begin making changes.

Express unconditional love and acceptance. Good friendships and solid marriages are always built on deep mutual acceptance communicated regularly in words and deeds. Small acts of kindness and loving words ("I love you just because you're you") allow a partner to grow and to love openly in return.

Encourage positive change for you both. Give up trying to change your partner or changing for your partner. Decide instead to make needed changes in yourself simply because it's the right thing to do.

Be willing to compromise. When divisive issues arise, assume that there are two valid points of view being expressed by friends who truly respect one another's viewpoints and values. Reject selfish solutions to the problem and look for mutually satisfying ways to resolve the issues at hand.

Friends Benefit from Their Relationships.

In a world where impersonality is growing and families are often isolated from one another, having at least one good friend is absolutely necessary. But many men and women overlook the most important source of friendship of all—their spouses.

If you make a commitment to one another to renew your marital friendship, not only will you bring the good life that you've always wanted much closer, but there will also be other benefits.

You won't be lonely anymore. Marriage can be a terribly lonely place without friendship. As you build your marital friendship, that "we're a team" feeling will return. No matter what happens, you will always be two close friends and partners working together for a good life.

You will have an emotional anchor. Good times are easy to handle, but during the bad times you need a friend. Knowing that your best friend and partner will always be there for you becomes a source of personal security. Knowing that you can get through anything together becomes an emotional anchor for you both.

Joy will return to your life. It's good to know with absolute certainty that your partner loves and cares about you. With this comes inner peace, a sense of personal fulfillment, and feelings of joy and contentment.

A special friendship is what a marriage relationship is all about. At its root, marriage is not sex, romance, emotional highs, or pleasure. All these things are part of the total relationship, but the core of marriage is a partnership built on emotional closeness, acceptance of one another, and fulfilling companionship. Read the vows you made to one another when you married. They are a wonderful description of a good friendship.

The Dance of Intimacy

A relationship is like a dance: to stay close without stepping on each other's toes takes practice. To make real music takes finesse. With insights from a renowned psychologist, you can bring out the best in each other and make your partnership soar.

Harriet Goldhor Lerner, Ph.D.

What does an intimate relationship require of us to be successful? For starters, intimacy means that we can be who we are in a relationship and allow the other person to do the same. By "being who we are," we can talk openly about things that are important to us, we can take a clear position on where we stand on significant emotional issues, and we can clarify the limits of what is acceptable and tolerable to us. If we allow the other person to do the same, we can stay emotionally connected to that other party, who thinks, feels, and believes differently, without needing to change, convince, or fix him.

An intimate relationship is one in which neither person silences, sacrifices, or betrays the self, and each expresses strength and vulnerability, weakness and competence, in a balanced way. Truly intimate relationships do not operate at the expense of the self, nor do they allow the self to operate at the expense of the other. This is a tall order, or, more accurately, a lifelong challenge. But it is the heart and soul of intimacy.

Only when we stay in a relationship over time—whether by necessity or choice—is our capacity for intimacy truly put to the test. Only in a long-term relationship are we called upon to navigate that delicate balance between separateness and connectedness, and only then can we confront the challenge of sustaining both, without losing either, in a way that works for each partner.

When Relationships Are Stuck

All of us develop our identities through emotional connectedness to others, and we continue to need close relationships throughout our lives. We get into trouble when we distance ourselves from friends, lovers, and kin; pretend we don't need people; ignore a relationship that begins to go badly; or put no energy into generating new options for change.

The challenge of change is greatest when a relationship becomes a source of frustration and our attempts to fix things only lead to more of the same. These stuck relationships are often "too distant," and/or "too intense," precluding real intimacy. Intense feelings—no matter how positive—are hardly a measure of true and enduring closeness. In fact, intense feelings may *prevent* us from taking a careful and objective look at the intimate dance we carry on with significant people in our lives. Intense togetherness can easily flip into intense distance—or intense conflict, for that matter.

Too much intensity means one person overfocuses on the other in a blaming or worried way or in an attempt to fix him. Or each person may be overfocused on the other and underfocused on the self.

Too much distance indicates there is little togetherness and real sharing of one's true self in the relationship. Important issues go underground rather than get aired and worked on. Many distant relationships are also intense, because distance is one way we manage intensity. If, for instance, you haven't seen your ex-husband in five years and can't talk with him about the kids without clutching yourself inside, then you have a *very* intense relationship.

Once a relationship is stuck, the motivation to change things is not enough to make it happen. For one thing, we may be so buffeted by strong feelings that we can't think clearly and objectively about the problem or our own part in it. When intensity is high we *react* rather than observe and think, we overfocus on the *other* rather than on the self, and we find ourselves in polarized positions where we are unable to see more than one side of an issue (our own) and find new ways to relate. We may navigate relationships in ways that lower our anxiety in the short run but diminish our capacity for intimacy over the long haul.

In addition, we may have a strong wish for change in a relationship but be unaware of, or unwilling to confront, the actual source of anxiety that is fueling a problem and blocking intimacy. How can we gain the courage to discover and confront the real issues? How can we unblock our intimate relationships?

Naming the Problem

A couple of years ago my sister came to me with a problem that illustrates this situation. Susan called me one day and confessed she was having a very rough time with her boyfriend, David. Although she felt entirely committed to the relationship, David said he needed more time to work through his own issues in order to make a decision about their living together. Susan and David lived in different cities, making for long and tiring weekend trips; however, this long-distance arrangement (and David's indefiniteness) was nothing new—it had been going on for quite some time.

What was new was my sister's sudden feeling of panic, resulting in her pressuring David for a decision he was not yet ready to make. Because Susan had been working for some time on altering her pattern of pursuing men who were distancers in romantic relationships, she was able to see her behavior like a red warning flag. She was unable, however, to tone down her reactivity and stop pursuing. By the time Susan called me, she was feeling terrible.

While thinking about my sister's situation, I was particularly struck by the *timing* of the problem. Susan's sense of desperation and her heightened reactivity to David's wish for more time and space followed a trip we took to Phoenix to visit our parents and to see our uncle Si, who was dying from a fast-moving lung cancer. Si's diagnosis had been a shock to us—he'd always been such a vibrant, active man. Seeing him sick reminded our family of past losses, impending losses, and some recent health scares on the family tree. Of all these stresses, the closest to home for Susan and me was the earlier diagnosis of our father's rare, degenerative brain disease. Because our father surprised everyone by regaining his functioning, this devastating diagnosis was replaced with a more hopeful one—but the experience had been very hard on our family.

During our phone conversation, I asked Susan if there might be a connection between her anxious focus on David and all the emotions that were stirred up by our recent visit to Phoenix. This made intellectual sense to her, but it also seemed a bit abstract, since Susan did not feel any connection at a gut level.

A few weeks later Susan visited me for a long weekend and decided to consult a family systems therapist. Afterward, she began to more fully appreciate the link between recent health issues in our family and her anxious pursuit of David. Simply *thinking* about this connection helped Susan to de-intensify her focus on David and reflect more calmly and objectively on her current situation.

Only when we stay in a relationship over time—whether by necessity or choice—is our capacity for intimacy truly put to the test.

Susan was also challenged to think about the pursuer-distancer pattern she was stuck in. It was as if 100 percent of the anxiety and ambivalence about living together was David's. And as if Susan was just 100 percent raring to go—no worries at all, except how they would decorate the apartment. Such polarities (she stands for togetherness, he for distance) are common enough, but they distort the experience of self and other and keep us stuck.

Finally, Susan confronted the fact that she was putting so much energy into her relationship with David, she was neglecting her own family and her career. On the one hand, Susan's attention to this relationship made sense because insuring its success was her highest priority. On the other hand, focusing on a relationship at the expense of one's own goals and life plan overloads that relationship. The best way Susan could work on her relationship with David was to work on her own self. This kind of self-focus is a good rule of thumb for all of us. While Susan's energy was overfocused on David, another woman might find herself overfocusing on another kind of relationship; she might dwell too intensely on a co-worker who undermines her or on a troubled sibling.

Breaking the Pursuit Cycle

Susan had gained insight and understanding of her problem, but her next challenge was translating what she had learned into action. What could she do differently when she was back home to lower her anxiety and achieve a calmer, more balanced relationship with David? By the time Susan left, she had formulated a plan. Whenever we are feeling very anxious, it can be enormously helpful to have a clear plan, one based not on reactivity and a reflexive need to "do something—anything!" but rather one based on reflection and a solid understanding of the problem.

Susan enacted her plan. First, she shared with David that she had been thinking about their relationship during her trip and had gained some insight into her own behavior. "I came to realize," she told him, "that the pressure I was feeling about our living together had less to do with you and our relationship and more to do with my anxiety about some other things." She filled David in on what these were—family issues related to health and loss. David was understanding and clearly relieved.

Susan also told him that perhaps she was letting him express the ambivalence for both of them, which probably wasn't fair. She reminded David that her own track record with relationships surely provided her with good reason to be anxious about commitment, but she had avoided this pretty well by focusing on *his* problem and *his* wish to put off the decision.

This statement was the hardest for Susan, because when we are in a pursuer-distancer polarity, pursuers are convinced that all they want is more togetherness, and distancers are convinced that all they want is more distance. Sometimes only after the pursuit cycle is broken can each party begin to experience the wish we all have for both separateness and togetherness.

Finally, Susan told David that she had been neglecting her work projects and needed to put more time and attention into them. "Instead of driving up next weekend," Susan said, "I'm going to stay at home and get some work done." For the first time in a while, Susan became the spokesperson for more distance, *not in an angry, reactive manner but as a calm move for self.*

The changes Susan made were successful in breaking the pursuer-distancer pattern, which was bringing her pain. If we are pursuers, such moves can be excruciatingly difficult to initiate and sustain in a calm, nonreactive way. Why? Because pursuing is often an unconscious reaction to anxiety. If it is our *usual* reaction, we will initially become *more* anxious when we keep it in check.

From where, then, do we get the motivation and the courage to maintain such a change? We must get it from the conviction that the old ways simply do not work.

Before Susan returned home, she considered another option aimed at helping her to calm things down with David. Whenever she found herself feeling anxious about the relationship and slipping back into the pursuit mode, she would contemplate sitting down and writing a letter to our father instead, or calling home.

This may sound a bit farfetched at first, but it makes good sense. If Susan managed her anxiety about family issues by distancing, she would be more likely to get intense with David. If, instead, she could stay connected to the *actual source of her anxiety,* she would feel more anxious about our parents' failing health, but the anxiety would be less likely to overload her love relationship. Indeed, learning how to stay in touch with our relatives and working on key emotional issues at their source lays the groundwork for more solid intimate relationships in the present or future.

A Postscript on Partners Who Can't Make Up Their Minds

What if *your* partner can't make a commitment? What if he's not ready to think about marriage, not ready to give up another relationship, not sure he's really in love? He may or may not be ready in two years—or 20. Does Susan's story imply that we should hang around *forever,* working on our own issues and failing to address our partner's uncertainty? Does it mean that we should never take a position on our partner's distancing or lack of commitment? Certainly not. A partner's long-term ambivalence *is* an issue for us—that is, if we really want to settle down.

We will, however, be *least successful* in

An intimate relationship requires a level of communication that allows each person to be comfortable with who they are and not feel it necessary to sacrifice their own identity.

addressing the commitment issue, or any other, when we feel reactive and intense. Working to keep anxiety down is a priority, because anxiety drives reactivity, which drives polarities. (*All* he can do is distance. *All* she can do is pursue.) The more we pay attention to the different sources of anxiety that affect our lives, the more calmly and clearly we'll navigate the hot spots with our intimate other.

A Calm Bottom Line

Let's look at a woman who was able to take a clear position with her distant and ambivalent partner, a position relatively free from reactivity and expressions of anxious pursuit. Gwenna was a 26-year-old real estate agent who sought my help for a particular relationship issue. For two and a half years she had been dating Greg, a city planner who had had disastrous first and second marriages and couldn't make up his mind about a third. Gwenna was aware that Greg backed off further under pressure, yet she didn't want to live forever with the status quo. How did she ultimately handle the situation?

As a first step, Gwenna talked with Greg about their relationship, calmly initiating the conversation in a low-keyed fashion. She shared her perspective on both the strengths and weaknesses of their relationship and what her hopes were for their future. She asked Greg to do the same. Unlike earlier conversations, she conducted this one without pursuing him, pressuring him, or diagnosing his problems with women. At the same time, Gwenna asked Greg some clear questions, the answers to which exposed his own vagueness.

"How will you know when you *are* ready to make a commitment?" she asked. "What specifically would need to change or be different than it is today?"

"I don't know," Greg responded. When questioned further, the best he could come up with was he'd "just feel it."

"How much more time do you need to make a decision one way or another?"

"I'm not sure," Greg replied. "Maybe a couple of years, but I really can't answer a question like that. I can't predict or plan my feelings."

And so it went.

Gwenna really loved this man, but two years (and maybe more) was longer than she could comfortably wait. So, after much thought, she told Greg that she would wait until the fall—about ten months—but she would move on if he couldn't commit himself to marriage by then. She was open about her own wish to marry and have a family with him yet equally clear that her first priority was a mutually committed relationship. If Greg was not at that point by fall, then she would end the relationship—painful though it would be.

Having set up a waiting period, Gwenna was able *not* to pursue Greg, and *not* become distant or otherwise reactive to his expressions of ambivalence. In this way, she gave him emotional space to struggle with his dilemma, and the relationship had its best chance of succeeding. Her bottom line position (a decision by the fall) was not a threat or an attempt to rope Greg in, but rather a true definition of self and a clarification of the time limits she could live with. Gwenna would not have been able to proceed this way if the relationship were burdened with baggage from her past and present that she was not paying attention to.

Unfortunately, doing our part right does not insure that things turn out as we wish. While my sister and David now live together happily, Gwenna's story has a different ending.

When fall arrived, Greg told Gwenna that he needed another six months to make up his mind. Gwenna deliberated a while and decided she could live with that. But when the six months was up, Greg was still uncertain and asked for more time. It was then that Gwenna took the painful but ultimately empowering step of ending their relationship.

Getting to the Source

We all know that anxiety impacts on everything from our immune system to our closest relationships. How can we identify the significant sources of emotional intensity in our lives? How can we know when anxiety from source *A* is causing "stuckness" in relationship *B*?

Sometimes it's obvious: there may be a recent stressful event, a negative or even positive change we can pinpoint as a source of the anxiety that is overloading a relationship. If *we* miss it, others may see it for us ("No wonder you've been fighting with Jim—you moved to a new city just three months ago and that's a major adjustment!").

Sometimes we think that a particular event or change is stressful, but we aren't fully aware just how stressful it really is. Our narrow focus on one intimate relationship obscures the broader emotional field from our view. For example, we may downplay the emotional impact of significant transitions—a birth, wedding, job change, promotion, graduation, child leaving home, ill parent—because these are just normal things that happen in the course of the life cycle. We fail to realize that "just normal things," when they involve change, will profoundly affect our closest ties.

Paradoxically, couples become less able to achieve intimacy as they stay focused on it and give it their primary attention. Real closeness occurs most reliably not when it is pursued or demanded in a relationship, but when both individuals work consistently on their own selves. By working on the self, I do not mean that we should maintain a single-minded focus on self-enhancement or career advancement; these are male-defined notions of selfhood, which women would do well to challenge. Working on the self includes clarifying beliefs, values, and life goals; staying responsibly connected to people on one's own family tree; defining the self in key relationships; and addressing important emotional issues as they arise.

The Challenge of Independence

For women, this presents an obvious dilemma. Only a few of us have been encouraged to put our primary energy into formulating a life plan that neither requires nor excludes marriage. In fact, we may have received generations of training to *not* think this way. Yet this kind of self-focus not only insures our well-being, it also puts us on more solid ground for negotiating in our intimate relationships. *We cannot navigate clearly within a relationship unless we can live without it.*

Having a life plan means more than working to insure our own economic security. It also means working toward clarifying our values, beliefs, and priorities and then applying them to our daily actions. It means thinking about what talents and abilities we want to develop over the next two—or 20—years. Obviously, a life plan is not written in stone but is instead open to constant revision over time.

Finally, having a life plan does not mean adopting masculine values and pursuing goals single-mindedly. Some of us may be striving to lighten our work commitments so we can spend more time with our friends and family or in other pursuits, such as spiritual development or the world peace movement. What *is* significant about a life plan is that it can help us live our own lives, not someone else's, as well as possible.

When we do not focus our primary energy on working on a life plan, our intimate relationships suffer. We begin to look to others to provide us with meaning or happiness, which is not their job. We seek a partner who will provide self-esteem, which cannot be bestowed by another. We set up a situation in which we are bound to get overinvolved in the other person's ups and downs because we are underfocused on ourselves.

Intimate relationships cannot substitute for a life plan. And, to have any meaning at all, a life plan must include intimate relationships. Only through our connectedness to others can we really know and enhance the self. And only through working on the self can we begin to enhance our connectedness to others. There is, quite simply, no other way.

Dynamics of Personal Adjustment: The Individual and Society

The passing of each decade brings changes to society. Some historians have suggested that changes are occurring more rapidly. In other words, history appears to take less time to happen. How has American society changed historically? The inventory is long. Technological advances, for example, can be found everywhere. A decade ago few people knew what "user-friendly" or "8MB RAM" signified. Today these terms are readily identified with the rapidly expanding computer industry. Fifteen years ago Americans felt fortunate to own a thirteen-inch television that received three local stations. Now people feel deprived if they cannot select from 100 different worldwide channels for their big, rear-screen sets. Today we can "fax" a message to the other side of the world faster than we can propel a missile to the same place.

In the Middle Ages, Londoners worried about the

Unit 5

plague. Before vaccines were available, people worried about polio and other diseases. Today much concern is focused on the transmission and cure of AIDS, the discovery of more carcinogenic substances, and the greenhouse effect. In terms of mental health, psychologists see few hysterics, the type of patient seen by Sigmund Freud in the 1800s. Depression, psychosomatic ulcers, and alcohol and drug addiction are more common today. In addition, issues about the changing American family continue to grab headlines. Nearly every popular magazine carries a story or two bemoaning the passing of the traditional, nuclear family and declining "family values." And if these spontaneous or unplanned changes are not enough to cope with, some individuals are purposely trying to change the world. Witness the changes in Eastern Europe, for example.

This list of societal transformations, while not exhaustive, reflects society's continual demands for adaptation by each of its members. However, it is not just society at large that places stress on us. Smaller units within society, such as our work group or our family, also demand continual adaptation by individuals. Families change as children leave the proverbial nest, as parents divorce, and as new babies are born. Work groups expand and contract with every economic fluctuation. Even when group size remains stable, new members come and go as turnover takes place; hence, changes in the dynamics of the group occur in response to the new personalities. Each of these changes, welcome or not, places stress on the individual who then needs to adjust to or cope with the change.

This unit of the book addresses the interplay between the individual and society in producing the problems each creates for the other. The first two articles describe our society in general. In "The Pace of Life," Robert Levine's research that measured life in the fast and slow lanes of different regions of the United States is explored.

The next three articles relate to society's reaction to masculinity and femininity. The first article in this series is about men: "The American Man in Transition" examines how the model of the ideal American man has changed according to both men and women. The image of the ideal man has shifted from an aggressive and tough fighting man to a sensitive and family-oriented gentleman. The companion article, "Blame It On Feminism," discusses how, despite the women's movement, American women have made few actual gains when hard data are analyzed. Despite equal opportunities, women often face the so-called "glass ceiling." The third article in this series examines how black women, who are the victims of both sexism and racism, fare in our society. The article interestingly is entitled "Taking Sides Against Ourselves."

The next set of articles describes social conditions related to smaller groups within society, groups that also experience their own share of problems. Groupthink is an interesting phenomenon, group decision-making gone wrong, and it is discussed in the article by Alison Bass aptly titled "Groupthink: Taking Easy Way Out of a Tough Decision." Similarly, bystander apathy is a situation in which witnesses to a crime or other misfortunes do not assist the victim; R. Lance Shotland describes the causes and effects of this bystander effect in his article, "When Bystanders Just Stand By." In "How Much Is Enough? Alan Durning discloses his opinion that Americans are creating waste and environmental destruction in search of happiness, a crisis he wants to see reversed.

Looking Ahead: Challenge Questions

Is society today more stressful than it was a century ago? How so? Are there changes from the previous decade that make our living easier? Harder?

Do you think researcher Robert Levine used the best measures of pace of life? Can you think of others? Which pace do you prefer?

Do you think men's and women's roles have changed in the last few years? How so? For better or worse?

What is groupthink? What are the symptoms and consequences of groupthink? Can you think of personal or public disasters that seem to have been the result of groupthink? How can groupthink be avoided?

Why don't people readily come to the aid of others? Can people be trained to be more altruistic? Should helping behavior be legislated; that is, should it be against the law to ignore a victim? What motivates volunteerism?

The Pace of Life

It can be measured in simple ways, such as by noting the accuracy of public clocks and the speed of postal clerks

Robert V. Levine

Robert V. Levine is professor of psychology at California State University, Fresno. Last year he was named the university's Outstanding Professor. Address: Department of Psychology, California State University, Fresno, CA 93740.

When I was teaching in Brazil some years ago, I noticed that students there were more casual than those in the United States about arriving late for class. I was puzzled by their tardiness, since their classroom work revealed them to be serious students who were intent on learning the subject. I soon found, however, that they were likely to be late not only in arriving for class but also in leaving it afterward. Whatever the reason for the students' lateness, they were not trying to minimize their time in the classroom.

In my classes in the United States I do not need to wear a watch to know when the session is over. My students gather their books at two minutes before the hour and show signs of severe anxiety if I do not dismiss them on time. At the end of a class in Brazil, on the other hand, some students would slowly drift out, others would stay for a while to ask questions, and some would stay and chat for a very long time. Having just spent two hours lecturing on statistics in broken Portuguese, I could not attribute their lingering to my superb teaching style. Apparently, staying late was just as routine as arriving late. As I observed my students over the course of a year, I came to realize that this casual approach to punctuality was a sign of some fundamental differences between Anglo-American and Brazilian attitudes toward the pace of life.

My experience in Brazil inspired an ongoing research program whose aim is to devise ways of measuring the tempo of a culture and to assess peoples' attitudes toward time. Every traveler has observed that the pace of life varies in different parts of the world, and even from place to place within a single country, but it is not obvious how to quantify these differences. We could question individuals about their concern with time and about the course of their days, but this method yields subjective descriptions that do not allow for systematic comparisons between groups. Without a suitable basis for comparison, it becomes difficult to gauge the meaning of "fast" or "slow."

In the past few years my colleagues and I have attempted to develop reliable, standardized measures of the pace of life. Our measurement techniques are based on simple observations that require no equipment more elaborate than a stopwatch. Much of the field work has been done by students in the course of their travels on summer vacation or during breaks between semesters.

Pace and Culture

There is value in describing and appreciating another culture's sense of time. We might, for example, begin to understand the source of some of the difficulties we experience when we are exposed to another culture. Adjusting to an alien pace of life may present almost as many difficulties as learning a foreign language. This was revealed most dramatically in an investigation into the roots of culture shock among Peace Corps volunteers returning from overseas assignments. James Spradley of Macalester College and Mark Phillips of the University of Washington found that two of the three greatest adjustment difficulties were the "general pace of life" and the "punctuality of the people." Only the "language spoken" proved to be a more stressful change. The temporal aspects of life may even be thought of as a silent language. As the American anthropologist Edward Hall has noted, these informal patterns of time "are seldom, if ever, made explicit. They exist in the air around us. They are either familiar and comfortable, or unfamiliar and wrong."

Misinterpreting this silent language may lead to serious difficulties in communication. In 1985, for example, a group of Shiite Muslim terrorists hijacked a TWA jetliner, holding 40 Americans hostage with the demand that Israel release 764 Lebanese Shiite prisoners being held in Israeli prisons. The terrorists handed the hostages over to Shiite Muslim leaders who assured the American negotiators that nothing would happen to the hostages if all demands were met. At one point during the delicate negotiations one of the leaders of the Shiite militia Amal said that the hostages would be returned to the hijackers in two days if there were no movement toward meeting their demands. The American negotiators knew that neither they nor the Israelis would be able to forge a settlement in such a short time. By setting a limit of two days, the Shiites made a compromise unlikely and elevated the crisis to a very dangerous level. But when the Shiite leader realized how his statement was being interpreted, he quickly backed off: "We said a couple of days but we were not necessarily specifying 48 hours" (United Press International, June 23, 1985). Forty lives were put in jeopardy by a misinterpretation of the word *day*.

A society's pace of life may have consequences for the health of the inhabitants as well. This idea has been widely publicized in the wake of the observation that individuals with a constant sense of time urgency, described as type-*A* behavior, may be more susceptible to heart disease than individuals who have a more relaxed attitude toward time.

With these considerations in mind, my colleagues and I have carried out a series of studies across and within cultures over the past 15 years. Our results indicate that differences in the pace of life exist not only between the Northern and Southern hemispheres but also between the Eastern and Western worlds; indeed, important differences can be perceived between the regions of a single country.

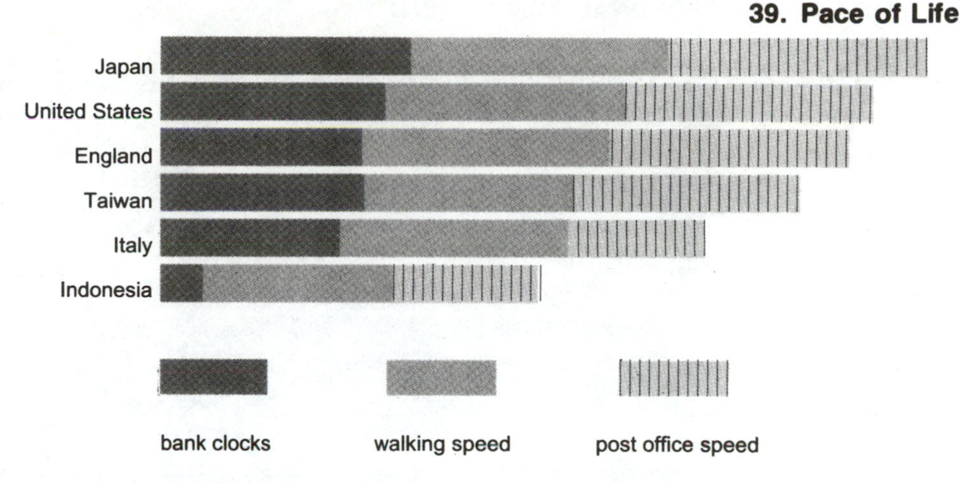

Figure 1. Three readily measured quantities were used to gauge the overall pace of life in six countries: the walking speed of pedestrians on downtown streets, the speed at which postal clerks fulfilled a standard request, and the accuracy of outdoor clocks on bank buildings. In each country the same measurements were made in the largest city and in one other, medium-size city. The results indicate that the pace is fastest in Japan and slowest in Indonesia. In the graph a longer bar corresponds to greater accuracy in public clocks, faster pedestrians and faster postal clerks.

The Pace of World Cities

In collaboration with Kathy Bartlett of California State University, Fresno, I have attempted to extend and refine our understanding of cross-cultural differences in the perception of time. Rather than focus on some single dimension such as punctuality, we used several objective measures that assessed the more general issue of the pace at which people live their lives. We collected our data from six countries: Japan, Taiwan, Indonesia, Italy, England and the United States. The selection of these countries allowed for comparisons between Eastern and Western cultures with varying degrees of economic development. In each country we collected data from the largest city and from one medium-size city (the populations ranged from 415,000 to 615,000).

We examined three indicators of tempo in each city. First, we measured the accuracy of a sample of outdoor bank clocks in the main downtown area. Fifteen clocks were checked and their times compared to that reported by the telephone company; deviations from the "correct time" were measured to the nearest minute.

Second, we measured the average walking speed of randomly chosen pedestrians over a distance of 100 feet. The measurements were made on clear summer days during business hours in at least two locations on main downtown streets. We avoided crowded or congested areas, so that the pedestrians could potentially walk at their own preferred maximum speed. In order to control for the effects of socializing, only pedestrians walking alone were timed. Subjects with obvious physical handicaps, and those who appeared to be window-shopping, were excluded from the survey.

Third, as an indicator of working pace, we measured the speed with which postal clerks fulfilled a standard request for stamps. In each city we presented clerks some paper money (the nearest equivalent of a five-dollar bill) and a note in the native language requesting a common denomination of stamp. We then measured the elapsed time between the passing of the note and the completion of the request.

Our results revealed a number of significant differences between the six countries. The Japanese cities rated the highest on all three measures: They had the most accurate bank clocks, the pedestrians there walked the fastest, and their postal clerks were the quickest to fulfill our request. In contrast, the Indonesian cities had the least accurate public clocks and the slowest pedestrians. The distinction of having the slowest postal clerks went to the Italian cities, where buying a stamp took nearly twice as long as it did in Japan.

There were also a number of differences between the large and the medium-size cities within each country. In particular, we found that people in the larger cities walked faster than those in the smaller communities. The difference was greatest in the least-developed countries in our sample, namely Indonesia and Taiwan. This may reflect the persistence of a traditional village life style among people in the smaller cities of those countries. (It would be interesting to investigate the pace of life in rural areas and small towns, but a different set of measures would be needed; there are few bank clocks in farming villages.)

What impressed us most about these findings was the high correlation between the three pace-of-life measures for each city. The accuracy of the bank clocks is strongly correlated with walking speed; the correlation coefficient, r, is .82. (An r value of 1 indicates perfect correlation.) There is also a strong correlation between clock accuracy and the speed of the postal clerks ($r = .71$). Finally, walking speed is positively correlated with postal-clerk speed ($r = .56$). The high correlation between these distinct measures supports the notion that a city has a definable overall pace, which manifests itself in the behavior of the inhabitants. It appears reasonable, then, to speak of a characteristic

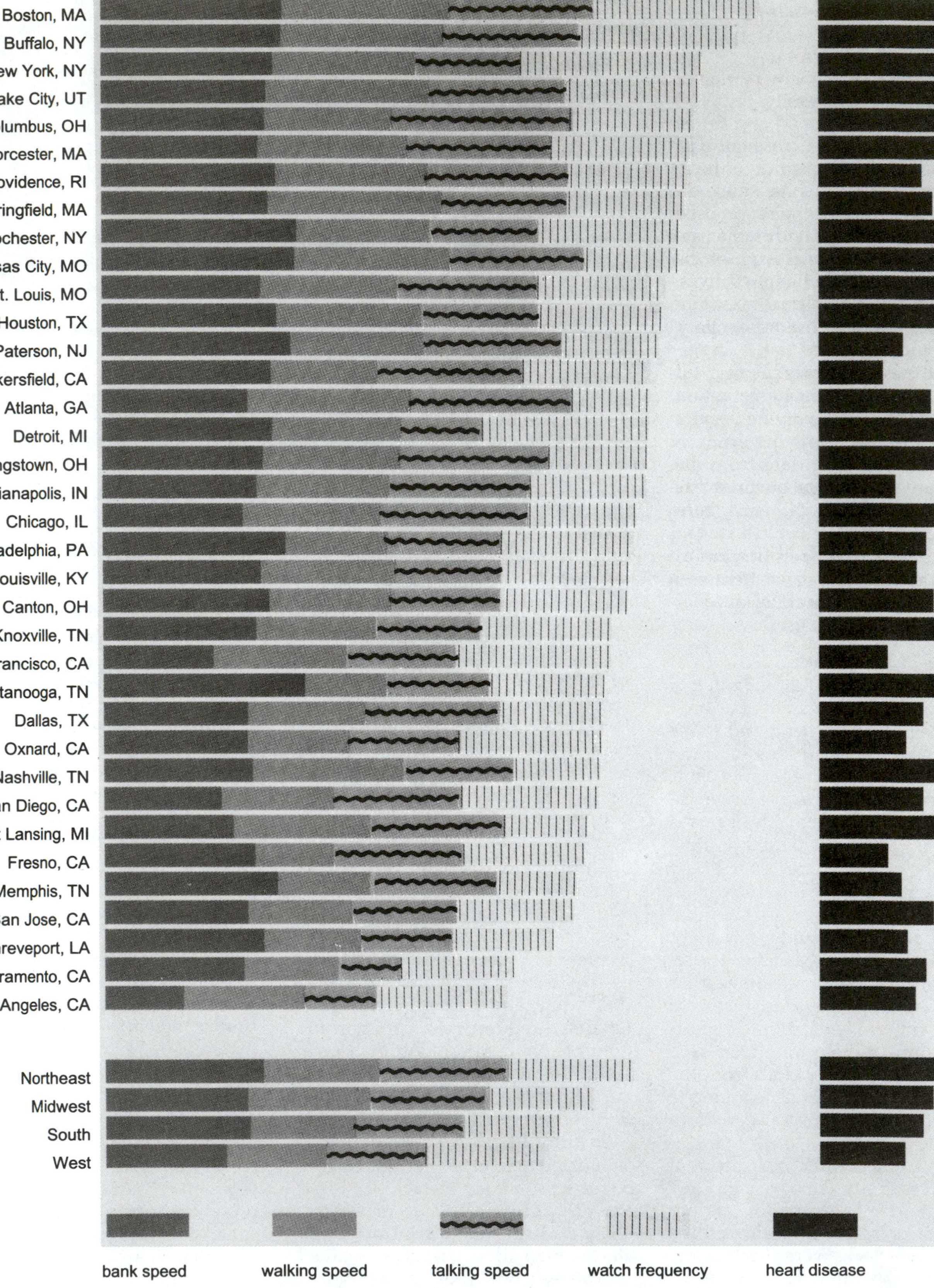

Figure 2. American cities were ranked on four pace-of-life measures: the speed at which bank tellers were able to fulfill a request for change, the walking speed of downtown pedestrians, the talking speed of postal clerks, and the proportion of people wearing wristwatches. In each case a longer bar corresponds to a faster pace. There is a significant and positive correlation between the overall pace of life for a city and the incidence of heart disease in that city. Data from nine cities in each of the four regions of the U.S. were pooled to express the average pace of life for each region.

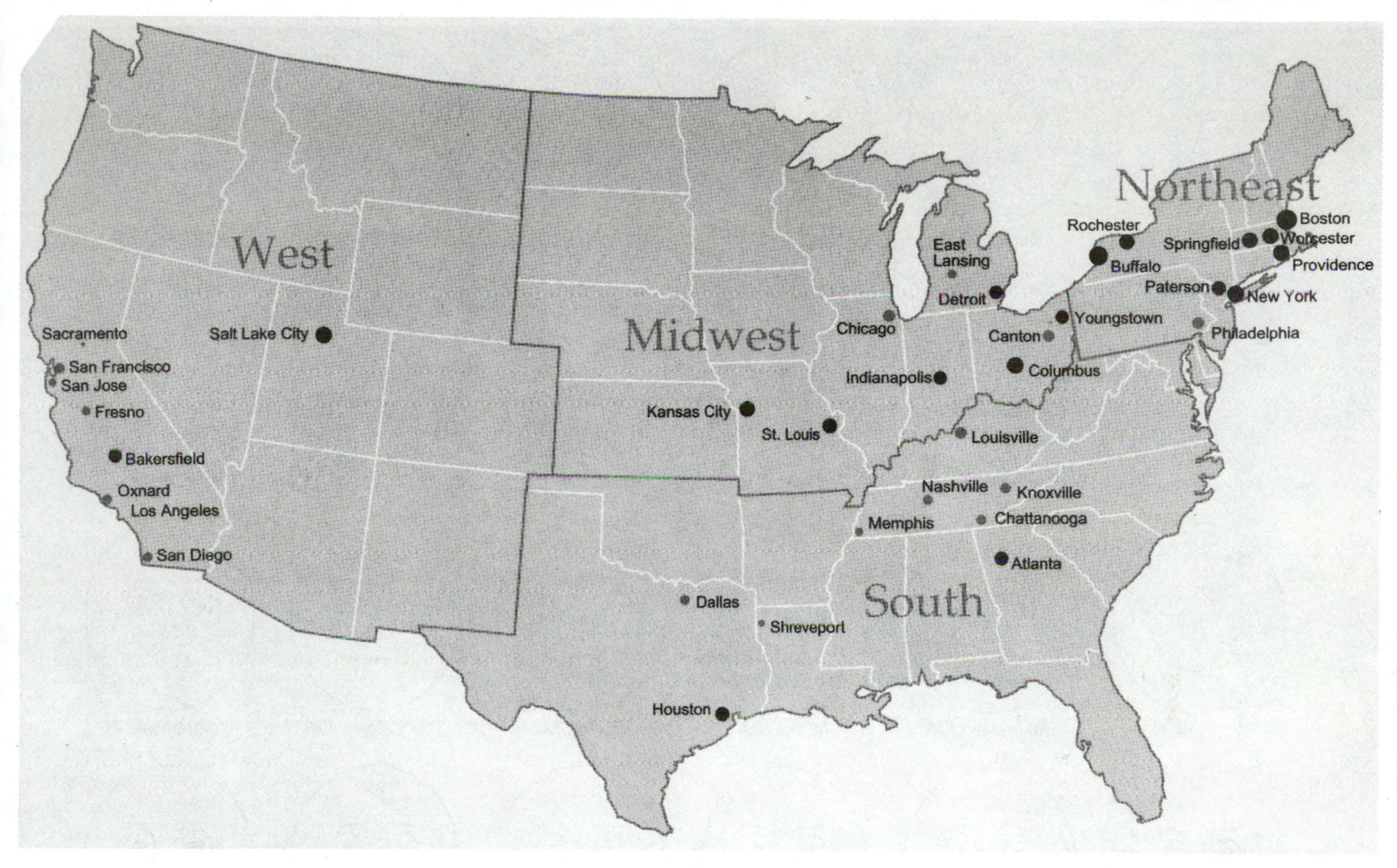

Figure 3. Regional differences in the pace of life are apparent in a map showing the 36 cities included in the American study. A faster pace corresponds to larger dots; the 18 fastest cities are represented by black dots, whereas the 18 slowest cities are represented by gray dots. Within each region measurements were made in nine cities—three large, three of medium size and three small.

pace of life for a particular area and to distinguish between cultures on the basis of this characteristic.

The Pace of U. S. Cities

Intrigued by our findings that various world cities have a particular pace of life, we decided to take a closer look at the cities of the United States. Are Californians really more laid-back than people in other parts of the country? Do New Yorkers live up to their reputation of living in the fast lane? What we learned confirmed many of our general preconceptions, but we also found some surprises.

Our methods were similar to those we employed in our studies of world cities. We examined nine cities in each of four regions of the United States: the Northeast, Midwest, South and West. Within each region, we studied three large metropolitan areas (population greater than 1,800,000), three medium-size cities (population between 850,000 and 1,300,000) and three smaller cities (population between 350,000 and 550,000).

Within each city we measured four indicators of the pace of life. First, we determined the walking speed of pedestrians over a distance of 60 feet. The speeds were measured during business hours on a clear summer day along a main downtown street. We applied the same restrictions on the selection of subjects and locations as in our international study.

Second, in order to gauge the speed of working life, we measured how long it took bank clerks to complete a simple request: We asked a teller in each of at least eight downtown banks to make change for two $20 bills or to give us two $20 bills for change.

Our third indicator of pace was talking speed. We asked postal clerks to explain the difference between regular mail, certified mail and insured mail; we recorded their responses and calculated their speaking rate by dividing the total number of syllables by the total time of their response.

Fourth, as a measure of the population's concern with time, we counted the proportion of men and women in downtown areas during business hours who were wearing a wristwatch.

Each of these measures considered individually has certain quirks. The number of people wearing a watch, for example, reflects not only a society's preoccupation with time but also its sense of fashion and perhaps its level of affluence. Basing measurements on interactions with postal clerks and bank tellers puts undue emphasis on these rather specialized subpopulations; furthermore, the performance of the clerks and tellers depends on their skill and knowledge as well as on their general tendency to hurry or tarry. To compensate for

Figure 4. Multidimensional data on the pace of life and the incidence of heart disease are presented in an alternative format devised in 1973 by Herman Chernoff of Stanford University. Chernoff noted that the human perceptual system is particularly sensitive to facial expression, and so he suggested that encoding data in facial features might help the viewer to detect patterns, groupings and correlations. Here measurements of various factors in 36 American cities—the same data presented in Figure 2—determine the appearance of simple cartoon faces. Walking speed is encoded in the angle of the eyebrows, talking speed in the width of the mouth, the frequency of watch-wearing in the height of the eyes, and the speed of bank transactions in the size of the pupils; a final factor, the death rate from heart disease, determines the curvature of the mouth. It is not suggested that the facial expressions reflect the mood of the corresponding cities, but perceived similarities and differences in the faces may offer clues to the nature of life in the cities. (The illustration was devised by the editors, not the author.)

these distortions we combined the scores from the four sets of measurements, creating an overall index of the pace of life in each city. First we normalized the scores, so that they all extended over the same range (an operation that has the effect of assigning equal weight to all four factors); then we added the normalized values.

In general, our results confirmed the widespread impression that the Northeastern United States is fast-paced, whereas the West Coast is a little more relaxed. We found that people in the Northeast walk faster, make change faster, talk faster and are more likely to wear a watch than people in [other parts of the country. In] fact, seven of the nine fastest cities are in the Northeast. Boston, Buffalo and New York are the fastest overall; a big surprise was that New York does not lead the list. (Manhattan residents might be excused a couple of steps, however, in order to watch the local events; during an interval of an hour and a half, our observer on one New York street corner reported an improvised concert, an attempted purse-snatching and a capsized mugger.)

The slowest pace is on the West Coast, and the slowest city overall is Los Angeles. The residents of that city scored 24th out of 36 in walking speed, next to last in speech rate and far behind everyone else in the speed of the bank tellers. The Los Angelenos' only concession to the clock was to wear one: the city was 13th highest in the proportion of the population wearing a watch.

Pace and Consequences

These temporal measures serve not only to inform us of differences between peoples, but they may also be used to examine relations between the pace of life and other traits of a population. One trait that has long been suspected of being associated with the pace of life is psychological and physical health. Of particular note is the reported association between a fast-paced life and a high incidence of heart disease.

In 1959 Meyer Friedman and Ray Rosenman reported that men who exhibit a behavior pattern characterized by a sense of time urgency, hostility and competitiveness are seven times more likely than others to have evidence of heart disease and are more than twice as likely to have a heart attack. People who exhibit this behavior pattern, which Friedman and Rosenman called type *A*, tend to walk quickly, eat quickly, do two things at once, and take pride in always being on time. The study seemed to support suspicions that behavior patterns can affect the incidence and course of a disease.

Since that first report, however, the association between type-*A* behavior and heart disease has become increasingly controversial. A number of authors have not been able to reproduce the results found by Friedman and Rosenman. The nature of our own studies suggested that we might be able to shed some light on this issue by investigating the relationship between the pace of life and the incidence of heart disease for particular populations. We were especially struck by the similarities between type-*A* behavior and those traits that we measured as indicators of a fast pace of life. Our research provides a unique perspective on the question, since most studies linking heart disease with a sense of time urgency have focused on individuals, not on geographic areas.

We began with the hypothesis that the faster a city's overall pace of life, the higher will be its rate of death from heart disease. To test the hypothesis we compared the overall pace of life measured in our 36 American cities with the death rate in each city from ischemic heart disease (a decreased flow of blood to the heart). The death rates were those reported by the Department of Health and Human Services for the year 1981. Since age is positively correlated with the incidence of heart disease, we statistically adjusted the death rates for the median age of each city's population. In this way we hoped to isolate the effects of social factors on heart disease.

Briefly, our results reveal a significant correlation between the pace of life and the rate of death from ischemic heart disease. The magnitude of the correlation ($r = .50$) is higher than that usually found between heart disease and measures of type-*A* behavior in individuals. In other words, our data suggest that the pace of a person's environment is at least as good a predictor of heart disease as his or her score on a type-*A* personality test. This was true whether we corrected for age or not.

Why are people in fast environments more prone to heart disease? In large part, we suspect that fast environments attract fast-moving, type-*A* people. The psychologist Timothy Smith and his colleagues at the University of Utah have shown that type-*A* individuals both seek and create time-urgent environments. The fastest cities in our study may represent both the dreams and the creations of people who live under a sense of urgency.

The development of a fast-paced city could be explained by the following scenario. First, type-*A* people are attracted to fast-paced cities. In turn, the greater proportion of type-*A* residents serves to maintain and further promote a fast-paced way of life. Meanwhile, slower, type-*B* individuals tend to migrate away from fast-paced cities to environments more compatible with their temperament. Smith's research suggests that the temporal expectations of fast-paced cities demand time-urgent behavior in all people—type *A*'s and type *B*'s alike. The result is that type-*B* individuals act more like type *A*'s, and type *A*'s strive to accelerate the pace still more.

The precise mechanism linking time-urgent behavior to heart disease is not known. Nevertheless, some recent statistics from the Department of Health and Human Services hint at one possibility: the incidence of cigarette smoking follows the same regional pattern as that of ischemic heart disease and the pace of life. That is, the rates for cigarette smoking and ischemic heart disease are highest where the pace of life is fastest: the Northeastern United States. The Northeast is followed by the Midwest, the South and then the West on all three variables.

Cigarette smoking has been identified as the single most important preventable cause of heart disease. It is also well documented that cigarette smoking is often related to psychological stress. These correlations suggest, but do not confirm, the possibility that a causal relation exists between these variables. One possibility is that stressful, time-pressured environments lead to unhealthy behaviors such as cigarette smoking and poor eating habits, which in turn increase the risk of heart disease. Our model of the fast-paced "type-*A* city" may provide a basis for examining this hypothesis.

[Closer examinations of] modern life offer an interesting perspective on our way of living, but a caveat is also in order here. Although we have come to view the choice between rushing and leisurely activity as a trade-off between accomplishment and peace of mind, we should note that time pressure is not always stressful; it may also be challenging and energizing. The optimal pressure seems to depend on the characteristics of the task and the personality of the individual. Similarly, what we have characterized as a type-*A* environment will affect different people in different ways. What may be most important is fitting people to thier environment. Although a type-*A* setting may be stressful to a type-*B* individual, a type-*A* person may experience more distress in a type-*B* environment. Given that heart disease remains the single largest cause of death in the United States, the search for a healthy person-environment fit takes on great importance.

Bibliography

Amato, P. R. 1983. The effects of urbanization on interpersonal behavior. *Journal of Cross-Cultural Psychology* 14:153-367.

Booth-Kewley, S., and H. Friedman. 1987. Psychological predictors of heart disease: A quantitative review. *Psychological Bulletin* 101:343-362.

Bornstein, M. H. 1979. The pace of life: Revisited. *International Journal of Psychology* 14:83-90.

Chernoff, Herman. 1973. The use of faces to represent points in k-dimensional space graphically. *Journal of the American Statistical Association* 68:361–368.

Cohen, J. B., S. L. Syme, C. D. Jenkins, A. Kagan, and S. J. Zyzanski. 1975. The cultural context of Type A behavior and the risk of CHD. *American Journal of Epidemiology* 102:434.

Freedman, J., and D. Edwards. 1988. Time pressure, task performance, and enjoyment. In J. E. McGrath (ed.), *The Social Psychology of Time: New Perspectives* (pp. 113-133). Newbury Park, CA: Sage.

Friedman, A. P., and R. H. Rosenman. 1974. *Type A Behavior and Your Heart*. New York: Knopf.

Hall, E. T. 1959. *The Silent Language*. New York: Doubleday.

Lauer, R. H. 1981. *Temporal Man: The Meaning and Uses of Social Time*. New York: Praeger.

Levine, R. 1988. The pace of life across cultures. In J. E. McGrath (ed.), *The Social Psychology of Time: New Perspectives* (pp. 39-62). Newbury Park, CA: Sage.

Levine, R., and K. Bartlett. 1984. Pace of life, punctuality and coronary heart disease in six countries. *Journal of Cross-Cultural Psychology* 15:233-255.

Levine, R., K. Lynch, K. and M. Lucia. 1989. The type A city: Coronary heart disease and the pace of life. *Journal of Behavioral Medicine* 12:509-524.

Levine, R., L. West and H. Reis. 1980. Perceptions of time and punctuality in the United States and Brazil. *Journal of Personality and Social Psychology* 38:541-550.

Marmot, M. G., and S. L. Syme. 1976. Acculturation and coronary heart disease in Japanese-Americans. *American Journal of Epidemiology* 104:225-247.

Matthews, K. 1988. Coronary heart disease and Type A behaviors: Update on an alternative to the Booth-Kewley and Friedman (1987) quantitative review. *Psychological Bulletin* 104:373-380.

McGrath, J. E. 1989. The place of time in social psychology: Some steps toward a social psychological theory of time. Paper presented at the Seventh Conference of the International Society for the Study of Time, July, 1989, Glacier Park, Montana.

Reid, D. D. 1975. International studies in epidemiology. *American Journal of Epidemiology* 102:469-476.

Smith, T., and N. Anderson. 1986. Models of personality and disease: An interactional approach to Type A behavior and cardiovascular risk. *Journal of Personality & Social Psychology* 50:1166-1173.

Spradley, J. P., and M. Phillips. 1972. Culture and stress: A quantitative analysis. *American Anthropologist* 74:518-529.

Werner, C. M., I. Altman and D. Oxley. 1985. Temporal aspects of homes: A transactional perspective. In I. Altman and C. M. Werner (eds.), *Home Environments: Human Behavior and Environment. Advances in Theory and Research*. (Volume 8, pp. 1-32). New York: Plenum.

Wright, L. 1988. The type A behavior pattern and coronary artery disease. *American Psychologist* 43:2-14.

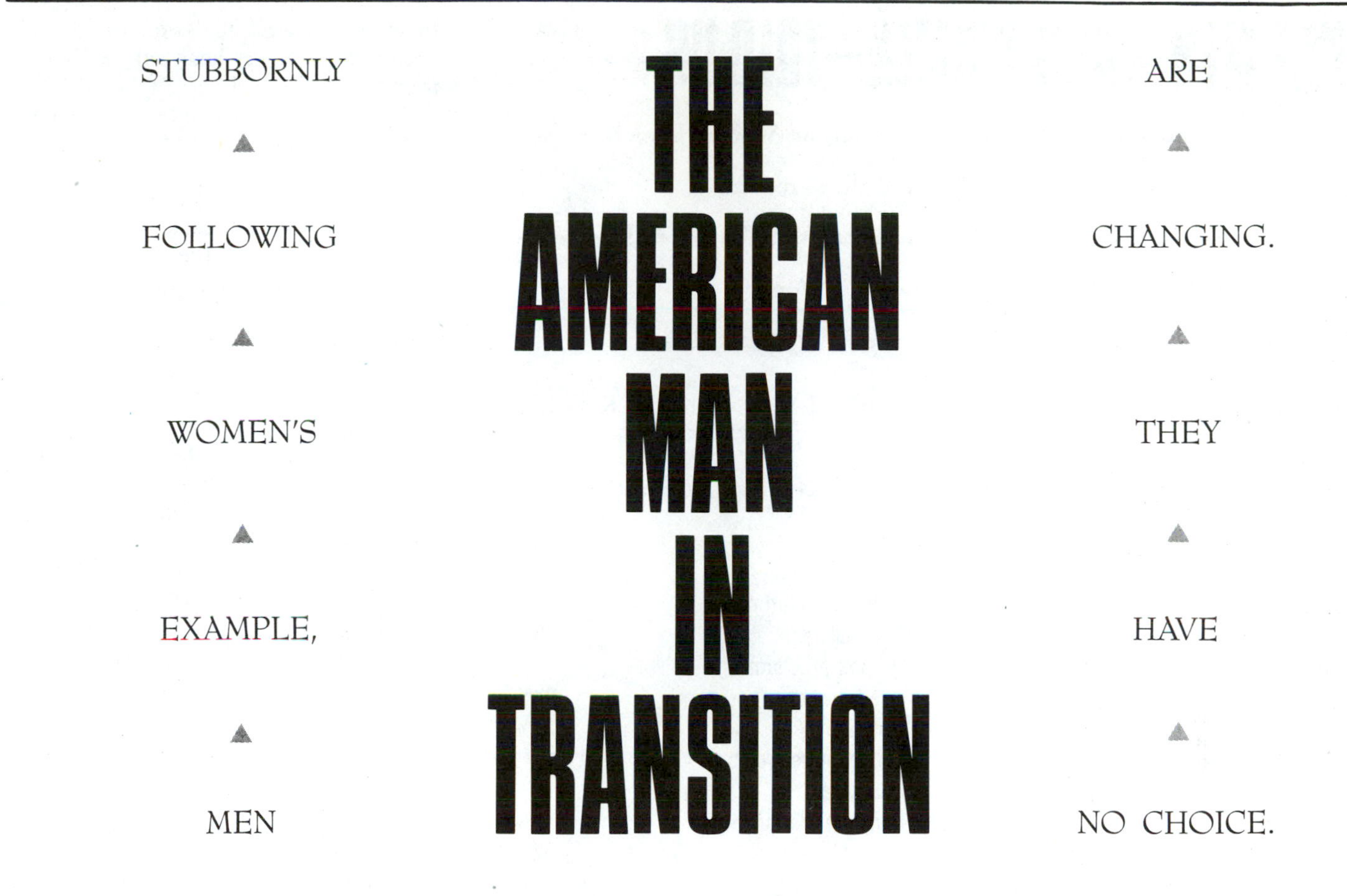

THE AMERICAN MAN IN TRANSITION

STUBBORNLY FOLLOWING WOMEN'S EXAMPLE, MEN ARE CHANGING. THEY HAVE NO CHOICE.

PROJECT EDITOR MICHAEL SEGELL

Men are doing a lot of soul-searching these days. The old role models—taciturn John Wayne, macho Stallone, sensitive Alda, workaholic Iacocca—simply have no relevance now. Inspired by women, who have radically redefined their roles in America, men are casting about for an identity that is comfortably, and truly, masculine. They're in transition, and they're finding it a wrenching, lonely business.

One thing is certain. American men must do something to change—and women have to help them, or risk losing them. On average, men die seven years younger than women. Biology isn't the full explanation—the gap used to be smaller. By one estimate, only two of those years can be clearly attributed to hard-wired differences in male and female biology. The traditional male sex role, characterized by a roll-with-the-punches stoicism and isolation, fraught with stress, anxiety and ambivalence, is hazardous to men's health. The body, that exacting taskmaster and teacher, is telling men to find a new way to be. It's a matter of life and death.

The American man's emotional life is crying out for change, too. Just as feminism encouraged women to enrich their lives by looking outward, the gains women have achieved have indirectly suggested to men the benefits of looking inward. Not only is the old male model physically destructive, it's emotionally stultifying—and unacceptable to many women. The sorry condition of men's interpersonal skills is reflected in a few telling data: At no time in history have there been so many divorced men, so many single fathers—and this at a time when men claim to cherish family and home life more than any other facet of their lives. That they are so inept at it is tearing them apart.

Their current failure to integrate their lives, though, may be temporary—a transition before they reach their ultimate transformation. A new *American Health*/Gallup survey has turned up a remarkable finding: Men and women are in very close agreement on the characteristics that make up an ideal man ("Perfection Incarnate"). Does this signal an end to the battle of the sexes? . . . Many men, by changing themselves, are at least moving toward a rapprochement. Like the early feminists, these men herald a shift, however gradual, in the American male psyche. Some—optimistically, perhaps—are calling the trend a men's movement.

Our survey documented not only evidence of that shift, but the ambivalence, reticence and discomfort accompanying it. Both men and women agree, for instance, that it's most important for an "ideal man" to be a good husband and father, have a sense of humor and be intelligent. That ideal traveled well even with single people, particularly men, who also rated qualities associated with being a family man near the top of the list.

The rise of this new ideal may signal the demise of the old: Both married and single men and women feel that conventionally "male" attributes like physical strength, aggressiveness, toughness and earning power are no longer as important as they once were.

Our poll did, however, highlight

WHAT MEN—AND WOMEN—TOLD US

When It Comes to Defining the Ideal Man, Men and Women Largely Agree; the Characteristics They Choose, and the Percentage Choosing Each, Are Shown in "Perfection Incarnate." But When They're Talking With Friends of the Same Sex, Men and Women Differ Tremendously, as "Shop Talk and Jock Talk" Makes Clear.

PERFECTION INCARNATE

Qualities of an "Ideal Man"

Quality	%
Being a good husband and father	68%
Intelligence	48%
Sense of humor	46%
Emotional sensitivity	31%
Ambition	30%
Rationality, not being overly emotional	17%
Earning power	17%
Being a good lover	11%
Aggressiveness	9%
Physical strength	7%
Physical attractiveness	5%
Toughness	4%
Sports ability	4%

(Total is more than 100% because respondents could give more than one answer.)

SHOP TALK AND JOCK TALK

Men talk with best friends about:

Topic	%
Work issues	43%
Sports	42%
Goals for the future	28%
Their children	26%
Personal problems and self-doubts	23%
Politics	21%
Books, movies, cultural activities	14%
Romantic relationships	13%
Religion	2%

(Total is more than 100% because respondents could give more than one answer.)

Women talk with best friends about:

Topic	%
Their children	47%
Personal problems and self-doubts	41%
Work issues	27%
Books, movies, cultural activities	23%
Goals for the future	22%
Romantic relationships	15%
Politics	10%
Sports	8%
Religion	2%

(Total is more than 100% because respondents could give more than one answer.)

some differences of opinion among various segments of the population. 45% of college graduates, for instance, think it's good for a man to be emotionally sensitive, compared with only 23% of non-college-graduates. The finding suggests that even though men know they have to abandon their old distant, authoritarian style, they're not quite ready to adopt a demeanor that could label them as wimps.

Men are lonely, too, our poll found. We asked men what they talk about when they get together with their closest friends (see "Shop Talk and **Jock Talk"). In contrast to women, who talk mostly about their children and personal problems, men talk about work and sports. Men *say* their families are the most important things in their lives, yet seem unable to talk about them with their best friends. In that sense, men truly may be isolated from sharing what they really care about.**

Men may also be more isolated from their families—or more specifically, their wives—than they would like. Our poll found, for instance, that 29% of men think their best male friend understands them better than their wife or girlfriend. (High as that figure may seem, it falls short of its counterpart among women: 39% of women say their best friend understands them better than their husband or boyfriend.)

The isolation our poll found may be rooted in men's earliest, most primary male relationship. Most sons—daughters, too—feel closer to their mothers than to their fathers. On average, both men and women rate their relationship with their father a 7.5, on a 10-point scale, while mom rates almost a full point higher. The American man may cherish his family, but his children are more attached to his mate.

Perhaps that's one reason why more than half the fathers we polled (51%) would quit their jobs and stay home with their children, if money were not a problem. Clearly, men feel torn between being able to provide their families with more of themselves and being, simply, good providers. The pressures of a two-career family are especially disturbing—70% of married men would prefer that their wives not work, despite the many proven benefits to health and self-esteem that a job provides.

The American male, in short, is in flux. He's trying to shake the old rigid macho values, but he'd still like to be the sole breadwinner and keep his wife in the kitchen. Some college-educated trendsetters think men should feel more emotion, but the rest of the population—particularly men, and to a lesser degree, women—is terrified by the idea. Men still can't share their feelings with other men, preferring to rehash ball games or dissect the nuances of office politics with their best friends rather than reach for what really matters. The "lonely guy" is real.

But some men are breaking down the old models and reconstructing the male role. Men are seeking each other's counsel, healing wounded relationships with their fathers, and exploring, with the help of poetry, myths and fairy tales, what it means to be masculine. Finally, men's groups are meeting with women's groups—a summit of sorts of the sexes—in an effort to raise everyone's consciousness and understanding.

It's an effort to go beyond feminism, beyond "masculinism," toward humanism—a noble direction, whatever your gender.

Blame it on Feminism

What's wrong with women today? Too much equality.

Susan Faludi

To Be A Woman In America at the Close of the twentieth century—what good fortune. That's what we keep hearing, anyway. The barricades have fallen, politicians assure us. Women have "made it," Madison Avenue cheers. Women's fight for equality has "largely been won," *Time* magazine announces. Enroll at any university, join any law firm, apply for credit at any bank. Women have so many opportunities now, corporate leaders say, that they don't really need opportunity policies. Women are so equal now, lawmakers say, that they no longer need an Equal Rights Amendment. Women have "so much," former president Ronald Reagan says, that the White House no longer needs to appoint them to high office. Even American Express ads are saluting a woman's right to charge it. At last, women have received their full citizenship papers.

And yet . . .

Behind this celebration of the American woman's victory, behind the news, cheerfully and endlessly repeated, that the struggle for women's rights is won, another message flashes: You may be free and equal now, but you have never been more miserable.

This bulletin of despair is posted everywhere—at the newsstand, on the TV set, at the movies, in advertisements and doctors' offices and academic journals. Professional women are suffering "burnout" and succumbing to an "infertility epidemic." Single women are grieving from a "man shortage." The *New York Times* reports: Childless women are "depressed and confused" and their ranks are swelling. *Newsweek* says: Unwed women are "hysterical" and crumbling under a "profound crisis of confidence." The health-advice manuals inform: High-powered career women are stricken with unprecedented outbreaks of "stress-induced disorders," hair loss, bad nerves, alcoholism, and even heart attacks. The psychology books advise: Independent women's loneliness represents "a major mental-health problem today." Even founding feminist Betty Friedan has been spreading the word: She warns that women now suffer from "new problems that have no name."

How can American women be in so much trouble at the same time that they are supposed to be so blessed? If women got what they asked for, what could possibly be the matter now?

The prevailing wisdom of the past decade has supported one, and only one, answer to this riddle: It must be all that equality that's causing all that pain. Women are unhappy precisely because they are free. Women are enslaved by their own liberation. They have grabbed at the gold ring of independence, only to miss the one ring that really matters. They have gained control of their fertility, only to destroy it. They have pursued their own professional dreams—and lost out on romance, the greatest female adventure. "Our generation was the human sacrifice" to the women's movement, writer Elizabeth Mehren contends in a *Time* cover story. Baby-boom women, like her, she says, have been duped by feminism: "We believed the rhetoric." In *Newsweek*, writer Kay Ebeling dubs feminism the "Great Experiment That Failed" and asserts, "Women in my generation, its perpetrators, are the casualties."

In the eighties, publications from the *New York Times* to *Vanity Fair* to *The Nation* have issued a steady stream of indictments against the women's movement, with such headlines as "When Feminism Failed" or "The Awful Truth About Women's Lib." They hold the campaign for women's equality responsible for nearly every woe besetting women, from depression to meager savings accounts, from teenage suicides to eating disorders to bad complexions. The *Today* show says women's liberation is to blame for bag ladies. A guest columnist in the *Baltimore Sun* even proposes that feminists produced the rise in slasher movies. By making the "violence" of abortion more acceptable,

From *Mother Jones*, September/October 1991, pp. 24-29. Excerpt from *Backlash, The Undeclared War on American Women*, published by Crown Publishers.

the author reasons, women's-rights activities made it all right to show graphic murders on screen.

At the same time, other outlets of popular culture have been forging the same connection: In Hollywood films, of which *Fatal Attraction* is only the most famous, emancipated women with condominiums of their own slink wild-eyed between bare walls, paying for their liberty with an empty bed, a barren womb. "My biological clock is ticking so loud it keeps me awake at night," Sally Field cries in the film *Surrender,* as, in an all-too-common transformation in the cinema of the eighties, an actress who once played scrappy working heroines is now showcased groveling for a groom. In prime-time television shows, from *thirtysomething* to *Family Man,* single, professional, and feminist women are humiliated, turned into harpies, or hit by nervous breakdowns; the wise ones recant their independent ways by the closing sequence. In popular novels, from Gail Parent's *A Sign of the Eighties* to Stephen King's *Misery,* unwed women shrink to sniveling spinsters or inflate to firebreathing she-devils; renouncing all aspirations but marriage, they beg for wedding bands from strangers or swing axes at reluctant bachelors. Even Erica Jong's high-flying independent heroine literally crashes by the end of the decade, as the author supplants *Fear of Flying*'s saucy Isadora Wing, an exuberant symbol of female sexual emancipation in the seventies, with an embittered careerist-turned-recovering-"codependent" in *Any Woman's Blues*—a book that is intended, as the narrator bluntly states, "to demonstrate what a dead end the so-called sexual revolution had become and how desperate so-called free women were in the last few years of our decadent epoch."

Popular psychology manuals peddle the same diagnosis for contemporary female distress. "Feminism, having promised her a stronger sense of her own identity, has given her little more than an identity *crisis,* the best-selling advice manual *Being a Woman* asserts. The authors of the era's self-help classic, *Smart Women/Foolish Choices,* proclaim that women's distress was "an unfortunate consequence of feminism" because "it created a myth among women that the apex of self-realization could be achieved only through autonomy, independence, and career."

In the Reagan and Bush years, government officials have needed no prompting to endorse this thesis. Reagan spokeswoman Faith Ryan Whittlesey declared feminism a "straitjacket" for women, in one of the White House's only policy speeches on the status of the American female population—entitled "Radical Feminism in Retreat." The U.S. attorney general's Commission on Pornography even proposed that women's professional advancement might be responsible for rising rape rates: With more women in college and at work now, the commission members reasoned in their report, women just have more opportunities to be raped.

Legal scholars have railed against the "equality trap." Sociologists have claimed that "feminist-inspired" legislative reforms have stripped women of special "protections." Economists have argued that well-paid working women have created a "less stable American family." And demographers, with greatest fanfare, have legitimated the prevailing wisdom with so-called neutral data on sex ratios and fertility trends; they say they actually have the numbers to prove that equality doesn't mix with marriage and motherhood.

Finally, some "liberated" women themselves have joined the lamentations. In *The Cost of Loving: Women and the New Fear of Intimacy,* Megan Marshall, a Harvard-pedigreed writer, asserts that the feminist "Myth of Independence" has turned her generation into unloved and unhappy fast-trackers, "dehumanized" by careers and "uncertain of their gender identity." Other diaries of mad Superwomen charge that "the hardcore feminist viewpoint," as one of them puts it, has relegated educated executive achievers to solitary nights of frozen dinners and closet drinking. The triumph of equality, they report, has merely given women hives, stomach cramps, eye "twitching" disorders, even comas.

But what "equality" are all these authorities talking about?

If American women are so equal, why do they represent two-thirds of all poor adults? Why are more than 70 percent of full-time working women making less than twenty-five thousand dollars a year, nearly double the number of men at that level? Why are they still far more likely than men to live in poor housing, and twice as likely to draw no pension? If women "have it all," then why don't they have the most basic requirements to achieve equality in the work force: unlike that of virtually all other industrialized nations, the U.S. government still has no family-leave and child-care programs.

If women are so "free," why are their reproductive freedoms in greater jeopardy today than a decade earlier? Why, in their own homes, do they still shoulder 70 percent of the household duties—while the only major change in the last fifteen years is that now men *think* they do more around the house? In thirty states, it is still generally legal for husbands to rape their wives; and only ten states have laws mandating arrest for domestic violence—even though battering is the leading cause of injury to women (greater than rapes, muggings, and auto accidents combined).

The word may be that women have been "liberated," but women themselves seem to feel otherwise. Repeatedly in national surveys, majorities of women say they are still far from equality. In poll after poll in the decade, overwhelming majorities of women said they need equal pay and equal job opportunities, they need an Equal Rights Amendment, they need the right to an abortion without government interference, they need a federal law guaranteeing maternity leave, they need decent child-care services. They have none of these. So how exactly have women "won" the war for women's rights?

Seen against this background, the much bally-hooed claim that feminism is responsible for making women miserable becomes absurd—and irrelevant. The afflictions ascribed to feminism, from "the man shortage" to "the infertility epidemic" to "female burnout" to "toxic day care," have had their origins not in the actual conditions of women's lives but rather in a closed system that starts and ends in the media, popular culture, and advertising—an endless feedback loop that perpetuates and exaggerates its own false images of womanhood. And women don't see feminism as their enemy, either. In fact, in national surveys, 75 to 95 percent of women credit the feminist campaign with *improving* their lives, and a similar proportion say that the women's movement should keep pushing for change.

If the many ponderers of the Woman Question really wanted to know what is troubling the American female population, they might have asked their subjects. In public-opinion surveys, women consistently rank their own *inequality,* at work and at home, among their most urgent concerns. Over and over, women complain to pollsters of a lack of economic, not marital, opportunities; they protest that working men, not working women, fail to spend time in the nursery and the kitchen. It is justice for their gender, not wedding rings and bassinets, that women believe to be in desperately short supply.

As the last decade ran its course, the monitors that serve to track slippage in women's status have been working overtime. Government and private surveys are showing that women's already vast representation in the lowliest occupations is rising, their tiny presence in higher-paying trade and craft jobs stalled or backsliding, their minuscule representation in upper management posts stagnant or falling, and their pay dropping in the very occupations where they have made the most "progress."

In national politics, the already small numbers of women in both elective posts and political appointments fell during the eighties. In private life, the average amount that a divorced man paid in child support fell by about 25 percent from the late seventies to the mid-eighties (to a mere $140 a month). And government records chronicled a spectacular rise in sexual violence against women. Reported rapes more than doubled from the early seventies—at nearly twice the rate of all other violent crimes and four times the overall crime rate in the United States.

The truth is that the last decade has seen a powerful counterassault on women's rights, a backlash, an attempt to retract the handful of small and hard-won victories that the feminist movement did manage to win for women. This counterassault is largely insidious: in a kind of pop-culture version of the big lie, it stands the truth boldly on its head and proclaims that the very steps that have elevated women's position have actually led to their downfall.

The backlash is at once sophisticated and banal, deceptively "progressive" and proudly backward. It deploys both the "new" findings of "scientific research" and the dime-store moralism of yesteryear; it turns into media sound bites both the glib pronouncements of pop-psych trend-watchers and the frenzied rhetoric of New Right preachers. The backlash has succeeded in framing virtually the whole issue of women's rights in its own language. Just as Reaganism shifted political discourse far to the right and demonized liberalism, so the backlash convinced the public that women's "liberation" was the true contemporary American scourge—the source of an endless laundry list of personal, social, and economic problems.

But what has made women unhappy in the last decade is not their "equality"—which they don't yet have—but the rising pressure to halt, and even reverse, women's quest for that equality. The "man shortage" and the "infertility epidemic" are not the price of liberation; in fact, they do not even exist. But these chimeras are part of a relentless whittling-down process—much of it amounting to outright propaganda—that has served to stir women's private anxieties and break their political wills. Identifying feminism as women's enemy only furthers the ends of a backlash against women's equality by simultaneously deflecting attention from the backlash's central role and recruiting women to attack their own cause.

Some social observers may well ask whether the current pressures on women actually constitute a backlash—or just a continuation of American society's long-standing resistance to women's equal rights. Certainly hostility to female independence has always been with us. But if fear and loathing of feminism is a sort of perpetual viral condition in our culture, it is not always in an acute stage; its symptoms subside and resurface periodically. And it is these episodes of resurgence, such as the one we face now, that can accurately be termed "backlashes" to women's advancement. If we trace these occurrences in American history, we find such flare-ups are hardly random; they have always been triggered by the perception—accurate or not—that women are making great strides. These outbreaks are backlashes because they have always arisen in reaction to women's "progress," caused not simply by a bedrock of misogyny but by the specific efforts of contemporary women to improve their status, efforts that have been interpreted time and again by men—especially men grappling with real threats to their economic and social well-being on other fronts—as spelling their own masculine doom.

The most recent round of backlash first surfaced in

the late seventies on the fringes, among the evangelical Right. By the early eighties, the fundamentalist ideology had shouldered its way into the White House. By the mid-eighties, as resistance to women's rights acquired political and social acceptability, it passed into the popular culture. And in every case, the timing coincided with signs that women were believed to be on the verge of a breakthrough.

Just when women's quest for equal rights seemed closest to achieving its objectives, the backlash struck it down. Just when a "gender gap" at the voting booth surfaced in 1980, and women in politics began to talk of capitalizing on it, the Republican party elevated Ronald Reagan and both political parties began to shunt women's rights off their platforms. Just when support for feminism and the Equal Rights Amendment reached a record high in 1981, the amendment was defeated the following year. Just when women were starting to mobilize against battering and sexual assaults, the federal government cut funding for battered-women's programs, defeated bills to fund shelters, and shut down its Office of Domestic Violence—only two years after opening it in 1979. Just when record numbers of younger women were supporting feminist goals in the mid-eighties (more of them, in fact, than older women) and a majority of all women were calling themselves feminists, the media declared the advent of a younger "postfeminist generation" that supposedly reviled the women's movement. Just when women racked up their largest percentage ever supporting the right to abortion, the U.S. Supreme Court moved toward reconsidering it.

In other words, the antifeminist backlash has been set off not by women's achievement of full equality but by the increased possibility that they might win it. It is a preemptive strike that stops women long before they reach the finish line. "A backlash may be an indication that women really have had an effect," feminist psychiatrist Dr. Jean Baker Miller has written, "but backlashes occur when advances have been small, before changes are sufficient to help many people. . . . It is almost as if the leaders of backlashes use the fear of change as a threat before major change has occurred." In the last decade, some women did make substantial advances before the backlash hit, but millions of others were left behind, stranded. Some women now enjoy the right to legal abortion—but not the forty-four million women, from the indigent to the military worker, who depend on the federal government for their medical care. Some women can now walk into high-paying professional careers—but not the millions still in the typing pools or behind the department-store sales counters. (Contrary to popular myth about the "have-it-all" baby-boom women, the largest percentage of women in this generation remain in office support roles.)

As the backlash has gathered force, it has cut off the few from the many—and the few women who have advanced seek to prove, as a social survival tactic, that they aren't so interested in advancement after all. Some of them parade their defection from the women's movement, while their working-class peers founder and cling to the splintered remains of the feminist cause. While a very few affluent and celebrity women who are showcased in news stories boast about going home to "bake bread," the many working-class women appeal for their economic rights—flocking to unions in record numbers, striking on their own for pay equity, and establishing their own fledgling groups for working-women's rights. In 1986, while 41 percent of upper-income women were claiming in the Gallup poll that they were not feminists, only 26 percent of low-income women were making the same claim.

Women's advances and retreats are generally described in military terms: battles won, battles lost, points and territory gained and surrendered. The metaphor of combat is not without its merits in this context, and, clearly, the same sort of martial accounting and vocabulary is already surfacing here. But by imagining the conflict as two battalions neatly arrayed on either side of the line, we miss the entangled nature, the locked embrace, of a "war" between women and the male culture they inhabit. We miss the reactive nature of a backlash, which, by definition, can exist only in response to another force.

In times when feminism is at a low ebb, women assume the reactive role—privately and, most often, covertly struggling to assert themselves against the dominant cultural tide. But when feminism itself becomes the tide, the opposition doesn't simply go along with the reversal: it digs in its heels, brandishes its fists, builds walls and dams. And its resistance creates countercurrents and treacherous undertows.

The force and furor of the backlash churn beneath the surface, largely invisible to the public eye. On occasion in the last decade, they have burst into view. We have seen New Right politicians condemn women's independence, antiabortion protesters firebomb women's clinics, fundamentalist preachers damn feminists as "whores." Other signs of the backlash's wrath, by their sheer brutality, can push their way into public consciousness for a time—the sharp increase in rape, for example, or the rise in pornography that depicts extreme violence against women.

More subtle indicators in popular culture may receive momentary, and often bemused, media notice, then quickly slip from social awareness: A report, for instance, that the image of women on prime-time TV shows has suddenly degenerated. A survey of mystery fiction finding the numbers of tortured and mutilated female characters mysteriously multiplying. The puzzling news that, as one commentator put it, "so many hit songs have the B word [bitch] to refer to women that some rap music seems to be veering toward rape music." The ascendancy of violently misogynist comics like Andrew Dice Clay, who calls women "pigs" and "sluts," or radio hosts like Rush Limbaugh, whose broadsides against "femi-Nazi" feminists helped make his syndicated program the most popular radio talk show in the nation. Or word that, in 1987, the American Women in Radio and Television couldn't award its annual prize to ads that feature women positively: it could find no ad that qualified.

These phenomena are all related, but that doesn't mean they are somehow coordinated. The backlash is not a conspiracy, with a council dispatching agents from some central control room, nor are the people who serve its ends often aware of their role; some even consider themselves feminists. For the most part, its workings are encoded and internalized, diffuse and chameleonic. Not all of the manifestations of the backlash are of equal weight or significance, either; some are mere ephemera thrown up by a culture machine that is always scrounging for a "fresh" angle. Taken as a whole, however, these codes and cajolings, these whispers and threats and myths, move overwhelmingly in one direction: they try to push women back into their "acceptable" roles—whether as Daddy's girl or fluttery romantic, active nester or passive love object.

Although the backlash is not an organized movement, that doesn't make it any less destructive. In fact, the lack of orchestration, the absence of a single string-puller, only makes it harder to see—and perhaps more effective. A backlash against women's rights succeeds to the degree that it appears *not* to be political, that it appears not to be a struggle at all. It is most powerful when it goes private, when it lodges inside a woman's mind and turns her vision inward, until she imagines the pressure is all in her head, until she begins to enforce the backlash, too—on herself.

In the last decade, the backlash has moved through the culture's secret chambers, traveling through passageways of flattery and fear. Along the way, it has adopted disguises: a mask of mild derision or the painted face of deep "concern." Its lips profess pity for any woman who won't fit the mold, while it tries to clamp the mold around her ears. It pursues a divide-and-conquer strategy: single versus married women, working women versus homemakers, middle versus working class. It manipulates a system of rewards and punishments, elevating women who follow its rules, isolating those who don't. The backlash remarkets old myths about women as new facts and ignores all appeals to reason. Cornered, it denies its own existence, points an accusatory finger at feminism, and burrows deeper underground.

Backlash happens to be the title of a 1947 Hollywood movie in which a man frames his wife for a murder he's committed. The backlash against women's rights works in much the same way: its rhetoric charges feminists with all the crimes it perpetrates. The backlash line blames the women's movement for the "feminization of poverty"—while the backlash's own instigators in Washington have pushed through the budget cuts that have helped impoverish millions of women, have fought pay-equity proposals, and undermined equal-opportunity laws. The backlash line claims the women's movement cares nothing for children's rights—while its own representatives in the capital and state legislatures have blocked one bill after another to improve child care, slashed billions of dollars in aid for children, and relaxed state licensing standards for day-care centers. The backlash line accuses the women's movement of creating a generation of unhappy single and childless women—but its purveyors in the media are the ones guilty of making single and childless women feel like circus freaks.

To blame feminism for women's "lesser life" is to miss its point entirely, which is to win women a wider range of experience. Feminism remains a pretty simple concept, despite repeated—and enormously effective—efforts to dress it up in greasepaint and turn its proponents into gargoyles. As Rebecca West wrote sardonically in 1913, "I myself have never been able to find out precisely what feminism is: I only know that people call me a feminist whenever I express sentiments that differentiate me from a doormat."

The meaning of the word feminism has not really changed since it first appeared in a book review in *The Athenaeum* on April 27, 1895, describing a woman who "has in her the capacity of fighting her way back to independence." It is the basic proposition that, as Nora put it in Ibsen's *A Doll's House* a century ago, "Before everything else I'm a human being." It is the simply worded sign hoisted by a little girl in the 1970 Women's Strike for Equality: "I AM NOT A BARBIE DOLL." Feminism asks the world to recognize at long last that women aren't decorative ornaments, worthy vessels, members of a "special-interest group." They are half (in fact, now more than half) of the national population, and just as deserving of rights and opportunities, just as capable of participating in the world's events, as the other half. Feminism's agenda is basic: It asks that women not be forced to "choose" between public justice and private happiness. It asks that women be free to define themselves—instead of having their identity defined for them, time and again, by their culture and their men.

The fact that these are still such incendiary notions should tell us that American women have a way to go before they enter the promised land of equality.

Taking Sides Against Ourselves

Caught between conflicting loyalties to race and gender, Anita Hill faced a predicament that has tormented black women for more than a century.

Rosemary L. Bray

Rosemary L. Bray is an editor of The New York Times Book Review. *She is working on a book of essays on black identity.*

The Anita Hill-Clarence Thomas hearings are over; Judge Thomas is Justice Thomas now. Yet the memories linger on and on. Like witnesses to a bad accident, many of us who watched the three days of Senate hearings continue to replay the especially horrible moments. We compare our memories of cool accusation and heated denial; we weigh again in our minds the hours of testimony, vacuous and vindictive by turn. In the end, even those of us who thought we were beyond surprise had underestimated the trauma.

"I have not been so wrenched since Dr. King was shot," says Jewell Jackson McCabe, the founder of the National Coalition of 100 Black Women, an advocacy group with chapters in 21 states and the District of Columbia. "I cannot begin to tell you; this thing has been unbelievable."

The near-mythic proportions that the event has already assumed in the minds of Americans are due, in part, to the twin wounds of race and gender that the hearings exposed. If gender is a troubling problem in American life and race is still a national crisis, the synergy of the two embodied in the life and trials of Anita Hill left most of America dumbstruck. Even black people who did not support Clarence Thomas's politics felt that Hill's charges, made public at the 11th hour, smacked of treachery. Feminist leaders embraced with enthusiasm a women whose conservative political consciousness might have given them chills only a month earlier.

Even before the hearings began, the nomination of Clarence Thomas had taken on, for me, the quality of a nightmare. The particular dread I felt was one of betrayal—not a betrayal by President Bush, from whom I expected nothing—but by Thomas himself, who not only was no Thurgood Marshall but also gradually revealed himself to be a man who rejoiced in burning the bridges that brought him over.

I felt the kind of heartbreak that comes only to those of us still willing to call ourselves race women and race men in the old and honorable sense, people who feel that African-Americans should live and work and succeed not only for ourselves but also for our people.

The heated debates about gender and race in America have occurred, for the most part, in separate spheres; the separation makes for neater infighting.

But black women can never skirt these questions; we are their living expression. The parallel pursuits of equality for African-Americans and for women have trapped black women between often conflicting agendas for more than a century. We are asked in a thousand ways, large and small, to take sides against ourselves, postponing a confrontation in one arena to address an equally urgent task in another. Black men and white women have often made claims to our loyalty and our solidarity in the service of their respective struggles for recognition and autonomy, understanding only dimly that what may seem like liberty to each is for us only a kind of parole. Despite the bind, more often than not we choose loyalty to the race rather than the uncertain allegiance of gender.

Ours is the complicity of guilty survivors. A black man's presence is often feared; a black woman's presence is at least tolerated. Because until recently so much of the work that black women were paid to do was work that white men and women would not do — cleaning, serving, tending, teaching, nursing, maintaining, caring — we seem forever linked to the needs of human life that are at once minor and urgent.

As difficult as the lives of black women often are, we know we are mobile in ways black men are not — and black men know that we know. They know that we are nearly as angered as they about their inability to protect us in the traditional and patriarchal way, even as many of us have moved beyond the need for such protection. And some black men know ways to use our anger, our sorrow, our guilt, against us.

In our efforts to make a place for ourselves and our families in America, we have created a paradigm of sacrifice. And in living out such lives, we have convinced even ourselves that no sacrifice is too great to insure what we view in a larger sense as the survival of the race.

That sacrifice has been an unspoken promise to our people; it has made us partners with black men in a way white women and men cannot know. Yet not all of us view this partnership with respect. There are those who would use black women's

commitment to the race as a way to control black women. There are those who believe the price of solidarity is silence. It was that commitment that trapped Anita Hill. And it is a commitment we may come to rue.

As I watched Hill being questioned that Friday by white men, by turn either timid or incredulous, I grieved for her. The anguish in her eyes was recognizable to me. Not only did she dare to speak about events more than one woman would regard as unspeakable, she did so publicly. Not only did she make public accusations best investigated in private, she made them against a man who was black and conservative, as she was — a man who in other ways had earned her respect.

"Here is a woman who went to Sunday school and took it seriously," says Cornel West, director of the African-American Studies department at Princeton University and a social critic who felt mesmerized by what he called "the travesty and tragedy" of the hearings. "She clearly is a product of the social conservatism of a rural black Baptist community." For black women historically, such probity, hard-won and tenaciously held, was social salvation. For white onlookers, it suggested an eerie primness out of sync with contemporary culture.

In the quiet and resolute spirit she might very well have learned from Sunday school, Hill confronted and ultimately breached a series of taboos in the black community that have survived both slavery and the post-segregation life she and Clarence Thomas share. Anita Hill put her private business in the street, and she downgraded a black man to a room filled with white men who might alter his fate — surely a large enough betrayal for her to be read out of the race.

BY SUNDAY EVENING, Anita Hill's testimony lay buried under an avalanche of insinuation and innuendo. Before the eyes of a nation, a tenured law professor beloved by her students was transformed into an evil, opportunistic harpy; a deeply religious Baptist was turned into a sick and delusional woman possessed by Satan and in need of exorcism; this youngest of 13 children from a loving family became a frustrated spinster longing for the attentions of her fast-track superior, bent on exacting a cruel revenge for his rejection.

These skillful transformations of Anita Hill's character by some members of the Senate were effective because they were familiar, manageable images of African-American womanhood. What undergirds these images is the common terror of black women out of control. We are the grasping and materialistic Sapphire in an "Amos 'n' Andy" episode; the embodiment of a shadowy, insane sexuality; the raging, furious, rejected woman. In their extremity, these are images far more accessible and understandable than the polished and gracious dignity, the cool intelligence that Anita Hill displayed in the lion's den of the Senate chamber. However she found herself reconstituted, the result was the same. She was, on all levels, simply unbelievable.

> 'Incidents in the Life of a Slave Girl' would have made more instructive reading for the Senate Judiciary Committee than 'The Exorcist.'

Anita Hill fell on the double-edged sword of African-American womanhood. Her privacy, her reputation, her integrity — all were casualties of an ignorance that left her unseen by and unknown to most of those who meant either to champion or abuse her. As credible, as inspiring, as impressive as she was, most people who saw her had no context in which to judge her. The signs and symbols that might have helped to place Hill were long ago appropriated by officials of authentic (male) blackness, or by representatives of authentic (white) womanhood. Quite simply, a woman like Anita Hill couldn't possibly exist. And in that sense, she is in fine historical company.

More than a century earlier, black women routinely found themselves beyond belief, and thus beyond help, solace and protection. In 1861, the most famous of the few slave narratives written by a black woman, "Incidents in the Life of a Slave Girl," was published. (The book was regarded as fiction for more than 100 years, until in 1987 Jean Fagin Yellin of Pace University completed six years of painstaking research substantiating the existence of its author, Harriet Jacobs, and her harrowing story.) Writing under the pseudonym "Linda Brent," Jacobs outlined for the genteel white woman of the 19th century the horrors, both sexual and otherwise, that awaited the female slave. Jacobs spent close to seven years hiding from her master ensconced in a garret, with food smuggled in by her recently freed grandmother.

In the story of Harriet Jacobs, the powerful man she fears is white. In the story of Anita Hill, the powerful man she fears is black. But the vulnerability of each woman is a palpable presence in the stories they tell. Jacobs's tale is enlivened by the dramatic structure of the 19th-century sentimental novel, Hill's accounts are magnified through the image of her presence on television. Indeed, Jacobs's first lines are a plea to her audience to be taken seriously. "Reader, be assured this narrative is no fiction. I am aware that some of my adventures may seem incredible; but they are, nevertheless, strictly true."

Later she recounts the beginning of her owner's pursuit of her, the year she turned 15: "My master began to whisper foul words in my ear. Young as I was, I could not remain ignorant of their import. I tried to treat them with indifference or contempt. . . . The other slaves . . . knew too well the guilty practices under that roof; and they were aware that to speak of them was an offense that never went unpunished. . . . I longed for some one to confide in. I would have given the world to have laid my head on my grandmother's faithful bosom, and told her all my troubles. . . . I dreaded the consequences of a violent outbreak; and both pride and fear kept me silent."

Harriet Jacobs had good reason to fear; even free African-American women of the 19th century possessed no rights that anyone was bound to respect. Regarded as immoral and loose, black women spent an inordinate amount of time in the years after slavery in attempts to establish themselves as virtuous women, as a rebuke to the rash of hypersexual images that flooded contemporary consciousness in those days, images that rationalized the routine sexual abuse of black women — both slave and free — by white men.

It was a stereotype that had consequences for black men as well: "Historically, the stereotype of the sexually potent black male was largely based on that of the promiscuous black female," explained Paula Giddings, in "When and Where I Enter," her history of black women in America. "He would have to be potent, the thinking went, to satisfy such hot-natured women."

Such myths of sexual potency and promiscuity, written and disseminated by trained 19th-century historians, fueled the widespread fears of black men as rapists of white women — and provided the engine for a campaign of terrorism against newly freed black people that included a rash of lynchings. Thus, it was especially troubling that Clarence Thomas should refer to the second round of hearings as "a high-tech lynching."

Thomas evoked one of the most emotional images in African-American consciousness, flinging himself across history like Little Eva clinging to an ice floe and, at the same time, blaming a black woman for his troubles. A century earlier, it was the courageous and single-minded investigative reporting of a black female journalist, Ida B. Wells, that finally galvanized a recalcitrant United States into taking lynching seriously.

"Incidents in the Life of a Slave Girl" would have made far more instructive reading for the Senate Judiciary Committee than "The Exorcist." It was, after all, the Senate's appalling lack of familiarity with what it feels like to be powerless, vulnerable and afraid that rendered Anita Hill and her behavior incomprehensible to most of them. In her preface, Jacobs writes that she has "concealed the names of places and given persons fictitious names. I had no motive for secrecy on my own account, but I deemed it kind and considerate toward others to pursue this course." It is likely that she is more fearful than she lets on.

But it is just as likely that Jacobs evokes a way of seeing the world that transcends 19th-century female gentility, that Jacobs is acting out of Christian charity to those who have persecuted her. And it is just as likely that she held on to her fragile dreams of connection, however slight, to home and friends, however frightening the context in which she enjoyed them.

STUDYING THIS CONNECTED way of seeing the world has been the work of Carol Gilligan's professional life. The author of "In a Different Voice: Psychological Theory and Women's Development," she has written extensively on women's psychological development and the issues of justice and care that characterize the relationships of many women, both personal and professional. Thus she did not find it implausible that Anita Hill might have experienced the events she described, yet continued to work with Judge Thomas.

"It amazed me that no one understood the underlying logic of what she did," Gilligan says. "Her basic assumption was that you live in connection with others, in relationship with others. Now, her experience of that relationship was one of violation; it was offensive to her. But she was making the attempt to work it through in the relationship; trying to resolve conflict without breaking connection." The possibility that such an ethic might have motivated Anita Hill in her choices is rarely voiced in discussions about her.

It may be that this low-key approach does not fit the image of the black woman who stands ready to challenge and confront offensive behavior. The surly black wife with a frying pan in her hand is the flip side of the nurturing mammy, and it is abundantly clear to millions by now that Anita Hill is neither.

Thus her profound self-possession, particularly in the face of the behavior she ascribed to Thomas, seemed impossible to observers—in large part because her response was not the conditioned one for black women. Hill showed no signs of the Harriet Tubman Syndrome, the fierce insistence on freedom or death that made Tubman an abolitionist legend. Anita Hill grabbed no blunt objects with which to threaten her superior, she did not thunder into his office in righteous anger or invoke the power to bring suit. She was not funny, or feisty, or furious in response to the behavior she described. She was disgusted, embarrassed and ambivalent. Therefore, it must have been a dream.

"IT WAS QUITE FITTING that the bulk of the hearings took place on the weekend that Redd Foxx died," says Stanley Crouch, a cultural critic and author of "Notes of a Hanging Judge: Essays and Reviews 1979-1989." "A bunch of the material sounded like stuff from a Redd Foxx-Richard Pryor-Eddie Murphy routine."

But few people were laughing. That week in October, my phone rang nonstop. Friends called to talk about their stories of sexual harassment, their memories of vengeful, jealous women who lie, their theories of self-loathing black men who act out their hostility toward black women while lusting after white women. My sister, Linda, called from Chicago the night before the vote, then used her conference call feature to add her good friend to the line, with whom she had been arguing for an hour already. "I already know you believe her," Linda announced to me. "I just want to hear you tell me why."

The buses and trains and elevators were filled with debates and theories of conspiracy. Hill set up Thomas to bring a black man down. Thomas was a man; what man didn't talk about his prowess? In a Harlem restaurant where I sat with a cup of tea and the papers that Saturday, the entire kitchen staff was in an uproar. The cook, an African woman, wanted to know why Hill waited 10 years to bring it up. The waitress, an African-American woman, said she couldn't tell what to think.

A young black man in his 20's announced he had a theory. "Clarence got jungle fever, and she got mad," he said with a laugh. Jungle fever is the code term, taken from the Spike Lee film of the same name, for a black man's desire to sleep with a white woman. Clarence Thomas's second wife is white, therefore Anita Hill was overcome with jealous rage and hungry for revenge.

"We all know that the animosity of black women toward black men who marry white women is on the level of the recent fire in Oakland," Stanley Crouch said. "That's a major fact. They might be as racist about that as white people used to be."

Then again, some black women might not care at all — a reasonable assumption, given the statistics indicating that interracial relationships between black women and white men have more than tripled in the last 20 years.

Some black women may feel rejected or betrayed by black men lured by a white standard of beauty few of them could emulate. Some may just hate white women. But there is no real evidence to suggest that any of these scenarios apply to Anita Hill and her galvanizing testimony. Most people with an opinion about why she stepped forward regard it as a matter of ideology not, as some people still want to think, romance.

Yet the issues of race and sex illuminated by the hearings remain. So, too, do the myriad ways in which race and gender combine to confuse us. But for the first time in decades, the country has been turned, for a time, into a mobile social laboratory. A level of discussion between previously unaligned groups may have begun with new vigor and candor.

Segments of the feminist movement have been under attack for their selective wooing of black women. Yet many of these same women rallied to Hill with impressive speed. Some black women who had never before considered sexism as an issue serious enough to merit collective concern have begun to organize, including a group of black female academics known as African American Women in Defense of Ourselves. And even in brusque New York, people on opposite sides of this issue, still traumatized by the televised spectacle, seem eager to listen, to be civil, to talk things over.

"I am so pleased people are starting to ask questions, not only about race and gender, but about the America that has frustrated and disappointed them," says Jewell Jackson McCabe. "People who had become cynical, people who have not talked about issues in their lives are talking now. I think the experience was so bad, it was so raw. I don't know a woman who watched those hearings whose life hasn't been changed."

"It was an international drama," says Michael Eric Dyson, assistant professor of ethics, philosophy and cultural criticism at Chicago Theological Seminary. "Anita Hill has put these issues on the American social agenda. She has allowed black men and women to talk freely for the first time about a pain that has been at the heart of our relationships since slavery. Black wives are beginning to tell their husbands about the kind of sexism they have faced not at the hands of white men, but black men."

What was most striking about the hearings, in the end, was the sense of destiny that surrounded them. There was something rewarding about seeing what began as a humiliating event become gradually transformed only in its aftermath. Two African-Americans took center stage in what became a national referendum on many of our most cherished values. In the midst of their shattering appearances, Anita Hill and Clarence Thomas each made us ask questions that most of us had lost the heart to ask.

They are exactly the kinds of questions that could lead us out of the morass of cynicism and anger in which we've all been stuck. That is an immensely satisfying measurement of the Hill-Thomas hearings. It would not be the first time that African-Americans have used tragedy and contradiction as catalysts to make America remember its rightful legacy.

GROUPTHINK: Taking easy way out of a tough decision

Alison Bass
GLOBE STAFF

At a time when the United States and other nations are desperately seeking a way out of the Iraqi crisis, America's leaders are at enormous risk of making a bad decision, psychologists who study group decision-making say.

In fact, if history is any guide, now is the time when President Bush and his advisers are most vulnerable to the kind of noncritical decision-making that has led to disastrous policy decisions in some previous administrations.

This kind of decision-making gave us the Bay of Pigs invasion and the escalation of the Vietnam War, these psychologists say, and they add that the conditions that set up the Kennedy and Johnson administrations for failure in those crises exist now.

"It's at times like these that you feel the power of needing a consensus," said Clark McCauley, a professor of psychology at Bryn Mawr College in Pennsylvania who studies group dynamics. "The situation in the Middle East right now is like sitting on a burning stove with no relief in sight. There is no easy answer."

McCauley and other specialists interviewed last week say they have no idea how the Bush administration is making decisions about the Iraqi crisis, and thus cannot speculate about how the president and his advisers are proceeding.

But they can say something about forces of human nature that drive group decision-making, and how those forces have sometimes conspired to produce ruinous decisions.

Researchers who study social behavior have long known, for example, that members of a group are often under strong pressures to conform to the majority view. When they don't conform, they risk being isolated or cast aside.

More recently, they have discovered that human beings, whenever they meet in groups, also feel a compelling need to reach consensus. They do so both to preserve the friendly atmosphere and cohesiveness of the group and to continue to be accepted by the group and its leader.

"In all these groups, members tend to evolve informal objectives to preserve friendly intragroup relations, and this becomes part of the hidden agenda at their meetings," wrote Irving Janus, an emeritus professor of psychology at Yale University in his landmark book, "Victims of Groupthink."

Janus studied many different groups in assembling his theory about this unconscious need to reach consensus, which he labeled "groupthink." He and other scholars have expanded their understanding of groupthink through a growing body of experimental studies.

The researchers found, for example, that groupthink almost always interferes with critical thinking. And they discovered that the phenomenon is especially intense in elite, high-prestige groups, which represent the pinnacle of success for their members.

Groupthink is quite different from the more blatant pressures for conformity. Groups that fall prey to the phenomenon are not consciously worried about losing their jobs if they dissent. Rather, they are more concerned about resolving the particular problem or uncertainty at hand without losing the group's clubby atmosphere.

Mutual assurance

"Groupthink is a group-coping mechanism, in the sense that people need to reassure each other and themselves that they are doing the right thing," explained Alexander George, a professor of political science at Stanford University and an expert on decision-making. "In the process, they drown out their own and others' inhibitions and uncertainties, and you get a much stronger consensus as a result. It's almost a mutual admiration society."

Groupthink is a more subtle psychological phenomenon than conformity pressures, and researchers believe it may be particularly prevalent in high-level government and corporate decision-making.

In his book, first published in 1972 and revised in 1982, Janus described five cases of major US policy decisions that were dictated (either entirely or in part) by "groupthink" and became unmitigated disasters. Among them were the Bay of Pigs invasion, the escalation of the Vietnam War and Watergate.

He also described two equally important cases where groupthink was avoided and the results were highly successful: the 1962 Cuban missile crisis and the development of the Marshall plan for restoring Europe after World War II.

In both cases, Janus said, the pivotal difference was a leader who had learned to encourage differences of opinion and alternative solutions, without insisting on his own.

"The successful examples come when the president doesn't provide a solution and urges alternative solutions and even appoints a devil's advocate to knock down each solution," agreed McCauley, who expanded on Janus' seminal work in a recently published article. "That seems to increase support and rewards for those in the group who want to think and express thoughts different from the others."

In addition to leadership style, Janus

Reprinted courtesy of *The Boston Globe,* September 10, 1990, pp. 29, 30.

discovered two other conditions that are especially conducive to groupthink: a decision-making group that is homogeneous in social background and ideology and a crisis that appears to have no easy way out.

Those were the conditions in what Janus termed the "perfect failure": the CIA-inspired invasion of Cuba in 1961, widely known as the Bay of Pigs invasion. Led by 1,400 Cuban exiles and aided by the US Navy, Air Force and the CIA, that military disaster left 200 dead, 1,200 exiles as Cuba's prisoners of war and the United States looking like an inept tyrant in the eyes of the world.

Both Janus and McCauley call the decision to invade Cuba a "prototype example" of groupthink. To begin with, there is evidence from later accounts by those who were there that President John Kennedy, even before he consulted his advisers, had decided to aid the anti-Castro rebels.

Despite the president's views, historical documents show, at least two of his advisers harbored serious doubts: Secretary of State Dean Rusk and Harvard historian Arthur Schlesinger, who had been called in by Kennedy as a special adviser. Schlesinger later released a memo he had written to the President at the time expressing his doubts.

But during the crucial meetings, neither Rusk nor Schlesinger voiced their concerns, paving the way for a quick consensus. In his [1989] article, McCauley speculated that both groupthink and conformity pressures played a role in silencing Rusk and Schlesinger.

McCauley noted that there is evidence that all the advisers felt some external pressure to support the plan. At one point, Robert Kennedy took Schlesinger aside and told him the President had made up his mind and it was time for his friends to support him.

But there is also evidence from Schlesinger's later accounts that the advisers desperately wanted to reach a consensus and remain a cohesive group, McCauley and Janus wrote.

Changed approach

By contrast, the same advisers under the same President did express their opinions forcefully in resolving another major test for the Kennedy administration: the Cuban missile crisis. In 1962, after discovering that the Soviets were building missile sites on Cuba, the administration decided to set up a naval blockade around Cuba to prevent Soviet ships allegedly carrying nuclear armaments from getting through. Although the crisis brought the United States and Soviet Union to the brink of nuclear war, it ended successfully when the Soviet ships turned back and Soviet Premier Nikita Khrushchev agreed to remove the missiles.

Kennedy's approach made all the difference in how those crises were handled, according to Janus. In the Bay of Pigs decision, Kennedy thrust a decision on his advisers; in the Cuban missile crisis, although he made an initial decision to respond with some kind of coercive action, he left it up to his advisers to decide what that action would be.

Perhaps, the researchers speculate, Kennedy had learned his lesson from the Bay of Pigs fiasco.

"He asked his advisers for consideration of all possible forms of coercion, deliberately absented himself from some of the earlier meetings of his advisers and appointed Robert Kennedy as devil's advocate to question and attack every proposal offered," McCauley wrote in the August 1989 issue of the Journal of Personality and Social Psychology. "The result was strain, lost sleep, impatience, and anger as the group argued on and on, until finally a majority agreed to recommend a naval blockade of Cuba."

McCauley said struggling to this kind of true consensus is much more arduous for the participants than groupthink, which is why it happens much more rarely. Yet Kennedy's advisers themselves later said the strain of the adversarial procedure itself was crucial in producing the detailed recommendations and contingency planning that made the blockade successful.

George Kennan, a State Department official and architect of the Marshall Plan, voiced similar sentiments in recalling the process that led to that highly successful plan. Given three weeks to come up with a broad plan to extend economic aid to European nations suffering from the aftermath of World War II, Kennan encouraged an open "no-holds-barred" group discussion in which his own proposals were heavily criticized.

"Kennan reported that he went home every night feeling like he had been beat up, but he got a good result out of his group," McCauley said. McCauley and Janus say the group's action was another example of a leader's being able to avoid groupthink.

President Johnson, Janus said, was not as farsighted. He said Johnson took dissent from his war policy as "personal disloyalty" and effectively isolated those who criticized his desire to escalate the Vietnam War. A number of key advisers and senior cabinet members, such as Robert McNamara, McGeorge Bundy and George Ball, left the administration during this time, further evidence that the pressures to conform were enormous.

"If people feel they are going to pay a social cost for expressing their feelings, most won't," McCauley explained. "You have to understand what belonging to the most powerful insiders' group in the world means. It means being invited to the best dinners in Washington, to the best country clubs; it's worth chairmanships on major corporations and big money. It's worth a lot of girls, or boys, if that's what you want."

In the revised version of his book, Janus added yet another example of disastrous decision-making to his list: the Watergate coverup. Even as evidence accumulated that too many people knew too much for the effort to succeed, President Nixon and his close advisers remained unanimous in supporting the coverup. Transcripts from the Nixon tapes show that the president time and again let everyone in the group know which policy he favored. He also discouraged any debate. It was not until John Dean began to be worried more about his own future than about the president's that the consensus unraveled, Janus said.

Pressures always there

Reached at his retirement home in Santa Rose, Calif., Janus said he has no idea how the Bush administration is making decisions about the Iraqi crisis.

"The present administration is extremely secretive," he said. "There is no indication of how they arrived at their decision [to commit troops] and whether they're really setting us up for war or just want a strong presence in the Middle East."

Both Janus and McCauley, however, say the potential for groupthink always exists, along with other pressures to conform to the president's will.

"I'm sure you'll find lots of people who have grave doubts about what's going on in the Mideast, but they're not talking up," McCauley said. "And that's not good. Whenever you do something without thinking about all the possible consequences of what could go wrong, that is bad decision-making."

When Bystanders Just Stand By

WHY DO SOME PEOPLE HELP CRIME VICTIMS WHILE OTHERS WON'T LIFT A FINGER OR EVEN A PHONE?

R. LANCE SHOTLAND

R. Lance Shotland is a professor of psychology at Pennsylvania State University. He and Melvin M. Mark coedited the book Social Science and Social Policy, *published by Sage Publications Inc.*

Twenty-one years ago, Kitty Genovese was brutally murdered as her cries in the night went unanswered by 38 of her neighbors. That infamous incident riveted public attention on just how helpless and alone crime victims may be without the support of their fellow citizens.

In fact, bystanders often do play a crucial role in preventing street crimes when they serve as extended "eyes and ears" of the police. Arrests occur more frequently when bystanders are present than when they are not. More than three-fourths of all arrests result from reports by bystanders or victims, while relatively few come from police surveillance alone. In more than half of all criminal cases, bystanders are present when the police arrive. These citizens may be important information sources, potential witnesses and influences on the victim's decision to report the crime.

Bystanders can also help control crime directly. In some cases, they leap in and rescue crime victims, or even form spontaneous vigilante groups that catch and punish offenders. Yet at other times they are peculiarly passive, neither calling the police nor intervening directly. What accounts for these differences?

The death of Kitty Genovese intrigued the press, the public and social psychologists, all of whom wondered how 38 people could do so little. In 1968, psychologists John Darley and Bibb Latané started a torrent of research by discovering experimentally that a person is less likely to help someone in trouble when other bystanders are present.

As Latané and Steven Nida have noted, by 1981 some 56 experiments had tested and extended this observation. These studies examined the reactions of unwitting subjects who witnessed a staged emergency—either alone or in the presence of actors instructed to ignore the incident. In 48 of the studies, bystanders helped less when someone else was present. People who were alone helped 75 percent of the time, while those with another person helped just 53 percent of the time. After close to 20 years of research, the evidence indicates that "the bystander effect," as it has come to be called, holds for all types of emergencies, medical or criminal.

The effect occurs, the studies show, because witnesses diffuse responsibility ("Only one person needs to call the police, and certainly someone else will") and because they look at the behavior of other bystanders to determine what is happening ("If no one else is helping, does this person really need help?"). As a result, membership in a group of bystanders lowers each person's likelihood of intervening.

This phenomenon does not completely explain the behavior of bystanders, however. In the Genovese murder, for example, even if each bystander's probability of helping had dropped appreciably, with 38 witnesses we would expect several people to attempt to help. Other factors must be involved.

When the witnesses in the Genovese case were asked why they did not intervene, they said, "Frankly, we were afraid," or, "You don't realize the danger," or, "I didn't want to get involved," and even, "I was tired." In other words, in deciding whether to help, they considered the cost to themselves. When direct intervention might lead to physical harm, retaliation from the criminal or days in court testifying, consideration of such costs is understandable. However, the deterrent effects of other costs, such as intervention time, are more surprising. Some of my own work indicates that if helping is likely to take approximately 90 rather than 30 to 45 seconds, the rate is cut in half.

Ambiguity also lowers the intervention rate. In a simulated rape, many more bystanders intervene if they glimpse a struggle than if they only hear the incident. In a simulated accidental electrocution, researchers Russell Clark and Larry Word found that more people intervene if they see a victim being "electrocuted" than if they see and hear only the flashes and sounds of a presumed victim's electrocution.

At times, people misinterpret rare events such as crimes even if they see them. A young woman recently told me about an incident in which she had intervened. She and her friends had met three young men in a bar. After some friendly conversation, the young men left, and the women left shortly afterwards. From a distance, the woman saw her recent acquaintances in the parking lot and thought they were simply horsing around. It wasn't until she reached her car, which was closer to the scene, that she realized the young men were being assaulted in a robbery attempt.

Even if they interpret the situation correctly, bystanders may still be unsure about what they are seeing. People who see a crime, an accident or other unlikely event may wonder, "Did it really happen?" and freeze while they try to figure it out. Latané and Darley were the first to observe that if people are going to intervene, most do it in the first few seconds after they notice the emergency.

Certain types of crime, such as a man's attack on a woman, have unique features that may particularly invite misinterpretation and inhibit intervention. One Genovese witness said, "We thought it was a lovers' quarrel." Bystanders frequently reach similar conclusions when a man attacks a woman. Nine years after the Genovese incident, this story was carried by the Associated Press:

"A 20-year-old woman who works for the Trenton [New Jersey] Police Department was raped yesterday in full view of about 25 employees of a nearby roofing company who watched intently but did not answer her screams for help. . . . [One witness explained], 'Two people did that up there about a year ago but it was mutual. We thought, well, if we went up there, it might turn out to be her boyfriend or something like that.' "

IN 48 OF 56 STUDIES, BYSTANDERS HELPED CRIME OR ACCIDENT VICTIMS LESS WHEN SOMEONE ELSE WAS PRESENT THAN WHEN THEY WERE ALONE.

Some of my own research conducted with Gretchen Straw, a former graduate student, shows that bystanders behave very differently if they assume a quarreling man and woman are related rather than strangers. For example, bystanders who witnessed a violent staged fight between a man and a woman and heard the woman shout, "Get away from me, I don't know you!" gave help 65 percent of the time. But those who saw the fight and heard the woman scream, "Get away from me, I don't know why I ever married you!" only helped 19 percent of the time.

People interpret fights between married people and between strangers quite differently. In our study, the nonresponsive bystanders who heard the "married" woman scream said they were reluctant to help because they weren't sure their help was wanted. They also viewed the "married" woman as much less severely injured than was the woman attacked by the "stranger," despite the fact that the two fights were staged identically. Hence, a woman seen as being attacked by a stranger is perceived as needing help more than is one fighting with a spouse. Furthermore, people expect the husband to stay and fight if they intervene, while they expect a stranger to flee. This makes intervention with fighting strangers seem safer and less costly. Unfortunately, if bystanders see a man and a woman fighting, they will usually assume that the combatants know each other.

What role do individual characteristics play in bystander behavior? Researchers have identified only a few personality factors that differentiate helpers from nonhelpers. Psychologist Louis Penner and his colleagues at the University of South Florida have found that people with relatively high scores for "sociopathy" on a personality test (although not clinically sociopaths) are less likely to help and are less bothered by others' distress than are people with low scores. On the other side of the coin, Shalom Schwartz and his colleagues at the Hebrew University in Jerusalem have shown that people who have a sense of moral obligation to the victim are more likely to help than those who do not.

Psychologist John Wilson of Cleveland State University and his colleagues have found that those concerned with achieving a sense of security are less likely to help than those who feel secure but need to build their sense of self-esteem.

These personality characteristics, combined with all the situational factors described earlier, go a long way in explaining the behavior of bystanders. But there are other factors as well. Consider those rare individuals who intervene directly when a crime is in progress:

Psychologists Ted Huston of the University of Texas at Austin and Gilbert Geis of the University of California at Irvine and their colleagues, who interviewed 32 of these people, found them to be quite different from the ordinary person. Active interveners were very self-assured and felt certain they could handle the situation by themselves. Further, they were likely to have specialized training in police work, first aid or lifesaving, and almost all were male. These people were more likely to have been victimized themselves and to have witnessed

SHOULD HELPING BE LEGISLATED?

Given the important role of citizen participation in crime control, Vermont, Rhode Island, Massachusetts and Minnesota have attempted to compel "good samaritanism" through legislation. Other states are considering passing such laws. Under such legislation, citizens who do not respond after witnessing a serious crime against a person could be fined, jailed or sued, depending on how the law is written.

Such laws, if enforced vigorously, might make inaction more "costly" in bystanders' minds than involvement. They might reduce diffusion of responsibility by making bystanders realize that they will be held personally responsible for their inaction. The laws might also tip the balance toward intervention if bystanders find the situation ambiguous, since they may feel it is safer to guard against a penalty by intervening rather than walking away.

Whether these presumed benefits actually occur is unstudied and unknown. But since they require strong enforcement to occur at all, such outcomes are unlikely. In the four states with duty-to-assist legislation, enforcement seems minimal, and to my knowledge, only one person is being or has even been prosecuted.

If such laws were vigorously enforced, the disadvantages might well outweigh the benefits. Consider how bystanders in the Kitty Genovese case might have been affected: The first attack occurred sometime after 3 a.m. The neighbors were in their apartments when they heard the sounds of the struggle and went to their windows. Not all remained passive spectators; some were ineffective helpers, turning on their lights, opening their windows and shouting. They did scare the killer away—twice. But no one went down to rescue her, an act that might have saved her life. One person called the police after considerable soul-searching about what action to take. His response was too late, however. The remainder did nothing.

Would the law have changed anyone's behavior? Perhaps, but not necessarily for the better. These bystanders had an easy escape: the claim that they were sound sleepers and heard nothing. Research shows that a sizable percentage of bystanders will use such excuses. Would they have told the police what they saw and risk a fine, jail or a legal suit for their nonintervention? Will there needlessly be more victims of rape and murder and more criminals going free because witnesses, fearing legal reprisal, will not provide information? Unfortunately, intimidation through such a law seems as likely as enlisting greater bystander participation. In those rare cases having many witnesses, even if some are intimidated, others are likely to report, so little information is lost. But in cases with only one witness, can we afford the risks of intimidation and lost information?

I doubt that a citizen can be effectively prosecuted with such a law, because it has an implicit time frame within which the authorities must be notified. As an example, take the Genovese witness who finally did call the police. How soon should he have acted to avoid prosecution? We know—and a jury trying his case would know—that he did not call in time. But could he have known?

Laws might avoid the specific time question by specifying that a bystander must report the crime within a "reasonable" amount of time, leaving the definition of reasonable up to prosecutor, judge or jury. When did the Genovese helper first become aware of the attack? Could it ever be determined reliably without his cooperation?

A bystander would have to act very quickly to aid in apprehending a criminal. Research conducted in Kansas City suggests that if crimes are reported while in progress, an arrest related to the response occurs just 35 percent of the time. If bystanders report the crime in less than a minute after the event ends, the chance of capture drops to 18 percent. Waiting a full minute to report lowers the capture rate to 10 percent, and delaying by one to five minutes brings it down to 7 percent. Again, what is reasonable?

Or consider the case of the young woman, mentioned earlier, who thought at first that the parking-lot assault she saw was a case of highjinks by friends. Had her car been parked farther from the crime scene, she might have simply ignored it and gone home. With a duty-to-assist law in effect, she could have been fined, sued or jailed. Should there be a penalty for an innocent mistake, and how can it be distinguished from deliberate shirking of civil duty? Given the huge monetary and emotional costs of a trial, do we want to leave these decisions to a prosecutor? These are but a sampling of the questions raised by prospective duty-to-assist legislation.

I believe such laws will be unenforceable as part of the criminal code and will create a nightmare in civil court similar to the excesses that have accompanied auto-accident litigation. The basic benefit from such laws, then, is likely to be symbolic, pointing out what society expects of its citizens. But I believe that Americans already know that. Such an unenforced law does a disservice by making people believe that a serious problem has been solved when a viable solution is still desperately needed.

I believe that workable solutions are at hand, but they will take time to institute. Social psychologist Jane Piliavin and her colleagues at the University of Wisconsin suggest that school training at an early age may be part of the answer. We also need more effective strategies for reporting crimes. For example, we know that eyewitness identification has many shortcomings. In a property crime such as burglary, which is likely to have physical evidence, perhaps we should teach people to focus on and report characteristics of the getaway car instead of concentrating on the criminal. Whatever the details of the program, we do desperately need new approaches in order to return the balance of fear to favor the citizenry.

more crime in the prior 10 years than were people in general.

From other research, we know that when direct interveners were asked why they did not seek help, they answered that "there wasn't enough time" and boasted that they could "handle the situation." In addition, many either had training in physical defense or boxing or possessed—and were willing to use—a knife.

Not everyone is born or trained to be a hero. Some bystanders help indirectly, by reporting the incident to authorities and/or providing information concerning the crime. Unlike those who leap into the fray, these people do not feel competent to intervene. A typical comment: "I couldn't do anything myself so I went to get help." Such people may also see the potential cost of intervention—injury or death—as too high. A bungled rescue attempt may not help the victim and may harm the rescuer.

Even indirect intervention calls for a quick response. Otherwise the criminal act may be over and the attacker gone. But sometimes the crime happens too suddenly for anyone to comprehend and react in time. The *New York Daily News* reported an example a few years ago.

"A plumber was shot dead on a sunny Brooklyn street last weekend in full view of about 50 of his friends and neighbors. But not a single witness has come forward to tell the police exactly what happened.... Treglia was about to get into his truck when a car pulled up alongside him. A man in the car shot him four times and drove off, leaving him dead in the street."

The bystanders were willing to cooperate with the police, but there were no firsthand accounts. Almost every piece of information was based on what the bystanders had heard from others. The police found this hard to believe, but they did not interpret the behavior as a fearful cover-up of mob murder. The bystanders' reactions are understandable if you look closely at how the situation probably developed:

The incident itself must have been over in seconds. Bystanders had no reason to look at the victim until they heard the shots. It would only have taken a second or two to realize that the man was shot, but by then, where was the gunman? Eyewitness testimony would have been impossible for most people. The great majority would not have seen the man fall, or been certain that shots were fired, or known their source. After talking to their neighbors, however, bystanders could have pieced the event together and told the police what they collectively knew.

Another response, a rare one, is spontaneous vigilantism, in which bystanders not only apprehend a criminal but mete out punishment themselves. For example, *The Washington Post* reported:

"...in the fashion of a Mack Sennett comedy, 29 cab drivers from the L&M Private Car Service and the No-Wait Car Service chased three men who had robbed and stolen one of No-Wait's taxis. Alerted over radio by their dispatcher, the cab drivers chased the suspects from 162nd Street and Amsterdam Avenue through two boroughs, finally cornering their prey in the Bronx. There, they collared two of the suspects, beat them and held them until the police arrived. Both were admitted to Fordham Hospital. One of the drivers, ..., a Vietnam veteran, said after the incident, 'We've got to stick together.' "

Research shows that spontaneous vigilantism happens only in response to certain types of crimes under definable conditions: First, the crimes generate strong identification with the victim (as in the case of the taxi drivers), leaving community members with a strong sense of their own vulnerability. Second, the crimes are particularly threatening to the local community's standards; bystanders would be especially motivated to prevent any recurrence. Third, bystanders are certain (even if sometimes mistaken) both about the nature of the crime and the identity of the criminal. Although people who resort to spontaneous vigilantism usually do not witness the incident directly, the details seem unambiguous because they are interpreted unambiguously to them by someone they view as credible. Fourth, spontaneous vigilantism usually occurs in neighborhoods that are socially and ethnically homogeneous, factors that enhance communication and trust as well as identification with the victim. Poor areas with high crime rates also breed vigilantes motivated by frustration with crime and by the apparent ineffectiveness of the legal system in deterring it.

When vigilantes join together to take illegal action, each person's share of the responsibility is proportionately lessened. Thus, unlike its usual effects in fostering inaction in bystander groups, the diffusion of responsibility in a vigilante group leads to action.

Bystanders can prevent crime by their very presence on the streets. Interviews with convicted felons confirm that, when planning a crime, they view every bystander as a potential intervener and take steps to avoid being seen by potential witnesses. For example, they avoid heavily traveled commercial districts and favor sparsely used residential streets where potential victims often park. Similarly, victimization on subways is highest when there are few riders, and crime rates are higher in areas that offer the greatest possibilities for concealment.

If bystanders decrease the likelihood of crime, then keeping pedestrians on the street should help to reduce it. Unfortunately, people who fear crime are likely to stay behind locked doors and avoid the streets. The greater their fears, the more they stay off the streets, thereby increasing the risks for those who do venture out.

The prevalence of crime in a community can be viewed as the result of a delicate balance between criminals' fear of bystander intervention and possible arrest and bystanders' fear of criminal victimization. To maintain social control effectively, the balance must strongly favor the citizenry. If fear of crime gains ascendance in a neighborhood, residents lose control of criminals, who then rule the streets.

Districts in which social control has been lost need not remain this way. A major item on the public agenda should be developing strategies to help community members exert social control (see box, "Should Helping Be Legislated?"), thus returning the streets to law-abiding citizens.

How Much Is Enough?

Our hunger for more—more cars, more energy, more growth—has all but trashed the planet. Having less would not mean doing without. In fact, it could well make us richer in spirit.

Alan Durning

Alan Durning is a senior researcher at Worldwatch Institute in Washington, DC.

Early in the post–World War II age of affluence, an American retailing analyst named Victor Lebow proclaimed, "Our enormously productive economy . . . demands that we make consumption our way of life, that we convert the buying and use of goods into rituals, that we seek our spiritual satisfaction, our ego satisfaction, in consumption. . . . We need things consumed, burned up, worn out, replaced, and discarded at an ever increasing rate."

Americans have responded to Mr. Lebow's call: Since 1950, United States consumption has soared. Per capita, energy use climbed 60 percent, car travel more than doubled, plastics use multiplied 20-fold, and air travel jumped 25-fold. And much of the world has followed suit. The Japanese speak of the "new three sacred treasures": color television, air-conditioning, and the automobile. Indeed, we are wealthy beyond the wildest dreams of our ancestors. The average person today is four-and-a-half times richer than were his or her great-grandparents at the turn of the century. Needless to say, this new global wealth is not evenly spread among the Earth's people. One billion live in unprecedented luxury; one billion live in destitution. American children under the age of thirteen have more pocket money—$230 a year—than do the half-billion poorest people alive.

Increasingly, the cost of this lopsided affluence is becoming clear. The world's richest billion people have created a form of civilization so acquisitive and profligate that the planet itself is in danger. The lifestyle of this top echelon—the car drivers, beef eaters, soda drinkers, and throwaway consumers—constitutes an ecological threat unmatched in severity by anything save perhaps population growth. The surging exploitation of resources threatens forests, soils, water, air, and climate.

Ironically, abundance has not even made people terribly happy. The time-honored values of integrity of character, good work, friendship, family, and community have often been sacrificed in the rush to riches. Thus, many in the industrial lands have a sense that their world of plenty is somehow hollow—that, hoodwinked by a consumerist culture, they have been fruitlessly attempting to satisfy what are essentially social, psychological, and spiritual needs with material things.

Of course, the opposite of overconsumption—poverty—is no solution to either environmental or human problems. It is infinitely worse for people and equally bad for the environment. Dispossessed peasants slash-and-burn their way into the rainforests of Latin America, and hungry nomads turn their herds out onto fragile African rangeland, reducing it to desert.

If environmental destruction results when people have either too little or too much, we are left to wonder how much is enough. What level of consumption can the Earth support? When does having more cease to add appreciably to human satisfaction? Answering these questions definitively is impossible, but for each of us in the world's consuming class, asking is essential nonetheless. Unless we see that more is not always better, our efforts to forestall ecological decline will be overwhelmed by our appetites.

Some guidance on what the Earth can sustain emerges from an examination of current consumption patterns around the world. Consider three of the most ecologically important types of consumption—transportation, diet, and use of raw materials.

DONKEYS, BIKES, AND AUTOMOBILES

About 1 billion people do most of their traveling—aside from the occasional donkey or bus ride—on foot, many of them never going more than a hundred miles from their birth places. Unable to get to jobs easily, attend school, or bring their complaints before government offices, they are severely hindered by the lack of transportation options.

The great number of people falling in the middle of the economic spectrum—some 3 billion residents of places such as China, Latin America, and the Middle East—travel by bus and bicycle. Mile for mile, bikes are cheaper than any other vehicles, costing less than a hundred dollars new in most of the Third World and requiring no fuel. The world's automobile class is relatively small; only 8 percent of humans, about 400 million people, own cars. But these cars are directly responsible for an estimated 13 percent of carbon dioxide emissions from fossil fuels worldwide, along with air pollution, acid rain, and a quarter-million traffic fatalities a year.

Car owners also bear indirect responsibility for the far-reaching impacts of their chosen vehicle. The automobile makes itself indispensable: Cities sprawl, public transit atrophies, shopping centers multiply, workplaces scatter. As suburbs spread, families start to need a car for each driver. One fifth of American households own three or more vehicles, more than half own at least two, and 65 percent of new American houses are built with two-car garages. Today, working Americans spend nine hours a week behind the wheel. To make these homes-away-from-home more comfortable, 90 percent of new cars have air-conditioning, which adds emissions of gases that aggravate the greenhouse effect and deplete the ozone layer.

Some 93 percent of American teenage girls surveyed in 1987 deemed shopping their favorite pastime.

Ironies abound: More "Eagles" drive America's expanding road network, for instance, than fly in the nation's polluted skies, and more "Cougars" pass the night in its proliferating garages than in its shrinking forests.

OUR DAILY BREAD

The global food-consumption ladder also has three rungs. At the bottom, according to the latest World Bank estimates, some 630 million people are unable to provide themselves with a healthy diet. On the next rung, the 3.4 billion grain eaters of the world get enough calories and plenty of plant-based protein, giving them the healthiest basic diet of the world's people. They typically receive less than 20 percent of their calories from fat. The top of the ladder is populated by the meat eaters, those who obtain close to 40 percent of their calories from fat. These 1.25 billion people eat three times as much fat per person as do the remaining 4 billion, mostly because they eat so much red meat. The meat class pays the price of its diet in high death rates from the so-called diseases of affluence—heart disease, stroke, and certain types of cancer.

But the Earth also pays for the high-fat diet. Indirectly, the meat-eating quarter of humanity consumes nearly 40 percent of the world's grain—grain that fattens the livestock they eat. Meat production is behind a substantial share of the environmental strains induced by the present global agricultural system, from soil erosion to overpumping of underground water. In the extreme case of American beef, producing two pounds of steak requires ten pounds of grain and the energy equivalent of a half-gallon of gasoline, not to mention the associated soil erosion, water consumption, pesticide and fertilizer run-off, ground-water depletion, and emissions of the greenhouse gas methane.

Beyond the effects of livestock production, the affluent diet rings up an ecological bill through its heavy dependence on shipping goods over great distances. One fourth of the grapes eaten in the United States are grown 7,000 miles away in Chile, and the typical mouthful of food travels more than 1,000 miles from farm field to dinner plate. Processing and packaging add further resource costs to the way the affluent eat. The new generation of microwave-ready instant meals, loaded with disposable pans and multilayer packaging, require ten times the resources of preparing the same dishes at home from scratch.

Global beverage consumption reveals a similar pattern. The 1.75 billion people at the bottom are clearly deprived: They have no option but to drink water that is often contaminated with human, animal, and chemical wastes. Those in the next group up, in this case nearly 2 billion people, take more than 80 percent of their liquid refreshment in the form of clean drinking water, with the remainder coming from commercial beverages such as tea, coffee, and, for children, milk. At the quantities consumed, these beverages pose few environmental problems; they are packaged minimally, and transport-energy needs are low because they are moved only short distances or in a dry form.

In the top class once again are the billion people in industrial countries. At a growing rate, they imbibe soft drinks, bottled water, and other prepared commercial beverages that are packaged in single-use containers and transported over great distances—sometimes even across oceans. Ironically, where tap water is purest and most accessible, its use as a beverage is declining. It now typically accounts for only a quarter of drinks in industrial countries. Americans now drink more soda pop than water from the kitchen sink.

THE STUFF OF LIFE

As for raw-material consumption, about 1 billion rural people subsist on local biomass collected from the immediate environment. Most of what they use each day—about a half-pound of grain, two pounds of fuel wood, and fodder for their animals—could be self-replenishing renewable resources. Unfortunately, because these people are often pushed by landlessness and population growth into fragile, unproductive ecosystems, their minimal needs are not always met.

These materially destitute billion are part of a larger group that lacks many of the benefits provided by modest use of nonrenewable resources—particularly durable things such as radios, refrigerators, water pipes, high-quality tools, and carts with lightweight wheels and ball bearings. More than 2 billion people live in countries where per capita consumption of steel, the most basic modern material, falls below 100 pounds a year. In those same countries, per capita energy use—a fairly good indirect indicator of overall use of materials—is lower than 20 gigajoules per year (the equivalent of less than 150 gallons of oil).

Roughly 1.5 billion live in the middle class of materials use. Providing each of them with durable goods every year uses between 100 and 350 pounds of steel and between 20 and 50 gigajoules of energy (between 150 and 345 gallons of oil). At the top of the heap is the throwaway class, which uses raw materials like they're going out of style. A typical resident of the industrialized fourth of the world uses 15 times as much paper, 10 times as much steel, and 12 times as much fuel as does a resident of the developing world. The extreme case is again the United States, where the average person consumes most of his or her own weight in basic materials each day—40 pounds of petroleum and coal, 30 pounds of other minerals, 26 pounds of agricultural products, and 19 pounds of forest products.

In transportation, diet, and use of raw materials, as consumption rises on the economic scale, so does waste—both of resources and of health. Bicycles and public transit are cheaper, more efficient, and healthier transport options than are cars. A diet founded on the basics of grains and water is gentle to the Earth and the body. And a lifestyle that makes full use of raw materials for durable goods without succumbing to the throwaway mentality is ecologically sound while still affording many of the comforts of modernity. Yet despite these arguments in favor of modest consumption, few people who can afford high consumption levels opt to live simply. What prompts us, then, to consume so much?

"THE AVARICE OF MANKIND IS INSATIABLE," wrote Aristotle twenty-three centuries ago, describing the way that as each of our desires is satis-

fied a new one seems to appear in its place. That observation, on which all of economic theory is based, provides the most obvious answer to the question of why people never seem satisfied with what they have. If our wants are insatiable, there is simply no such thing as enough.

What distinguishes modern consuming habits from those of Aristotle's time, some would say, is simply that we are much richer than our ancestors, and consequently have more ruinous effects on nature. There is no doubt a great deal of truth in that view, but there is also reason to believe that certain forces in the modern world encourage people to act on their consumptive desires as rarely before.

In the anonymous mass societies of advanced industrial nations, daily interactions with the economy lack the face-to-face character that prevails in surviving local communities. Traditional virtues such as integrity, honesty, and skill are too hard to measure to serve as yardsticks of social worth. By default, they are gradually supplanted by a simple, single indicator—money. As one Wall Street banker put it bluntly to *The New York Times,* "Net worth equals self-worth." Under this definition, consumption becomes a treadmill, with everyone judging their status by who is ahead and who is behind.

Psychological data from several nations confirm that the satisfaction derived from money does not come from simply having it. It comes from having more of it than others do, and from having more this year than last. Thus, the bulk of survey data reveals that the upper classes in any society are more satisfied with their lives than the lower classes are, but that they are no more satisfied than the upper classes of much poorer countries—nor than the upper classes were in the less-affluent past.

More striking, perhaps, is that most psychological data show the main determinants of happiness in life to be unrelated to consumption at all: Prominent among them are satisfaction with family life, especially marriage, followed by satisfaction with work, leisure, and friendships. Indeed, in a comprehensive inquiry into the relationship between affluence and satisfaction, social commentator Jonathan Freedman notes, "Above the poverty level, the relationship between income and happiness is remarkably small." Yet when alternative measures of success are not available, the deep human need to be valued and respected by others is acted out through consumption. Buying things becomes both a proof of self-esteem ("I'm worth it," chants one advertising slogan) and a means to social acceptance.

Beyond social pressures, the affluent live completely enveloped in proconsumption advertising messages. The sales pitch is everywhere. One analyst estimates that the typical American is exposed to between 50 and 100 advertisements each morning before nine o'clock. Along with their weekly twenty-two-hour diet of television, American teen-agers are typically exposed to three to four hours of TV advertisements a week, adding up to at least 100,000 ads between birth and high school graduation.

Ad expenditures in the United States rose from $198 per capita in 1950 to $498 in 1989. Total global advertising expenditures, meanwhile, rose from an estimated $39 billion in 1950 to $237 billion in 1988, growing far faster than economic output. Over the same period, per-person advertising expenditures grew from $15 to $46. In developing countries, the increases have been astonishing. Advertising billings in India jumped five-fold in the '80s, and South Korea's advertising industry has recently grown 35 to 40 percent annually.

The proliferation of shopping centers has, in a roundabout way, also promoted the compulsion to consume. Many critics believe mall design itself encourages acquisitive impulses. But perhaps more important, suburban malls and commercial strips suck commerce away from downtown and neighborhood merchants. Shopping by public transit or on foot becomes difficult, auto traffic increases, and sprawl accelerates. In the end, public places such as town squares and city streets are robbed of their vitality, leaving people fewer attractive places to go besides the malls that set the whole shopping process in motion.

Particularly in the United States, shopping seems to have become a primary cultural activity. Americans spend six hours a week doing various types of shopping, and they go to shopping centers on average once a week—more often than they go to church or synagogue. Some 93 percent of American teen-age girls surveyed in 1987 deemed shopping their favorite pastime. The 32,563 shopping centers in the country surpassed high schools in number in 1987. Just between 1986 and 1989, total retail space in these centers grew by 78 million square yards, or 20 percent. Shopping centers now garner 55 percent of retail sales in the United States, compared with 16 percent in France and 4 percent in Spain.

Countless government policies also play a role both in promoting high consumption and in worsening its ecological impact. Urban and transport planning favor private vehicles—and motorized ones—to the exclusion of cleaner modes. Most governments in both North and South America subsidize beef production on a massive scale. Tax law in the United States allows virtually unlimited deductions for purchases of houses: The more homes a family buys, the more taxes they save. Partly as a consequence, 10 million Americans now own two or more homes, while 300,000 (at bare minimum) are homeless.

Land use and materials policies in most of the world undervalue renewable resources, ignore natural services provided by ecosystems, and underprice raw materials extracted from the public domain. More fundamentally, national economic goals are built squarely on the assumption that more is better. National statistics, for example, refer to people more frequently as consumers than as citizens. Economic policy, because it is based on modern economics' system of partial accounting, views as healthy growth what is often feverish and debilitating overconsumption.

Finally, the sweeping advance of the commercial mass market into realms once dominated by family members and local enterprise has made consumption far **more wasteful than in the past. Over the past century, the mass market has taken over an increasing number of the productive tasks once provided within the household.** More and more, flush with cash but pressed for time, households opt for the questionable "conveniences" of prepared, packaged foods, miracle cleaning products, and disposables. All these things, while saving the householders time, cost the Earth dearly, and change households from the primary unit of the economy to passive, consuming entities. Shifting one economic activity after another out of the home does boost the gross national product—but that is largely a fiction of bookkeeping, an economic sleight of hand.

Like the household, the community economy has atrophied—or been dismembered—under the blind force of the money economy. Shopping malls, superhighways, and "strips" have replaced corner stores, local restaurants, and neighborhood theaters—the very things that help to create a sense of common identity and community in an area. In the United States, where the demise of local economies is furthest advanced, many neighborhoods are little more than a place to sleep. Americans move, on average, every five years, and develop little attachment to those who live near them.

All these things nurture the acquisitive desires that everyone has. Can we, as individuals and as citizens, act to confront these forces?

When Moses came down from Mount Sinai he could count the rules of ethical behavior on the fingers of his two hands. In the complex global economy of the late-twentieth century, in which the simple act of turning on an air-conditioner affects planetary systems, the rules for ecologically sustainable living could run into the hundreds. However, the basic value of a sustainable society—the ecological equivalent of the Golden Rule—is simple: Each generation should meet its needs without jeopardizing the prospects of future generations. What is lacking is the thorough practical knowledge—at each level of society—of what living by that principle means.

Ethics, after all, exist only in practice, in the fine grain of everyday decisions. When most people see a large automobile and think first of the air pollution it causes rather than the social status it conveys, environmental ethics will have arrived. In a fragile biosphere, the ultimate fate of humanity may depend on whether we can cultivate deeper sources of fulfillment, founded on a widespread ethic of limiting consumption and finding nonmaterial enrichment. Moreover, an ethic becomes widespread enough to restrain antisocial behavior effectively only when it is encoded in culture, in society's collective memory, experience, and wisdom.

For individuals, the decision to live a life of sufficiency—to find their own answer to the question "How much is enough?"—is to begin a highly personal process. The goal is to put consumption in its proper place among the many sources of personal fulfillment, and to find ways of living within the means of the Earth.

One great inspiration in this quest is the body of human wisdom passed down over the ages. Materialism was denounced by all the sages, from Buddha to Muhammad. "These religious founders," observed historian Arnold Toynbee, "disagreed with each other in the pictures of what is the nature of the universe, the nature of the spiritual life, the nature of ultimate reality. But they all agreed in their ethical precepts. . . . They all said with one voice that if we made material wealth our prarmount aim, this would lead to disaster." The Christian Bible echoes most of human wisdom when it asks, "What shall it profit a man if he shall gain the whole world and lose his own soul?"

Realistically, voluntary simplicity is unlikely to gain ground rapidly against the onslaught of consumerist values. As historian David Shi of North Carolina's Davidson College has noted, the call for a simpler life has been perennial through the history of North America, from the Puritans of Massachusetts Bay to the back-to-the-landers of the '70s. None of these movements ever gained more than a slim minority of adherents. Elsewhere, entire nations such as China and Vietnam have dedicated themselves to rebuilding human character—sometimes through brutal techniques—in a less self-centered mold, but nowhere have they succeeded with more than a token few of their citizens.

It would be hopelessly naïve to believe that entire populations will suddenly experience a moral awakening, renouncing greed, envy, and avarice. The best that can be hoped for is a gradual widening of the circle of those practicing voluntary simplicity and a weakening of the consumerist ethos. The challenge before humanity is to bring environmental matters under cultural controls, and the goal of creating a sustainable culture—a culture of permanence—is best thought of as a task that will occupy several generations. Just as smoking has lost its social cachet in the United States in the space of a decade, conspicuous consumption of all types may be susceptible to social pressure over a longer period.

Ultimately, personal restraint will do little, though, if it's not wedded to bold political steps against the forces promoting consumption. Beyond the oft-repeated agenda of environmental and social reforms necessary to achieve sustainability—such as overhauling energy systems, stabilizing population, and ending poverty—action is needed to restrain the excesses of advertising, to curb the shopping culture, to abolish policies that push consumption, and to revitalize household and community economies as human-scale alternatives to the high-consumption lifestyle. Such changes promise to help both the environment, by reducing the burden of overconsumption, and our peace of mind, by taming the forces that keep us dissatisfied with our lot.

Efforts to revitalize household and community economies may prove the decisive element in the attempt to create a culture less prone to consumption. At a personal level, commitment to nonmaterial fulfillment is hard to sustain without reinforcement from family, friends, and neighbors. At a political level, vastly strengthened local institutions may be the only counterweight to the colossus of vested interests that currently benefit from profligate consumption.

Despite the ominous scale of the challenge, there could be many more people ready to begin saying "enough" than the prevailing opinion suggests. After all, much of what we consume is wasted or unwanted in the first place. How much of the packaging that we put out with the household trash each year would we rather never see? How much of the rural land built up into housing developments, "industrial parks," and commercial strips could be left alone if we insisted on well-planned land use inside city limits? How many of the miles we drive would we not gladly give up if livable neighborhoods were closer to work, a variety of local merchants closer to home, streets safe to walk and bike, and public transit easier and faster?

The satisfaction derived from money does not come from simply having it. It comes from having more of it than others do.

In the final analysis, accepting and living by sufficiency rather than excess offers a return to what is, culturally speaking, the human home: to the ancient order of family, community, good work, and good life; to a reverence for excellence of skilled handiwork; to a true materialism that does not just care *about* things but cares *for* them; to communities worth spending a lifetime in.

For the luckiest among us, a human lifetime on Earth encompasses perhaps a hundred trips around the sun. The sense of fulfillment received on that journey—regardless of a person's religious faith—has to do with the timeless virtues of discipline, hope, allegiance to principle, and character. Consumption itself has little part in the playful camaraderie that inspires the young, the bonds of love and friendship that nourish adults, the golden memories that sustain the elderly. The very things that make life worth living, that give depth and bounty to human existence, are infinitely sustainable.

Enhancing Human Adjustment: Learning to Cope Effectively

On each college and university campus a handful of students experiences overwhelming stress and life-shattering crises. One student learns her mother, living in a distant city, has terminal cancer and about two months to live. Another receives the sad news that his parents are divorcing; the student descends into a deep depression that lowers his grades. A sorority blackballs a young woman whose heart was set on becoming a sister; she commits suicide. Now all of the sorority sisters sense the heavy burden of responsibility. Fortunately almost every campus houses a counseling center for students; some universities even offer assistance to employees. At the counseling service, trained professionals such as psychologists are available to offer aid and therapy to troubled members of the campus community.

Knowing what assistance to provide is not the first step, however. The first difficulty with treatment or therapy is not *how* to intervene but *when* to intervene. There are as many definitions of mental illness and its reciprocal, mental health, as there are mental health professionals. Some practitioners define mental illness as "whatever society cannot tolerate." Others define mental illness in terms of statistics: "if a majority do not behave that way, then the behavior is deviant." Some professionals suggest that an inadequate self-concept is a sign of mental illness while others cite a lack of contact with reality as an indicator of mental illness. A few psychologists claim that mental illness is a fiction: to call one individual ill suggests that the rest are healthy by contrast, when in fact there may be few real distinctions between people.

Because mental illness is difficult to define, it is sometimes difficult to treat. For each definition, each theorist develops a different treatment strategy. Psychoanalysts press clients to recall their dreams, their childhoods, and their intrapsychic conflicts in order to empty and analyze the contents of the unconscious. Humanists encourage clients to explore all facets of their lives in order for the clients to become less defensive and more open to experience. Behaviorists are not concerned with the psyche at all, but rather are concerned with observable and, therefore, treatable symptoms or behaviors. No underlying causes such as intrapsychic conflict are postulated to be the roots of adjustment problems. Other therapists, namely psychiatrists, who are physicians by training, may utilize these therapies and add somatotherapies such as drugs and psychosurgery as well.

This brief list of therapeutic interventions raises further questions. For instance, is one form of therapy more effective, less expensive, or longer-lasting than another? Should a particular diagnosis be treated by one form of therapy when another diagnosis is more amenable to a different treatment? Who should make the diagnosis? If two experts disagree on the diagnosis and treatment, who is correct? Should psychologists be allowed to prescribe

Unit

psychoactive drugs? Researchers are studying these questions now. Some psychologists question whether therapy is effective at all. In one well-publicized but highly criticized study, researcher Hans Eysenck was able to show that spontaneous remission rates were as high as therapeutic "cure" rates. You, yourself, may be wondering whether professional help is always necessary. Can people be their own healers? Is support from friends as useful as professional treatment?

The first series of articles provide a general discussion of the issues related to mental health, mental disturbance, and treatment. In the first article, "Mental Health Checkup," Andrea Atkins reviews the differences between "normal" and "abnormal" symptoms. By so doing, she assists the reader in differentiating quirks from real mental disorders. The companion article, "The Listening Cure," pertains to a new form of treatment that focuses on our mental health rather than our problems.

"The Revolution in Psychiatric Care" describes the sometimes devastating effects of cutbacks for treatment of mental illness by health insurance companies. Findlay also assists the reader in evaluating various mental health facilities. In "What Good Is Feeling Bad?" Randolph Nesse suggests that there are reasons we experience psychic pain; not all physical or mental pain is bad, then. Psychic pain, he explains, may have evolutionary significance.

In "Managing Stress and Living Longer," Jerome Murray prefers that we avoid stress, but, when it is unavoidable, as it often is in modern life, we need stress management programs. Murray explains that these programs can become added sources of stress if they are not properly managed.

The remaining articles in this unit of the book describe various forms of mental disorders, one at a time. Many of these articles also offer advice about treatment. Two common disorders are tackled first. Clinical depression is the focus of "Winning the War Against Clinical Depression," while sexual desire disorders (such as low desire) is the focus of "Sexual Desire."

In "The Secret Illness: Obsessive-Compulsive Disorder," by Isabel Forgang, an individual's overwhelming preoccupation with certain thoughts and behaviors is described. Multiple personality, a rare but fascinating disorder in which the individual's identity fragments into multiple identities, is the disorder discussed in "Who Am I?"

Information about schizophrenia is not left out of this unit either. Not to be confused with multiple personality, schizophrenia signifies a split with reality and is highlighted in "Awakenings: Schizophrenia—A New Drug Brings Patients Back to Life."

The next article in this unit is "Hitting Bottom Can Be the Beginning." Although criminality is not a disorder per se, many felons have mental disorders or problems relating to others. Incarceration as a form of treatment for commission of a crime often decreases an individual's self-esteem that, in turn, creates problems when the individual is released from prison. In this article the success of "Delancy Street," a successful treatment service for ex-cons, is described.

Finally, in "Healthy Pleasures," Robert Ornstein and David Sobel chide the average American for forgetting that life's small pleasures, such as a good nap or fine food, bring large rewards in terms of physical and mental health.

Looking Ahead: Challenge Questions

There are a myriad of definitions for mental illness. Catalog and discuss the pros and cons of each one. Is it possible that mental illness is a fiction created by society to repress a minority? Is mental health the absence of mental illness?

Each profession (medicine, law, teaching, etc.) has its own code of ethics. What are the ethical guidelines under which psychotherapists ought to operate? Do you think some therapists are unethical or incompetent?

How have changes in insurance coverage, new forms of treatment, and the self-help movement altered how we treat the mentally disordered as well as the average citizen in our society?

Do you think adjustment problems are exclusively the realm of mental health professionals? What do you think society at large should do about problems such as crime and alcoholism?

Sexual problems, substance abuse, and crime can cause distress even in the mentally healthy. What other everyday situations are stressful, and how can people cope effectively with them? Is professional help the best answer?

For each of these disorders, define the major symptoms as well as a form of treatment: clinical depression, sexual desire disorder, obsession-compulsion, multiple personality, and schizophrenia.

MENTAL HEALTH CHECKUP

Do Your Quirks Have You in a Quandary?

Andrea Atkins

Have you ever asked yourself "Am I nuts?" Though usually spoken in jest, questions about our mental health sometimes reflect deeper worries.

"Why can't I stop thinking about food?"
"Is it normal to be sad all the time?"
"When will I get over needing these fantasies?"

It's sometimes hard to tell when you, or someone you care about, has crossed the line between an endearing behavior quirk and a problem in need of professional help. But that's a decision at least one in three of us will have to make at some time.

Acting odd is normal. Many of us behave "strangely" at times—entertaining unusual thoughts, taking unconventional actions, or developing odd habits. Most mental health experts say that unless your thoughts, actions, or fears either hurt someone else or are keeping you from functioning in life, they are probably not worrisome. But if you're not producing at work, not socializing with friends and family, or otherwise not enjoying life, then you should seek professional help.

"If you're having patterns in your life that are troubling you, then you should get help," says Ken Thompson, M.D., assistant professor of psychiatry at the University of Pittsburgh School of Medicine.

And getting that help is nothing to be ashamed of. According to the American Psychiatric Association, during any six-month period, nearly 30 million people in this country suffer from a diagnosable mental illness that keeps them from their job, school, or just daily life.

Still wondering about where you or a loved one stand? Let's look at some common forms of mental illness, along with signals that indicate the need for professional help.

Depression. Sad feelings brought on by the loss of a loved one, loss of a job, or the dissolution of a relationship affect all of us. But when those feelings of sadness overwhelm your life, you may be suffering [from] clinical depression. More than 8 percent of all Americans will suffer this serious depression in their lifetime. The APA defines depression as lowered mood accompanied by feelings of helplessness, hopelessness, and irritability. Depressed people lose interest in life, have low self-esteem, don't sleep or eat well, can't concentrate, feel tired, and have recurring thoughts of death or suicide.

No one knows what causes depression, but researchers now point to chemical imbalances in the brain, which can be treated with a range of drugs. Talk therapy has also proven effective in the treatment of depression.

Depressed folks often talk to a friend, cleric, or family doctor. "If you have a problem and you're feeling anxious and depressed, and you haven't figured out how to deal with it, seek help," says Harvey Ruben, M.D., a psychiatrist and host on NBC Radio's Talknet. "It does not mean you need long-term psychotherapy."

Thompson notes, however, that some forms of depression can be so debilitating that a person feels unable or unwilling to seek help. That's when a caring friend or relative can do a great service by helping to get assistance.

Another sort of depression, manic depressive disorder, is characterized by mood swings from deep depression to extreme euphoria. It strikes most people before age 35, and studies have pointed to a genetic predisposition to the illness. According to the APA, manic depressive disorder is one of the most treatable mental health disorders; a combination of medication and psychotherapy can help many sufferers regain control of their lives.

Anxiety disorders. You may have heard of arachnephobia, claustrophobia, and agoraphobia. You may even claim to suffer from them. But having an extreme dread of spiders (arachnephobia) is one thing—refusing to leave your house for fear of running into one is another matter.

Phobias are but one form of anxiety disorder, a condition that the APA says affects about 12 percent of Americans. Other anxiety disorders include generalized anxiety disorder, a state of chronic nervousness; panic disorder, a temporary feeling of intense terror with no apparent cause; and obsessive/compulsive disorder, repeated, unwanted thoughts or behaviors that nearly take over one's life.

As with other mental illnesses, anxiety disorders are considered dangerous when they threaten to keep you from enjoying life. "If a person takes four showers a day, and his life is happy and satisfactory, then who cares?" says Judith Rapoport, M.D., author of "The Boy Who Couldn't Stop Washing," a study of obsessive/compulsive disorder. "But if this person is exhausted because he's fighting the urge to take all those showers, then that's something else."

Any ritualistic behavior that you cannot control warrants discussion with a doctor. Ruben says if you find that you are checking things over and over again, you might want to get help preemptively. "If you're checking the stove five times a day, in two weeks it might be 10 times a day. And the more severe a problem becomes, the harder it is to treat."

"FALSE" ALARMS

President George Bush had all the signs of anxiety disorder: Heart palpitations, feelings of extreme anxiety, problems in sleeping, shortness of breath. But what his doctors found was a thyroid condition called Grave's Disease.

"Not all that wheezes is asthma," warns Mark Gold, M.D., author of *The Good News About Depression.*

The first thing a psychiatrist or other mental health professional should do on listening to your symptoms is order a complete physical and neurological examination, Gold contends. He has seen hundreds of cases of patients being treated for a mental health disorder when in fact they were suffering from allergies, thyroid conditions, medication side effects, or some other physical ailment.

"The most important thing is to have as much understanding as possible about a disease," Gold says. "Also ask about what other conditions might cause your symptoms."

Similarly, if you are so frightened of something that you cannot face it at all, talk to someone. While some people manage phobias by simply avoiding the object or situation that causes them fear, others become prisoners to them. Agoraphobia, for example, the fear of open spaces, imprisons its sufferers in their home.

Panic disorder is one of the less predictable anxiety disorders, striking for no apparent reason. Sufferers feel heart palpitations, trembling, hot or cold flashes, a choking sensation, shortness of breath, chest discomfort, and sweating. They cannot pinpoint what is causing the problem. Panic attacks can progressively take over a person's life. "The attack may occur while they're driving," Thompson says, "so then they avoid driving. The next one may be in a crowded place, so they'll avoid crowded places. These attacks will sneak up until they're hemmed in."

Anxiety disorders are most often treated with a mix of drugs and psychotherapy.

Substance abuse. You may be surprised to see this heading in a story about mental illness. "The truth is," says Thompson, "the biggest mental health problem in America is addiction and substance abuse. Substance abuse is increasing most rapidly in women."

Why is substance abuse considered a mental illness? Often because it is brought on by psychological and environmental factors that are responsive to counseling. During their lifetime, 16 percent of Americans suffer substance abuse, Ruben says. That's more than 25 million, according to the APA. Researchers have found that substance abusers seem to share certain biological characteristics that may predispose them to addiction. Alcoholics, for example, have a liver enzyme that functions improperly, early studies have shown.

The first indication that you've crossed the border from normal behavior to addiction is lack of control. If you cannot get through the day—or even the week—without your substance of choice, you are probably in danger. Be aware of changes in the patterns of your life. "An alcoholic will frequently think that drinking is not a problem," Thompson says. "But an alcoholic may notice that he or she is fighting more with a spouse."

The APA distinguishes between substance abuse and substance dependence. A person who can't stop using drugs or alcohol daily, weekly, or in binges, is considered an abuser. He or she finds that job performance, relationships, and life in general are affected by drug use. Drug dependence has the same characteristics as abuse, plus the sufferer needs more and more of the drug to feel the effects.

Treatment may include psychotherapy or participation in one of many addiction self-help support groups.

Sexual deviance. "People have all sorts of sexual fantasies," says Bernie Zilbergeld, Ph.D., a sex therapist and author of *The New Male Sexuality* (Bantam, 1992). And that's OK. "Any fantasy you have is fine unless it takes away from your partner."

As a sex therapist in Oakland, California, Zilbergeld says he's heard about people who could have sex only with a woman wearing high-heels, people who needed sex three times a night, a man who could be aroused only by a woman who looked a certain way.

One man who consulted him worried because he masturbated four or five times a day. The psychologist told the man that as long as his needs didn't interfere with his work or his relationship with his wife, there was no need for concern.

"But if you have a fantasy and you think you're going to lose control of it—you think you might give in to something that's illegal or immoral, or that could hurt someone—then you better get help," Zilbergeld says.

You don't need to seek a sex therapist, necessarily. Any licensed mental health professional will be able to help, he says.

SEEKING HELP

Whether or not you recognize yourself in the descriptions here, don't be shy about getting help if you feel your life is not right. "The best thing is to get help as soon as symptoms are present," Ruben says. "I've heard it said that if you don't treat depression, it will go away in six months—but you may kill yourself first."

Where should you go? Start with your family doctor, who can refer you to a mental health professional. A trusted cleric can also provide a referral. Whomever you select, make sure you feel comfortable with him or her. Above all, don't give up.

For more information on mental illnesses, write The American Psychiatric Association, Public Affairs Division, Dept. BHG92, 1400 K Street, NW, Washington, DC 20005. Specify the disorder that concerns you.

The listening cure

Psychology of mind urges clients to heal old wounds by living in the present

Teo Furtado

Teo Furtado is a free-lance writer living in San Francisco.

What's the problem? In therapy sessions, this is a critical question, right? Wrong, say therapists who advocate a controversial new therapy called psychology of mind. These therapists believe that dwelling on painful experiences of the past keeps people from experiencing the innate mental health we all possess. This simplistic-sounding approach is aimed at a wider audience than the typical middle-class psychotherapeutic clientele: It's being used to help poor blacks in Miami, Native Americans in Minnesota, and victims of alcohol and drug abuse nationwide.

To Stan and Leslie Miller, it was nothing short of a miracle. After five years of marriage, the two had reached a point where every conversation became a battle of wills, every attempt to start anew was thwarted by grudging unforgiveness. By the time they showed up in therapist George Pransky's office, they were on the brink of divorce. They had seen therapists before—to no avail. Now they once again prepared to parade out the problems of their marriage.

Stan chose to wait outside while Pransky talked with Leslie. Tense and so nervous that she was almost twitching, Leslie sat down on a couch and explained why the marriage wasn't working. He wanted children; she did not. He was a workaholic; she admitted to having an affair. Pransky listened politely, but didn't probe further. Leslie was frankly startled by his lack of interest in the problems underlying their marital conflict. Didn't he want to get to the bottom of this?

Instead he began to tell her stories. Your mind is like a car, he said, you just need to learn how to drive it. Negative thinking is like a burr under a saddle, he told her. The longer it's there, the more irritation it causes. But thoughts have no life of their own. They gain importance only because you choose to give it to them.

Suddenly, something in what he said—and neither Pransky nor Leslie can say exactly what it was—clicked. It struck her as so true, and yet so obvious, that she sat up straight in her chair. *Of course*, she thought. "I couldn't stop laughing," Leslie says. "In less than an hour, my whole world changed. I looked around me and thought, They must be pumping nitrous oxide [laughing gas] in here."

Pransky had come to expect quick results from his clients, but even he was taken aback by the suddenness of the change. "What did you hear me say?" he asked.

"I don't know. I guess I heard you say that I'd been caught in my own mental devices," she responded. Her head felt clear, as if she'd had a heavy cold and could breathe freely for the first time in a long while. The marriage could work, she knew. When Pransky called Stan in, she embraced and kissed him. Puzzled, he walked her outside, then came in and closed the door behind him.

"What did you do to her?" Stan asked.

"I just talked to her about mental health," Pransky said.

But Stan now says something had changed in his wife. She seemed excited again, and her excitement affected him as well. The Millers came back for another session the following week, but it was merely a formality. Whatever had been troubling them, they say, had already vanished.

If only everyone's problems could be solved so simply. George Pransky thinks they can. When we meet for brunch at San Francisco's Sheraton-Palace Hotel, the 50-year-old former stockbroker tells me about the Millers as an example of how *psychology of mind*—a relatively new approach that he and approximately 500 other therapists around the country are using—works.

I'm intrigued, but skeptical. As a journalist who frequently writes on psychological topics, I'm familiar with dozens of different varieties of therapies—all of them promising to fix the human mind. How are people supposed to evaluate the validity of all these therapies, much less decide which kind of therapist to visit when they're unhappy or mentally ill?

Pransky, whose broad Boston accent is surprisingly unpretentious, explains how psychology of mind is different from other therapeutic approaches by telling me how the major branches of psychology would have dealt with Leslie and Stan. A psychodynamic therapist, one in the tradition of Freud, would most likely have tried to help them understand the deep-seated conflicts underlying their problems: Was Stan afraid of intimacy because of his own unresolved relationship with his remote parents? Was Leslie acting out some deep insecurity about her attractiveness?

A behavioral or cognitive therapist, on the other hand, would offer a more pragmatic approach: He or she might suggest that the couple improve their communication skills, or give positive enforcement when their partner was acting loving, or try to find a way of coping with undesired behavior. But such advice would still be based on overcoming their problems.

The simple secret to psychology of mind, Pransky explains, is that therapists who use this approach don't focus on your problems. They focus on your health. Psychology of mind assumes that your most natural state is one of mental health, security, and self-esteem. To be happy, you only need to stop overanalyzing your problems and realize how your thinking is infecting the way you feel. "Problems are merely mirages that seem to exist when viewed from a low state of mind," Pransky says. Not only are we all essentially healthy, but we're also inherently innocent and good. Bad behavior results not from malice, but from insecurity. The best way to deal with your problems is not to analyze them.

It sounds a little escapist, I tell Pransky. He takes my criticism in stride. After a hundred years of Freud's reign over psychology, he says, it's hard to give up the idea that it's good to get to the bottom of our problems. The infiltration of Freudian language—words like *ego, unconscious, subliminal,* and *oedipal*—show precisely how imbedded in our understanding of mental health his ideas have become. Psychology of mind represents a brash challenge to that model. And it goes further. The model is not just wrong, says Pransky, it's harmful. If we insist on searching for the roots of our problems, not only will we not feel better, we'll actually get worse.

But it's not just our allegiance to Freud that makes psychology of mind hard to swallow. Its emphasis on childlike innocence and inherent healthy-mindedness smacks of the kind of New Age philosophy that's lately gotten a bad name. People like Werner Erhard made millions when est (Erhard Seminars Training) promised to supply the secret to happiness, and L. Ron Hubbard and his disciples used scientology to build a highly lucrative pyramid stairway to heaven.

The language of psychology of mind sounds uncannily similar to these and other pop psychology movements. Has psychology of mind simply borrowed the most palatable items from the menu of New Age psychology movements and presented it as a new recipe for happiness? Like David Viscott—the guru of self-help writers—it proffers the notion that mental health is not a complex issue; as in co-counseling, it assumes that every person is decent and that the natural relationship between people is one of love and cooperation; and like est, psychology of mind insists that the past has little reality beyond what our thoughts tell us about it. Est told its estimated 750,000 adherents that thoughts are things that can be discarded or accepted just as we might pick up or reject a book.

Thoughts have no life of their own. They gain importance only because you choose to give it to them.

I'm not surprised, however, that psychology of mind shares so much with New Age approaches. Its founder, Sydney Banks, was a welder with no training in traditional psychotherapy. And its best-known advocates—Pransky, Roger Mills (a former partner of Pransky's who has been applying the principles of psychology of mind in community development projects around the country), and Bill Pettit (a psychiatrist at the Cherokee Mental Health Institute in Cherokee, Iowa)—were all previously associated with a New Age technique called Lifespring, a wrenching encounter-group session that became popular in the '70s and '80s. Pettit even served as the organization's national director and resident psychiatrist before his conversion to psychology of mind in 1983.

Pransky assures me that such similarities are incidental. These other approaches have had intimations of the truth, but they've all been trapped in their own thought processes. "Est is nothing more than a distilled form of traditional psychology," he says dismissively. "It still tries to get you in touch with the memories you have. It has you express your emotions in the form of 'telling the truth.'

What Is Psychology of Mind?

Drawing on spiritual springs and shaped by the American vernacular, a new form of psychotherapy has grown with little attention from either the popular or the professional media. Called "psychology of mind," this new approach is now being applied to a wide range of problems from substance abuse to marital discord.

Although psychology of mind was once identified as neocognitive therapy, it is not to be confused with the increasingly popular cognitive therapy of Aaron Beck at the University of Pennsylvania. Psychology of mind aims less at disentangling particular patterns of thought (as cognitive therapy does) than at teaching clients how to stop identifying with the process of thinking itself. In this way, the new approach echoes spiritual teachings.

Psychology of mind begins with four deceptively simple postulates. As explained by Minneapolis therapist Joe Bailey in his book *The Serenity Principle* (Harper & Row, 1990), these axioms state that:

- thought creates our psychological experience and thus we each live in a separate reality,
- thinking is a voluntary function,
- emotions indicate our level of psychological functioning, and, in particular,
- low moods are a sign that we are identifying with our thoughts, rather than witnessing them.

The *Dhammapada,* an ancient Buddhist scripture, encapsulates these sentiments in its beginning declaration: "Our life is shaped by our mind; we become what we think." But how does this bear on what happens in psychotherapy sessions?

Instead of treating emotions as primary, as somehow "deeper" than thought, psychology of mind regards negative emotions as what therapist George Pransky calls "warning lights on the dashboard"—a signal that we have overidentified with momentary thoughts by "taking them too seriously."

"Suffering follows an evil thought," the *Dhammapada* continues, "as the wheels of a cart follow the oxen that draw it." If a cart is going the wrong way, the driver does not try to manipulate the wheels; he turns the oxen. In therapy based on psychology of mind, this means not dwelling on trauma or the usual presenting symptoms. It means focusing instead upon natural good feeling as it emerges in our flux of moods.

This approach differs from "the power of positive thinking" (Norman Vincent Peale) and from New Age "affirmations" (Shakti Gawain, or *The Course on Miracles*). The point is not to affirm that the world is the way you wish it were. Instead, you notice that at some moments you are happier than at others, then discover the choices you (as the thinker) have to let go of thoughts that create discomfort in your life.

Although psychology of mind differs from positive thinking, it does exemplify what William James, in *The Varieties of Religious Experience,* called "healthy-mindedness." Its pragmatic goal is not truth, analysis, or depth, but enjoyment of life. It assumes that the natural state of mind is positive, until it is "contaminated" by self-defeating patterns of thought.

Therapists inspired by psychology of mind tend to avoid detailed analysis of the past. Why require clients to reimmerse themselves in traumas, or root through the trash of their most distressing moments? To a conventional therapist, this attitude smacks of outright denial. But the new approach, says Bailey, "believes that painful memories lower mood states to the point where insights and discoveries are less likely to occur" to the client.

Recalling Einstein's dictum about problems that cannot be solved on the level on which they were created, Bailey explains that psychology of mind seeks to facilitate a "vertical shift" in consciousness. "The new therapy reacquaints clients with their natural health and common sense and teaches them to bring their innate wisdom (as well as intellect) to bear on problems."

In the view of many practitioners, psychology of mind offers an answer to the question that is now troubling 12-step programs: "Is there a next step after being 'in recovery'?" The new therapists say yes. The next step is to find a way back to our birthright, which is natural good feeling. Psychology of mind seeks to offer clients direct access to good feelings, thus dissolving the need for substitute gratifications such as alcohol or cocaine. To recover serenity, they say, we first of all need to understand how it was obscured from us.

—Craig Comstock
Special to *Utne Reader*

For more information on psychology of mind, write MIMH Communications, 1409 Willow St., Suite 500, Minneapolis, MN 55403 or call 612/870-1084.

"I helped to design Lifespring training," he says. "And I can tell you that Lifespring and John Bradshaw's 12 steps and other so-called state-of-the-art counseling techniques are to psychology of mind what medieval medical practices are to medicine today."

This is not a cult, he adds. No one's making money off of this—not any more than they'd make if they chose to practice any of the other therapies. "Sure, I make a good living [Pransky and his wife, Linda, charge couples $3,000 for an intensive four-day therapy session at their home in La Conner, near Seattle], but I was probably making a lot more before I started doing psychology of mind," he says. There's no pyramid scheme here, he says. There's no guru, and no followers.

Interviews with dozens of therapists who use the approach bear this out. "You don't see psychologists of mind riding around in Jaguars," says Eugenia Perez, a therapist in San Francisco who was trained in developmental child psychology. Perez considers herself a conservative when it comes to choosing therapeutic approaches. She first heard of psychology of mind when she began working for Kaiser Permanente, the largest health maintenance organization in the country.

At the time, like most therapists, Perez relied on a mixture of psychodynamic and cognitive approaches. When Pransky first came to talk to the therapists at Kaiser, to Perez his message sounded similar to cognitive approaches that focused on the bad "tapes" people played in their heads. But Pransky wasn't suggesting that clients should exchange bad tapes for good ones—the old positive thinking idea. Instead, he just told people to pay attention to the fact that they were playing tapes at all. And he asked them to compare the quality of the tapes they played when they were in good and bad moods. If you could make people aware of that, Pransky said, their problems would be solved.

"At first, I was skeptical," says Perez. "I heard his claims and thought, nothing can be that simple." After further exposure to the approach, and hearing more stories of its effectiveness from other therapists and patients, she decided to give it a try. Now she uses nothing else.

Clearly, Pransky is telling therapists and patients something that they want to hear. "Psychology of mind cuts out the diagnosis," says Sheila Krystal, a former behaviorist who now practices psychology of mind therapy in Berkeley. "Its language is secular and commonsensical. Patients don't need to keep coming to therapy for years—sometimes one session alone is enough. And there's something true about the notion that illness is a sign that our thoughts have distracted us from health."

But Pransky is also making some people nervous with extraordinary (and some say dangerous) claims. At a time when psychiatrists are leaning toward prescribing more drugs to deal with an ever-increasing number of mental illnesses, psychology of mind practitioners are advocating just the opposite. "All mental illness has the same cause—insecurity and lack of self-esteem," Pransky says. "Only the symptoms differ. People simply lose their bearings." That sounds innocent enough, but its implications are radical. It means, for one thing, that psychology of mind should be able to treat paranoid schizophrenia and manic depression, illnesses that the medical community insists are physiological.

Pransky isn't shy about the claim. He describes Bill Pettit's work with patients other psychiatrists had given up as hopeless. He describes his own successful treatment of a manic depressive who'd been found by the police trying to direct street traffic in his underwear. "We show such patients that their problems stem from misunderstanding or misinterpretating what's going on in their minds," Pransky says. "And we teach them how to be happy. That's what it means to be mentally healthy."

Perhaps so. But some skeptics—even those inclined to believe that there is something to the approach—feel that such claims are false, even foolhardy, and damaging. Every therapeutic approach, no matter how bogus or how sound, be it est, primal scream, or Jungian analysis, can buttress its arguments with any number of sensational anecdotes and testimonials. Doubters point to the very real possibility of an institutionalized placebo effect in

Psychology of mind forcefully challenges conventional views of mental health. We expect this material to be controversial; it provoked a wide range of responses here in our own office. Psychology of mind is such a new and unusual approach to therapy that it has not been debated outside of a small but growing circle of advocates. We decided to publish [this and other articles (see Utne Reader, *January/February 1992, pp. 97–99)], in part, to open a wide-ranging discussion on what constitutes psychological well-being and how to attain it. We invite our readers—both lay people and psychotherapeutic professionals—to write us with your comments.*

—The Editors

which the therapist's skill and the patient's need combine to bring about an apparently miraculous cure.

"You can't make too much of any one example," warns Tom Deiker, Bill Pettit's boss at the Cherokee Mental Health Institute. "About one-third of all cases get better spontaneously anyway."

Perhaps the most prominent critic is Rick Suarez, a renegade former psychology of mind therapist who is largely credited with trying to place the

Can Self-Esteem Fight Poverty and Drugs?

Psychology of mind cites successes in unexpected places

The people at the Modello Housing Project—a poor, crime-infested neighborhood in Miami that's among the worst in America—had never met anyone quite like Roger Mills. He didn't look or sound like a crusader. Instead of talking about raising more money to rid the neighborhood of its pimps and prostitutes, its hustlers and crack houses, Mills talked about mental health. Instead of directing people to act, he talked to them about changing the way they felt about themselves. To Modello's residents, Mills' words sounded like the remote feel-good mouthings of a man out of touch with the crude truths of the ghetto.

Here's this white man coming in with his little ideas about, you know, feeling good about yourself and all that crap," said Virene McCreary when she first heard about Mills. What could he do in a neighborhood where more than 65 percent of the families took or sold drugs? Where 85 percent of the families were headed by a single parent, where the school dropout rate was over 50 percent, and child abuse and neglect were an everyday fact of life?

"I went to the first class he held, and here he was saying that regardless of what was happening in your unit, if your self-esteem is high then it don't matter," McCreary continued. "And right away I said, well, he ain't too bright and I ain't got time for what he's talking about."

But Mills won her over, along with most of the other residents. He was nonjudgmental, but persistent. If one of the women could not attend a meeting, Mills would volunteer to discuss his ideas at her home. When another claimed not to be able to find a baby-sitter, no problem, he told her. He'd be right over. The important thing was for the residents to hear what he had to say. Once they heard it, he felt, they'd recognize the truth of his message.

Mills did not work alone. He sought and got cooperation from the local department of Housing and Urban Development (which rebuilt 120 housing units in the project), the Metro-Dade Team Police, and a crime prevention organization. His approach was to offer community leadership training classes, to invite parents and teachers to come together in a PTA format, to form student workshops, to contact community service programs, and to keep on talking. The root of the problem, he told them, was their self-image.

"People's lives become what they think is possible," he said. "Only when the residents began to feel hope was there a possibility for change.

"Mental health is like a cork rising to the surface from under water," he said. "You can hold it under, but because it's buoyant it'll rise to the top once you let go."

The community responded to his message of confidence and hope. Within two years, school delinquency dropped by 80 percent. Severe child neglect decreased by 60 percent. Parent involvement in schools increased by 500 percent. More than half of the parents involved in the project began to work toward a high school equivalency degree; another 21 percent decided to attend a job training program through Miami-Dade Community College. Drug trafficking dropped by 75 percent. "The changes were quite remarkable," says Curtis Ivy, chief of the Homestead Police Department, "especially in conjunction with the efforts of HUD and other local organizations."

Elsewhere in the country, psychology of mind therapists are claiming unrivaled success in dealing with a slew of different problems. In Minneapolis, for example, Mavis Karn and Joe Bailey use the approach to work with drug and alcohol dependency and sexual abuse. Just outside the city, the Second Chance Ranch applies psychology of mind to help so-called incorrigible kids. Eugenia Perez in San Francisco says her success with trauma patients illustrates what can be done using the approach. Educators in Florida, Colorado, and Minnesota have reported success in using psychology of mind techniques to improve students' grade point averages and attendance. If the reports are true, something significant is happening.

"The real answer to problems of deviance, school failure, truancy, delinquency, and welfare dependence is to teach people how they're using their thinking to keep themselves in an insecure pattern of thinking about their lives," Mills says. "Psychology of mind teaches them to become conscious of their inner power for self-esteem. Once they have that, the possibilities are limitless."

—Teo Furtado
Special to *Utne Reader*

approach within the context of cognitive psychology. His book, *Sanity, Insanity, and Common Sense* (Ballantine,1987), offers a good description of psychology of mind. "Applying psychology of mind to schizophrenia is like trying to put out a forest fire with a squirt gun," he says bluntly. Suarez worries about using psychology of mind techniques for seriously disturbed patients or those who are suicidal, and is also concerned about the therapy's bias against using medicine. (Practitioners such as Joe Bailey, president and therapist at the Minneapolis Institute of Mental Health, say that medication should be continued in appropriate cases, but that therapists work toward eventually getting their clients off medication.) Suarez is skeptical about the accreditation of some—not all—psychology of mind practitioners, such as Pransky, whose doctorate from Columbia Pacific University is of the correspondence variety. (Pransky is licensed as a family and marriage counselor.)

Illness is a sign that our thoughts have distracted us from health.

Suarez warns about exaggerated claims and the possibility of oversimplification. "Psychology of mind is neither a cure-all for every psychological disorder nor immune from misuse by unscrupulous or unethical people," he says. "Psychiatric disorders are anything but simple."

Suarez has disassociated himself from psychology of mind and now calls his own approach "neo-cognitive psychotherapy." While he has not renounced psychology of mind's effectiveness—"These ideas represent a genuine contribution," he says—he objects to the cult of personality that he fears is forming around psychology of mind's founder, Sydney Banks.

George Pransky makes no bones about his debt to Sydney Banks, a reclusive welder with little formal education whose insight 17 years ago led to the development of psychology of mind. Banks and a friend were taking a walk on the beach in Sault Spring Isle, Canada. His life was in a rut, Banks complained. His marriage was in trouble; his job was leading nowhere; he lacked direction. He was an unhappy man. "You're not unhappy," his friend said. "You just *think* you are." It was the kind of truism we hear every day. But it hit Banks with the force of a religious conversion.

"Did you hear what you just said?" he asked. "It's all in our minds." Like Paul on the road to Damascus, Banks would never be the same again. At home, his wife wondered what had gotten into him. He blamed her less and seemed more accommodating and helpful. His friends noticed the change and were puzzled by it. Banks shared his discovery with them; they changed. Word of what was happening in Sault Spring eventually reached Pransky and his partner, Roger Mills.

The two had been disenchanted with what they saw as the low success rate of traditional psychology and were using various strains of popular psychology in their practice. The common thread to most of these "New Age" psychologies was the idea that you must confront your problems head on, "get in touch with your feelings," and relive past traumas to achieve some sort of catharsis.

But when Mills and Pransky met up with Banks, it wasn't long before their own methods began to wilt under his quiet assault. Banks questioned the effectiveness of *all* psychology, from Freud to behaviorism to any one of the pop psychologies that proliferated in the '70s. "You mean, you try to achieve mental health by having your patients live through their most painful experiences?" Banks asked incredulously. "Isn't that a bit like trying to heal a wound by poking at it? How can you reduce anxiety by first increasing it?" Pransky and Mills were as astonished by the audacious simplicity of his words as by their inability to confound him. After several visits to Sault Spring Isle, they began to apply in their practice what they were learning from Banks.

Pransky, Mills, and others now hope to convince mainstream psychologists of psychology of mind's value, but they meet plenty of resistance. For example, when Pransky spoke to a group of psychiatrists and nurses at Pettit's hospital last spring, he was received courteously, though less than enthusiastically. Several professionals said that they would suspend judgment until they had proof that the approach worked. At this point, no one has prepared double-blind trials in which patients matched by age, background, and illness are divided into two groups, half to be treated by a traditional psychologist and half by a psychology of mind practitioner.

Critics worry about using psychology of mind techniques for seriously disturbed patients.

Is psychology of mind everything that Pransky and others say it is? After many interviews and much thought, I remain skeptical. For me, no amount of talking about moods or mind or thought or feeling or innocence can dispel the notion that it's just, well, talk. As a recipe for a good, productive relationship between therapist and client, it sounds fine. As a therapeutic way of imparting practical advice in a setting that increases its chances of being heard, all right. Even as an effective antidote to our preoccupation with ourselves and our "problems," well and good. But can claims like one I heard from one psychiatrist—"This is a revolution in thought as significant as Einstein's theory of relativity"—be true? I don't see it.

Clearly, though, the commonsense advice that Pransky and other psychology of mind advocates offer their troubled clients has an effect, sometimes powerful enough to induce significant changes. A placebo effect? Perhaps.

Psychiatrist Tom Deiker frames his hesitance this way: "It's hard to talk a schizophrenic out of his schizophrenia. Can this approach cure the frustration of having cancer? I believe so. Can it cure cancer? Schizophrenia and other bipolar disorders are physical, genetic, biochemical diseases just like cancer. If this approach claims to cure such diseases, it'll probably be dismissed for promising more than it can deliver."

For professionals such as Deiker, psychology of mind remains what it most wants to avoid: just another promising technique that may be reaching far, far beyond its grasp.

But for people such as the Millers, who feel that their marriage has been given a second chance after a few sessions with Pransky, it doesn't matter if the therapy is "valid" or not. As to how the larger psychotherapy establishment will receive psychology of mind, only time will tell.

THE REVOLUTION IN PSYCHIATRIC CARE

Quality treatment is harder to gauge than it is with other illnesses. Here's what to look for

Psychiatric hospitals used to evoke images of evil nurses and gray fortresses where empty-eyed patients stared endlessly into space. But few treatment centers these days much resemble the "One Flew Over the Cuckoo's Nest" stereotype. The average person who requires hospitalization for emotional problems will likely encounter a caring well-trained staff and a clean, modern ward that looks more like a college dorm than a prison.

But the problems for people seeking competent, compassionate psychiatric care have not disappeared. Cutbacks in mental-health insurance coverage, for example, are restricting access to inpatient and outpatient care as well as forcing many middle-income Americans to pay more for both. A typical employer-based plan today sets a lifetime cap of $20,000 to $75,000 on hospital care for mental illness and often limits stays to 45 days. And the plan may cover only 50 percent of the costs of outpatient care and cap them at $2,000 to $5,000 a year. Health maintenance organization coverage is stricter, too, with many plans limiting outpatient therapy visits to fewer than 20 per year.

A family caring for a severely mentally ill person who may be hospitalized several times and need lengthy outpatient care can easily exhaust insurance benefits in a year or two. "Mental illness has become a second-class passenger in our health-care system," says Steven Mirin, psychiatrist-in-chief at McLean Hospital in Belmont, Mass., which ranked highest among U.S. facilities in a *U.S. News* survey of psychiatrists.

Hospitalization used to be routine in any significant mental crisis. But the combination of insurance pressures, the development of effective psychiatric drugs and greater understanding of emotional disorders has now made a hospital stay the exception rather than the rule. In 1955, for example, three fourths of all psychiatric patients were hospitalized. Today, 90 percent receive only outpatient care in any given year. Hospital stays today also are months shorter than they used to be, now averaging under 30 days. But at the same time, the number of people seeking treatment for mental illnesses has soared. Some 20 million U.S. adults now receive mental-health care each year, triple the number of the early 1960s. Of the 2 million out of that group who are hospitalized, 43 percent suffer from schizophrenia, 22 percent are severely depressed and 10 percent have alcohol or drug-related problems.

The demand for services has set off a boom in treatment programs. There are about 450 private psychiatric hospitals in the nation, up from 180 in 1979. And about 1,700 of the nation's roughly 6,700 hospitals have psychiatric wards, double the number 20 years ago.

A place to regroup. The "science" of mental-health treatment has advanced significantly in the past 20 years, but its practice is still less well-defined than those of other medical specialties. There is, for example, no clear-cut criterion for hospitalization. People who pose imminent harm to themselves or others obviously are candidates, but, beyond that, decisions are made case by case. Patients may wind up in the hospital because their living situation or family problems aggravate their illness, or because they need a safe, controlled environment in which to regroup. Many patients have simply failed to get better as outpatients.

Mental illness respects no boundaries of class, income or education. "I was surprised at how many people were 'normal'—bankers, artists, professors," says Rebecca Millman, a 21-year-old former McLean patient.

Since the early 1900s, wealthy patients seeking mental-health care have traveled to exclusive private hospitals such as the Menninger Clinic in Topeka, Kan., McLean or Baltimore's Sheppard and Enoch Pratt Hospital, sometimes spending years as inpatients. Today, such long-term treatment is rare, and increasingly limited to those with very comprehensive insurance coverage or fat bank accounts. But such world-class centers still draw out-of-town patients for stays that may last months. At

Menninger, for example, 92 percent of inpatients last year came from outside Kansas, and a majority stayed an average 200 days.

Private hospitals, both big and small, treat patients like valued customers. Many have specialized programs for senior citizens, adolescents or other groups such as patients with eating disorders. McLean, for example, offers both art- and dance-therapy sessions and has a gym. Sheppard Pratt has a summer camp for patients.

Team treatment. But a hospital is only as good as its staff. The best facilities use a team approach that brings together psychiatric nurses, social workers, occupational therapists, psychologists and psychiatrists, each with a unique perspective that results in more well-rounded treatment. The vast majority of hospitals also use psychiatric drugs like antidepressants or antipsychotics. While a few hospitals still resist using drugs except in the most severe cases, staff psychiatrists typically evaluate patients for drug treatment soon after they have signed in.

Drugs are only part of the program. A good psychiatric unit offers a comprehensive mix of psychotherapy, counseling, family meetings, activities and discharge planning. Patients soon learn the benefits of simply sorting through problems regularly with other patients.

As a home away from home, a hospital should feel comfortable to patients, too. And the only way to see whether a hospital has a distinctly unhospital-like atmosphere—one that seems supportive and open—is to visit. Confidentiality is important in psychiatric settings, however, and the staff may be unwilling to let visitors talk to patients. Indeed, if a staff member reveals intimate details about a patient, it's probably not a place you'd want to be. But visitors can learn a lot simply by observing. Are most patients dressed and involved in activities, or are they lying in bed or watching television? A good hospital keeps all but the most severely disturbed patients busy from early morning to evening. An activity chart, usually posted near the nurses' station, lists scheduled activities for the day. Has the hospital staff planned outings for patients such as trips to the movies, the mall or a museum?

Reading a hospital's promotional literature can also provide clues. But boasts about cure rates can be misleading; no study shows that one type of hospital, or one specific hospital, can help cure psychiatric patients any better than another. One hospital claim that does carry weight is university affiliation. Your chances of receiving state-of-the-art care are better at a university-connected hospital or one that sponsors training of psychiatric residents.

The best hospitals realize that psychiatric care does not end once patients pack their bags. Continuing care helps cement the recovery started in the hospital and eases reentry into the community. Better hospitals will offer patients the choice of spending a few hours each day at the hospital but living at home, moving to a halfway house or undergoing counseling in community-based mental-health centers. Many of the leading hospitals even own their own halfway houses, which some patients swear by. "I would not have been able to go back to living on my own right away," says Rebecca Millman, who now lives at a halfway house owned and operated by McLean Hospital. The key is how long the programs last. A 1988 study found that only 15 percent of hospitals—usually privately owned—typically continued to treat patients for up to a year, and 46 percent offered programs that lasted only a few weeks. Psychiatrists say that after-care programs should last at least a few months.

Since most hospitals are eager to tout themselves, an independent check is wise. Groups like the National Alliance for the Mentally Ill, (800) 950-6264, can provide useful information. Based in Arlington, Va., the alliance, which provides support for the mentally ill and their families, has some 1,000 chapters nationwide. It is staffed mostly by former psychiatric patients or their families, many of whom have firsthand knowledge of facilities in their area.

Pocketbook concerns creep into hospital choices, too. Except in emergencies, virtually all private and comprehensive-care community hospitals require proof of insurance coverage for admission. But some insurers and employers are becoming more accommodating in the face of complaints about coverage limits. Both may be willing to "flex" coverage, for example, by picking up the tab for more outpatient care or time spent in a halfway house if the hospitalization is short. Even so, chances are you'll have to dip into your own pocket.

To many observers, such insurance limitations testify to a lingering stigma. Notwithstanding the advances of the past decade, it probably will still take years before people with mental illnesses are treated with the same degree of compassion—and insurance protection—as are victims of, say, heart disease or cancer.

Steven Findlay

What Good Is Feeling Bad?

The Evolutionary Benefits of Psychic Pain

Randolph M. Nesse

Randolph M. Nesse is an associate professor of psychiatry at the University of Michigan in Ann Arbor, where he directs the adult ambulatory care division and the evolutionary psychiatry project. He is also associate director of the anxiety disorder program there.

Most people come to me for the treatment of anxiety, but recently a new patient came in with only a simple request. "All I really need is a refill," she said, handing me a nearly empty bottle of an antidepressant medication. She had just moved from another city, and for the previous year she had been taking fluoxetine for weight loss, one of the side effects of the drug. "I lost a few pounds," she said, "but I want to keep taking it mainly because it makes me feel better." She denied feeling unusually depressed before, but she insisted that the drug made her more confident and energetic. "I used to be uncomfortable with strangers at parties, but now I can go up to anyone and say anything I want to," she said. "I don't feel nervous or worried about what people think of me. Also, I am more decisive, and people say I am more attractive. I'm usually even eager to get out of bed in the morning. Everything is just—well, better. I hardly ever feel bad anymore."

A routine psychiatric examination uncovered no history of clinical depression. In fact, even before taking fluoxetine she had had relatively few days of feeling down. She reported no family history of mood disorders, no unusual personal or family conflicts. She had sometimes felt uncomfortable in social situations, but she had not avoided giving speeches or going to parties. She denied abusing drugs or alcohol. As far as I could determine, she was a normal person whose normal feelings of distress were blocked by the drug.

Fluoxetine, commonly known as Prozac, has been on the market for slightly more than a year. In that short time it has become the most prescribed antidepressant, because it does not cause dependency and its side effects are, for most patients, few and mild. My patient had only minor insomnia and occasional nausea—and she lost those few pounds. For others, some 15 percent of patients, the side effects are intolerable, and in a few extreme cases patients reportedly became suicidal or began behaving uncontrollably after starting treatment with the drug; studies have not verified the extreme reactions in large, controlled samples of people who use the drug.

Whatever may eventually be discovered about fluoxetine, it is clear that psychopharmacology is entering a new era. In the old days—three or four years ago—all antidepressants had side effects so annoying that normal people would not take them. Fluoxetine is one of the first effective agents with only minor side effects in a class of drugs the psychiatrist Peter D. Kramer of Brown University has called mood brighteners. Several more will be introduced within the next few years, some from whole new classes of drugs that promise even more specific actions than fluoxetine with still fewer side effects.

"So what do you think, doctor?" my patient asked. "All I really want is another prescription—unless there's some danger. Do you think it's safe for me to keep taking this?" I wrestled with the question. If the drug makes her feel better, why not give it to her? Maybe it is relieving a subclinical depression. Then again, it might have unknown side effects, despite its approval by the Food and Drug Administration and a year of clinical experience. But a separate possibility gave me pause: Are bad feelings somehow useful? If they are, is blocking them wise?

Consider pain and anxiety. Much as people want to avoid those feelings, each is essential in a dangerous world. Pain motivates people to avoid actions that might cause injury or death. Anxiety induces changes that make it easier to protect oneself from physical or social threats. The capacity for such feelings must have conferred an advantage in the course of human evolution. Do other bad feelings, such as jealousy and sadness, also serve worthwhile, possibly crucial purposes? If emotions did indeed come about through natural selection—whereby nature selects characteristics if they help organisms survive longer or reproduce more—then bad, as well as good, feelings are probably useful. And though specific experiences or environmental influences may modulate feelings differently in each individual, the basic capacity for the various emotions must somehow have assisted human survival. The task of understanding the evolutionary functions of emotions is a scientific frontier, one that urgently needs exploration, especially if psychotropic drugs are to be used wisely.

One day in the sixth grade, when I was on the playground, a friend pointed out

This article is reprinted by permission of *The Sciences* and is from the November/December 1991 issue, pp. 30-37. Individual subscriptions are $18.00 per year. Write to *The Sciences*, 2 East 63rd Street, New York, NY 10021 or call 1-800-THE-NYAS.

a boy who could not feel pain. This bit of information was not a mere curiosity but a valuable warning: if the boy wanted to give someone a good drubbing, he would be undeterred by counterpunches, no matter how solidly planted. Getting up my nerve, I asked the fellow about his unusual condition. Obviously embarrassed, he said he had no concept of pain, just as someone who is color-blind cannot fathom color. Yet he seemed to feel guilt and social rejection like everyone else. Later it came to light that his mother had to check over his entire body inch by inch every night to make sure he had not been injured. My playground group made fun of him for that, but always behind his back.

Today he is almost certainly dead. People who cannot feel pain are extremely rare and usually die in early adulthood. Their joints fail from excess strain, caused in part by the lack of the normal discomfort that makes most people shift position from time to time. The effects of multiple injuries accumulate rapidly, infections and appendicitis go unnoticed, and death from one cause or another comes prematurely. The disease syringomyelia also illustrates the utility of pain. A degeneration of the center of the spinal cord, the condition selectively eliminates pain in various parts of the body, especially the hands. Smokers with syringomyelia repeatedly let cigarettes burn down to nubbins, unaware that their fingers are being charred.

Physical pain is essential to the body's defense against future, as well as immediate, tissue injury. Years ago, a hook impaled my brother's ear while he was fishing. The acute pain moved him to extract the hook immediately (even though the fish had just started biting). And the memory of the pain arouses enough anxiety to ensure that, while fishing, he always wears a hat.

Why is pain painful? If a person simply noticed when tissue was being damaged, would the same purpose not be served? Why must suffering be involved? Surprisingly enough, there is an answer. Pain must be aversive in order to arouse the motivating mechanisms of the mind. Those mechanisms ensure that eliminating the source of pain gets the highest priority in the body's regulation of behavior, for rarely is anything more important to an individual's Darwinian fitness than stopping tissue damage. Patients with chronic pain, who are at the opposite end of the pain-arousal spectrum from my school-yard mate, know only too well the near futility of trying to ignore pain. Its urgent call for attention is crucial to its evolutionary function.

To gain a broader perspective on the defensive systems of the body, consider some of the other, more elaborate mechanisms that have evolved. Many of them are triggered by disease; they include nausea, vomiting, cough, diarrhea, fever, fatigue and anxiety. Each is called forth when specialized detectors in the body warn of a threat. Nausea, vomiting and diarrhea eliminate toxins detected in the gastrointestinal tract, and coughing expels harmful matter in the respiratory tract. Fever counters infection, and fatigue prevents damage from overexertion. Anxiety protects the organism from a wide range of dangers.

Such defenses are analogous to the low-oil pressure light on an automobile dashboard. In that case it is clear the glowing light itself is not the problem; instead, the light is a protective response to the problem of low oil pressure. The dashboard indicator is one component of a system carefully designed to warn of dangerous conditions: an oil-pressure sensor set to respond at an appropriate threshold, wires for transmitting the signal, and a light bulb, positioned for visibility on the dash. If the driver has sense enough to stop, the defense system works. If instead the driver responds, say, by cutting the wire to the light, the engine is likely to be irreparably damaged.

It is important to note, however, that not all manifestations of disease are defenses; many are a result of a defect in the body's machinery. Paralysis, seizures, tumors and jaundice, for example, serve no function; they merely reflect a breakdown in the workings of the body. They are analogous to a clank in the transmission, a plume of steam from an overheated radiator or the silence one gets when turning the ignition key of a car with a dead battery.

The distinction between defenses and defects calls attention to the usefulness of defenses—and the dangers of blocking them. Physicians well know that suppressing a cough can turn a routine pneumonia into a life-threatening illness. It is also true—though not so commonly known—that blocking diarrhea can aggravate certain infections and increase complications. And forcing a fever down can prolong an illness. Even low iron levels in the blood, which often accompany chronic infections, counteract bacteria by depriving them of a crucial mineral. Physicians unaware of that defensive role may unwittingly aid a pathogen by prescribing iron supplements.

Defects, in contrast, are useless. Physicians need have no trepidation about trying to stop seizures, paralysis or jaundice. Furthermore, defects in themselves are not painful, except when they disrupt normal function. Most tumors come to medical attention only after they form noticeable lumps or when they interfere with a bodily function. Kidney failure can be quite advanced before a person notices anything wrong. And a person may be alerted to a weak leg muscle only by scuffs on the toe of one shoe. The capacity for pain is present only where, in an evolutionary sense, it has been able to help. As the evolutionist George C. Williams of the State University of New York at Stony Brook pointed out in his 1966 book *Adaptation and Natural Selection*, damage to the heart or the brain was so often fatal in the natural environment that the capacity for pain or even repair in those tissues would have been irrelevant to survival.

Thus the presence of bad feelings is most reliably associated with defenses, not defects. Nausea, diarrhea, cough, fatigue and anxiety all are distressing; they must be to carry out their protective functions. Indeed, one can argue that all bad feelings are components of defenses. Natural selection has molded each kind of bad feeling to help protect against a specific threat. A person who does not experience nausea as aversive is liable to eat the same toxic food again and again; a person who does not get fatigued will suffer damage to muscles and joints.

Emotional suffering can be just as useful as physical discomfort. Emotions adjust a person's response to the task at hand. In that sense they are similar to computer programs, which adjust the setup of the computer to carry out a certain kind of task. The program may change what appears on the screen, the functions of certain keys, how memory is allocated, or the way information is processed. Like computers, living organisms are faced with a variety of challenges. The behavioral, physiological and cognitive responses that help a person elude a tiger are different from those that help woo a lover or attack a competitor. Thus fear, love and anger are highly distinct psychological subroutines gradually shaped by natural selection to improve the person's ability to cope with each challenge.

All emotions can help in certain situations but hinder in others. Anxiety is welcome when it aids escape from a pack of wild dogs, but it can become a clumsy intruder at delicate moments in courtship. Conversely, though romantic fantasizing may enhance courtship, it can fatally distract a person fleeing wild dogs. Emotions are excellent examples of the "Darwinian algorithms" described by Leda Cosmides and John Tooby, psychologists at the University of California at Santa Barbara, in the 1987 book *The Latest on the Best: Essays on Evolution and Optimality*:

> When a tiger bounds toward you, what should your response be? Should you file your toenails? Do a cartwheel? Sing a song? Is this the moment to run an uncountable number of randomly generated response possibilities through the decision rule? . . . How could you compute which possibility would result in more grandchildren? The alternative: Darwinian algorithms specialized for predator avoidance, that err on the side of false positives in predator detection, and, upon detecting a potential predator, constrain your responses to flight, fight or hiding.

Why are emotions always positive or negative, never neutral? As the biologists Randy and Nancy Thornhill of the University of New Mexico have pointed out, circumstances that pose neither opportunity nor threat arouse no emotion. Why should they if they are unrelated to Darwinian fitness? A falling leaf rarely stirs any feeling, unless perhaps it is seen as a symbol of mortality. A tree leaning precariously over one's bedroom, however, arouses anxious apprehension that is quite unpleasant. If anxiety were pleasant, would people not seek out bedrooms under large, dead, leaning trees, instead of avoiding them?

There are more negative emotions than positive ones—twice as many, by one count. The imbalance arises because people encounter only a few kinds of opportunity, and so—in the Darwinian sense, again—they need only a small number of positive emotions. Happiness, excitement, joy and desire motivate people to take full advantage of each opportunity. Threats, however, come in many forms—predators, poisonous small animals, disease, exposure, starvation, exclusion from a group, loss of allies, loss of stored food, loss of territory, loss of a mate and on and on. Consequently, many distinct patterns of response have been developed to contend with those threats.

Of all the negative emotions, anxiety is the most obviously useful. Although there are many kinds of anxiety, the well-known fight-or-flight response, first described by the American psychologist Walter B. Cannon in 1915, best exemplifies the value of anxiety. In the dangerous environment of early humans the response was highly beneficial for the frequent occasions when life was in danger. The strong, rapid heartbeat that accompanies panic anxiety brings extra nutrition and oxygen to muscles and speeds the removal of wastes. Muscle tension prepares for flight or physical defense. Shortness of breath induces rapid breathing, hyperoxygenating the blood. Sweating cools the body in anticipation of flight. Greater production of blood glucose also helps bring more nutrition to the muscles. Secretion of adrenaline into the blood makes it clot faster, should injury occur. Blood circulation shifts from the digestive system to the muscles, leaving a cold, empty feeling in the pit of the stomach and a tense readiness in the muscles.

Accompanying all those physiological changes are psychological and behavioral ones. A person having a panic attack puts aside concerns about paying debts and fantasies about having sex to focus all mental energy on assessing the danger and determining the best means of escape. Often, even before finding out what the danger is, the person makes behavioral adjustments, standing ready to take headlong flight at the slightest provocation.

Social dangers pose equally severe threats. Many of my patients tell me they are too sensitive to social pressures; they are deathly afraid of being left out of a group, and they feel they must always please people. Typically, they have tried hard, sometimes with the help of a therapist, to overcome those "insecurities." They often think they should have high self-esteem regardless of social opinion. But imagine what would happen to a relentlessly self-confident person in the natural environment. Such a person would have no qualms about challenging the leader or doing other things that would cause exclusion from the group. Then the outcast might well walk off confidently onto the savanna, a response that would almost certainly end in death.

The political scientist Robert Axelrod of the University of Michigan has described some of the many ways individual human relationships depend on the exchange of favors and the adherence to certain rules. Within any network of social obligations one has many chances to violate the rules to gain a short-term advantage over one's fellows. In my view, it is the conscience that advocates following the rules and accepting the short-term costs of rule compliance for a chance at greater long-term benefits. But primitive unconscious drives lobby for violating the rules to exploit the immediate opportunity. People usually forgo ephemeral gains to avoid risking the relationship, thanks in large part to anxiety that arises out of guilt or fear of punishment. According to one of the more widely accepted findings of psychoanalysis, anxiety is aroused by socially unacceptable unconscious wishes. It thus inhibits actions that would give immediate pleasure but cause the loss of long-term rewards. Anxiety, even the vague kind that seems to have no specific source, is often useful.

Of course there are circumstances in which anxiety is excessive and serves no purpose. Although the capacity for the state came about through natural selection, environmental variables—early childhood experiences, for instance—and genetic differences affect the individual's susceptibility to anxiety. Those influences are widely recognized. But psychiatry has yet to fully acknowledge the value and evolutionary origins of anxiety and other bad feelings, though the psychiatrists Isaac M. Marks of the University of London and Brant Wenegrat of Stanford University have begun leading the field in that direction.

Another emotion that often seems useless and damaging is jealousy. In a cross-cultural study of sexual jealousy the psychologists Martin Daly and Margo Wilson of McMaster University found such jealousy present in every culture they investigated. Moreover, it was consistently more intense for males than females. Male sexual jealousy is simpler than anxiety in that it defends against a fairly circumscribed threat—sexual infidelity; hence it need not arise in a variety of forms. In another sense, though, it is more complex, because it is a swirl of diverse, conflicting emotions—anger, loneliness, sadness and unworthiness, among others. For all the research on it, jealousy is still widely misunderstood.

Several years ago a patient came to me because he felt he was excessively jealous. "I am constantly jealous of my wife," he told me. "I even follow her to find out what she is doing. I know it is wrecking the relationship, but I can't help it." When I asked him whether he had any reason to be jealous, he said, "Well, she goes out a few nights a week with another man, but she says they are just friends, and that she will leave me unless I can be less jealous and give her more freedom."

He felt jealousy was abnormal and had never considered that it might be valuable. As the anthropologist Donald Symons of the University of California at Santa Barbara has pointed out, in the course of human evolution a man who did not experience jealousy would risk his wife's becoming impregnated by other men and thus having fewer children of his own. Without jealously guarding his mate, he could never be certain about who was the father of her babies. He would then run the further risk of investing effort in the parenting of other men's children, diverting effort from his own. In present times, as women achieve more power, male jealousy is becoming less beneficial to fitness, since fewer women will tolerate an intensely jealous spouse. Furthermore, there is no doubt that jealousy in the extreme has provoked men to behave destructively and abuse their mates. Nevertheless, in the long run and on average, the moderately jealous man has had more children. Jealousy in women has different cues and other motivations, which would require a separate, lengthy discussion; suffice it to say, it is directed primarily toward ensuring survival of her offspring by keeping a male provider from deserting her for another woman.

Elucidating the evolutionary origin of sadness poses a special challenge. It is easy to see how happiness can be beneficial; it motivates people to seek out and meet new people, attempt difficult tasks and persist in the face of adversity. But sadness is another story. Not only does it seem maladaptive; it also is increasingly viewed as a socially unacceptable result of wrong thinking or of bad genes. When I lecture on the utility of emotions, the question invariably arises: What benefit could sadness possibly confer?

The hypothesis I favor is that mood regulates the allocation of resources. High mood allocates energy, time and social resources to the enterprises most likely to pay off. Low mood withdraws investments from wasted enterprises. According to the principles of resource allocation developed by workers in behavioral ecology, every animal must decide at every moment what to do next—sleep, forage, find a mate, dig a den. All those activities are important, but each must be done at the right time and in proper proportion. Even a single activity such as foraging requires complex decisions about which foods to pursue and how to divide the effort among the accessible patches of land. Any animal, whether wolf or wasp, that pursues less than optimal prey or does not choose the best time to pursue it will lose out in the long run.

People also must make decisions about where, when and how to invest their resources. Shall I write a paper, paint the living room, read a book or clean the basement? At every moment people are deciding. Life's important decisions are usually questions about whether to maintain the status quo or to change patterns of resource allocation.

Making changes is not easy. The life circumstances people fashion for themselves generally require substantial investments in education, physical skills, social skills, relationships and reputation. Changing long-term strategies—gaining, leaving or changing a mate; switching careers; setting new life goals—is risky business. It requires, at the least, giving up on major life investments and starting anew, usually at a lower level, in some new arena. Such a change also usually entails a period of uncertainty, as one experiments with new possibilities. Because of the risks, it is wise not to undertake such changes lightly; it is often better to persist in an enterprise that is, for the moment, not paying off. A mechanism that induces people to stay with their current life strategies despite fallow periods might be quite useful.

Evidence of such a mechanism appears in recent research showing that most people are consistently overly optimistic. Shelley Taylor, a psychologist at the University of California at Los Angeles, has reviewed extensive work showing that, on average, normal people believe that they are more highly skilled than they really are and that they have more control over their environment than they actually do. Furthermore, other work shows that people generally think fewer bad things will happen to themselves than to others. Many depressives, in contrast, seem to be brutally accurate in their assessments of themselves—not pessimistic, merely accurate. Normally, people see the world through rose-colored glasses. That optimism is just what is needed to get people to persist in temporarily unprofitable enterprises and to stay with good relationships that are not going well at the moment.

When efforts fail repeatedly, however, the rose tint fades, and people become harshly realistic about the future and their friends, abilities and problems. When things are bad enough long enough, illusions must be abandoned to make major changes possible. If a farmer plants a field three years in a row and it washes out every year, it is time to stop. If a man is turned down by every beautiful woman he asks for a date, it is time he consider other types. If a person is repeatedly passed over for a promotion, it may be time to change goals or look for another position. As the Swedish psychiatrist Emmy Gut has pointed out, depression often arises when a primary life strategy is failing and no alternatives seem available. She argues that the withdrawal and rumination characteristic of depression help motivate a deep reassessment of life goals and strategies.

The loss of a relationship through death or separation brings on a special form of sadness: grief. Although it can motivate people to prevent such losses, grief is an unusually harsh teacher. An adequate explanation of its function does not yet exist; the links between behavior and psychodynamics must first be more clearly defined and the complexities of attachment taken into account.

Another school of thought argues that mood helps people adapt to their social position. In the 1960s the English psychiatrist John Price proposed that primates exhibit low-mood characteristics when their continued membership in a group demands that they submit to others. The idea has been supported in experiments by the psychiatrists Michael T. McGuire and Michael J. Raleigh of the University of California at Los Angeles, who showed that the dominant males in the social hierarchy of vervet monkeys have high levels of blood serotonin, a chemical that acts as a messenger between neurons in the brain. When the dominant male is removed from the colony, however, and can no longer rule the others, his serotonin level plummets. He stops eating, huddles and appears to be deeply depressed. Intriguingly, many antidepressants, including Prozac, work by increasing serotonin in the brain. In another experiment the UCLA investigators removed the dominant monkey from each of twelve groups, and gave one of the two remaining males in each group a drug that increases serotonin. In each case the drugged monkey became dominant. The next experiment, it seems to me, is to give the drug to a submissive male while the dominant male remains in the group: I suspect the normally submissive monkey, spurred by raised serotonin levels, would foolishly challenge the leader and get beaten back into his usual place in the hierarchy. One can only wonder whether widespread use of antidepressants might similarly be tampering with the mechanisms that regulate human social hierarchies.

Several alternative explanations for sadness have been proposed. For example, perhaps it serves as a cry for help. Just like an infant's wail, sadness can elicit aid from relatives. Indeed, communication is an important function of sadness; after all, it is often marked by distinctive facial features and tears. But if the only purpose of sadness were communication, it should take place almost exclusively in public. That is evidently not the case; people often feel saddest when they are home alone at night. Some investigators think sadness may aid creativity by somehow giving people access to unconscious thoughts and feelings, but few conclusions can yet be drawn because of a lack of data and uncertainty about how creativity influences fitness. To get to the heart of sadness, the next step is to find people without the capacity for mood and to look for any disadvantages they share. If the resource-allocation hypothesis is correct, for instance, such people ought to waste substantial effort in useless enterprises and yet be unable to take full advantage of brief windows of opportunity.

An understanding of the functions of negative feelings would give psychiatry the tools it needs to treat patients more effectively. Currently the field often tacitly assumes that bad feelings are caused by some defect in the brain, and many investigators are preoccupied with finding the neurochemical mechanisms that mediate anxiety and depression. People do inherit susceptibilities to depression and anxiety. In some cases, the susceptibilities certainly come from brain defects. Such conditions are true diseases arising from faulty regulation and are comparable to an excessive immune response. But if sadness is useful, a tendency to depression might better be compared with a propensity to vomit readily or to get high fevers than with diseases such as epilepsy or tuberculosis. Some people may simply have their baseline level of mood set too low, a condition called dysthymia. For others the gain of the system is excessive, causing moods to fluctuate wildly in response to ordinary events. In the clinic that condition is described as cyclothymia or, if it is severe, manic-depressive disorder.

Rather than assuming that negative feelings are symptoms of a physical abnormality or a dysfunctional personality, family or society, the therapist can consider the possibility that some suffering is part of a vital mechanism shaped by natural selection to help people survive in their environment. For many of my patients it is a wonderful revelation to realize that there are benefits to the capacities for various kinds of unhappiness—that there is some sense to their suffering. The new perspective allows them to quit blaming themselves and others and to concentrate instead on making their lives better.

If the mechanisms that regulate the emotions are products of evolution, it might seem to follow that interfering with them will usually be unwise. After all, natural selection has had millions of years to shape the mechanisms, and so by now their thresholds should be set to near-optimum levels. But everyday medical practice contradicts that conclusion. People routinely take aspirin for pain and fever with few untoward consequences; antinausea and antidiarrhea medications relieve much suffering with only occasional complications; ten million Americans each year take anxiety medications, yet there is no epidemic of risky behavior. Nature may seem overly protective, in part because the earliest human environments presented many more dangers than modern industrial society does. People today face few tigers in the street. The readiness to panic may have been a great boon at the oasis, but it is a bane at the grocery store. Exclusion from a social group may have been fatal back then, but today it is not.

A changed environment may not be the only reason defenses seem overresponsive. Be it vomiting, fever or a panic attack, a defense is usually cheap in terms of calories lost and time taken from other activities. But if the defense is not expressed when it is needed, the cost can be enormous. The absorption of bacterial toxins into the stomach, a mauling by a tiger or rejection by a mate can exact huge costs. If the defense is to protect from every instance of danger, the threshold for response must be set low, so low that many false alarms will occur—thus the illusion that the defenses are overresponsive. Patients with agoraphobia, a fear of open places, say they feel silly avoiding a place where they once had a panic attack. But if they are asked what the best response would be if years ago they had been attacked by a tiger at that spot, most quickly realize that a hundred false alarms would be worth a single escape from an attack.

Emotions are set to maximize Darwinian fitness, not happiness. In that dismal conclusion is a kernel of optimism. If much suffering is unnecessary, there should be many occasions on which it can be safely blocked—throughout much of the lives of chronic depressives, for instance. Given the growing power of drugs to influence feelings, top priority should go to gathering the knowledge needed to distinguish the safe occasions from others, in which bad feelings are vital. If we continue to let only side effects or dependency dictate the use of psychotropic drugs, people will take new agents to change their feelings at will, with little idea of the purposes those feelings serve. It is time to make a vigorous study of the evolutionary functions of emotions.

Until that takes place, psychiatry is increasingly going to find itself in a quandary. Indeed, with little knowledge about when bad feelings are useful, I felt quite lost with my new patient, trying to decide whether to refill her prescription. I finally agreed to let her have a few more pills, but I also asked to see her again to explore her life in more detail. And I vowed to do whatever possible to further the understanding of the evolutionary functions of emotions.

MANAGING STRESS AND LIVING LONGER

"Every person is born with a genetically predetermined amount of stress-coping energy. . . . When it is depleted, death occurs."

Jerome Murray

Dr. Murray, a clinical psychologist, lecturer, and consultant from Santa Rosa, Calif., is author of From Uptight to All Right.

WARNING! Even though you rigorously follow a stress management program, stress still could be ravaging you and shortening your life. This is true because most people's definition of stress management is erroneous.

To the average person, it means learning to relax and enjoy life, taking time to mellow out in comfortable, stress-free environments, exercising regularly, and a healthy diet. Many, believing themselves to be engaged in pursuing greater health and self-fulfillment, energetically practice relaxation techniques, yoga, meditation, and biofeedback. They play tennis every weekend, jog faithfully, watch their cholesterol intake, and take pride in their enlightened lifestyle.

Millions of dollars are spent annually on gym memberships, exercycles, and other means of improving cardiovascular efficiency. Multimillion-dollar industries have been created to service these enthusiasts' need for clothing and shoes.

The problem is one of timing. Much of the damage attributable to stress has occurred before these stress management efforts even have begun. Permitting yourself to be bombarded by stressors during the day and trying to undo the damage evenings and weekends is the classic "too little, too late." Living a hectic and frenzied life compounded by pressure and frustration and punctuated by periodic attempts to relax and exercise is a parody of stress management. More accurately, it is an endeavor to manage *dis*tress, not stress.

While managing distress effectively is not to be decried, it is analogous to fighting a fire. Even with sophisticated apparatus, the best strategy is to avoid the conflagration in the first place. This means learning to prevent stress from becoming distress, expanding the range of one's coping skills, and not allowing stressors to continue unabated.

Even though distress management techniques have their place, they frequently are nothing more than expensive padlocks to put on a barn already empty of horses. The elimination of stress isn't the answer either. True stress management is distress *prevention*.

In an experiment to find out what would happen in a stress-free environment, subjects were placed in a deprivation tank, where they floated in water warmed to body temperature. The drug curare was used to paralyze muscle movement. Eyes were blindfolded, ears were plugged, and there was nothing to smell or taste, or sensations to which the subjects had to adjust. After a period of relaxation, they began to hallucinate and have delusional thoughts—they became psychotic. Lacking stimulation, the brain produced its own. The marvelous mechanisms of brain and body require stimulation to function. The issue is, how much, how frequent, and how long?

Stress is the body's non-specific response to stressors such as frustrations, conflicts, and pressures. In more general terms, they are known as adjustment demands. Every adjustment we make in life takes its toll in stress.

Yet, stressors, as the deprivation tank illustrates, can not and should not be avoided. They are essential to mental and physical health. Without the stress of learning, there would be no education. Without the stress of exercise, bodies would be flabby and unable to perform.

Stressors are inevitable and even necessary. They serve to condition our minds and bodies, enabling greater performance. Stressors can stimulate growth and confidence and actually assist in keeping us alive. The problem occurs when the stressors exceed our coping ability or continue too long. When that happens, stress becomes distress, and that is the issue of concern.

There are two human conditions having the greatest potential for producing distress—impotence and isolation. When they are experienced, the human organism is at its most vulnerable to stress.

Resist the impulse to jump to conclusions—this type of impotence refers to a psychological state in which we feel a demand to act, but lack the authority or ability.

If you took psychology in college, you may remember studying the "executive monkey" experiment, conducted at the Walter Reed Army Institute of Research. Two monkeys were strapped upright in a plastic box permitting limited movement, a console in front of each of them with a light and a button. The light was turned on 10 seconds before the monkeys received a jarring shock to their feet. The button would prevent the shock if it was pushed within the 10-second grace period. The monkeys learned this fact faster than most graduate students.

The researchers then added an inventive twist. They disconnected a wire to one of the buttons, reconnecting it to the other. Now, one monkey controlled the shock for both. Being responsible for another and having decision-making power, he was dubbed the executive monkey. After 23 days of this pressure, the executive monkey expired. A post-mortem revealed the beginning of atherosclerosis, incipient renal failure, and a perforated duodenal ulcer. The surviving non-executive monkey was sacrificed to the cause of science and found to be without physiological abnormality.

The moral was supposed to be that executives were prone to stress-related diseases because they have responsibility for others. At first examination, that interpretation had face validity, and overstressed executives sympathized with the deduction. It duly was printed in most general psychology textbooks and taught to undergraduates.

However, that conclusion was not supported by attempted replications. Every other attempt to duplicate the original results failed. Each time, it was the monkey whose button didn't work that developed ulcers. He knew he was going to get shocked, but was helpless to prevent it. This state is identified as responsibility without authority, better known in corporations as mid-level management.

The most devastating type of stress is not heavy responsibility—it is having a sense of responsibility without the power to do anything about it. Responsibility won't kill you as long as your buttons work, but feeling responsible for something over which you have no authority will send you to an early grave.

To avoid the distressful consequences of feeling impotent, limit your sense of responsibility to those areas over which you have authority. Parents who agonize over the behavior of children whose age precludes parental authority suffer from impotence. Employees who feel stymied in their careers because of the perceived inadequacies of their supervisors are making themselves impotent. Anyone who laments the quality of his or her life because of inability to control the actions of another suffers from distress. In effect, they are saying to others, "I am powerless to improve the quality of my life unless you change." That produces a feeling of impotence and heightened vulnerability to stress.

This does not suggest that attempts to influence the lives of others are inconsequential. Sometimes, efforts to influence others succeed, causing them to change in ways that enhance the complexion of your life. However, don't be misled—influence is not authority. If others do not respond positively to your efforts to modify their behavior, don't make yourself impotent by persisting in your efforts. Keep the responsibility where the authority is. Ask yourself: "What can I do to live a more successful life even though this other person is not cooperating with my pursuit of happiness?"

That is the only effective question to ask. It focuses the issue on what *you* do—not what others do or don't do. By concentrating on the authority you have to enrich your own life, you will minimize feelings of impotence. This reduces susceptibility to distress and has another important benefit—you'll be happier and more productive.

Isolation

There is ample evidence that vulnerability to stress is intensified by the lack of close, bonded relationships. Social research confirms that we derive something from attachments that, in effect, serve to immunize us from stress. This "need for nearness" is manifested in strivings to feel wanted, needed, and valued. It is met by establishing intimate social bonds and involves the feeling of belonging and being loved. Even the need for self-esteem is an expression of the necessity for nearness. When we feel good about ourselves, it strengthens our confidence that we are worthy of belonging.

Historically, marriage and family have been the prime source for meeting nearness needs. In this age of anxiety, when tranquilizers are the most frequently prescribed medicine, it is not surprising that these institutions are less secure than ever before. Broken families seem to be the rule, not the exception. Sadly, family and marriage do not offer the stability and support they once did.

Actuarial statistics reveal that married people live longer than single people. We simply don't do as well alone as we do when we have intimacy. As the divorce rate escalates, so does vulnerability to stress.

Increasingly, health specialists are adopting the attitude that disrupted social bonds affect the body's immune system, increasing susceptibility to disease. The California Department of Mental Health found the following correlation between social ties and health:

- People who isolate themselves from others face two to four times the risk of premature death.
- Terminal cancer strikes isolated people more often than those with bonded relationships.
- The rates of mental hospitalization are five to 10 times greater for separated, divorced, and widowed persons than for married people.
- Pregnant women under stress and without supportive relationships have three times the number of complications than expectant mothers with intimate ties who are equally stressed.
- Women who can confide in a close friend are much less likely to become depressed.

Moreover, studies indicate the mortality rate of widowers is 40-60% higher during the first six months of bereavement. If remarriage occurs, mortality rates return to normal.

The health risk vulnerability of people lacking committed social bonds is dramatized further by a study examining death rates for smokers and non-smokers. Not surprisingly, those who smoke have higher death rates than people who don't. The most revealing statistic is that, in both smoking and non-smoking populations, single, widowed, and divorced men had the highest rates. Divorced men who smoked had the highest rates of all. Being alone is bad enough; feeling unwanted is worse. If the loss of established relationships increases stress vulnerability, creating loving, committed relationships is the best safeguard against it.

Several microcosmic population groups have been found with high percentages of centenarians. Efforts to discover the secret of their long lives have been inconclusive. The first, in the U.S.S.R. area of Georgia, led physically active lives, which led to the acceptance of cardiovascular fitness as the explanation. This conjecture was weakened by the discovery of a similar group in India that had a high percentage of its populace living past 100 years of age despite being extremely sedentary in lifestyle. Eventually, the revelation of their high-fiber diet led to its attribution as the genesis of their longevity. In still another community in the Peruvian Andes, the aged not only weren't active, their diet was primarily home-made beer.

Further reflection on these populations reveals only one common tie—in every instance, the communities valued and respected their elders. There were no mandatory retirement age or convalescent homes. There was no segregation by age at all. The older members of each group were involved in community activities, including meaningful work, and were valued for their experience and knowledge. They felt needed, wanted, and loved.

Every person is born with a genetically predetermined amount of stress-coping energy. Using this energy exacts a physiological toll known as aging. When it is depleted, death occurs. The most rapid depletion occurs in conditions of distress.

Think of yourself as a vehicle and the stress-coping energy as gas in your car. The size of your gas tank, set at birth, and how well your engine is tuned determine how much mileage your vehicle will get. Many people treat their lives just like cars. They "run out of gas" long before they should because they don't take care of their "engine" or "drive" sensibly. While you can't change the size of your gas tank, you can do two things to maximize your mileage—keep your engine tuned and don't take any unnecessary trips.

The next time you impotently rage at the "idiot" going 40 in the fast lane, ask yourself: Is it worth it? It could cost you seconds of your life. Do you really want to waste your finite stress-coping energy on someone you don't even know?

Permitting the feeling of responsibility without a corresponding authority to act is like revving the car's engine with the brakes on. It may sound impressive, but it's a waste of gas.

The next time you decide to "write off" any of the people in your life because they have offended you, ask yourself: Can I afford it? Do you really want to lose the potential support and nourishment represented by that relationship? Doesn't it make more sense to salvage it?

As important as diet and exercise are to "tuning up your engine," they are not as crucial as avoiding the feeling of isolation. Making and maintaining loving relationships is the single most important way to stress-proof your personality. Minimizing feelings of impotence and isolation are the philosophical heart of stress management.

Winning the War Against CLINICAL DEPRESSION

"Although we still cannot prevent people from becoming clinically depressed, today's treatments can speed their recovery from an episode of illness and help prevent subsequent ones."

Alan I. Leshner

Dr. Leshner is acting director, National Institute of Mental Health, Rockville, Md.

CLINICAL DEPRESSION is one of the most widespread and debilitating of all mental disorders. Unlike the blue moods and passing periods of sadness and unhappiness everyone experiences, clinical depression is a severe and frequently lifelong mental disorder that recurs and upsets both body and brain functions. It makes life hellish for at least 11,500,000 adult Americans and drains over $27,000,000,000 from our national economy annually, with more than 75% of that sum due to lost social and economic productivity, not the costs of treatment. (Americans miss an estimated 177,000,000 days from work each year due to the ravages of this disorder.) Clinical depression is as debilitating as a chronic heart condition and it, too, can be a killer; it is a factor in up to 70% of all cases of suicide in the U.S.

What is most appalling is that much of the enormous suffering, expense, and loss of life it causes is unnecessary, given the current availability of diagnostic procedures as well as treatment approaches. Although we still can not prevent people from becoming clinically depressed, today's treatments can speed their recovery from an episode of illness and help prevent subsequent ones. We now have a wealth of effective and specific treatments for depression, including many types of medications, several forms of psychotherapy, and their combination. Indeed, as many as 80% of patients with this disorder are likely to respond if they are diagnosed and treated properly.

That is a big "if," however. A major national epidemiological survey sponsored by the National Institute of Mental Health (NIMH) has revealed that, in the U.S., only one-third of people with clinical depression receive any professional treatment for their illness. According to a 1986 Roper poll, 78% of respondents said they would live with depression until it passes, and most people who develop the disorder appear to do just that. The NIMH survey also found that some individuals try unwittingly to self-treat their symptoms by abusing drugs and/or alcohol.

Neither approach is prudent, because ignoring clinical depression or subjecting it to inappropriate remedies is an invitation to prolonged suffering and even more severe problems later. Although a single episode eventually will remit, this disorder recurs in 50-60% of cases and is chronic in 15-20%. When clinical depression is untreated, episodes of illness often return, becoming longer and more frequent over time, until most of a person's life is spent being severely mentally ill. For those who become psychotic or suicidal, repeated rounds of expensive inpatient hospitalization—possibly for months on end—may be required.

Given the magnitude of clinical depression—its personal, social, psychological, and economic costs, as well as its potential lethality—why do so many people with this severe mental disorder go untreated? The reasons include the general public's ignorance about the nature of depression and the likelihood of successful treatment; stigmatization of mental illness, which makes many unwilling to seek help, however much they hurt, and often leads family members and associates to consider depressed individuals lazy or somehow character-flawed, rather than ill; lack of adequate and equitable health insurance coverage for mental disorders, making treatment financially unavailable for some people; the geographic inaccessibility of many health and mental health services, especially in rural areas; and the inability of many health professionals and general medical practitioners to recognize and diagnose depressive illness in their patients—an essential step for appropriate referral or treatment.

Many individuals and organizations, both public and private, are attempting to overcome these problems. Of particular importance is the recent upsurge in organizations focused on advocacy for those with mental illnesses such as depression.

We at the National Institute of Mental Health also have been doing our part. In 1986, we launched a pioneering national campaign to educate the general public as well as health and mental health professionals about the nature of clinical depression and its treatment. The NIMH Depression Awareness, Recognition, and Treatment (D/ART) program, based on the best available scientific information about the disorder, has developed and distributed a wide array of educational materials and has worked closely with local and national groups to stimulate greater public and professional understanding of depression.

The program is conducted cooperatively with D/ART Community Partners—networks coordinated under the leadership of a single nonprofit mental health agency and dedicated to enhancing public awareness of the symptoms and treatment of depression. Partners are active in 24 states and the District of Columbia, organizing a variety of community programs that include speakers bureaus, telephone hotlines, media appearances, public forums, support groups, and professional training.

The latter are addressed to health and mental health practitioners as well as those still in training. Particular attention is given to providing education and mental health consultation for primary care physicians and nurses in rural areas where mental health professionals may be scarce.

In addition to the D/ART Public Education Campaign and its Professional Training Program, a new thrust is focusing on the workplace as a key site for recognizing clinical depression and providing treatment and referral through employee assistance plans. The D/ART Worksite Program also seeks to encourage corporate leadership to adopt health insurance plans and policies that provide appropriate and equitable mental health benefits for treatment outside the workplace.

We have found employers extremely receptive because they recognize that the considerable toll depression takes in absenteeism and reduced productivity can be lowered through appropriate treatment as well as programs and benefits packages that encourage it. One study revealed, for example, that, at the First National Bank of Chicago, inpatient psychiatric charges were reduced by 32% after a comprehensive mental health program was initiated that included prevention and early intervention programs as well as the redesign of mental health benefits.

In addition to efforts to encourage widespread adoption and application of knowledge about the diagnosis and treatment of depression, NIMH is supporting a comprehensive research program that focuses on understanding how psychological and biological factors interact to produce clinical depression, how to treat it more effectively, and how eventually to prevent it. Together, these are helping people with clinical depression spend less time despairing, being impaired and ill, and more time being fulfilled, productive, and healthy. However, removing many of the deeply ingrained barriers to appropriate care will take many more years of consistent, dedicated effort. Making a visible change in the costly pattern of underrecognition and undertreatment we now see will need more than the efforts of a single Federal agency, or a handful of advocacy organizations and their grassroots supporters. It will require all Americans, wherever they live or work, to make an extra effort to learn about clinical depression, encourage people who appear to be ill to seek treatment, and motivate employers to offer benefit plans that provide adequate coverage for mental health as well as health care.

Origins of depression

The causes of depression are many and complex. However, their fundamental mechanisms are becoming increasingly understood, thanks to growing sophistication in the science of mental disorders. Usually, a combination of biological and social/psychological factors is involved, although their specific proportions will vary considerably from one person to another.

Biological factors can be sufficiently powerful—such as inheriting a very strong genetic predisposition toward the disorder, or being exposed to certain drugs or medical procedures—that they alone can precipitate depression. Conversely, disastrous environmental events sometimes can bring on clinical depression virtually by themselves. Most often, however, we believe that a combination of factors is at play.

The role of genetics is a matter of intense research study, but, as yet, the picture remains cloudy. It is known that depression runs in families, and scientists currently are searching for the genetic basis of the disorder. At present, the best that can be said is that some people appear to inherit a predisposition to depression. No specific genetic marker has been found that would allow us to identify who is at particularly high risk of developing this disorder.

Some theorists have argued that depression has its roots in childhood trauma or poor parenting, but there is no well-substantiated long-term research evidence to support this view. Studies have shown, however, that, on average, the offspring of depressed parents are more likely to be depressed than other children. This hardly is surprising. Those of depressed parents face not only the genetic risk of illness, but the environmental possibility of being exposed to an abnormal style of childrearing.

Depression can be a devastating mental disorder, but it also is a very treatable one. We now have a broad array of effective biological and psychological treatments and steadily are improving the ones now available, making it possible for most patients to recover relatively quickly from a depressive episode. These treatments also can help prevent recurrent episodes of depression—an especially important achievement in dealing with a chronic mental disorder. The net effect is that people with clinical depression—many of whom once might have spent most of their lives in a mental hospital—now can be treated on an outpatient basis and lead normal, indeed highly productive, lives.

Studies of depressed people make it clear that depression affects the entire person—thoughts, feelings, and social relationships, as well as the body and brain. In its mental and emotional symptoms, it produces profound despair about the present and a sense of extreme helplessness and hopelessness about the future. Many of the distorted thought patterns of depressed people that help to perpetuate their illness and contribute to suicidal behavior appear to be learned. With therapy, these tendencies can be reversed.

People with clinical depression may develop additional layers of psychological and social problems that can complicate their illness and their recovery. For example, an episode severely may strain or upset a person's relationship with a spouse, child, or lover, and may wreak havoc in the workplace due to absenteeism and severely lowered performance. If hospitalization is required, the person later may suffer the additional burdens of stigmatization as a former mental patient. Often, psychotherapy can help patients—hospitalized or not—cope more effectively with the difficulties of getting their lives back together.

Depressed people have many physical as well as mental symptoms—including disturbances of sleep, appetite, sexual drive, and physical energy—and, when given laboratory tests, reveal additional biological abnormalities. For example, in many depressed patients, the stress hormone cortisol is regulated abnormally, indicating that a key hormone system linking the hypothalamus in the brain, the pituitary just below it, and the adrenal is not functioning properly.

Research also has shown that one or more chemical messenger systems in the brain might be altered during depression. Communication systems that rely upon the neurotransmitters dopamine and serotonin seem to be particularly relevant, as are those involving certain hormone-like brain peptides. Many medications that have been developed can treat depression effectively, normalizing these pathological processes to a certain degree, but through different mechanisms of action. However miraculous the effects of many of these medications may be, it is clear that, at present, the fundamental biological processes underlying depression are just beginning to be understood.

Treatment approaches for clinical depression need to be tailored to meet the specific diagnosis and needs of individual patients. Mild cases of depression may respond well to psychotherapy. Medication often is used, however, during the early stages of an episode, especially if it is severe and there is a strong risk of suicide. (Notwithstanding its unpopularity, electroconvulsive therapy frequently proves to be lifesaving for some severely depressed and suicidal patients who do not respond to medication.) As acute symptoms begin to lessen, psychotherapy may be added to help them understand their illness, strengthen their capacity to cope with its social and psychological consequences, and lessen their vulnerability to situational stressors. Recent evidence from research at the University of Pittsburgh suggests that if, once the episode is over, the patient continues to take standard antidepressant medication on a regular basis, often coupled with periodic psychotherapy services, the likelihood of future episodes is decreased significantly.

For more information on the diagnosis, treatment, and prevention of clinical depression, write: Depression/USA, Rockville, MD 20857.

SEXUAL DESIRE

Whether it's dull appetite or ravenous hunger, millions of Americans are unhappy with their intimate lives

She won't look at him. Keeps staring out the window, even though there's nothing to see but the black Minnesota night and a car speeding past, headlights sliding along the glass. "I thought it would just go away," the petite woman says finally, in a small, tired voice. "That it was just a phase I was going through. I would make excuses."

The muffled thuds and shouts of playing children drift from the basement. Her wiry husband, seated on the Early American sofa, is a machinist in his late 30s. She is a homemaker. And all that matters now is that they haven't had sex in eight months. "He'd start a little foreplay. I'd say '*No.* Just leave me alone!' "

"Boy, would that put me away," says her husband, his bearded face stony above a red T-shirt. "I was already feeling hurt. I'd roll over and go to sleep."

"Sometimes, every three to four months, I'd force myself," she confesses. "Grit my teeth and get through it."

Neither partner looks at the other, and a hesitant hush hovers over the room. Finally, the husband turns to psychologist Eli Coleman, who runs a sex-therapy clinic in nearby Minneapolis. "There's just one thing I want to know," he says, frowning. "Is this a common situation?"

Common? Try epidemic. The problem under discussion is sexual desire, an instinct that should flow as freely and unself-consciously between two loving humans as the urge for a fine meal or a good night's sleep. This is a story about what happens when desire goes askew. It is a tale of people who typically are articulate, competent and to all appearances quite ordinary, yet they cannot enjoy one of humankind's most basic pleasures. Madonna may be falling out of her bustier on MTV, Prince may be singing the joys of masturbation on FM and the latest sex-and-gore thriller may be packing them in at the Cineplex, but in the bedroom, an estimated 1 in 5 Americans—some 38 million adults—don't want sex at all. As many as 9 million more, meanwhile, suffer almost uncontrollable sexual desire, compulsively masturbating or prowling a surreal landscape of massage parlors and rumpled beds in a frenzied quest for loveless sex.

To be sure, sexual-desire disorders date back a lot further than "The Devil and Miss Jones," or even Don Juan. What's new is that such complaints now constitute the No. 1 problem bringing clients to sex therapists. Women without orgasms and men who ejaculated prematurely once dominated the practice; now—because of the pioneering research of Dr. William Masters and Virginia Johnson in the 1960s—people with such common conditions seek do-it-yourself solutions. "The simpler cases can go out and get self-help books," says Dr. Constance Moore, head of the Human Sexuality Program at Houston's Baylor College of Medicine. "Today, sex therapists are seeing the more complicated problems."

No one is sure whether the onslaught of Americans seeking help reflects a real rise in desire disorders or whether such problems are simply more visible. In the 1960s, public expectations of sex began to shift in profound ways. Thanks to the birth-control pill, women could for the first time in history separate sex from the fear of pregnancy. Suddenly, it was not only OK for women to enjoy sex—it was *de rigueur.* The 1953 Kinsey report that as many as 29 percent of single women were sexually unresponsive now seemed as old-fashioned as stiff petticoats and white gloves.

At the same time, new cultural messages glorified casual sex. More than 80 percent of women and 90 percent of men now engage in premarital intercourse, compared with 50 percent of women and 80 percent of men in the 1920s. And from seductive Calvin Klein–jeans ads to the estimated 176 monthly sex scenes on prime-time TV, free sex has emerged as the presumptive symbol of the good life. Sexual health has become a right.

And so they come for help: A man who, after pursuing his bride-to-be for months, shuts down sexually on his wedding night in their $200-a-day bridal suite. A school administrator with five boyfriends who sandwiches frenzied appointments for sex between dashes to office and supermarket. They are farmers and salesmen, consultants and lawyers, homemakers and clerks. In the sanitized confines of therapists' offices, they haltingly reveal their secrets—it's hard, after all, to confess even to a best friend that one masturbates five times a day or hasn't slept with one's spouse in a year. Eyes downcast, voices leaden, they evoke the anguish of abusive fathers, of religiously suffocating mothers, of families where sex, if discussed at all, was shameful and dirty and where dad sometimes slipped into bed with the kids.

What unites them is fear. As children, they learned that caring too much for others was risky. As adults, they found they could control their fear by controlling sex. Instead of an intimate and loving act, sex became a tool to manipulate those who might get too close. And while no one can properly distinguish why some people channel childhood anxieties into food or booze while others fasten on sex, it may be that what eating disorders were to the '80s, desire disorders will be in the '90s: the designer disease of the decade, the newest symptom of American loneliness and alienation. "Sex isn't just sex," explains Raul C. Schiavi, head of the Human Sexuality Program at Mount Sinai Medical Center. "It's an avenue to express many more needs: intimacy, support, self-esteem or whatever."

Given that baggage, it's no wonder that the treatments for sex problems are neither identical nor tidy. In the past three years, researchers have discovered that antidepressants like Prozac can markedly improve symptoms in sexual compulsives. But for victims of low desire, the results are sketchier. The quest for an aphrodisiac, of course, is ancient: King Tut gulped licorice root before romancing his queen, and other love potions, from powdered rhinoceros horn to bees' wings, have proved just as disappointing. But for most cases, treatment involves counseling and therapy, beginning with an attempt to define when things went wrong.

WHAT IS NORMAL?

*At first it was fun: feverish kisses in his red Chevy, giggly nights of passion in the apartment. But then came marriage, two kids, and suddenly her husband's hands on her flesh felt like tentacles, and the sight of him approaching made her body stiffen with revulsion. Then the disagreements began, hurtful scenes ending with each of them lying wedged against opposite sides of the bed, praying for sleep. "I didn't know what to do—look in the yellow pages?" recalls Karen, 35, a clerk-cashier in suburban Minneapolis. Her husband didn't know, either. "We finally got a phone number from our family doctor," he says. "It was three more months before we called."**

It wasn't so long ago that low sexual desire was considered a good thing—at least in women. Madame Bovary scandalized 19th-century France with her extramarital fling in Gustave Flaubert's novel. And no one ever said that the remote Estella of Dickens's "Great Expectations" had a low-desire problem. Indeed, from Eve's seduction of Adam, women's sexuality outside of procreation was often considered evil, and early Christian thinkers were just as unsparing toward men—a philosophy that found particularly fertile ground in the New World. As recently as 1907, Dr. John Harvey Kellogg developed his popular corn flakes in an unsuccessful effort to curb desire.

Nor were men and women always physically able to enjoy sex. In late 17th-century England, for instance, people suffered from long bouts of crippling illness, not to mention bad breath from poor dentistry, running sores, ulcers and skin diseases. Without antibiotics, women endured repeated vaginal and urinary tract infections that made sex painful.

Then came marriage, two children, and suddenly her husband's hands felt like tentacles. His approach made her stiffen with revulsion.

In fact, the idea of "normal" sexual appetite is such a 20th-century artifice that few experts are comfortable defining it. Clinically, hypoactive sexual desire means having sexual urges, fantasies and/or activity less than twice a month. But even that is the loosest of definitions, since if both partners are happy, once a month may be as "proper" as once a day. "I make the diagnosis [of HSD] if there's been a definite change in desire," says sexologist Moore, "and if it's causing the patient some distress." In Karen's case, the distress was acute: Each night she huddled on her side of the bed, tormenting herself with guilt and dread that her marriage was slipping away.

More typically, though, it's the patient's *partner* who is in distress. Consider Tom, 35, a Midwestern advertising executive whose wife has HSD. "I would try to ignore it as long as I could," he says. "Then she'd give in [and have sex]. But she'd lie limp, waiting for me to get it over with. She could have been downtown. I felt terrible afterward, very guilty."

Prodded by their mates, victims of desire disorders often show up for therapy complaining of impotence or lack of orgasm. But in the mid-1970s, therapists began to notice that the real problem was often that, as in Karen's case, they didn't truly *want* to have sex. In her groundbreaking 1979 work, "Disorders of Sexual Desire," Dr. Helen Singer Kaplan found that unlike sexual arousal, desire exists primarily in the mind. As a result, Kaplan concluded, HSD stems not from a lack of ability to perform but from a lack of motivation. Even so, the fact that HSD may be "all in your mind" doesn't make living with it any easier. "The most important part of sex," Kaplan says, "is the emotional, subjective part. Without that, mechanical function is not gratifying."

Therapists have found that HSD appears to be about twice as prevalent in women as in men. While no national samples are available, one 1978 study of 100 nonclinical American couples found that 35 percent of the women reported lack of sexual interest, compared with 16 percent of the men. But despite this gap, the causes of HSD for both men and women are the same, and the problem usually begins with the emotions.

*Like many desire disorder victims quoted here, Karen is a client of the University of Minnesota's Program in Human Sexuality. All names and identifications have been changed.

CAUSES OF LOW DESIRE

The memories started coming after two years in therapy: gauzy, not quite distinct, yet so haunting that tears slowly squeezed from her eyes right in front of the therapist. Jeanine was 8 years old, lying in bed in her Wisconsin home, watching the door creak open. Suddenly, her father was silently over her, breathing heavily. She never told anybody. How could she? There were crucifixes in every room of the house, and her father led the family in the rosary nightly during Lent. Her mother once lectured her on how little girls who "touched themselves" must confess to the priest. Years later, after she got married, Jeanine never had an orgasm with her husband, Tom. Later, she shut down altogether. She and Tom last had sex 4 1/2 years ago.

The roots of desire disorders often lie between the "Sesame Street" years and junior high. Some adults, like Jeanine, report having been sexually abused as children; for others, the abuse was more emotional. John Money, who has pioneered treatments for deviate sexuality at Johns Hopkins University, says children raised in homes where sex is viewed as evil and harmless activities like "playing doctor" are cruelly punished are likely to grow up with warped sexual identities. "In girls, often you extinguish the lust completely, so that they can never have an orgasm, and marriage becomes a dreary business where you put up with sex to serve the maternal instinct," says Money. "In boys, sex gets redirected into abnormal channels."

Jeanine was 8 years old, lying in bed, watching the door creak open. Suddenly, her father was silently on her, breathing heavily.

Not surprisingly, women like Jeanine, who learn as children not to trust those closest to them, often have trouble melding passion and intimacy. Although victims of low desire may be drawn to hit-and-run encounters with strangers, when they get close to a partner, it's too dangerous to let themselves go sexually. Many men suffer from Freud's famous "Madonna-whore complex," whereby a man endows his partner with the "Madonna-like" qualities of his mother. "You find a sudden cessation of interest in sex right after the wedding, even on the night the engagement was announced," says Harold Lief, professor emeritus of psychiatry at the University of Pennsylvania. "These men can't lust after someone they love, or vice versa."

Then there are the tangled cases, where the core problem is not so much historical as personal: The husband and wife detest each other. Marital difficulties, say Lief and other therapists, underlie as many as half of desire disorder cases. Often the problem stems from suppressed anger. "If a couple comes into my office," says Kaplan, "and they fight about where they're gonna sit, and the only question is who's gonna complain about the other more, I know why they're not having sex."

Childbirth, stress and depression can also precipitate low sexual desire. But only in a minority of cases—roughly 15 percent—are the causes medical, such as hormone deficiencies or diseases like diabetes. Some antidepressants and antihypertensives can also squelch desire. The good news is that such problems usually have a medical solution, sparing patients lengthy hours on an analyst's couch. But the story is not so simple for most HSD sufferers.

TREATMENT FOR HSD

"I just can't do this," Karen announced, midway through the first "homework" session. The kids were asleep in the next room, and the suburban Minneapolis woman and her husband, Bruce, lay naked on the bed. For 15 minutes, according to their therapist, Bruce was to gently explore her breasts and genitals, while she told him what felt good. But as she guided his hand across her rigid body, it might have been made of marble: She felt nothing. Devastated she thought: "This is a waste of time. Nothing's going to change." Later, she told Bruce, "I don't want to go back to therapy." He replied: "We have no choice. We've got to go back."

Reversing low desire takes time. "I went into therapy thinking I'd get an instant fix," says Karen, who has seen a psychologist for a year but still has not had intercourse with her husband. Many therapists estimate the cure rate for low desire is 50 percent at best, and can take months or years of therapy. Nor do desire disorders lend themselves to any standard formula. "It's not a cookbook," says Kaplan. "We work out a different program for each."

Take Jeanine, the Wisconsin woman who was abused by her father. At first, her therapist assigned a set of widely used "homework" exercises based on the work of Masters and Johnson. The program aims to demystify the sex act by having couples practice mutual, noncoital "pleasuring" at first. Therapists emphasize that the practice is not strictly mechanical—a loving atmosphere is considered crucial. In Jeanine's case, the exercises helped her experience the first orgasm of her life by masturbating. And while sex with her husband hasn't yet improved, she has begun in therapy to deal with long-suppressed memories of childhood sexual abuse.

It would be a lot simpler, of course, if scientists could somehow find that elusive "sex pill"—a notion that might not be as farfetched as it seems. Researchers know desire is triggered in the brain by the male hormone testosterone, with the help of chemicals like dopamine that act as "messengers" between nerve cells in the brain. In recent years, doctors have begun using testosterone to stimulate desire in menopausal women, as well as in men with low hormone levels. And the pharmaceutical giant Eli Lilly & Co. has had promising preliminary results with drugs that affect dopamine; the results of a full-scale study are due out next year. But for now, drugs hold far more promise for treating people who have too much desire, not too little.

WHEN SEX BECOMES COMPULSIVE

Gary's pattern was always the same: first, the unbearable anxiety, never feeling good enough to handle the latest stress at his architect's job. Then, the familiar response—a furtive scanning of newspaper ads, a drive to a strip show, two straight Scotches to catch a buzz, and finally a message parlor. He would park about a block away, slip off his wedding ring and dart through the door, where $100 bought a massage, sex and momentary relief. Afterward, he'd sit naked on the edge of the bed, his thoughts roiling in disgust: "I must be sick . . . I can't change." But a few days later, the anxiety would begin again and he'd pore over the ads.

Too *much* sex? For many Americans, especially young men, the notion sounds like an oxymoron. In fact, the downside of sexual compulsiveness has been largely overshadowed throughout history by a romanticized view of the rake, from Casanova to basketball legend Wilt Chamberlain, with his claims of 20,000 affairs. Compulsive sexual behavior is perhaps easiest to define by what it is not: It does not include someone who masturbates occasionally, periodically rents an X-rated video or engages in a limited period of promiscuity following the breakup of a relationship. As best therapists can tell, those prey to CSB alternate between profound anxiety and all-embracing self-loathing.

But these are not perverts in raincoats. Gary, the architect described above, wears a well-cut tweed sports jacket and speaks in measured tones. "I was two different people," he says quietly, seated in a psychologist's office in Minneapolis. "Most people who knew my wife and me would say we were a good couple. But when I was home I wasn't really there. I felt like a dirty person, rotten." Indeed, one hallmark of compulsive sexual behavior is secrecy: Gary's wife didn't find out about his clandestine visits to porn shops and prostitutes until she discovered a phone bill listing multiple calls to a "900" sex line.

After $100 bought a massage, sex and momentary relief, he'd sit naked on the bed, his thoughts roiling in disgust: "I must be sick."

So secret are their escapades that CSB victims have never even been counted, and experts' figures—they estimate roughly 5 percent of the adult American population—are the merest guess. But if the figures are flimsy, the portrait is precise. To the sexual compulsive, sex is not about love or intimacy or even pleasure. It is mainly about relief. "These are highly anxious people who respond to stress by attempting to 'medicate' their pain through sex," says Eli Coleman, director of the University of Minnesota's Program in Human Sexuality, and a pioneer in treating CSB. Just as the obsessive compulsive washes his hands 100 times in a row, the sexual compulsive turns to a vast erotic menu that might include compulsive masturbation, feverish cruising and anonymous sex, frenzied multiple affairs or insatiable demands within a relationship.

A small proportion of CSB victims cross the criminal divide into hard-core deviations: voyeurism, obscene phone calls, pedophilia, exhibitionism and others. But the majority prefer ordinary sex—taken to an extreme. What they share is an overwhelming sense of powerlessness. Like the alcoholic, the sexual compulsive is so intent on diverting his pain that he often doesn't even *see* a choice. "If I saw a prostitute on the street, that was it," says Jeff, 36, a public-relations executive from St. Paul, Minn. "It was impossible to not do it."

THE CAUSES OF CSB

His parents were strict Catholics who said the rosary every night and sent their 11 kids to parochial school. The messages about sex began early. Once, at age 12, Jeff overheard his 19-year-old sister tell his father. "Sex is fun." His father shouted. "Don't you ever say that!" Jeff's mother didn't even like hugging and protested loudly on the rare occasions that her husband kissed her in front of the children. As for the nuns, Sister Frances told Jeff's third-grade class: "One should never be naked for longer than necessary." The little boy worried that he had condemned his soul to hell by dawdling in the bathroom. "The message was: 'Lord I am not worthy,' " says Jeff, who became hooked as an adult on compulsive phone sex, masturbation and prostitutes. "I took all of it to heart."

Though he has never cheated on his wife, Karl has spent much of his adult life obsessing about sex: fantasizing, masturbating, demanding sex.

Certainly most people survive strict religious upbringing without becoming "Fantasy Hotline" junkies. Yet over and over, as CSB victims have recounted their stories, therapists have seen a disturbing pattern: As children, these men and women learned that sex was anything but a loving, natural experience. Their parents were rarely able to nurture them or allow them to express feelings in healthy ways. In some cases, they simply neglected the kids: Jeff remembers going weeks without a bath and wearing his clothes to bed. Other parents expected their kids to toe some unattainable line of perfection. "My dad yelled at me, taunted me," says Kevin, 32, a professional from the Midwest who started cruising for anonymous sex in public bathrooms at 16. "Sometimes, he would shake me or choke me. He called me Sissie, told me I was worthless, a mess."

In recent years, family therapist Patrick Carnes—author of the 1983 book "Out of the Shadows"—has gained thousands of followers for his claim that CSB is not an anxiety-based disorder but an addiction, much like alcoholism. It is a spiritual disease, he believes, as well as an emotional and physical one, and his plan for recovery involves belief in a higher power. But while the addiction model has spawned four popular nationwide AA-style support groups, many researchers are skeptical, maintaining that it's impossible to be "addicted" to sex since there is no addictive substance involved. Both the chemical and spiritual explanations, they maintain, grossly oversimplify a complex phenomenon. "It's also sex-negative and moralistic," argues Howard Ruppel of the Society for the Scientific Study of Sex. "They confuse normal activity like masturbating with addiction."

TREATMENT OF CSB

Karl is a Wisconsin farmer, a beefy guy of 42 with sharp blue eyes and hands as big as pie plates. "If I went into town here and told them I was a sexual compulsive," he says, "they'd probably shoot me dead." Instead, he went once a week for group therapy. Though he has never cheated on his wife, Karl has spent months obsessing about sex: fantasizing, masturbating, demanding sex two or three times a day. When he eventually sought help, his therapist prescribed the antidepressant Prozac, which immediately "seemed to take the edge off" his craving. The deeper work came in therapy, where Karl found it was safe to talk—even laugh—about his "problem"; no one condemned or ridiculed him, the way his father had. The turning point came when a group member agreed to role-play Karl's dad and Karl shouted back, finally venting his rage at the way his father always put him down. When his dad died, Karl sat by the coffin at the funeral home and told him haltingly that he knew he'd done the best he could. And then he wept.

"It is so inspiring watching people recover—because they *do,*" says Minneapolis psychologist Anne J. McBean. "I can see someone in my office who's an utter wreck, depressed, anxious, and I know that two years later, the same person is going to be sitting here saying, 'I can't believe it—I've got my life back.' "

For years, psychiatrists treated sex offenders with antiandrogens, compounds that partly block the action of the male sex hormones. But because such drugs have potential side effects and are not government-approved for treating CSB, therapists considered them unsuitable for widespread use. In 1989, when Judith L. Rapoport published groundbreaking studies on obsessive compulsive disorders, researchers who had been attempting to link sexual compulsivity with OCD got a boost. Rapoport and others found that drugs that affect the brain chemical serotonin seem to help many people reduce their obsessive-compulsive behaviors, such as constant hand washing.

Sexologists like Coleman have applied the same principle to CSB. In small studies and clinical trials, they tested the effects of both lithium carbonate, which is also used to treat manic depression, and Prozac, which enhances serotonin activity in the brain. Both drugs, they found had some success interrupting the compulsive sexual cycle.

But drugs are only half of the answer. By the time CSB victims seek help, they need therapy as well. Typically, sexual compulsives are largely disconnected from the childhood loneliness and shame that drive their behavior. After Karl, the farmer, saw his farm sold at auction a few years ago, he began obsessing about sex constantly—even driving his pickup or feeding the hogs. In fact, one of the first aims of therapy—once medication had relieved his compulsive symptoms—was to bring back for Karl memories of his father's intolerance, so that he could begin to release them. Within two years of entering therapy, Karl was virtually cured.

Ultimately, the problem with treating both extremes of sexual desire is that researchers still struggle with their own ignorance. The most comprehensive national survey of American sexual behavior is still the Kinsey report, completed nearly 40 years ago. Such studies are expensive and inevitably controversial. Just in the past year, for instance, the Bush administration, under pressure from conservatives, has derailed two planned surveys of American sexual practices. Yet in the absence of such research, knowledge about HSD and CSB is based largely on privately funded studies requiring heroic extrapolations from small samples. Key research—studying the areas of the brain that control sexual behavior or the effects of drugs on desire—awaits funding. "We have almost no information about how people form their sexual habits," says psychologist Elizabeth Allgeier, co-author of "Sexual Interactions," a widely used college text. "If we don't know how it develops, we can't change it."

Still, for millions of Americans it is reassuring to know that no one is doomed to a life of torment by sex. At the very least, educating and encouraging adults to have more enlightened sexual attitudes might enable children to grow up with healthier feelings toward sex. Psychologist John Money says that sexually repressive attitudes now force "at least 50 percent of the nation [to] get 57 cents to the dollar on their sex lives." When Americans are less imprisoned by public expectations and a private sense of sexual shame, perhaps more couples will earn their full satisfaction.

The American Academy of Clinical Sexologists (202-462-2122) and the American Association of Sex Educators, Counselors and Therapists (send an SASE with $2 to 435 North Michigan Ave., Suite 1717, Chicago, IL 60611) will provide names of qualified local sex therapists.

Lynn Rosellini

THE SECRET ILLNESS: OBSESSIVE-COMPULSIVE DISORDER

Fran Sydney, forty-five, had always been compulsively neat. But at age twenty-two, when her first child died at birth, Fran's need for perfection grew all-consuming. Towels had to be folded just so, and the labels on the canned food in her cupboards had to face the same way and be the same distance apart.

As her three children were growing up, her need to "protect" them through neatness and perfection intensified. "We couldn't have visitors, because they would disturb the order of things," she recalls, "and I didn't allow the kids to play with their toys because of the mess. If clothes touched the side of the washing machine when I was taking them out, they had to be washed all over again.

"I was a cleaning machine. Cleaning became a way of controlling something that wasn't controllable," she explains. "It made me feel safe—for about two seconds."

As freakish as Fran's situation sounds, it's all too typical among sufferers of obsessive-compulsive disorder (OCD), an anxiety condition that afflicts millions of Americans. People with OCD experience persistent, unpleasant thoughts, or obsessions, such as preoccupation with dirt and disorder, fear of acting on violent impulses or feeling overly responsible for the safety of others. To offset their anxiety, they feel forced to repeat meaningless actions, or compulsions, such as constant washing, cleaning, checking, counting and arranging. They know their obsessions and compulsions are irrational and excessive, yet they cannot control them.

Although the disorder has been recognized for more than one hundred fifty years, no one knew how prevalent it was until recently. Fearing they would be labeled as crazy, many victims tried to conceal their affliction from others. However, in 1988, a three-year survey by the National Institute of Mental Health found that an estimated 4.5 million adults suffered in secret from this disease.

RECOGNIZING THE SIGNS

"Everyone has occasional fleeting bizarre thoughts," says Michael Liebowitz, M.D., director of the Anxiety Disorder Clinic at the New York State Psychiatric Institute in Manhattan. "You know you won't act on them, so you dismiss them. What is abnormal is if the thought becomes recurrent and intrusive, affecting your ability to function."

A second characteristic of OCD is the sheer amount of time it consumes—often hours a day. "A lot of everyday situations can bring out compulsiveness in many people," says Wayne Goodman, M.D., chief of the OCD clinic at the Yale University School of Medicine. "You may check a couple of times to see that you locked the front door, for example. For someone with OCD, this compulsiveness follows them everywhere. They'll check the lock again and again. At work they're still concerned, so they'll call a neighbor to check."

These pathological doubts separate a person with OCD from someone with an obsessive-compulsive personality, says psychologist Fred Penzel, Ph.D., a member of the science advisory board of the Obsessive Compulsive Foundation, in New Haven, Connecticut. "In OCD, repetitive behaviors are attempts to eliminate anxiety and fear that harm will come to oneself or to others," he explains. "An obsessive-compulsive personality, on the other hand—one that is superclean or superorganized—sees its actions as positive. There is no distress or doubt associated with the behavior."

OCD afflicts both men and women alike. Although researchers don't know why, it often begins in adolescence or the early twenties. However, there are cases of children as young as two years old with the disorder. And while some people may be only compulsive washers or checkers, others are afflicted with multiple symptoms. In short, says Michael A. Jenike,

M.D., director of the Obsessive Compulsive Disorder Clinic and Research Unit at Massachusetts General Hospital, "there's nothing consistent about this disorder."

THE LATEST BREAKTHROUGHS

Definitive knowledge about the cause and treatment of OCD has also been elusive, but experts are making progress. Current research points to a biochemical imbalance in the brain involving the neurotransmitter serotonin, a chemical that affects sleep, appetite, anxiety and repetitive behavior. Exactly how serotonin is implicated, though, remains a mystery. Genetics may also play a part. Studies show that about 25 percent of OCD sufferers have an immediate family member with the disorder.

Researchers have discovered that drugs that act on serotonin seem to be the most effective treatment. Recently, one such prescription drug, clomipramine, which has been available abroad for more than twenty years, was approved by the Food and Drug Administration. Sold under the trade name Anafranil, it's the only drug approved for the treatment of OCD. Two antidepressants, fluvoxamine (or Faverin) and fluoxetine (or Prozac), are being used experimentally to treat OCD. Almost 60 percent of patients are dramatically helped with medication, reports Jenike. But, he and other doctors caution, medication is a treatment, not a cure.

The best answer for most victims, say experts, combines drugs and behavior therapy. With therapy, OCD sufferers are exposed to increasingly large doses of what they fear, while discouraged from performing their anxiety-reducing rituals. Over 90 percent of people with OCD can be helped with this two-pronged treatment, adds Jenike.

For Fran Sydney, medication marked the turning point in her battle with OCD. Today, she says, "I'm able to have a normal life. I can leave things disorganized for a while. I can cope as well as any mother. It's just the normal life cycle that gets to me now!" —ISABEL FORGANG

For more information about OCD, or for a referral to support groups and treatment centers nationwide, contact the Obsessive Compulsive Foundation, P.O. Box 9573, New Haven, CT 06535; 203-772-0565.

WHO AM I?

She is a wife, a mother—and the victim of one of the most baffling mental illnesses known. Forty-nine personalities—some of them violent—vie for control of her body; many are children, a few are men. And shocking as it is, this woman's condition may be more common than you think.

Nelly Edmondson Gupta

Vickie,* a round-faced brunet of thirty-six, looks like a typical suburban mother in her loose plaid jumper and pink T-shirt. To some extent, that's just what she is; in less than two hours, she will pick up her seven-year-old son, Toby, from school. But suddenly a chilling transformation takes place. She looks down, then shakes her head quickly. And when she starts to speak, she sounds eerily childlike. "I'm Roxette, and I'm seven," she says in a tiny voice. "I enjoy playing house and school. I like to read. I have a book about a unicorn and a book about a magic tree . . . and a bunch of others, too!"

Who is Vickie? She is the thirty-six-year-old mother, the seven-year-old child—and many, many others as well. Vickie suffers from multiple personality disorder (MPD), one of the most complicated psychiatric disorders known. Inside her psyche, forty-nine personalities battle for control of one body. In addition to Vickie and Roxette, there are Rose, the original, or birth, personality, so depressed that she wants only to die; Badla, an often sadistic male personality who usually decides which self will be "out," or in control of the body at any given moment; docile Suzy, who likes to clean house and cook; and Lila, the computer, who keeps track of all the personalities and their memories. There are other personalities, too, some children, some male. And all of them must cope with a painfully fragmented reality. As Vickie—the personality most often in control at this point—puts it, her body is like a lifeless glove; as each personality comes forward, it slips in like a separate, disembodied hand.

Often those changes can be frightening, and even dangerous. "One night when I was driving on the highway," Vickie says, "Badla suddenly put Suzy in control, knowing she can't drive. She hit a lamppost and almost went over a cliff."

Divided minds

Many MPD patients live in the shadows, terrified that others will discover their secret. But Vickie and her therapist, Pamela Hall, Ph.D., a clinical psychologist based in Perth Amboy, New Jersey, and affiliated with Pace University in New York, agreed to talk to the *Journal* to help others understand the condition. Although many of us already know about MPD through the best-seller *The Three Faces of Eve* (1957) and *Sybil* (1973), the disorder still is widely misinterpreted and misunderstood.

Documented reports of MPD go back for more than four centuries, yet it wasn't until 1980 that the American Psychiatric Association officially recognized it as a bona fide illness. Before that, about two hundred cases were reported; experts now speculate that in the United States alone there may be as many as sixteen thousand people with MPD.

"We now know that MPD is not rare," says Robert Benjamin, M.D., a psychiatrist affiliated with Eugenia Hospital, in Lafayette Hill, Pennsylvania. "Until recently, professionals didn't look for it." As a result, he says, the disorder has been misdiagnosed as everything from schizophrenia to plain old unhappiness.

(Even now, some psychiatrists are cautious about the diagnosis, warning that it may be faddish; severely disturbed people, they say, often exhibit extreme emotional and personality

*All the personalities' names have been changed to protect the patient's privacy.

Reprinted from *Ladies' Home Journal* magazine, March 1990, pp. 160-161, 233-237.

changes during therapy, which overeager practitioners may misinterpret.)

Contrary to the stereotype, only about 6 percent of MPD victims exhibit flagrant personality changes, according to Richard Kluft, M.D., director of the dissociative-disorders unit at the Institute of the Pennsylvania Hospital, in Philadelphia. "Many of the rest have long periods when they're switching off neatly without much strife. In other cases, a single personality may be out for long periods of time."

Experts are also careful to emphasize that MPD differs from schizophrenia, a mental disorder marked by bizarre thought and behavior patterns. For years, schizophrenics were popularly—and wrongly—believed to suffer from a "split personality." And while experts still do not know the cause of schizophrenia—which seems to have chemical or genetic roots—they do know that MPD patients do not usually appear to have the disturbed thought patterns of schizophrenia. For the most part, their internal entities exhibit reasonably clear, purposeful thinking within the context of each separate personality.

A survival strategy

The disorder actually begins as a mental survival strategy that helps children cope with horrendous sexual, physical or emotional abuse. In fact, many experts believe our new sensitivity to the prevalence of child abuse may contribute to the growing awareness of MPD.

"MPD develops when people have been so overcome by early traumas that they have to put up mental partitions in order to function in everyday life," explains Benjamin. MPD patients often have numerous childlike personalities, he says, precisely because much of the abuse occurred early in life and those memories become "frozen" at the ages when the traumas occurred.

Of all those diagnosed with MPD, about 90 percent are women. According to Elizabeth Bowman, M.D., assistant professor of psychiatry at Indiana University School of Medicine in Indianapolis, that may be because females are up to three times as likely as males to be sexually abused.

Some experts believe many undiagnosed male victims of MPD may be out on the streets—or in jail. While female multiples are likely to become depressed and suicidal, males seem more likely to direct their rage outward. "Many criminals—serial killers and others who commit seemingly senseless crimes—could be multiple personalities," says Hall.

Shattered lives

While Vickie has never had the urge to commit a crime, she has been forced into some painful choices because of her disorder. She decided to leave her job as a case supervisor in a child protective services agency after Badla began throwing childish Roxette out at work. "I'd get scared," says Roxette, as Vickie speaks in her little-girl voice. "Vickie had her own office, and I'd close the door. She kept crayons and a coloring book there for me, and I'd play until I could go back inside." Eventually, unable to take the pressure of working under such stressful circumstances, Vickie left. She lives now on medical-disability payments, and most of her former co-workers still do not know the real reason she resigned.

At home, Vickie's conflicting personalities sometimes lead to inconsistent parenting. One self will say, "No candy before dinner," and another, younger self will come out and say, "Let's go eat cupcakes together!" But the changes do not seem to affect Toby, Vickie says: "When Roxette or other child personalities are out with him, he just figures he's got this great mom who can really relate to him and play with him."

Luckily, Vickie has several close friends who are aware of her problem, and on the relatively rare occasions when she feels seriously depressed or self-destructive, she ensures Toby's well-being by having him spend a day or two at their homes. "Vickie would never hurt her child," says Hall. "She has made considerable efforts to be a good parent. He's a really terrific, intelligent kid."

In addition to behaving erratically, Vickie's alternate personalities display annoying physiological differences: For example, Vickie and some of the other adult personalities have asthma, while many of the younger ones don't. In addition, Vicki says doses of barbiturates that calm her make some of her other selves more aggressive. Doctors who work with MPD patients say such differences between personalities are actually quite common.

Roots of an illness

Vickie's childhood, in a rural working-class town on the East Coast, is typical of thousands of MPD sufferers. As far back as she can recall, her mother acted like two completely different people. "In front of others, she was the perfect, storybook mother. She acted very compassionate and loving, made Halloween costumes by hand—the whole nine yards. But when other people left, all hell would break loose. I was beaten unconscious, locked in the basement for entire days; she even put me in the oven with the gas on and nearly asphyxiated me. She was real good at not leaving too much evidence, but when it was there, she always had a good explanation: 'She fell off the stoop; she's uncoordinated; she bumped into my cigarette.' "

Looking back, Vickie says she was probably functioning as a multiple personality even before she learned to talk, although she didn't really understand what was going on. "We knew there were others inside, but we weren't fully aware we were parts of one person," she explains.

Because of the alarming shifts in her mother's behavior, Vickie thinks her mother might have been a multiple personality, too. She could be right. "It's common for MPD to be a familial, multigenerational problem," says Benjamin. Although there is no known genetic component to the disease, he adds, if parents grossly abuse their children, the disorder can be handed down from one generation to the next, especially in those who have a tendency to undergo self-hypnosis—put themselves into trance states—in stressful situations.

"You're a liar"

As a toddler, Vickie tried to tell her legal father about the abuse, but he refused to believe her. "He'd say, 'Your mother would never do that; you have to stop telling such lies,' " she recalls bitterly.

In fact, Vickie's unsuccessful attempts to seek help prompted her mother to abuse her even more. "There's one memory from age four of being tied up and put in a carton. She carried me out to the part of the yard where trash was burned, lit a match and threatened to set the box on fire. Finally, she took me out and said, 'See, I saved you. But if you tell on me again, next time I won't.' "

In school, Vickie found little respite from her troubles. "I was always being accused of lying because one personality would learn a lesson, and the next day another personality who did not know the material would be out," she says.

When she was twelve, Vickie's family moved, and the physical abuse finally stopped. At eighteen, she broke off contact with her relatives and entered college.

There, the personality system made a concerted effort to "pass" as an integrated individual, though her internal divisions were as strong as ever. Rose—the birth personality, who was then most often in control—continued to lose large chunks of time during which she could remember nothing.

"People she didn't know would often say hello to her," says Vickie. "Professors would greet her, but she didn't know she was taking their classes. This caused a lot of stress; in fact, she figured she was crazy."

What was actually happening, says Vickie, was that many of the other selves were often in control. Two personalities—Rose and Rosemary—attended classes. Meanwhile, Vickie worked as a nude model for art classes, and admits now that she was sometimes sexually promiscuous—facts of which Rose was unaware. At the same time, Rose and yet another personality, Marie, held down respectable part-time jobs as a statistics and psychology tutor and as a recreational aide in a group home for troubled teenagers.

After graduation, Vickie met her first husband, Roy, whom she married at age twenty-seven. Although she hid her situation from Roy, a new personality, Cookie, was soon created to cope with married life, and Suzy would often emerge to take care of household chores. But Roy was physically abusive, and in 1983, the couple sought marital therapy. After hearing about Vickie's past—the child abuse she'd suffered, her erratic behavior and the bouts of amnesia—the counselor sent Vickie to a psychologist who suggested that Vickie might be suffering from MPD. Upon receiving the diagnosis, Vickie says, there were many different reactions within the personality system. "Rose didn't believe she had MPD, and it was hard for some of the younger personalities to understand the condition," she says. "I [Vickie] didn't believe the diagnosis at first, though I do now." Badla, she adds, still considers himself a completely separate individual.

A family secret

Difficult as it was for Vickie to face the fact that she had MPD, worse was yet to come. In 1983, right after Toby's birth, she was hospitalized for depression and a psychiatrist gave her sodium amytal—a drug that induces a kind of chemical hypnosis—to help her recall key events from her past. In a trance, Vickie had a searing memory of being raped by her maternal grandfather at age eight. At the same time, says Hall, a younger personality emerged and recalled being told by her paternal grandfather that her mother's husband was not her real father. In fact, he said, Vickie was the product of an incestuous relationship between her other grandfather and her mother. The allegation was unbearable to Rose. "She couldn't deal with it," says Vickie. "So she left. Since then, the rest of us have pretty much been living her life for her."

Following her hospitalization in 1984, Vickie divorced her husband and tried to find a therapist. About two years ago, she called Kluft at the Pennsylvania Hospital and was referred to Hall, whom she now sees three times a week. "At this point, we're working on *not* splitting into new personalities as a way to deal with stress," says Vickie.

Strange as it sounds, however, she isn't sure at this point that she wants to give up her multiplicity. "My forty-nine personalities are all quite distinct and well developed; it's going to be very hard for them to accept integration," she says. "The real problem is that we're not all playing on the same team. What I want now is mutual cooperation."

Although Hall understands these fears, she hopes Vickie will someday feel differently. If Vickie can learn to accept all the disparate parts of herself, says Hall, "integration would be a natural progression."

A brighter future

These days, Vickie's life is far from easy, but she *is* making progress. About a year and a half ago, she became reacquainted with Tom, an old high-school classmate who returned to her town after seventeen years in Florida, where he worked at a series of jobs and eventually became a computer engineer.

During a phone call shortly after their reunion, Vickie told Tom about her MPD diagnosis. "She blurted it all out," he recalls. "In a way, I think it was sort of a test. I think she felt, 'Let's put this between us now so it won't be between us later.' "

Fortunately, Vickie's difficulties have not come between them; they were married last December. However, Tom does admit having mixed feelings about Vickie's multiplicity. "Sometimes I'm a little spooked; I think, Who is this person next to me?" he says. But he adds: "I really admire her strength; MPD is an indication of incredible resourcefulness and an ability to survive against all odds."

One of the most positive aspects of the relationship, says Hall, is that Tom tries to understand and deal with all of Vickie's selves as they emerge. When Roxette or another child personality is out, he's careful not to make a sexual advance. Tom has also saved Vickie from being hurt by some of the evil personalities.

The most frightening incident took place on May 26, 1988, Vickie's thirty-sixth birthday, when, luckily, she had sent Toby to a friend's house for the night. "She went into the bathroom and stayed there for a long time," Tom remembers. "I called through the door, asking if she was all right. She said, 'Leave me alone; I'm fine,' but her tone of voice made me suspicious, and I could smell something burning. Finally, I got a hammer and popped the door out of the frame."

What he saw then was terrifying: "Vickie was crouched on the floor burning some black candles and holding a giant kitchen knife. She—it may have been an evil child personality named Samantha—snarled, 'I'm going to hurt her.' I said, 'No. I won't let you do this.'

"I saw a look of indecision pass over her face," Tom continues, "so I grabbed the knife and threw it into the hallway behind me. Then I knelt down and asked if one of her other selves could take control. Eventually, another personality came forward and started weeping. Finally, I led her out of the bathroom. I was terrified for Vickie—and for myself."

Becoming whole

Both Vickie and Tom hope her evil personalities will stop their destructive behavior soon. They want to be able to focus all of their energies on building a better future together. "I want to raise happy kids, and I want to have a solid, nonabusive relationship with my husband," Vickie says. Someday she would also like to return to work at a child protective services agency, and hopes that society will become more alert to the problem of child abuse. "We must realize that people can be pretty horrific, and that parents aren't always what they appear to be on the surface," she says. Nor are patients—and therapists hope they will soon be able to reach out to more MPD sufferers like Vickie, to help them become whole and healthy persons.

Treating MPD

The prognosis for MPD is good—if a person can tolerate what Catherine Fine, Ph.D., program coordinator of the dissociative-disorders unit at the Institute of Pennsylvania Hospital, calls "one of the most difficult therapies a patient can undergo."

The primary treatment is intensive, long-term psychotherapy in which patient and therapist meet for at least an hour one or more times per week. Sometimes antidepressant, antianxiety and other drugs are used to ease symptoms.

Experts often divide therapy into several phases: beginning, middle and termination. During the first phase, the doctor makes the diagnosis, tries to gain the patient's trust and gets to know the personality system: the name, the purpose each serves and when each one split off from the birth personality.

During the second phase, patients must force themselves to go back and recall past traumas in detail. "They must mentally reexperience the abuse that caused their illness," explains Fine. This process, called abreaction, or "remembering with feeling," is so painful that patients sometimes scream, sob and flail about—just as they did during the real event.

As the process continues, the therapist helps the patient break down amnesiac barriers so the personalities can begin to know, understand and help each other. Sometimes, doctors make video- or audiotapes of the personalities, or have patients keep journals so alternate selves can establish a written dialogue. Therapists may also use hypnosis to gain access to buried memories and personalities that don't often emerge, and to encourage interpersonality communication.

Then the therapist must get the personalities to cooperate with each other to accomplish common goals, such as going to the office and making sure childlike personalities do not take control at work. For these constructive changes to occur, the patient must come to terms with all aspects of her self—including uncomfortable feelings such as rage, depression, guilt and shame. As the patient begins to accept herself, barriers between the personalities gradually become less rigid.

"Patients often develop a sense that whereas they used to live only in one room, they are now opening the doors of a large house," says Frank Putnam, M.D., chief of the unit on dissociative disorders at the laboratory of developmental psychology at the National Institute of Mental Health, in Bethesda, Maryland.

Finally, during the third, or postintegration treatment phase, patients learn how to function effectively in the world without creating new selves to cope with life.

Ultimately, say experts, the successfully integrated individual is the sum total of all the feelings, experiences, memories, skills and talents that were previously encapsulated in all of the different personalities. If the patient sincerely wants to integrate—and if she is able to stay in ongoing treatment for at least three to five years—this goal can often be achieved.

Awakenings

SCHIZOPHRENIA

A NEW DRUG BRINGS PATIENTS BACK TO LIFE

By CLAUDIA WALLIS and JAMES WILLWERTH

They are tormented by demons and at times lost to reality. Now, after years of madness, some schizophrenia patients are being "awakened" by a costly new drug.

FOR WEEKS THEY HAD PRACTICED dance steps, shopped for formals, fretted about hairstyles and what on earth to say to their partners. Now the Big City band was pumping up the volume, and the whole ballroom was beginning to shake. Brandon Fitch, wearing a pinstripe suit and an ear-to-ear grin, shimmied with a high-stepping blond. Daphne Moss, sporting a floral dress and white corsage, delighted her dad by letting him cut in. The usually quiet Kevin Buchberger leaped onto the dance floor and flat-out boogied for the first time in his life, while Kevin Namkoong grabbed an electric guitar and jammed with the band. The prom at Case Western Reserve University had hit full tilt.

But this was a prom that almost never was. Most of the 175 participants were in their 30s; they had missed the proms of their youth—along with other adolescent rites of passage. Don't ask where they were at 18 or 21. The memories are too bleak, too fragmented to convey. They had organized this better-late-than-never prom to celebrate their remarkable "awakening" to reality after many years of being lost in the darkness of schizophrenia. The revelers were, in a sense, the laughing, dancing embodiments of a new wave of drug therapy that is revolutionizing the way doctors are dealing with this most devilish of mental illnesses.

Daphne Moss, 30, can barely reconstruct her 20s, when she dwelt in a shadowy land of waking nightmares, fiendish voices and the alarming conviction that her parents were actually witches. What she can recall clearly is the moment two years ago when it all came down to one choice: Should she dive headfirst or feetfirst from the third-floor window ledge of her room in a Cleveland boarding house? Feetfirst, she decided. It meant a fractured hip, multiple bruises—and survival.

Buchberger, 33, also spent a decade wrestling with inner demons. He was hounded by a frightening spirit—a golden beam of light—that he believed, had previously haunted an executed murderer. The spirit never spoke. "It tormented me, but I never knew what it wanted," he recalls.

Fitch's memories are just as scary, but in his case the darkness descended at the tender age of eight. Fitch, now 19, spent his early years imagining that historical figures such as Czar Nicholas II lived at his home. He insisted on dressing formally at all times, in a coat and tie or in historical costumes, and he avoided the gaze of people pictured on magazine covers. Watching him boogie the night away at the prom, his mother recalled the last time she had seen her son near a dance floor, six years earlier: "We went to a wedding, and he hid in an alley most of the evening and begged me to take him home."

Moss, Buchberger, Fitch and their fellow promgoers were awakened from their long nightmare of insanity by a remarkable drug called clozapine (brand name: Clozaril). The dinner dance, organized with help from psychiatrists and counselors at Case Western Reserve's affiliated University Hospitals, in Cleveland, served as a bittersweet celebration of shared loss and regained hope. "Those of us who are ill travel on a different road," said prom chairman Fitch in a welcoming address to his fellow refugees from madness. "We would have liked to have gone to our senior proms, but fate didn't give us that chance."

Until quite recently, medicine didn't offer much of a chance either. While doctors and drugmakers have made impressive strides in treating other forms of mental illness, including depression and anxiety, progress against schizophrenia has been painfully slow. Fewer than half of America's 2 million to 3 million schizophrenics respond well enough to the standard treatment with Thorazine (chlorpromazine) and similar drugs to avoid further hospital visits. Most who do respond remain somewhat disabled, and about 80% are stuck with serious and humiliating side effects, including dulled emotions, a clumsy gait known as the "Thorazine shuffle," a compulsive foot-tapping restlessness and an irreversible syndrome called tardive dyskinesia, characterized by twitching and jerky movements of the facial muscles and tongue.

Clozapine is not perfect either. In some patients it causes seizures. A few develop a life-threatening blood defect and must be immediately taken off the medication. It is also extremely expensive, costing $4,160 annually for the drug itself and as much as $9,000 more for doctor-monitored treatment. But for some it brings miracles. Of 20,000 American schizophrenics who did not respond well to Thorazine and were given clozapine, more than half have shown significant improvement: they become less withdrawn, and the nagging inner voices grow hushed. One patient in 10 responds to the drug so dramatically that the effect is like being reborn. "You go from hating the sunshine in the mornings to loving it," says Daphne Moss, who after two years of treatment with clozapine is teaching public school part time and living independently. "In 15 years of practice, I've never seen anything like it," says Dr. Samuel Risch, a psychiatrist at Emory University in Atlanta.

The emergence into sunlight comes gradually. "You don't take something and wake up the next morning," cautions Dr. Herbert Y. Meltzer, director of the Biological Psychology Laboratory at Case Western Reserve's affiliated University Hospitals and one of the leading U.S. authorities on clozapine. "You see small, steady changes." Still, the 10% of patients who experience a dramatic awakening can be overwhelmed by the bright glare of reality and by the grief of having lost so much time to mental illness. To help patients with this "Rip Van Winkle syndrome," the Case Western group has learned that each small step forward with clozapine must be carefully nurtured with psychological counseling. Without it, the awakened patients can slip back into mental confusion, and the devilish inner voices may begin harping again.

For doctors, patients and anguished families who have coped for years with schizophrenia, the arrival of a new drug that can dramatically help even a portion of the victims is cause for elation. The nation at large should celebrate as well. According to a 1991 study by the National Institute of Mental Health (NIMH), mental illness costs the country $129 billion annually, and schizophrenia alone steals a disproportionate $50 billion—roughly equivalent to what the Federal Government spent last year on all Medicaid grants. Drugs and doctor bills, hospital beds and police problems add up to $29 billion; lost income and family crises account for the rest.

The cost of schizophrenia can be measured on several scales. By some estimates, fully a quarter of the nation's hospital beds

About a quarter of American hospital beds are occupied by patients with schizophrenia

are occupied by schizophrenia patients. Many are chronic abusers of drugs and alcohol, the result of desperate attempts to medicate themselves. The illness can therefore become a one-way ticket to the bottom of the socioeconomic ladder. A third of America's homeless are afflicted, as are about 3% of prison inmates and nearly 6% of those in maximum-security facilities (compared with 1% of the general population). The disease takes a mortal toll as well. About 1 in 4 schizophrenics attempts suicide, 1 in 10 succeeds.

Schizophrenia typically makes its appearance sometime between the ages of 15 and 25, a period when the frontal lobes of the brain are rapidly maturing. Contrary to popular belief, the disorder has nothing to do with "split personality." The term schizophrenia (Greek for split mind) was coined in 1908 by the Swiss psychiatrist Eugen Bleuler and refers to a splitting of the capacity for thought.

The onset is insidious. Victims may begin dressing strangely, sleeping at odd hours, withdrawing from friends and family, whispering to invisible companions or talking back to the television set. They become paralyzed by irrational fears or subject to suspicions that other people are monitoring their thoughts. Eventually the symptoms can no longer be dismissed as the moody vagaries of youth.

Felt from the inside, schizophrenia is terrifying. Here is how one 22-year-old victim described it: "Sometimes people are taking away parts of my body and putting them back. Sometimes I think they are going to kill me." The young man would see huge rats scurrying about his room, and believed others were reading his mind. He heard voices he attributed to "just God and Jesus, but sometimes they sound like my mom and dad."

For families who have watched a child grow and flower, the effect is devastating. "At 15 my son returned to the day of his birth," says a father in Brook Park, Ohio. "He crawled on the floor, and his mother had to diaper him. He withdrew to his room and wouldn't come out except to eat. Once, his voices told him to grab a little girl in a store and undress her. Many times I saw my wife with bruises. I've learned a lot about schizophrenia since she died. I think living with my son killed her."

What causes such bizarre behavior remains mysterious. For centuries schizophrenics were believed to be possessed by devils or even angels. St. Teresa of Avila was probably schizophrenic, and so perhaps was the prophet Ezekiel, who, in addition to his many apocalyptic visions, said he heard a divine voice command him to sleep on his right side for 390 nights and then switch to his left for 40. Some archaeologists believe that holes drilled in prehistoric skulls represent efforts to release the demons of madness. During the Middle Ages, those who heard voices were frequently burned at the stake. As recently as the 1950s, psychiatrists blamed the disorder on parents, specifically a cold, "schizophrenogenic" mother, though Freud himself had concluded that the illness had biological roots.

Freud, of course, was right. Modern research indicates that the tendency to develop schizophrenia is hereditary. While the average child has a 1% chance of being stricken, the child of a schizophrenic parent faces 10 times those odds, and if both parents are affected, the likelihood jumps to 40%. But genes do not tell the whole story. Children of parents with schizophrenia raised by adoptive parents who don't have the illness have a somewhat reduced risk. In addition, if one identical twin has the disorder, the odds are just 50% that the other will. Clearly, environmental factors—stress and possibly even a viral infection during infancy or gestation—also may play a role in triggering the disease.

The first useful treatment for schizophrenia was discovered by accident. A French surgeon serving in Vietnam in the 1950s noticed that Thorazine, then administered as a sedative, quieted ravings and hallucinations among soldiers awaiting

About 1 in 4 schizophrenics attempts suicide; 1 in 10 succeeds

surgery. That prompted a Paris psychiatrist to try the drug on schizophrenics. Thorazine calmed patients and reduced their symptoms. It was quickly proclaimed a miracle drug. Thorazine and related drugs such as haloperidol, fluphenazine and thiothixene soon eclipsed the brutal treatments previously in vogue: lobotomy, primitive electroshock and artificially induced insulin shock. Over the next two decades, nearly half a million patients were discharged from state hospitals in the U.S. and hundreds of thousands more from hospitals in Europe.

But the drawbacks soon became apparent. In addition to producing severe side effects, the drugs leave patients listless and indifferent. In short, while they alleviate the so-called positive symptoms of schizophrenia—the voices and the delusions—they do not touch the negative symptoms of apathy and social withdrawal. Furthermore, they provide this limited sort of recovery for just 40% of patients; 30% have flare-ups of madness and must be periodically hospitalized, while the remaining 30% are considered to be "treatment resistant" and are largely confined to mental institutions.

Thorazine works primarily by blocking dopamine, one of the many biochemical messengers used by the brain. This discovery, made by Dr. Arvid Carlsson of Sweden in 1967, led doctors to believe schizophrenia is caused by an excess of dopamine. That explanation has now been dismissed by many researchers as too simplistic.

Clozapine was developed by the Swiss pharmaceutical giant Sandoz as an alternative that avoids most of Thorazine's side effects. As a major bonus, it at least partly reduces the passivity of schizophrenics as well as their more blatant symptoms. In contrast to the Thorazine family of drugs, clozapine primarily blocks the neurotransmitter serotonin, though it also inhibits dopamine transmission to some degree. The fact that it influences both neurotransmitters may help explain its greater effectiveness. Still, "nobody completely understands why clozapine is a superior drug," says Dr. Luis Ramirez, chief of psychiatry at Cleveland's VA hospitals.

For all its superiority, the drug almost didn't make it to the U.S. market. Approved in several European countries in 1969, it was quickly withdrawn six years later, after Finnish doctors reported that eight patients taking the drug had died of agranulocytosis, a sudden loss of infection-fighting white blood cells. In the U.S., the Food and Drug Administration halted even preliminary tests. "We assumed it was a dead product," recalls psychopharmacologist Gilbert Honigfeld, who helped develop the drug for Sandoz and is now in charge of marketing it in the U.S. American

AFTER THE AWAKENING, THE REAL THERAPY MUST BEGIN

IN WASHINGTON IRVING'S CLASSIC FOLKTALE, RIP VAN WINKLE AWAKES FROM a 20-year nap to find his youth behind him, the world radically changed and his assumptions hopelessly outmoded. Schizophrenics roused to reality by clozapine endure much the same jolt. Re-entry is not merely a question of catching up with the arrival of rap music and the end of the cold war. It often means coming to terms with lost dreams: the chance to buy a house, build a career or perhaps start a family. On top of this, patients emerging from schizophrenia must acquire the skills needed to live independently while contending with the disorientation, neurological damage and emotional problems left behind by the disease. To manage all this takes more than a great drug; it demands months, even years, of painstaking therapy. "Clozapine gets their attention," says Sarah Burnett, supervisor of Case Western Reserve's Psychosocial Rehabilitation Clinic, "then counseling starts."

A counselor's first goal is to coax newly awakened patients out of the cocoon of their former life. "They are like children at first," says Burnett. "Everything frightens them." Once their trust is gained, they must learn the most fundamental, practical facts about how to organize their life. In a group session, for instance, participants are asked to make a pie chart of a typical day. How big a slice does sleep get? Work? Television? Many schizophrenics are accustomed to sleeping 16 hours a day. To enforce normal habits, Burnett often uses peer pressure. When new arrivals realize that other patients in the group have cut their sleep time to eight hours, she says, "a light goes on." The technique has also worked to convince an unkempt patient of the need for regular showers.

> "I can't drive a car. I can't follow a map. I have no idea what a computer is. It's really embarrassing."

Patients at the rehabilitation center practice social skills by calling each other on the phone and organizing excursions to restaurants and shops. They help one another set daily goals: cook breakfast, buy Mom a birthday card, look for a job. They also learn to do mundane chores: washing clothes in the hospital laundry room and cooking in a tiny employee kitchen. Nothing is easy. Soap goes into the washing machines, but clothes are often forgotten. Because schizophrenics have certain cognitive problems, they have trouble generalizing the principles behind the chores. Thus learning to fry chicken doesn't mean they will know how to cook a hamburger. Technical skills can be mastered only by constant repetition. "I can't drive a car. I can't follow a map," complains a 40-year-old female patient. "I have no idea what a computer is. It's really embarrassing. Just about everybody with an I.Q. over 70 can do things I can't do." Another problem: parents who have suffered through decades of caretaking have trouble letting go. "That can really slow things down," says Burnett. She and her team conduct therapy sessions with the patients' families to help them adjust.

Recovering patients must also cope with clozapine's side effects, which include drooling, drowsiness and possible seizures. Most adjust. But the risk of agranulocytosis is terrifying. Everybody at the center remembers a model patient who did so well on clozapine that she moved into her own apartment, got a job, found a boyfriend and bought a car. Then she lost it all, lapsing into homelessness and insanity, after she developed the dreaded blood-cell deficiency and had to be taken off the drug. Burnett remembers the woman begging to return to clozapine, insisting she'd "rather be dead" than endure madness again. She was ultimately killed in a street robbery.

But for some, even the fear of agranulocytosis cannot compare with the hollow ache of lost possibilities. Kevin Buchberger, a former Little League star, had to jettison his dreams of playing pro baseball. One patient returned to a favorite fishing hole—and found an apartment building. Women who have missed the chance to have children stare sadly at the enlarged girth of counselor Kathy Sinkiewicz, pregnant with her second child. Patients eventually have to confront and if necessary "mourn" these losses, says Sinkiewicz. Dancing at a belated high school prom was part of that process, but only the first of many intricate steps back toward life.

—By James Willwerth/Cleveland

and European research eventually showed that agranulocytosis occurred in 1% to 2% of clozapine patients and that it could be detected and nipped in the bud by conducting blood tests on a weekly basis.

In 1989 the FDA approved clozapine for patients who failed to benefit from Thorazine-type drugs, but required the weekly blood testing. Then Sandoz, with the agency's approval, added an unprecedented stipulation: only its representatives could administer the blood tests. Technicians representing Sandoz were prepared to travel hundreds of miles to draw a single patient's blood if necessary. The policy boosted the drug's price tag to an astonishing $8,944 a year and raised a fire storm of protest from families, mental-health advocates and state mental-health-department officials, who argued that local technicians could perform the blood tests at a much lower cost. Finally, the controversy was resolved when Sandoz agreed last summer to sell clozapine without company blood testing.

Now at $4,160 a year, clozapine still looms beyond the reach of most who need it. The stiff price has discouraged many state institutions and agencies, which are responsible for the care of the vast majority of American schizophrenia patients. While a few states have embraced the drug—Minnesota, for example, has provided clozapine to 1,000 of its 4,300 eligible patients—most have not made that commitment. California, for instance, with 60,000 potentially eligible patients, has treated only 1,300. Veterans hospitals, which treat as many as 9,000 eligible schizophrenia patients annually, have given clozapine to only 300.

In addition, many private insurance companies resist paying for the drug. "The miracle of clozapine has turned into a mirage," says Laurie Flynn, executive director of the National Alliance for the Mentally Ill. "You can see it. You can read about it. But you can't get it." The Flynn family, in Alexandria, Va., had to pay an extra $6,000 in insurance to obtain coverage that allowed their daughter Shannon, 24, to use clozapine. Once seriously ill, the young woman has recovered sufficiently to graduate from Georgetown University and hold a part-time job at NIMH.

Cases like Shannon's indicate that clozapine is a good investment. In fact, a soon-to-be published study by Case Western Reserve's Meltzer concludes that clozapine can save more than $30,000 a year in medical costs per patient, compared with Thorazine-type drug treatment, by greatly reducing the need for hospitalization and other intervention.

For patients who get the drug, the greatest drawback is the risk of developing agranulocytosis. So far, six of the 20,000 Americans who have been treated with clozapine have died from the condition. Although that is considered a low fatality rate, it is still enough to make mental-health professionals nervous. They worry that the uncertainty and risks might jump in 1994, when Sandoz loses its exclusive license to manufacture clozapine. The appearance of generic versions of the drug may be a boon for cash-strapped families, but it raises the specter of fewer controls—and more deaths.

The appearance of agranulocytosis—marked by a drop in white blood cells—is always tragic. Some patients, when informed that they must immediately go off clozapine, beg to remain on it rather than descend again into madness. Phil, 36, was awakened by clozapine after 13 years of suffering. Thanks to the drug, he was able to work part time in a grocery store and start up a social life. Then agranulocytosis struck, and he had to be taken off the drug. "He has his voices and moods again," his father reports sadly. "We'll just have to wait for something else to come along."

Researchers are working furiously to develop that something else. Janssen Pharmaceutica, a Belgium-based subsidiary of Johnson & Johnson, is in the lead with risperidone, a drug that so far appears to be safer than clozapine and works in the same way. Testing is incomplete, however, and the drug is at least 18 months away from the market. Abbott Labs, Eli Lilly and others are also developing successors to clozapine.

Research into brain chemistry is progressing so quickly that doctors in the frustrating field of schizophrenia finally have reason to be optimistic. "We can do for schizophrenia what we've done for so many major illnesses," insists Dr. Samuel Keith, head of NIMH's National Schizophrenic Plan. "We can dissect and demystify it. Then we can defeat it."

Hitting Bottom Can Be the Beginning

Stressing mutual support, self-discipline and responsibility, Mimi Silbert's Delancey Street program turns hard-core criminals into upstanding citizens.

Hank Whittemore

In his teens, Robert Rocha was selling drugs night and day to survive. He was a street kid in San Francisco—using and pushing heroin, sleeping wherever he could. His mother had been in and out of jail for robbing banks ever since he could remember, he says. He had been sent to foster homes from the age of 8. He lived on the edge, hustling and stealing.

Rocha carried a gun to pull holdups. He stabbed people too; and while still a juvenile, he was arrested and charged with 27 armed robberies.

His dream, to go to a big-time prison, came true at age 19, when he was sent to San Quentin. "I'd lost touch with everything," Rocha says, "and had no belief in myself. No hope. No trust in nothing or nobody. The reason I wanted to go to prison was because that's where I could be somebody. But when I got there, nothing in prison excited me, because I'd done everything by then. When I got back out on the street, I thought about changing my life. Then I got busted again—for selling heroin to an undercover cop."

That was in 1987. Today, at 26, the same young man is well-groomed, wears a business suit and carries himself with quiet pride. He has the warm, confident smile of a person with solid ground under his feet along with a future. In the four years since he went on parole, he has learned eight construction trades. He takes college courses in criminology. He tutors other ex-convicts in geometry, helping them earn high school diplomas. He has transformed his life on every level—not in some magical way, but through a painful process of taking one small step after another.

Robert Rocha is one of 10,000 men and women with similar stories of tragedy and triumph. Over the last two decades, these former felons, drug abusers and prostitutes have helped each other survive to become healthy, productive citizens. Each of them has spent an average of four years as part of the Delancey Street Foundation, based in San Francisco, which has received worldwide acclaim for its ability to mend even the most broken of lives.

At the heart of this unique "extended family" is the spirit and unswerving resolve of Dr. Mimi Silbert, 49, a criminologist who has dedicated her life since 1972 to keeping Delancey Street open and growing. An elfin woman weighing less than 100 pounds, she stands toe-to-toe with the meanest, toughest ex-felons until the shouting turns to laughter, tears and hard work, and deep wounds gradually heal.

"You want to quit?" she challenged Robert Rocha and other Delancey Street residents while they were building their new San Francisco complex on the waterfront. Despite their lack of experience, they were doing the job by themselves. "Well," Silbert told them, "that's what you've *always* done—given up every time it has gotten difficult! I know you're hammering away and thinking that this isn't worth it, but you're hammering away on your *lives*.

"You're building your *own* foundation. If you make a mistake with that wall, tear it down and rebuild it! That's what we're doing at Delancy Street, for *ourselves*—tearing down bad things and making good things to replace 'em. And if you're too guilty and angry and hopeless to fight for yourself, then do it for the next guy. Because he's counting on you. Meanwhile, you're learning new skills. You're getting something that nobody can take away from you. You're building your lives."

There are 500 current residents at the San Francisco complex that opened in late 1990. About 500 others are going through this same rigorous program in Brewster, N.Y.; in Greensboro, N.C.; and in San Juan Pueblo, N.M. With neither funding nor a permanent staff other than Silbert herself, Delancey Street is almost entirely self-supporting. Its business enterprises, run by residents, net $3 million a year.

"We're trying to prove that the 'losers' in our society can, in fact, be helped," Silbert says, "and also that they, in turn, can help. Essentially they make up an underclass. A third of our population was homeless. The average resident is four or five generations into poverty and two or three generations into prison. They've been hard-core dope fiends. They're unskilled and functionally illiterate. They've had horrible violence done to them, and they've been violent.

"Most people would rather see them locked up for the rest of their lives, but our point is the opposite—that they can be taught to help themselves. They can learn to be responsible and self-reliant. And we believe that helping these same people is a critical part of turning around all the rest of society."

"You want to quit?" Dr. Silbert challenged a group of ex-felons. "That's what you've always done—given up when it got difficult. If you're too angry and hopeless to fight for yourself, then do it for the next guy."

Last fall Silbert was among six recipients of the second annual America's Awards, sponsored by the Positive Thinking Foundation, of which Dr. Norman Vincent Peale is co-founder. "These unsung heroes personify the American character and spirit," Dr. Peale says. "They are ordinary people who are extraordinary examples of values that make our country great."

Over the years, Silbert has been besieged by requests from groups around the country wanting to learn about Delancey Street in order to duplicate it. Now, with typically large vision, she plans to create a "training institute" that would include up to several months of internship. Delancey Street could become a model for the nation.

"There's no way I'd go back to my old life," says Shirley LaMarr, 43, a resident for nearly three years. "I went through the whole siege of drugs and prostitution, getting beat up and having guns drawn on me, getting raped and carried out on pills, you name it. I've robbed people, all kinds of stuff, and each year I'd feel more disgusted. I lived on the street, with my own space on the sidewalk. When I was arrested, I sent a letter to Delancey Street. I was at the bottom, with a choice of coming here or going back out to die."

Those who enter Delancey Street invariably are filled with bitterness and despair. Having lost all trust and hope, they are angry and defensive. To be admitted, however, they must go through the motions of writing and asking to be let in.

Although they must promise to stay at least two years, the doors are not locked—so they can leave at any time, and few believe they will remain longer than a couple of months.

"But we already *know* that," Silbert says, laughing because the pattern is repeated so often, "and we're up front about it right away. I tell a new person who's scowling at me with utter contempt, 'Hey, we know you're trying to manipulate us. Our job is to out-manipulate you! And we're better at it than you are.'

"They always play the victim: 'It wasn't my fault.' We ask them to explain: 'Somebody tied you down and injected a needle into your arm? Someone forced you to take a gun and bash that old lady on the head? Is that what happened? Who actually did those things?' Finally they admit, 'Well, yeah, it was me. I did it.' We don't care that they don't mean what they say, just as long as they say it. Then we remind them of it every day that they're here!"

New arrivals at Delancey Street are given maintenance chores at the bottom of a long, intricate chain of command that includes every resident. A drug addict who wakes up in the lobby is given a broom to push and told, "Now you're no longer an addict. Why? Because we don't allow drugs in here. So the question for you is how you're going to live your life without drugs."

This "outside-in" approach is central to the Delancey Street process. "Image is important to them, so we start there," Silbert says. "They have to cut their hair, get into a suit and even change the way they walk. We ask them to act as if they were upstanding citizens or successful executives, even though they feel the opposite. Through external imitation, something gets internalized."

The same person also is told to be responsible for the next arrival, and so forth up the tightly structured chain of interaction, based on the premise that people will change simply by "doing" for somebody else.

"For my first eight months here," Robert Rocha remembers, "I didn't believe in anything that Mimi and the others were saying. I had such a hard attitude that nobody could tell me nothing. I'd say, 'Get away from me,' because there was no way that I could trust anybody with my feelings. Nobody had ever cared about me, so why should I care about anyone else?

"Then one day I saw that one of the guys was going to leave, and I found myself shouting at him. I got hysterical, trying to get him to listen to me. Some people told me, 'Hey, Robert, stop. We've taken care of it. But you know what? You're starting to care.' And when I realized that it was true—that I did care—I almost broke into tears."

Delancey Street's rules forbid alcohol or drugs and prohibit threatening—much less committing—violence. In two decades, there has never been a violent incident, and the few residents who have made threats were thrown out. Eighty percent have kept their promise to stay at least two years. Graduates, with an average residency of four years, today include attorneys, business people, technocrats, construction workers and others who represent an extraordinary record of transformation.

Mimi Silbert came from an immigrant neighborhood of Boston, where her father ran the corner drugstore. "Delancey Street functions the way my own family did," she says. "I've duplicated here what worked for me in that neighborhood, where everybody looked out for everybody else as we struggled upward. It was like holding hands while climbing a mountain. Together we rise or together we fall. And that's what happens here every day."

Although her family moved to the Boston suburbs when she was in sixth grade, Mimi Silbert never forgot the supportive structure of that immigrant neighborhood and its values of hard work and self-reliance. A cheerleader who was voted "nicest girl" in the class of 1959 at Brookline High School, Silbert majored in English and psychology at the University of Massachusetts. After that came a doctorate in criminology from the University of California at Berkeley.

"I interned as a prison psychologist," she recalls, "and it was clear to me that this system of punishment doesn't work. The people who wind up there are given everything, all paid for by the taxpayers, and they are responsible for nothing. And then we wonder why, when they come out, they're no different."

Silbert was approached in 1971 by John Maher, a former felon who invited her to join him in creating a center for criminal rehabilitation and vocational training. It would be *for* ex-cons and run *by* ex-cons.

When they joined forces, Maher and Silbert agreed on a system of total self-sufficiency. All residents would work to support the group, with no outside funds. They would follow strict rules of behavior and be self-governing. Each resident would develop at least three marketable skills as well as earn a high school equivalency diploma.

Named for the section of New York City's Lower East Side where immigrants congregated at the turn of the century, Delancey Street started with four addicts in a San Francisco apartment. By late 1972, about 100 former felons were jammed into that single space. Yet, by helping each other, and by working and pooling their incomes, they were able to buy an old mansion—formerly housing the Soviet consulate—in fashionable Pacific Heights.

"Delancey Street functions the way my own family did," Silbert says. "Everybody looked out for everybody else as we struggled upward. That's what happens here every day. Together we rise or fall."

Silbert and Maher fell in love. "We shared a life and a dream," she says. For a decade, as their work continued to gain recognition, Maher helped Silbert raise her twin sons from an early marriage. However, personal problems took up more and more of Maher's time, and he resigned from Delancey Street in 1984. Four years later, at age 48, he died of a heart attack.

Since then Mimi Silbert has emerged not only as the driving force behind Delancey Street's continued success but also as a leader. One testament to her drive and ability is the foundation's new Italian-style complex in San Francisco. Because it was constructed almost entirely by the residents, the spacious complex—assessed at $30 million—cost only half that figure to build.

Called the Embarcadero Triangle, it contains 177 apartments, along with meeting rooms, a movie theater, a swimming pool and space for some businesses—such as printing, picture-framing and catering—run by residents. At street level is an upscale restaurant, also operated solely by Delancey Street people, and Silbert is now getting major businesses to set up discount retail stores, which residents will learn to run.

Meanwhile she has begun a new alliance with the California Department of Corrections, through which Delancey Street people are interviewing San Quentin prisoners before their release. The purpose is to give them alternatives to going directly back out on the street, including the option of entering Delancey Street itself—before, instead of after, they hit rock bottom.

Aside from the new programs and businesses, daily life at Delancey Street continues at an intense pace. Activities include frequent "games" held for residents to develop their interpersonal skills. For those at the one-year mark, there are marathon sessions called "dissipations" to help them get rid of the tremendous guilt over what they did in the past. And a final area of education involves volunteer community or social work, with residents engaged in numerous projects, from helping the elderly to working with young people in poor neighborhoods.

"We're coming together to make things happen," Silbert says, "not just with good results but also with a good process. Because life itself is a process. If you fall apart, it doesn't have to end there. Hitting bottom can be the beginning. And I think, right now, that America itself has the same problem that brings people to Delancey Street.

"At one time, we all believed we were going up as a country, but now we've started to feel like losers. There's a sense of being powerless, an attitude of fear and distrust. We're on the way down. Maybe we have to hit bottom before we can wake up the spirit of hope in America. But there's tremendous good in being able to get excited that rebuilding is possible. Once you know it's possible, you can take the risk of starting again. Then the best part of life is the struggle."

For further information, write to: Delancey Street Foundation, Dept. P, 600 Embarcadero St., San Francisco, Calif. 94107.

HEALTHY PLEASURES

ROBERT E. ORNSTEIN, PH.D., AND DAVID S. SOBEL, M.D.

Robert E. Ornstein, Ph.D., *teaches psychology at the University of California, San Francisco, Medical School.* **David S. Sobel, M.D.,** *is regional director of patient education and health promotion at the Kaiser Permanente Medical Care Program in northern California.*

A PROVOCATIVE NEW BOOK SAYS FEELING GOOD IS GOOD FOR YOU

Imagine the world without pleasure. Life would appear colorless and humorless. A baby's smile would go unappreciated. Food would be tasteless. The beauty of a Bach concerto would fall on deaf ears. Joy, delight, ecstasy, elation and happiness would disappear. The touch of a mother would not soothe; a lover could not arouse. Interest in sex and procreation would disappear. The next generation would wait unborn.

Fortunately, our life is not like that. There is a pleasure machine within our heads: Several brain centers respond to gratifying stimulation. Nerve pathways speed satisfying sensations to the brain, and packets of chemicals stand ready to transmit pleasure signals from one nerve cell to another.

This didn't happen by accident; human beings evolved to seek enjoyment to enhance survival. What better way to assure healthy, lifesaving behavior occurs than to make it pleasurable?

So evolution has connected health-promoting acts to pleasure. Enjoying food, sex, work and family is the innate guide to health. People recognize what is healthful by the joys of life, by their pleasurable feelings—a delicious nap, a full stomach, the gratification of sex. These sensations signal our brains that we are on the right track and should keep going. Good feelings and pleasures reward us twice: in immediate enjoyment and improved health.

Think about the healthiest, most robust people you know. What makes them vital? The most hardy people we know do not follow all the "correct" advice about health. Some assault the U.S. Senate Dietary Guidelines at nearly every meal. Many forgo regular medical checkups. They don't lead bland, "stress-free" lives. They simply expect good things of the world. They expect things to work out well; they expect their world to be orderly; they expect people to like and respect them. Most important, *they expect pleasure in much of what they do.*

The positive mood and expectation of pleasure in healthy people was so striking to us that we decided to find out how these people live. As a rule, they enjoy simple pleasures and stolen moments: watching the sun rise, building a model classic car, silly talk with their spouses, kids and pets. They highlight minor things that please them: a shotgun collection, playing the violin passionately (though terribly), cooking their favorite meals. These pursuits seem somehow to absorb some of the troubles of their active lives.

Most of the people we've talked to are passionate about their work, families and hobbies. Little troubles don't frazzle them. When his car was stolen,

From *American Health,* May 1989, pp. 53-58, 60, 62. From *Pleasures,* by Robert E. Ornstein and David S. Sobel.

Many people are not getting their minimum daily requirement of sensual pleasure

one said: "Can you drive me home? I wanted to talk more to you this afternoon."

Many robust people enjoy a good, hearty laugh—more often than not at themselves. Others bring an unbridled enthusiasm to everything they do and everyone they touch. They care more for people, animals, political causes or volunteer organizations than for micro-managing their blood chemistries or fiber intake. They see themselves as a part of life, not apart from it.

Don't get us wrong. We recognize well that exercising, not smoking, not drinking to excess, wearing seat belts, avoiding extreme sunburn, all contribute to a long, healthy life. Even so, the sum total of all these "good health habits" still doesn't add up to as much as we might believe, and it doesn't explain the essential vitality of some people. The healthiest people seem to be pleasure-loving, pleasure-seeking, pleasure-creating individuals.

There appears to be a physiology of hope, optimism and happiness that speaks to the heart, the immune system—in fact, the entire body. In one study, people who felt that many positive things would happen to them reported fewer physical signs of ill health and better physical well-being. Compared with optimists, pessimists also have measurable deficiencies in critical immune functions. And an optimistic way of viewing the world can promise better health and survival over the course of 20 to 30 years.

So Pollyanna was right: There are important reasons to believe in the best.

CIVILIZATION AND ITS DISPLEASURES

If pleasure is so health-enhancing, then why do we give ourselves such a bad time about feeling good? No one tries to prove to cats that they really should nap, purr and chase mice, or point out to puppies the joys of romping, sniffing or gnawing on a bone. Yet humans have a surprising and deeply rooted resistance to anything that smacks of simply offering a good time.

Our culture seems to have lost a vital perspective on what is *natural* for a human being to be, do and feel. Our health, as well as our quality of life, suffers greatly. Despite visible excesses by so-called pleasure-seekers, we haven't really learned to enjoy ourselves.

Or, more accurately, we've just forgotten.

If we think back to our pre-industrial ancestors, there were marked alternations between periods of intense effort and moments of complete idleness. The farmer might strain during planting and certainly during harvest, but there was little need to work in fallow times. One could live long parts of the year at one's own tempo—playing with the kids, watching geese fly, soaking up the morning sun, and taking (literally) a roll in the hay in the middle of the afternoon.

During the Industrial Revolution factory life became common. But our ancestors didn't happily relinquish control over their time. Historical records show that people hated taking up a tethered, regulated life. Their natural urges to seek pleasure had to be subjugated to the appetites of the industrial machine.

With the modern work ethic has come an almost involuntary dismissal of healthy sensuality and play. We have so learned to delay sensual gratification and curb our passions that many find it difficult to indulge themselves even when the time is right. The idea of napping, lovemaking, taking a walk, sitting idly watching the natural world, or just playing catch with a child somehow seems nonproductive. This view is needlessly shackling 20th-century society: Simple pleasures contribute to real productivity as well as health.

The work ethic is not the only cultural barrier to pleasure. Many religious leaders exhort us to view pleasure, particularly the sensual kind, as morally suspect and corrupting. Banishment from Paradise awaits those who indulge in the flesh, and a flaming hereafter is promised. The body is to be denied, passions reigned in, the mind disciplined.

Redeeming a natural and healthy sensuality requires us to buck strong historical forces. But our health, happiness and future depend upon understanding and reversing this deep-rooted cultural denial of sensual pleasures and leisure.

We need to restore some sensibility, too, to the pursuit of health. People increasingly view themselves as fragile and vulnerable, ready to develop cancer, heart disease or some other ailment at the slightest provocation. In the name of health people give up many of life's enjoyments.

The important point is that *worrying* too much about anything—including calories, salt, cancer and cholesterol—is bad for you. Living optimistically, with pleasure, zest and commitment, is good. Medical terrorism shouldn't attack life's pleasures.

It is time, now, to break the conspiracy against healthy pleasures. Feeling good pays off not only in immediate enjoyment but also in better health.

COMING TO OUR SENSES

Human beings evolved to find pleasure in sensory experiences: the sweetness of a peach, the swelling satisfactions of sex, the peaceful flow of a river, the view stretching from a mountaintop all the way to the horizon.

The human world has changed, though. Many sensual pleasures we're primed to receive are blunted in the modern world. City dwellers miss the glory of the sunrise and sunset as they hustle in their commutes. The synthetic foods in our markets bear little resemblance to the tasty real foods we were built to eat. Our ancestors heard the pleasant sounds of a stream and wind rustling in the trees, but for us it's the din of traffic.

Many people aren't getting their minimum daily requirement of sensual pleasures. Modern life has deprived us of too many of our sensory requirements. We need to regain a balance.

Some pleasures are close at hand.

TOUCHING THE HEART

We speak of something being "touching," implying a close link between physical contact and the emotional reactions of the heart. It's more than a metaphor: Our skin does speak to our hearts. And our hearts respond.

The result of touch depends on how someone is touched and how it feels to him or her. While tender hand-holding can slow the heart rate, pulse-taking by a nurse—if it provokes anxiety—can increase heart rate and prompt irregular beats.

For the most part, however, we find touching, especially light stroking of the arms, legs, back or chest, relaxing and pleasurable. From the pressure points of Oriental massage techniques to the kneading, stroking and gentle pummeling of Swedish massage, the various forms of skin stimulation have been credited with nearly every conceivable health benefit. Unfortunately, science has found little to support most of these claims.

Massage does seem to benefit patients with chronic anxiety, however. In one study, a group of patients with chronic muscle tension, body aches and pain got massage treatment. All had failed to respond fully to anti-anxiety medications, antidepressants and muscle relaxants, as well as standard relaxation training exercises. The researchers measured heart rate, muscle tension and skin resistance (a measure of stress) before and after deliberately stressing the subjects with blaring loud noises.

Then came the fun part. Each patient was treated to 10 sessions, each lasting 30 to 45 minutes, of deep massage. When the physiological measurements were repeated after the massages, each person improved in at least one of the measures: slower heart rate, lower muscle tension, decreased arousal. Most reported less tension, pain and need for medication.

The massage also apparently loosened their tongues. After the massage the patients seemed to speak much more freely and at greater length about their problems. Given our focus on psychotherapy or medication for mental problems, we might consider these touching alternatives.

Our society distances us from others; we don't give each other baths, hugs or massages much and today's parents don't carry their young long distances as their ancestors did. But touching helps us feel close to others. It may be as simple as scheduling a massage instead of a coffee break (companies that provide office rubdowns are springing up), or it may be the realization that it's been too long since you've caressed your child or lover.

Of course, our skin communicates much more than the pleasurable sensations of touch. We also have sensors for temperature, and when it comes to heat. . . .

SOME LIKE IT HOT

Most people like to get hot. We seek out sunny, warm climates, saunas, steam baths, hot tubs and solariums. Yet most research with respect to heat ignores our love of hot spots, focusing instead on the damaging effects of extreme heat.

One of the few areas in which heat's potential health benefits have been studied is the sauna. Exposure to high temperatures for brief periods produces major physiological changes: Stress hormones are released, the heart rate accelerates, respiration and sweating increase, and the skin flushes as the body struggles to maintain a normal body temperature.

Many people find saunas pleasurably relaxing; a brief sauna can decrease muscle and joint pain. One intriguing study in Czechoslovakia demonstrated that sitting in a sauna for 30 minutes increased blood levels of beta-endorphins, the internally produced chemicals that relieve pain and produce a sense of well-being and euphoria. So it may not be so far-fetched to speak of "sauna bathers' high."

Heat may also deplete our body stores of stress hormones. This makes us less likely to respond to stress later—a beneficial type of "burnout."

The healthy pleasures of saunas and hot baths may go well beyond physiological benefits. A dip in the heat is a great excuse for a protected, quiet rest period in an otherwise harried life.

LOOKING AT LIFE

We have an appetite for visual feasts. When given a choice between viewing a natural scene rich in foliage or an urban landscape devoid of vegetation or water, human beings nearly always favor the nature scene. This may come as no surprise, but there is now mounting evidence that such choices may be more than simple aesthetic preferences. Flooding our brains with rich, natural visual stimulation helps us recover from surgery, tolerate pain and manage stress.

When people view photographic slides of natural scenes, they report more positive feelings such as friendliness and elation, and fewer feelings of sadness and fear than those looking at manmade, urban scenes. Compared with cityscapes, natural scenes produce lower levels of arousal and more alpha brain waves, a brain state associated with wakeful relaxation.

We prefer certain types of landscapes, perhaps as a result of deep-rooted evolutionary experience. So try to include some elements from the natural environment in your home and at work. Plants, pets, windows with views of natural scenes, paintings or photographs of outdoor scenes, even an aquarium, can transform a lifeless manmade environment and reconnect you with nature.

MUSICAL MEDICINE

You are sitting in a darkened room. At moments you feel intense spine-tingling thrills that seem to begin at your neck and radiate up over your head and all the way down to the toes. You actually shiver with pleasure, get goose bumps; you may even weep. What could possibly be the source of such delicious sensations? Fabulous sex? A well-wrought movie? A glorious painting? The birth of a great idea?

Had you participated in this study at Stanford University, you would have been responding to music. Music is an ardent as well as healthy pleasure. One survey showed that some people find music more thrilling than anything else—including sex (which tied with "nostalgic moments" for sixth place on the all-time thrill scale).

Be it Bach, jazz, rock, gospel or pop, music is a mood mover. The right music at the right time brings us joy and serenity, soothes frazzled nerves, lifts us when we're down.

There seems to be a built-in response to certain tones: People uniformly describe high-pitched music as happy and playful, low-pitched music as sad and serious. On the other hand, tempo may be the most important factor for our hearts and our heads. Our hearts normally beat 70 to 80 times per minute. Most Western music is set (coincidentally?) to this tempo. Some studies have shown heart rate will synchronize with the beat.

Music therapy is useful in the treatment of many illnesses. It can ease pain, calm anxiety and lift the spirits of the terminally or chronically ill. It's now being used extensively for treating headaches, digestive problems, depression and other diseases with a strong emotional component.

THE EVOLUTION OF TASTE

Food is, fortunately, not one of the sensory pleasures that has disappeared from the world we've inherited. All animals feed, but only human beings savor food with such passion. We eat to nourish, to celebrate, to commemorate, but most of all, we eat for pleasure. Why else would we go to such trouble and expense in gathering, storing, preparing and finally, in one gustatory orgy, consuming our food?

We love variety and crave different taste sensations. This has led some experts to recommend that the road to weight loss is paved only with monotony. At least in the short run, facing a limitless smorgasbord of food is more likely to result in an orgy of calories than is choosing from a more limited menu. Yet there may be ways to indulge our craving for taste without overdoing it in the calorie department.

One researcher has increased dieters' satisfaction and the amount of weight they lose by boosting the *flavor*, but not the calories, in food. Here's where spices can be a boon for calorie counters (and others who want to enhance their taste sensations). Many tasty, low-calorie foods satisfy as much as high-calorie fare.

Eating slowly also allows time for satiety signals from the stomach to do their job. If you gulp down your food you may rush past the optimal level of satisfaction and into that postprandial stuffed feeling. Dieters who slowly sip a bowl of soup at the start of a meal feel satisfied earlier in the meal. For every additional calorie in the soup, dieters consume about two fewer calories in the main meal.

Remember, too, that you don't always have to eat when you crave food; even going for a walk instead may help to distract you.

GOOD SCENTS . . .

Smell is perhaps the most ignored and underappreciated of the human senses. Ever since our remote ancestors stood upright and headed for the trees, the two "distance senses"—sight and sound—have been our predominant means of gathering information about the threats and opportunities in our environment. Nevertheless, smell, because of its connection with the brain's emotion-generating areas, has a great, though often subconscious, influence on our moods and memories.

Egyptian papyrus fragments suggest that in the time of the Pharaohs the aroma of spices such as cinnamon was regarded as medicinal. In the traditional herbal medicines of ancient Greece, Rome, India and the Far East, too, perfumes were thought to have medicinal properties.

Fragrances inspire us. While savoring a pleasant fragrance we take slow, deep breaths and become relaxed. A strong aroma focuses our awareness, distracting us from less pleasant thoughts. Pleasant smells may also invoke positive memories or emotions with their associated beneficial physiological effects.

People with insomnia, anxiety, panic attacks, back pain, migraines and food cravings are now being treated with modern aromatherapy. For example, some patients with chronic pain are taught deep muscle relaxation while inhaling peach fragrance. Later, the patient simply takes a whiff of peach, and the relaxed state is quickly induced.

. . . AND GOOD SEX

Good sex puts a spring in your step, a sparkle in your eye, a glow in your skin. Some people claim sex helps them relax; others swear it helps them sleep better, eases menstrual cramps and other aches and pains, or even cures the common cold. We were surprised to find very little in the scientific literature when we researched the effect of a healthy sex life on happiness and well-being. But there is growing evidence that singer Marvin Gaye was right: There is such a thing as "sexual healing."

Testosterone is the hormone primarily responsible for the sex drive in both men and women. Female testosterone levels—and desire—are highest around the middle of a woman's menstrual cycle, when ovulation takes place and conception is most likely. Some women produce up to 10 times more testosterone than others, and these women tend to make love more often and enjoy it more.

Testosterone also has its tender side: It may help a man and woman bond together as a couple. In the long term, couples' testosterone levels tend to synchronize, and so does their desire for each other. This tends to make for a more contented, harmonious relationship.

Indeed, one of the most important benefits of sex may be psychological in nature. We're the only primates that engage in sex throughout the reproductive cycle, even at times when conception isn't likely. This sexual bond is basic to us as a species, and to our ability to raise more children.

Sexual fulfillment may help reduce the impact of certain stresses in a marriage. In a fascinating study, married couples monitored sexual intercourse and arguments on a daily basis. The result could be dubbed the "F Index": the frequency of fornication minus the frequency of fights. The higher the F index, the more likely they were to consider their marriages to be happy ones. For example, if a couple fights 10 times a month, but engages in sex 12 times a month, their F index is plus two, which points toward happiness.

Remember that sex fulfills many needs: being touched, being caressed, feeling close to others. Unfortunately, many erroneous beliefs—from upbringing, cultural traditions, media images—can interfere with sexual pleasures. Sex may be the first thing to go during times of physical and mental stress, from illness, pregnancy, parenting and aging. If your sexual relationship is a problem for you, give this essential pleasure the attention it needs to make it nourishing.

MAKING WORKOUTS PLAYFUL

"No pain, no gain" may at last be on its way to the graveyard of outdated health slogans. Human beings didn't evolve to run 26 miles at a time, but to walk. We didn't evolve to bench press 200 lb., but to carry 20 lb. to 30 lb. long distances.

So ease off. You don't have to kill yourself to save your life.

The exercise necessary to be healthy is much less than most people think, and doesn't have to involve burdensome regimens. It should be part of life. Gardening alone—hoeing, digging, pulling weeds and pushing a lawn mower—can boost heart rates by 20% to 25%. For a sedentary person that may be enough to improve health.

In a long-term study of nearly 17,000 Harvard alumni, those who burned as few as 500 calories a week in exercise had a 20% lower death rate. That modest workout could be achieved by a 15-minute walk each day, just over an hour of bicycling or a one-hour volleyball game per week! Granted, you might get even more benefit by burning 2,000 or more calories a week (death rates dropped another 10% to 20%). But the bulk of the benefit accrued to those who went from being complete couch potatoes to modest movers.

More important, gentle exercise makes you feel terrific. When you begin an exercise program you improve your mood and boost your confidence and sense of self-mastery.

Start by looking for opportunities to include more physical activity in the everyday things you do. You may not have time to "exercise," but you can build energetic activities into your life. Take the stairs instead of the elevator. Climb a hill. Walk through the park. Instead of driving to the store all the time, walk, and carry a bag of groceries home. Take seriously dancing, bowling, gardening, playing with children, or golf.

If you do enjoy the feeling of strenuous workouts, fine. But remember this is supposed to be *fun*.

LIFE-SAVING SIESTAS

Winston Churchill, a confirmed napper, wrote, "Nature had not intended man to work from eight in the morning until midnight without the refreshment of blessed oblivion, which, even if it lasts only 20 minutes, is sufficient to renew all vital forces." Most people imagine the natural sleep pattern is a single long period at night, but science is proving the value of napping.

When people in a laboratory are allowed to sleep without restriction, an interesting pattern develops. In addition to normal hours of night sleep, they begin to prefer a midday nap. Outside the laboratory, napping is quite common among college students and the aged, two groups often liberated from work-time demands.

The napless day we usually experience is probably an unnatural, fairly recent invention. Our early ancestors may have slept through the darkness of the night, hunted in the early morning, then escaped the midday heat by napping in a shady spot. Our biological rhythms appear programmed for a midday rest.

A catnap can refresh—relaxing the body, clearing the mind, and offering a break from the pace and stresses of daily life. You probably don't have to sleep to get the rejuvenation from an afternoon lie-down. A group of students were invited to either nap, rest quietly in a darkened room, or watch a video program on nature for one hour. After either napping *or* resting, they reported being more alert and clearheaded, and less anxious and fatigued.

ALL PLEASURES—GREAT AND ESPECIALLY SMALL

Which frames of mind and experiences really make human beings happy? Is it necessary to have intense moments of pleasure, or are little pleasures more important? Is happiness built up from many small occurrences or does it spring from a few fantastic events, such as one's first love, a long-awaited job promotion or a once-in-a-lifetime trip to Europe? The answers may surprise you.

In one study, a psychologist asked people to observe their moods over six weeks. Each person carried a beeper that recorded how he or she felt at any moment, and also rated happiness over the six-week period. Happiness, it was concluded, springs from *how much of the time* a person spends feeling good, not from momentary peaks of ecstasy. Simple pleasures—hours spent walking on a sunny day, gardening, running with the dog, or helping someone less fortunate—are more allied with happiness than strong feelings.

Don't bet your whole life on the big events—winning the lottery, becoming president of the company, or doubling your income. Instead, make sure you attend to the daily healthy pleasures of smells, tastes and sounds, rewarding relationships and meaningful work. The good feelings are likely to add up to a more optimistic view of your future and, perhaps, a longer, healthier life.

Glossary

This glossary of psychology terms is included to provide you with a convenient and ready reference as you encounter general terms in your study of psychology and personal growth and behavior that are unfamiliar or require a review. It is not intended to be comprehensive, but taken together with the many definitions included in the articles themselves, it should prove to be quite useful.

Abnormal Irregular, deviating from the norm or average. Abnormal implies the presence of a mental disorder that leads to behavior that society labels as deviant. There is a continuum between normal and abnormal. These are relative terms in that they imply a social judgment. *See* Normal.

Accommodation Process in cognitive development; involves altering or reorganizing the mental picture to make room for a new experience or idea.

Acetylcholine A neurotransmitter involved in memory.

Achievement Drive The need to attain self-esteem, success, or status. Society's expectations strongly influence the achievement motive.

ACTH (Adrenocorticotropic Hormone) The part of the brain called the hypothalamus activates the release of the hormone ACTH from the pituitary gland when a stressful condition exists. ACTH in turn activates the release of adrenal corticoids from the cortex of the adrenal gland.

Action Therapy A general classification of therapy (as opposed to insight therapy) in which the therapist focuses on symptoms rather than on underlying emotional states. Treatment aims at teaching new behavioral patterns rather than at self-understanding. *See* Insight Therapy.

Actor-Observer Attribution The tendency to attribute the behavior of other people to internal causes and the behavior of yourself to external causes.

Acupuncture The technique for curing certain diseases and anesthetizing by inserting needles at certain points of the body, developed in China and now being studied and applied in the West.

Adaptation The process of responding to changes in the environment by altering one's responses to keep one's behavior appropriate to environmental demands.

Addiction Physical dependence on a drug. When a drug causes biochemical changes that are uncomfortable when the drug is discontinued, when one must take ever larger doses to maintain the intensity of the drug's effects, and when desire to continue the drug is strong, one is said to be addicted.

Adjustment How we react to stress; some change that we make in response to the demands placed upon us.

Adrenal Glands Endocrine glands involved in stress and energy regulation.

Affective Disorder Affect means feeling or emotion. An affective disorder is mental illness marked by a disturbance of mood (e.g., manic depression.)

Afferent Neuron (Sensory) A neuron that carries messages from the sense organs toward the central nervous system.

Aggression Any act that causes pain or suffering to another. Some psychologists believe that aggressive behavior is instinctual to all species, including man, while others believe that it is learned through the processes of observation and imitation.

Alienation Indifference to or loss of personal relationships. An individual may feel estranged from family members, or, on a broader scale, from society.

All-or-None Law The principle that states that a neuron only fires when a stimulus is above a certain minimum strength (threshold), and that when it fires, it does so at full strength.

Altered State of Consciousness (ASC) A mental state qualitatively different from a person's normal, alert, waking consciousness.

Altruism Behavior motivated by a desire to benefit another person. Altruistic behavior is aided by empathy and is usually motivated internally, not by observable threats or rewards.

Amphetamine A psychoactive drug that is a stimulant. Although used in treating mild depressions or, in children, hyperactivity, its medical uses are doubtful, and amphetamines are often abused. *See* Psychoactive Drug.

Anal Stage Psychosexual stage, during which, according to Freud, the child experiences the first restrictions on his impulses.

Animism The quality of believing life exists in inanimate objects. According to Piaget, animism is characteristic of children's thinking until about age two.

Antisocial Personality Disorder Personality disorder in which individuals who engaged in antisocial behavior experience no guilt or anxiety about their actions; sometimes called sociopathy or psychopathy.

Anxiety An important term that has different meanings for different theories (psychoanalysis, behavior theory); a feeling state of apprehension, dread, or uneasiness. The state may be aroused by an objectively dangerous situation or by a situation that is not objectively dangerous. It may be mild or severe.

Anxiety Disorder Fairly long-lasting disruptions of the person's ability to deal with stress; often accompanied by feelings of fear and apprehension.

Applied Psychology The area of psychology that is most immediately concerned with helping to solve practical problems; includes clinical and counseling psychology, and industrial, environmental, and legal psychology.

Aptitude Tests Tests which are designed to predict what can be accomplished by a person in the future with the proper training.

Arousal A measure of responsiveness or activity; a state of excitement or wakefulness ranging from deepest coma to intense excitement.

Aspiration Level The level of achievement a person strives for. Studies suggest that people can use internal or external standards of performance.

Assertiveness Training Training which helps individuals stand up for their rights while not denying rights of other people.

Assimilation Process in cognitive development; occurs when something new is taken into the child's mental picture of the world.

Association Has separate meanings for different branches of psychology. Theory in cognitive psychology suggests that we organize information so that we can find our memories systematically, that one idea will bring another to mind. In psychoanalysis, the patient is asked to free associate (speak aloud all consecutive thoughts until random associations tend of themselves to form a meaningful whole). *See* Cognitive Psychology; Psychoanalysis.

Association Neurons Neurons that connect with other neurons.

Associationism A theory of learning suggesting that once two stimuli are presented together, one of them will remind a person of the other. Ideas are learned by association with sensory experiences and are not innate. Among the principles of associationism are contiguity (stimuli that occur close together are more likely to be associated than stimuli far apart), and repetition (the more frequently stimuli occur together, the more strongly they become associated).

Attachment Process in which the individual shows behaviors that promote the proximity or contact with a specific object or person.

Attention The tendency to focus activity in a particular direction and to select certain stimuli for further analysis while ignoring or possibly storing for further analysis all other inputs.

Attitude An overall tendency to respond positively or negatively to particular people or objects in a way that is learned through experience and that is made up of feelings (affects), thoughts (evaluations), and actions (conation).

Attribution The process of determining the causes of behavior in a given individual.

Autism A personality disorder in which a child does not respond socially to people.

Autonomic Nervous System The part of the nervous system (the other part is the central nervous system) that is for emergency functions and release of large amounts of energy (sympathetic division) and regulating functions such as digestion and sleep (parasympathetic division). *See* Biofeedback.

Aversion Therapy A counterconditioning therapy in which unwanted responses are paired with unpleasant consequences.

Avoidance Conditioning Situation in which a subject learns to avoid an aversive stimulus by responding appropriately before it begins.

Barbiturates Sedative-hypnotic, psychoactive drugs widely used to induce sleep and to reduce tension. Overuse can lead to addiction. *See* Addiction.

Behavior Any observable activity of an organism, including mental processes.

Behavior Therapy The use of conditioning processes to treat mental disorders. Various techniques may be used, including positive reinforcement in which rewards (verbal or tangible) are given to the patient for appropriate behavior, modeling in which patients unlearn fears by watching models exhibit fearlessness, and systematic desensitization in which the patient is taught to relax and visualize anxiety-producing items at the same time. *See* Insight Therapy; Systematic Desensitization.

Behaviorism A school of psychology stressing an objective approach to psychological questions, proposing that psychology be limited to observable behavior and that the subjectiveness of consciousness places it beyond the limits of scientific psychology.

Biofeedback The voluntary control of physiological processes by receiving information about those processes as they occur, through instruments that pick up these changes and display them to the subject in the form of a signal. Blood pressure, skin temperature, etc. can be controlled.

Biological (Primary) Motives Motives that have a physiological basis; include hunger, thirst, body temperature regulation, avoidance of pain, and sex.

Biological Response System System of the body that is particularly important in behavioral responding; includes the senses, endocrines, muscles, and the nervous system.

Biological Therapy Treatment of behavior problems through biological techniques; major biological therapies include drug therapy, psychosurgery, and electroconvulsive therapy.

Bipolar Disorder Affective disorder that is characterized by extreme mood swings from sad depression to joyful mania; sometimes called manic-depression.

Body Language Communication through position and movement of the body.

Brain Mapping A procedure for identifying the function of various areas of the brain; the surgeon gives tiny electrical stimulation to a specific area and notes patient's reaction.

Brain Stimulation The introduction of chemical or electrical stimuli directly into the brain.

Brain Waves Electrical responses produced by brain activity that can be recorded directly from any portion of the brain or from the scalp with special electrodes. Brain waves are measured by an electroencephalograph (EEG). Alpha waves occur during relaxed wakefulness and beta waves during active behavior. Theta waves are associated with drowsiness and vivid visual imagery, delta waves with deep sleep.

Bystander Effect Phenomenon in which a single person is more likely to help in an emergency situation than a group of people.

Cannon-Bard Theory of Emotion Theory of emotion that states that the emotional feeling and the physiological arousal occur at the same time.

Catatonic Schizophrenia A type of schizophrenia that is characterized by periods of complete immobility and the apparent absence of will to move or speak.

Causal Attribution Process of determining whether a person's behavior is due to internal or external motives.

Cautious Shift Research suggests that the decisions of a group will be more conservative than that of the average individual member when dealing with areas for which there are widely held values favoring caution (e.g., physical danger or family responsibility). *See* Risky Shift.

Central Nervous System The part of the human nervous system that interprets and stores messages from the sense organs, decides what behavior to exhibit, and sends appropriate messages to the muscles and glands; includes the brain and spinal cord.

Central Tendency In statistics, measures of central tendency give a number that represents the entire group or sample.

Cerebellum The part of the brain responsible for muscle and movement control and coordination of eye-body movement.

Cerebral Cortex The part of the brain consisting of the outer layer of cerebral cells. The cortex can be divided into specific regions: sensory, motor, and associative.

Chaining Behavior theory suggests that behavior patterns are built up of component parts by stringing together a number of simpler responses.

Character Disorder (or Personality Disorder) A classification of psychological disorders (as distinguished from neurosis or psychosis). The disorder has become part of the individual's personality and does not cause him or her discomfort, making that disorder more difficult to treat psychotherapeutically.

Chromosome *See* Gene.

Chunking The tendency to code memories so that there are fewer bits to store.

Classical Conditioning *See* Pavlovian Conditioning.

Client-Centered Therapy A nondirective form of psychotherapy developed by Carl Rogers in which the counselor attempts to create an atmosphere in which the client can freely explore herself or himself and her or his problems. The client-centered therapist reflects what the client says back to him, usually without interpreting it.

Clinical Psychology The branch of psychology concerned with testing, diagnosing, interviewing, conducting research and treating (often by psychotherapy) mental disorders and personality problems.

Cognitive Appraisal Intellectual evaluation of situations or stimuli. Experiments suggest that emotional arousal is produced not simply by a stimulus but by how one evaluates and interprets the arousal. The appropriate physical response follows this cognitive appraisal.

Cognitive Behavior Therapy A form of behavior therapy that identifies self-defeating attitudes and thoughts in a subject, and then helps the subject to replace these with positive, supportive thoughts.

Cognitive Dissonance People are very uncomfortable if they perceive that their beliefs, feelings, or acts are not consistent with one another, and they will try to reduce the discomfort of this dissonance.

Cognitive Psychology The study of how individuals gain knowledge of their environments. Cognitive psychologists believe that the organism actively participates in constructing the meaningful stimuli that it selectively organizes and to which it selectively responds.

Comparative Psychology The study of similarities and differences in the behavior of different species.

Compulsive Personality Personality disorder in which an individual is preoccupied with details and rules.

Concept Learning The acquisition of the ability to identify and use the qualities that objects or situations have in common. A class concept refers to any quality that breaks objects or situations into separate groupings.

Concrete-Operational Stage A stage in intellectual development, according to Piaget. The child at approximately seven years begins to apply logic. His or her thinking is less egocentric, reversible, and the child develops conservation abilities and the ability to classify. *See* Conservation.

Conditioned Reinforcer Reinforcement that is effective because it has been associated with other reinforcers. Conditioned reinforcers are involved in higher order conditioning.

Conditioned Response (CR) The response or behavior that occurs when the conditioned stimulus is presented (after the conditioned stimulus has been associated with the unconditioned stimulus).

Conditioned Stimulus (CS) An originally neutral stimulus that is associated with an unconditioned stimulus and takes on its capability of eliciting a particular reaction.

Conditioned Taste Aversion (CTA) Learning an aversion to particular tastes by associating them with stomach distress; usually considered a unique form of classical conditioning because of the extremely long interstimulus intervals involved.

Conduction The ability of a neuron to carry a message (an electrical stimulus) along its length.

Conflict Situation that occurs when we experience incompatible demands or desires.

Conformity The tendency of an individual to act like others regardless of personal belief.

Conscience A person's sense of the moral rightness or wrongness of behavior.

Consciousness Awareness of experienced sensations, thoughts, and feelings at any given point in time.

Consensus In causal attribution, the extent to which other people react the same way the subject does in a particular situation.

Conservation Refers to the child's ability to understand laws of length, mass, and volume. Before the development of this ability, a child will not understand that a particular property of an object (e.g., the quantity of water in a glass) does not change even though other perceivable features change.

Consistency In causal attribution, the extent to which the subject always behaves in the same way in a particular situation.

Consolidation The biological neural process of making memories permanent; possibly short-term memory is electrically coded and long-term memory is chemically coded.

Continuum of Preparedness Seligman's proposal that animals are biologically prepared to learn certain responses more readily than others.

Control Group A group used for comparison with an experimental group. All conditions must be identical for each group with the exception of the one variable (independent) that is manipulated. *See* Experimental Group.

Convergence Binocular depth cue in which we detect distance by interpreting the kinesthetic sensations produced by the muscles of the eyeballs.

Convergent Thinking The kind of thinking that is used to solve problems having only one correct answer. *See* Divergent Thinking.

Conversion Disorder Somatoform disorder in which a person displays obvious disturbance in the nervous system, however, a medical examination reveals no physical basis for the problem; often includes paralysis, loss of sensation, or blindness.

Corpus Callosum Nerve fibers that connect the two halves of the brain in humans. If cut, the halves continue to function although some functions are affected.

Correlation A measurement in which two or more sets of variables are compared and the extent to which they are related is calculated.

Correlation Coefficient The measure, in number form, of how two variables vary together. They extend from −1 (perfect negative correlation) to a +1 (perfect positive correlation).

Counterconditioning A behavior therapy in which an unwanted response is replaced by conditioning a new response that is incompatible with it.

Creativity The ability to discover or produce new solutions to problems, new inventions, or new works of art. Creativity is an ability independent of IQ and is opened-ended in that solutions are not predefined in their scope or appropriateness. *See* Problem Solving.

Critical Period A specific stage in an organism's development during which the acquisition of a particular type of behavior depends on exposure to a particular type of stimulation.

Cross-Sectional Study A research technique that focuses on a factor in a group of subjects as they are at one time, as in a study of fantasy play in subjects of three different age groups. *See* Longitudinal Study.

Culture-Bound The idea that a test's usefulness is limited to the culture in which it was written and utilized.

Curiosity Motive Motive that causes the individual to seek out a certain amount of novelty.

Cutaneous Sensitivity The skin senses: touch, pain, pressure and temperature. Skin receptors respond in different ways and with varying degrees of sensitivity.

Decay Theory of forgetting in which sensory impressions leave memory traces that fade away with time.

Defense Mechanism A way of reducing anxiety that does not directly cope with the threat. There are many types, denial, repression, etc., all of which are used in normal function. Only when use is habitual or they impede effective solutions are they considered pathological.

Delusion A false belief that persists despite evidence showing it to be irrational. Delusions are often symptoms of mental illness.

Dependent Variable Those conditions that an experimenter observes and measures. Called "dependent" because they depend on the experimental manipulations.

Depersonalization Disorder Dissociative disorder in which individuals escape from their own personalities by believing that they don't exist or that their environment is not real.

Depression A temporary emotional state that normal individuals experience or a persistent state that may be considered a psychological disorder. Characterized by sadness and low self-esteem. *See* Self-Esteem.

Descriptive Statistics Techniques that help summarize large amounts of data information.

Developmental Norms The average time at which developmental changes occur in the normal individual.

Developmental Psychology The study of changes in behavior and thinking as the organism grows from the prenatal stage to death.

Deviation, Standard and Average Average deviation is determined by measuring the deviation of each score in a distribution from the mean and calculating the average of the deviations. The standard deviation is used to determine how representative the mean of a distribution is. *See* Mean.

Diagnostic and Statistical Manual of Mental Disorders (DSM) DSM-III was published in 1980 by the American Psychiatric Association.

Diffusion of Responsibility As the number of witnesses to a help-requiring situation—and thus the degree of anonymity—increases, the amount of helping decreases and the amount of time before help is offered increases. *See* Bystander Effect.

Discrimination The ability to tell whether stimuli are different when presented together or that one situation is different from a past one.

Disorganized Schizophrenia A type of schizophrenia that is characterized by a severe personality disintegration; the individual often displays bizarre behavior.

Displacement The process by which an emotion originally attached to a particular person, object, or situation is transferred to something else.

Dissociative Disorders Disorders in which individuals forget who they are.

Distal Stimuli Physical events in the environment that affect perception. *See* Proximal Stimuli.

Distinctiveness In causal attribution, the extent to which the subject reacts the same way in other situations.

Divergent Thinking The kind of thinking that characterizes creativity (as contrasted with convergent thinking) and involves the development of novel resolutions of a task or the generation of totally new ideas. *See* Convergent Thinking.

DNA *See* Gene.

Double Bind A situation in which a person is subjected to two conflicting, contradictory demands at the same time.

Down's Syndrome Form of mental retardation caused by having three number 21 chromosomes (trisomy 21).

Dreams The thoughts, images, and emotions that occur during sleep. Dreams occur periodically during the sleep cycle and are usually marked by rapid movements of the eyes (REM sleep). The content of dreams tends to reflect emotions (sexual feelings, according to Freud) and experiences of the previous day. Nightmares are qualitatively different from other dreams, often occurring during deep or Stage 4 sleep.

Drive A need or urge that motivates behavior. Some drives may be explained as responses to bodily needs, such as hunger or sex. Others derive from social pressures and complex forms of learning, for example, competition, curiosity, achievement, *See* Motivation.

Drive Reduction Theory Theory of motivation that states that the individual is pushed by inner forces toward reducing the drive and restoring homeostasis.

Drug Dependence A state of mental or physical dependence on a drug, or both. Psychoactive drugs are capable of creating psychological dependence (anxiety when the drug is unavailable), although the relationship of some, such as marijuana and LSD, to physical dependence or addiction is still under study. *See* Psychoactive Drug; Addiction.

Drug Tolerance A state produced by certain psychoactive drugs in which increasing amounts of the substance are required to produce the desired effect. Some drugs produce tolerance but not withdrawal symptoms, and these drugs are not regarded as physically addicting.

Effectance Motive The striving for effectiveness in dealing with the environment. The effectance motive differs from the need for achievement in that effectance depends on internal feelings of satisfaction while the need for achievement is geared more to meeting others' standards.

Efferent Neuron (Motor) A neuron that carries messages from the central nervous system to the muscles and glands.

Ego A construct to account for the organization in a person's life and for making the person's behavior correspond to physical and social realities. According to Freud, the ego is the "reality principle" that is responsible for holding the id or "pleasure principle" in check. *See* Id.

Egocentrism Seeing things from only one's own point of view; also, the quality of a child's thought that prevents her or him from understanding that different people perceive the world differently. Egocentrism is characteristic of a stage that all children go through.

Electra Complex The libidinal feelings of a child toward a parent of the opposite sex. *See also* Oedipus Complex

Electroshock Therapy A form of therapy used to relieve severe depression. The patient receives electric current across the forehead, loses consciousness, and undergoes a short convulsion. When the patient regains consciousness, his or her mood is lifted.

Emotion A complex feeling-state that involves physiological arousal; a subjective feeling which might involve a cognitive appraisal of the situation and overt behavior in response to a stimulus.

Empathy The ability to appreciate how someone else feels by putting yourself in her or his position and experiencing her or his feelings. Empathy is acquired normally by children during intellectual growth.

Empiricism The view that behavior is learned through experience.

Encounter Groups Groups of individuals who meet to change their personal lives by confronting each other, discussing personal problems, and talking more honestly and openly than in everyday life.

Endocrine Glands Ductless glands that secrete chemicals called hormones into the blood stream.

Equilibration According to Piaget, the child constructs an understanding of the world through equilibration. Equilibration consists of the interaction of two complementary processes, assimilation (taking in input within the existing structures of the mind, e.g., putting it into mental categories that already exist) with accommodation (the changing of mental categories to fit new input that cannot be taken into existing categories) and is the process by which knowing occurs. One's developmental stage affects how one equilibrates.

Ethnocentrism The belief that one's own ethnic or racial group is superior to others.

Experiment Procedures executed under a controlled situation in order to test a hypothesis and discover relationships between independent and dependent variables.

Experimental Control The predetermined conditions, procedures, and checks built into the design of an experiment to ensure scientific control; as opposed to "control" in common usage, which implies manipulation.

Experimental Group In a scientific experiment, the group of subjects that is usually treated specially, as opposed to the control group, in order to isolate just the variable under investigation. *See* Control Group.

Experimental Psychology The branch of psychology concerned with the laboratory study of basic psychological laws and principles as demonstrated in the behavior of animals.

Experimenter Bias How the expectations of the person running an experiment can influence what comes out of the experiment. Experimenter bias can affect the way the experimenter sees the subjects' behavior, causing distortions of fact, and can also affect the way the experimenter reads data, also leading to distortions.

Extinction The elimination of behavior by, in classical conditioning, the withholding of the unconditional stimulus, and in operant conditioning, the withholding of the reinforcement.

Extrasensory Perception (ESP) The range of perceptions that are "paranormal," (such as the ability to predict events, reproduce drawings sealed in envelopes, etc.).

Fixed Interval (FI) Schedule Schedule of reinforcement in which the subject receives reinforcement for the first correct response given after a specified time interval.

Fixed Ratio (FR) Schedule Schedule of reinforcement in which the subject is reinforced after a certain number of responses.

Fixed-Action Pattern Movement that is characteristic of a species and does not have to be learned.

Forgetting The process by which material that once was available is no longer available. Theory exists that forgetting occurs because memories interfere with one another, either retroactively (new memories block old) or proactively (old memories block new); that forgetting occurs when the cues necessary to recall the information are not supplied, or when memories are too unpleasant to remain in consciousness. *See* Repression.

Formal Operational Stage According to Piaget, the stage at which the child develops adult powers of reasoning, abstraction, and symbolizing. The child can grasp scientific, religious, and political concepts and deduce their consequences as well as reason hypothetically ("what if . . .").

Frequency Theory of Hearing Theory of hearing that states that the frequency of vibrations at the basilar membrane determines the frequency of firing of neurons that carry impulses to the brain.

Frustration A feeling of discomfort or insecurity aroused by a blocking of gratification or by unresolved problems. Several theories hold that frustration arouses aggression. *See* Aggression.

Functionalism An early school of psychology stressing the ways behavior helps one adapt to the environment and the role that learning plays in this adaptive process.

Gene The unit of heredity that determines particular characteristics; a part of a molecule of DNA. DNA (dioxyribonucleic acid) is found mainly in the nucleus of living cells where it occurs in threadlike structures called chromosomes. Within the chromosomes, each DNA molecule is organized into specific units that carry the genetic information necessary for the development of a particular trait. These units are the genes. A gene can reproduce itself exactly, and this is how traits are carried between generations. The genotype is the entire structure of genes that are inherited by an organism from its parents. The environment interacts with this genotype to determine how the genetic potential will develop.

General Adaptation Syndrome (GAS) The way the body responds to stress, as described by Hans Selye. In the first stage, an alarm reaction, a person responds by efforts at self-control and shows signs of nervous depression (defense mechanisms, fear, anger, etc.) followed by a release of ACTH. In stage 2, the subject shows increased resistance to the specific source of stress and less resistance to other sources. Defense mechanisms may become neurotic. With stage 3 comes exhaustion, stupor, even death.

Generalization The process by which learning in one situation is transferred to another, similar situation. It is a key term in behavioral modification and classical conditioning. *See* Classical Conditioning.

Generalized Anxiety Disorder Disorder in which the individual lives in a state of constant severe tension; continuous fear and apprehension experienced by an individual.

Genetics The study of the transfer of the inheritance of characteristics from one generation to another.

Genotype The underlying genetic structure that an individual has inherited and will send on to descendants. The actual appearance of a trait (phenotype) is due to the interaction of the genotype and the environment.

Gestalt Psychology A movement in psychology begun in the 1920s, stressing the wholeness of a person's experience and proposing that perceiving is an active, dynamic process that takes into account the entire pattern of ("gestalt") of the perpetual field. *See* Behaviorism; Associationism.

Glia Cells in the central nervous system that regulate the chemical environment of the nerve cells. RNA is stored in glial cells.

Grammar The set of rules for combining units of a language.

Group Therapy A form of psychotherapy aimed at treating mental disorders in which interaction among group members is the main therapeutic mode. Group therapy takes many forms but essentially requires a sense of community, support, increased personal responsibility, and a professionally trained leader.

Growth The normal quantitative changes that occur in the physical and psychological aspects of a healthy child with the passage of time.

Gustation The sense of taste. Theory suggests that the transmission of sense information from tongue to brain occurs through patterns of cell activity and not just the firing of single nerve fibers. Also, it is believed that specific spatial patterns or places on the tongue correspond to taste qualities.

Habit Formation The tendency to make a response to a stimulus less variable, especially if it produced successful adaptation.

Hallucination A sensory impression reported by a person when no external stimulus exists to justify the report. Hallucinations are serious symptoms and may be produced by psychoses. *See* Psychosis.

Hallucinogen A substance that produces hallucinations, such as LSD, mescaline, etc.

Hierarchy of Needs Maslow's list of motives in humans, arranged from the biological to the uniquely human.

Higher Order Conditioning Learning to make associations with stimuli that have been previously learned (CSs).

Hippocampus Part of the cortex of the brain governing memory storage, smell, and visceral functions.

Homeostasis A set of processes maintaining the constancy of the body's internal state, a series of dynamic compensations of the nervous system. Many processes such as appetite, body temperature, water balance, and heart rate are controlled by homeostasis.

Hormones Chemical secretions of the endocrine glands that regulate various body processes (e.g., growth, sexual traits, reproductive processes, etc.).

Humanism Branch of psychology dealing with those qualities distinguishing humans from other animals.

Hypnosis A trancelike state marked by heightened suggestibility and a narrowing of attention that can be induced in a number of ways. Debate exists over whether hypnosis is a true altered state of consciousness and to what extent strong motivating instructions can duplicate so-called hypnosis.

Hypothalamus A part of the brain that acts as a channel that carries information from the cortex and the thalamus to the spinal cord and ultimately to the motor nerves or to the autonomic nervous system, where it is transmitted to specific target organs. These target organs release into the bloodstream specific hormones that alter bodily functions. *See* Autonomic Nervous System.

Hypothesis A hypothesis can be called an educated guess, similar to a hunch. When a hunch is stated in a way that allows for further testing, it becomes a hypothesis.

Iconic Memory A visual memory. Experiments suggest that in order to be remembered and included in long-term memory, information must pass through a brief sensory stage. Theory further suggests that verbal information is subject to forgetting but that memorized sensory images are relatively permanent.

Id According to Freud, a component of the psyche present at birth that is the storehouse of psychosexual energy called *libido,* and also of primitive urges to fight, dominate, destroy.

Identification The taking on of attributes that one sees in another person. Children tend to identify with their parents or other important adults and thereby take on certain traits that are important to their development.

Illusion A mistaken perception of an actual stimulus.

Imitation The copying of another's behavior; learned through the process of observation. *See* Modeling.

Impression Formation The process of developing an evaluation of another person from your perceptions; first, or initial, impressions are often very important.

Imprinting The rapid, permanent acquisition by an organism of a strong attachment to an object (usually the parent). Imprinting occurs shortly after birth.

Independent Variable The condition in an experiment that is controlled and manipulated by the experimenter; it is a stimulus that will cause a response.

Inferential Statistics Techniques that help researchers make generalizations about a finding based on a limited number of subjects.

Inhibition Restraint of an impulse, desire, activity, or drive. People are taught to inhibit full expression of many drives (for example, aggression or sexuality) and to apply checks either consciously or unconsciously. In Freudian terminology, an inhibition is an unconsciously motivated blocking of sexual energy. In Pavlovian conditioning, inhibition is the theoretical process that operates during extinction, acting to block a conditioned response. *See* Pavlovian Conditioning.

Insight A sudden perception of useful or proper relations among objects necessary to solve the problem.

Insight Therapy A general classification of therapy in which the therapist focuses on the patient's underlying feelings and motivations and devotes most effort to increasing the patient's self-awareness or insight into his or her behavior. The other major class of therapy is action therapy. *See* Action Therapy.

Instinct An inborn pattern of behavior, relatively independent of environmental influence. An instinct may need to be triggered by a particular stimulus in the environment, but then it proceeds in a fixed pattern. The combination of taxis (orienting movement in response to a particular stimulus) and fixed-action pattern (inherited coordination) is the basis for instinctual activity. *See* Fixed-Action Pattern.

Instrumental Learning *See* Operant Conditioning.

Intelligence A capacity for knowledge about the world. This is an enormous and controversial field of study, and there is no agreement on a precise definition. However, intelligence has come to refer to higher-level abstract processes and may be said to comprise the ability to deal effectively with abstract concepts, the ability to learn, and the ability to adapt and deal with new situations. Piaget defines intelligence as the construction of an understanding. Both biological inheritance and environmental factors contribute to general intelligence. Children proceed through a sequence of identifiable stages in the development of conceptual thinking (Piaget). The degree to which factors such as race, sex, and social class affect intelligence is not known.

Intelligence Quotient (IQ) A measurement of intelligence originally based on tests devised by Binet and now widely applied. Genetic inheritance and environment affect IQ, although their relative contributions are not known. IQ can be defined in different ways; classically it is defined as a relation between chronological and mental ages.

Interference Theory of forgetting in which information that was learned before (proactive interference) or after (retroactive interference) the material of interest causes the learner to be unable to remember the material.

Interstimulus Interval The time between the start of the conditioned stimulus and the start of the unconditioned stimulus in Pavlovian conditioning. *See* Pavlovian Conditioning.

Intrauterine Environment The environment in the uterus during pregnancy can affect the physical development of the organism and its behavior after birth. Factors such as the mother's nutrition, emotional, and physical state significantly influence offspring. The mother's diseases, medications, hormones, and stress level all affect the pre- and postnatal development of her young.

Intrinsic Motivation Motivation inside of the individual; we do something because we receive satisfaction from it.

Introspection Reporting one's internal, subjective mental contents for the purpose of further study and analysis. *See* Structuralism.

James-Lange Theory of Emotion Theory of emotion that states that the physiological arousal and behavior come before the subjective experience of an emotion.

Labeling-of-Arousal Experiments suggest that an individual experiencing physical arousal that she or he cannot explain will interpret her or his feelings in terms of the situation she or he is in and will use environmental and contextual cues.

Language A set of abstract symbols used to communicate meaning. Language includes vocalized sounds or semantic units (words, usually) and rules for combining the units (grammar). There is some inborn basis for language acquisition, and there are identifiable stages in its development that are universal.

Language Acquisition Linguists debate how children acquire language. Some believe in environmental shaping, a gradual system of reward and punishment. Others emphasize the unfolding of capacities inborn in the brain that are relatively independent of the environment and its rewards.

Latency Period According to Freud, the psychosexual stage of development during which sexual interest has been repressed and thus is low or "latent" (dormant).

Law of Effect Thorndike's proposal that when a response produces satisfaction, it will be repeated; reinforcement.

Leadership The quality of exerting more influence than other group members. Research suggests that certain characteristics are generally considered essential to leadership: consideration, sensitivity, ability to initiate and structure, and emphasis on production. However, environmental factors may thrust authority on a person without regard to personal characteristics.

Learned Helplessness Theory suggests that living in an environment of uncontrolled stress reduces the ability to cope with future stress that *is* controllable.

Learned Social Motives Motives in the human that are learned, including achievement, affiliation, and autonomy.

Learning The establishment of connections between stimulus and response, resulting from observation, special training, or previous activity. Learning is relatively permanent.

Life Span Span of time from conception to death; in developmental psychology, a life span approach looks at development throughout an individual's life.

Linguistic Relativity Hypothesis Proposal by Whorf that the perception of reality differs according to the language of the observer.

Linguistics The study of language, its nature, structure, and components.

Locus of Control The perceived place from which come determining forces in one's life. A person who feels that he or she has some control over his or her fate and tends to feel more likely to succeed has an internal locus of control. A person with an external locus of control feels that it is outside himself or herself and therefore that his or her attempts to control his or her fate are less assured.

Longitudinal Study A research method that involves following subjects over a considerable period of time (as compared with a cross-sectional approach); as in a study of fantasy play in children observed several times at intervals of two years. *See* Cross-Sectional Study.

Love Affectionate behavior between people, often in combination with interpersonal attraction. The mother-infant love relationship strongly influences the later capacity for developing satisfying love relationships.

Manic-Depressive Reaction A form of mental illness marked by alternations of extreme phases of elation (manic phase) and depression.

Maternalism Refers to the mother's reaction to her young. It is believed that the female is biologically determined to exhibit behavior more favorable to the care and feeding of the young than the male, although in humans maternalism is probably determined as much by cultural factors as by biological predisposition.

Maturation The genetically-controlled process of physical and physiological growth.

Mean The measure of central tendency, or mathematical average, computed by adding all scores in a set and dividing by the number of scores.

Meaning The concept or idea conveyed to the mind, by any method. In reference to memory, meaningful terms are easier to learn than less meaningful, unconnected, or nonsense terms. Meaningfulness is not the same as the word's meaning.

Median In a set of scores, the median is that middle score that divides the set into equal halves.

Memory Involves the encoding, storing of information in the brain, and its retrieval. Several theories exist to explain memory. One proposes that we have both a short-term (STM) and a long-term memory (LTM) and that information must pass briefly through the STM to be stored in the LTM. Also suggested is that verbal information is subject to forgetting, while memorized sensory images are relatively permanent. Others see memory as a function of association—information processed systematically and the meaningfulness of the items. Debate exists over whether memory retrieval is actually a process of reappearance or reconstruction.

Mental Disorder A mental condition that deviates from what society considers to be normal.

Minnesota Multiphasic Personality Inventory (MMPI) An objective personality test that was originally devised to identify personality disorders.

Mode In a set of scores, the measurement at which the largest number of subjects fall.

Modeling The imitation or copying of another's behavior. As an important process in personality development, modeling may be based on parents. In therapy, the therapist may serve as a model for the patient.

Morality The standards of right and wrong of a society and their adoption by members of that society. Some researchers believe that morality develops in successive stages, with each stage representing a specific level of moral thinking (Kohlberg). Others see morality as the result of experiences in which the child learns through punishment and reward from models such as parents and teachers.

Motivation All factors that cause and regulate behavior that is directed toward achieving goals and satisfying needs. Motivation is what moves an organism to action.

Motor Unit One spinal motoneuron (motor nerve cell) and the muscle fibers it activates. The contraction of a muscle involves the activity of many motoneurons and muscle fibers. Normally we are aware only of our muscles contracting and not of the process producing the contraction, although biofeedback can train people to control individual motor units. *See* Biofeedback.

Narcotic A drug that relieves pain. Heroin, morphine, and opium are narcotics. Narcotics are often addicting.

Naturalistic Observation Research method in which behavior of people or animals in the normal environment is accurately recorded.

Negative Reinforcement Any event that upon termination, strengthens the preceding behavior; taking from subject something bad will increase the probability that the preceding behavior will be repeated. Involves aversive stimulus.

Neuron A nerve cell. There are billions of neurons in the brain and spinal cord. Neurons interact at synapses or points of contact. Information passage between neurons is electrical and biochemical. It takes the activity of many neurons to produce a behavior.

Neurosis Any one of a wide range of psychological difficulties, accompanied by excessive anxiety (as contrasted with psychosis). Psychoanalytic theory states that neurosis is an expression of unresolved conflicts in the form of tension and impaired functioning. Most neurotics are in much closer contact with reality than most psychotics. Term has been largely eliminated from DSM-III.

Nonverbal Behaviors Gestures, facial expressions, and other body movements. They are important because they tend to convey emotion. Debate exists over whether they are inborn or learned.

Norm An empirically set pattern of belief or behavior. Social norm refers to widely accepted social or cultural behavior to which a person tends to or is expected to conform.

Normal Sane, or free from mental disorder. Normal behavior is the behavior typical of most people in a given group, and "normality" implies a social judgment.

Normal Curve When scores of a large number of random cases are plotted on a graph, they often fall into a bell-shaped curve; there are as many cases above the mean as below on the curve.

Object Permanence According to Piaget, the stage in cognitive development when a child begins to conceive of objects as having an existence even when out of sight or touch and to conceive of space as extending beyond his or her own perception.

Oedipus Complex The conflicts of a child in triangular relationship with his mother and father. According to Freud, a boy must resolve his unconscious sexual desire for his mother and the accompanying wish to kill his father and fear of his father's revenge in order that he proceed in his moral development. The analogous problem for girls is called the Electra complex.

Olfaction The sense of smell. No general agreement exists on how olfaction works, though theories exist to explain it. One suggests that the size and shape of molecules of what is smelled is a crucial cue. The brain processes involved in smell are located in a different and evolutionally older part of the brain than the other senses.

Operant Conditioning The process of changing, maintaining, or eliminating voluntary behavior through the consequences of that behavior. Operant conditioning uses many of the techniques of Pavlovian conditioning but differs in that it deals with voluntary rather than reflex behaviors. The frequency with which a behavior is emitted can be increased if it is rewarded (reinforced) and decreased if it is not reinforced, or punished. Some psychologists believe that all behavior is learned through conditioning while others believe that intellectual and motivational processes play a crucial role. *See* Pavlovian Conditioning.

Operational Definitions If an event is not directly observable, then the variables must be defined by the operations by which they will be measured. These definitions are called operational definitions.

Organism Any living animal, human or subhuman.

Orienting Response A relatively automatic, "what's that?" response that puts the organism in a better position to attend to and deal with a new stimulus. When a stimulus attracts our attention, our body responds with movements of head and body toward the stimulus, changes in muscle tone, heart rate, blood flow, breathing, and changes in the brain's electrical activity.

Pavlovian Conditioning Also called classical conditioning, Pavlovian conditioning can be demonstrated as follows: In the first step, an *unconditioned stimulus* (UCS) such as food, loud sounds, or pain is paired with a neutral *conditioned stimulus* (CS) that causes no direct effect, such as a click, tone, or a dim light. The response elicited by the UCS is called the *unconditioned response* (UCR) and is a biological reflex of the nervous system (for example, eyeblinks or salivation). The combination of the neutral CS, the response-causing UCS, and the unlearned UCR is usually presented to the subject several times during conditioning. Eventually, the UCS is dropped from the sequence in the second step of the process, and the previously neutral CS comes to elicit a response. When conditioning is complete, presentation of the CS alone will result in a *conditioned response* (CR) similar but not always the same as the UCR.

Perception The field of psychology studying ways in which the experience of objects in the world is based upon stimulation of the sense organs. In psychology, the field of perception studies what determines sensory impressions, such as size, shape, distance, direction, etc.

Physical events in the environment are called distal stimuli while the activity at the sense organ itself is called a proximal stimulus. The study of perceiving tries to determine how an organism knows what distal stimuli are like since proximal stimuli are its only source of information. Perception of objects remains more or less constant despite changes in distal stimuli and is therefore believed to depend on relationships within stimuli (size *and* distance, for example). Perceptual processes are able to adjust and adapt to changes in the perceptual field.

Performance The actual behavior of an individual that is observed. We often infer learning from observing performance.

Peripheral Nervous System The part of the human nervous system that receives messages from the sense organs and carries messages to the muscles and glands; everything outside of the brain and spinal cord.

Persuasion The process of changing a person's attitudes, beliefs, or actions. A person's susceptibility to persuasion depends on the persuader's credibility, subtlety, and whether both sides of an argument are presented.

Phenotype The physical features or behavior patterns by which we recognize an organism. Phenotype is the result of interaction between genotype (total of inherited genes) and environment. *See* Genotype.

Phobia A neurosis consisting of an irrationally intense fear of specific persons, objects, or situations and a wish to avoid them. A phobic person feels intense and incapacitating anxiety. The person may be aware that the fear is irrational, but this knowledge does not help.

Pituitary Gland Is located in of the brain and controls secretion of several hormones: the antidiuretic hormone that maintains water balance, oxytocin that controls blood pressure and milk production, and ACTH that is produced in response to stress, etc. *See* ACTH.

Placebo A substance that in and of itself has no real effect but which may produce an effect in a subject because the subject expects or believes that it will.

Positive Reinforcement Any event that, upon presentation, strengthens the preceding behavior; giving a subject something good will increase the probability that the preceding behavior will be repeated.

Prejudice An attitude in which one holds a negative belief about members of a group to which he or she does not belong. Prejudice is often directed at minority ethnic or racial groups and may be reduced by contact with these perceived "others."

Premack Principle Principle that states that of any two responses, the one that is more likely to occur can be used to reinforce the response that is less likely to occur.

Prenatal Development Development from conception to birth. It includes the physical development of the fetus as well as certain of its intellectual and emotional processes.

Preoperational Stage The development stage at which, according to Piaget, come the start of language, the ability to imitate actions, to symbolize, and to play make-believe games. Thinking is egocentric in that a child cannot understand that others perceive things differently.

Primary Reinforcement Reinforcement that is effective without having been associated with other reinforcers; sometimes called unconditioned reinforcement.

Probability (p) In inferential statistics, the likelihood that the difference between the experimental and control groups is due to the independent variable.

Problem Solving A self-directed activity in which an individual uses information to develop answers to problems, to generate new problems, and sometimes to transform the process by creating a unique, new system. Problem solving involves learning, insight and creativity.

Projective Test A type of test in which people respond to ambiguous, loosely structured stimuli. It is assumed that people will reveal themselves by putting themselves into the stimuli they see. The validity of these tests for diagnosis and personality assessment is still at issue.

Propaganda Information deliberately spread to aid a cause. Propaganda's main function is persuasion.

Prosocial Behavior Behavior that is directed toward helping others.

Proximal Stimulus Activity at the sense organ.

Psychoactive Drug A substance that affects mental activities, perceptions, consciousness, or mood. This type of drug has its effects through strictly physical effects and through expectations.

Psychoanalysis There are two meanings to this word: it is a theory of personality development based on Freud and a method of treatment also based on Freud. Psychoanalytic therapy uses techniques of free association, dream analysis, and analysis of the patient's relationship (the "transference") to the analyst. Psychoanalytic theory maintains that the personality develops through a series of psychosexual stages and that the personality consists of specific components energized by the life and death instincts.

Psychogenic Pain Disorder Somatoform disorder in which the person complains of severe, long-lasting pain for which there is no organic cause.

Psycholinguistics The study of the process of language acquisition as part of psychological development and of language as an aspect of behavior. Thinking may obviously depend on language, but their precise relationship still puzzles psycholinguists, and several different views exist.

Psychological Dependence Situation when a person craves a drug even though it is not biologically necessary for his or her body.

Psychophysiological Disorders Real medical problems (such as ulcers, migraine headaches, and high blood pressure) that are caused or aggravated by psychological stress.

Psychosexual Stages According to Freud, an individual's personality develops through several stages. Each stage is associated with a particular bodily source of gratification (pleasure). First comes the oral stage when most pleasures come from the mouth. Then comes the anal stage when the infant derives pleasure from holding and releasing while learning bowel control. The phallic stage brings pleasure from the genitals, and a crisis (Oedipal) occurs in which the child gradually suppresses sexual desire for the opposite-sex parent, identifies with the same-sex parent and begins to be interested in the outside world. This latency period lasts until puberty, after which the genital stage begins and mature sexual relationships develop. There is no strict timetable, but, according to Freudians, the stages do come in a definite order. Conflicts experienced and not adequately dealt with remain with the individual.

Psychosis The most severe of mental disorders, distinguished by a person being seriously out of touch with objective reality. Psychoses may result from physical factors (organic) or may have no known physical cause (functional). Psychoses take many forms, of which the most common are schizophrenia and psychotic depressive reactions, but all are marked by personality disorganization and a severely reduced ability to perceive reality. Both biological and environmental factors are believed to influence the development of psychosis, although the precise effect of each is not presently known. *See* Neurosis.

Psychosomatic Disorders A variety of body reactions that are closely related to psychological events. Stress, for example, brings on many physical changes and can result in illness or even death if prolonged and severe. Psychosomatic disorders can affect any part of the body.

Psychotherapy Treatment involving interpersonal contacts between a trained therapist and a patient in which the therapist tries to produce beneficial changes in the patient's emotional state, attitudes, and behavior.

Punishment Any event that decreases the probability of the preceding behavior being repeated. You can give something bad (positive punishment) to decrease the preceding behavior.

Rational-Emotive Therapy A cognitive behavior modification technique in which a person is taught to identify irrational, self-defeating beliefs and then to overcome them.

Rationalization Defense mechanism in which individuals make up logical excuses to justify their behavior rather than exposing their true motives.

Reaction Formation Defense mechanism in which a person masks an unconsciously distressing or unacceptable trait by assuming an opposite attitude or behavior pattern.

Reactive Schizophrenia A type of schizophrenia in which the disorder appears as a reaction to some major trauma or terribly stressful encounter; sometimes called acute schizophrenia.

Reality Therapy A form of treatment of mental disorders pioneered by William Glasser in which the origins of the patient's problems are considered irrelevant and emphasis is on a close, judgmental bond between patient and therapist aimed to improve the patient's present and future life.

Reflex An automatic movement that occurs in direct response to a stimulus.

Rehearsal The repeating of an item to oneself and the means by which information is stored in the short-term memory (STM). Theory suggests that rehearsal is necessary for remembering and storage in the long-term memory (LTM).

Reinforcement The process of affecting the frequency with which a behavior is emitted. A reinforcer can reward and thus increase the behavior or punish and thus decrease its frequency. Reinforcers can also be primary, satisfying basic needs such as hunger or thirst, or secondary, satisfying learned and indirect values, such as money.

Reliability Consistency of measurement. A test is reliable if it repeatedly gives the same results. A person should get nearly the same score if the test is taken on two different occasions.

REM (Rapid-Eye Movement) Type of sleep in which the eyes are rapidly moving around; dreaming occurs in REM sleep.

Repression A defense mechanism in which a person forgets or pushes into the unconscious something that arouses anxiety. *See* Defense Mechanism; Anxiety.

Reticular Formation A system of nerve fibers leading from the spinal column to the cerebral cortex that functions to arouse, alert, and make an organism sensitive to changes in the environment. *See* Cerebral Cortex.

Retina The inside coating of the eye, containing two kinds of cells that react to light: the rods that are sensitive only to dim light and the cones that are sensitive to color and form in brighter light. There are three kinds of cones, each responsive to particular colors in the visible spectrum (range of colors).

Risky Shift Research suggests that decisions made by groups will involve considerably more risk than individuals in the group would be willing to take. This shift in group decision depends heavily on cultural values. *See* Cautious Shift.

Rod Part of the retina involved in seeing in dim light. *See* Retina.

RNA (Ribonucleic Acid) A chemical substance that occurs in chromosomes and that functions in genetic coding. During task-learning, RNA changes occur in the brain.

Role Playing Adopting the role of another person and experiencing the world in a way one is not accustomed to.

Role Taking The ability to imagine oneself in another's place or to understand the consequences of one's actions for another person.

Schachter-Singer Theory of Emotion Theory of emotion that states that we interpret our arousal according to our environment and label our emotions accordingly.

Schizoid Personality Personality disorder characterized by having great trouble developing social relationships.

Schizophrenia The most common and serious form of psychosis in which there exists an imbalance between emotional reactions and the thoughts associated with these feelings. It may be a disorder of the process of thinking. *See* Psychosis.

Scientific Method The process used by psychologists to determine principles of behavior that exist independently of individual experience and that are untouched by unconscious bias. It is based on a prearranged agreement that criteria, external to the individual and communicable to others, must be established for each set of observations referred to as fact.

Secondary Reinforcement Reinforcement that is only effective after it has been associated with a primary reinforcer.

Self-Actualization A term used by humanistic psychologists to describe what they see as a basic human motivation: the development of all aspects of an individual into productive harmony.

Self-Esteem A person's evaluation of oneself. If someone has confidence and satisfaction in oneself, self-esteem is considered high.

Self-Fulfilling Prophecy A preconceived expectation or belief about a situation that evokes behavior resulting in a situation consistent with the preconception.

Senses An organism's physical means of receiving and detecting physical changes in the environment. Sensing is analyzed in terms of reception of the physical stimulus by specialized nerve cells in the sense organs, transduction or converting the stimulus' energy into nerve impulses that the brain can interpret, and transmission of those nerve impulses from the sense organ to the part of the brain that can interpret the information they convey.

Sensitivity Training Aims at helping people to function more effectively in their jobs by increasing their awareness of their own and others' feelings and exchanging "feedback" about styles of interacting. Sensitivity groups are unlike therapy groups in that they are meant to enrich the participants' lives. Participants are not considered patients or ill. Also called T-groups.

Sensorimotor Stage According to Piaget, the stage of development beginning at birth during which perceptions are tied to objects that the child manipulates. Gradually the child learns that objects have permanence even if they are out of sight or touch.

Sensory Adaptation Tendency of the sense organs to adjust to continuous, unchanging stimulation by reducing their functioning; a stimulus that once caused sensation no longer does.

Sensory Deprivation The blocking out of all outside stimulation for a period of time. As studied experimentally, it can produce hallucinations, psychological disturbances, and temporary disorders of the nervous system of the subject.

Sex Role The attitudes, activities, and expectations considered specific to being male or female, determined by both biological and cultural factors.

Shaping A technique of behavior shaping in which behavior is acquired through the reinforcement of successive approximations of the desired behavior.

Sleep A periodic state of consciousness marked by four brain-wave patterns. Dreams occur during REM sleep. Sleep is a basic need without which one may suffer physical or psychological distress. *See* Brain Waves; Dreams.

Sleeper Effect The delayed impact of persuasive information. People tend to forget the context in which they first heard the information, but they eventually remember the content of the message sufficiently to feel its impact.

Social Comparison Theory proposed by Festinger that states that we have a tendency to compare our behavior to others to ensure that we are conforming.

Social Facilitation Phenomenon in which the presence of others increases dominant behavior patterns in an individual; Zajonc's theory of social facilitation states that the presence of others enhances the emission of the dominant response of the individual.

Social Influence The process by which people form and change the attitudes, opinions, and behavior of others.

Social Learning Learning acquired through observation and imitation of others.

Social Psychology The study of individuals as affected by others and of the interaction of individuals in groups.

Socialization A process by which a child learns the various patterns of behavior expected and accepted by society. Parents are the chief agents of a child's socialization. Many factors have a bearing on the socialization process, such as the child's sex, religion, social class, and parental attitudes.

Sociobiology The study of the genetic basis of social behavior.

Sociophobias Excessive irrational fears and embarrassment when interacting with other people.

Somatic Nervous System The part of the peripheral nervous system that carries messages from the sense organs and relays information that directs the voluntary movements of the skeletal muscles.

Somatoform Disorders Disorders characterized by physical symptoms for which there are no obvious physical causes.

Somesthetic Senses Skin senses; includes pressure, pain, cold, and warmth.

Species-Typical Behavior Behavior patterns common to members of a species. Ethologists state that each species inherits some patterns of behavior (e.g., birdsongs).

Stanford-Binet Intelligence Scale Tests that measure intelligence from two years of age through adult level. The tests determine one's intelligence quotient by establishing one's chronological and mental ages. *See* Intelligence Quotient.

State-Dependent Learning Situation in which what is learned in one state can only be remembered when the person is in that state.

Statistically Significant In inferential statistics, a finding that the independent variable did influence greatly the outcome of the experimental and control group.

Stereotype The assignment of characteristics to a person mainly on the basis of the group, class, or category to which he or she belongs. The tendency to categorize and generalize is a basic human way of organizing information. Stereotyping, however, can reinforce misinformation and prejudice. *See* Prejudice.

Stimulus A unit of the environment that causes a response in an individual; more specifically, a physical or chemical agent acting on an appropriate sense receptor.

Stimulus Discrimination Limiting responses to relevant stimuli.

Stimulus Generalization Responses to stimuli similar to the stimulus that had caused the response.

Stress Pressure that puts unusual demands on an organism. Stress may be caused by physical conditions but eventually will involve both. Stimuli that cause stress are called stressors, and an organism's response is the stress reaction. A three-stage general adaptation syndrome is hypothesized involving both emotional and physical changes. *See* General Adaptation Syndrome.

Structuralism An early school of psychology that stressed the importance of conscious experience as the subject matter of psychology and maintained that experience should be analyzed into its component parts by use of introspection. *See* Introspection.

Sublimation Defense mechanism in which a person redirects his socially undesirable urges into socially acceptable behavior.

Subliminal Stimuli Stimuli that do not receive conscious attention because they are below sensory thresholds. They may influence behavior, but research is not conclusive on this matter.

Substance-Induced Organic Mental Disorders Organic mental disorders caused by exposure to harmful environmental substances.

Suggestibility The extent to which a person responds to persuasion. Hypnotic susceptibility refers to the degree of suggestibility observed after an attempt to induce hypnosis has been made. *See* Persuasion; Hypnosis.

Superego According to Freud, the superego corresponds roughly to conscience. The superego places restrictions on both ego and id and represents the internalized restrictions and ideals that the child learns from parents and culture. *See* Conscience; Ego; Id.

Sympathetic Nervous System The branch of the autonomic nervous system that is more active in emergencies; it causes a general arousal, increasing breathing, heart rate, and blood pressure.

Synapse A "gap" where individual nerve cells (neurons) come together and across which chemical information is passed.

Syndrome A group of symptoms that occur together and mark a particular abnormal pattern.

Systematic Desensitization A technique used in behavior therapy to eliminate a phobia. The symptoms of the phobia are seen as conditioned responses of fear, and the procedure attempts to decondition the fearful response until the patient gradually is able to face the feared situation. *See* Phobia.

TAT (Thematic Apperception Test) Personality and motivation test that requires the subject to devise stories about pictures.

Taxis An orienting movement in response to particular stimuli in the environment. A frog, for example, always turns so its snout points directly at its prey before it flicks its tongue. *See* Orienting Response.

Theory A very general statement that is more useful in generating hypotheses than in generating research. *See* Hypothesis.

Therapeutic Community The organization of a hospital setting so that patients have to take responsibility for helping one another in an attempt to prevent patients from getting worse by being in the hospital.

Token Economy A system for organizing a treatment setting according to behavioristic principles. Patients are encouraged to take greater responsibility for their adjustment by receiving tokens for acceptable behavior and fines for unacceptable behavior. The theory of token economy grew out of operant conditioning techniques. *See* Operant Conditioning.

Traits Distinctive and stable attributes that can be found in all people.

Tranquilizers Psychoactive drugs that reduce anxiety. *See* Psychoactive Drug.

Trial and Error Learning Trying various behaviors in a situation until the solution is hit upon; past experiences lead us to try different responses until we are successful.

Unconditioned Response (UR) An automatic reaction elicited by a stimulus.

Unconditioned Stimulus (US) Any stimulus that elicits an automatic or reflexive reaction in an individual; it does not have to be learned in the present situation.

Unconscious In Freudian terminology, a concept (not a place) of the mind. The unconscious encompasses certain inborn impulses that never rise into consciousness (awareness) as well as memories and wishes that have been repressed. The chief aim of psychoanalytic therapy is to free repressed material from the unconscious in order to make it susceptible to conscious thought and direction. Behaviorists describe the unconscious as an inability to verbalize. *See* Repression.

Undifferentiated Schizophrenia Type of schizophrenia that does not fit into any particular category, or fits into more than one category.

Validity The extent to which a test actually measures what it is designed to measure.

Variability In statistics, measures of variability communicate how spread out the scores are; the tendency to vary the response to a stimulus, particularly if the response fails to help in adaptation.

Variable Any property of a person, object, or event that can change or take on more than one mathematical value.

Weber's Law States that the difference threshold depends on the ratio of the intensity of one stimulus to another rather than an absolute difference.

Wechsler Adult Intelligence Scale (WAIS) An individually administered test designed to measure adults' intelligence, devised by David Wechsler. The WAIS consists of eleven subtests, of which six measure verbal and five measure performance aspects of intelligence. *See* Wechsler Intelligence Scale for Children.

Wechsler Intelligence Scale for Children (WISC) Similar to the Wechsler Adult Intelligence Scale, except that it is designed for people under fifteen. Wechsler tests can determine strong and weak areas of overall intelligence. *See* Wechsler Adult Intelligence Scale (WAIS).

Whorfian Hypothesis The linguistic relativity hypothesis of Benjamin Whorf; states that language influences thought.

Withdrawal Social or emotional detachment; the removal of oneself from a painful or frustrating situation.

Yerkes-Dodson Law Prediction that the optimum motivation level decreases as the difficulty level of a task increases.

Source for the Glossary:

The majority of terms in this glossary are reprinted from *The Study of Psychology*, Joseph Rubinstein. © by The Dushkin Publishing Group, Inc., Guilford, CT 06437.

The remaining terms were developed by the Annual Editions staff.

Index

Credits/ Acknowledgments

Cover design by Charles Vitelli

1. Becoming a Person

Facing overview—WHO photo by J. Mohr.

2. Determinants of Behavior

Facing overview—WHO photo. 48—Illustration by Lewis E. Calver. 49—(top right) Hank Morgan—Rainbow; (middle left and bottom right) Buchsbaum; (middle right) Dan McCoy—Rainbow; (bottom right) Howard Sochurek. 50—(top & middle) Courtesy Haier & Buchsbaum; (bottom) courtesy Buchsbaum.

3. Problems Influencing Personal Growth

Facing overview—The Dushkin Publishing Group, Inc.

4. Relating to Others

Facing overview—United Nations photo by John Isaac. 154—United Nations photo by Margot Granitsas.

5. Dynamics of Personal Adjustment

Facing overview—United Nations photo.

6. Enhancing Human Adjustment

Facing overview—United Nations photo by John Isaac.

PHOTOCOPY THIS PAGE!!!*

ANNUAL EDITIONS ARTICLE REVIEW FORM

■ NAME: ___________________________________ DATE: ___________________________________

■ TITLE AND NUMBER OF ARTICLE: ___________________________________

■ BRIEFLY STATE THE MAIN IDEA OF THIS ARTICLE: ___________________________________

■ LIST THREE IMPORTANT FACTS THAT THE AUTHOR USES TO SUPPORT THE MAIN IDEA:

■ WHAT INFORMATION OR IDEAS DISCUSSED IN THIS ARTICLE ARE ALSO DISCUSSED IN YOUR TEXTBOOK OR OTHER READING YOU HAVE DONE? LIST THE TEXTBOOK CHAPTERS AND PAGE NUMBERS:

■ LIST ANY EXAMPLES OF BIAS OR FAULTY REASONING THAT YOU FOUND IN THE ARTICLE:

■ LIST ANY NEW TERMS/CONCEPTS THAT WERE DISCUSSED IN THE ARTICLE AND WRITE A SHORT DEFINITION:

*Your instructor may require you to use this Annual Editions Article Review Form in any number of ways: for articles that are assigned, for extra credit, as a tool to assist in developing assigned papers, or simply for your own reference. Even if it is not required, we encourage you to photocopy and use this page; you'll find that reflecting on the articles will greatly enhance the information from your text.

Annual Editions revisions depend on two major opinion sources: one is our Advisory Board, listed in the front of this volume, which works with us in scanning the thousands of articles published in the public press each year; the other is you—the person actually using the book. Please help us and the users of the next edition by completing the prepaid article rating form on this page and returning it to us. Thank you.

ANNUAL EDITIONS: PERSONAL GROWTH AND BEHAVIOR 93/94

Article Rating Form

Here is an opportunity for you to have direct input into the next revision of this volume. We would like you to rate each of the 57 articles listed below, using the following scale:

1. **Excellent: should definitely be retained**
2. **Above average: should probably be retained**
3. **Below average: should probably be deleted**
4. **Poor: should definitely be deleted**

Your ratings will play a vital part in the next revision. So please mail this prepaid form to us just as soon as you complete it.
Thanks for your help!

Rating	Article
	1. The Last Interview of Abraham Maslow
	2. Hey, I'm Terrific!
	3. Self-Esteem: The Keystone to Happiness
	4. Oedipus Wrecked
	5. Erikson, in His Own Old Age, Expands His View of Life
	6. Personality: Major Traits Found Stable Through Life
	7. Embattled Giant of Psychology Speaks His Mind
	8. The Town B. F. Skinner Boxed
	9. Same Family, Different Lives
	10. What a Child Is Given
	11. Born or Bred?
	12. Mapping the Brain
	13. 1990–2000, The Decade of the Brain
	14. A Pleasurable Chemistry
	15. The Face as Window and Machine for the Emotions
	16. Tapping the Healing Power of Positive Thinking
	17. Doctors Find Comfort Is a Potent Medicine
	18. Barriers to Success
	19. Clipped Wings
	20. Is Your Baby Getting Enough Stimulation?
	21. Putting Children First
	22. I'm OK, They're OK
	23. Children After Divorce
	24. Girls' Self-Esteem Is Lost on Way to Adolescence, New Study Finds
	25. Children in Gangs
	26. Reaching the Child Within Us
	27. Silent Saviors
	28. The Miracle of Resiliency
	29. Bright Lights, Big Mystery
	30. Euthanasia: What Is the "Good Death"?
	31. Art of Anger Difficult for Women to Master
	32. Do You Know Who Your Friends Are?
	33. How Anger Affects Your Health
	34. Resolving Conflicts: Step by Step
	35. No Life to Live
	36. What Happy Couples Do Right
	37. Friends Forever
	38. The Dance of Intimacy
	39. The Pace of Life
	40. The American Man in Transition
	41. Blame It on Feminism
	42. Taking Sides Against Ourselves
	43. Groupthink: Taking Easy Way Out of a Tough Decision
	44. When Bystanders Just Stand By
	45. How Much Is Enough?
	46. Mental Health Checkup
	47. The Listening Cure
	48. The Revolution in Psychiatric Care
	49. What Good Is Feeling Bad?
	50. Managing Stress and Living Longer
	51. Winning the War Against Clinical Depression
	52. Sexual Desire
	53. The Secret Illness: Obsessive-Compulsive Disorder
	54. Who Am I?
	55. Awakenings: Schizophrenia—A New Drug Brings Patients Back to Life
	56. Hitting Bottom Can Be the Beginning
	57. Healthy Pleasures

(Continued on next page)

ABOUT YOU

Name _______________ Date _______
Are you a teacher? ☐ Or student? ☐
Your School Name _______________
Department _______________
Address _______________
City _______________ State _______ Zip _______
School Telephone # _______________

YOUR COMMENTS ARE IMPORTANT TO US!

Please fill in the following information:

For which course did you use this book? _______________
Did you use a text with this Annual Edition? ☐ yes ☐ no
The title of the text? _______________
What are your general reactions to the Annual Editions concept?

Have you read any particular articles recently that you think should be included in the next edition?

Are there any articles you feel should be replaced in the next edition? Why?

Are there other areas that you feel would utilize an Annual Edition?

May we contact you for editorial input?

May we quote you from above?

No Postage Necessary if Mailed in the United States

ANNUAL EDITIONS: PERSONAL GROWTH AND BEHAVIOR 93/94

BUSINESS REPLY MAIL

First Class Permit No. 84 Guilford, CT

Postage will be paid by addressee

DPG **The Dushkin Publishing Group, Inc.**
Sluice Dock
Guilford, Connecticut 06437